EUROPE IN

TRANSITION

EUROPE IN

TRANSITION

1300—1520

WALLACE K. FERGUSON
University of Western Ontario

HOUGHTON MIFFLIN COMPANY · BOSTON

To Peggy

Preface

This book has been a long time in the making. In the process the original plan was somewhat altered, for books, I find, can take on a life of their own, and have a way of writing themselves. Nevertheless, the ideas I had in mind when I began to write have remained essentially unchanged, except, of course, for such shifts in emphasis as have resulted from further study and thought. These ideas were formulated a little more than a decade ago in an article entitled "The Interpretation of the Renaissance: Suggestions for a Synthesis."[1] Stated in the briefest terms, and without much necessary qualification, it was there my contention that the period from about the beginning of the fourteenth century to the end of the sixteenth witnessed the transition from medieval to modern civilization, that is, the gradual shift from one type of civilization to another, radically different in almost every respect. Further, if we consider the civilization of Western Europe as a whole, it was this transitional process, involving as it did the co-existence of medieval and modern elements in a constant state of flux, which gave to the period we know as the Renaissance its special character, and which justifies us in regarding it as a distinct historical period. Much of the controversy over the chronological scope and essential nature of the Renaissance, it seemed to me, has arisen as a result of concentrating attention upon one aspect of culture or upon one limited geographical area. While granting that the rate of change varied from one form of culture to another and from one country to another, I felt that a truer perspective might be attained by taking into consideration all the major countries of Western Europe and by regarding their civilization from as many points of view as possible.

As the book wrote itself, the program thus outlined was altered principally in chronological scope. In the first place, I have felt it necessary, in accordance with my conception of the transitional character of the period following the years around 1300, to begin with a preliminary essay

[1] *Journal of the History of Ideas*, XII (1951), 483-495.

on the economic, political, social, religious and cultural structure of the High Middle Ages, as a means of establishing the norm in relation to which the nature and extent of change could be assessed. In the second place, I became increasingly convinced of the need for a fuller treatment of the period from about 1300 to about 1520 than I had originally planned. Too often the fourteenth and fifteenth centuries have been dealt with either as an epilogue tacked on to a history of the Middle Ages or as a cursory introduction to the history of modern Europe. The need for another general history of the sixteenth century or the Age of the Reformation seemed to me less pressing. While still of the opinion that a complete discussion of the transition from medieval to modern civilization would have to be carried through to the end of the sixteenth century or beyond, I was thus forced to the conclusion that the years around 1520 might well serve as the *terminus ad quem* for the present work. The transition was still incomplete at that time, but it had already progressed far enough to make its general direction apparent. To go beyond that point, in any case, would necessitate the writing of another volume involving a whole new set of problems.

Even this somewhat shortened period seemed too long to be treated as a single unit. I have, therefore, divided it into two periods at about 1450. Within each of these sub-periods I have discussed the various aspects of civilization in parallel chapters, following roughly the same order as in the introductory section. This process has resulted in a somewhat artificial separation of elements of what was in fact a coherent whole; but it seemed necessary as a means of analysis and as a method of organizing data. At times the scheme of organization I have adopted has seemed too rigid, and I have departed from it when it did not conform to the nature of the material under discussion. Chapters vary greatly in length in accordance with my sense of what had to be included. On the whole, however, the structural framework of the book remains clearly visible, and it will, I hope, serve to guide the reader through the intricacies of a peculiarly complex age. A certain amount of repetition has resulted from the necessity of discussing the same developments from different points of view in successive chapters, and there has been some unavoidable overlapping at the dividing points between the chronological periods. I have tried, however, to avoid repetition except where it seemed essential to clarity or to making explicit the relation between the various aspects of civilization discussed in different parts of the book. I have regretfully confined foot-notes almost entirely to the acknowledgment of direct quotations. To have indicated all the sources upon which I have drawn would have been impossible without overloading every page, and to have noted some while ignoring others would have resulted in invidious discrimination. Finally, after a lifetime of reading, I can in some instances no longer remember to what author I am indebted for suggestions which have influenced my own interpretation. I can do no more here than make a blanket acknowledgment of my debt to those innumerable scholars, specialists in their field, without whose work this attempted synthesis would clearly have been impossible. A representative selection of their writings will appear in the bibliography.

I am more immediately and personally indebted for counsel and encouragement to my friend Professor John Rowe, as well as to Monsignor Lester Wemple and Professor George Black, who read sections on scholastic philosophy and music respectively. Above all I am indebted to my wife who read the manuscript at each stage of its composition, tirelessly questioning passages that seemed unclear or infelicitous, and who finally read both galley and page-proof and assisted in the preparation of the index. To her patient checking of orthography, capitalization and usage the book owes such consistency in matters of form as it possesses.

WALLACE K. FERGUSON

London, Ontario

Contents

Contents

Contents

Plates

The Medieval Background

I

The Economic Foundation

Feudal society in all its branches was founded upon an economic base of landholding and agriculture. This is the primary economic fact of early medieval civilization. An agricultural economy, such as that of the ninth and tenth centuries — the formative age of feudalism — furnishes no market for the sale of produce. Production was thus directed toward consumption by the tillers or owners of the soil. It was, in short, a subsistence economy, dominated throughout by the ideal of self-sufficiency. It was also in large degree a moneyless economy, its simple needs satisfied by barter or the exchange of services. But by the eleventh century the revival of commerce began to introduce into the feudal world the alien elements of city markets, foreign goods, the products of skilled industry, and, as a necessary result of a more complicated economic activity, the constant use of money as a medium of exchange or a standard of value. Feudal society still operated within a framework shaped by its agrarian origins, but the economic foundation of the great age of medieval civilization was no longer purely agricultural. The commercial and industrial economy of the towns was a minority phenomenon, though with an influence out of proportion to its volume, and its most characteristic institutions still bore the marks of its origin in the midst of a hostile feudal world. Both rural and urban economy, however, ex-

3

panded enormously during the eleventh, twelfth, and thirteenth centuries, and with expansion the character of both was changing. Before the end of the latter century, signs of the coming transformation were evident on every hand, though the characteristically medieval forms of economic life still remained, their major outlines as yet unimpaired.

A. LANDHOLDING AND AGRICULTURE: THE MANORIAL SYSTEM

This brief survey of the economic structure of the High Middle Ages is not the place for a discussion of the causes of that decline of commerce which in the preceding period had reduced Western Europe to a state of almost complete dependence on agriculture. Whatever the causes, the fact is that from the eighth century to some point, varying from country to country, in the eleventh century regular commerce had practically ceased. An occasional wandering peddler might still bring to isolated rural communities necessities that could not be produced in the locality, but this thin trickle of trade could have had little effect upon the organization of economic life. In these centuries, land and its produce were for all practical purposes the sole form of wealth. This condition, as will be noted later, contributed to the disintegration of the state and to the formation of political feudalism. But the failure of central government in turn was an important factor in shaping economic and social organization. One major consequence of this failure was the partition of the powers of the state, either by theoretical delegation or outright usurpation, among the great landholders. The landholder thus became a lord with sovereign powers over those living on the land. Conversely, the workers on the land became entirely dependent on their lord and in varying degrees lost their freedom. Only the possession of a considerable estate with its dependent workers could enable a landholder to maintain his position as a member of that military aristocracy which was the ruling class in the feudal system. The domain, or great estate, thus became a necessary economic unit, and by virtue of the lord's sovereign powers it was also a political unit, while its isolation from the rest of the world made it equally, for the peasants at least, a self-contained social unit. Forms of agricultural organization varied greatly in detail, but there was, nevertheless, a remarkable uniformity in all parts of Western Europe. Everywhere the rural community was shaped by the same factors: the lack of outside markets, the resultant ideal of self-sufficiency, and the integrating domination of the workers by the landholding lord.

The great estate, known in Latin as *villa*, in English as a manor, was not, it is true, the only form of agricultural organization in the Middle

4

Ages. In mountain country, in grazing areas, or wherever the topography of the countryside made it impractical, other forms might be found. And here and there occasional "allods" — independent farms held by freemen — might still be found in the eleventh century. The manor was nevertheless the normal unit of agrarian life. It was in essence a self-sufficient estate, containing the fortified residence of the lord or his agent and a village community composed of more or less unfree workers. The size of manors varied, but it was held within certain limits by practical circumstances. A manor should be large enough to maintain a knight as its lord, with his attendants and the equipment of a mounted warrior. It should also be large enough to justify the construction of a fortified manor house for the protection of the villagers whose huts clustered close about its walls. On the other hand, a manor must not be so large that it could not be worked from the village center. A lord who held more land than could be worked from one village would divide it into more than one manor. A great lord, indeed, might have many manors and these might be widely scattered, but each would be organized as a separate unit, governed by a bailiff as the lord's representative if the lord himself were not in residence. For the organization of agricultural economy and peasant life it mattered little whether the lord, who might be king, baron, bishop, or simple knight, had one manor or many. For our discussion of the manorial system, which formed the economic basis of feudal society, we can therefore concentrate attention upon the individual manor and ignore for the time being the relative power of its lord and his place in the system of political feudalism.

The large estate was no new development. It antedated the beginnings of feudalism by centuries. But it was its adaptability to the conditions of early feudal society that made it an almost universal institution. When land was the only form of wealth, the lord, whether he was a lay noble or an officer of the Church, needed land to maintain him in the style to which he had become accustomed. Land, however, is worthless without workers, and where there is no cash market for agricultural produce there is no money to pay them. The manorial system offered the simple solution. Part of the land of the manor was retained as demesne for the lord's use. The remainder was divided among the peasants who, in return for protection and the use of the land assigned them, worked the lord's demesne and also contributed part of the produce from their own land. The lord thus acquired unpaid workers, and the peasants paid with services and produce for the use of enough land to feed themselves and their families. The jurisdictional powers of the lord protected him against the loss of workers, but if the tenants were bound to the soil they were by that very fact protected from fear of eviction. What they lost in freedom they gained in the security of hereditary tenure and protection from attack which alone made life possible for the poor and unarmed in the violent days of early feudalism.

The manorial system was also well adapted to the primitive methods of agriculture practised throughout the feudal age. To maintain its fertility, part of the land had to be left uncultivated each year. In most parts of Europe a three-year rotation was followed, with one third of the land left fallow each year. The fallow field was allowed to grow up in natural grass on which cattle were turned in to graze. It would have been almost impossible for each peasant to put this system into effect independently on his own small holding. The general practice, therefore, was to divide the arable land of the manor into large fields, some of which might be retained exclusively as demesne, but in the rest of which the peasant holdings together with demesne land were scattered in narrow strips or plowlands. Moreover, few if any peasants owned the four or six oxen needed to make up a plow team. Plowing thus became a communal enterprise. So long as the manor retained its original form, the whole peasant community worked together to cultivate and harvest the manorial fields, though each peasant, as well as the lord, took the produce only of his own land. In addition to the arable fields, the manor also contained meadows and large stretches of waste land and woods. In all of these the lord and the peasants had certain "common" rights, determined by age-old custom. To complete its self-sufficiency, the manor usually had a mill, a communal oven, a blacksmith's shop, and a church. These, even in a sense the church, belonged to the lord, and the peasants paid for their use in kind.

A tightly knit little community, each manor had its own body of custom, which regulated the activity of its inhabitants at every turn and determined their relation to each other and to their lord. This custom, believed to be of immemorial antiquity, was the peasants' only substitute for state-enforced law. Less flexible than legislation, custom tended to make peasant society conservative and to impede technical or social progress. To the modern age, it seems an intolerable hindrance to individual enterprise. But in no other way, probably, could communal cultivation of the soil have been made to function. And the semi-legal character of custom had, from the peasants' point of view, the inestimable advantage that it limited to some degree the lord's ability to exploit his dependents. The power of the lord, unchecked as it was by any higher authority, was arbitrary and oppressive enough, especially in relation to the more servile class of peasants who were taxable at the lord's will. The labor services demanded by the lord in any case imposed a constant hardship upon the peasants, who needed all their time and strength to wrest a living with inadequate tools from a few strips of poorly fertilized soil. Nevertheless, the manorial system, with its deeply rooted custom, gave to the peasant class a fair amount of security and a reasonably stable organization, in contrast to the generally chaotic condition which prevailed in the upper brackets of feudal society.

What has been described above is the ideal manor, as it exists in the minds of historians and more or less as it existed, with infinite variation of detail, in the period before the revival of commerce and the rise of the towns. It is the norm from which we shall have to trace the gradual transition to modern methods of landholding and farming. That transition had, in fact, already begun in the High Middle Ages. The stimulus to agriculture furnished by growing town markets, as well as by the restoration of some degree of order in the feudal state, led to an immense expansion of cultivation in the twelfth and thirteenth centuries. Everywhere waste lands, woods and marshes were cleared or drained and brought under the plow. This process of clearance or "assarting" brought under cultivation large amounts of land to which no customary conditions of tenure were attached. Much of the new land was reclaimed from the woods and waste land of old manors, but much of it, too, was carved out of the forests and swamps that still covered a large part of Europe in the eleventh century. In any case, it was heavy, grubbing work, and the pioneers who undertook it had to be offered more favorable terms than obtained on old manorial land. Assarted land was usually held on relatively free tenure, free at least from labor services. This, in turn, led to a gradual improvement in the condition of the peasants on the older estates. In order to retain their tenants, lords were forced to mitigate the labor services and other hereditary or customary obligations of their unfree tenants. Commutation of labor services for payments in money or kind became increasingly common. At the same time, as the opportunity to sell produce in the town markets introduced money into the manorial system, lords sometimes found it easier or more profitable to rent part or all of the demesne than to farm it directly. Where this occurred, the need for labor services became less apparent and lords were often quite willing to commute them for cash. These developments occurred at different times and at varying rates of speed in different places, and they were still minority phenomena in the thirteenth century. But before the end of that century the closely coordinated manor, which had been the economic foundation of feudal society as well as the social framework of peasant life, was clearly losing its integrity.

The manorial system, like the political feudalism to which it was so closely related, was from the economic point of view a method of organizing an agrarian society without markets or money. The introduction of these latter elements into feudal society acted at first as a powerful stimulus. The total wealth of both the landholding and landworking classes was greatly increased. The majority of the peasants profited by the acquisition of a slightly higher standard of living and greater personal freedom. The lords profited by an increased income in spendable form. At the same time, however, the economic balance of feudal society was gravely imperilled and its essential structure weakened from within. The townspeople not only bought agricultural produce, they also offered for sale the products of distant lands or of skilled industry. Luxuries tend, by a kind of evolutionary mutation, to become necessities. And the nobles, tempted to buy goods of which their more primitive ancestors had been happily ignorant, found that their increased income seldom kept up with the rising cost of living. The ever pressing need for more money led improvident nobles to various expedients, such as the commutation of services, the renting or leasing of the demesne, or even the mortgaging of their estates. But these expedients were no more than a temporary solution. The money paid as commutation or for long term leases declined in value as prices rose. There is ample evidence that in the long run the new economy, together with the reckless extravagance it fostered, was undermining the economic stability of the whole noble class.

In still other ways the new economy acted as a solvent, disintegrating the foundations of the feudal system. In proportion as the lords abandoned demesne farming and their claims upon the labor services of their tenants, or alienated portions of their prerogatives for money, they lost direct contact with the soil and its workers. As a result, that network of personal relations and mutual obligations binding all classes together, which was the essence of feudalism, was gradually loosened. Money economy, indeed, worked like a drug in a system that had never been designed for it. The first effects were stimulating, even exhilarating. The constitution of feudal society, however, could not long endure that stimulus without deleterious effects. In the High Middle Ages only the stimulating effect was as yet clearly apparent, but signs of the future disintegration were already present.

B. COMMERCE AND INDUSTRY

It was from the towns that money economy spread through the feudal world. And the towns owed their existence, in the first instance, to the revival of trade. Here again we must pass lightly over the question of origins. Documentary evidence for the beginnings of medieval commerce is deplorably meager, for the early merchants could not write, and those monks and churchmen who could write were not interested in them or their nefarious dealings. It is clear, however, that the tenth century witnessed a stirring of trade in Italy and the Netherlands. In the eleventh century, commercial activity grew in volume and spread inland, finally penetrating every part of Western Europe in the twelfth. Once begun, the commercial revival set in motion a series of chain reactions, in which cause and effect were inextricably mixed. Where groups of merchants settled, towns grew up and furnished a market for the agricultural surplus of the countryside. This, in turn, added to the purchasing power of the landed classes and so expanded the market for the merchants' goods. Increasing wealth was accompanied by an increase in the population of both town and country, and these, together with the activity of the merchants, created in every town a market for the products of skilled industry. Artisans, finding it possible to make a living by a specialized trade, flocked to the towns and so swelled the urban population. The great economic expansion of the High Middle Ages was fostered throughout by a profitable exchange of goods and services between town and country. The gradual settling down of feudal society, which resulted in a greater security for life and property, undoubtedly contributed to this movement. The initial impetus, however, came from the revival of commerce.

Though the supplying of a local market absorbed more and more of the activity of medieval townsmen, it was the carrying of goods from distant parts that offered the first opportunities for profitable trade and continued to produce the largest profits throughout the period. Goods that could not be produced in most parts of Western Europe, especially those luxury goods brought by Italian merchants from the Levant, could always command a high price. And it is probable that large profits were needed, in the beginning, to lure merchants into their hazardous profession. The clearly traceable radiation of trade from Italy and the Netherlands, and the abnormally early economic development of these two focal centers, at any rate suggests that the initial stimulus to the revival of commerce came from foreign trade, as the decline of Moslem power in the Mediterranean and the cessation of Viking raids in the North Atlantic combined to reopen Europe's trade lines to her most important distant markets.

Even in the darkest period of the Early Middle Ages, Venice had maintained commercial contact with Constantinople, the greatest commercial and industrial city of the Near East. By the beginning of the eleventh century, Genoa and Pisa were fighting for their share of the Mediterranean trade, and by the end of that century all three of the great Italian trading cities were ready to take full advantage of the crusaders' conquest of the Syrian coast. The highest profits in the Levantine trade came from the luxuries of the fabulous East: spices, silks, ivory, precious stones, dyes, drugs, and condiments, brought by Arab merchants through the Persian Gulf or the Red Sea and deposited on the doorstep of Christian Europe. In addition, however, the Italian merchants imported many valuable products of the Levant itself: cotton, silk, the alum that was essential for the finishing of cloth, sugar, and a great variety of luxury articles from the workshops of Byzantine or Moslem artisans. In return they exported European products: olive oil, wine, woollen cloth, metals, armor and weapons.

The northern trade, which centered in the Netherlands, offered less brilliant opportunities for the accumulation of profit. The northern merchants dealt mostly in goods for which there was a steady demand, but which were less valuable, in proportion to bulk and weight, than the eastern luxuries. Aside from the Baltic herring, which by itself could have maintained a flourishing commerce, the principal imports from the North were furs, timber, pitch, tar, iron and copper ore, grain, and a few luxury items such as amber. These were exchanged for olive oil and wine from the South, the woollen cloth of Flanders, and various kinds of manufactured goods. As trade spread inland, binding the whole of Western Europe together in a network of trade routes, the volume of commerce was greatly increased by interchange between North and South and by the handling of raw materials or manufactured goods that were for one reason or another the specialty of a particular region. This inter-regional trade operated within a more limited geographical range than the trade with the East or the North, but it still involved the carrying of goods by road and river over considerable distances.

Throughout the medieval period, the typical merchant was a far-wandering man, a dusty-footed citizen of the roads. By land or sea the hazards of travel made his life an uncertain one, and his only possible guarantee of safety lay in association with his fellows. Merchants, therefore, commonly sailed in fleets or travelled the roads in caravans. From this fact resulted two of the primary characteristics of medieval trade: the institution of the periodic fairs and the international merchant law, the *jus mercatorium*. Caravans of merchants needed a concentrated market, larger than could be furnished by any but the biggest cities. They also needed an opportunity to exchange goods with caravans from other regions. The periodic fairs offered the solution of this problem. Until the end of the thirteenth century, the fairs established in the County of Champagne were the chief meeting places of Italian and northern merchants, but fairs were also established at strategically placed points in every country by kings or feudal lords, where merchants might meet at the same time each year to exchange goods or to sell a year's supply to local shopkeepers or to the magnates of the countryside. These fairs might be situated in or near a town, but they were outside the jurisdiction of the town government and so free from the monopolistic regulations by which the medieval towns strove to protect their citizens from foreign competition. For the duration of the fair the assembled merchants were under the protection of the lord of the fair. His interest in the fair, however, was limited to the levying of tolls. He left to the merchants themselves the regulation of trade and the settling of disputes. They formed their own courts, those "pie powder" courts that have so long amused English-speaking students, and there judged cases as they arose, in accordance with laws of their own making. This merchant law was not the product of legislation, but developed by a kind of amateur jurisprudence from decisions based on the customary procedure of merchants from all parts of Christendom. Until the rising power of central government in the Later Middle Ages introduced national economic policy and regulation, medieval commerce was completely international in character. It was as universal in its customs as were the Church, the manorial system, and the institutions of feudalism.

If the sphere of itinerant commerce was supra-national, that of retail commerce and industry was much less than national. It was confined within the city walls. National government was no more concerned with the economic activity of the urban worker or shopkeeper than it was with the wandering merchant. Each town formed a more or less autonomous economic unit, subject only to the jurisdiction of its immediate lord. The rise of urban self-government is a complicated story, which will be touched upon later. Enough for the present that by the twelfth century most towns had succeeded in winning the right to regulate and control their own economic life. Here, as in the case of itinerant commerce, similar institutions arose everywhere to meet the need for security. The medieval town was a tiny citadel of protection for men whose way of life was alien to the feudal world about them. Only through a close corporate union could the non-noble townsmen gain the collective strength that was their sole guarantee of some measure of security. But that mutual dependence implied much self-imposed discipline and the rigid regulation of individual action in the interest of the common weal. The right to buy, sell, or ply a trade within the city was a privilege which must be paid for by service to the community. The medieval burgher would have regarded the doctrine of *laissez faire*, if it had ever occurred to him, as not merely immoral, but positively suicidal. The ideal inspiring the economic legislation of the medieval towns was to protect the interest of both buyer and seller, since both were members of the community, to guarantee to each citizen the opportunity to make a living commensurate with his social status, to maintain for all the citizens an adequate supply of food and other necessities at a reasonable price, and, finally, to preserve for the town's own citizens a monopoly of the town's trade or at least a privileged position in their dealings with foreigners from without. Between the ideal and the reality, no doubt, fell a number of shadows, but in an effort to achieve the ideal each town undertook, not only to prevent fraud, profiteering, and unfair competition, but also to regulate prices, the quality of goods, conditions of sale, methods of manufacture, wages, hours of labor, and volume of output.

This regulation of urban economy was in the last analysis the responsibility of the city government. In many places, however, guilds supplied much of the administrative machinery by which it was put into effect. In some places a voluntary association of all who bought or sold in the town, merchant and artisan alike, preceded the acquisition of some form of town government and, indeed, might be a preliminary step in that direction. But, as the towns grew in size, such merchant guilds tended to become exclusively mercantile, while the individual crafts formed smaller and more specialized organizations. Craft guilds were by no means universal, though the regulation of commerce and industry was. They were, however, sufficiently typical to have won notice in even the most elementary textbooks. Their form of organization, with its tripartite division into classes of apprentices, journeymen, and masters, is too well known to need full description here.

The craft guild was in essence a publicly regulated association of workers in a more or less specialized branch of industry or retail commerce. Whether it had its origins in free association or was imposed upon the workers by the city government, the guild operated under the supervision of the city's authorities. It had, then, a double purpose: on the one hand, to protect the interests of the members and, on the other, to protect the interest of the consuming public. For both purposes detailed regulation was essential. Regulation in the interest of the consumer might work to the disadvantage of the guildsmen, but they were compensated by reasonable prices and by a monopoly of their trade. Similarly, the internal regulation of the guild might work to the disadvantage of the most industrious or enterprising, but for this too they were compensated by the prevention of competition which might deprive the individual of his fair share in a limited market. For the guildsmen, as for the whole burgher community, security was more important than the opportunity for unlimited individual enterprise. The guild organization also served a number of other purposes, encompassing the whole life of its members. The system of apprenticeship offered supervised training for future masters and, at the same time, prevented the formation of a permanent class distinction between employers and workers. Until capitalism began to invade the guilds in the fourteenth and fifteenth centuries, apprentices, journeymen, and masters were of the same social class, for each master had passed through the preliminary stages and each apprentice had a reasonable expectation of becoming a master. As a fraternal society, the guild provided a framework for its members' religious and social life and offered them aid and comfort when they were stricken by illness, death, or disaster. Finally, it gave the guildsman a status in the community, more limited and hence more personal than that offered by mere citizenship. It made him a privileged person, whose rights were publicly recognized and would be defended by both the law and his fellow guildsmen.

Medieval economic theory grew out of the experience of the burghers. It was shaped by the conditions of urban life in a feudal society. But to the formulation of the theory, the Church and Christian doctrine added a strongly moral tone. Legislation designed to restrain individual greed was largely the work of lay authorities and was in full accord with burgher opinion. However, the regulation of commerce and industry would probably not have worked as well as it did if the burgher had not been assured that profiteering and usury, or taking advantage of his fellows in any other way, imperilled his immortal soul. The doctors of the Church, recruited for the most part from the landholding classes and conditioned by monastic ideals, generally took a dim view of commercial activity. In a society devoted to the pursuit of gain, and gain, moreover, computed in monetary terms, they saw greed and devotion to the things of this world in their most naked form. Profit, they felt, could be morally justified only in terms of wages; that is, it should not be more than was required to pay the merchant or artisan enough to furnish him with a decent living as compensation for his labor. Working from premises of Christian morality, the Church doctors thus arrived at the theory that there is a "just price" for every commodity, a theory which coincided closely enough with the burghers' recognition of price control as a social necessity. The idea that profit could be justified only so far as it was necessary to making a decent living also fitted well enough with the aspirations of craftsmen and shopkeepers, who had little opportunity or incentive to accumulate more profit than the needs of subsistence demanded.

Both the doctrines of the Church and the social attitudes underlying the economic legislation of the cities were in closer accord with the realities of local trade and industry than with the practice of the merchants engaged in distant commerce. It is among these latter that we find the first deviations from an economic system directed primarily toward subsistence, stability, security, and mutual aid. The actions of the travelling merchant, it is true, were limited in many ways by the demands of corporate responsibility. But he could not be closely controlled by city regulations when travelling abroad, and he had fewer scruples about taking advantage of foreigners than of fellow-citizens. For merchants handling goods from distant parts, the doctrine of the "just price" could have little meaning. They would, indeed, have been hard put to compute it. In distant trade, most notably in the Italian luxury trade with the Near East, both risks and profits were great. The merchant became an adventurer, who might easily be ruined or might make profits far in excess of the needs of subsistence. With growing opportunities for the accumulation and reinvestment of profits, business enterprise became larger and more varied. Before the end of the High Middle Ages, partnerships and other forms of commercial association, moneylending, various systems of credit, and all the techniques of a nascent capitalism had made their appearance in Italy and along the main routes of inter-regional commerce. The Church might still brand the lending of money at interest as usury, but as merchants found it to their advantage to borrow money at interest for investment in profitable enterprise, moneylending lost much of the moral stigma that had attached to it in a society where such opportunities were few and where money was most often borrowed as a result of some personal disaster or for unproductive purposes. No survey of the economy of the High Middle Ages would be accurate without mention of these evidences of early capitalism, but it would be equally misleading to represent them as typical of medieval business. Just as, in this period, the money economy introduced by the towns stimulated rural economy but had not as yet materially altered the feudal system of landholding, so the early forms of capitalism developed in distant commerce served to stimulate local industry and trade, but still left the conservative spirit and the regulated economic life of the towns largely undisturbed.

II

Political Organization

The political life of the High Middle Ages was still shaped in all its major outlines by that somewhat chaotic system known as feudalism. But it was no longer the undiluted and untrammeled feudalism of the earlier period. The feudal system had taken shape during the ninth and tenth centuries as a *modus vivendi* under the compulsion of the twin necessities imposed by an exclusively agrarian economy and the collapse of central government. By the middle of the eleventh century, however, the reintroduction of money economy and the gradual reassumption of authority by central government in Church and state were beginning to impose restrictions and some degree of stability upon the feudal chaos. But, if the ruling class in feudal society had outlived its first fine careless rapture, what was lost in uninhibited action was compensated for by the crystallization of rights and privileges through the sanction of long-continued custom. The monarchy, the Church, and the cities — the three institutions of non-feudal origin — were forced as yet to accommodate themselves more or less to the feudal system. And the inner decay, which before the end of the thirteenth century had fatally, if imperceptibly, weakened the structure of feudalism, was for the time being hidden by the efflorescence of feudal culture.

The Medieval Background

A. THE FEUDAL STATE AND THE MONARCHY

The roots of political feudalism, like those of the manorial system, may be traced far back into the pre-feudal period. The concept of an institutional state was foreign to early Germanic thought. The government of the Frankish kings was essentially personal. They made no distinction between their public and private property, rights, or functions. The counts, who were the officers of local government, though appointed by the king and responsible to him, governed their territories in the same personal way in which the king governed the kingdom. Central government was assured, therefore, only so long as the king could maintain his personal control over his officers. The giants of the Carolingian house succeeded in checking the tendency of the counts to regard their office as a personal and hereditary right, but they did so only with the greatest difficulty. Anything that served to weaken further the authority of the king would make central government almost impossible.

The most serious menace to royal authority was the centrifugal force inherent in the exclusively agricultural economy to which Western Europe had been reduced by the eighth century. With the practical disappearance of money from circulation, the king was forced to pay his administrative officials with grants of land which constituted the only remaining form of wealth. Land thus granted was not given in outright ownership, but in temporary tenure. Such tenure, however, tended to become hereditary under any but a powerful and vigilant ruler, and where that happened the office also became hereditary and so escaped, more or less, from royal control. When to the constant strain imposed by the lack of financial resources was added during the ninth century the shock of civil war among the descendants of Louis the Pious and the destructive raids of Northmen, Magyars and Saracens, the central government of the Frankish state ceased to function. The only possible solution to the problem of maintaining some kind of order and security under such circumstances was to permit each landholder to exercise the functions of government in his own land. Whether by a theoretical grant of powers from the monarchy or by a *de facto* seizure of power on the part of the landed proprietors, the duties and privileges of government thus fell into private hands and became identified with the tenure of land. All that the king saved from the wreckage of the state was the concept of monarchy and the oath of loyalty from those great lords who held land directly from him. Nor did the decentralization of government and the identification of sovereignty with land tenure end with those lords who were titular officials of the crown or held land directly from the king. In order to maintain their power, the great landholders needed fighting men and, like the king, they could pay for military service only by granting land. The land thus granted became a fief, which time and custom would eventually make hereditary. The fief might be large enough to support more than one knight. In that case the holder of the fief would re-grant parts of it to knights who became his men and were pledged to follow him to battle, thus making up the force required from their lord's fief. In this period the mounted and heavily armed knights were the only effective military force. But such expensively equipped warriors needed an estate with its dependent workers to support them and give them the leisure to devote their time entirely to fighting, and, like the greater lords, they exercised jurisdiction over the dependent workers on their land.

While the decentralization of government was thus working downward through the ranks of the military class to form a succession of descending lordships, the general state of insecurity was working from the bottom of society to force each individual to find for himself a place in a system in which protection could be secured only at the price of subjection and service. Every feudal relation worked two ways. It involved a *quid pro quo:* subjection and service for protection and land. In short, the need to find a security which the king could no longer guarantee forced all those who were not already dependent to seek protection from some large landholder. Driven by sheer necessity, each man made the best bargain he could, but generally with the result that he became the man of some lord, and his land, if he had any, became the lord's land. In return for his services, he received from the lord enough land to maintain him. For the vast majority, the services to be rendered were manual — the working of the lord's demesne — and the amount of land received was the bare minimum required for subsistence. These found a more or less servile niche within the manorial system described in the preceding chapter. For those whose services were military, the land received formed an estate large enough to support them in leisure. These happy few became members of the military aristocracy and, by virtue of their tenure of land with dependent workers, were themselves lords. It is with this minority of landholders who owed military service that the system of political feudalism is chiefly concerned.

The feudal system was a spontaneous, unplanned development, created by voluntary agreements or by coercion, the product of innumerable personal bargains. The contracts which bound man to lord and formed the framework of feudal society were characterized, accordingly, by an infinite variety of detail. But everywhere they were the product of similar conditions and similar needs, so that certain essential features were common to all. Economic necessity — the lack of any other form of wealth

17

— made tenure of land the indispensable material factor in the feudal contract. From top to bottom of the feudal scale, each member of the military aristocracy held land as a "fief" from the king or some intermediate lord. By the fact of accepting or inheriting a fief he became the "vassal" of his lord. As a vassal, he owed loyalty and military service, as well as various forms of aid in times of stress. In return he was promised protection and justice. The lord, meanwhile, gained the military force which enabled him to maintain his own status and to protect his vassals and dependents and, in general, to perform the functions of government which the state had been forced to relinquish.

It is not necessary here to describe the terms of the normal feudal contract. They are familiar enough. What is important for our purpose is a consideration of the general structure of political feudalism and of the forces that brought it into being, for only by an understanding of these can we assess the factors that later led to its disintegration and to the transition from feudalism to the modern state. Enough for the present, then, that under the combined effect of an exclusively agrarian economy, the failure of central government, and a shocking state of insecurity, there emerged a system in which ownership of land was replaced by hereditary tenure, in which the direct relation of the individual to the state was replaced by a complex of personal relations determined by land tenure, and in which the functions of government were transferred from the state to landholding lords. In this system, the fief was the nexus of both political and economic relations, and the feudal contract between vassal and lord — a contract symbolized by the dual ceremony of homage and investiture — was the sole instrument by means of which society could continue to function.

Had the theory and practice of feudalism come approximately close to coinciding, society might have functioned well enough under the feudal system. As rationalized by late feudal lawyers, feudal society formed a pyramidal hierarchy, bound together by a series of mutual obligations. From the king at the apex of the pyramid a chain of authority passed downward through a series of lords, each of whom had sovereign authority over his vassals, until it reached the knight who had too little land to enfeoff any part of it to a vassal, but who was at least the lord of a manor with jurisdiction over the peasants who inhabited it. In actual fact, however, the system of sub-infeudation never bore any recognizable relation to the symmetrical picture presented by feudal theory. It had grown up, in the first instance, as the result of a vast number of individual bargains which conformed to no preconceived plan. Moreover, with each passing generation, fiefs were divided or expanded by the accidents of inheritance. Every feudal marriage, too, implied the transfer of some land as dowry from the bride's family to her husband. Fiefs might thus come to comprise land held from several lords, including lords of inferior status in the feudal hierarchy. A vassal, under such circumstances, could not do full military service, much less accord complete obedience, to all his lords. But even the service and obedience a vassal owed to his primary lord — his *liege* lord as the French termed it — could not always be enforced. It would be unjust to the feudal nobles to assert that the oath of fealty, which bound them to serve and obey their lords, had no meaning for them. Yet, all too often, they fulfilled their obligations as vassals only when and in so far as their lord's power and their own interests forced them to do so. The principle that "every baron is sovereign in his own barony" which, though not formulated in so many words till rather late was implicit in the system from the beginning, bred in the feudal lord an arrogant sense of his own independent power and made him constitutionally loath to submit to any authority. In the chain of command extending from the king down through the ranks of sub-infeudation, every link had a potential flaw on which any untoward circumstance might impose too great a strain. The weakness of the early feudal state was in fact more real than apparent. Hereditary tenure tended to make each vassal regard his fief as his own property rather than as compensation for services rendered, and the fact that it could not be readily taken from him made it difficult to force him to fulfill his obligations. Finally, among the most cherished rights of the feudal lord was the right to declare war on his neighbors. Private warfare was, in fact, one of the principal causes of the insecurity and violence that cursed the early period of feudalism and made the feudal state a kind of organized anarchy. Such wars, though small in scale, were in the aggregate immensely destructive. They might be caused by disputes arising from the feudal contract, by conflicting claims to land, by sheer greed, by blood feuds, or by simple bad temper. Whatever the cause, they constituted something like the normal condition of early feudal society.

That any reasonable degree of order should have emerged from this chaotic system is perhaps more remarkable than that its early phases were so violent. A good deal of credit for the gradual evolution of feudal society toward a more peaceful condition must be accorded to the Christian religion, dimly comprehended though it was by half-civilized warriors whose piety could do no more than make them pious barbarians. The clergy labored with some success during the eleventh century to impose various limitations — Peace of God or Truce of God — upon feudal warfare. At the same time, a growing prosperity had the effect of softening manners and of placing a higher value upon peace and security.

Even before the monarchy began to recover sufficient authority to impose order on the feudal state, there were signs, though faint, that a more stable condition was evolving within feudal society itself.

The circumstances that made feudalism necessary lasted throughout the ninth and tenth centuries and were still largely present in the eleventh. During the course of the latter century, however, the revival of commerce and city life began to free society from the limitations of a purely agrarian economy and was in process of reintroducing the money economy that would make central government possible. But feudalism could not be replaced as soon as, or in proportion as, it ceased to be indispensable. The sovereign authority of the lords and the hereditary relations centering about the fiefs had by then been sanctioned by immemorial custom. Yet it was a system that could be justified only by necessity. The rapacity, the continuous private wars, and the irresponsible egoism of the feudal nobles had been compensated in the beginning by the protection which they alone could provide. In proportion as they lost that excuse for their existence they became simply public nuisances, endowed with a vested interest in social chaos. In the High Middle Ages, the dynamic currents of economic, social, and political development were already setting against them. It is the distinguishing characteristic of the period from about the middle of the eleventh century to the end of the thirteenth that the structure of political feudalism still stood apparently unshaken upon its foundation of custom and vested interest, while the new or resurgent forces of monarchy and money were actually draining it of substantial content.

In its purely political aspects, feudalism had but one serious rival: the monarchy. During the early feudal period, the monarchy had for all practical purposes abdicated its sovereign rights in favor of the feudal nobles. The king had ceased to be a sovereign and had become a suzerain, a lord of lords, the titular apex of the feudal pyramid. Yet, despite the abdication of actual powers, the monarchy retained a large part of its theoretical claims, simply because these were not challenged by feudal theory. The concept of monarchy was not a feudal concept, and so it maintained a shadowy existence outside the structure of the feudal régime. Powers abandoned by the king in practice had never been formally surrendered, although they might have been more or less legally delegated. A feudal suzerain in fact, in theory the king remained the king. The monarchy may have survived chiefly because the king's position as the ultimate lord was necessary to complete the feudal hierarchy, but survive it did. And with it survived, if only in a dormant state, the principle of royal authority.

The methods employed by the monarchy to recover some of its lost authority varied from country to country and were successful in markedly different degree. In France, the feudal state *par excellence*, the kings of the Capetian House were still at the beginning of the twelfth century mere feudal suzerains, whose effective power was limited to the royal domain. This area, the Île de France, which surrounded the city of Paris, the king ruled as any feudal lord ruled his fief. It had been, in fact, the fief of the ancestors of the Capetian kings. The rest of France was divided into fiefs, some larger than the royal domain, held by vassals-in-chief who could seldom be forced to obedience. To make matters worse, the Duchy of Normandy and later a whole collection of fiefs, extending down the western coast to the Pyrenees, were held by English kings of the Norman and Angevin dynasties. But if the king's power was limited in practice to a rather vague feudal over-lordship, his material weakness was balanced by the imponderable moral authority and prestige attached to the royal title. As king, he was always something more than a feudal lord and, most important of all, his authority was strengthened by a religious sanction such as no mere feudal lord possessed. He was consecrated at his coronation, as was Saul by the prophet Samuel. He was "the Lord's anointed." It was by virtue of this moral authority that Louis VI, that great-bodied "justicier de fer vêtu," acted as the champion of justice and defender of the oppressed. As the twelfth century progressed, townsmen and clergy, in short all those elements in society that were opposed to the lawless violence of the feudal lords, were drawn to support the monarchy. Meanwhile, by a consistent policy of expanding the royal domain at every opportunity and using the growing financial resources made possible by money economy to supplement the feudal levy with mercenary troops, the French kings from Louis VI to Louis IX were gradually adding to moral authority the effective weight of material force. Louis IX, the saintly king who died on the last Crusade in 1270, still operated within the feudal system, but the monarchy had travelled a long way since the days of the early Capetians. At the end of the thirteenth century the stage was set in France for the transition from the feudal to the centralized national state.

In England, the fact of the Norman conquest created a situation in many ways unique. William the Conqueror introduced a feudal system modelled on that of France, but the very fact of its having been introduced by a conquering king made it essentially different from its continental prototype. Norman feudalism in England was a planned creation, not a spontaneous development. The fiefs held by William's Norman followers were actually granted them by the king, and never in large contiguous blocks of territory. England had no great territorial fiefs comparable to Normandy, Anjou, Aquitaine, or Burgundy. At the same time, William retained the old Saxon shire organization with the sheriffs acting as royal officers, and through it a system of royal taxation. Finally, he was able to establish the extra-feudal principle that all members of the military class, whether vassals-in-chief or not, owed their first loyalty to the crown. Building upon that foundation, his successors were able, before the end of the twelfth century, to make the king's law the common law of the land and to establish firmly-organized institutions of royal government. When the barons rebelled against the king in the following century their aim was not to secure independence of royal control, as it would have been under similar circumstances in either France or Germany. The Great Charter, wrung by rebellious barons from King John, bound the king only to obey the laws and to respect the rights of his vassals as both had been established in the days of his powerful father, Henry II. And when barons and commons made common cause against Henry III, under the leadership of Simon de Montfort, their aim was to gain control of royal government in order to save it from abuse by a weak and foolish king.

The development of feudalism and the monarchy in Germany followed from the beginning a course very different from either the French or the English types. Formed out of the East Frankish Kingdom, much of which had been acquired as recently as the reign of Charlemagne, Germany retained more of the primitive forms of Germanic local government than was true of the more Romanized western kingdom. Personal freedom and free or "allodial" tenure of land lasted here much longer. Indeed, the feudalism which emerged from the anarchy of the ninth century in the older parts of the Frankish state left Saxony and the eastern marches almost untouched. There were dangers to central government in the existence of a free aristocracy, but the slower development of feudalism was nevertheless in all probability one of the reasons why the German kings of the tenth and eleventh centuries were able to establish a stronger royal government than could their French contemporaries. In this period the counties in Germany were still centers of royal administration and the counts functioned, more or less, as royal agents. From the time of Otto the Great, moreover, till the middle of the eleventh century, the German monarchs maintained complete control of the Church in Germany, nominated the bishops and abbots, endowed them with extensive lands, and used them as administrative officers of the central government. But the German monarchy was not left free to work out its destiny along these promising lines. The revival of the Roman Empire in its medieval form by Otto the Great in 962 bound the history of Germany to that of Italy and the papacy. It was that close connection that made impossible any peaceful settlement of the conflict between the imperial policy in relation to the German Church and the reform program of Gregory VII. The Investiture Controversy gave the German nobles the opportunity to shake off the centralizing authority of the monarchy, and they seized it eagerly. In the half-century of civil war after 1075, the system of royal government in Germany broke down completely. In place of the old counties a new system of local government grew up around the castles of practically independent nobles, who reduced the surrounding population to feudal subjection. So far as Germany was concerned, the real victors in the Investiture Controversy were the great German nobles, the "princes" as they were generally called thereafter. German society was now completely feudalized. From the political and social revolution of these years the German monarchy never recovered. When Frederick Barbarossa (1152–90) reasserted royal authority it was as a feudal monarch, ruling by feudal means. Even so, his position did not compare unfavorably with that of Louis VII, his contemporary in France. There was still hope for the growth of German monarchy had not the imperial entanglement with Italy and the papacy once more intervened, this time with permanently disastrous results. The union of the Kingdom of Sicily with the Empire under Henry VI in 1190 committed his successors to an Italian, anti-papal policy which, after another half-century of conflict, ended in the destruction of the Hohenstaufen dynasty and the permanent weakening of imperial government. Once more, the real victors were the German princes. Thenceforward the forces that worked for the disintegration of feudalism worked, in Germany, to the advantage of the territorial principalities rather than the imperial government.

For the history of Italy, too, the revival of the Empire was an event of decisive importance. Equally decisive, however, was the fact that in the center of Italy the pope ruled a secular state stretching across the peninsula from coast to coast, while the South formed a separate kingdom under Norman conquerors. These three facts together made the rise of a feudal monarchy of national scope impossible. Imperial authority had never been firmly established in Italy, and the emperors of the first half of the eleventh century, who did so much to strengthen central government in Germany, did little or nothing to improve administration in their southern kingdom. Such imperial administration as existed in Italy was, in fact, left almost entirely in the hands of the bishops. This policy had the effect of making the episcopal cities the centers of governmental authority, thus drawing the feudal nobility into the sphere of urban organization, while at the same time it forced the emperors to maintain control of the bishops as their sole effective agents. But this was the period when in the northern Italian cities, under the impulse of the com-

mercial revival, the communes were struggling to wrest from their episcopal rulers greater freedom and rights of self-government. When
Gregory VII and his reforming successors strove to break the emperor's
control of the bishops, they therefore found vigorous allies in the communes which were always ready to rebel against the bishops in the
interest of their own freedom. The civil wars of the Investiture Controversy gave the Italian communes an opportunity comparable to that
seized by the princes in Germany. In Italy they were the real victors.
Even the vigorous imperialism of Frederick Barbarossa could not restore
the lost authority over the rich cities of Lombardy and Tuscany. When,
in the following century, imperial government in Italy was destroyed
with the fall of the Hohenstaufen dynasty, these cities became independent city-states, ruling the land around them. Feudalism died out earlier
and more completely in northern and central Italy than it did anywhere
north of the Alps, but it perished as a result of the growing power of
the communes rather than of the central government.

B. The Church and the Feudal States

Like the monarchy, the medieval Church was an institution with traditions of centralized government centuries older than the feudal system.
But it, too, was forced to accommodate itself more or less to the *mores*
and forms of organization of a feudal society.

The internal government of the Church had been formed within the
framework of the Roman Empire. From early times bishops had exercised authority over the Christian community in each Roman *municipium*,
and by the third century a further development of the hierarchy took
place when the bishops of each Roman province formed the habit of
meeting in a provincial synod, presided over by the bishop of the capital
city — the metropolitan bishop or archbishop. Finally, during the troubled years of the fifth century the hierarchical evolution of Church government was completed by the universal recognition of the Bishop of
Rome — in common parlance the pope — as head of the Latin Church.
Thanks to the tradition which ascribed the foundation of the Church
of Rome to St. Peter, the Roman bishops could claim as his successors
the authority of Vicars of Christ. They profited, too, by the prestige of
the capital city of the Roman state, the city to which for centuries men
had looked for government. Finally, the activity and character of a long
line of able and devoted popes from Leo the Great to Gregory the Great
had established the "papal monarchy" on a firm basis in the days before continued economic decline and the beginnings of feudalism made

the exercise of practical authority over a large area extremely difficult.

The period following the break up of the Roman Empire in the West witnessed a great extension of the activity of the Church's officers into the field of secular government. After the disappearance of the imperial administration, the bishops were for practical purposes the only officers remaining in the cities to whom the people could turn for aid and government, for the Germanic counts in general remained in the country and left the cities pretty much to themselves. This *de facto* authority was later given royal sanction and a semi-legal status by the Frankish rulers, who used the bishops as unpaid administrators and found in them a useful counterweight to check the threatening independence of the counts. In these centuries, too, the Church was gradually acquiring vast quantities of land through the accumulation of pious gifts. The Church had begun to grow wealthy as soon as it was freed from persecution; but, as Western Europe drifted further and further toward a purely agrarian economy, this wealth came to consist increasingly of land. By the dawn of the feudal era, the Church was by far the largest landholder in Europe, and the bishops and abbots, as the local officers of the Church, were already great landed proprietors.

With the officers of the Church holding large quantities of land and accustomed to exercising governmental functions, it was inevitable that they should be drawn into the feudal system. When all land tenure became feudalized, Church lands could not escape the universal tendency. They assumed the character of fiefs, and the bishops and abbots who held them as officers of the Church became vassals, usually of the monarch though sometimes of a lesser feudal lord. As vassals, bishops and abbots owed fealty, military service, aid and counsel, and all the other obligations customarily embodied in the feudal contract. The only significant differences between the status of an ecclesiastical and that of a lay vassal were that the former could not be required to do military service in person and that he held his fief by virtue of his office rather than by hereditary tenure. At the same time, the possession of a fief made the bishops and abbots feudal lords with vassals of their own and with sovereign powers over the peasants living on their estates.

In their capacity as great lords and vassals, the officers of the Church were inevitably burdened with a multitude of worldly cares. What was worse, from the point of view of a centralized Church government, the emperors and kings could scarcely resist the temptation to interfere in ecclesiastical elections and help to choose the only vassals they had who did not hold their fiefs by hereditary right. In the Empire, particularly, Otto the Great and his successors had adopted the policy of conferring large fiefs upon their ecclesiastical vassals simply because they could choose them and hence be better able to depend upon their loyalty. Bishops and abbots, selected primarily with a view to their suitability as vassals, might well be men of stainless character and possessed of the highest spiritual qualifications, but the odds were against it. So long as these shepherds of the flock were forced to divide their services somewhat unequally between God and Mammon, the hungry sheep would continue to look up and not be fed. In any case, the higher officers of the Church were almost invariably recruited from the upper ranks of the feudal nobility, and shared many of the attitudes and points of view of their class. Accustomed to thinking of all social and political problems in feudal terms — and in this period feudalism had become a kind of Kantian category of the mind — ecclesiastical vassals were likely to regard their obligations to their immediate feudal lord as more binding than their duty of obedience to a distant central Church government. There were in this situation obvious dangers both to the spiritual character of the Church and to the authority of its papal head.

Despite this obvious clash of interests, there was little real conflict between the papacy and the monarchies during the early feudal period. Both the Church and the feudal states were too decentralized to bring the conflict of authority into sharp relief. Effective central government of the Church, like that of the state, was rendered almost impossible by lack of mobile financial resources and by the extreme difficulty of communications. By the middle of the eleventh century, however, the beginnings of the commercial revival, together with the restoration of greater security in feudal society, had made the reassertion of papal authority throughout the Church more nearly possible. At the same time, the wave of agitation for reform that spread from the monasteries of the Congregation of Cluny gave to papal policy a new, vigorous motivation and widespread popular support. The reform of the papacy itself owed much to the emperor, Henry III who, like Otto the Great, used his imperial authority to secure the election of a series of reforming popes. But, though Henry's action had greatly strengthened the papacy, it had certain sinister connotations. It was, in fact, an extension of the imperial control of ecclesiastical affairs, long established in Germany, to the central government of the Church. This threat to papal independence was met during the minority of Henry IV by the Election Decree of Nicholas II (1059), which secured the free election of the pope by the cardinals. The next step in the reform program was to re-establish free, canonical elections throughout the Church and so emancipate the bishops and abbots from control by secular princes. It was the conviction of the reform party that this step was an essential prerequisite not only to the restoration of the purely spiritual character of the clergy, but also to the reassertion of papal authority over the officers of the Church by means of which alone practical reform could be put into effect. Such a program could not be carried out, however, without seriously weakening the government of every feudal monarch, but most especially that of the emperor who, more than any other ruler, depended on the support of his ecclesiastical vassals. This fact, together with the continuous threat of imperial domination over the papacy itself, goes far to account for the peculiar bitterness with which the Investiture Controversy was fought out in Germany and Italy. Elsewhere, a compromise solution was reached without open conflict.

The medieval popes were never more than half successful in their struggle to free the officers of the Church from secular control, though they wrecked the Holy Roman Empire in the attempt. They were more successful in asserting the principle of papal sovereignty within the Church and in tightening up administrative control over the bishops and the monasteries. The greatest triumph of the medieval papacy, however, was the unprecedented degree to which, building upon the doctrines of papal supremacy enunciated by Gregory VII, the popes were able to exercise a practical authority over secular rulers and lay society in general. Under Innocent III, the papacy was without question the greatest political power in Western Europe. And the Church had become, for all practical purposes, a universal state, superimposed upon all secular states. It had an administrative hierarchy and a fiscal system, both more highly centralized than those of any feudal kingdom. It had its own courts and its own laws, with exclusive jurisdiction over the clergy as well as extensive jurisdiction over laymen in a variety of cases which in modern times would be regarded as entirely the concern of the state. Its officers, on the other hand, the whole body of the clergy, claimed immunity from the jurisdiction of all secular courts whatever. Finally, to round out the picture of a universal state, the Church had its own language, the Latin of liturgy, law, and learning; and it directed and controlled all institutions of higher education.

Though it seems a paradox, the Church of the High Middle Ages owed its vast political authority in part to the feudal system. The universal character of the Church was, in a sense, the complementary opposite to the local particularism which was the essence of feudalism. Between these two principles there could be no real conflict. The personal and local loyalties of the feudal regime did not conflict with the larger loyalty to a universal Church. The interests of both the feudal nobility and the papal monarchy were opposed to those of centralized national governments, a fact demonstrated by the incongruous alliance of the German princes — all of them "great despoilers of churches" — with the papacy in the Investiture Controversy. In the early days of feudalism, it is true, the general tendency toward decentralization had weakened even the Church government, but from this stage the Church recovered more rapidly than did the secular states. From the time of Gregory VII, however deleterious the involvement of the Church in the feudal system might be to the spiritual character and religious functions of its officers, the Church continued to grow in power so long as it was opposed only by states which, like the Holy Roman Empire, were weakened by feudalism. It would meet more effective opposition when central government began to triumph over feudal decentralization in the great national states.

C. Urban Government: the Cities and the Feudal States

The medieval cities, unlike the monarchy and the Church, were a new phenomenon. But, like these, they were essentially extra-feudal institutions, though forced by the fact of their existence in the midst of a feudal society to accommodate themselves to the feudal system. One characteristic, indeed, they shared with feudalism: they arose spontaneously as the result of economic, social, and political necessity. The revival of commerce and industry brought into being a new class of merchants and artisans, whose way of life was alien to that of the agricultural and landholding classes which made up feudal society. It was this new class which formed the cities and won for itself by corporate action an established status in a society that had no place for its individual members.

The exact process by which cities came into existence, as well as the juridical origin of urban institutions, has been the subject of much scholarly debate. Since cities were formed by independent action under a variety of local circumstances, the whole movement of urban development could scarcely have been a uniform process. Everywhere, however, the needs of the city dwellers were much the same, and the resultant institutions were fundamentally similar. If we except the later *villes neuves* founded outright by kings or feudal lords, it seems likely that most cities were formed in the first instance by the congregation of merchants about any focal center of protection — cathedral, monastery, or feudal castle — that was conveniently located in relation to the routes of trade. Many of them grew up on the site of old Roman cities, a fact accounted for by the survival of these cities as centers of episcopal administration, even after they had lost the commercial and industrial economy essential to any truly urban community. They were for the most part situated on natural trade routes, and the bishops offered to those who sought their protection the double security afforded by their status as both Church officials and feudal lords. Begun as a little community of merchants, whose houses were huddled about the castle or cathedral close, the infant city acquired a more distinct existence when its growth demanded the building of a new encircling wall. There was thus formed a new "burg," whence its inhabitants came to be known as burghers or *bourgeois*.

At first the merchants, together with the skilled artisans who soon came to swell their ranks, lived of necessity under the jurisdiction of the feudal lord whose protection they sought. But feudal custom, designed to meet the needs of an agricultural economy, made no provision for men who lived by commerce and industry, just as the hierarchical organization of feudal society had no place for men who were neither serfs nor vassals, and whose status was not determined by tenure of land with its accompanying services, either manual or military. The merchants' way of life made freedom an absolute necessity, not only the personal freedom which most merchants probably had to start with, but also freedom from seigneurial claims upon their services or profits. More positively, the burghers needed laws suitable to commerce, industry, and an urban society, and a degree of security which, in the feudal world, could be acquired only by attaining an established status with recognized rights and privileges and the force to defend them. These necessary conditions could never have been created by the burghers acting as individuals. Nor could they look to the state to do it for them, for the feudal monarchy cared for none of these things. The only hope of security for the individual burgher lay in association with his fellows. Collective strength alone could compensate for individual weakness.

The need for collective security led to innumerable forms of association — religious confraternities, merchant guilds, and so forth — but for the burgher group as a whole the most essential form of association was the commune. This was in origin a sworn association of all the burghers of a city, bound by oath to mutual support and defense. As a corporate entity, it treated with the lord under whose jurisdiction the city had grown up and acquired, by agreement, purchase, armed rebellion, or simple seizure, the right to organize the city government and to make and administer its laws and regulations. It was as a corporation, too, that the commune paid to the lord such fiscal dues as were necessary. The personal relation between the individual burgher and the lord under whose jurisdiction he lived was thus broken. At the same time the burgher acquired free ownership of his house and land in place of the hereditary tenure which had left the lord a vested interest in it. The burgher of an established commune was a free man, and he owned his property in freehold, to be willed, sold, or mortgaged at his discretion. Henceforth his economic, social, and political life would all function within the framework of the commune. And the place in the feudal hierarchy, which the burgher could not have acquired for himself, was taken by the commune as a collective personality. Once well established as communal corporations, as they were almost everywhere by the twelfth century, the cities acted as collective vassals and even as collective lords. Paradoxical as it may seem, then, the more completely the commune was enfranchised, the more closely it fitted into the feudal hierarchy.

While thus becoming a feudal entity in its relations with the world outside the walls, the city in its internal organization assumed the character of a more or less autonomous republic. The degree to which the self-government of the cities was free from interference on the part of their lords varied greatly. But, even where the lord retained some voice in the conduct of its affairs or the choice of its officers, the city was governed by a council and executive officers chosen from among the burghers. As an administrative body with delegated powers, the city council directed the daily life of the city's inhabitants, watched over their interests, and issued statutes which formed a distinct body of municipal law. One of the important functions of the council was the collection of taxes to pay whatever tribute the city owed its lord, to maintain the walls and other public works, and to keep up the city's military defenses. These taxes were collected from all the burghers and, so far as possible, in proportion to their ability to pay. The system of taxation and administration of public funds worked out by the city government was a new creation, the first rational fiscal system known to the feudal age. Growing out of the conditions of urban life, it was a remarkably skillful adaptation of means to ends, as was also the city government's regulation of food supply, commerce and industry.

Beside the council, from which emerged the body of administrative law necessary to maintain the regulation of urban life, the city also possessed courts or tribunals with jurisdiction over civil and criminal cases. These courts were composed of burghers; and the law they enforced was exclusively the city's law. It applied to all inhabitants of the city, but it operated only within the city walls. Born of the experience and needs of city life, it was an original creation, without precedent in the feudal world. Urban criminal law was exceptionally harsh and the punishments brutal, for crime throve in the crowded quarters of the city and the burghers had property to protect; but convictions were based on evidence and a rational procedure rather than on the ancient customs of ordeal and compurgation. Urban civil law was equally original in content and procedure. In each city it formed a carefully worked out body of jurisprudence designed to meet the needs of a trading society.

By virtue of its laws, its government, and the pledge of mutual aid which was the essence of the commune, the medieval city was at once a juridical and an administrative entity, a political, social, and economic unit. In short, it had in a minute but intense form all the fundamental characteristics of a state. The burghers, whose security and status depended entirely upon it, felt for their city a deeply rooted patriotism, which, like the national patriotism of a later day, had as its obverse side suspicion and hostility toward all outsiders. This exclusively local patriotism goes far to explain the varying policy of the cities in relation to the feudal state and the monarchy. In England and France, where the gradual strengthening of central government promised to mitigate the perils to trade represented by the lawlessness of the feudal nobility, the burghers were generally favorable to the monarchy. There, too, the kings reciprocated by protecting the towns and hastening their enfranchisement. Feudalism was the common enemy of both the towns and the monarchy, a fact that made these two essentially extra-feudal institutions natural allies. But, if the burghers threw their growing political weight into the scales on the side of royal authority it was simply because they hoped for greater security from a strong government. They were as innocent of national sentiment as were the feudal lords themselves; and they generally resented royal control when the central government grew strong enough to impose a national economic policy.

The purely local character of burgher patriotism was even more evident in Italy, where the cities played a decisive rôle in preventing the growth of a national state. There, the fact that the bishops, who governed the cities, were the emperor's agents of administration and were supported by him forced the cities to turn against the emperor in their struggle for self-government. The enthusiasm for reform of the Church which spread among the burghers of northern Italy enabled them to combine piety with patriotism in their revolt against the authority of simoniacal bishops. It also gained for them the moral support of the papacy in their struggle for freedom from imperial control. Taking advantage of the paralysis of imperial government during the Investiture Controversy, the northern Italian communes succeeded in achieving almost complete independence during the twelfth century, and became for all practical purposes city-states, ruling the land around them. The situation in Italy was unique in that the cities were themselves able to suppress or absorb the feudal nobility of the surrounding countryside.[1] They had, then, no need for the monarchy as an ally against feudal chaos.

In Germany, on the other hand, the cities were too small and the feudal nobility too numerous and too powerful for any such solution. The German cities might well have proved valuable allies of the central government, as indeed they were during the Investiture Controversy, had it remained strong enough to justify their support. With the practical collapse of the Empire in the thirteenth century, however, the imperial cities were forced to depend on themselves. Though they never succeeded in dominating the surrounding nobles and becoming city-states on the Italian model, those German cities which were directly under the emperor won for themselves a status as "free imperial cities" and a greater degree of autonomy than was enjoyed by any city in France or England.

[1] Otto of Freising, Frederick Barbarossa's uncle, wrote of Italy in his day: "almost the whole country pertains to the cities, each of which forces the inhabitants of its territory to submit to its sway, and there is hardly a man of rank or importance who does not recognize his city's authority. They surpass all other cities of the world in riches and power, and the long absence of the ruler across the Alps has contributed to their independence." Otto of Freising, *Gesta Friderici*, II, 13–15.

III

Social Organization and Social Life

"For as we have many members in one body, and all members have not the same office: so we, being many, are one body in Christ, and every one members one of another" (Romans, XII, 4–5). With these sage words of St. Paul to the Romans, coupled with the admonition in the preceding verse: "to every man that is among you, not to think of himself more highly than he ought to think," the doctors of the medieval Church sought to rationalize in accordance with Christian morality and to justify by divine sanction a caste-bound society. As so often in its social theory, the Church was here striving to inject an ennobling ideal into the grim realities of a social system which had been shaped by economic and political circumstance. Feudal society was in fact divided into three clearly distinguished classes, each with its peculiar function: the clergy who cared for the souls of men; the nobles who fought and governed; and the peasants whose sole duty was to work so that the whole body politic might be nourished. In a society that was at once Christian and agrarian and almost totally lacking in effective state government, only the cleric and the warrior had any conceivable function to perform other than tilling the soil. And they could play their necessary rôle only if they controlled enough land and subject workers to maintain them without themselves having to labor. The rise of the cities introduced into medieval society

33

a new class of merchants and artisans who were neither noble nor servile and whose membership in the social body was more difficult to rationalize. The burghers were essentially a non-feudal class, and they remained stubbornly outside the normal pattern of feudal society.

A. THE NOBLES

The existence of a noble class, separated from the common herd by a hereditary barrier, found justification in Church doctrine, in legal and political theory, and in the presuppositions nourished by contemporary literature and the cult of chivalry. These ideal factors, reinforced by social snobbery, enabled the nobles to retain a privileged position in society and the state long after they had ceased to perform any necessary function and, indeed, perpetuated far into modern times the odd conviction that noble blood was of a more azure tint than that of common men. In the Middle Ages, however, the theory of the noble class was in close accord with the actual state of society, and its privileges and powers rested upon a concrete foundation of fact.

The medieval noble was, first of all, a warrior; and warfare was in medieval opinion an honorable occupation, whereas manual labor was regarded as degrading. But there was more than popular opinion involved in the attribution of an aristocratic status to the knight. A change in military technique, which had begun in the eighth century when Charles Martel found it necessary to create a force that could meet the mounted Saracens on their own level and which developed further because of the virtual disappearance of the class of small freemen who would naturally have fought on foot, had left to the knights — the mounted, armored and heavily armed horsemen — a monopoly of the field of battle. Under the economic conditions of the feudal age, the tenure of a fief was necessary to support a knight, with all his appurtenances and attendants, and to give him the necessary leisure for training and the pursuit of his calling. From economic necessity, then, the military class was a landholding class. And the landholding class, after the collapse of central government, was *ipso facto* a governing class, since each landholder exercised jurisdiction over the tenants on his land. He was in a very real sense *dominus*, a lord, even though he himself held his land in fief from some higher lord whose vassal he was. The noble was noble because his wealth, his occupation, his way of life, and his jurisdictional powers raised him in the social scale far above the poverty-stricken, laboring, and half-servile peasant. All of these social attributes in the last analysis depended on his tenure of land in fief; and as feudal tenure of land became hereditary, the status of the noble also became in fact hereditary. The belief that nobility of birth was a prerequisite to noble function or status was thus, so long as this situation endured, in full accord with social reality.

The noble class had won its dominant position in the early age of feudalism — the ninth, tenth, and eleventh centuries — and retained it, despite the growing power of the monarchy in France and England, for two centuries longer. In Germany, indeed, the nobility established their status more firmly than ever during the twelfth and thirteenth centuries. Only in Italy, where they were drawn into the cities, were the nobles losing their feudal character and something of their unique place in society. It was in these two centuries that the noble class, everywhere north of the Alps, attained to the fullest development of a social life peculiarly and characteristically its own, while still in accord with practical reality. In the transitional period that followed, the ornamental aspects of noble society might become more elaborate, but they would no longer rest upon such a solid foundation of real power. We may concentrate attention, therefore, upon the twelfth and thirteenth centuries for the study of the medieval nobility at the most ideal stage of its development.

The economic revival, which swept across Europe following the reintroduction of commerce and city life, furnished the landholding classes with the means to elevate their standard of living. It is true that money economy held hidden dangers for the feudal nobility,[1] but its immediate effect was to enable them to turn part of their wealth into cash, with which they could acquire both the appurtenances of a more civilized existence and the improved castles, armor, and weapons that would enable them for a while longer to maintain their privileged status. The possession of a fortified stronghold and of body armor and equipment had been, from the beginning of the feudal age, the essential factor in enabling the nobles to maintain both their independence in relation to the monarchy and their dominant position in relation to their dependents. In the general poverty of the earlier centuries, however, castles and armor had been of a very crude sort. The great age of the stone castle began after the economic revival had made such elaborate structures practicable, and at the same time body armor attained the most perfect balance between skillful construction and practical usefulness.

It would be difficult to exaggerate the importance of the stone castle for the life of the medieval noble. Its walls, towers, and battlements dominated the countryside and symbolized the temporal power of the lord, much as the towering spires of the Gothic cathedral symbolized the spiritual authority of the Church. But its importance was less symbolical

---

[1] See above, p. 8, and below, pp. 133–141.

than practical. The castle was the means by which the noble protected — and frequently oppressed — his dependents. It was the focal center of feudal government. From it the lord exerted his authority over the surrounding country. In Germany, in particular, the castellany became in the twelfth century the normal area of jurisdiction, and noble families regularly took their names from the castles they held. The fact that a well-constructed castle was almost impossible to take by storm or by anything but a long and generally impracticable siege was also the chief reason why nobles were able to engage so lightheartedly in war with their fellow lords or to defy their king with relative impunity. At a time when little progress was made in weapons of offence, the defensive fortifications of the castles were immensely improved. In a baronial castle of the twelfth or thirteenth century, the original stone tower — the donjon or keep — was generally surrounded by one or two lines of walls reinforced by towers and enclosing courtyards, stables, servants' quarters, the lord's "palace" and a chapel. A moat filled with water or the skillful use of a hilltop site further strengthened the castle and attested to the engineering ability of the builders. The defenses of the gateway — drawbridge, portcullis, and flanking towers — are likewise evidence of an ingenuity and power of invention that could have been inspired only by urgent necessity.

When the nobles fought in the open field, their body armor gave them a fair degree of immunity from the fatal hazards of war. The armor characteristic of this period was the product of skilled industry and was admirably suited to the demands of practical warfare. It consisted of a steel helmet, usually conical in shape and with a nasal or visor to protect the face, and a hauberk of flexible mail reaching from neck to knees. These, together with mailed gauntlets and leg coverings, furnished adequate protection while still permitting full freedom of movement. The period had yet to come when the frantic race between armor and improved weapons of offence led to the use of plate-covering from head to foot and came close to immobilizing the knight therein encased.

Wherever we meet the medieval noble in the pages of contemporary chronicles or romance, we find him presented as a fighting man, perpetually concerned with the problems, techniques, and hazards of war. He was trained to the use of arms from his youth up. Fighting was his trade and when, for some reason, there was no war available, he fought in tournaments which were made to resemble real battle as closely as possible. But, by the twelfth century, the noble was no longer the complete barbarian, the ferocious and irresponsible bully, that he had been in the iron age of feudalism. The institution of chivalry had begun to place some restraint upon his warlike activity and to inject into his bellicose life some modicum of ennobling ideal. The term "chivalry," originally applied in the sense of our word "cavalry" to any body of armed horsemen, had by the High Middle Ages been restricted in its application to those nobly born warriors who had been accorded the honor of knighthood. Collectively, these formed the "order of chivalry." Though lacking the formal organization which was characteristic of the later national orders such as the Garter or the Golden Fleece, medieval chivalry possessed a body of customs and ideals which set the knight apart as a member of a distinct social order of international scope. At the same time, by extension, the term "chivalry" was frequently applied to those virtues, obligations, and ideals of conduct which were regarded as the exclusive property of the knightly class. It is in this latter sense that the term has survived in modern times.

Since the knight was first of all a feudal warrior, the primary virtues required of him were courage, loyalty, and a rigid sense of honor. The first two of these were the qualities naturally to be encouraged in a feudal vassal; the last, however, was rather the product of the class consciousness of the knights. The knight must do nothing to disgrace his order. He must keep his word, be ever ready to resent an insult, and show himself courteous and generous to those of his enemies who were fellow members of the order of chivalry. The ideal knight should at all times be lordly in his relations with his inferiors, open-handed, high of heart and nothing common do or mean. These virtues were, of course, balanced by complementary vices. The ideal knight might be described with equal aptness by an unfriendly critic as extravagant and vain, arrogant, quarrelsome, and cruel. These were the virtues and vices bred by his social position and by his habitual preoccupation with mayhem and homicide. They represent, however, only one aspect of the chivalrous ideal and, indeed, the virtues at least could scarcely have developed without the action of other factors which tended to make the knight something more than a feudal warrior.

The first of these extraneous influences was religion. The Church, indefatigable in its efforts to moderate the brutality of feudal society, labored mightily to make the knight, if not a man of peace, at least a Christian warrior. The institution of chivalry offered an opportunity to inculcate Christian virtues along with those that came more naturally to the medieval noble. Ecclesiastical writers of the twelfth century claimed for the Church a prominent place in the ceremony by which knighthood was conferred, and seized every opportunity to impress upon the knights their duty to defend the Church and its faith and to protect widows, orphans, the poor and the oppressed. The Crusades were the practical expression of this religious aspect of chivalry, which found its

37

most perfect embodiment in the union of chivalry with monasticism in the great crusading orders: the Templars, the Knights Hospitallers, and the Teutonic Knights.

While the Church thus sought to consecrate chivalry and to instill into the knight a sense of responsibility toward the faith and of mercy toward the weak, a very different force was working, with perhaps more notable success, to improve the manners of the knight and to give him an object in life other than fighting. It was the influence of the ladies that made courteous behavior the third essential attribute of the perfect gentle knight. In the period of growing prosperity that followed the commercial revival, the baronial donjon became a court and its inhabitants began to develop the manners of courtesy. Warfare, though still endemic, was no longer so nearly continuous. Knights had the leisure and means to cultivate a more refined social life. In a sense scarcely applicable in the early days of feudalism, the noble's castle was his home. And in this more spacious and leisured domestic scene, the noble lady began for the first time to assume an important place. Veneration for the Virgin Mary, the Church's admonition to protect the weak, and the conspicuous place accorded to courtly love in the romantic literature of the period all aided in the emancipation of the noble lady. Women were still far from being regarded as equals; but the knight's deeply rooted conviction of the inferiority of women was now balanced by an equally exaggerated reverence for the nobly born and reasonably attractive members of the sex. The emergence of women from the thralldom that had been their lot in an earlier age had a revolutionary effect on chivalrous society. Once they had been accorded a place of honor, the ladies began to work with invincible optimism upon their self-appointed task of making silk purses out of sows' ears. Under their tutelage the chivalrous barbarian gradually acquired the manners and some of the more inherent attributes of a gentleman.

That there was some divergence between the ideals of chivalry and the realities of feudal life is obvious and amply attested. Contrast between ideal and reality was, of course, common to all branches of medieval society — and to the society of other ages as well — but it seems particularly noticeable in the case of the chivalrous class. It might also be added that the elements out of which the ideal of chivalry was compounded were of a nature so essentially disparate that they could be held together only in a rather uneasy union. Medieval Christian morality, with its emphasis upon humility, pity, and chastity accorded ill with either the bellicose or the amorous aspects of the chivalrous life. The cult of courtly love itself, though it undoubtedly softened the manners of the knights, had a slightly unreal quality. It had no solid foundation in family life; for in feudal society marriage was primarily a matter of political expediency — the union of two fiefs. The love that inspired the knight to noble deeds was normally a publicly expressed devotion to another lord's wife, and was conventionally assumed to have no private consummation. Despite all that the Church and the ladies could do, the knight remained a fighting man, first and last. Perhaps the most that can be said for the relation of chivalry to social reality is that it was admirably suited to the technique of contemporary warfare. It provided a rigid system of training and developed just those qualities most needed in an age when hand-to-hand combat between armor-clad horsemen was the normal order of battle.

B. The Clergy

The clergy formed a distinct class in medieval society, as clearly distinguished by their function as were the nobility, and like the latter they enjoyed a privileged status. They were endowed with lands, tithes, and other income, and in consideration of the sacred character of their calling they were exempt from all secular jurisdiction. One of the most important privileges of their class was the right to be tried only in an ecclesiastical court and in accordance with canon law. In the comparison of the body politic with the human body, which haunted the minds of medieval political theorists, the clergy represented the soul and were therefore to be revered by those members of society who represented parts of the inferior physical body. The clergy were, ideally, subjects of the Church rather than of the state and owed obedience only to their superiors in the hierarchy. Ideally, too, the clergy were all of the same social class, their ranks distinguished by office, function, and degree of authority rather than by inherited social status. The son of a peasant or artisan might, and occasionally did, become a bishop, abbot, or even pope. Nicholas Breakspeare (Pope Adrian IV), the only English pope, was born of a humble burgher family. But here as elsewhere in medieval society the ideal and the actual were often widely separated. The possession of lands, wealth, and political power drew the officers of the Church into the feudal system as lords and vassals, forced them to divide their allegiance between their ecclesiastical and their secular superiors, and created a social gap between them and the lower clergy which corresponded closely in fact to the gap that separated noble from common in lay society. In the vast majority of instances, those of the clergy who by virtue of their office enjoyed wealth and power were recruited from the class which possessed wealth and power as a hereditary right.

Among the upper clergy, if we exclude the pope, the cardinals and the officers of the papal curia who held a unique position at the apex of the Church's administrative system, the highest-ranking officers of the hierarchy were the bishops. Among these we may include the archbishops who exercised a certain supervisory authority over the other bishops in their ecclesiastical province. In the twelfth and thirteenth centuries the bishops' powers were being impaired by encroachments from all directions, so that they no longer possessed the unlimited authority over the clergy in their dioceses or the vassals on their lands that they had enjoyed in earlier centuries. Papal authority was growing steadily and was being enforced increasingly in matters of diocesan administration. Many monasteries had secured exemption from the authority of their bishop and were subject directly to the pope. Appeals to Rome transferred an increasing number of cases from the episcopal courts to the papal curia. Within the diocese, cathedral chapters were growing more independent and the archdeacons frequently usurped in practice many of the bishop's jurisdictional functions. Finally, the growing power of central government was seriously cramping the bishops' feudal sovereignty over their fiefs. Nevertheless, the bishops held an exalted place both in the Church and in secular society, and the episcopal office was eagerly sought after by men of the noblest birth. Aside from the fact that their position in the ecclesiastical hierarchy gave them wide administrative and jurisdictional power, the bishops were great feudal lords and behaved accordingly. They maintained a baronial household; held court among their noble vassals; occupied a place of honor in the king's councils; acted as royal ministers and ambassadors, and even served as generals commanding armies in the field. Despite the partial success of the reform movement begun by Gregory VII, emperors, kings and great nobles still exerted a decisive influence in many episcopal elections, and it was inevitable that men whose office would make them feudal lords should be chosen largely from the noble class. If they shared many of the tastes and something of the violent temper of their noble brethren, the bishops were nevertheless as a rule men of superior ability and character, well-educated, hardworking, and endowed with a higher sense of responsibility than were the majority of the lay lords.

Next in dignity to the bishops, although they did not hold a place of independent authority in the hierarchy, were the canons. These were the priests and deacons attached to a cathedral and organized in a chapter under the presidency of a dean. The individual canonries or prebends, as well as the chapter as a whole, were endowed with land and other forms of income, and the canons could exercise considerable power through their right to elect the bishops. As a result they were recruited largely from the noble class, since the wealth and dignity attached to their offices was sufficient to attract the younger sons of noble families. The chapter, indeed, formed a kind of exclusive club. Their primary duty was to assist in the liturgical services that were a daily, almost hourly, requirement in these great churches, but when this duty became too arduous they frequently hired vicars-choral to take their places in the choir. Another of their important functions was to maintain a school for the teaching of the diocesan clergy, and the resulting need for qualified teachers tended to modify the aristocratic character of the chapters by opening prebends to commoners who had graduated from one of the newly founded universities. By the thirteenth century the degree of Master of Arts was a commonly accepted stepping-stone to a canonry.

When we turn from these dignitaries of the Church to the mass of the lower clergy, we descend to a quite different social stratum. Among the lower clergy were included parish priests, chaplains, and a variety of clerics in minor orders, deacons, sub-deacons, and the like. Of these, the first named performed by far the most important function. The parish clergy were of crucial importance to the religious life of the people. It was they who furnished what religious instruction the ordinary layman received, heard confessions, administered the sacraments, and in general exercised the cure of souls. The indelible character conferred upon priests by their ordination entitled them to a special reverence. Their social status and material prosperity, however, varied considerably. The priest who was rector of his parish and entitled to the major share of the tithes, fees, and income from parish lands held a position of authority in the community and was reasonably prosperous. On Church lands, however, the title and emoluments of the rectorate were frequently retained by the bishops, monks or canons to whom the land belonged, and a vicar was appointed to perform the functions of the parish priest. Living on a small salary or a minor share of the parish income, the vicars were con-siderably less well endowed with either means or authority than the rectors. Of still more uncertain status were the chaplains who served the numerous endowed chapels in large churches, or were attached to noble households. This variety of function and status makes any gen-eralization hazardous, but even the most fortunate of the lower clergy ranked well below the dignitaries of the Church, not only in office, but in wealth and social standing. They were recruited mainly from the non-noble classes and even the sacred character of their office could not free them, in the eyes of the nobility at least, from the stigma of in-herited social inferiority.

Just as the character and social relations of the upper clergy were determined in part by their involvement in the feudal system, so those of the parish clergy were determined in part by their involvement in the manorial economy and manorial jurisdiction. The lord of the manor, whose predecessors had built and endowed the parish church, was the patron of the parish and claimed a share of the income from tithes, fees, and parish land, in much the same way as he claimed a share of the income from the manorial mill. More important, the patron claimed the right to nominate — to "present" — the parish priest, though only the bishop could ordain him and install him in his office. That priests, thus casually nominated by lay lords, and the underpaid vicars employed by absentee rectors were not always men of great learning or strong religious vocation was no more than could be expected, and goes far to explain the charges of ignorance, greed, and immorality so frequently brought against the parish clergy throughout the Middle Ages. The reforming preachers and the satirists, who form our chief sources of opinion concerning the character of the lower clergy, were interested in calling attention to abuses and undoubtedly exaggerated both the number of priests who were unworthy and the degree of their unworthiness. There were certainly good priests as well as bad in the Middle Ages, and not a few indifferent. Nevertheless, what objective evidence in the form of records of episcopal visitations has survived bears out the impression that the mass of the parish clergy were little better educated than their parishioners and that many of them were of doubtful moral character. There is considerable evidence that the reverence the peasants felt for their priest's spiritual authority was coupled with contempt for his person, resentment against his financial exactions, and a very grudging payment of the tithes.

The secular clergy, considered in the preceding paragraphs, played an active rôle in society and their social status can be determined with some measure of assurance. It is rather more difficult to describe the social position of the regular clergy, those living by a monastic rule. Ideally, the monks and nuns, who lived by the ancient rule of St. Benedict or belonged to one of the more recent reformed foundations, had withdrawn from the world and lived apart from lay society. Legally they were regarded as dead. When lived in full accordance with the spirit as well as the letter of the rule, the monastic life was too severe to attract any but those devoted souls who were prepared to forswear forever the pleasures of the flesh and the spiritual comforts of social intercourse. In theory it was open to any free man or woman who chose to adopt it. But again, practice and theory frequently parted company. Most religious houses were amply endowed with land, for the sanctity of their profession made the monks the most common recipients of pious gifts. Though vowed to poverty, the monks as a community were rich, and their abbots were, like the bishops, feudal lords, much concerned with worldly cares. Periodic reforms restored individual monasteries to a stricter observance of the rule, and there were always many monks whose lives demonstrated a true monastic vocation; but the weight of the evidence bears out the impression that as a general rule the monks and nuns lived well and not uncomfortably. The relative security and wealth of the religious houses attracted the younger sons of noble families who could not be provided for adequately from the family lands. In practice, many monasteries and convents were all but closed to any candidate not of noble birth or unable to bring a dowry.

What made the relaxation of monastic rules almost unavoidable was the fact that many monks and nuns had not entered the monastic life of their own volition, or had embraced it for a variety of reasons quite irrelevant to the monastic ideal. Aside from those superfluous sons and daughters of noble families who were dedicated to the cloister from birth, the unfit and the unwanted found a refuge within the monastic walls from the hazards of a very imperfect society. To such, the ascetic demands and the social isolation of the ideal monastic life made little appeal. They sought in every possible way to avoid its rigors, both by making life within the cloister more comfortable and sociable, and by escaping from it on any conceivable pretext for brief sojourns in the world. Monks were to be met with on every road, going on pilgrimages, on their way to study at distant universities, visiting their families, supervising the monastic estates and otherwise attending to monastic business, or engaged in embassies in the interest of their feudal superiors. At the same time, the obligation to extend hospitality to travellers, which was one of the important social functions of the monastery, brought into the cloister many quite worldly folk and might be stretched to include the entertainment of friends and relatives. Nunneries very frequently added to their income by taking as paying guests secular ladies who were for some reason temporarily homeless. Bishops making their official visitations complained constantly of the monks and nuns that the world was too much with them. The friars of the Franciscan and Dominican orders fall into a different category. The purpose of their orders took them out into the world to mingle with the people, teaching and preaching. Recruited mostly from the urban classes, poor and homeless, begging for their daily bread, the friars of the first generation or two won the respect of the populace and were the instruments of a great revival of lay piety. But for these, too, popular reverence brought wealth and well-endowed houses in every city, and with these came a tendency to relax the spirit if not the letter of their rule.

Aside from their purely religious duties, the clergy of all kinds performed a number of social functions now left to the state or to members of the lay professions. They were almost solely responsible for poor relief. Monasteries, in particular, regularly fed throngs of the indigent. Regulars and seculars alike served when necessary as ministers of government, as secretaries, lawyers, physicians, and teachers. One reason for this was the monopoly of higher education which the clergy maintained, with a few exceptions, to the end of the thirteenth century. Not only the cathedral and monastery schools, but also the new universities, which had been called into being by that great revival of learning known as the Twelfth Century Renaissance, were controlled by the Church, and both teachers and students were clerics.

The students, indeed, formed one of the most distinctive as well as most interesting social groups among the medieval clergy. The majority of those who attended the universities of Paris, Bologna, Oxford or other centers were youngsters who were as yet only clerics in minor orders. Among them, however, there were also a number of secular priests, canons, monks, and friars, on leave, as it were, and engaged in completing their education. Among them, too, were feckless and indigent wandering scholars who had little or no professional future and were to be distinguished from common rogues and vagabonds only by their wit and their tonsure. The students at a university like Paris came from every part of Europe, but their common clerical status, their common familiarity with the Latin tongue, and their immunity from secular jurisdiction gave them a homogeneity and an *esprit de corps* that could scarcely be found in a modern university. Faculty and students together formed a distinct corporate body, in the city but not of it. So long as they remained at the university, students were under the sole jurisdiction of the faculty. The fact that the students were clerics, most of whom would seek a career in the Church, did much to determine the choice of subjects to be studied and the general character of the curriculum, but it apparently did not do much to make the medieval students more orderly or law-abiding than their modern counterparts. The impression left by even such sympathetic studies of student life as Charles Homer Haskins's charming lectures, *The Rise of the Universities*, is that the Latin Quarter was in those days a gay and frequently riotous place with well-frequented taverns, and that, though such worldly-minded clerics as those who wrote the Goliardic songs were the exception rather than the rule, the general run of students bore their tonsure lightly.

C. THE PEASANTS

Despite great variation in wealth, function, and status, the nobles and clerics were all alike members of privileged classes. When we turn to the peasants, who formed by far the largest proportion of the population, we enter the world of the unprivileged. Here, too, there were significant variations in wealth and status, or perhaps one should say in poverty and lack of status, but one may safely say that in general the peasant's lot was not a happy one. Even at the best of times and in the most fortunate situation, the medieval peasant lived close to the margin of subsistence. He was born to labor as the sparks fly upward, and his life was cribbed, cabined, and confined by restrictions, varying in degree, upon his freedom. Though there were "free" peasants, and the number of these increased somewhat during the twelfth and thirteenth centuries, the entire population of a manor lived under its lord's jurisdiction and most of the peasants were still serfs or quasi-serfs, bound to land and lord. For this servile or semi-servile condition, it is true, the peasants were compensated by the security from eviction which their hereditary tenure of their land implied. For all the peasants, too, free and unfree, the manorial organization with its closely knit corporate life and its customary rights and regulations provided a considerable stability and a relatively effective guarantee against either the unlimited exploitation or the necessity of facing the world alone, which has been the lot of so many modern poor. But there were other hazards, which made the peasant's life uncertain.

Of these, the most frequent and disastrous were disease, famine, and war, and these three frequently struck together. The ravages of disease, indeed, worked havoc among all classes in the Middle Ages to a degree almost inconceivable in modern times, but were most deadly to the undernourished. In good times the peasants had enough to eat to maintain health, though the food was usually of poor quality and lacking in variety, but any unfortunate weather condition could create a serious local famine, for agricultural methods were still very primitive and the imperfect state of communications made the shipping of food over long distances prohibitively expensive. Even when the crops were good, they might be destroyed at any time by warring nobles. When their lord's land was invaded, the peasants were fortunate to escape with their lives. The best they could expect was an artificially produced famine.

But hard and degrading as were the conditions of peasant life, they were at least improving steadily during the twelfth and thirteenth centuries. This was a period of general prosperity in Western Europe, and in this prosperity the peasants shared. The assarting of new lands opened the way to greater freedom, while the opportunity to sell surplus produce in the town markets was introducing money economy into the manorial system and facilitating the commutation of labor services for payments in money or kind. Even where these advances were not achieved, the unlimited exactions to which the most servile class had been subject tended to become fixed and limited by customary right. Differences in local custom and the variety of connotations given to such terms as "serf" and "villein" make it difficult to distinguish clearly between classes of unfree peasants or to generalize about the degree of freedom enjoyed by the masses at any given time. All that can be said with any assurance is that the actual condition as well as the legal status of the unfree peasants was improving and that the improvement was probably most pronounced among those who had been least free. Servile status was still, however, personal and hereditary. Free peasants were the exception rather than the rule, and even these were subject to the lord's jurisdiction and often to a number of vexatious manorial exactions.

In any case, whatever their degree of freedom or servitude, the peasants were all without exception regarded as members of an inferior social class. The mounted knight, helmeted and armor-clad, looking down from his great war horse upon the bent back of the peasant as he grubbed in his field, shaggy-haired, unwashed, and clothed in filthy homespun rags, symbolizes without exaggeration the social distance which separated the noble from the peasant. The lord in his stone castle lived in a different world from the villagers whose huts clustered about the castle gate. Every reference to the peasants in feudal literature reflects the contempt of the noble for the base-born. Nobles, like other people, varied in personal character, and there were no doubt kindly lords who took a paternal interest in the welfare of their peasants. The more common attitude, bred by the actual social situation, was to regard the peasants as property, economically valuable and, therefore, to be protected and cared for within reason. They were, in short, a superior form of livestock. This conception of the peasants was, of course, mitigated in many ways by the Church, which always recognized the peasant's humanity and his possession of an immortal soul. If anything gave dignity to the peasant's life it was his right to take communion and to participate in the same religious services as his betters. And if anything gave him hope for the future, it was the promise of an immortal life in which the first shall be last and the last shall be first. But beyond treating the peasant as a human being with a soul, and doing what could be done by preaching and moral suasion to protect him from violence and oppression, the Church did little to improve the social position or legal status of the peasant class. The doctors of the Church were agreed that it was the divinely ordained function of the peasants to toil; and on well-regulated episcopal or monastic estates they toiled, if anything, more diligently and rose more slowly toward freedom than on the more carelessly administered estates of lay lords.

D. THE BURGHERS

Compared with the peasants, the burghers were a privileged class. They were privileged also in the absolute, legal sense of the word, for they enjoyed an exceptional status with rights and immunities peculiar to their class. Though non-noble, the burghers were free, and through the strength gained by corporate organization they had won for themselves almost everywhere the right to govern themselves and to make and enforce their own laws. The city, as a corporate entity, had its place in the feudal system, but its citizens, alone among laymen, enjoyed a non-feudal status. Even less than the clergy were they individually involved in feudal relations. At a time when, in theory and to a large extent in practice, every man had his lord, the burghers called no man master. If they owed allegiance to the king or to the lord on whose land the city had grown up, it was a citizen's allegiance, not a personal homage. They were not a military class, but they had the free man's right and the free man's ability to defend themselves and their rights by force of arms. They were, indeed, the first commoners to infringe the nobles' monopoly of the art of war. The burgher militia proved its worth on the fields of Legnano in 1176 and Bouvines in 1214 and in innumerable minor conflicts with noble enemies. The turreted walls of the city made it as much a fortress as any castle, and through its narrow, crooked streets the wind of freedom blew as strongly as it did around the tower of any noble keep. The proud boast of the German cities, *Stadtluft macht frei* (city air makes free), could have been echoed with equal validity by any city in western Europe.

Franchise, privilege, immunities, preoccupation with commerce and industry, and an urban way of life all combined to make the bourgeoisie as clearly distinguishable a class as were the nobility or the clergy. Within the burgher class, however, there were variations of wealth, occupation, social position, and political power that prevented them from being an entirely homogeneous group, though these variations were not so marked in the early period of city life as they became in the later Middle Ages. Except in a few centers of woollen cloth manufacturing, like Florence and the Flemish cities, where a nascent capitalism had already begun to transform industry, the cities of the High Middle Ages had no industrial proletariat in the modern sense of the word. Neverthe-

47

less, a considerable proportion of the urban population was composed of propertyless men — household servants, porters, unskilled workers, hewers of wood and drawers of water. These shared in the city's freedom and immunity from outside jurisdiction and were protected by the city's "peace," that is, its special laws and courts; but they were seldom accorded political rights in the self-governing communes. In small market towns of purely local importance, there were burghers who made the greater part of their living by cultivating the soil of the *banlieu* — the land surrounding the town which fell within its jurisdiction — and many more of the burghers supplemented their income by cultivating a plot of land and by pasturing livestock on the town commons. The air of these small country towns was not only free; it was also redolent of the odors of the farmyard. Even when engaged in a peasant's occupation, however, the burghers still remained distinct from the peasant class. They were freeholders, who owed no manorial dues or services. Agriculture, however, was not the characteristic occupation of the townsman, nor was it the economic force that had created the cities. It was commerce and industry that made city life possible and had called into being the burgher class. Except for the semi-rural burghers mentioned above, a few landed proprietors living on rents, and an occasional member of the few professions open to laymen, the burghers were merchants, shopkeepers, or artisans.

In small towns, serving only the local countryside, these must have formed a fairly homogeneous group. But in all the larger cities there existed from the beginning a decided social cleavage between the well-to-do merchants who travelled abroad and the retail shopkeepers, most of whom were also skilled artisans manufacturing the goods which they sold across the counters of their shops. With the passage of time and the continued growth of the cities, the distance between the merchant class and the local tradesmen tended to widen still further and to be reinforced by a corresponding divergence of political rights and powers. In many places, the craftsmen withdrew or were excluded from the merchant guild and formed smaller and politically less powerful guilds of their own. Even where guild organization did not exist, the merchant class tended to monopolize the offices of city government and to exercise a disproportionate influence on the shaping of city policy. As a recognized urban aristocracy, the merchant patriciate frequently took steps to protect its exclusive social rank by sumptuary legislation, designed to prevent the poorer classes from wearing clothing of the same quality as their betters. By the end of the thirteenth century there were signs of a growing strain between the merchant oligarchy and the mass of craftsmen in many cities, a strain that in the following period frequently bred open violence and revolution.

By the very fact of their existence as an urban population engaged in commerce and industry, the burghers were a dynamic element in medieval society. Their introduction into the relatively static agrarian life of feudal Europe greatly accelerated the rate of social and cultural change. The effect of their appearance was to raise the standard of living of all classes, to hasten the emancipation of the unfree, to strengthen central government, and to make possible the full growth of chivalric culture, the revival of learning, and the efflorescence of Gothic art that distinguished the High Middle Ages, but these were not aims that the burghers themselves consciously pursued. What they achieved, they achieved in the pursuit of their own interests. To a very large extent, their dynamic influence on medieval society resulted from their economic activity, an activity inspired by a simple, unspoiled desire for gain. If they fought for freedom, it was freedom for themselves. They made no attempt to improve the condition of the servile classes in the surrounding countryside. Their direct contribution as a class to the intellectual and aesthetic culture of the High Middle Ages, too, was relatively small. It could scarcely have been otherwise, for the struggle to make a living and to protect their rights in a society still dominated by feudalism absorbed almost all the burghers' energies. The material nature of their interests was qualified only by a deeply rooted religious sense. As a class, the burghers were profoundly pious, though their piety sometimes harmonized none too well with an authoritative Church. They sometimes showed a disturbing tendency to do their own thinking, and they were generally more open to the infection of heresy and of various forms of semi-heretical mysticism than were the rural populace. In assessing their contribution to contemporary culture, it must not be forgotten that, despite their very great indirect influence on the development of medieval civilization, the burghers were still only a very small minority of the population. Medieval cities were small, almost ridiculously small, by modern standards. Moreover, though privileged, the burghers were still a socially inferior class, marked by the stigma of ignoble birth. Even their wealth could arouse no respect, only resentment, in the minds of the socially dominant classes. And the burghers themselves had not yet acquired either the means or the self-confidence needed to take a leading rôle in shaping the culture of their age. The future was theirs, but that they could not know.

I V

Religion and Culture

The twelfth and thirteenth centuries may be called the classic period of the Middle Ages, for in this period the peculiarly medieval forms of religion and culture ripened to maturity. In this age feudal Europe, its economic and political life stimulated by the revival of commerce and the rise of the cities, shook off the provincialism to which an exclusively agrarian economy had condemned it, and expanded both its physical and its intellectual horizons. It was an age of intense activity in every area of culture. It opened with a great movement of monastic reform and the vigorous assertion of papal supremacy. As it progressed, the revival of learning that had begun in the eleventh century passed through a period of clerical humanism to the full development of scholastic philosophy and theology. This was, indeed, the great age of the Church's domination of European civilization. Art, literature, and learning served the Church and flourished under its patronage. The clergy held a practical monopoly upon higher education and even contributed considerably to the secular, vernacular literature, which reflected the coming-of-age of feudal society and was the only significant exception to the generally ecclesiastical tone of medieval letters. The culture of the High Middle Ages was, in short, feudal and ecclesiastical in all its main outlines, and reflected the interests, presuppositions, and prejudices of the

two classes whose dominant position in society is the peculiar characteristic of medieval civilization. The dynamic force that stimulated the new
activity may have had its origins in the commercial revival and the rise
of the cities and the bourgeoisie, but its immediate effect was to enable the
previously existing and still dominant classes and institutions to develop
their characteristic potentialities rather than to turn the current of cultural evolution into other channels.

A. RELIGION

The religious life and thought of the High Middle Ages was held
within a unified framework by the universal Church. This unity, which
is in marked contrast to the heterodoxy of the modern world, rested upon
certain fundamental assumptions, so deeply rooted that few people ever
thought to question them. The first of these is that there is but one form
of truth and that it has been made manifest by divine revelation; the
second, that the Church is the temporal custodian of truth, the sole
divinely ordained interpreter of revelation. To this unity of belief the
Church, as an institution necessary to the salvation of men and endowed
with the power to enforce obedience through its courts, added a further
unity of organization. The Church was an international institution, its
beliefs, customs, and forms of organization much the same from one end
of Europe to the other. It was this fact, together with the supremely
important nature of its function, that made the Church in this period the
matrix in which the civilization of Western Christendom was cast.

But, though medieval religion had a unity which has since been lost, it
was at the same time an extremely complex phenomenon. On close examination it presents a great variety of facets, each an aspect of the whole,
yet each with its own peculiar character. For purposes of analysis, then,
we may treat the major aspects of medieval religion separately, though
with a constantly watchful eye for their mutual interrelation and with
the full realization that they are all parts of an organic whole.

At the very core of medieval religion lay an unshaken faith in personal
immortality, and with it the problem of salvation. No medieval man
doubted for a moment the existence of an eternal future world, to which
man's mortal life is but a brief, though terribly decisive, prelude. To the
thoughtful Christian, the chief significance of life in this world is that it
determines man's eternal fate. According to the doctrine of original sin,
all men have inherited the sin of Adam which corrupts their nature.
They are born in sin and, as a result of their fallen nature, will inevitably
be guilty of sins of omission and commission. Of himself, then, no man

can merit salvation. Only through the operation of Divine Grace, the product of Christ's saving sacrifice, can sinful man hope to be forgiven his sins, to do good works, and to win eventually the eternal bliss of Heaven or — what was probably more vividly present to the minds of most medieval men — to escape from the torments of Hell. And Divine Grace, the essential means of salvation, is channelled through the sacraments. This not only made the sacraments a fundamentally important element in religious thought and practice; it also lent emphasis to the sacerdotal aspect of religion by making the Church an indispensable institution and giving to the clergy, who alone possessed the power to administer the sacraments, a monopoly upon the most precious commodity known to man.

Sacraments are as old as the Church, but their number and function was not clearly defined until the great age of scholastic theology that began with the twelfth-century revival of learning. Of the seven sacraments, five were administered only under specific circumstances, but together they combined to bring every man into contact with the Church at the most important stages of his life. Baptism freed the newly born child from the guilt of original sin. In the exceptional case of converted infidels, it was also administered to adults; it then absolved the convert from all sins previously committed while in a state of ignorance, and made him a naturalized citizen of the *Respublica Christiana*. Confirmation, which could normally be administered only by a bishop, was not a sacrament essential to salvation, but was valuable as imparting additional grace and thus completing and confirming baptism. Ordination, invariably administered by a bishop, conferred upon the priest his indelible character and his power to perform the sacraments. The sacrament of matrimony consecrated marriage and made it an unbreakable union under the jurisdiction of the Church. Extreme unction was the last sacrament for the dying. The two remaining sacraments — penance and the Eucharist — were more frequently received by the faithful and were regarded as the most important parts of the sacramental system. The sacrament of the Eucharist, surrounded as it was by all the dramatic and awe-inspiring liturgy and ceremonial of the Mass, was at once the central element of public worship and the means by which the faithful partook of the saving grace of Christ. It was founded upon the Gospel story of Christ's last supper with His disciples (Matthew 26:26–28; Mark, 14:22–24; Luke, 22:17–21), when He gave them the bread to eat and the wine to drink, saying, "this is my body" and "this is my blood." According to the doctrine of transubstantiation, long held but not officially established by the Church until the Fourth Lateran Council (1215), the priest, in the process of consecrating the elements of the sacrament, causes the bread and wine to be transformed into the substance of the body and blood of Christ. With all its emotional as well as theological implications, the sacrament of the Eucharist became the focal point of religious devotion and, more than anything else, distinguished the priest as a person who, by virtue of his power to perform the act of transubstantiation, possessed a special character that made him superior to even the most pious layman. The sacrament of penance was equally vital to the life of the Christian and to the authority of the Church, for it was through this sacrament, which included the acts of contrition, confession, absolution, and the imposition of penance, that the sinner was forgiven his sins and restored to a state of grace. The crucial importance of the sacrament of penance for the individual Christian is clear from the fact that it was the essential instrument of salvation, the only means of escape from the eternally damning consequences of sin. It was also of fundamental importance for the authority of the Church. It was the power to absolve the sinner that made the priest the essential personal minister of salvation, while the confessional gave him a direct supervision of individual conscience, and the imposition of penance invested him with a disciplinary power equivalent to that of a court of law. This sacrament thus became one of the principal means by which the Church was able to enforce its moral and ethical doctrines.

Because it was so dependent upon the priesthood and so indissolubly related to the Church as an institution, the sacramental system was the main support of the sacerdotal and hierarchical element in medieval religion. More than anything else, it made the Church an authoritative institution, with jurisdiction over all moral acts, and justified both the privileged status of the sacerdotal class and the Church's claim to supremacy over all merely worldly and temporal governments. It furnished the Church with its most effective weapons for dealing with its opponents: excommunication — the power to expel the recalcitrant sinner from the Church and to deny him the sacraments — and the interdict, which withdrew the services of the Church from a whole community. The doctrine which maintained that the sacraments operated *ex opere operato,* by virtue of the power inherent in them regardless of the personal worthiness of the officiating priest, also protected the Church from the consequences of any unfavorable criticism of the morals of the clergy. At the same time, the authoritative character of the Church was reinforced by its claim to be the sole interpreter of revealed truth and by the fact that the clergy were the only learned class and hence alone capable of wrestling with the intricacies of doctrine. Accepting the implications of the belief that there was no salvation possible outside the Church and no true faith outside the Church's doctrine, the officers of the Church could scarcely avoid the responsibility for keeping all Christians within the fold, by force if necessary, and for extirpating heresy by all possible means, including the extirpation of the heretics.

The authority of the Church was in practice vested in its official hierarchy. Within it authority descended from above, having its source in the pope who, as the successor of St. Peter and the Vicar of Christ, received his authority directly from God. The growth of the "papal monarchy" within the Church and of the papal supremacy over secular governments in the period from Gregory VII to Innocent III was no doubt made possible by a fortunate combination of circumstances. The expanding money economy and improved means of communication that followed the commercial revival made the exercise of central government throughout the Church more feasible than it had been in the Early Middle Ages. At the same time, the secular states, which might oppose the exercise of papal authority in matters temporal, were as yet divided and weakened by feudalism. Still, the vast authority exercised by the great popes of the High Middle Ages cannot be explained solely by temporary material circumstance. It had its real and indispensable basis in the sacramental system, the sacerdotal monopoly of both the means of salvation and the interpretation of revealed truth, and the hierarchial conception of the source of authority.

The domination of worldly by spiritual authority found support also in the otherworldliness and dualism that are the basic elements of asceticism, but the ascetic current in medieval religion may be regarded as a distinct phenomenon which had its most obvious embodiment in monasticism, though exercising a widely-diffused influence upon both Church doctrine and lay piety. Christian asceticism had its origins in the rejection by the early Church of the pagan world of the Roman Empire. Later it was reinforced by the dualism that was one of the elements of Neoplatonic philosophy as it developed under the influence of oriental mystery religions in Alexandria during the first three centuries A.D. The Platonic distinction and contrast between the temporal world of the senses and the eternal world of the spirit here developed into a concept of the body as a hindrance to the ascent of the soul toward God, as something that must be transcended through rejection of all physical appetites and passions. In the same way, anything that attaches men's interests to this mortal world must be rejected and transcended lest it hinder the soul's ascent toward the eternal world of the spirit in which the soul may be united with God. The conception of man's physical nature as a hindrance to the ascent of the soul and hence as inherently evil could be brought into accord with Christian doctrine through the story of Adam's fall and the resultant inheritance by all men of original sin; and St. Augustine, through whom Neoplatonist ideas exercised their strongest influence on the theology of the Latin Church, underlined all the consequences of man's congenitally sinful nature. Against the temptations of the world and the flesh all Christians must struggle constantly; but the struggle was the professional concern only of the monks, the "athletes of Christ," who labored by the renunciation of self-will and of all worldly affections and desires, by prayer, fasting and mortification of the flesh, for the salvation of their souls, while at the same time contributing by vicarious atonement to the salvation of their fellow Christians.

It is often forgotten that the monks, while cutting themselves off from human society, still fulfilled a social function by performing services that were as essential to the common weal as were the more material services of the noble, peasant, or bourgeois classes. This was one of the reasons why the monks were not only revered by laymen but also richly endowed — with results that were often injurious to the ascetic spirit. But, however much wealth and human frailty might tend to corrupt monastic practice, the ascetic spirit was constantly revived, and never more vigorously than in the great movements of monastic reform that marked the beginning of the High Middle Ages. Though in its purest form it could be the possession of only a few, it served as a perpetual source of religious inspiration and renewal. It was, as might be expected, the driving force behind every monastic reform, but it was also one of the most important factors inspiring the reform of the entire church undertaken by Pope Gregory VII. If there is an apparent contradiction involved in the fact that the temporal power of the Church, which resulted from the Gregorian reform and left it deeply enmeshed in worldly concerns, was supported by the more ascetic of the monastic orders, the contradiction is readily resolved by the dualistic conception of the Church as the embodiment of the City of God which must be made to triumph over the sinful worldly state.

Closely related to asceticism, yet distinguishable from it, the strain of mysticism formed still another aspect of medieval religious life. Of all the varieties of religious experience, mysticism is the most difficult to define or explain, for by its very nature it goes beyond reason. It is purely subjective and defies objective analysis. The mystic cannot communicate his experience to others except by the use of symbols, the sense of which is incommunicable to those who have no inward ear for it, just as the sense of music is incommunicable to the tone-deaf. The tendency to mysticism, indeed, seems to be an innate personal trait, not something that can be acquired by study or an act of will. The inherent tendency of men to rationalize their experience did, it is true, provide Christian mysticism with a body of traditional doctrine, a mystical theology drawn mostly from Neoplatonic sources; but fundamentally the mystic depended on direct intuition and personal experience. Perhaps mysticism may be defined most comprehensively as the satisfaction through imaginative experience of the soul's yearning for a sense of identity with the divine essence of the universe. There have been mystics in nearly all religions to whom this definition would apply. In the Christian mystics the emotional force of mysticism was derived from a passionate love of God and an equally passionate desire to be united with Him. It was most commonly found among ascetics, whose whole being was concentrated on contemplation of the divine. Medieval mystics gravitated naturally toward the cloister, where they could find unique opportunities for the contemplative life, but the identification of mysticism with ascetic monasticism tended to give to much of medieval mysticism a dualistic character in which yearning for the divine was coupled with fear and hatred of the world. Such a mystic was St. Bernard, whose passionate love of God was equalled only by his passionate hatred of all things worldly. Among the less intellectual mystics extreme asceticism sometimes produced states of hysterical ecstasy that bordered on the pathological. Many of the ecstatic mystics were nuns, much given to visions and trances. Despite occasional eccentricities, however, mysticism, like asceticism, was a source of spiritual energy. It helped to make monasticism at its best one of the most potent forces of spiritual awakening throughout the Middle Ages.

So long as they remained within the monastic walls, however, both the ascetic and the mystic could influence the piety of the lay world only indirectly and intermittently. Not till the founding of the Franciscan order in the early thirteenth century was mysticism brought directly to the people in terms that they could understand, and then it became the agent of a great revival of lay piety, which may well have saved the populace of the crowded Italian cities for the Church. Franciscan mysticism, though still coupled with asceticism, was of a very different sort from that of the older monks and hermits. There was in it little dualism and less of intellectual symbolism. St. Francis loved Christ quite simply and directly, and with equal simplicity and directness loved all God's creatures. Here was no unintelligible yearning for harmony with a divine essence, but a love of Christ and identification with Him that was incomprehensible to the pious layman only in its intensity. The asceticism of St. Francis was in the same way different from the tortured fear of the world that drove the monastic ascetic to seek isolation from his kind. It was rather a cheerful disregard for worldly things which quite literally counted them as nought. Thanks to his own simple faith and the wisdom of the Church, St. Francis escaped the fate of the heretic;

but his intensely personal, subjective religious emotion, his literal reading of Christ's teaching, and his emphasis upon direct, personal relation to God were all implicitly antagonistic to the sacramental-sacerdotal aspect of medieval religion as embodied in a hierarchical Church endowed with wealth and worldly power.

By its very nature as a universal institution, which encompassed that great majority of the human race whose life was inescapably bound up with the material problems of earthly existence, the Church could not, of course, shape its doctrines and practices solely for the needs of the mystic or the ascetic. It could not have maintained its dominant position for so long, nor have served its people so well, had it not made room for the worldly as well as the otherworldly life. Medieval doctrine, as stated by the great scholastic doctors of the twelfth and thirteenth centuries, recognized the worldly life as necessary and, therefore, as divinely ordained, though on a lower level than the spiritual. It could thus rationalize the existing social organization by assigning to each class a function necessary to the existence of the whole social body. By emphasizing service as the aim of social life and the sole justification for the possession of wealth or power, the Church strove to direct economic and social activity, so far as possible, into channels consonant with Christian morality. This was a doctrine especially well suited to a simple and largely agrarian economy and to the feudal organization of society and the state. The manorial and feudal tenure of land was in fact founded upon an exchange of services and, ideally at least, upon sentiments of loyalty and mutual trust.

It was more difficult to bring the economic activity of the newly revived towns into this scheme. Money economy tended to emphasize the pursuit of gain rather than the ideal of service and to make all social relations more complex. The service to society of the merchant who bought cheap and sold dear was somewhat less clear than that of the peasant who produced the necessities of life. Nevertheless, there were many elements in the economic life of the early towns that could be brought within the Church's doctrine of mutual service and brotherly aid. Thus, while taking a generally jaundiced view of commercial activity, the Church found congenial elements in the corporate solidarity of commune and guild, in the regulation of individual enterprise for the good of the whole community, in the concept of the just price, and the condemnation of usury, and to these elements of urban policy it gave the support of its moral authority. Later, as an incipient capitalism began to revolutionize commerce and industry, the Church found it increasingly difficult to keep its doctrine in step with changing conditions. The social doctrine of the medieval Church was, in fact, essentially conservative. In effect, it recognized the *status quo* as divinely ordained and strove only to bring practice within reasonable reach of the ideal. It stressed each man's obligation to serve in the position in which God had seen fit to place him, and hence opened no doors to social revolution. Finally, the concept of a hierarchy of values, which was fundamental to all scholastic thought, together with the hierarchical organization of the Church, fitted a hierarchical organization of society and provided a justification for it.

It is difficult to think of medieval religion apart from the Church, yet there were large areas of what might be called popular religion in which the institutional Church played a secondary rôle. In these areas doctrines or practices sanctioned and, indeed, fostered by the Church were adapted to the comprehension and spiritual capacity of men who were neither saints nor scholars. The scope of religion in daily life was by no means limited to the problem of salvation nor to the direction of social ethics, the areas in which the Church was most directly active. Medieval men lived daily, hourly, in the presence of the supernatural. For good or evil, supernatural forces animated all the natural phenomena with which they had to deal in the daily struggle for existence. The majority of medieval men lived close to the soil, and their lives depended upon the capricious and to them inexplicable operation of natural forces. Drought, thunderstorms, hail or high water, human disease or a murrain on the cattle — all of these evils were regarded as supernatural in origin and could be met only by appeal to supernatural aid. And on these occasions men turned to the saints as an ever present help in time of trouble.

The veneration of saints, culminating in the cult of the Virgin Mother of Christ, formed, indeed, one of the most vital parts of popular religion. Though in full accord with orthodox belief, encouraged and in part directed by the Church, the veneration of saints belonged in a peculiar way to the people rather than to the Church as an institution, and was colored more by popular imagination than by the theology of the schoolmen. From it came much of the warmth and color of medieval religion. The legends of the saints formed a kind of religious folklore. They were the stuff that dreams are made on. They filled the imagination of medieval men, inspired their art, and furnished an inexhaustible theme for the tales told on winter evenings. At the same time, the saints brought to men much-needed comfort and what sense of security was possible in a terrifying world. They were endowed with miraculous powers, and, having been themselves human beings on this earth, their sympathy was readily enlisted for the succor of human ills and troubles. Mary was at once the most potent and the most compassionate of the saints, and hence the most frequently invoked. She also appealed in a special way to the chivalrous instincts of the medieval knight. Other saints, whose aid was frequently invoked, were particularly effective in healing certain diseases, aided those in peril on the sea, or were adept in finding lost articles. Others still were the patron saints of particular towns, fiefs, or countries, and might be expected to show special interest in their welfare. Every guild or craft had its patron saint, as did each individual. No one thought it beneath the dignity of a saint to take a practical interest in a toothache or the inopportune souring of milk in the dairy. Nor did there seem any incongruity in using the name of St. George or St. Denis as a battle cry. Even the felon when engaged in his employment might seek the aid of a saint in carrying out his felonious little plans. For in the somewhat confused ethical thinking of simple men, the sinner's desperate need might seem sufficient to justify the saint's becoming an accessory before or after the fact. In any case, the miracle-working power of the saint was often transformed in the thought of literal-minded men into a magical power to be invoked by the formula of prayer or oblation regardless of the nature of the aid sought or the deserts of the seeker.

But even more than in dealing with the immediate problems of this world, medieval men turned to the saints for aid in the one great problem of human existence: the problem of escaping eternal punishment for sin. Here, it is true, the saints were of secondary importance. The primary factor was the sacrament of penance, which loomed large in popular religion as it did in the more sacerdotal aspect of religious organization and doctrine. In the popular mind, however, the sacrament of penance lost much of its spiritual quality and frequently became little more than a magical incantation which automatically freed the sinner from the consequences of sin. For the mass of men afflicted more or less with spiritual myopia, the winning of salvation tended to degenerate into a mechanical process, a matter of keeping one's books balanced. But however meticulous one's accounting, a doubt might still remain, and when in doubt the sinner turned to the saints to intercede with a just and implacable God. To humble men God was too distant, too unapproachable to be reached by direct prayer. It was on the whole better to leave the matter in the hands of subordinates whose attention and sympathy was more easily attracted and who were in a position to intercede effectively. This tendency to think in terms of a hierarchy of intermediate authorities came the more naturally to men whose whole life was conditioned by a hierarchical feudal society and a hierarchical Church.

There was, indeed, a good deal of literal-minded prose as well as poetry in the medieval attitude toward the saints. One might chaffer, drive a hard bargain, or even trick them into giving aid. A similarly matter-of-fact attitude characterized the popular conception of those extremely concrete personifications of the forces of evil, the devil and his ministers

Ever eager to trick men's souls into hell, the devil was the ever present enemy, full of wiles and stratagems, and even, in his eternal busyness, not above making a nuisance of himself in minor but irritating ways. Witches and wizards were his human agents, against whose black magic one's best protection was the white magic of the sign of the cross. Given the hourly action of the supernatural in daily life, it was perhaps inevitable that men should have reduced it to understandable, concrete terms and have worked out practical ways of dealing with it. And it was equally inevitable that in a half-civilized society, men who were unable to grasp the transcendental, or to comprehend the spiritual significance of the symbol, should have endowed the physical symbol and the literal word with miraculous powers inherent in themselves. This tendency goes far to explain the value placed upon the relics of the saints, which formed one of the most profitable commodities in medieval trade. Such relics — a bone, a piece of the clothing worn by the saint, or some article personally associated with him — were not merely collectors' items to be treasured for their rarity or sentimental value. They were valued for their practical power to work miracles. These various elements of popular religion were not, of course, limited to the uneducated laity. Saints and doctors of the Church envisaged the devil in equally concrete fashion, and the veneration of both saints and relics was given support by Church doctrine and practice. Still there is a difference, if not in belief, yet in intellectual and imaginative grasp, between the doctrine as held by schoolmen and mystics and that as understood by untrained and naturally unspiritual men. If the majority of the medieval clergy were in this respect nearer to the latter than to the former, it is but proof that they were products of their society and not always more spiritually gifted than the laity they served.

One final aspect of medieval religion still remains to be considered, namely heresy. In the Age of Faith, this was a minority phenomenon, but one of sufficient proportions to alarm the authorities of the Church and move them to drastic action. The growth of heresy in the eleventh and twelfth centuries was a symptom of the general quickening of intellectual and spiritual activity that followed the revival of trade, and it was closely connected with the rise of an urban class. The most serious heresies of the High Middle Ages flourished chiefly in the cities of northern Italy and southern France, where the growth of an urban population was at that time most rapid. The fanatical Cathari — called Patarini in Italy and Albigenses in Provence — and the Waldeneses whose doctrine spread from Lyons, differed from one another in the manner and degree of their deviation from orthodox belief, but all represented the revolt of urban groups against the worldliness of the clergy and against dependence for salvation upon priest and sacrament. For this revolt, the neglect of the spiritual needs of the people in crowded and overpopulated parishes was partly responsible. But the discontent that centered in the cities was also a reflection of the deeply pious, but also vigorously independent spirit of the burghers. Men who had thrown off the yoke of feudalism and who had battled with their bishops for political freedom were prone to question authority and to assert their independence in spiritual as well as temporal affairs. In Italy, this anti-clerical wave of lay piety was directed during the thirteenth century into orthodox channels by the subjective, half-mystical piety of the early Franciscan movement. Yet St. Francis was in thought and act not very different from Peter Waldo, the "poor man of Lyons," who had sold his goods and given his money to the poor and had gone forth to preach the Gospel. The failure of the Church authorities to recognize what was essentially Christian in Waldo's teaching and to direct and utilize it drove the Waldenses into heresy. Their mild evangelical piety, coupled though it was with a strong anti-sacerdotal feeling, was not so far removed from orthodoxy as to justify drastic suppression. Despite intermittent persecution, Waldensian sects survived until the Reformation. The more eccentric and fanatical heresy of the Albigenses — a recrudescence of primitive Manichaean dualism that was essentially unchristian — was a more serious menace. It was destroyed by fire and sword, and much of the fair land of Provence with it, in the Albigensian Crusade (1207). What survived was exterminated by the newly founded papal Inquisition and the preaching of the Dominican Order. By the middle of the thirteenth century, heresy had ceased to be a serious threat to the Church, though the motives for it remained to emerge in different forms in the following century.

Because of the important rôle played by the Dominicans and Franciscans in combatting heresy and meeting the spiritual needs of the new urban classes something more should be said about these two great orders of friars. We shall have to return to them again frequently in dealing with the fourteenth and fifteenth centuries. The friars represented a radical departure from the traditional forms of monasticism. Their vocation was apostolic: to go out into the world and preach the Gospel. Their life was to be spent among the people, particularly among the poor of the crowded city quarters; and to the poor they could speak the more effectively because they themselves were poor, without possessions, dependent for their living on begging for their daily bread — whence the term "mendicant orders" applied to them. Such poverty was, at least, the ideal envisaged by their founders and laid down in the rules, although, as their later history showed, it proved very difficult to put into effect in actual practice. In both their freedom from enclosure and their lack of permanent endowment they differed from the monastic orders. They differed, too, in being attached to no fixed place of abode. Although they soon acquired convents in which to live, they were not bound to any one house, but wandered freely from convent to convent, from town to town, subject only to the authority of their superior officers. Both orders were highly centralized, with a hierarchy of officers and a central government responsible only to the pope. Their immunity from episcopal jurisdiction and their close relations with the papacy were, incidentally, an important factor in reinforcing papal authority throughout the Church.

In all these respects the two great mendicant orders were alike, but there were also differences between them, especially in their early years, which reflected the radical differences in the characters and aims of their respective founders. It was the personality of St. Francis of Assisi (1182–1226) that gave the order he founded its special character. That gay, humble little man, who had been born to wealth and luxury, gave away all that he had and embraced poverty joyfully because it was for him the only road to spiritual freedom. A layman without theological training or much formal education, he preached the simple Gospel of Christ because he could not help imparting to others the emotion that filled his soul. His aim, and that which he envisaged for his order, was to revitalize the spiritual life of the people by focusing their religious emotion upon the person of the incarnate Christ. He had little interest in dogma and, while humbly accepting the authority of the Church in matters of doctrine, he felt that theology and much learning were a hindrance rather than a help in the evangelical mission which he wished his brothers to undertake. It is significant that the official name given by the *Poverello* to his followers was the Order of Friars Minor. The new order, as St. Francis conceived it, was less an institution than a way of life. But it was a way of life beyond the reach of ordinary men, however sincere, and before long the institution prevailed over the spirit. It could scarcely have been otherwise. The life of absolute, vagrant poverty which Francis and his earliest followers had led, giving no thought to the morrow, was impracticable for a great order with hundreds of members in every country of Western Europe. Nor could the lay character of the order and the unlettered simplicity of the early Franciscan preaching survive the intrusion into the order of great numbers of university-trained men — clerics, lawyers, philosophers and theologians. Before the end of the thirteenth century the Franciscans were the dominant force at Oxford and other universities and included among their distinguished doctors St. Bonaventura, Roger Bacon, Duns Scotus and, in the following century, William of Ockham. Meanwhile the rule of absolute corporate poverty had been evaded with full papal connivance, and the Franciscans had been furnished by the overwhelming generosity of the faithful with the use, if not the technical ownership, of the houses, furniture, churches, and financial means they needed to carry on their work. The memory of the glowing personality of the *Poverello*, however, did not die out altogether in the order he founded. Despite the compromises demanded by the institutionalization of an ideal, there was always a faithful minority of zealots who strove to follow the example and injunctions of their founder in the most literal sense. The result was a long internal conflict and an eventual split in the order.

If the Franciscan order was the spontaneous product of a unique personality, the Dominican order was the conscious creation of a great organizer, whose personality is almost lost behind the institution he founded. St. Dominic was a Spaniard of Castile, an Augustinian canon who travelled in southern France on the eve of the Albigensian Crusade and was profoundly shocked by the prevalence of heresy there. He felt that there was a desperate need for more preachers, well educated and trained in theology, to win the people back to the Church and to orthodox belief. The order he founded, and to which he gave the significant name, *Ordo Praedicatorum*, the Order of Preachers, was designed to meet that need. The Dominican friars were clerics from the beginning, priests whose main function was preaching, and their whole organization was designed to make them as efficient as possible. Unlike St. Francis, Dominic had a high regard for learning, for only the trained theologian could meet the arguments of the heretics. The rule provided that in each Dominican convent a lecturer in theology should instruct the novices for three years before they were licensed to preach, while the most promising were sent for further study to a university. They were soon the most active group in the University of Paris, and to indicate the importance of their contribution to orthodox theology and philosophy one need only mention the names of St. Albertus Magnus and St. Thomas Aquinas. Like the Franciscans, the Dominicans were mendicants, but St. Dominic thought of poverty as a means to an end, not as an end in itself. With sound practical sense he realized that his preachers could win the sympathy and confidence of the people better if they avoided the wealth which had brought so many of the monks and the secular clergy into disrepute. The Dominicans never entirely abandoned the rule of personal poverty and the practice of mendicancy, but the order was never torn by internal conflict or open schism as a result of the inevitable relaxation of a too strict rule.

While the first enthusiasm lasted, the two great mendicant orders were the most vital force in the religious life of Western Europe. They spread rapidly to every country of Catholic Christendom, bringing religious inspiration and sound doctrine to towns and villages ill-served by their parish clergy, exerting a direct personal influence as confessors, and injecting new intellectual energy into the universities. Aside from the thousands who joined their ranks, and the orders of nuns who were affiliated with them, numbers of lay men and women, living at home under rules which exacted a strict piety, became members of the Third Order which grew up around each of the orders of friars. These lay groups formed religious confraternities or guilds which carried the ideals of the parent order into the lay world and were a constant stimulus to lay piety. It would be difficult to exaggerate the influence of the friars on the religious life and the culture of the thirteenth century, but, as so often happens in movements of religious reform, success and expansion were accompanied by a lowering of the spiritual level and loss of the original inspiration. Before the end of the thirteenth century the two orders had become more alike, each having lost something of the peculiar character bequeathed to it by its founder. A remnant of the dedicated remained, and always would remain, but the average friar asked of himself no more than the average man could fulfill.

B. CLERICAL CULTURE: LITERATURE AND LEARNING

The time has long since passed when historians could regard the whole of the Middle Ages as a period of cultural darkness. Learned research in the past half-century or so has thrown light upon many dark places and has demonstrated that much of the apparent darkness was the product of modern ignorance and misunderstanding of medieval culture. Some recent medievalists may have discovered, in their enthusiasm to redress an ancient wrong, more enlightenment in the Middle Ages than actually existed. But no historian would now deny that there was a great revival of literature and learning in the Latin tongue, a "Twelfth Century Renaissance," as Charles Homer Haskins called it, nor that the period from about the middle of the eleventh century to the end of the thirteenth witnessed an intense, if somewhat restricted, intellectual activity. This vigorous culture was the product of the clerical class and was restricted in scope by the range of clerical interests. Yet it was an infinitely broader culture than that of the Early Middle Ages, inspired and enriched by the recovery of large portions of antique Latin literature and of antique Greek philosophy and science as well as by contact with the highly developed civilization of the Moslem world.

Knowledge of the Latin classics had, of course, never been completely lost. Even in the darkest periods before and after the Carolingian revival, when few people read and those who did preferred the late patristic writers or the encyclopedic transmitters of ancient culture, like Isidore of Seville, there were always a few scholars who read the great authors of the past with wonder and admiration. It was not till the middle of the eleventh century, however, that scholars in Italy and in the great cathedral schools of the North began to show signs of a sympathetic comprehension of the classics and learned from them the art of expressing their own thoughts and emotions in polished literary form. From then on, for about a century, a vital current of clerical humanism ran parallel to that of scholastic logic and metaphysics and in conflict, more or less, with the current of monastic asceticism that characterized the great age of the Gregorian reform. It was, perhaps, a minority phenomenon, but it cannot be ignored as it has so often been by historians who saw in medieval culture nothing but the transcendental and the metaphysical. This clerical humanism, which is best represented by the long series of scholars, culminating in John of Salisbury, who frequented the cathedral school at Chartres, was entirely Christian and most of it deeply religious. The piety and clerical training of the medieval humanists, as well as the preconceptions they brought from a feudal society which was so very different from that of ancient Rome, may have prevented them from absorbing classical culture as unconditionally as did the urban laymen of the fifteenth and sixteenth centuries; but the influence of the classics can be seen clearly enough in the value they placed upon literary form, in their interest in human emotion, coupled as it was with a heightened power of self-expression, and in a new appreciation of the beauties and the pleasures of this present world. As Helen Waddell has demonstrated with innumerable examples, "with every rediscovery of antiquity comes the discovery of the goodness of the earth."[1] It was this tendency to arouse an undue interest in the world of nature, rather than the fact that it was pre-Christian, that made the ancient poetry an object of suspicion to the ascetic mind. The strongest denunciation of the study and imitation of the ancient poets came not from those who were incapable of appreciating them, but from those who had themselves felt their insidious charm. Both St. Peter Damiani and the good abbot, Guibert de Nogent, repented bitterly the misspent youth in which they had immersed themselves in the ancient poetry and had vied with Ovid in turning a verse.

The most deadly enemies of humane letters, however, were not asceticism and otherworldliness, but logic and philosophy. By the middle of

[1] H. Waddell, *The Wandering Scholars* (7th ed., London, 1947), p. 100.

the twelfth century these dominated the curriculum of the schools and left little room for the study of literature. Latin, however, continued to be the sole language of the universities and though literary form was cramped by the syllogism and vitiated by the technical jargon of philosophy, it was still a living language capable of adaptation to the needs of contemporary thought. Latin, too, was the language of the students in their hours of ease, the colloquial tongue of the Latin Quarter. It was, in short, the language of every literate cleric. Latin prose was his natural medium for the communication of ideas, and to Latin he turned when driven by religious or secular emotion to express his feelings in verse. Largely independent of either classical humanism or scholastic learning, the Latin poetry of the Middle Ages holds an honored place in the history of the world's literature, though it has not been appreciated at its full value by modern critics until fairly recent times. Classically trained scholars from the Renaissance to the eighteenth century could not forgive the medieval poet's disregard for classical norms, their substitution of an accented meter for the quantitative meter of classical Latin verse and their use of rhyme. Nevertheless, it was this very rejection of classical standards that, by drawing Latin poetry closer to the vernacular, gave it the spontaneity and vitality of a living tongue.

The most characteristic forms of medieval Latin poetry were intended to be sung, and the religious aspiration of the age found one of its most congenial forms of expression in the sequences and hymns that did so much to enrich the liturgy of the Church. Not all the Latin songs of the Middle Ages, however, were of this sort. Medieval people loved to sing, and they did not always sing church music. Even clerics had their less pious moments, when hymns seemed inadequate to express the fullness of life that was in them. This was especially true of those technical clerics — or clerics in the making — the university students. In the taverns of the Latin Quarter, the verse forms of the Latin hymns were adapted joyously to the expression of a variety of unsanctified emotions, and were set to music drawn indiscriminately from liturgical tunes and vernacular songs. Drinking songs, amorous lyrics, parodies on sacred themes, bitter comments on the lot of unendowed scholars, these "Goliardic" songs possessed a verve and variety that time cannot wither nor custom stale. Most of them were anonymous, though here and there we can distinguish the shadowy figure of the "Archpoet" or of some other wandering scholar, grown gray in sin, refusing to settle down in any academic or ecclesiastical niche and expressing in ribald verse an inveterate hatred of all propriety. The student songs were international, like the language in which they were written. They were the songs, not of a nation, but of a class; and that this was the same class that produced the great hymns and the most fervent expressions of mystical exaltation but serves to demonstrate the variety as well as the vigor of clerical culture. For medieval Latin poetry, whether sacred or profane, was the product of the clerical class, a class which formed an aristocracy of privilege, self-consciously distinguished from the rest of society by the possession, among other things, of a language of its own.

Learning rather than literature was, however, the major preoccupation of the clerical class in the Middle Ages. From the beginning of the revival of learning, the schools in which the clergy studied and taught concentrated attention more and more exclusively upon dialectic, philosophy, and theology. Scholastic learning, cast within this framework, was the most significant intellectual achievement of the clerical class through three centuries of vigorous reasoning. Much of it is extremely difficult for the modern student to grasp, unless he has been thoroughly trained in one of the neo-scholastic schools that have done so much in recent years to revive an interest in medieval thought. Scholastic philosophy was a highly developed discipline, with a technical terminology that falls strangely on modern ears. Its ways of thinking are not ours, and its aims, methods, premises, and basic problems are largely alien to us. Even that part of philosophy which included the natural sciences was based upon premises and a way of thinking very different from ours.

Medieval learning, like its modern counterpart, was conditioned by the interests of the age and by the data available. The medieval school-man desired to know, first of all, the things that were most important for him to know: the essential natures of God and man, and the means by which man can achieve salvation. Secondly, he strove to understand the universe in which he lived, but that universe, unlike the universe of the modern scientist, was one in which the natural order was subordinate to the supernatural. For these purposes the most important data were furnished by revealed truth as embodied in the Bible and the works of the Fathers of the Church, and next to this by the authoritative works of ancient Greek science, enriched as they were by Moslem commentators. Medieval scholasticism represented a revival of learning in the strictest sense of the word, and its first task was to recover, assimilate, and adapt to its own uses a body of knowledge already existing. It was natural, then, that the schoolmen should begin their thinking on any subject with an authoritative text, and that the method they used should be that of deductive logic. Given their strong orientation toward theology, it was natural, too, that they should be more interested in the metaphysical than the physical. The schoolmen sought to know first of all the abstract essence of things, and this tendency was powerfully reinforced by the fact that the elements of Greek thought first recovered were formal logic and the more abstract portions of Greek philosophy. Until nearly the end of the twelfth century, the scholastic thinkers had only a fragmentary knowledge of Platonic philosophy, and of Aristotle they knew little except the works on logic. Continued contact with the Byzantine and Moslem worlds, however, brought an increasing store of Greek and Arabic philosophy and science. During the thirteenth century, the complete Aristotle and nearly everything that had survived of Greek and Hellenistic mathematics, astronomy, cosmology, physics and medicine, together with all that had been added by Arabic commentators, was translated into Latin, either directly from the Greek or from Arabic and Hebrew intermediary sources.

The introduction of antique Greek philosophy with Moslem trimmings into the world of Christian thought inevitably posed new problems. Of these, one of the most crucial was that of reconciling reason with revelation. What the schoolmen gained from their newly acquired learning was not so much a body of knowledge, important though that was, as a way of thinking, and that way of thinking consisted primarily of formal logic. It furnished their minds with a new tool, which they manipulated with unspoiled delight and with unshaken faith in its powers. It inspired them to discover whatever could be known by the light of natural reason. At the same time, however, they were in possession of a body of revealed truth, which reason must strive to understand but never to challenge. When employed in the service of the faith, logic and philosophy might prove valuable allies to theology, but when pursued for their own sake they might become subtly subversive forces within the commonwealth of Christian thought. According to the way in which they solved the problem inherent in the relation of reason to revelation, the scholastic doctors may be divided into groups, or families as Étienne Gilson calls them.

The earliest of these, and one having many influential adherents throughout the whole scholastic period, may be called the Augustinian. Despite manifold variations of method, the philosophers of this family shared with the great Father of the Church the conviction that revelation must come first, reason second. As formulated by St. Anselm of Canterbury at the end of the eleventh century, their creed was "I do not seek to understand that I may believe, but I believe in order that I may understand (*credo ut intelligam*)." This was no denial of the potency of reason. It merely asserted that reason can achieve valid results only when informed by faith. Anselm's confidence in reason, which he identified with logic, was indeed so great that he believed it possible to demonstrate by pure dialectic the truth or necessity of many of the articles of the Christian faith. Later, the recovery of the complete works of Aristotle tended to undermine the Platonic Realism on which Anselm had based his arguments and to diminish the number of articles of faith regarded as susceptible to logical demonstration.

During the thirteenth century the translation into Latin of the commentaries on Aristotle of the great Arabic philosopher, Averroës, brought into existence a new family of scholastic philosophers. Averroës not only regarded Aristotelian philosophy as identical with natural reason and its conclusions as necessary, but also pointed out that in many respects it conflicted with theological doctrine, as, for example, in denying the individuality and immortality of the soul. The Latin Averroists, as clerics teaching in Church schools and bound to orthodox faith, were thus faced by a dilemma which forced them to abandon the attempt to reconcile reason with revelation. Many of them were forced to the unsatisfactory compromise solution that there are truths demonstrated by philosophy and others, frequently contradictory, founded upon revelation. The former must be regarded as necessary conclusions in philosophy, the latter as necessary conclusions in theology. The conflict between the two could be avoided, they felt, only by keeping philosophy and theology in separate watertight compartments. With most of the Latin Averroists, the absolute truth of the Christian faith and the superiority of revelation over reason was no doubt sincerely maintained. But there were also some, increasing in number toward the end of the thirteenth century, whose rationalist philosophy was no more than superficially qualified by formal recognition of the superior truth of revealed doctrine.

Averroists and Augustinians represented the opposing poles of opinion concerning the primacy of reason or revelation. The Thomists strove to establish a middle ground which would give to each its due in a single comprehensive system. It was the necessity of preserving the unity of the faith against the dangers implicit in Averroism, yet without returning to the pure Augustinianism of Anselm, that led St. Thomas Aquinas (c. 1225–74) to construct his masterly synthesis. It was founded upon a clear distinction between knowledge and faith as two different forms of cognition, each valid in its own sphere. But, unlike the Averroists, Thomas saw no necessary conflict between the two, nor would he keep philosophy, which is dependent on natural reason, and theology, which is dependent on revelation, in separate compartments. Instead he would place the findings of each in an ordered system, in which the things that can be known either by reason or faith are placed in an ascending hierarchy of essences, reaching from the material upward toward the spiritual. The coherent synthesis of social theory, moral philosophy, metaphysic and theology which it contained may well be regarded as the supreme achievement of scholastic thought, and the attacks made upon it in the fourteenth century as symptoms of the disintegration of scholasticism.

Throughout its whole course, the scholastic argument concerning the relation of reason to revelation was inseparably bound up with a philosophical debate over the nature of reality and our knowledge of it. The question of what has real existence is fundamental to the issue because the definition of a reality determines both how reality can be known and also the limits beyond which reason cannot go unaided by revelation. In accordance with their position in relation to this basic question the schoolmen can be classified as either Realists or Nominalists, although there were numerous variations of opinion within each group. Both positions were stated in extreme form in the late eleventh century, by Anselm and Roscelin of Compiègne respectively. Realism was for the moment triumphant and it continued to be maintained by most philosophers of the Augustinian family. It was challenged and modified in the twelfth century, however, by Abelard, and in the following century Thomas Aquinas gave the weight of his authority to a modified Realism, more Aristotelian than Platonic, which, though avoiding the extreme position of Anselm, was still positive enough to furnish the foundation for a synthesis of philosophy and theology. The triumph of Nominalism came only in the fourteenth century, and with it the disintegration of the synthesis.

In extreme form, Realism consisted in a belief that the only realities are the "universals" which, like the Platonic Ideas, have an independent existence apart from the individual things which are their imperfect and temporary manifestations. For example, what is ultimately real is not this man, this stone, this red-colored object, but man, stone, redness. This conception of reality was originally borrowed from Plato and applied to the understanding of Christian doctrine by St. Augustine and later revived and extended by Anselm. It gave invaluable support to rational proof of the articles of faith by asserting the reality of intangible substances, which can be perceived by a direct intuitive act of the intellect. The thought of the extreme Realist dealt only with the world of immutable, absolute Ideas or Forms which exist in the mind of God and can be perceived by the mind of man when illuminated by Divine Grace. The gradual recovery of Aristotelian philosophy and science in the twelfth and thirteenth centuries turned attention more toward concrete individual things and a theory of knowledge in which the physical senses played a larger part. The modified Realism of St. Thomas, and in a somewhat different sense that of Abelard, recognized that the universals exist only in particular things, not apart from them. Yet the universals are real. They are not merely names for categories of similar objects, as the Nominalists maintained. The universals are perceived by a process of active thought, which abstracts from the variety of individual phenomena within a given species what is the common principle, the "essence" of all. For example, while our knowledge of man is founded upon sensory perception of individual men, the intellect can discern through a process of abstraction what is the essence of man, as distinct, for example, from other animals. Though that essence, which is universal, not particular to the individual, does not exist apart from men, it is a real thing and can be known. It serves to place man in his proper relation to the other essences, including the supernatural, which make up the intelligible universe. Nominalism, on the other hand, flatly denied the reality of universals and so limited knowledge to direct perception of individual things which alone have real existence. The full effect of this theory as developed by William of Ockham, however, belongs to a later period and will be discussed within the context of late scholasticism.

Without a certain amount of Realism, philosophy is powerless to deal with the intangible substances of a metaphysical universe, and therein lay its importance for medieval Christian thought. But, as a way of thinking, it was by no means limited to the problems posed by theology and metaphysics. It pervaded every aspect of medieval thought, including social and political theory, and it goes far to explain the subordination of the individual to the corporate or ideal institution that was so characteristic of medieval society.

> Corporations were prior to individuals, as the universal was prior to its particulars. Dominating all activities there was the pervasive and unifying reality of the Church. And numerous institutions, the papacy, the great monastic orders, the ecclesiastical schools, the universities, the towns, the guilds, the manors, and many other corporate personalities expressed the medieval confidence in Realist principles. In our own day there has been a portentous revival of extreme Realism in European politics.[2]

To this summary by Meyrick Carré of the political and social implications of Realism might be added Haskins's corollary comment on the results of Nominalism when applied to political theory:

> Apply the Nominalist doctrine to the Church, and the Church ceases to be a divine institution with a life of its own and becomes merely a convenient designation for the whole body of individual Christians. Apply it to the state, and where does political authority reside, in a sov-

2 M. H. Carré, *Realists and Nominalists* (Oxford, 1946), p. 38.

ereign whole or in individual citizens? In form, at least, the problem is still with us.[8]

It is with us indeed. And it is the impossibility of limiting the Realist way of thought to metaphysics and theology that makes many modern liberals — unconscious Nominalists — find the atmosphere of the Neo-Thomist philosophy uncongenial.

Realism and the habit of thought it engendered also served to make the intellectual atmosphere of the medieval schools inhospitable to empirical science. Extreme Realism tended to ignore the world of concrete appearances almost entirely, and even the moderate Realism of the Aristotelians reinforced the schoolmen's ingrained tendency to seek through deductive logic to find the abstract essences of things, rather than to weigh or measure or otherwise study individual things concretely. Medicine was the only science that had its own professional schools, and even in them the principal intellectual tool was deductive logic, and the method of instruction was exposition of authoritative texts with little attention to clinical observation or experiment. The other sciences found their way into the universities only in a subordinate position in the curriculum of the Faculty of Arts, where they were not only overshadowed by logic and philosophy, but studied by the methods of the one and used to serve the interests of the other. Mathematics was valued chiefly for its logical concepts, and cosmology for its contribution to a metaphysical construction of the universe. Recent research has demonstrated that there was much more natural science in the medieval schools than earlier historians had supposed, but the fact remains that the most vigorous and constructive thought of the schoolmen was devoted to the subjects of their greatest professional interest: philosophy and theology.

The subordination of all systematic speculation to Christian doctrine, and with that the subordination of physical science to metaphysics and of concrete to abstract realities, was in part, no doubt, the natural result of the overpoweringly strong religious interests of the age, and in part resulted from the fact that the scientific knowledge available, for all its richness, was still inadequate to furnish an explanation for most of the operations of the physical universe. At the same time, it must not be forgotten that the primary function of the medieval schools was to educate the clergy. Both teachers and students were clerics and, though clerics might have worldly interests, they had ideally no professional concern with the things of this world. The curriculum of instruction was designed to train members of a professional class whose function in so-

[8] C. H. Haskins, *The Renaissance of the Twelfth Century* (Cambridge, Mass., 1927), p. 352.

ciety was the cure of souls and the interpretation of Christian doctrine. Even in modern times, the natural sciences play a very small part in the curriculum of schools devoted exclusively to the training of the clergy.

So much of medieval scholarship was concentrated in the schools and universities that the unacademic forms of clerical learning are sometimes overlooked. One of the most important of these, the writing of history, flourished almost entirely outside the academic halls in monasteries or cathedral chapters. The medieval historians were, with very few exceptions, clerics. Though many of them were educated at the universities, they did not learn their craft there, for history had no place in the medieval curriculum. The most common forms of medieval historiography — the annals, chronicles, and lives of the saints — had originated in the Early Middle Ages; but they made tremendous advances in scope, erudition, and style after the middle of the eleventh century. The most primitive form, the annals, were originally little more than jottings of memorable events on the yearly calendar kept in monasteries and cathedrals to record the Church festivals and holy days. From these grew the monastic and episcopal chronicles. Later, the yearly records were in many places collected, revised, and expanded by a single author to form a coherent history. The chronicles were at first restricted largely to local events. With the revival of learning, however, and with the expansion of the writers' horizon made possible by the economic and political growth of the crusading era, the best of them became universal histories, thrusting far back into the past and expanding their view of recent events to the limits of Christendom. The history of the distant past contained in these chronicles, usually beginning with the creation, the flood, and the Tower of Babel, was mostly lifted straight from the Bible or from the works of Eusebius, the Venerable Bede, and other early Christian writers. It adds little to our knowledge of history. But for their own times and the more immediate past, the chronicles are invaluable sources. When written by men of the caliber of Otto of Freising, Matthew Paris, or Vincent of Beauvais, they contain a wealth of information concerning current political events, illuminated by much acute observation.

For all their interest in secular history, however, the point of view of the chroniclers was unmistakably clerical and their philosophy of history profoundly theological. Their conception of world history was shaped in the first place by belief in the Divine creation of the world and in the continuous direction of human affairs by Divine Providence. This gave to history a definite starting-point in time and one all-pervasive causal force. The medieval philosophy of history was also dominated by a dualistic conception of the contrast between the eternal City of God and the temporal city of man, and it was given a teleological

73

direction by the conviction of the eventual triumph of the former. This was the contribution of St. Augustine, whose great essay on the meaning of history, the *De civitate Dei*, furnished clerical historians with most of their leading ideas. Under his influence, history became almost a branch of theology. It was theology teaching by examples. Many of the clerical historians were practical statesmen, or at least lived under the rule of bishops or abbots who were great figures in contemporary political life, and they were profoundly versed in secular affairs. Yet their histories could never be entirely secular. Like Augustine they believed that the worldly state was founded in sin by fallen man, and they were profoundly convinced of its inferiority in relation to the Church, which they envisaged as the earthly embodiment of the City of God. The clerical chronicle was always in greater or lesser degree *historia ecclesiastica*. And, for all the provincialism inherent in the chronicle of a particular monastery or bishopric, the local scene and the contemporary event were set against the background of world history. Every action was significant only as a part of the great human drama for which God has set the stage, outlined the plot, and determined the final curtain. Medieval historiography, then, no less than scholastic philosophy, represented the ideas of the clerical class and bore the marks of its authors' professional training.

C. Feudal Culture: Vernacular Literature

The medieval nobles were not a learned class. Few, indeed, were literate, and those who could read generally preferred not to. Latin, the language of all learned writing, was a closed book to all but a very few, and they were mostly men who had been originally dedicated to the Church by their families, but had, through some shift in the family fortunes, remained in the lay world. If the nobles did not form a reading public, however, they did become, under the influence of a more luxurious, leisured, and courtly way of life, an avidly listening public for the song, story, and lyric poetry of minstrel and troubadour. It was primarily for the feudal nobility that literature in the rising national languages was created in the same period which saw the revival and apotheosis of clerical learning. Except for the knightly authors of the Provençal love lyrics or of the German *Minnesang*, the creators of feudal literature were for the most part not themselves lay nobles. Some were clerics; the majority were professional minstrels or *jongleurs*. Whatever their origin or social status, however, they wrote for a noble audience and their work reflects the preoccupations, the ideals and prejudices of the feudal and chivalrous classes.

Despite the use of national languages, feudal literature was almost as international as the society it mirrored. The same story material and the same lyric motifs appeared wherever feudalism and chivalry flourished. By far the greater part of it, however, originated in France, the feudal and chivalrous land *par excellence,* or in those lands to which the conquering Normans had introduced French language and culture. The *Nibelungenlied* and the tale of the Spanish hero, the Cid, are perhaps the most notable exceptions. This literature was of two quite different kinds: stories in verse or prose, most of which first appeared in nothern France, and lyric poetry, the seeds of which were first sown in the hothouse atmosphere of the chivalrous Provençal courts. The most widely disseminated story material consisted of two great cycles which had as their focal point the figures of Charlemagne and King Arthur respectively. Other lesser cycles dealt with the Trojan War, Alexander the Great, or the Crusades. There was also a group of miscellaneous romances, like the story of Floire and Blanchefleur which was retold in nearly every European language, and the charming tale told in alternate prose and verse of the star-crossed lovers, Aucassin and Nicolette.

The stories of the Charlemagne cycle, the *chansons de geste,* have a particular value for the historians, for they present the most realistic picture of French feudal society as it was in the crusading era. That the great emperor and his peers are the nominal heroes and that some of the stories refer to faintly traceable historical events, such as the slaughter of Charlemagne's rear guard at Roncesvalles in the *Chanson de Roland,* is largely irrelevant. For all practical purposes the *chansons* are straight fiction. They are action stories in a twelfth-century feudal setting. Charlemagne's barons are the contemporaries of Godfrey of Bouillon and Louis VII, though it may be that Roland in his earliest literary appearance was rather the contemporary of William the Conqueror. The *Chanson de Roland* is at any rate almost certainly the oldest, as it is certainly the greatest, of the *chansons.* The plots of these stories are feudal plots. They turn on the motives of loyalty, rebellion, treachery, and endless feud over disputed fiefs, together with the ever present motive of the Crusade against the vile Paynim, all resulting in vast effusion of blood. Whatever the plot, it leads inevitably to warfare, but for reasons entirely comprehensible to any feudal noble. The campaigns, too, are realistic, often brutally so, for these stories were composed for an audience of experts. If there is exaggeration it is in the numbers slain by the paladins. The noble audience was not composed of statisticians, and it did not worry them, apparently, that the mortality rate reported in the *chansons* would shortly have led to race suicide. Every knight in the *chansons* was endowed with superhuman strength, capable of cleaving an armored enemy from brow to waist. Like Saul they slew their thousands and like David their tens of thousands. But, if they were in this way idealized — figments of wish-fulfillment — they were otherwise not all ideal figures. There is real tenderness in the friendship of Roland for Oliver, and honest grief in his mourning for the good knights slain as a result of his own bullheaded courage and stubborn honor. There are numbers of loyal, truehearted vassals; but there are also numerous examples of every feudal vice. The titular heroes of *Garin de Lorain* and *Raoul de Cambrai* were bestial in their ferocity, cruel, treacherous, and guilty of every impiety. The monotonously repeated accounts of rapine and pillage and the mutilation or massacre of prisoners who were not worth holding for ransom have a matter-of-fact tone that chills the blood. Sheer love of carnage is, indeed, the prevailing tone throughout the *chansons*. Of tenderer sentiments there is only occasional evidence.

Love and romance, myth and the fairy world of imagination entered feudal story from the Celtic twilight of Wales and Brittany, rather than from the lusty and bellicose tradition of old France. The origin of the Arthurian legends is lost in the mists of Celtic folklore, whence they brought with them a dark undercurrent of primitive myth, the significance of which was probably not recognized by the French poets who made them over into tales of chivalry and romance. As they made their appearance in the feudal literature of the twelfth and thirteenth centuries, the heroes of King Arthur's Round Table were, in fact, contemporary French knights. But in these tales, the emphasis has shifted from feudalism to chivalry, and chivalry as it was conceived under the influence of troubadour poetry and the cult of courtly love. They reflect the ideals of a courtly society, in which the ladies have begun to occupy a prominent and highly idealized place. Chrétien de Troyes, the most famous of the northern French poets and largely responsible for introducing the Arthurian material, wrote at the request of the cultured Countess Marie de Champagne, daughter of the brilliant Eleanor of Aquitaine and like her a recognized authority on the code of courtly love. There are recognizable feudal elements in these stories, and there is an abundance of mayhem and homicide; but the adventures recorded are mostly those of knights-errant, who set out to rescue distressed damsels or to prove by tournament-like encounters with other knights or by wholly fanciful conflicts with giants and monsters their devotion to their ladies. With their background of myth and magic and their improbable plots, the romances lack the realistic quality of the *chansons*. They do, however, reflect the ideals and even something of the way of life of a society in which chivalry was still a vital reality and had not yet degenerated into preciosity. Love is here the major theme, with that convention of absolute, unswerving devotion to the lady's slightest whim which the cult of courtly love demanded. Yet for all the rigid, almost legalistic code of devotion to the knight's chosen lady — usually someone else's wife — which the romances owed in large part to Provençal influences, they display a much more delicate analysis of sentiment and a far more sophisticated tone than can be found in the ruder *chansons de geste*. And their influence was more widely spread. The most psychologically profound as well as most artistically integrated of all the Arthurian poems were produced in Germany: the *Tristan and Iseult* of Gottfried von Strassburg and the *Parsifal* of Wolfram von Eschenbach.

While northern France gave birth to the largest body of feudal story, it was in the southern lands of Provence and Languedoc that the lyric poetry, which embodied chivalrous love in quintessential form, was first born. The twelfth century was the great age of Provençal culture, before the Albigensian Crusade struck it down. The revival of trade in the Mediterranean stimulated the economy of southern France and made possible a more luxurious and sophisticated social life for the upper classes at an unusually early date. Far removed from royal control, the feudal nobles of the south retained their practical autonomy, so that the land was dotted with the castles of semi-independent lords. To these courts thronged the lord's vassals, together with landless knights and minstrels, to become courtiers in much the sense in which the word was used three hundred years later by Castiglione. They paid feudal homage to the lord and an almost equally feudal homage to his lady and to the damsels of her entourage. To these latter their homage took the form of romantic love, of a sort unknown to antiquity or to the Early Middle Ages, but which has never since entirely disappeared. Shorn of its excesses and adapted to other social environments, it has continued, like the chivalry from which it sprang, to shape the ideals and inspire the poetry of every century since. In its pristine form, chivalrous love had, it is true, certain qualities that seem rather odd by modern standards. It was, as C. S. Lewis put it, "love of a highly specialized sort, whose characteristics may be enumerated as Humility, Courtesy, Adultery, and the Religion of Love."[4] For reasons inherent in the feudal system, courtly love could seldom lead to marriage. The lover pledged his absolute loyalty, obedience, and unswerving constancy. He hoped for little in

[4] C. S. Lewis, *The Allegory of Love* (Oxford, 1936), p. 2.

return and asked for less. He suffered audibly and, on the whole, melodiously. Love became the mainspring of his life. Acting as a substitute for religious emotion it inspired him to all worthy deeds.

The troubadours who wrote the lyrics of courtly love were many of them — at least half of the five hundred-odd whose names we know — of the noble class, though their songs were carried from court to court throughout Europe by professional *jongleurs*. Contemporary with the Latin lyrics of the wandering scholars, these poems used many of the same strophic forms, though from which direction the borrowing occurred is a matter of much scholarly debate. In general, the vernacular verse displayed greater variety and ingenuity, at times an almost perverse ingenuity, in the complication of rhyme schemes. It would be difficult to find any strophic form in modern lyric poetry that could not be duplicated from the work of the troubadours. But it was less the form, not always translatable, than the sentiment of the Provençal lyric that made it the seed-bed from which was transplanted or seminally derived so much of medieval and modern verse. Suppressed at home by the fury of the heresy hunters, it spread like a contagion through all the courts of Europe. As early as the reign of Philip Augustus (1180–1223) it was introduced into the northern French court of Champagne in the train of the Countess Marie. There it inspired the lyric song of the *trouvères*, who were the northern counterparts of the troubadours. In the early thirteenth century it also gave the initial impetus to one of the greatest periods of German poetry, the age of Walther von der Vogelweide and the *Minnesinger*. From Provence Dante later drew his *dolce stil nuovo* and Petrarch the models for his songs to Laura. Without the seeds sprung from Provence, Chaucer would not have written as he did, nor would a host of later English lyric poets. Finally, it was the Provençal religion of love that blossomed in northern France into that peculiarly medieval phenomenon, the allegory of love. In that most widely read of all medieval poems, the *Roman de la Rose*, especially in the first part written early in the thirteenth century by Guillaume de Lorris, all the subtleties, all the nuances of courtly love were set forth in an allegorical form scarcely intelligible to the modern mind but filled with meaning for the medieval. When the bourgeois Jean de Meung completed the poem at the end of the century the great age of courtly love was already passing. It continued to exert its influence for centuries to come, but in its pure form the love poetry of the troubadours and *trouvères* faded with the chivalrous society that produced it.

The greater part of feudal literature in this period was in verse — fit to be memorized and sung or recited. Prose belongs by nature more to book-learning and demands a reading public. By the thirteenth century, however, lettered if not learned members of the noble class were becoming less rare. More of the romances of that century were written in prose, and an occasional noble turned his hand to prose composition. As might have been expected, the military memoir offered unusual opportunities for the noble author, and at least two of these have won for themselves a place in the world's literature. In the early years of the thirteenth century, Count Geoffroy de Villehardouin wrote, or at least dictated, an eye-witness account of the Fourth Crusade, and at the end of the century Jean, Sire de Joinville, set down in French prose his memories of the ill-fated crusades of St. Louis. But these men were pioneers and exceptions to the rule. The age of lay learning was just beginning to dawn at the end of the thirteenth century, and it began in Italy rather than France, among the urban rather than the feudal classes.

D. Architecture and Art: the Age of High Gothic

The age which embodied its loftiest intellectual aspirations in scholastic philosophy and theology found expression for its aesthetic sense in religious architecture and art. This is no more than might be expected of an age in which religion exercised a more pervasive influence upon thought and emotion than, perhaps, at any other period. The almost exclusively religious character of medieval art, however, cannot be accounted for so simply. Religious art reigned supreme for the same reason that scholasticism dominated intellectual life: it had no serious competitors. Just as higher learning was a monopoly of the clergy, the only educated class, so the higher forms of art were a monopoly of the Church, the only institution with both the need for art and the means to pay for it. Barons and burghers, as well as priests and prelates, contributed their wealth to the building and decoration of churches and shared, according to their capacity, in the enjoyment of the results; but neither the fortress-like castles of the nobles nor the utilitarian homes of the merchants and artisans as yet furnished a suitable setting for works of art or were themselves designed with an aesthetic purpose. Only the church — constructed *ad majorem Dei gloriam* — called forth the artistic skill and vision of the age to clothe the House of God in imperishable beauty. From this primary purpose of erecting a suitable edifice to house Divinity there resulted a domination of architecture over sculpture and painting which reduced the figurative arts to a subordinate position. With the exception of miniature painting in illuminated manuscripts, these arts could exist only within the framework of the building.

The new style which began to replace Romanesque in the second half of the twelfth century, and which a later age, imbued with classical standards of taste, contemptuously dubbed "Gothic," made its first appearance in the cities of the Île de France. Elements of the new structural form had already been introduced tentatively in the Romanesque churches of Normandy, Burgundy, and other parts of France; but true Gothic was born in Paris in the abbey church of St. Denis, which Abbot Suger, the great minister of Louis VI and Louis VII, began to build in 1137. Here for the first time the pointed arch and the cross-ribbed vault were used systematically and with revolutionary effect. All that was needed thereafter was the addition of the flying buttress to complete the evolution of the Gothic style and to create a radically new method of construction, which during the following century spread to almost every part of Western Europe, leaving only Italy comparatively untouched.

Reduced to its essentials, the Gothic building was simply a balanced system of basic structural units, varying in size but similar in construction. Each unit was composed of a four-sided bay with piers or pillars at each of the four corners. These were connected by arched ribs on all four sides and by diagonal ribs which crossed to form the center of the vault. Unlike the round arches of the Romanesque, the pointed arches of the Gothic ribs made it possible to vault over rectangles or the wedge-shaped bays of the curved apse. A series of high and wide bays running down the center of the church formed the nave and choir and were crossed by a similar series of bays, extending to left and right between nave and choir, to form the transepts which gave the floor plan the form of a cross. These central bays were flanked by a corresponding series of smaller and lower bays to form the side aisles. These, after the break caused by the transepts, continued in a curve around the apse to form the ambulatory embracing the choir. In some of the early Gothic buildings the structure was strengthened by double aisles, with a matching series of bays built on top of the inner aisle to form a gallery. Throughout the building the downward thrust of the pointed arches was carried from the ribs down through the piers or pillars to the floor, while the lateral thrust of the ribs was counterbalanced by the corresponding lateral thrust of the ribs of the adjoining bays. Finally, the outward thrust of the ribs of the side aisles against the outer wall was stopped against massive buttresses, while that of the nave arches, rising high above the aisles, was met by the leaping counterthrust of the flying buttresses. The essential elements of the entire structure thus made up a skeleton of ribs, piers and buttresses, the dynamic thrust of each balanced by a corresponding counterthrust, so that a current of latent force seems to run through it from end to end and side to side. At the same time, since only this skeleton carried weight, the vaults between the ribs could be filled in with lighter stone and, most important of all, the walls could be practically eliminated and replaced with glass. Thus the Gothic architect was able to raise the diaphanous structure of his nave to unprecedented heights — 138 feet at Amiens — with the vertical lines extending from the piers through the supports to the pointed arches, and leading the eye constantly upward.

Brilliant as was the technical innovation that made it possible, the Gothic cathedral was more than a technical achievement. It was at once the expression of a vision and the embodiment of a habit of thought peculiar to the age: an age that expressed transcendental ideas in tangible symbols, that conceived the church as an earthly analogy of the Heavenly City, and that strove to construct it in accordance with the number and proportion which had governed the construction of the universe by the Divine Architect. The vision was in the first instance that of Abbot Suger and the habit of thought that of scholasticism, but the rapid spread of the Gothic style demonstrates how perfectly it fitted the mentality of the period.

It may always be an open question whether the discovery of rib construction led to the opening up of the walls or whether it was the desire to illuminate the sanctuary that inspired the architects to develop the potentialities of the ribbed vault. The account left by Suger of the construction of his prototype church suggests the latter alternative. As Abbot of St. Denis, Suger's attention was drawn to the writings of that fifth-century Neoplatonist whom tradition had identified with St. Paul's Athenian convert, Dionysius the Areopagite, who in turn had been traditionally identified with the martyred St. Denis, patron saint of France, in whose honor Suger raised his great church. In these writings he found a metaphysical conception of light, drawn from Platonic and Biblical sources, which identified it with divinity and regarded it as the nearest analogy to God who is the True Light. According to the pseudo-Dionysius, light is at once the creative principle in all things and the means by which our minds are illuminated to perceive truth. Heaven itself is bathed in light, and the beauty of all things and their place of dignity in the cosmic hierarchy depends upon the degree to which they possess it. This conception of light, at once metaphysical and aesthetic, runs through medieval thought from the mystical theology of Hugh of St. Victor to the poetry of the *Divine Comedy*, but nowhere is it made more immediately visible than in the pervading luminosity of the Gothic cathedral. Suger was explicitly thinking of his church as an analogy of Heaven when he opened up the walls of the apse to allow light to pour into the sanctuary and so arranged the vaults that all the great windows were directly visible from a place before the high altar. What distinguishes the Gothic from the Romanesque building is not so much the pointed arches and ribbed vaults — these are but technical devices — as the substitution of a diaphanous for an opaque wall. At the same time, the development from Early to High Gothic can be traced by the progressive opening up of the walls as the gallery was eliminated and the clerestory brought down almost to the top of the side aisles.

In still another way, the Gothic church was constructed to represent an analogy of the cosmos as God had created it. From the mystical significance attributed to numbers by Pythagoras and transmitted through St. Augustine and Boethius, medieval schoolmen evolved a theory that the universe owes its beauty and its stability to "perfect" proportion. The ratios which determine this perfect proportion can be arrived at by geometrical means, and also conform to the ratios of the musical consonances which reflect the cosmic harmony. Geometrical ratios thus acquired for medieval thinkers a metaphysical significance. Working under clerical direction the architect was bound to use these ratios in laying out his ground plan and designing the elevation. It may be true that the masterbuilder found it more convenient to work out a series of ratios by the manipulation of squares, triangles or other geometrical figures than by arithmetical calculations. Whatever the motive, the conception of architecture as applied geometry and the systematic adherence to certain metaphysically justified ratios guaranteed a harmoniously constructed building, even though the work might be interrupted and two or three generations might elapse before it was completed; while at the same time it made the building an analogy of the divine order in the cosmos, through contemplation of which the mind might be drawn to perception of the nature of the Divine Architect.

Finally, as Erwin Panofsky has argued,[5] the Gothic architects, through contact with the scholastically trained clergy under whose direction they worked, acquired a habit of thought that found expression in the systematic logic by which all parts of the building were related and in the clarity with which the relation between form and function was made explicitly visible. Scholastic thought was nothing if not systematic, and in the logical structure of the *summa* no step in the argument was taken for granted. Like the scholastic *summa* the Gothic building was composed of a system of similarly constructed parts, while the visible articulation of ribs to supporting shafts enabled the viewer to follow the logic of the architect's thought with all the explicit clarity of a syllogism.

The extent to which the architects were influenced by scholastic habits of thought may be difficult to prove, but there can be no doubt that scholastic love of system and synthesis and the theologians' habit of

[5] E. Panofsky, *Gothic Architecture and Scholasticism* (New York, 1957).

NAVE LOOKING WESTWARD FROM THE SANCTUARY.

CHURCH OF ST. DENIS, PARIS

1

FAÇADE.

CATHEDRAL OF REIMS

APSE, WITH FLYING BUTTRESSES.

CATHEDRAL OF NOTRE-DAME, PARIS

4

WEST PORTAL.

CATHEDRAL OF CHARTRES

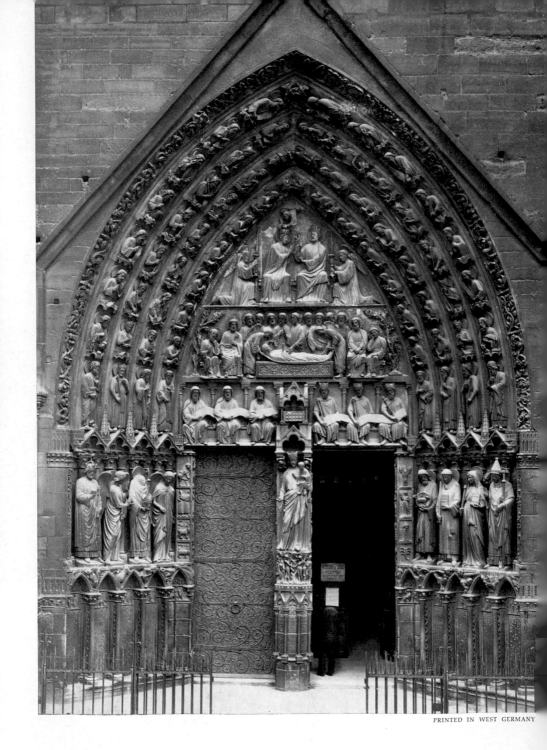

PORTAL OF THE VIRGIN.

CATHEDRAL OF NOTRE-DAME, PARIS

6

VIRGIN OF THE NORTH PORTAL.

CATHEDRAL OF NOTRE-DAME, PARIS

LA VIERGE DORÉE.

CATHEDRAL OF AMIENS

expressing abstract truth in symbol and allegory was directly reflected in the iconographical program of sculpture and stained glass, which made the cathedral in a quite literal way a *summa* of Christian knowledge, theological, moral, natural and historical. In thousands of statues and carved reliefs, framing the portals or dotting the façades, and in the design of the stained glass windows there appeared Biblical scenes and figures, from the Nativity to the Last Judgement, prophets, apostles and saints, kings and patriarchs, choirs of angels, allegorical figures representing the vices and virtues, the seven liberal arts, philosophy and theology, the Church and the Synagogue, the various trades and types of labor, the months of the year and a host of symbolic beasts. The choice and arrangement of these was clearly not left to the discretion of the master-builder, but was dictated by the bishop or the canons of the cathedral, many of whom were deeply versed in scholastic theology. The decoration of the cathedral was, in fact, intended to form a kind of scripture, which could be read by those who could not read written words, for the meaning of the scenes and figures was made familiar and intelligible by the tradition that bound the artists to specific ways of representing them.

At the same time, however much tradition and scholastic learning might prescribe what the artist must do, they could neither direct his hand nor control completely his vision of the external world. In Gothic art the ideal is expressed in the total effect of the figure or the scene, while a new realism, product of the concrete vision of the lay artist, makes its appearance in the detail, and triumphs uninhibited in the purely ornamental flower and leaf designs that crowned the pillars. Even in the ideal figures there is a clarity of line and a suggestion of solidity that was foreign to the monastic vision of the Romanesque artists. Yet this dichotomy of idealism and naturalism does not in fact impair the essential unity of the decorative scheme. Rather it corresponds to that unity which the moderate Realism of St. Thomas Aquinas achieved in his great synthesis, the fundamental principle of which was that the universal exists *in* the particular. It has real existence, as does the ideal in Gothic art, but it does not exist apart from the concrete thing made intelligible through the senses.

A similar movement in the direction of detailed naturalism was evident in painting, although painting was in this period a distinctly minor art which could scarcely claim any independent existence at all. The Gothic building offered little or no surface for mural paintings or mosaics, such as had decorated the earlier Byzantine or Romanesque churches, their place being taken by the stained-glass windows. Painting was therefore restricted almost entirely to the illumination of manuscripts, where it had not yet freed itself from cramping dependencies on the setting provided by capital letters and the margins of the page. Nevertheless, the age of the High Gothic witnessed the beginnings of a revolution in the illuminators' art that foreshadowed the exquisite miniatures of the two following centuries. With a growing demand for books of devotion on the part of royal and noble patrons or wealthy ecclesiastics, illumination ceased to be confined to the *scriptoria* of the monasteries. Lay craftsmen brought to their painting a professional skill and training and added the touches of naturalism in detail that were already making their appearance in the work of the sculptors and workers in stained glass. The influence of stained glass, the major pictorial art of the period, is clearly evident in the iconographical scheme of the illuminations, in the architectural framing frequently provided for the pictures, in the rather cramped grouping of the figures, the preference for solid colors and, above all, in the setting of the figures against a solid background, with gold taking the place of the colored glass. The limitations of the stained-glass medium, thus transferred to painting, tended to retard the development of three-dimensional figures moving freely in space, but this was compensated by an increasingly graceful use of line, more natural gestures and a general air of aristocratic elegance.

Throughout Gothic art a high level of craftsmanship was combined with a subservience to tradition that limited the expression of individual genius. That this should be so was rendered inevitable, not only by the control over the spirit and form of art exercised by ecclesiastical patrons, but also by the social status and organization of the artists. The Gothic age marked the passing of art from the monastery into the hands of lay artists, for nearly all the men who built and decorated the Gothic churches, as well as the illuminators who developed the Gothic style of painting, were laymen. We cannot deny them the title of artist; but in the eyes of their contemporaries — and doubtless in their own conception of themselves — they were simply artisans, that is, skilled craftsmen, not in any special way different from the masters of other trades. The architect or master-builder might be a man of some education. He was highly respected and comparatively well paid. He was, however, an exceptional figure, a man of authority as well as unusual skill and knowledge, but even he had begun his career as a mason, learning the fundamentals of his trade. The ordinary masons, the sculptors and the workers in stained glass had no opportunity to rise above the level of the artisan. Like other craftsmen, they served their apprenticeship, then worked for some years as journeymen and finally achieved the rank of master. In large cities like Paris they were organized in corporations; but, unlike the workers in other trades, the masons were frequently forced by the intermittent nature of work on large buildings to travel from place to place seeking employment. When on the job, these wandering artisans lived in the masons' lodge and were subject to its hierarchical discipline. In the course of time they developed something like an international guild, with secret signs by which journeymen and masters might identify themselves as qualified according to their grade. The strong corporate organization of the lodge did much to guarantee sound workmanship and uniformity of style, while the itinerant nature of the masons' life assisted the spread of new developments from such advanced centers as the Île de France to other parts of Europe.

Gothic art was pre-eminently urban. The cathedral rose from the city square to proclaim the burghers' civic pride as well as the power of the Church. It was the money economy introduced by the growing cities that made it possible to turn landed wealth into money to pay workers and buy materials. It was the cities, too, that furnished the reservoir of skilled workers. But it would be an error to regard Gothic as in any real sense bourgeois art. It grew in the midst of a pre-capitalist economy and a society still dominated by feudalism and the Church. It was the Church that provided the patronage and the direction. What the urban artisan contributed was only his skill, his pride in his craft, and occasional glimpses of his earthy vision of external reality.

E. Music of the Early and High Middle Ages

The cathedrals and churches which arose all over Western Europe in the twelfth and thirteenth centuries furnished the setting not only for the visual arts of the period, but also for the greater part of its music. From the eleventh century the cathedrals and collegiate churches were beginning to replace the monasteries as the most important centers of musical activity. Beneath the Gothic arches of their choirs music swelled to fill the church at almost every hour of the day and to furnish an increasingly elaborate setting for the liturgy of the Mass and the offices of the canonical hours. This was a period of decisive importance in the history of Western music as in that of learning, literature, architecture and art, a period marked by a great revitalization of intellectual and aesthetic energy. Despite much innovation, however, it represented not so much a break with the past as the acceleration of a course of development begun centuries earlier. Just as we cannot understand the music of the fourteenth and fifteenth centuries with which this book is principally concerned, or estimate the magnitude of its achievement, without some knowledge of the music of the High Middle Ages which formed its point of departure, so we cannot understand the advances made from the eleventh to the thirteenth centuries without relating them to the evolution of musical forms in the preceding period. It will be necessary, therefore, to review here at what may seem disproportionate length, though also at the risk of much oversimplification, the development of Western music from the beginning of the Christian era, the more so because much of it was until recent years almost unknown and hence neglected in general histories of culture.

The history of music in Western Europe, as we know it, begins with Christian chant, that is, with musical forms which originated for the most part in the Hebrew synagogues, from which they were carried over into the infant Christian churches and spread with the expansion of Christianity. These musical forms were introduced into the West as settings of Greek texts, but before the end of the third century they had been adapted to the Latin tongue, which was thereafter to remain the language of the Western Church. The freeing of Christianity from persecution by Constantine in 313 ushered in a period of rapid growth of liturgical music so prolific and varied that the Church authorities soon felt it necessary to restrict and codify it in the interest of orthodoxy and uniformity. Such a codification was undertaken in northern Italy before the end of the fourth century by St. Ambrose, Bishop of Milan. Other forms of chant, however, continued to flourish for several centuries in Gaul and Spain. All of these, with the exception of the Ambrosian chant which still survives in Milan, were eventually replaced by the chants which had developed under papal authority in the *schola cantorum* at Rome. Although several early popes played an important part in this process, the decisive event was the reform undertaken under the direction of Gregory the Great (590–604), and the resultant body of Gregorian chant has remained with remarkably little change the official chant of the Roman Catholic Church to this day. Despite the great authority of Gregory, the Roman music was not universally adopted for some time, nor did the composition of new chants cease. The triumph of Gregorian chant over its rivals was in fact not finally assured until the formation of the Carolingian Empire reinforced the unity of the Western Church and added the authority of Charlemagne to that of the pope in support of the Roman usage. Britain, it is true, lay outside the Empire, but there Gregorian music had been introduced directly by the missionaries sent by the great pope himself. The turn of the eighth century thus marked the end of the first period in the history of Gregorian chant — its Golden Age — by which time the three thousand-odd melodies that make up the official Gregorian corpus were nearly all established in the form they still retain.

The music thus codified was a monodic setting of psalms, prose excerpts from the Scriptures and hymns. Although not without form, it had no fixed rhythm but ebbed and swelled with a free wave-like motion, nor was there any measured variation in the length of the notes. The relation of text to music varied greatly depending on its sense and liturgical purpose. In long passages where the meaning was all important, as in the Credo, there was usually a syllable to every note. In other cases there might be groups of two to four notes to a syllable, while in those shorter phrases in the liturgy which seemed to call for special jubilation, like the Alleluia, a long melismatic series of notes might be set to a single syllable. The relation of notes to syllables was fixed at an early period, probably before the Gregorian reform, by writing the notes in groups called "neumes," which indicated the number of notes to a syllable, but not as yet their pitch or time value.

One further characteristic of Gregorian music must be noted. Its tonality was determined in accordance with one of a number of melodic "modes," of which only two, corresponding to our major and minor scales, survive in modern music. This also remained true of nearly all medieval music and goes far to explain why it sounds strange to modern ears. The theorists of the ninth and tenth centuries, who classified the chants in accordance with the modes, regarded these as rooted in Greek musical practice and took over the names of the Greek *tonoi*. In theory there were twelve modes, divided into two groups of six "authentic" modes beginning on the tonic or key-note and six corresponding "plagal" modes beginning on the dominant or fifth of the octave below. In Gregorian music only the first eight, the so-called "ecclesiastical modes," were used. The modes differed from modern practice in that no accidentals were theoretically permitted and that the half-tone interval, occurring at a different place in each pair of modes, falls at what seems to us unexpected places. Perhaps the simplest way to envisage the modes is to play scales beginning on each of the white notes of the piano and using only the white notes.

Gregorian chant, which was in its origins an importation from the East, was not the spontaneous expression of Western musical taste, but was imposed by the authority of the Church. Had that authority been completely effective the creative impulse without which music cannot live would have been permanently frustrated. This was of course impossible. The history of music from the ninth century to the end of the Middle Ages is, in fact, largely the history of successive efforts first to embellish and vary the official chants and then to create new and more independent music. These efforts took several different forms which follow one another more or less logically, but not necessarily in chronological sequence.

The first method of embellishment, and one which continued to flourish in luxuriant profusion for three or four centuries, was to insert new melodies with or without new words into any portion of an official chant that seemed to offer an opportunity for expansion. These additions or interpolations, which were purely optional and merely tolerated by the Church, were called "tropes." The first step was apparently to add a melody without words as a melisma on one syllable; the next to fit a text, usually taken from the Scriptures, to the new melody, a syllable to each note, perhaps as a help in memorizing the lengthened melismatic passage. Such tropes were eventually introduced into almost every part of the Mass except the Credo as well as into the liturgy of the Offices, thus lengthening the service, adding variety, and finally so overloading it that the Council of Trent was forced to forbid them.

Of all the portions of the Mass, the one best adapted to free and almost unlimited embellishment was the Alleluia following the Gradual. Here the melisma on the final syllable could be extended indefinitely. To fit this a special kind of trope developed, possibly as early as the ninth century: the sequence. It was at first a series of matching prose couplets, sometimes with a single line at the beginning or end, each couplet having a different melody and varying in length. Later, in the twelfth century, sequences began to be written in regular verse forms with accented meter and rhyme. The sequence offered a tempting opportunity to introduce new poetical and musical material into the Mass. Great numbers of them were written before the end of the Middle Ages, but since the drastic reforms of the Council of Trent only five survive in official use.

The addition of new words and melodies might add variety to the Gregorian corpus, but need not in itself have changed the musical character of the chant. The effort to enrich Gregorian music, however, also took a musically more important direction: the addition of one or more voices. This was a change of fundamental significance, since it broke the tradition of exclusively monodic composition. The first step was to add a second voice moving parallel to the first at the interval of the fifth or the fourth. These intervals, together with the octave, were the only ones recognized by early medieval theorists as consonances, another reason why much of medieval music sounds strange to us. The earliest form of polyphony, which consisted simply of the addition of a voice or voices to an established melody was called "organum." The simplest form, parallel organum, was well established before the end of the ninth century. By that time, or shortly thereafter, a more complex free organum also made its appearance, in which the added voice moved more independently, in oblique or contrary motion as well as parallel, the preferred intervals being still the fourth and fifth although other intervals might occur in passing from one consonance to another. Such elaboration might be added to official Gregorian chants, but seems to have been more commonly used for the newer tropes and sequences.

As the use of organum, particularly the freer forms with irregular intervals, grew in popularity it became necessary to find a system of notation that would indicate the relative pitch of the notes. This need was met at first by grouping the neumes around a single line in such a way as to show their approximate height. Later other lines were added, on or between which the neumes were written as are the notes on a modern staff. It was now possible to write music with precise intervals and pitch, although as yet there was no means of indicating rhythm or the duration of notes. The introduction of the staff dates from at least as early as the first half of the eleventh century, as it is fully described in the *Micrologus* of Guido of Arezzo (c. 995–1050), one of the most remarkable musical theorists of the Middle Ages.

The twelfth century opened a period of more intensive activity in music as in other areas of cultural life. The surviving manuscripts indicate two leading centers of experimentation and composition: the monastery of St. Martial at Limoges in the first half of the century, and later the Cathedral of Notre Dame in Paris. In both places a new type of organum appeared, which served as the basis for many later developments. In this type the lower voice stretched out a pre-existing melody in very long notes (hence called the "tenor" from *tenere*, to hold), while the upper voice or voices sang an independent melismatic melody in short notes, sometimes as many as thirty or forty to one note in the tenor. The tenor thus became a kind of drone bass serving as an anchor, whence it was also called a *cantus firmus*. The earlier form of free organum, in which the voices moved in step, note against note, did not, however, die out, and toward the end of the century it developed into a distinct form known as *conductus*, distinguished from organum in that the principal voice was a newly composed melody, not a borrowed Gregorian chant. This had hitherto been rarely done, one of the few known examples being the charming *Mira lege* composed at Limoges in the first half of the century. Another form, which made its appearance at Paris in the last decades of the century, added variety to the organum by introducing *clausulae*, sections in which the long-held notes of the tenor were replaced by shorter notes arranged in a definite rhythmic pattern.

The new preoccupation with fixed rhythms which characterized musical composition around the turn of the century is particularly evident in the work of Perotinus (d. 1235), the leader of the Notre Dame school and the most famous composer of the High Middle Ages. The more complex forms of polyphony developed during the twelfth century had by this time made it necessary to establish rhythm and determine the length of notes so that two, three or even four voices, each moving at a different speed, could keep together and avoid the chaos of dissonances that would otherwise result. The problem thus posed was solved by Perotinus and his colleagues with an intellectual energy and a feeling for mathematically determined order that reminds us that they were the contemporaries of the great scholastics and the builders of the Gothic cathedrals. The method they worked out was to organize music in fixed rhythms or "rhythmic modes," which were based on the six recognized meters of classical verse (trochaic, iambic, dactylic, and so forth), with long and short notes corresponding to the long and short syllables of the metrical patterns. To make it possible to fit any two or more of these patterns one above the other, so that they could be sung simultaneously, it was necessary that all should be divisible into the same number of short notes. The first two modes (the trochaic short-long and the iambic long-short) could be divided into three short notes, but to fit this pattern the fourth and fifth (the dactylic and anapaestic) had to be altered by adding a half to the long and doubling the second short, so that the resulting pattern could be divided into six and set against two groups of three. The reason given by contemporary theorists for the division of all modes into groups of three or triple time was that three is a perfect number corresponding to the triune nature of the Holy Trinity; but it seems more likely that it was found in practice to be easier to set a voice in one rhythmic mode above a voice in another if all could be reduced to triple time. The next necessary step was to evolve a system of notation which would indicate the long and short notes. This was achieved by the expedient of taking over the normal Gregorian notation, but with the neumes bound together in ligatures which differed for each rhythmic mode, with pauses at fixed intervals depending on the mode and the number of rhythmic patterns in each phrase or *ordo*. It was thus possible to determine which rhythmic mode was being used and to read the notes as long or short depending on their place in the pattern of the mode.

With the introduction of fixed rhythms and relative note-values in addition to polyphony, music had departed decisively from the Gregorian prototype, and it is not surprising that the thirteenth century was a period of unrestrained experimentation. The composers of the mid-century not only added melodic lines above the slower-moving tenor, which was still usually borrowed from a Gregorian chant, but supplied these lines with texts as well. Thus was born the "motet," so called because of the added words (*mots*) in the upper voices. For two centuries or more this remained the most important form of musical composition, used indiscriminately for sacred and secular music. When used as a setting for the liturgy of the Mass and the Offices the upper voices were usually in Latin, and some attempt was made to keep them congruent to the liturgical theme, but in secular motets one or more vernacular lines were common. As the century progressed, the need for a means of subdividing the notes of the rapid upper voices led to further experiments with notation, preparing the way for the refinements and innovations of the following century.

The polyphonic music of the period from the middle of the twelfth century to the end of the thirteenth corresponded not only in time but also in many of its essential characteristics to the great period of Gothic architecture and art. It might well be described, indeed, as Gothic music, although the term has not been generally adopted by historians. Certainly, it represents a method of construction as distinct from that which preceded it as Gothic architecture was from Romanesque, though in neither case was the new form a complete break with the past. Above all, the composers of this period show their kinship to the builders of the Gothic cathedrals in their preoccupation with mathematical ratios and in their capacity to organize disparate parts into a coherent, symmetrical whole. The purely linear construction of music in this period, lacking as it is in chordal depth, seems also to suggest an affinity with the two-dimensional linearity of Gothic painting.

Thus far we have considered chiefly the music of the Church, for it is here that the lines of musical development can be seen most clearly. Moreover, medieval people, casually at home in the church as they were, made less distinction than we do between sacred and secular music and the two evolved in close relation to one another. We cannot, however, ignore the great outpouring of lyric song of the twelfth-century troubadours of Provence and their successors the northern French *trouvères* and the German *Minnesinger*. Although much influenced by Gregorian melody, these songs were primarily intended for a solo voice and avoided the general trend in the direction of polyphony until the mid-thirteenth century when they began to succumb to the all-embracing form of the motet. Solo song required a less careful notation of time values than did polyphony, and the rhythm of such songs may have remained fairly free. Rhythm, on the other hand, was essential to dance music, and little of it was written until the thirteenth century developed a system of notation capable of recording it. There is ample evidence, however, of the existence of dance music throughout the Middle Ages, and from the beginning of the thirteenth century dance tunes, called *estampies*, frequently in polyphonic settings, appear with increasing frequency in the surviving manuscripts.

It is obvious that only a small fraction of all the music that was played and sung in these centuries has come down to us, and by no means all of it in a form that can be interpreted with any degree of certainty. Still, thanks to the devoted labours of musicologists who have struggled tirelessly with the problems presented by obscure notation and a *materia musica* in many ways different from ours, a respectable amount of medieval music has been made available in published form and in recorded performance. Those who have attuned their ears to it have also learned to appreciate its beauty and to value it for its own sake and not merely as a primitive stage in the evolution of modern music.

The First Period of Transition

(c.1300–c.1450)

V

The Growth of Capitalism and the Disintegration of Manorial Economy

For the economy of Western Europe as a whole the period from the end of the thirteenth century to the middle of the fifteenth was not an age of expansion and steady growth, such as had characterized the two preceding centuries. The reversal of the upward trend struck different countries at different times. In some of the northern countries there was evidence of a slackening in the rate of growth early in the fourteenth century. In Italy it did not assume serious proportions until the 1340's. After the middle of the century Europe entered upon a prolonged depression, which lasted well into the fifteenth century, and during which the volume of production and exchange of goods remained relatively stable or may even have declined. The clearing of new land for cultivation practically ceased, as did also the great movement of expansion by colonization in eastern Germany. In many places land that had been cultivated was allowed to return to waste. With the data now available neither the causes nor the extent of this recession can be determined with certainty. It seems probable that in the great expansion of the thirteenth century marginal land had been put under cultivation and after a time wore itself out and had to be abandoned. The long devastation of France during the Hundred Years' War, persistent warfare between the Italian states, and the chronic anarchy that plagued the Holy Roman Empire were certainly contributing factors. The most serious blow to Europe's economy, however, was the radical decline in population which began with the widespread famines of 1315–17, but did not assume serious proportions until mid-century when the Black Death (1348–50) cut the population of Western Europe by a third or more. Thereafter recurrent visitations of the same plague, together with the devastation caused by war, prevented the normal recouping of losses until the second half of the fifteenth century. Yet, despite the general recession, or perhaps because of it, this was a period of decisive change in economic institutions and of extreme social tension.

The vigorous growth which had characterized both rural and urban economy in the High Middle Ages had been contained, if somewhat uneasily, within the framework of typically medieval institutions. In these centuries money economy won a partial but decisive victory over the older and simpler forms of barter and the exchange of services; but in town and country alike economic life still retained a strongly communal or corporate character. The normal commercial and economic activity of the cities was strictly regulated and designed primarily to provide itinerant merchants, shopkeepers and artisans with a decent living according to their status in society. Yet, in the great centers of international commerce, merchants trading at a distance in precious goods had already introduced the dynamic and disruptive elements of a nascent capitalism. The date scholars assign to the beginnings of capitalism depends very much on their definition of the term. Some have discovered elements of capitalism in the prehistoric economy of the pastoral nomads; others would limit it to the era of industrial exploitation that began with the nineteenth century. Here the term is used in the more commonly accepted sense of a system of private business enterprise characterized by the accumulation and reinvestment of capital in relatively large amounts, by a widening and more or less permanent differentiation in status between employer and worker, and by complex forms of business organization, bookkeeping, credit and exchange. A further essential characteristic is the pursuit of profit as an end in itself over and above the amounts required to meet the needs of subsistence. So far as medieval Europe is concerned, capitalism, thus defined, made its first appearance in the twelfth and thirteenth centuries in a few limited areas. It was fairly well advanced in Italy and Flanders before the end of the thirteenth century; but it was in the following period that its forms were most fully developed. In the century and a half we are here considering, changing trade routes and intensified competition for limited markets combined to force the development of more complex and more rational methods and to bring into being that essentially un-medieval type of businessman — the sedentary entrepreneur.

Capitalism, in any reasonable sense of the word, was in this period limited almost entirely to wholesale commerce, large-scale industry and finance. With some partial exceptions, notably in Italy, it left agriculture largely untouched. Yet, even before the end of the thirteenth century, the expansion of money economy, as distinct from capitalism, had begun to place an intolerable strain upon the feudal and manorial organization of landholding and agriculture and to initiate changes as radical as those which capitalism was introducing into the economy of the cities. In the following century and a half that strain was intensified by depopulation and depression and by such political factors as the growing power of central governments. The weight of tradition still lay heavy upon the land, and change came slowly among men whose life was geared to the slow rhythm of the changing seasons. Nevertheless, the process by which leases, rents and wages replaced hereditary tenures and labor services continued inexorably and by the middle of the fifteenth century it had revolutionized the social and economic organization of the rural classes, both peasant and noble.

A. The Growth of Capitalism in Italian Commerce, Finance and Industry

The history of early capitalism is to a very large extent the history of Italian commerce. Thanks to her geographical position, Italy became the entrepôt of trade between the eastern Mediterranean region and Western Europe, as early as the eleventh century. At the end of that century the conquest of Syria by the crusaders gave an additional impetus to the trade between East and West, and furnished opportunities for profit which the Italian merchants exploited to the full. A century later, after the Fourth Crusade had ended in the conquest of Constantinople and the founding of a Latin Empire in the East, the Venetians gained a privileged position in the old Byzantine capital and founded colonies in the islands of the Aegean as well as on the mainland. Genoa, too, established colonies in the Aegean and on the Black Sea. For a century or more before its disintegration around 1340 the great Tartar Empire kept the trade routes of central Asia open, so that the Italian colonies on the Black Sea coast were the terminal points of an overland trade route from China. The most valuable trade, however, came from the Indian Ocean through the Persian Gulf to Syria or through the Red Sea to Egypt, where the Italian merchants acquired priceless stores of spices, silks and other oriental luxuries. The Levantine countries themselves also produced numerous luxury goods: cotton, sugar, alum, dyestuffs, and the products of skilled Moslem or Byzantine workmanship. These goods were brought by sea to Italy and then carried overland to southern Germany, to the headwaters of the Rhine or to the Champagne fairs in northeastern France. In return the Italians exported to the East woollen cloth and other products of the growing Italian industries. Italian commerce was from the beginning predominantly a matter of importation and exportation, with local consumption absorbing only a relatively small part of the total volume. Moreover, it was to an extraordinary degree a luxury trade. The fact that the Italian merchants operated so largely in foreign markets enabled them to evade the restrictive regulations characteristic of medieval economic policy. At the same time, the abnormally high value of their goods opened the way to large profits and to the expansion of individual enterprise.

Capitalism thus developed at an unusually early date in Italy. Most of the techniques of capitalist business were well established there before 1300. Nevertheless, changing conditions around the end of the thirteenth century make it possible to regard the following century and a half as the classic period of early Italian capitalism. One of the most important of the new developments was a shift in the trade routes between Italy and the West, when the fiscal policies of Philip the Fair ruined the Champagne fairs and forced the Venetians and Genoese to open a maritime trade route through the Straits of Gibraltar to the Netherlands and England. Italian commerce was thus brought into direct contact with the focal center of northern trade, to which the luxury goods from the East and the products of the Mediterranean area could now be shipped direct, while Italian industry was fed by the direct importation of wool from England and unfinished cloth from Flanders. The result was not only an unprecedented boom in Italian industry and commerce, which lasted till the crisis of the 1340's, but also the more lasting domination of northern banking and finance by colonies of Italians settled in Bruges and London. Safe transportation and the possibility of regular correspondence with partners or agents resident in the centers of northern trade also accelerated the development of new methods of conducting business, as the itinerant merchant of the overland routes was replaced by the sedentary merchant who directed his business through correspondence with his agents abroad. "This evolution," to quote Raymond de Roover, "involved such a drastic change in the methods of doing business that the transition from one system to the other could be called, without exaggeration, 'the commercial revolution of the end of the thirteenth century'."[1]

The new Atlantic route was made possible by two simultaneous improvements in the character of Italian merchant ships, improvements which also contributed notably to the speed and safety of transportation throughout the whole Mediterranean area. Shortly after 1303, when Basque pirates entered the Mediterranean and demonstrated the advantages of the square-rigged ships which had been developed to cope with the rough waters of the western ocean and the northern seas, most Italian merchants abandoned the small lateen-rigged ships that were characteristic of Mediterranean sailing in favor of the larger, more seaworthy northern type. The "cog," as the single-masted square-rigger was called, cut costs by doubling the freight capacity of the earlier type while using less than half the crew. For bulky merchandise, the cog of around three hundred tons' burden remained the common carrier till the second half of the fifteenth century.

It was not bulky merchandise, however, that made the largest profits for the Italian merchants. Their fortunes were made principally by handling luxury goods which had a very high value in proportion to bulk and weight, and they could afford to pay high freight rates to have these precious cargoes transported swiftly and safely. The "great galley," introduced by the Venetians in the last years of the thirteenth century, was designed specifically to meet this need. Light, fast galleys, dependent entirely on oars, had long been used as fighting ships in the Mediterranean; but their long, low, narrow shape and the use of the entire deck space for the banks of the oarsmen prevented their carrying any considerable cargo. The new type of heavy merchant galley was much larger and was built to ride the rougher seas of the Atlantic. Designed originally to carry some 140 tons of freight below decks, they were constantly enlarged until by the middle of the fifteenth century a capacity of 250 tons or more was considered normal. Unlike the naval galleys, these merchant ships used sail on the open sea to carry them from port to port, but they were also equipped with oars which could be used for short distances in an emergency. This was especially important for getting in and out of harbor. Where a sailing ship might be held up in port for days or weeks, or be forced to hover off a treacherous coast waiting for a favorable wind, the galley could manoeuvre under its own power. The use of oars demanded a larger crew which, together with the bowmen carried exclusively for defense, made up a formidable fighting force, some two hundred men in all. The great galley was, in fact, an armed

[1] R. de Roover, *Money, Banking and Credit in Medieval Bruges* (Cambridge, Mass., 1948), p. 11.

merchantman, capable of repelling any piratical attack. Though more expensive to operate than ordinary sailing ships, the great galleys were so much safer and faster that they maintained for nearly two centuries a monopoly on the shipping of precious cargoes. So secure were they, indeed, that many merchants thought it unnecessary to insure goods carried on them. In Venice the galleys were built, equipped, and manned by the state, and they were considered so important to the economy of the republic that their sailing was directed and controlled by governmental policy. Each year Venetian fleets sailed to Flanders and England, calling at North African and Spanish ports on the way, as well as to the Black Sea, the Aegean area, Syria, and Egypt.

What made the Italian merchants the pioneers of modern business, and in the field of capitalist enterprise the schoolmasters of Western Europe, was not, however, so much the volume or value of the goods handled by their merchant fleets as the forms of business association and the techniques of credit and exchange which they developed in the course of their search for profit, and which they extended from commerce into the adjacent areas of industry and finance. It is worth while, then, to examine in some detail the character and organization of Italian business during this transitional period, for it was the model followed at a later date and with local variations by the economy of the other European countries.

The history of Italian capitalism may be said to have begun when both the accumulation of profits beyond the needs of subsistence and the possibility of augmenting capital by various forms of credit presented opportunities that could not be exploited adequately by the early medieval type of itinerant merchant who travelled with his goods, traded on his own capital, and kept his books, presumably, in his head. The Italians had passed that point a century or more before 1300, but, as we have already noted, it was around this date that the most decisive changes in the organization of Italian business took place. The successful Italian merchant of the fourteenth and fifteenth centuries was no longer the dusty-footed frequenter of the fairs, nor the ship-wise mariner of the middle sea. Rather, he was the earliest representative of a new type of businessman, the sedentary merchant whose normal habitat was his countinghouse in his native city or the branch office of his firm at one of the terminal points of international trade. Working with capital inflated by credit and extending his personal management through the activity of partners and agents, the sedentary merchant, like his successor the modern entrepreneur, recognized no limits to the size and variety of his enterprise. He no longer encountered the personal dangers that made the itinerant merchant's life hazardous by land and sea; but he ran great risks of financial loss or of failure through overstrained credit. The era of the great early fourteenth-century fortunes was also the era of crashing bankruptcies. After the middle of the fourteenth century the restriction of markets and profits forced a still more careful adaptation of means to ends and a closer calculation of the margin of profit or loss. The merchant who would win and keep the golden fruits of trade must be both adventurous and cautious. He must be prepared to risk his capital in distant places, but at the same time guard against the chance of ruinous loss, so far as possible, by spreading his investment among a number of enterprises. For this purpose, as well as to achieve the concentration of capital needed for large undertakings, forms of business organization were needed that would add flexibility and scope to the activity of the individual merchant.

One of the earliest forms of business association, designed to meet the need for a means of concentrating capital, extending the sphere of personal activity and splitting the risks through variety of investment, was the temporary partnership or *commenda*. Begun apparently in Genoa in the twelfth century to exploit the sea-borne trade with Syria, partnerships of the *commenda* type, with many variations, came to be widely used and were adapted to such overland trade as that to the fairs of Champagne. In this type of partnership, one or more silent partners contributed the greater part of the capital. An active partner, to whom the capital was entrusted and who contributed only a small share or none himself, conducted the venture and was awarded a share in the profits for his services. At the end of the venture, the partnership would be liquidated, each partner receiving his allotted share of the profits. Though lacking continuity of direction, these temporary partnerships were extremely flexible and presented a number of advantages. They enabled a man with little capital beyond his adventurous spirit and calculating mind to raise the funds necessary for trade and thus edge his way into the merchant class. At the same time they enabled the merchant with a small amount of idle capital to put it to work without having to raise the full amount needed for a venture or to devote his full time to its management. By dividing his available assets among a number of such partnerships he could also diminish the risk of being ruined by the failure of a single venture. These strictly temporary partnerships, however, were better suited to the conditions of early trade, when it was still necessary for someone to travel with the goods, than to the later period when commerce was both safer and better organized. During the fourteenth century, Italian merchants more and more frequently shipped goods to a resident agent who would sell them and use the funds accruing from the sale to purchase goods for a return cargo. Such an agent might be the active or managing partner of a profit-sharing partnership organized for a term of years rather than for a single venture. Such "terminal partnerships" became more common as management became more sedentary, but many small merchants found it simpler to employ resident agents abroad to buy and sell for them on a commission basis. By the end of the fourteenth century commission agencies had practically supplanted the temporary partnerships as a means of conducting single ventures.

Another early form of organization of capital, and one which persisted through the fourteenth and fifteenth centuries and beyond, was the family firm. This was in its original form a pooling of the family's resources, managed by the head of the family in cooperation with his sons and other kinfolk, who acted as agents to carry on the firm's business in the far corners of the world. Such a firm might trade simultaneously in Cairo and Constantinople, in Valencia, Bruges and London. It might also vary its risks and keep its capital constantly at work by lending money to other merchants or to governments, by dealing in foreign exchange, by investing in land or in industrial production. Once launched upon a successful career with its credit well established, the firm could greatly increase its working capital by accepting deposits on which it paid interest. Volume of capital, continuity of direction, and a widespread network of branch offices made this type of firm especially suited to the combination of commerce with international banking and exchange operations, and most of the great Florentine banking houses of the early fourteenth century were of this type. As the family firms grew in size they frequently took into partnership trusted outsiders, who were allowed to secure shares in the firm's capital. The capital of the great Florentine firm of the Bardi, for example, in 1331 was divided into fifty-eight shares, of which thirty-six and three-quarters were held by six members of the family, the remainder by five outsiders. In 1312, the shares of the rival firm of the Peruzzi were divided among eight members of the family and nine outsiders. By 1331 the outsiders had gained control by acquiring more than fifty per cent of the capital. All the branch houses were owned by the firm and were managed by salaried factors or by partners sent out to act as managers under directions from the home office. The Florentine chronicler Giovanni Villani, for example, was a partner of the Peruzzi and was sent for a time to act as branch manager in Bruges. Although policy-making decisions were usually left to the head of the family, disagreement among the partners in the home office sometimes led to divided counsels and may have contributed to the collapse of the Bardi, Peruzzi and other firms of this type.

After the series of bankruptcies that wiped out most of the old Tuscan firms in the 1340's, other less highly centralized forms became more common. In some family firms, of which that of the Medici was typical,[2] each separate branch or industrial concern was organized as a distinct partnership, in which members of the family held a controlling interest. A somewhat similar form of organization, save that his was a personal rather than a family business, characterized the numerous enterprises of that remarkable merchant, Francesco Datini of Prato, whose career, thanks to the preservation of his records, we can follow in some detail. Beginning as a young man in 1356 on little more than a shoestring, Datini before his death in 1410 had built up a personally directed commercial empire with branch houses in Avignon, Pisa, Florence, Genoa, Barcelona, Valencia and Majorca. Each of these branches was organized as a separate partnership. The resident partner or partners contributed their services and usually some capital; but the largest share of the capital was supplied by Datini, and he controlled the entire enterprise, framing general policy and, so far as possible at a distance, directing the activity of his junior partners.

The complex business arrangements of firms, partnerships and commission agencies demanded a vast quantity of written records. Bills of sale, contracts, a constant flow of letters to business associates, and systematic entries in journals and ledgers kept the pen of the merchant, or those of his clerks and agents, perpetually busy. As Leo Battista Alberti wrote in the *Trattato della cura della famiglia*, "It befits a merchant always to have ink-stained hands." Without some form of systematic bookkeeping, indeed, the expansion of business enterprise which marked this period would have been impossible. The details of scores of ventures, involving partners, agents and depositors, could not be entrusted to even the most retentive memory or to haphazard notations on scraps of paper. During the fourteenth century double entry bookkeeping, which embodied the basic principle of all modern accounting, was gradually replacing the simpler form of single entry, and by the beginning of the following century it was standard practice in Genoa, Venice, Florence and other centers of large-scale business. Bookkeeping made possible not only the expansion of enterprise, but also a degree of rational direction and accurate calculation unknown to medieval commerce. The double entry system, with its balancing of debits and credits, enabled the merchant to estimate precisely his profits or losses on each venture and served to remind him daily that profit is the aim and bankruptcy the end of business. Some notion of the volume of business records a merchant might accumulate can be gathered from the Datini archives in Prato in which can still be found the books and correspondence of Francesco Datini's home office and branch houses, which at his death he ordered

[2] See below, pp. 428–430.

to be collected and stored in his house, in all some five hundred ledgers and more than 150,000 letters, as well as hundreds of deeds, insurance policies, bills of exchange and other commercial papers. Among these priceless records are the handsomely bound, double entry *Libri grandi* of each of the partnerships, each headed, as was Datini's pious and hopeful custom: "In the name of God and of profit."[3] These, together with the less complete but still numerous records of various Genoese, Venetian and Florentine merchants, like those of that typical merchant of Venice, Andrea Barbarigo, made available in F. C. Lane's brilliant study,[4] enable us to reconstruct in some detail the inner workings of early capitalist enterprise.

The use of written records was made necessary not only by the size and complexity of business organization, but even more by the fact that large commercial transactions were normally conducted on credit rather than by an exchange of hard money. The available supply of coinage, which increased but little during this entire period, was hopelessly inadequate to meet the demands of an expanding commerce. Moreover, merchants engaged in the kind of periodic trade dictated by the fairs or the semi-annual sailing of fleets to the Levant could not have enough money with them at all times to take advantage of unforeseen opportunities, whereas they could arrange to take on their next trip enough goods or money to meet known obligations. From very early times, then, it was a common practice to buy on a promise to pay at the next fair or to settle debts at the end of a fair by an exchange of credits among the merchants present. Payment for credit purchases was guaranteed more or less by the necessity all merchants felt of maintaining their credit, and also by the right of reprisal, that is, the creditor's right to recoup bad debts by seizing the goods of any fellow-citizen of the defaulting debtor. Credit transactions were often given a further legal guarantee by registering bills of sale and letters of indebtedness with the public authorities of city or fair.

As business organization became more complex with the rise of the type of sedentary merchant who bought and sold through agents in distant places, it became increasingly necessary to transfer capital quickly and safely from place to place. The inadequate supply of bullion, the merchant's unwillingness to tie up his stock of coinage during the period of transportation, the danger of loss by shipwreck or theft, and the policy of forbidding the exportation of gold and silver followed by many fourteenth-century governments, all conspired to make some technique for

---

[3] I. Origo, *The Merchant of Prato, Francesco di Marco Datini* (London, 1957), p. 114.

[4] F. C. Lane, *Andrea Barbarigo, Merchant of Venice, 1418–1449* (Baltimore, 1944).

the handling of international exchange by written instruments or book-keeping an absolute necessity. The fiscal needs of the papal curia, which collected income from all parts of Europe, had also to be met by some system of transporting large sums from country to country. The Italian merchants met this need by developing an elaborate system of bills of exchange and by transferring credits from one account to another on the books of the great firms. As past masters of this art, the Italians gained something like a monopoly of the handling of international exchange, a business which was not only lucrative in itself, but opened the way to other profitable enterprises.

The business of dealing in bills of exchange combined the elements of moneylending, speculation, and the service to international trade or finance involved in the transference of funds from place to place. The bill of exchange or *lettera di cambio* was in effect an order drawn upon a partner or agent to pay to a designated person a sum of money at a future date (whence it becomes a credit transaction), in another country, and in another currency. In the hands of the skillful Italians it became an exceedingly flexible instrument capable of meeting a variety of needs. It might enable a Venetian merchant to send money to an agent in Bruges to buy goods there or he might use it to bring back to Venice the proceeds of a sale in London. In either case he would employ the services of a banker who had branch offices in Bruges or London. To send money to Bruges, the Venetian merchant would buy a bill of exchange from a banker in Venice drawn on the banker's partner in Bruges, who, when the bill reached him some two months later, would turn over the equivalent sum to the merchant's agent there. The bill of exchange might also be used as a means of raising a short-term loan without running foul of the laws against usury. In this case, the merchant would raise the money by selling a bill of exchange drawn on his partner in Bruges, who would meet it by selling another bill drawn on the merchant in Venice. Between the time when he sold the first bill and the time when he had to meet the returning bill some four months would elapse, during which time he had the use of the money. The banking firm which handled the bills would expect to make a profit by the differential in the rate of exchange between Venetian and Flemish coinage in Venice and Bruges. The banker's profit would be roughly equivalent to interest on a loan for that time. Since exchange rates fluctuated, the banker's profit was not certain and was therefore permissible by canon law. It was not regarded as usury, as a fixed interest rate would have been. There was some sophistry in the argument which freed exchange dealings from ecclesiastical censure, for in normal times the banking firm which handled the bill received more than it had paid out. Nevertheless, there was a genuine element of risk involved. Wars, the eccentric policies of state governments, and the inevitable time lag between the inception of a transaction and its completion in a distant country, all combined to introduce so many uncertainties into dealings in international exchange that only the superb skill and organization of the Italian firms enabled them to embark upon it with any reasonable hope of profit.

In addition to the great merchant-banking firms, which handled international exchange and large financial operations, and clearly to be distinguished from them, there were also money-changers, whose business originated in the manual exchange of coins of different currencies, but who also accepted money on deposit and performed the function of local transfer banks. Italian money-changers had performed both of these useful functions at the Champagne fairs, but their services were equally necessary in the day to day business of the Italian cities. The bewildering variety of medieval coinage made their expert services necessary in any transaction involving actual transfer of coins and, for the same reason, businessmen preferred if possible to conduct their business without having to resort to the use of hard money. They found it convenient, therefore, to keep deposits in a current account with a money-changer and make payments by simply ordering him to transfer funds from their account to that of their creditor, who, if a businessman himself, would normally have an account with the same money-changer or another in the same city. Since neither checks nor paper money were in common use in this period, such book transfers served an even more useful function than does a current account in a bank today. As for the money-changer, he could make a profit, not only on the exchange of coins, but also by investing the money deposited with him, provided he kept a sufficient cash reserve to meet current demands for withdrawal in cash.

To the difficulties inherent in the exchange of money and credits the chaotic state of medieval coinage added a confusion thrice confounded. Not only kings, but cities and feudal lords, and in Germany even bishops and abbots, claimed the right to mint coins, and used it to their profit. In the fourteenth and fifteenth centuries, the extension of royal power gave wider circulation to national coinages, especially in England, but the usefulness of these as standards of value was vitiated by their chronic instability. Poor workmanship in the mint and the erosion of coins by enthusiastic amateurs, who clipped silver from around the edges, made the value of medieval coins at the best of times uncertain. The most serious confusion arose, however, from the common practice of re-minting coins at frequent intervals, with an altered and usually lowered standard of weight and fineness. In the fourteenth century this became one of the regular ways by which kings, princes, and even city governments added to their income and lowered their obligations. Philip the Fair repeatedly debased the French royal coinage, and John II, at a low point of French fortunes during the Hundred Years' War, is said to have altered the coinage eighty-six times in fourteen years. The Viennese silver penny was altered on an average of once a year from 1250 to 1400, and the *denar* of Cologne, which had been one of the best German coins in the thirteenth century, depreciated at a rate of 2.8% a year from 1280 to 1380. Italian money-changers, who did a thriving business at the great fairs, made fortunes from this miracle of the confusion of coins; but Italian bankers and merchants, whose business depended on the exchange of credits, early realized the need for an invariable and generally accepted standard of value. To meet this need, both Florence and Venice coined gold pieces — the florin and ducat respectively — in the second half of the thirteenth century, and for the next two centuries maintained these at a very high standard of stability. During that period the florin and ducat were almost universally accepted as standards of value, thereby greatly facilitating all exchange and credit manipulations. By relating the current value of other coins to the florin or ducat it became possible to calculate the fluctuations of exchange with reasonable certainty, and, above all, it became possible to assure the merchant who sold on credit in distant places, or the moneylender who made a long term loan, that he would be repaid in money of a value roughly equivalent to the original debt.

In addition to other forms of credit, moneylending was an important ingredient in the mobilization of capital for commercial enterprise, while at the same time commercial loans furnished merchants with a relatively safe field for the investment of their surplus profits. Loans at interest were, of course, prohibited by canon law and frequently by civil law as well. The Church's doctrine on usury had been authoritatively stated at a time when lending for productive purposes was rare — it was permanently defined by the Second Lateran Council in 1139 — and it was difficult to modify it to meet changing conditions. However, as merchants learned by experience that money can be made to make money, the ethical objection to taking interest on loans lost much of its force. If the moneylender's conscience was troubled, and there is evidence that it was, it seems to have been so troubled only intermittently and usually *in articulo mortis*. In any case, there were loopholes in the doctrine that could be exploited, and the law itself could be circumvented by various rather transparent subterfuges. Canon law permitted interest in the form of damages for belated repayment on a loan, so that borrower and lender might enter into a collusive agreement to set the term of the loan for an impossibly short period. Payment of a fixed interest was also permitted when, as in the early "sea loans," the lender shared the risk by forfeiting his claim if the goods in which the capital was invested were lost. The risk involved in such loans was, however, largely fictitious, since it was usually covered by some form of marine insurance. The easiest means of evading the law, and one commonly practised, was to write into the contract a larger sum than that actually paid, so that repayment of the nominal debt included the actual loan plus interest. Where evasions of this sort were impractical, as in the payment of a regular interest on deposits, the law was simply ignored, and generally with impunity. Both Church and state governments borrowed money at interest too frequently to take a firm stand. The demand of the merchants for working capital could not, in fact, be denied, and throughout this period borrowing at interest, whether open or thinly disguised, was a normal ingredient in Italian trade.

Moneylending was also a normal part of almost every merchant's activity, and it did not necessarily involve large sums. The handling of large deposits and loans, the manipulation of international exchange and loans to foreign governments were, however, usually left to the great commercial firms which had the capital and the organization to undertake them. During the fourteenth and fifteenth centuries, nearly all the largest Italian firms might be described as banking houses. But banking and finance were seldom, if ever, the original sources of a firm's capital or its sole preoccupations. As a general rule, capital was accumulated first in trade and later diverted in part into moneylending or banking operations. Diversity of investment and the continuous turn-over of capital were the secrets of success in this period, rather than specialization in a single field of activity. The combination of commercial operations with banking and exchange added greatly to the opportunities for profit from both. Lending to governments might serve to secure valuable privileges for trade, while commercial transactions might equally facilitate the profitable business of handling international exchange. An example of the combination of commercial and finance capitalism characteristic of this period is afforded by the ambidextrous activities of the Florentine houses of Bardi and Peruzzi, which handled the collection of papal income from England in the first half of the fourteenth century. Their agents collected the taxes due to the pope in England, invested the money in wool, and shipped the wool to Florence. The firms then sold the wool or manufactured it for re-export as cloth, meanwhile satisfying the papal claims by a simple transfer of funds or credits from Florence to Rome or Avignon. They were thus in a position to make a three-fold profit: first, from the commission charged for their services as agents; second, from the exchange of English into Italian currency; and, finally, by carrying on their own wool-importing business on papal capital.

The same two firms also furnish the classic example of the ruinous risks which might be attached to the profitable business of lending money to state governments. Edward III borrowed largely from both to aid in financing his invasion of France at the opening of the Hundred Years' War. When in 1343 he repudiated his debts — some 900,000 gold florins owed to the Bardi and 600,000 owed to the Peruzzi — both firms were ruined, and numbers of other Florentine firms were shaken by the ensuing panic. In the period of transition from feudal to centralized state government, royal income seldom succeeded in keeping up with growing expenses. As mercenary armies replaced the feudal levy, the cost of warfare was immensely increased and could seldom be met by taxation or other normal forms of fiscal income. The kings of England and France, and lesser princes everywhere, were forced again and again to turn to the Italian bankers for loans to tide them over a financial crisis. To secure such loans, they had necessarily to offer very favorable terms, so that the profit expected from public loans was high. But sovereign princes were uncertain debtors, against whom it was difficult to enforce legal claims. They could usually count on popular support for refusal to repay the hated Italian moneylenders, or, when it suited their purpose, they might fall back upon canon law for moral and legal justification in disowning their obligations. The Bardi and Peruzzi were not the only early fourteenth-century firms to put their trust in princes with disastrous results. The brothers Francesi made the fatal mistake of lending too much money to Philip the Fair, and involvement in the finances of the Kingdom of Naples ruined both the house of Scali and the ancient firm of Buonaccorsi.

The financial operations of these great firms of merchant-bankers should be clearly distinguished, as they have not always been, from the openly usurious moneylending of the "Lombards." This generic term was used all over Europe to designate the pawnbrokers and petty moneylenders, who originated for the most part in the cities of Asti and Chiesi in Piedmont. Unlike the merchant-bankers, the Lombards were professional usurers, seldom seriously engaged in commerce, and their loans were almost all made to people who borrowed for consumption rather than investment. Usually they took as security jewels, household equipment, tools, clothing, or any article that could conceivably be sold at a profit. People of every rank and class borrowed from the Lombards, but the majority of their dealings consisted of small loans to small people. The risks involved in a business that was never more than barely legitimate, as well as the cost of storing pledges and selling those not redeemed, made it necessary to charge very high interest rates. This was usury in the full canonical sense, and it was condemned by Church and public alike. Yet the perpetual demand for consumer credit was so great that the Lombards had to be tolerated. In Flanders they were licensed by the government and permitted to charge twopence in the pound per week, or 43 1/3 per cent per annum, which was, in fact, the generally recognized rate everywhere. Considering the expense and the risks this rate was probably not unduly high. It is, in fact, not much higher than the interest charged on small loans by pawnbrokers today. But to the journeyman who was forced to pawn his tools, or the widow who was forced to pawn her household belongings, this looked very much like grinding the faces of the poor. The Lombards were hated and feared by their victims, and the popular resentment they aroused frequently spread to include, rather unjustly, their fellow countrymen who were engaged in the less morally reprehensible dealings in commercial credit and exchange or in public finance.

Next to commerce, moneylending, banking, and state finance, the most profitable area for capitalist exploitation was that opened up by the growth of a few large industries. Capitalist industry, however, was still the exception rather than the rule. By far the greater part of industrial production was carried on, as it had been in the High Middle Ages, by master craftsmen, who manufactured the goods of their trade and sold them across the counters of their shops. This type of retail manufacturing lent itself to guild organization and regulation by city governments, and it remained throughout our period almost untouched by capitalism. Only when the volume of production was far in excess of the local demand, so that the greater part of it was destined for a foreign market, did capital enter the picture, and then it was almost entirely commercial capital. But even when the merchants controlled both the importation of raw materials and the exportation of the finished product, they were not always able to control the process of manufacturing itself. In crafts where a high degree of skill and training was needed, the artisans usually succeeded in retaining a fair degree of independence. Makers of luxury articles for the world market, such as the goldsmiths and jewellers, or the armorers who formed one of the largest industrial groups in Milan, manufactured their product from beginning to end, and much of its ultimate value was the result of their skilled labor. Even though dependent on the merchants for supplies and a market, they could not be reduced to the position of wage earners. The merchants' opportunity to gain control of industry occurred chiefly where division of labor and a relatively low standard of required skill enabled them to retain ownership of the material and put it out to a series of workers at piece-rate wages. In such industries, indeed, the merchants were almost forced to become industrial entrepreneurs in order to keep their import-export trade moving. To an even greater extent, then, than was true in banking and money-lending, capitalism in industry was an outgrowth of commercial capitalism and was carried on by merchants as an adjunct to their normal business.

Division of labor, the primary factor in opening the way for capitalist exploitation of large industries, operated in the manufacture of some kinds of leather goods and in shipbuilding; but it was nowhere so highly developed as in the textile trades, and it was in these that merchants found the most numerous and most profitable openings for entrepreneurial activity. Silk-weaving was a flourishing capitalist industry in Lucca, Florence, Arezzo, Siena, Genoa, Venice and elsewhere. It was far surpassed, however, both in volume of production and degree of capitalist control, by the making and finishing of woollen cloth. Despite the lack of an adequate supply of native raw materials, wool-weaving was developed at an early date in many Tuscan and Lombard cities. In Florence, where it was most highly developed, it became the city's major industry and was the solid foundation on which Florentine prosperity rested. In the early fourteenth century, it furnished a living, by Giovanni Villani's reckoning, for some 30,000 people, about one-third of the city's population. According to the same chronicler, who was himself a cloth merchant, Florence produced in 1338 seventy to eighty thousand pieces of woollen cloth, worth more than a million gold florins.

The wool industry of Florence was organized under two great guilds: the *Arte della Lana*, whose members manufactured cloth, and the *Arte di Calimala*, which specialized in finishing cloth imported from Flanders. But these were not guilds of master artisans in the medieval manner. They were rather associations of merchant-industrialists, who used the guild organization as a means of maintaining monopolies, of exercising political influence to shape the economic policies of the state, and above all, of controlling their workers. Through their political power, they were able to obtain state laws to prevent any kind of organization among the workers themselves, and to crush strikes or concerted demands for higher wages. In these guilds no vestige remained of that homogeneity which had characterized the medieval craft guilds. It had been replaced by a clear division into two classes of capitalist employers and proletarian workers. Until the end of the thirteenth century, the *Arte di Calimala*, which imported unfinished cloth from Flanders through the fairs of Champagne and produced a finely finished cloth for export, was the richer and more influential of the two guilds. It included a number of the great banking firms among its members. The balance shifted, however, in the early fourteenth century, when the opening of a direct sea route to England and the activity of Florentine merchants as collectors of papal revenue there, made possible the importation of fine English wool in quantity. Though more expensive than the North African or Spanish product, it made a much more valuable cloth and so produced higher profits for the manufacturer. It also demanded a larger capital investment and more extensive business organization, so that it favored the large firms as against their smaller competitors.

The division of labor involved in the making of fine cloth on a large scale forced the merchants of the *Arte della Lana* to develop the most complex form of industrial capitalist organization known to this period. The wool passed in the process of manufacture through about twenty stages, each of which required the specialized labor of a different set of workers. The poorest and least skilled of these were the wool-beaters, combers and carders, who worked in the merchant–employer's shop preparing the wool for spinning. The spinners were mostly women, many of whom lived in the surrounding countryside. Agents of the manufacturer distributed the wool among them and brought back the spun yarn to be put out again to the weavers. These were men who lived in the poorer quarters of the city and, like the spinners, worked at home. They were, however, completely dependent on the merchant–employer, and their wages seldom rose above the bare minimum of subsistence. From the weavers, the cloth was passed on to fullers, dyers, and stretchers in turn. These required a plant with a certain amount of machinery and employees of their own, so that they were themselves minor capitalists. Finally, the cloth was turned over to finishers of various kinds, whose skill was sufficient to win for them better wages and more favorable treatment than the other workers. From beginning to end of the process, the merchant-industrialist retained ownership of the material and functioned in a purely managerial capacity.

The growth of capitalism changed not only the forms of economic activity, but also in varying degrees the social and political organization and the cultural interests of Italy. True, it left the numerous middle class of city dwellers, who were engaged in shopkeeping or small industry, relatively untouched. But it wrought a profound revolution in the social status and living conditions of all those engaged in distant trade or large industry. It brought about drastic changes, as we shall see, in the system of landholding and agriculture and in the condition of the rural population. It concentrated unprecedented wealth in the hands of a socially and politically dominant minority. It created a new class of *rentiers*, passive investors who lived off their capital while enjoying the leisure to pursue intellectual or aesthetic interests. To this class, and to the patronage made possible by concentrated wealth, the Italian Renaissance owed much of its cultural brilliance. But, if the development of capitalist business brought wealth and a more enjoyable life to many, it brought poverty and hardship to many more. It created another new class in the industrial proletariat, a class underprivileged and profoundly discontented. By reshaping the social structure of Italy, capitalism created new social strains and tensions and aggravated those already existing. It also exercised an indirect but potent influence on the evolution of new political institutions. But of all this more hereafter.

B. NORTHERN COMMERCE AND INDUSTRY

During the period we are here considering, the Italian merchant-bankers still dominated the European money markets and controlled much of the trade between the Mediterranean and the North Sea. Their incomparable mastery of the techniques of capitalist enterprise still gave them an advantage over their northern competitors. The evolution of capitalism was slower, on the whole, in the transalpine lands than in Italy, and medieval elements lingered longer in the ways of thinking as well as in the business practices of the northern merchants. But, if in the field of business administration the Italians were still the schoolmasters of Western Europe, the northerners were proving themselves apt pupils, and by the middle of the fifteenth century were prepared to compete on even terms. The variety of geographical and political circumstances, however, makes it difficult to generalize about the economic development of this period, more difficult than in the High Middle Ages, when trade practices were more uniform and less subject to national variation. A reasonably accurate picture of Western European economy can be presented only by considering each country in all its local peculiarity.

Both the economic balance of the Western European states and the methods of capitalist enterprise were profoundly affected by a series of events which occurred in the last years of the thirteenth century and the first two decades of the fourteenth. The decline of the fairs of Champagne and the opening by the Genoese and Venetians of an all-water trade route from Italy to the Netherlands and England shifted the bulk of trade between the two focal points of medieval commerce from the overland route through France to the Atlantic coast. As a result, Italian firms established permanent branches in Bruges and London, and introduced into the North the peculiarly capitalist techniques of the sedentary merchant. In about the same period, the North German cities of the

Hanseatic League were opening up a regular sea-borne trade between the lands bordering on the Baltic and those bordering on the North Sea, and this too was trade carried on by sedentary merchants through agents permanently settled in the London Steelyard or in the great *kontor* of the Hanse at Bruges. The settling of the English wool staple on the continent, war between Edward I and Philip the Fair, and the revolt of Flanders which broke trade relations between the Flemish cities and France and opened an era of social conflict, were further factors tending to give a new orientation to the economy of northwestern Europe.

Each of these events had the most direct repercussion upon the economic life of the Netherlands. The territories that were referred to collectively as the Netherlands or Low Countries in the Middle Ages corresponded roughly to the present kingdoms of Belgium and Holland. Until they were united under the dukes of Burgundy at the end of the fourteenth century, they formed a group of separate principalities, owing a vague allegiance to either France or the Empire. The most important for the economic history of the fourteenth and fifteenth centuries were the County of Flanders, the Duchy of Brabant, the County of Hainault, and the Bishopric of Liége. The commercial growth of Holland and Zeeland, which made the Dutch Netherlands a great maritime power in modern times, had scarcely begun in the period we are now considering. Flanders and the other states of the southern Netherlands, on the other hand, had been flourishing centers of industry and commerce since the Early Middle Ages. Favored by their geographical position on the North Sea, and close to the mouths of the Rhine and the Meuse which drained the commerce of western Germany and northern France, blessed, too, with rich agricultural land capable of supporting a large population, these territories occupied a place in the economic life of northern Europe comparable to that of Italy in the Mediterranean. A very fair economic history of Europe from the eleventh to the sixteenth century could be written from a detailed study of the trade that flowed through these two small but crucially important areas.

The prosperity of the Netherlands did not, however, depend solely upon commerce, but rather upon the combination, rare in the Middle Ages, of commerce with large industrial production. Wool-weaving furnished a living to thousands of workers in Bruges, Ghent, Ypres, and a score of other cities. It also furnished the basic commodities for a huge export trade, with ramifications reaching out to every market touched by European traders. Until the end of the thirteenth century, a large part of the import-export trade of the Netherlands was handled by native merchants. English wool, the essential raw material of Netherlandish industry, was imported largely by Flemish merchants who were members of the Hanse of London, an amalgamation of the merchant guilds of some fourteen wool-weaving towns. These merchants also exported finished cloth to England, and, as sidelines to a profitable trade, imported Cornish tin and lead to feed the bronze foundries of Dinant, and, in return, carried to the English fairs all the miscellaneous goods that found their way from south, east, and north to the Flemish ports. Flemish merchants, too, were engaged in a profitable three-cornered trade in cloth, wine, and wool, from their home ports to Gascony, England and back. To northern Germany they exported cloth in return for furs, fish, and other northern products. By far the largest part of their trade, however, was directed toward the Champagne fairs, where they exchanged cloth for the spices and luxury goods brought there by Italian merchants. At these fairs, the men of the Low Countries held a privileged position, protected by a federation of merchant guilds known as the Hanse of the Seventeen Cities.

This widespread commercial activity ended with the thirteenth century. After that time, the Flemish merchants went no more a-roving. It is a fact of the utmost significance for social and cultural as well as economic history that the Netherlanders, unlike the Italians, did not continue to exploit actively the opportunities afforded by their central position, but allowed the carrying trade which passed through their ports to slip out of their hands. Of the several factors which contributed to this strange development, perhaps the most important was the general shift in the center of gravity of European trade from the inland fairs to the ports of the northern and western coast. After the turn of the century, Flemish merchants ceased to frequent the Champagne fairs, which had dwindled away, smothered by the fiscal solicitude of Philip the Fair. Flemish cloth still travelled south in great quantities, but it went in Venetian or Genoese galleys, and these same galleys now brought the rich and varied products of the Far East and the Mediterranean area directly to Bruges or Antwerp. On the way they also stopped to pick up a fair share of the trade with intermediate points in Spain, Gascony, France, and England. At the same time, the sea-borne trade of the Hanseatic cities was replacing the older overland routes to northern and eastern Germany. By the end of the thirteenth century, Hansard cogs were carrying the herring, wheat, timber, and furs of the Baltic area directly to Bruges and were carrying back Flemish cloth for distribution throughout northern Europe. Finally, the action of the English government in establishing a staple for the wool trade on the continent, in or near the Netherlands, gave the bulk of the trade between the wool-growing and wool-weaving countries to English merchants. It was now no longer necessary for Flemings to cross the narrow seas in search of the basic raw material for their industry, and the Hanse of London disappeared. In the fourteenth and fifteenth centuries, the Low Countries were, more than ever, the essential connecting link between the great trade routes of Western Europe; but the rôle of the native merchants had changed drastically. The travelling merchants of the earlier period were replaced by "drapers," who were small industrial entrepreneurs and local dealers in cloth, or by "courtiers," that is, brokers, who made a good living by acting as intermediaries for the foreign merchants who visited the ports of Bruges and Antwerp.

The change in the character of Netherland commerce, though largely the result of external developments, was also in part both cause and effect of an alteration in the ecomonic and social balance within the Flemish cities themselves. During the thirteenth century, the great weaving cities of Flanders were dominated by the merchants who formed a patrician oligarchy, bent on controlling the cloth trade to their own advantage. Through the organization of commercial guilds they were able to control both the economic and political life of the cities and to keep the working classes in subjection. But in the last years of the century, the merchant oligarchy was losing its grip. The scions of the old patrician families, their initiative blunted by inherited wealth, lacked the energy to compete with the foreign traders and were withdrawing their capital from the carrying trade and putting it into urban real estate, rents, and other less exacting forms of investment. The weavers and fullers and the masters of the minor industrial crafts were meanwhile growing increasingly restless. A series of riots and revolts culminated in 1302 in a triumphant rising of the crafts, led by the weavers of Bruges, against both the patriciate and the King of France, who had succeeded temporarily in gaining control of Flanders. This revolt left the guilds of wool-workers and the minor crafts in control of the government of the Flemish cities. It destroyed the old patrician hanses and left the cities with a strongly anti-French sentiment which the English kings later exploited to good advantage. Deprived of the political power to protect their monopolies, the merchant patriciate declined, to be replaced by the newly risen classes of drapers and courtiers. The latter, though large and prosperous groups, and comfortably wealthy, were prevented by their concentration on the local market from making the great fortunes that had been characteristic of the older merchants, or the still greater fortunes made by the Florentine cloth dealers through the combination of industrial with commercial and financial enterprise.

Under the democratic régime, the minor crafts — guilds engaged in production for the local market — reinforced their exclusive monopolies and became a tightly organized class of privileged artisans and shopkeepers. But the workers in the woollen industry were bitterly disillusioned by the failure of political revolution to achieve the economic revolution they had hoped for. True, the share in city government, which their overwhelming numbers and strong *esprit de corps* gave them under the new régime, won for them the right to organize autonomous guilds and with it greater security and more favorable conditions than were enjoyed by the proletariat of the woollen industry in Florence. Otherwise the Flemish cloth industry followed pretty much the pattern we have already noted in Florence, except that the Flemish drapers were smaller operators than the great merchants of the *Arte della Lana*. By its very nature as a large export industry, it was doomed to capitalist control, and the weavers, fullers, dyers, and other workers continued to be wage earners, working under the putting-out system, and entirely dependent on the entrepreneurial draper. Embittered by the failure of their hopes, the cloth-workers remained discontented and rebellious. Again and again during the fourteenth century they broke out in bloody revolts in Ghent and elsewhere, revolts that were crushed with merciless severity by the Count of Flanders, now supported by both the merchant class and the masters of the minor crafts who had learned to fear the violence of the turbulent weavers. The social struggle died down only with the decline of the weaving industry in the old manufacturing cities.

That decline began in the last quarter of the fourteenth century, and by 1450 the woollen industry of the old cities was ruined. This catastrophe was not, however, primarily a result of either the commercial revolution that had given the import-export trade into the hands of foreigners or the political revolution and social struggle that disturbed the peace of the Flemish cities. Flemish weaving continued to flourish throughout the greater part of the fourteenth century, despite foreign wars and malice domestic, while the cloth industry of inland Brabant grew to unprecedented volume. Under the strong rule of its dukes, who maintained consistently friendly relations with France, Brabant enjoyed internal and external peace, and its merchants had free access to the markets of northern France. After the decline of the Champagne fairs, Brabançon merchants continued to frequent Paris, and the fairs of the Île de France, the Duchy of Burgundy, and Geneva, as well as the markets of Cologne, the great center of distribution for the upper Rhine. They carried the fine and richly dyed cloths of Brussels, Louvain, and Malines, products that had gained an international reputation as luxury goods and that held their place in the world market until the general decline of the Netherlands fine-cloth industry in the fifteenth century.

What ruined the ancient industry of both Flanders and Brabant was the failing supply of the essential raw material, the fine wool shorn from

English sheep. To this failure several factors contributed. Since the opening of a direct sea route to England, the Florentine merchants of the *Arte della Lana* had taken a considerable portion of the English wool and had also deprived the Low Countries of a part of the Mediterranean market for fine cloth. Meanwhile, economic and social changes in England, which will be discussed later, reduced the production of wool or, at least, held it in a state of stability. Finally, and by far the most important factor, the English weaving industry was advancing with rapid strides and was using more and more of the native wool. What chance the Flemings had of competing with English industry was wrecked by the fiscal policy of the English kings, who placed an enormous export tax on wool. As a result English merchants could sell their cloth in Antwerp cheaper than the Netherlanders, who had to buy wool at prices swollen by the export tax. There was, of course, other wool available. It was produced in great abundance in the uplands of central Spain. But Spanish wool was drier, inferior in quality, and required different weaving techniques from those prescribed by the traditional guild regulations. These regulations were bound up with the monopolies and privileges won by the weavers' guilds in the fourteenth century, and rather than abandon them the guilds preferred to commit suicide. By the second half of the fifteenth century, the thousands of weavers in Bruges, Ghent and Ypres had shrunk to a miserable handful, whose labor served only the local market. Ypres, with an economy dependent almost entirely on the weaving industry, was the hardest hit. There the population dropped from more than twenty thousand in the early fourteenth century to less than eight thousand toward the end of the fifteenth. In 1486, a third of the remaining inhabitants were reported to be destitute and reduced to begging.

The other old cities were more fortunate. Bruges was saved by her commerce and finance, Ghent by her grain trade, while the smaller cities and rural areas founded a new prosperity on newly established industries. In these newer industries, the capitalist entrepreneur had a freer hand and operated on a larger scale. While the guilds of the old cities were starving for lack of English wool, merchant-industrialists from Antwerp were putting out Spanish wool to be woven into cheap, light cloth in villages and small towns where no guild organizations existed and labor was cheap. Here, unhampered by tradition, the entrepreneur was free to adapt production to the condition of the market. An incidental result of the new rural industry was a decided shift in the balance of population, which tended to deprive the old cities of the dominant position they had held in the preceding centuries. Even in the old cities, however, new industries, which, simply because they were new, were free from guild restrictions, attracted capital and helped to restore a general prosperity. Linen-weaving both in cities and in rural districts grew to be a large export industry all through Flanders, Brabant, and Hainault. Fine linens, like the "cambric" cloth of Cambrai, soon won a place in the world's markets comparable to that held in the preceding period by fine Flemish and Brabançon woollens. Another important new industry was the making of tapestries, many of them designed by distinguished artists, for which Brussels, Tournai, Malines, and especially Arras, acquired an international reputation. By Shakespeare's time, as the sad fate of Polonius reminds us, "arras" was a common synonym for tapestry.

The textile industries rightly occupy the most prominent place in any discussion of the economy of the Low Countries, but they were not the only important ones. From the Early Middle Ages, copper-beating and bronze-founding were highly developed in the inland region around Dinant, and the wares of that district were sold along all the trade routes of Europe. After the middle of the fourteenth century, Liége, too, became the center of a large iron industry, which in the next century specialized in the manufacture of firearms. Like most industries producing largely for export, these metal industries were controlled by merchant entrepreneurs. Though the workers succeeded in gaining a share in city government during the democratic movement of the fourteenth century, they remained a wage-earning proletariat, dependent for employment on the merchant capitalists who handled the export trade.

Much more might be said about the commerce that made the Netherlands the central market of Western Europe, but so much of it was handled by foreigners after the beginning of the fourteenth century that it can be discussed most effectively in connection with the countries from which the alien merchants came. We have already noted the activity of the great Italian firms which made Bruges the terminal point of their sea-borne trade. From the end of the thirteenth century, permanent colonies of Genoese, Venetian, Lucchese, Florentine, and Milanese merchants were established in Bruges and organized under the jurisdiction of their own consuls. Though barred from local trade, they were free to carry on a large import-export business through the mediation of native agents. These Italian firms deserve further mention here, however, because their contribution to the economy of the Low Countries was not limited to commerce and was, indeed, out of all proportion to their share in the Netherlands' trade. The larger firms were all bankers as well as merchants, and it was their dealing in international exchange that made Bruges in this period the greatest money market of Western Europe.

Next to the Italians, the most important group of merchants trading with the Netherlands were the Hansards, who founded a *kontor* at

Bruges before the end of the thirteenth century and made it the southwestern terminus of the Baltic trade, as the Italians had made it the northwestern terminus for the commerce of the Mediterranean. Bruges thus became the vital link in a great semicircle of trade routes extending from the Levant to the Gulf of Finland.

For three hundred years, the history of northern commerce was very largely the history of the German Hanse. The foundations of the Hanseatic trade were laid in the period between the middle of the twelfth and the middle of the thirteenth century by the great movement of commercial colonization, the *Drang nach Osten* of the German burghers, which spread a network of German towns through the thinly populated Slavic lands from the Elbe to East Prussia. Founded by free merchants in areas where there was no strong state government, these North German towns early acquired a high degree of municipal autonomy; and the fact that they grew as the result of successive migrations lent a marked social and cultural uniformity to cities scattered all the way from Lübeck to Riga. Before the end of the thirteenth century, merchants from these cities had united with those of Hamburg, Bremen, Cologne, and other cities of western Germany to form Hanses in London and Bruges, similar to the Flemish Hanse of London. At the other end of their trade routes, the Germans also united to establish trading posts at Bergen on the west coast of Norway and at Novgorod, the great commercial center of northwestern Russia. Meanwhile, groups of North German cities were also uniting under the leadership of Lübeck and Hamburg to clear the North Sea and the Baltic of pirates. From these early experiments in cooperation at home and abroad, the Hanseatic League finally emerged in the middle of the fourteenth century as a federal union which at its height included some seventy or eighty cities. The League soon became the greatest naval power in the North, a potent political entity, capable of dealing with national governments on terms of equality. In 1367 it opened war on Denmark to free transportation through the narrow Sound that leads from the Baltic to the North Sea, and also to break the hold of Denmark on the rich herring fisheries of Scania. The Peace of Stralsund, which ended the war in 1370, left the Hanseatic League the dominant power in the Baltic area. Thereafter, for a century and a half the League maintained the practical monopoly of the northern trade which the Hansard cities had won in the preceding years. So long as they held that monopoly, the Hansards were the indispensable middlemen between the industrial production of Flanders and England and the vast forests, fisheries, and grain lands of the North. They were thus able to maintain the privileged position they had won in non-German countries at the terminal points of their trade. Even in

England, where there was bitter opposition from native merchants, they paid lower customs duties than the English themselves, while their settlement in London, the Steelyard, enjoyed a kind of extra-territorial status, largely immune from municipal jurisdiction.

The main axis of Hanseatic trade ran northeast from London and Bruges to Novgorod. A secondary axis ran north from Bruges to Bergen, while a third ran from Cologne through Bruges to London. These were water routes in the main, but each was connected by roads with a large inland area. The trade of the Cologne circle consisted of a great variety of goods. From the lands drained by the Rhine and its tributaries, the Cologners carried westward wines, canvas, linen, metal goods, madder and woad for dyeing cloth, and on their way to England they picked up the varied objects of world-wide trade to be found in the markets of Bruges. In return, they imported wool, cloth, tin, and lead from England and cloth from the Netherlands. The north-south trade which terminated in Bergen consisted largely of an exchange of cloth, manufactured articles, wine, and other southern produce, for fish, fish oil, furs, and timber. By far the most important part of the Hanseatic trade, however, was that which flowed along the main line from Bruges and London to Novgorod, with tributaries leading off to the North German, Prussian, Polish, and Scandinavian regions along the way. Until the clearing of the Sound in 1370, and to a considerable extent thereafter, this route ran through the North Sea to Hamburg and thence across the narrow isthmus at the base of the Danish peninsula to Lübeck on the Baltic, a fact which accounts for the crucial position of these two cities in the early history of the Hanse. The vast area served by this trade route formed a balanced economic unit, within which industrial products and southern goods were exchanged for raw materials and northern products. The eastbound trade consisted of metal wares, wine, Biscayan salt, spices and all the luxury goods of the Mediterranean, brought by Italian galleys to Bruges, and, above all, English and Flemish cloth. The records of the Oldesloe tolls indicate that in 1368 at least 23,000 pieces of Flemish cloth were carried from Hamburg on the overland route via Oldesloe to Lübeck for distribution in the Baltic. At a later time the English customs accounts show the Hansards exporting from England an annual average of 6,000 "cloths" from 1406 to 1427 and 10,000 from 1438 to 1459. For the westbound trip, the big Hansard cogs were loaded with timber and forest products, such as pitch, tar and ashes, grain from the flat lands of northern Germany and Prussia, furs, hides, honey and wax from Russia and Scandinavia, Swedish iron, and, most important of all, the indispensable herring, which fed a large part of Europe during Lent and the other numerous fast days prescribed by the Church. Other foodstuffs, too, were important articles of commerce, even in this period when the great majority of Europe's population still practised agriculture. Grain was imported from the Baltic in large quantities to the thickly populated Low Countries and also to the Gascon area where the rich land was given over almost entirely to producing wine.

The forms of business organization in Hansard commerce had developed by the fourteenth century along lines similar to those followed a little earlier by Italian capitalist enterprise. The typical fourteenth-century Hansard trader no longer travelled with his goods. He had become a sedentary merchant, directing by correspondence the activity of junior partners, factors, or commission agents resident in Novgorod, Bergen, Bruges, or London. Family firms, *commenda*-like partnerships, and commission agencies, as well as bookkeeping and written instruments of credit and exchange, though not in such advanced form, were as essential parts of Hansard as of Italian business. A large carrying trade between widely separated localities, in each of which goods had to be disposed of and shipments gathered together for the return voyage, could scarcely have been conducted in any other way. The fact that almost all buying and selling was done on credit, and involved a complicated system of time payments, would alone have made necessary the continuous activity of resident agents. It goes far to account for the relatively large Hanseatic communities in the *kontor* at Bruges or the London Steelyard. But, well-developed as were their business methods, the Hansard capitalists did not accumulate as large capital resources as did the contemporary Italians. Although the total volume of Hanseatic trade probably equalled, if it did not surpass, that of Italy, the commodities handled by the Hansards were mostly goods of relatively low value in proportion to bulk and weight as compared to the spices, silks, and finely manufactured goods that made up the Italian luxury trade. Even the roomy cogs, great square-rigged tubs, could not carry timber or fish of a value equivalent to the cargo of the much smaller Italian galleys. The profits made by individual merchants, though fairly regular and secure, were therefore relatively small. They contributed to a solid prosperity but did not create great fortunes. Moreover, the Hansard merchants concentrated their attention exclusively on commerce. They did not supplement their capital by entrepreneurial profits from industry or by the manipulation of international exchange and finance. The social and cultural implications of Hanseatic capitalism were thus very different from the Italian equivalent.

In all the Hanseatic cities, the merchants formed a patrician upper class, which dominated the city government and controlled both economic and political activity. In the early days of Hanseatic expansion, these solid, hard-headed burghers had shown themselves to be adventurous, enterprising, and at times ruthless protagonists of a kind of economic imperialism. But with the triumph of 1370, a change came over the spirit of their dream. The Peace of Stralsund marked the high point of Hanseatic power. Thereafter, the Hanseatic patricians became more conservative, bent on holding the dominant position they had won. That position was threatened during the first half of the fifteenth century by English merchants, who succeeded for a time in establishing direct trade with Danzig and the Prussian cities, and also by growing Dutch competition. This trade was not entirely unwelcome to the Danzig merchants, who were more interested in the inland trade with the Prussian hinterland than in the long-distance sea-borne commerce. The interlopers were bitterly resented, however, by the central Hanseatic cities, which lived chiefly by the carrying trade. Lübeck, in particular, was strongly opposed to any trade that followed the all-water route through the Sound, since it bypassed the overland short cut from Lübeck to Hamburg which was vital to her existence. Convinced that from their point of view, any change would be for the worse, the Lübeckers fought stubbornly against change of any kind, and after much friction succeeded in imposing their conservative policy upon the Prussian cities as the price of unity. The business methods, regulations, and policies of the Hanseatic cities thus tended to become set in an inflexible mold and could not easily be adjusted to meet changing conditions. But the "nemesis of creativity," which haunts those who adhere slavishly to the methods of a glorious past, did not overtake the Hanseatic League until well after the period we are here considering.

After the Italians and the Hansards, the most important carriers of the foreign trade of the Netherlands were the English merchants, whose emergence as a force in maritime commerce is one of the significant developments of this period. Economic relations between England and the Low Countries were particularly close during the whole medieval period. Flemish industry depended on English wool, while the English upper classes depended on the Flemish markets for fine cloth, Rhine wines, and all the luxury goods — weapons, armor, silks, spices, religious bijouterie and objects of art — brought by the Flemings from the fairs of Champagne. Until the beginning of the fourteenth century, most of this trade was in the hands of Flemings, many of whom were members of the Hanse of London, or of Cologners and other "Easterlings," as the Hansards were called in England. Thereafter, the Italian galleys took over most of the direct exchange of English wool for Mediterranean luxuries, while the exportation of wool to the Low Countries was taken over by the English "Merchants of the Staple."

The foundation of a "staple," or compulsory market for the sale of English wool on the continent, marked a significant stage in the development of English participation in foreign trade. The history of the English wool staple is complicated at best, and at worst obscure, despite the large amount of scholarly attention it has received. Much of the complication, and a certain amount of the obscurity, results from the fact that the staple was instituted, and its development directed, by the uneasy co-operation of the royal government and the merchants engaged in the trade. From the first its evolution was influenced less by rational economic policy than by the shifting political weight of various pressure groups at home, by the vagaries of royal diplomacy during the Hundred Years' War, and by the insatiable appetite of the royal government for easily collectable taxes. The king's interest in channelling all of England's most important export trade toward one port on the continent is fairly clear. It enabled him to collect with comparative ease a huge export tax on wool, a tax so important to the royal treasury that the Lord Chancellor sat, and by force of tradition still sits, enthroned upon a symbolical woolsack. It also furnished him with a priceless deposit of English money on the continent, which could be borrowed to pay troops or buy allies. Finally it gave him an invaluable diplomatic bait, with which to win friends and influence people in the weaving cities of the Low Countries. It was this diplomatic use of the staple that accounts largely for the frequent shifts in its location during the early period of its history. The first staple, apparently a voluntary one, was established by Edward I in 1294 at Dordrecht and later shifted to Antwerp. It was still at Antwerp when it was first made compulsory by Edward II in 1313. During the next fifty years the staple was moved from place to place. Most commonly it was situated at Bruges, Antwerp or St. Omer, though on three occasions it was brought back to England, because of opposition to a foreign staple on the part of up-country wool dealers and cloth makers. Finally, in 1363, the staple was established at Calais, then an English possession, and there it remained except for brief interludes until Calais was lost to England in 1558.

The staple system, however, involved more than a place to which all wool must be shipped. It involved also an organized company of merchants, founded by royal charter, exercising semi-public functions and jurisdictions, and enjoying a quasi-monopoly of the trade. From the beginning the king had dealt with the "mayor and commonality of the merchants," and had used them to help collect the export taxes and to enforce the regulations of the staple. Out of this rather vaguely defined association of native and alien merchants, the English Company of the Staple finally crystallized after the settlement of the staple at Calais. This was a "regulated company," composed of wool merchants who had been admitted either through apprenticeship or by purchase and had paid a rather high entrance fee. It held a state-guaranteed monopoly on the exportation of wool to Calais, a monopoly granted by the government as a *quid pro quo* for the burden placed upon the wool trade by heavy export taxes. Not that the Staplers themselves bore the actual burden of taxation, which, as middlemen, they contrived to distribute between the producer and the consumer. But only a monopoly and strict regulation of the volume of export could enable them to maintain a sufficient differential between prices at home and abroad to absorb the tax. The Staplers were merchant capitalists, each trading independently on his own capital, yet the Company of the Staple retained something of the medieval corporate tendency to regulate and limit the enterprise of its members for the good of the whole fellowship. Its effect was to create a fairly large class of solidly prosperous merchants, but at the same time to inhibit the rise of a few great financiers.

In its broader implications, the staple system affected English trade in a variety of ways, not all to the national advantage. It favored English over foreign merchants, and introduced larger numbers of Englishmen into the trade with the Low Countries. Flemish and Brabançon merchants now bought English wool on their own doorsteps and the Flemish Hanse of London went out of existence. Italian traders, especially great firms like the Bardi and Peruzzi who combined collecting papal income with the shipment of wool to Florence, still held a large part of the export trade until the financial crisis of the 1340's, frequently buying from the crown special licences to export wool "whithersoever they will." Thereafter their share of the wool trade declined. By the end of the fourteenth century, the Italians handled only about twenty per cent of the wool exported, and, after 1378, they were required to carry it directly by sea to the Mediterranean. The export of wool to the Low Countries was by that time entirely in the hands of the Merchants of the Staple. But if the staple system gave a protective monopoly to the Staplers, it was a monopoly that worked to the disadvantage of other English merchants as well as of aliens. Small traders and merchants dealing in other commodities, who might have added wool to their stock-in-trade, were excluded. In the same way, the provincial wool dealers were prevented from becoming exporters. Forced to sell their wool to the Staplers, they formed a class of secondary middlemen, taking a profit between the wool growers and the exporters. Wool exporting thus did less than it might have done to encourage English merchants to participate in foreign trade. On the other hand, the staple system, together with the export tax of around thirty-three per cent on wool, did a good deal to encourage the manufacturing and exportation of woollen cloth by making wool cheaper and more plentiful at home than abroad, so that English merchants could sell their cloth at Antwerp cheaper than the Netherlands producers who had to buy wool at Calais prices. This was certainly to the advantage of English economy as a whole, but it was disastrous to the staple trade. Since the production of wool remained fairly constant during this period, the exportation of wool inevitably declined in direct ratio to the increase in the native manufacturing of cloth. Customs figures show a decline in average annual export from 35,000 sacks of wool in the early fourteenth century to 8,000 sacks in the middle of the fifteenth century.

The transformation of England from a wool-exporting to a wool-weaving country was an event of epoch-making proportions, the magnitude of which can scarcely be exaggerated. Its repercussions upon the industry of the Low Countries have already been noted. Its effect on the economy of England was no less revolutionary. It marked the beginning of that process of industrialization which in the course of time made England the workshop of the modern world. Wool weaving, it is true, was not an entirely new industry in England in the fourteenth century. But English weavers hitherto had worked largely for the local market, in old towns where they enjoyed the protective monopolies and were subject to the detailed regulations characteristic of medieval urban economy. Production for export, however, was stimulated during the reign of Edward III by the immigration of Flemish weavers under royal protection in 1331 and 1337, and by the heavy export tax on wool. As English cloth makers acquired the skill needed to compete with the best foreign production, more and more wool was absorbed by native industry. One result of the growth of production for export was a revolutionary change in the character and organization of the industry. Like the large textile industries of Italy and the Netherlands, the new English export industry was thoroughly capitalist, controlled from beginning to end by merchant-industrialists who put out the wool to a series of workers.

The organization of the English industry, however, differed in certain important respects from that of the older industries in the great European textile centers. In the first place, it was not concentrated in large cities like Florence, Bruges, Ypres, or Ghent. It resembled more closely the new rural industry introduced into the Low Countries after the decline of the old weaving cities. Once their market began to expand, the English clothiers found it more profitable to put out their wool to workers in country districts, villages and small towns than to struggle with the monopolies, regulations and higher wages of the old guild cities. They were also attracted to country districts where water power was available for the operation of fulling mills. These mills, incidentally, by furnishing a mechanical substitute for the arduous process of trampling the cloth in troughs, greatly reduced the labor force required, and thus gave the English industry an additional advantage over that of the Netherlands where the use of water power was not practicable. In the second place, the clothiers who controlled the English industry were for the most part not importers and exporters like the great Florentine firms. Some were no doubt London merchants who engaged in foreign trade, but most of them were up-country middlemen who bought wool from the growers, manufactured it in the area in which it had been produced, and then took the cloth up to London or one of the other ports and sold it to the exporters. They correspond to the provincial wool dealers, who bought wool from the growers and sold to the Merchants of the Staple. It is worth noting, as a fact of considerable significance for the social and political history of England, that in both the wool and cloth trades, which were at this time the most important elements in English commerce and industry, the profits were split between two groups of capitalists. Behind the great exporters, concentrated in London and other seaports, there was a numerous class of prosperous provincial entrepreneurs scattered throughout the kingdom in small cities and market towns. These were the solid burgesses who sat with their landowning neighbors in the House of Commons and thus helped to make that body genuinely representative of the nation's interests.

England's exports generally exceeded her imports in value, leaving a favorable balance of trade. In the export trade, wool and cloth occupied an overwhelmingly dominant position. According to figures computed from the customs accounts of the years 1446–48, the wool and cloth exported were together valued at £172,000, while other miscellaneous merchandise was valued at only £11,000. No commodity occupied a comparable place in the import trade. Wine, the largest single import, accounted for less than a third of the total. Some wines came from the Rhine and the Mediterranean, but the greater part of the wine brought to England originated in the Gascon area of southwestern France and was shipped from Bordeaux. The trade with Bordeaux was made more easy, and more profitable to the government, by the fact that Gascony was a possession of the English kings until 1453, a fact that also had considerable bearing on the causes of the long conflict between the kings of England and France. The remaining imports were of a most varied sort and came chiefly from the three great areas that had a close economic relation with England — the Baltic, the Netherlands, and Italy.

At the beginning of the fourteenth century, foreign products were brought to England chiefly by aliens, who sold them wholesale to native merchants in the seaports or carried them up country to the fairs. The great fairs at Bristol, St. Ives, Boston, Stamford, and Winchester were still international gatherings, transient, polyglot communities subject to the speedy justice of the "pie powder" courts. As the century progressed, however, English merchants took over more and more of the import trade, and they acquired an almost complete monopoly of distribution inland. The great fairs were still important, though much less so than they had been; but they were apparently no longer much frequented by aliens. We know less, however, about the internal trade of England than about her foreign commerce, concerning which customs records give unusually full and accurate figures from the reign of Edward I. From these we can trace the steady growth of native participation in the import trade. English merchants imported in the years 1446–48 goods to the value of £85,800, while the Hansards' imports were valued at only £20,800 and those of all other aliens at £40,100. There were native importers in every English seaport, as well as in some inland cities, but during this period an increasingly large percentage of the import trade was being concentrated in London. It was the Mercers' Company of London which, in 1407, took the lead in founding the famous Company of Merchant Adventurers in the Low Countries, with permanent headquarters at Antwerp. This was a regulated company or "fellowship" of importers and exporters, who dealt in cloth and every kind of commodity except wool. Similar companies were founded at about the same time by the English merchants trading with Prussia and Norway, but after mid-century these were driven out of business by the exclusive policy of the Hanseatic League. The Antwerp organization thus became *the* Company of Merchant Adventurers. Like the Company of the Staple, it was founded by royal charter and exercised semi-public functions, though it did not secure a complete monopoly of the trade with the Low Countries until the last decade of the century. Like the Staplers, the Merchant Adventurers were independent capitalists, each trading on his own capital, but subject to regulations and limitations upon individual enterprise according to a common policy enforced by the company's officers and backed by governmental authority.

Though commercial activity was widely spread throughout England, the merchants of London were in this period acquiring a preponderant share of the import-export trade and were also taking over more and more of the wholesale distributive trade inland. Some special attention must therefore be given to the peculiar organization of its great merchant companies. Citizenship, "the freedom of the city," in London as in many other cities could be acquired only by enrolling as a member in one of the city's hundred-odd guilds, crafts, or mysteries, as they were variously called, and paying the necessary fees and dues. A high degree of specialization and a jealous preservation of monopoly characterized the artisan crafts and retail shopkeeping, but with the growth of wholesale trade the richer members of the mercantile crafts, or of those in which commerce could be combined with industry, traded freely in almost every kind of commodity. Most merchants, it is true, enrolled by preference in the craft most closely related to their principal line of trade, since there were quite definite advantages in being associated with men of similar interests. But, as long as a citizen maintained himself as a member in good standing in one of the mercantile guilds he was free to trade wholesale pretty much as he chose. The vintners held most of the wine trade, the fishmongers the trade in fish; the grocers specialized more or less in spices, metals, dyes and drugs; the mercers in fine fabrics such as cloth of gold, satin, silks, tapestries, linen, and also such luxury oddments as ivory, amber, and mirrors. But almost every rich merchant dealt wholesale in cloth. The Merchant Adventurers at Antwerp, all of whom handled cloth as their principal export, included, besides the mercers who had taken the lead in organizing the company, grocers, drapers, skinners, haberdashers, fishmongers, and tailors. Some of the same men exported wool to Calais. This, however, involved becoming a member of the Company of the Staple. Most Staplers concentrated on exporting wool, and were content to get their money back to England through bills of exchange drawn on the mercers, who needed money on the continent to buy their expensive wares in the marts of Bruges or Antwerp and were happy to give the Staplers bills on London at the cost of a reasonable interest concealed in the exchange differential. No other commodity was as well protected by monopoly as wool, and almost every wholesaler struck a bargain wherever opportunity offered in fish, metal goods, wine, grain, or spices.

Not all the members of the guilds mentioned above, however, were wholesalers. One of the striking developments in the London guilds during this period was the clear-cut and legally recognized distinction between those merchants whose business was mainly wholesale and the lesser masters who were engaged exclusively in retail shopkeeping or handicraft production. During the fourteenth and fifteenth centuries the wealthier merchants formed separate incorporated organizations within a dozen or so of the major crafts, the most important of which were the mercers, grocers, drapers, fishmongers, goldsmiths, skinners, salters, vintners, ironmongers, tailors, and haberdashers. Entrance to this inner circle involved the payment of high fees and the expense of a special costume or "livery" to be worn on all public occasions. It was an expense which could be borne only by merchants engaged mainly in wholesale transactions. Thanks to their separate organization, the members of the "livery companies" were able to control the whole policy of the guild in their own interest and to keep the lesser masters and journeymen in a subordinate position. They also formed a kind of merchant oligarchy which monopolized the offices of city government. Their advent marked a definite stage in the evolution of capitalism out of the guild organization of the Middle Ages.

The growth of capitalism in commerce and the export industries, described above, was limited almost entirely in the period before 1450 to the countries which maintained close trade relations with the great international markets of the Netherlands. The parts of Germany which lay outside the Hanseatic sphere of influence showed relatively little change from the condition of the preceding centuries. The Spanish kingdoms, too, remained largely outside the sphere of European capitalism, except for the growing exportation of wool from the vast merino flocks that roamed the Castilian uplands and the well-developed Mediterranean commerce of Aragon and Catalonia. Barcelona rivalled the Italian cities in the development of banking and commerce in the Mediterranean area, and there was also a fairly large Catalan merchant colony in Bruges. For France, the period from 1300 to 1450 was one of stagnation and, after the beginning of the Hundred Years' War, of actual economic decline in many places. Generation after generation, English armies and the companies of mercenary soldiers left unemployed during periods of truce devastated the whole western half of France, laying waste the countryside and impoverishing the towns. Moreover, France, or at least the parts of France then under royal control, had no large export industries, nor any considerable sea-borne trade except in the Mediterranean. The great wine-exporting area of the southwest was still a possession of the English monarchy, and the industrial and commercial center of the north, the County of Flanders, had become practically independent and was frequently hostile to France. Paris was a wealthy city with a prosperous luxury trade, fed by the demands of the nobles and upper clergy who flocked to the royal court. On the strength of that trade the mercantile crafts, the *Six Corps de Marchands* (drapers, spicers, furriers, mercers, money-changers, and goldsmiths), emerged from the ranks of the industrial *métiers* to form a kind of bourgeois aristocracy. These, however, were largely retailers and lacked the widespread commercial activity of the great London companies. Much of the importing was handled by Italian or Brabançon merchants, while the Italians still held a practical monopoly of banking and exchange.

In discussing the changes in economic life during this first period in the transition from medieval to modern civilization, it has been necessary to concentrate attention primarily upon wholesale commerce and export industries, for it was in these areas, together with banking and finance, that the transformation of medieval economy was most pronounced. It must not be forgotten, however, that in all the countries of Europe, even the most economically advanced, the great bulk of industrial production was still in the hands of master craftsmen, who manufactured chiefly for the local market and sold their goods at retail, mostly to the ultimate consumer. These, together with the retail shopkeepers, made up the conservative middle class of the cities. In contrast to the capitalists who operated on a larger scale and in a wider sphere, these local craftsmen and shopkeepers intensified rather than relaxed the exclusiveness and the rigid regulation of individual activity that had been characteristic of the medieval guilds. Strangely enough, it was in this period rather than in the High Middle Ages that the largest number of guilds was formed. All over Europe guilds appeared in cities where none had existed before or in crafts that had hitherto been regulated only by the city government. In France their numbers increased enormously, fostered by the royal policy of using the guilds as instruments of governmental control. But, if this seems on the surface to be the classic period of guild organization, there is nevertheless evidence that the character of the guilds was changing, that they were being warped from their original purpose, and that even in this conservative area an embryonic capitalism was beginning to rear its head. The most noticeable development, apparently common to all parts of Western Europe, was a tendency to restrict entrance to mastership by imposing high fees and requiring an elaborate "masterpiece," with preferential treatment for the sons and sons-in-law of masters. The cessation of economic expansion which characterized the greater part of this period was evidently forcing masters to cling more jealously to their share in a relatively stable market. Under these circumstances a great many journeymen were prevented from becoming masters. The social solidarity of the guilds was thus broken as a widening gap appeared between a semi-hereditary oligarchy of masters and a growing class of permanent wage earners. In many places organizations of journeymen — yeomen guilds or *compagnonages* — were formed to protect their interests by strikes or other means against the employing masters. These developments were accompanied, especially in the larger cities, by a partial disassociation of the commercial from the industrial function of the guilds. Where the volume of business warranted it, a master tailor or goldsmith might spend most of his time buying materials or dealing with his customers, while the actual production of goods was left to a group of apprentices and journeymen.

One further factor in the economic evolution of this period should be mentioned. There was a close relation of mutual dependence between the growth of capitalism and that of royal power. The increase in governmental and military expenses, which grew with the centralization of authority, frequently forced kings and princes to turn to the merchant-bankers for loans. They also employed these experts to aid them in handling the increasingly complex problems of state finance, with the result that a number of large fortunes were made out of the more or less legitimate opportunities that an office in the royal government afforded. Contracts for supplying the needs of the royal court and the royal army also presented new opportunities for large-scale enterprise. At the same time, the growth of central government tended to break down urban monopolies and open up freer inter-urban trade, thus expanding the scope of capitalist enterprise. Royal governments, too, could foster commerce by negotiating trade treaties with foreign powers. Economic nationalism, however, was as yet in its infancy; royal attempts to regulate commerce and industry were fitful; and the economic policies of kings and princes vacillated in accordance with shifting diplomatic or fiscal needs or as the result of hastily considered attempts to find remedies for economic ills, the causes of which were but dimly perceived.

C. RURAL ECONOMY IN TRANSITION: THE DISINTEGRATION OF THE MANOR

During the period from 1300 to 1450, in agriculture as well as in commerce and industry, cessation of that steady growth that had characterized the two preceding centuries was accompanied by decisive changes in economic organization and social institutions. Rural districts seem to have been more seriously affected than were the cities by the depopulation which resulted from the ravages of famine, warfare, and disease. The results, at any rate, were probably more lasting, for though the death rate during the Black Death and its recurrent manifestations may well have been higher in the crowded cities than in the open country, urban population was constantly recruited by immigration from the country, whereas there was relatively little movement of city people back to the land. Unprotected villages, too, suffered more than the walled towns from the homicidal violence of mercenary soldiers and from the wanton destruction that characterized the warfare of this period. A persistent labor shortage thus placed the agricultural worker in a stronger bargaining position than that enjoyed by workers in industry. The suffering of the peasants was at times acute, but in the long run the more fortunate of them, at least, emerged from the crisis with their economic, social, and legal status notably improved.

Certain political factors, as well as the catastrophic plagues and famines that depopulated the land, served to aggravate the crisis through which rural society passed in the century and a half after 1300; but the decisive cause of change was purely economic. It was in essence the transformation of a natural economy, in which produce and services were exchanged for the use of land, into a money economy characterized by rents and wages, buying and selling. And the most significant result was the disintegration of the manorial structure that had furnished the economic base of the feudal system. This process, it is true, was well begun before 1300 and was by no means complete in 1450, but the years between these two dates witnessed the most crucial stages in the transition from medieval to modern forms of agrarian organization. For a century or more before 1300, agricultural society had been gradually adjusting to an expanding money economy for which the institutions of feudalism were totally unsuited. The resulting social and economic stresses, however, had been eased by the opening up of new land and by a constantly growing consumer market. The twelfth and thirteenth centuries, in short, had been a period of fairly general prosperity for both lords and tenants, and the changes involved in the introduction of money economy had been achieved without too great strain and largely within the framework of traditional institutions. Before the end of the thirteenth century, however, most of the land that could be worked profitably with existing techniques had apparently been cleared. Thereafter, the expansion of the cultivated area ceased, and no improvement in agricultural methods occurred to make possible an expansion of production by more intensive cultivation. On the contrary, there is some evidence, though not conclusive, that average yields per acre in England declined during the fourteenth and fifteenth centuries, while in France large areas were laid waste and abandoned during the Hundred Years' War. Landlords were thus forced to meet the loss of real income, which resulted generally from the expansion of money economy, without the compensation of increasing production.

The rate of change was by no means uniform in all countries, and in any given region it varied greatly from manor to manor. But, wherever the manorial organization had existed, sooner or later two allied tendencies might be observed: the abandonment of direct farming of the demesne by the lord or his agents and the commutation of labor services to money payments. Since the manorial system had been created largely as a means of securing unpaid labor for the lord's demesne, these two processes struck at the very heart of the medieval organization of land and labor. When demesne farming and labor services were replaced by a system of rents and wages, the manor lost its principal reason for existence, and when the lord became a *rentier*, whose only interest in the land was the cash income he derived from it, he lost that close relation with his manorial tenants which was an essential part of the medieval system. For members of the noble landholding class as a whole, the economic crisis of the fourteenth and fifteenth centuries meant not only impoverishment, but also the loss of many jurisdictional powers, partial loss of control over their land and people, and a consequent loss of the political independence they had enjoyed during the flourishing days of feudalism.

As has been suggested, the demesne farm was originally the very heart of the manorial system. From it the lord drew the greater part of the produce to feed his family, his retainers and his servants. With the growth of towns and the corresponding expansion of agriculture in the twelfth and thirteenth centuries, however, lords began to regard their demesne land more as a source of revenue than of food. Surplus produce could be sold in the town markets and the money received could be used to buy foreign luxuries or the products of skilled industry. This might be very profitable for the lord, but it also had its inconvenient side. Great lords, both lay and ecclesiastical, who possessed widely scattered manors, had to manage their estates through bailiffs or stewards who could not always be trusted, while petty lords, who could not afford an administrative organization, were often too busy fighting or going on crusades to supervise the farming of their land. In any case, lords both large and small were generally poor financiers, perpetually in need of ready cash. More and more frequently, then, lords found it advisable to lease parts of the demesne to their own bailiffs, to religious corporations, to prosperous peasants, or to burghers with money to invest. This process seems to have begun earlier in France and Germany than in England, but even in England it was eventually forced upon lords by the labor shortage and high wages of the century following the Black Death. Many of the early leases were perpetual, so that the tenant became a hereditary proprietor, subject to the payment of a fixed rent in money or kind. Later, lords more generally guarded against the effects of monetary inflation by leasing what remained of the demesne for a term of years, so that the rent or portion of the crop they received could be readjusted at intervals. Though many lords kept a small demesne around the manor house or castle to serve the immediate needs of the household for fruits, vegetables or wine, demesne farming in the old manner had been abandoned almost everywhere by the middle of the fifteenth century, and the demesne had been dismembered, leased out to perpetual or temporary tenants, or might even have been alienated in whole or in part.

So long as the demesne remained under direct exploitation, however, the lord had to have labor to work it, and labor services had originally formed the most important part of what the lord received in return for the land allotted to his tenants. These services usually consisted of three days "week work" on the demesne land plus certain other *corvées* such as carting, hedging and ditching, performed by unfree tenants. Free tenants seldom owed more than special "boon works" at harvest time. It was the only practical system at a time when there was little or no market for produce and very little money in circulation; but it was in many ways inconvenient for both lord and tenants. The latter disliked it because it cut down the time they could spend on their own land, and also because the lord's land had to be ploughed, sowed, and reaped at the best time and under the best weather conditions, while their own land had to take second best. The lords, on the other hand, found that forced labor, grudgingly performed, was often unsatisfactory, and a complex administrative machinery had to be maintained to regulate it. During the thirteenth century, when a growing population made labor fairly plentiful, lords were frequently willing to commute services to money payments and to use part of what they received to hire cheaper labor from among the class of "cotters" who held only a few acres or a tiny "toft" on the fringes of the manor. Though commutation was generally to the immediate advantage of the lord, it was also at times forced upon them by the fear that their unfree tenants would run away to find land in newly cleared areas where labor services were usually light or nonexistent. In the century following the Black Death, the high price of labor made commutation much less advantageous to the lords, but it was increasingly forced upon them by the necessity of making concessions in order to keep tenants who could easily find higher wages elsewhere or better conditions on vacated land. Whether commutation was to the immediate advantage of the lord or not, however, it was the peasants who profited in the long run. They gained a greater degree of economic independence and were left free to make the most of their own land, while the payments they made their lord in lieu of services, having been fixed in money terms, decreased steadily with the universal and persistent depreciation of coinage in every European country. The tendency to commute labor services was, of course, closely related to the contemporaneous tendency on the part of the lords to abandon demesne farming. In the earlier period the lord's decision to lease parts of the demesne was probably his chief reason for being willing to commute services which he no longer needed. Later, when depopulation had created a drastic labor shortage, it was probably the difficulty of enforcing services as well as the high price of labor that made many lords decide to let their land out on lease. Both tendencies were in any case complementary aspects of a single process: the substitution of free contracts and a cash nexus for the intricate web of customary relations and personal services that were characteristic of the manor in its original form.

The commutation of labor services and the establishment of a monetary relation between the lord and his tenants did not of itself give freedom to the servile or semi-servile peasants, but it was a long step in that direction, for the necessity of doing forced labor was one of the most obvious marks of servitude and one of the principal reasons why lords were loath to grant freedom to their serfs. There were, however, other customary exactions which the lord imposed upon his unfree tenants, not so much as rent for their land as because, in legal theory, they were his property and their bodies and all their goods belonged to him. In many places the lord demanded an annual "tallage" from his serfs. This was originally an arbitrary tax imposed at the lord's will, but by the thirteenth century it had become an invariable sum fixed by the custom of the manor and paid in money or kind. In addition, the lord exacted "heriot" on the death of a serf. This consisted of the serf's best beast or chattel, though in some places it was a larger share of such goods as he left. By the fourteenth century it had generally been commuted to a money payment. The lord might also impose a fine when a serf's daughter married and a larger fine if she married off the manor, though the custom in this respect varied so widely that generalization is impossible. These and other dues which the lord received from his unfree tenants by virtue of their servile status were an important addition to his revenues from the land, and he would not forfeit them willingly or without compensation. The economic and social crises of the fourteenth and fifteenth centuries, however, created a situation which favored the spread of freedom among the peasants. The necessity of making concessions in order to keep their tenants, in addition to their own chronic need for money, sooner or later forced lords to grant freedom to their serfs, whether for a lump sum or for an annual payment added to the normal rent for the tenant's land. This change was facilitated by the fact that servile obligations had generally become fixed by custom in money terms and so could be more easily regarded as simply an additional charge upon the land. In many places servile obligations, having been attached to the land, might be assumed by a freeman who took the land as a tenant, without his thereby becoming a serf. This practice, together with the translation of servile obligations into money terms, tended to blur the distinction between bond and free and to accelerate the movement toward personal freedom which had already begun in the thirteenth century. By the end of the period we are here considering, serfdom had disappeared or was rapidly dying out in most parts of Western Europe. Where it remained it was distinctly a minority phenomenon. Freedom did not necessarily improve the economic status of the peasant in any marked degree, but it did give him greater independence, opened up new opportunities, and, above all, lifted from him and his children the social stigma of hereditary bondage, a stigma which had become all the more galling as it became the exception rather than the rule.

The revolution in agrarian life was international in scope, but the course it followed varied a good deal from country to country. At the risk of some repetition, then, it will be necessary to trace the main lines of development in each of the major countries of Western Europe. England may well be considered first, since it presents the clearest example of the operation of economic forces. Under the strong government of Norman and Angevin kings, the English lords lacked the irresponsible sovereignty over their lands enjoyed by the feudal nobles on the continent. They were thus encouraged at an earlier date to think of their land in economic terms, as a source of revenue rather than of military force and political power. England, too, was comparatively free from the curse of feudal warfare, which in France and Germany did so much to disrupt family estates and to make the exploitation of widely scattered lands difficult and hazardous. The general adoption of the principle of primogeniture during the thirteenth century also helped to protect the estates of the English landholding class from fragmentation by divided inheritance. Finally, the English landlords were enabled to make a reasonably advantageous adjustment to the introduction of money economy by the fact that they had a dependable source of cash revenue in the wool produced on their demesne lands. England, indeed, experienced something like a boom in demesne farming during the thirteenth century, at a time when it was already declining on the continent. Surviving records, especially those of the great monastic estates, give evidence of an extremely systematic and apparently very profitable exploitation of demesne lands through the agency of bailiffs and a whole staff of manorial officials.

Despite the healthy state of demesne farming in the thirteenth century, however, commutation of labor services had already begun and it continued at a more rapid pace in the following century. The appalling mortality and disruption of all social life resulting from the Black Death, here as elsewhere, accelerated the tendency to replace labor services by fixd rents in money or produce. Everywhere lords found themselves with vacant land on their hands, their fields unploughed or their crops rotting on the ground. Wages rose during the second half of the century by at least fifty per cent, despite the Statute of Laborers passed by Parliament in an effort to keep them static. Much against their will, then, lords were forced to make concessions, often in the hope that they would be only temporary. The disappearance of villein services, however, was neither immediate nor uniform. It was a very gradual process and was accompanied by much social unrest, which broke into open violence in the Peasants' Revolt of 1381. In some places labor services could still be found in the sixteenth century, but one can safely say that by 1450 they played an insignificant part in rural economy, and that by the end of the century the emancipation of the villeins was virtually complete.

The peasant who had commuted his labor services and secured his freedom now became a hereditary tenant, whose right to his land was guaranteed by custom or, more legally, by copy of the manor court rolls, and who paid a fixed annual quit-rent. Barring this fixed payment, which monetary inflation made progressively less onerous, the copyholder was practically a free proprietor, and could sell or bequeath his rights to his land. Meanwhile, the decline and eventual disappearance of demesne farming, which accompanied commutation of services, created another class of tenants, to whom landlords leased out blocks of the demesne in return for a money rent. English leases, unlike those used in many parts of France and Germany, were nearly always for a term of years, and the rent could be raised on the renewal of the lease. English landlords were thus partially protected from the loss involved in dependence on fixed rents in money of declining value.

The revolution in methods of landholding transformed the lord of the manor into a landlord, whose sole relation with his tenants was an economic one. As such he had no jurisdictional authority, although as a Justice of the Peace he might exercise jurisdiction in local affairs in the king's name. The breakup of the manorial organization also resulted in greater variation in the relative economic and social status of the English peasants than had existed in the earlier period. Although almost all were equally free, the substitution of cash rents for hereditary services caused some to lose their land and to sink to the class of hired laborers, while others, more fortunate or industrious, acquired additional property by purchase or lease and became well-to-do yeoman farmers, employing laborers to help them cultivate the land. Despite the prolonged agricultural depression, this seems to have been a period of unusual prosperity for the English tenant farmers and agricultural workers. Rents were low and wages high. A small flock of sheep guaranteed a cash income, for with the breaking up of the demesne most of the sheep-raising was now carried on by tenants rather than landlords. The growth of the rural weaving industry offered part-time employment to the landless workers. And the enclosure movement, which caused much hardship in the sixteenth century, had not yet become a serious menace.

In France, where feudalism flourished in all its anarchical vigor, the relation of lords to their land was more political and jurisdictional and less purely economic than in England. It was therefore more subject to the operation of non-economic forces. Sub-infeudation was here much commoner than in England. The necessity of keeping a large military force caused most great lords, both lay and ecclesiastical, to grant out large parts of their land to armed vassals, so that much of the land was held directly by petty lords, who were almost constantly engaged in warfare and whose economic condition was generally precarious. Moreover, the chaotic conditions of the eleventh and twelfth centuries frequently enabled manorial officials, or the *avoués* who served as lay protectors and judges in ecclesiastical estates, to usurp parts of the demesne. The insecurity caused by feudal warfare, together with the chronic financial embarrassment and general irresponsibility that seems to have characterized the French nobles, may also go far to explain why they resorted to the expedient of renting out the greater part of their demesne lands at an unusually early date. Whatever the cause, it seems clear that by the end of the thirteenth century demesne farming had virtually disappeared in many places, and with it the labor services of servile tenants. Since most leases in this period were perpetual, the demesne land thus leased out was permanently alienated, and was held by hereditary tenants who paid a fixed rent in money or produce or a fixed portion of the crop or both. During the fourteenth and fifteenth centuries, leases for a term of years became somewhat more common; but by that time the greater part of the demesne was already gone. French landlords suffered in these years not only from the labor shortage caused by plague, but also from the devastation of their lands by the mercenary soldiers employed in the Hundred Years' War. The necessity of resettling land that had been ravaged and abandoned thus forced them to grant perpetual tenures at fixed rents, to commute payments in kind, and to make other concessions to attract tenants. The result was a progressive impoverishment of the landholding nobility as monetary depreciation reduced the value of their fixed incomes.

The disintegration of the manorial system in France, as in England, was accompanied by the enfranchisement of the unfree peasants, but the process was not as universally effective. By the end of the fifteenth century there were only a few serfs left in France, but where serfdom survived it continued until the French Revolution. That the enfranchisement of the French peasantry stopped short of completion was largely because of the jurisdictional rather than economic powers retained by the French nobles. The *seigneurie*, in short, outlasted the manor. To a far greater extent than was true in England, the medieval nobles in France were lords in the full feudal sense of the word. During the fourteenth and fifteenth centuries, it is true, their independent authority was increasingly restricted by the growing power of royal government, but much still remained. Many nobles still retained the right to administer both high and low justice, which added to their practical authority and also to their income, though the income was declining as more and more cases were claimed by royal courts. By virtue of seigneurial authority, too, the French nobles exacted various dues from their tenants both free and unfree, in addition to the rents which they claimed simply as landlords. The whole system of *banalités* — payments for the use of the lord's mill, oven, and wine press, and all the other innumerable petty seigneurial monopolies — was much more fully developed in France than elsewhere, and it survived as a source of income long after the disintegration of the manorial structure. Most of these seigneurial dues had been commuted by the fourteenth century to fixed money payments and so declined with the value of the coinage, but they were still important enough to compensate slightly for the depreciation in value of ground rents and other income from the land. The nobles accordingly clung with great tenacity to their traditional seigneurial rights; but these were not enough to prevent the general decline in real income that undermined the position of the whole noble class during these crucial centuries. The feudal nobles were thus forced to meet the challenge of growing royal power, bourgeois competition, and new methods of warfare with sadly depleted resources. The feudal system, which had furnished the social and political framework for medieval civilization, was dying in the fourteenth and fifteenth centuries from lack of economic sustenance.

In Germany widely divergent political and social conditions make generalization particularly difficult; but there, too, rural society and property relations were being transformed by the spread of money economy and the dissolution of manorial institutions. To an even greater degree than in France, the political situation of the nobles influenced the course of economic development. After the collapse of imperial government with the fall of the House of Hohenstaufen in the thirteenth century, the lords who held fiefs directly from the emperor strove to establish themselves as independent princes with sovereign rights over their lands. The ensuing struggle for political power led to endless feuds, which hastened the disintegration of noble estates and the decline of the lords' real income from demesne lands and peasant tenures. The necessity of raising money to pay the mounted troops that were essential to survival in a state of political chaos forced lords to mortgage the income from their estates, to commute labor services and payments in kind into fixed money payments or to sell them outright for ready cash. The steady decline in the purchasing power of money thereafter might result in a lord getting only a paltry income from an estate that had once supported him or his ancestors in a fashion appropriate to his rank. The smaller lords were especially hard hit by dependence on fixed money incomes. Many were forced to mortgage and eventually lose their lands, or to sell them to wealthy burghers or city governments eager to extend their jurisdiction over the surrounding countryside. Those greater lords who succeeded in becoming territorial princes, on the other hand, used their governmental authority to impose taxes and judicial fees and so compensate for their loss of income as landlords. They also used their princely authority to maintain such servile and other obligations and dues owed by their peasants as still remained, and even to add to them. What the peasants gained by the commutation of their services and payments in kind was thus counterbalanced by the added burden imposed by their landlord in his capacity as a sovereign prince. The resentment thus aroused was all the more bitter because the new exactions imposed by the prince were not justified by immemorial custom. It was largely responsible for the innumerable revolts in which the peasants' rallying cry was a demand for return to the old customs.

This situation was especially characteristic of the south and southwest of Germany, where the struggle for princely power was most acute. In northeastern Germany, where territorial states developed more slowly and most of the land was held by great lay or ecclesiastical lords, the situation was different, and there something like a modern farming system grew up during the fourteenth and fifteenth centuries. Here the original direct farming of the demesne had at an early date been replaced by hereditary or life leases to the *Meier* or bailiff, who thus ceased to be the lord's agent and took over not only the demesne but also the services and dues of unfree tenants on payment of a fixed rent. This system would ultimately have proved disastrous to the lords had they not undertaken with unusual initiative and foresight to alter it before it was too late. During the fourteenth century they began systematically to regain control of the demesne and to lease it for short terms, in return for a rent in kind, the amount of which could be revised at the end of each lease. Having no need for the labor services of their unfree tenants, the lords then proceeded to free them, while at the same time depriving them of their hereditary right to their holdings. The old servile tenures were then consolidated into larger farms and rented, like the demesne lands, on short-term leases. The more fortunate peasants thus became tenants renting fair-sized farms, while others were forced to become hired laborers. In any case they gained freedom and a measure of economic independence, but at the cost of losing the security that the old manorial system had guaranteed.

Still another situation prevailed in central and eastern Germany, where land had been settled by forest clearing or by colonization at the expense of the original Slavic population during the twelfth and early thirteenth centuries. As was generally the case in land brought under cultivation by assarting in that period, the pioneers who cleared these forest lands had secured very favorable conditions of tenure. Personal freedom was the general rule, and though services existed, they were not common or onerous. The great majority of the peasants here were hereditary proprietors of their land, paying an annual quit-rent to the lord who was the ultimate owner. Under such circumstances, the expansion of money economy had relatively little effect upon the system of landholding or the organization of rural society.

Despite all regional variation, the evolution of agrarian economy followed a fundamentally similar course in all the European countries north of the Alps. In Italy, on the other hand, the unusually early and intensive growth of cities, money economy, and an embryonic capitalism created a situation in many respects unique. From the twelfth century, central and northern Italy were dominated both economically and politically by urban communes, which gradually evolved into city-states. As these city-states acquired governmental authority over the surrounding *contado*, the old noble landholding families were forced by economic and political pressures to leave their rural castles and move into the urban center. At the same time, wealthy burghers bought or foreclosed mortgages on the land of those indigent nobles who could not maintain a rising standard of living on their income from land. Rural land was sought by prosperous burghers not only as a secure and socially respectable form of investment for surplus capital, but also as the site of a villa to which the family might repair during the heat of summer, or at times when plague decimated the crowded population of the cities. Many nobles, too, having taken up commerce and merged with the upper bourgeois class, retained their old lands as an additional source of revenue. In either case, most of the arable land in central and northern Italy came to be owned by city dwellers, who regarded the land as primarily an investment and expected from it a cash income. The manorial organization, designed as it was principally to provide food for the lord and his retainers, did not serve the needs of urban owners and so disappeared at an early date. Demesne lands were leased, while peasant holdings were transformed into hereditary tenures, with the tenants paying a fixed rent, but enjoying all the rights of a free proprietor. Serfdom practically disappeared in the thirteenth century. In many places the peasants formed rural communes, which could bargain collectively with the landowners and so accelerated the movement toward enfranchisement.

Thus far the situation, except for the unusually early breakup of the manorial system, and the growth of absentee landlordism was not so very different from that in parts of the North. But, from the second half of the thirteenth century, urban landowners, whose attitude toward investment was being shaped by the growth of capitalism, began to exploit their land more rationally and systematically, with a view to making it produce as large a money income as possible. Grain crops were replaced, especially in hilly country, by olive trees and vineyards, which permitted more intensive cultivation and a larger cash return per acre. In the Lombard plain a system of irrigation was gradually developed, which made possible increased grain yields and the cultivation of rice, introduced from the Orient in the fourteenth century. At the same time, old village communities were broken up, and scattered holdings were regrouped to form consolidated estates. In the process, the old system of perpetual or long-term leases was commonly replaced by short-term, sharecropping contracts, in which the owner supplied the land and equipment and received in return half the crop. This system, known as *mezzadria*, became increasingly common during the fourteenth and fifteenth centuries and long remained the normal form of tenancy in many parts of Italy. It was particularly well suited to the exploitation of land where planting with vineyards or olive trees or extensive irrigation demanded considerable initial capital outlay. It thus offered some advantages for the peasant who had no capital and could contribute only his labor, but in general the introduction of the *mezzadria* meant a deterioration from the rather unusually favorable position achieved by the Italian peasants in the thirteenth century. The sharecropping tenant was legally free, but, having no capital and little chance of making more than a bare living on his small plot of land, he was in fact economically bound to the soil and more often than not in debt to the landlord. On the other hand, he had lost the security of perpetual tenure, since he could be evicted at the landlord's will.

The agricultural development of the Spanish peninsula, like that of Italy, was in some respects unique, but for different reasons. The Moslem occupation and the long struggle of the reconquest left its permanent mark on both methods of agriculture and the character of the Spanish rural classes. In the rich southern part of the peninsula, the Moslem invaders introduced many new semi-tropical fruits and vegetables and intensive methods of cultivation of a more scientific sort than could be found elsewhere in Western Europe. On the barren uplands of Castile, on the other hand, the perpetual warfare between Christian and infidel competed with an inclement climate in discouraging agriculture and in breeding into the Spanish character a greater fondness for military activity alternated with periods of idleness than for the peaceful pursuit of the plough. Agriculture in the great Castilian tableland was further discouraged by the vast flocks of merino sheep, which migrated each year hundreds of miles to summer pastures in the northern highlands and back again to winter quarters in the plains and valleys of the south. Organized in a great guild-like society, the *Mesta*, the sheep owners, most of whom were great lay or ecclesiastical lords, kept up a constant conflict with the settled communities that lay along the path of migration, and used their wealth and influence to prevent the enclosure or protection of arable land. During the reconquest, a good many small proprietors seem to have acquired a fairly free tenure of their land, but the normal method of peasant landholding seems to have been one or another of the forms of free or unfree tenantry with which we are familiar in other parts of Europe. Lack of data and of a sufficient volume of research makes it difficult to follow in detail the evolution of peasant society in Spain toward freedom and the transformation of tenant-landlord relations under the influence of money economy, but there is sufficient evidence to indicate that, aside from the special conditions imposed by intensive fruit-growing or migratory sheep-raising, it followed a course not unlike that common elsewhere in Western Europe.

VI

*The Decline of Feudal and Communal
Institutions and the Growth of the Centralized
Territorial States*

In the political as well as the economic history of Western Europe, the period from about 1300 to the middle of the fifteenth century represents the first decisive stage in the transition from medieval to modern forms. There is, indeed, a close causal relation between economic and political developments in this crucial period, and the current of influence did not always run in the same direction. For, if the expansion of money economy and the growth of capitalism acted as powerful solvents upon the feudal and communal institutions of the Middle Ages, it is equally true that the growing territorial or national states, which replaced feudal lordships and communal autonomy, furnished a milieu more favorable to the further development of the new economic forces.

Medieval political theory, always conditioned by the theologians' conviction that there was a divine plan for Christian society, had been deeply imbued with the concept of a universal *Respublica Christiana*. This concept found its material embodiment in the universality of the Roman Catholic Church and the Holy Roman Empire. But, powerful as was the ideal of universality, the effective institutions of medieval political, judicial and economic organization were almost wholly local. Founded within the limits of an agrarian economy, they could scarcely have been otherwise. Lacking adequate fiscal income, the central governments of the Early Middle Ages were forced to abdicate their sovereign rights and powers and to leave effective jurisdiction to each lord in his own land. And when cities arose once more, the burghers as a corporate group won for themselves a similar jurisdiction within their city walls, neither greatly helped nor hindered by a distant and impoverished state government. During the twelfth and thirteenth centuries, however, the economic conditions that had made local autonomy unavoidable were gradually disappearing. The revival of commerce and city life vastly increased the circulation of money and made possible the development of a monetary fiscal system and the concentration of fluid wealth in the royal treasuries. At the same time, itinerant merchants were opening up a network of trade routes along which the officers of state and Church could also travel with relative ease and security. By the end of the thirteenth century, the cumulative effects of economic change had made local autonomy not only unnecessary but increasingly impracticable. In the following two centuries, kings and princes gradually whittled away the independent jurisdictions of feudal lords, ecclesiastical authorities, and urban communes and step by step transformed a feudal suzerainty into an absolute monarchy. They were aided in achieving this end by the economic crisis that undermined the position of the landholding class and hampered the feudal nobles in their struggle to maintain their customary independence. They were aided also by the positive support of the growing class of capitalist entrepreneurs, whose business had outgrown the confined jurisdiction of the medieval communes and demanded the larger sphere of operation which only a territorial state could provide. In both economic and political spheres European society was in these centuries slowly emerging from a condition of practical isolation combined with theoretical universality, and was beginning to adjust itself to the more modern frame of reference furnished by the monarchical state.

A. Italy: from Commune to Territorial State

The political development of Italy, the land of cities and the birthplace of capitalism, was in many ways different from that of the great feudal kingdoms. Here, the early growth of urban communes, the inclusion of northern Italy in the Germanic Holy Roman Empire, the existence of a papal state stretching from coast to coast across the center of the peninsula, and of a kingdom ruled by foreign dynasties to the south, all had combined to make the evolution of a national state in Italy virtually impossible. After the fall of the imperial House of Hohenstaufen in the second half of the thirteenth century, Italy was irrevocably committed to particularism. Feudalism declined here earlier than in any other country; but there was here no national monarchy to utilize the moneyed wealth with which the Italian cities were so precociously supplied, or to rally the commercial classes in support of a central government that could maintain peace and order throughout the country. In northern and central Italy, on the contrary, feudalism was replaced by a host of autonomous communes, which absorbed the feudal nobility, extended their authority over the surrounding countryside and, by the second half of the thirteenth century, had become for all practical purposes city-states. But, though the feudal system was thus replaced by one equally localized and, in its republican communal form, equally medieval, economic and political forces were working here as in the larger states beyond the Alps toward the development of a state system that was less medieval than modern.

During the period from the late thirteenth century to the middle of the fifteenth, the political institutions of Italy underwent a profound transformation. In the first stage of this process, republican government gave way to the rule, more or less legitimate, of princes or despots in every important city-state except Venice, Florence and Siena. In the second stage, the wealthier and more powerful states absorbed their weakers neighbors, until by 1450 the dozens of little Lombard and Tuscan city-states had been replaced by three large territorial states — Venice, Milan and Florence — with three or four small states still maintaining a precarious independence. A few half-independent principalities still survived in the States of the Church, but the popes of the next half-century succeeded in crushing these and uniting their territory under a strongly centralized government. By the end of the period we are here considering, then, Italy acquired a system of territorial states, the prototype on a smaller scale of the state system that was developing out of feudalism and the *Respublica Christiana* in Western Europe as a whole.

Historians have frequently referred to this period in Italian history as "The Age of the Despots," and with some reason, for the rise of despots was in fact one of the most characteristic phenomena of the period of transition from commune to territorial state. The form of government represented by the despots — or, to use the less prejudiced Italian term, the *signori* — was peculiar to northern and central Italy. It had no parallel in the rest of Europe, for it could have developed only out of autonomous urban communes, such as scarcely existed elsewhere.

It was certainly no outgrowth of feudal institutions or of feudal ways of thinking. Though the *signoria* might become hereditary, it was not founded upon feudal loyalty to an established dynasty, nor was the despot hampered by any conception of reciprocal obligation to his hereditary dependents. The *signore's* government was purely personal. He had unlimited executive and legislative authority. His will was law and he himself was above the law. He could ignore or alter existing laws and customs and could issue statutes without consulting any representative body. At the same time, the *signore* was in a sense a constitutional ruler, since his office had been created in the first instance by the will of the people and was in most cases made legitimate by the formally expressed consent of the citizens on the accession of each new ruler. This consent, it is true, became in time a rather hollow formality, particularly when it took the form of the election of a hereditary prince, but it symbolized fairly enough the actual situation. For, even though a particular despot might have acquired his power by the assassination of a kinsman, by conquest or purchase, the *signoria* itself existed by virtue of the consent, whether active or passive, of the citizens. Disillusioned with a republican government that could not keep order or prevent ruinous civil strife, the people had in fact abdicated their sovereign power and, whether legally or not, had entrusted the government to one man whose authority, in order to be effective, must be unlimited. The *signoria* was the logical successor to a democracy that had committed suicide.

The failure of republican government in the communes was largely the result of economic and social tensions, of incurable class, party, and factional conflicts within the urban communities. It occurred earliest in the inland cities of Lombardy, where the balance between the opposing classes was most evenly maintained, and civil strife, therefore, the normal condition. Republican forms, on the other hand, lasted longest in the great commercial cities like Venice and Florence, where a merchant oligarchy was strong enough to monopolize the government. In most of the communes a relatively simple class distinction had crystallized in the twelfth century during the struggle for freedom from imperial or papal control. Leadership in that strenuous age was tacitly assured by the class of *milites* or knights, that is, those citizens who were wealthy enough to fight on horseback with a knight's equipment. This class was composed partly of prosperous merchants and partly of feudal nobles who had moved into the cities, where they built fortified towers and for a time maintained a semi-feudal way of life. Eventually, however, these nobles were forced to adapt themselves to the urban economy. They engaged in trade, intermarried with the merchant families and merged with them to form a purely urban patriciate, to which the term "noble," with all its feudal and chivalrous connotations, scarcely applies. They were more accurately described by contemporaries as magnates or *grandi*, though the term "noble" was also used rather indiscriminately. By the thirteenth century, this wealthy class, of mixed feudal and mercantile origin, had become an exclusive oligarchy, ruling the city in its own selfish interests. The remainder of the active citizens of the commune were the *pedites* who fought on foot and who were generally referred to simply as the *popolo*, the people. This class consisted chiefly of the master artisans and local shopkeepers, who made up the bulk of the city's middle class. In the larger cities where there was considerable foreign trade, there arose among these, to complicate the political situation, a growing class of newly rich entrepreneurs, who may be designated by the term felicitously applied to them by their Florentine contemporaries: the fat people, *popolo grasso*. Finally, wherever there were large export industries, the development of capitalist forms of business enterprise also created a propertyless industrial proletariat, with interests quite distinct from those of the privileged guildsmen of the lesser crafts. Though frequently referred to as the *popolo minuto*, these proletarian workers were not regarded as citizens and were, therefore, not included among the *popolo* strictly speaking. The term *popolo* had a definite political significance. It referred to all citizens who were not classed as magnates. By the end of the thirteenth century, in most communes, the *popolo* had a distinct political organization, founded upon membership in the greater and lesser guilds.

Had the *grandi* been willing to share their privileges with the newly arisen capitalist families they might have remained strong enough to prevent popular rebellion. Or had the *popolo grasso* been numerous and rich enough, as they were in Florence, they might have formed a new oligarchy on the ruins of the old. But in most of the communes the classes were too evenly balanced for the decisive victory of any one of them. In many places the mercantile guilds of the *popolo grasso* in alliance with the smaller guilds of local tradesmen and artisans succeeded in winning a popular victory. But the economic interests of the merchant capitalists, whose competition for foreign trade led them into constant conflict with other cities, and the tradesmen, whose activity was limited to the local market, were actually very different. Given a temporary victory of the popular party, this divergence of interest would soon become apparent, and would disrupt the unity of the *popolo*. The political situation was further complicated in many places by the traditional hostility between the Guelf and Ghibelline parties. These parties, which cut more or less across class lines, had lost their original reason for existence with the end of the papal-imperial conflict. In the fourteenth century they ceased to represent differences in general policy, but the old party names survived to differentiate local factions, which continued to involve the population of the cities in civil strife. Family feuds also divided the proud and quarrelsome magnates and, like that between the Montagues and the Capulets, might keep a whole city in turmoil. Finally, the oppressive economic regulations imposed by the cities on the surrounding countryside, and the suppression of all political rights in the rural communes and small towns of the *contado*, led to constant friction between city and country, and deprived any victorious party of support outside the city walls.

Under such circumstances, it is small wonder that the mass of the commercial and industrial populace of the cities lost confidence in the ability of republican government to maintain the peace and order, the security of life and property, that were essential to the conduct of business. During the thirteenth century, almost every city attempted to solve this problem by the temporary expedient of turning the government over to a *podestà* who, having been brought in from some other city, was supposed to be free from entanglement with any local party or faction and therefore capable of imposing order equally upon all. At first the authority of the *podestà* was limited by the necessity of conforming to existing law and it was also strictly limited in time to a year or two. But the political powers of any people tend to atrophy unless continuously exercised, and in course of time the *podestà* might be given wider and wider executive, legislative and judicial authority and his term of office lengthened to a term of ten years or life. A *podestà* who had secured a life tenure of his office was, in fact, practically a *signore*. In actual fact, only one of the great fourteenth-century lordships, that of the family of Este in Ferrara, grew directly out of the office of *podestà*. Nevertheless, the *podestà* was an important transitional figure in the evolution from republic to *signoria*. Surrender of governmental authority to him accustomed the people to being ruled by one man, and paved the way for the acceptance of a permanent *signore*.

In most places, however, the further development of the office of *podestà* was checked and eventually overshadowed by the rise of the equally dictatorial but more popularly supported office of *capitano del popolo*, "Captain of the People." Though theoretically above party, the *podestà* was frequently the creature of the patrician class. The *capitano del popolo*, on the other hand, grew to power as the chief executive of the combined guilds, which formed an organized party in opposition to the patrician government of the commune. When, in one city after another, a popular revolution, often led by merchants of the *popolo grasso,* placed the *popolo* in power, the *capitano* reduced the *podestà* to a subordinate position and took over the control of the government. Since it was necessary for the champion of the successful popular party to exercise unlimited extra-legal powers in order to carry out the suppression of the defeated *grandi,* and also to mediate between the two classes of large merchants and small shopkeepers who constituted the *popolo,* the *capitano* would be granted successively wider powers and his term of office would be indefinitely lengthened until, as in the case of the earlier *podestà,* his office might evolve into a hereditary lordship. It was in this way that Mastino della Scala became lord of Verona and his heirs became hereditary *signori.* In this way, too, the family of Carrara became lords of Padua, the Gonzaga of Mantua and the Della Torre and Visconti of Milan, not to mention numerous lesser dynasties in Lombardy and the Papal States.

Once established as hereditary rulers, however, the *signori* soon broke away from their democratic origins. The greater lords acquired a new claim to legitimacy by purchasing the title of imperial "vicar," which entitled them to act as deputy or vicegerent of the emperor. Although the imperial vicariate, purchased for cash from emperors who no longer exercised effective authority in Italy, may seem an empty honor, it served a significant purpose. It not only freed the *signore* from dependence on the theory of popular election; it also freed his title from dependence upon one particular commune, and left him free to expand his territory. Can Grande della Scala regarded his vicariate as sufficiently important to have it renewed by Frederick of Austria in 1317 and by Louis the Bavarian in 1329. So, too, it was the purchase of the title of vicar from Charles IV in 1348 that marked the solid establishment of the Carrara lordship in Padua. Later the great territorial *signori* achieved a still more independent status by purchasing the more resounding title of duke or marquis. Thus in 1395 Giangaleazzo Visconti bought from the Emperor Wenceslas the title of Duke of Milan for a hundred thousand florins. Francesco Gonzaga acquired the title of Marquis of Mantua in 1432 from the Emperor Sigismund, and Borso d'Este that of Duke of Ferrara from Pope Paul II in 1471. These titles carried with them legal recognition of hereditary succession by the rule of primogeniture as in the monarchical states. The *signori* had become princes, and the last shadow of popular sovereignty had faded from sight.

Scarcely were the *signori* firmly established than they entered upon a policy of territorial expansion, which led them into constant conflict with one another and culminated in the creation of a great territorial state in Lombardy under the Visconti. Conflict between city-states was no new phenomenon in Italy, but the motives which inspired the despots were somewhat different from those which led republics governed by merchant oligarchies like Venice and Florence to conquer their trade rivals. When the Scaligeri as lords of Verona conquered a large territorial state in the first half of the fourteenth century, and the Visconti as lords of Milan did the same in the second half of the century, this process did not signify the conquest of the other Lombard cities by Verona or Milan. At any rate, it did not involve the complete subordination of the economic interests of the conquered cities to those of the capital, as did the conquest of eastern Lombardy by Venice or of Tuscany by Florence in the fifteenth century. The expansion of the territorial state of a *signore* meant simply the extension of his personal rule to a larger area, and it was motivated by nothing more than dynastic ambition and personal lust for wealth and power.

Skilled opportunists as they were, the despots employed various means to expand their states. Sometimes they stirred up sedition and civil strife in a neighboring city, and then stepped in as peacemakers. Sometimes they were invited to interfere by citizens who suffered under a tyrannical lord or whose city was torn by factional conflict. In other instances the lordship of a city was purchased from the reigning *signore* for good hard cash. Thus, Obizzo d'Este in 1341 bought the lordship of Parma for a reputed 70,000 gold florins; Mastino della Scala bought and sold Lucca; and Giovanni Visconti purchased Bologna for 200,000 florins, only to lose it a few years later. More frequently the despots acquired additional cities by conquest, often aided by the treachery of disaffected elements among the citizens. However acquired, the lordship of a city was as a rule formally transferred to the new *signore* by the city council or by the acclaim of the *popolo*. Thereafter the city became part of the new lord's territorial state, and was subject to his laws and taxes, although it might retain its own municipal institutions and a fair degree of autonomy in regulating its own economic activity. The territorial state of a despot was, in fact, a kind of federation, bound together only by the personal rule of the prince. To the citizens, then, it made relatively little difference whether they were ruled by a local *signore* or by a more powerful and distant lord. There might be advantages or disadvantages either way.

The transformation of political institutions involved in the rise of the *signori*, and the expansion of the wealthier states at the expense of the poorer, was accompanied by an equally drastic change in the military organization of the Italian states. During the period of class and party conflict that followed the acquisition of communal autonomy, the citizen militia, which had fought the wars for freedom, gradually disintegrated. By the end of the thirteenth century citizen armies had practically disappeared in the Lombard cities that were drifting into despotism, and they lasted as effective military force only a little longer in the more vigorous republics of Tuscany. This is a fact of cardinal importance for the decline of republican government, the expansion of the wealthier states at the expense of the poorer, and the eventual conquest of a large part of Italy by foreign powers. The surrender on the part of the Italian people of the power to defend themselves and their liberties was very largely the result of the unhealthy political situation common to nearly all the city states of that period. Where an oligarchy of magnates still ruled a city seething with rebellion, they could no longer afford to call the *popolo* to arms. And when a successful revolution placed the popular party in power, the first concern of the victors was to disarm, disenfranchise or drive into exile the *grandi* who had formed the vitally important cavalry wing of the communal army. The *popolo grasso*, it is true, were rich enough to serve as mounted knights, but they had neither military training nor the soldierly spirit of the old patriciate. The newly risen capitalists found the pursuit of gain a more profitable and generally more congenial occupation than fighting, and they were probably aware that they would cut a rather sorry figure on horseback. The guildsmen, who had made up the rank and file of the infantry, had also lost much of their martial spirit. Their training had long been neglected, and they had little enthusiasm for wars against commercial rivals fought largely for the advantage of big business. No recruits could be counted on from the surrounding countryside either, for no urban government, popular or patrician, dared arm the oppressed and disaffected population of the *contado*. The same fundamental weaknesses, in fact, that led the declining republics to turn the business of government over to a hired *podestà* and later to the *signori* caused them also to turn the business of fighting over to mercenary soldiers. At the same time, the fact that the armed forces of the cities were composed of hired troops who would fight for any paymaster made it much easier for a party leader who had gained temporary control of the treasury to turn his office into an absolute lordship. And once established in power, the *signori* could count on the mercenaries to overawe the unarmed populace and crush any hint of rebellion.

The soldiers of fortune who fought the wars of the Italian states throughout the fourteenth and fifteenth centuries were led by commanders of a new type, the *condottiere*, a type as characteristic of this period in the history of Italy as was the capitalist entrepreneur, whom he resembled in many ways. As a military entrepreneur, the *condottiere* contracted with state governments to supply an armed force at a price, and his sole interest in the bargain was the profit to be derived therefrom. The successful *condottiere* was first of all a shrewd business man. He played off one state against another, accepted the highest bid, and as a rule was quite prepared to terminate the contract without notice if he was offered more money by the opposing government. He had no patriotic interest in destroying the enemy's army, and he was generally loath to waste the soldiers who were his stock-in-trade by engaging in unnecessarily sanguinary battles. A *condottiere* had to win a certain number of victories to maintain his credit, but he had no strong urge to win a decisive victory that would bring the war to an end and leave him unemployed. When trapped by a superior force he would generally prefer to surrender rather than fight a desperate engagement. Surrender, he knew, would mean no more than a bothersome financial loss, since a sort of gentlemen's agreement between members of the profession made it customary to release prisoners on payment of a moderate ransom.

Machiavelli has left us a sharply etched, if somewhat prejudiced, picture of the treachery, cowardice and general futility of the mercenary soldiers who plundered and impoverished Italy for two hundred years, betrayed every cause they served, and in the end left the country a helpless prey to foreign invaders. In justice to the military reputation of the *condottieri*, however, it must be noted that the uncertain nature of their employment made it impossible for them to maintain large forces of trained infantry, such as were revolutionizing the art of war in the national states. Their armies were composed largely of heavy cavalry, and the terrain of Italy is peculiarly unsuited to cavalry tactics. As a result, their campaigns consisted of endless marches and counter-marches and manoeuvres for position. In this kind of chess game the *condottieri* developed a great deal of skill. Their conduct of battles and campaigns was on the whole more rational than that of the semi-feudal commanders of the north. Machiavelli to the contrary, the *condottieri* who had to meet the foreign invasions at the end of the fifteenth century were well-trained professional soldiers, and when the conditions were favorable and the incentive sufficient they were capable of effective action. Their forces, however, were too small to cope with the much larger and better balanced armies of the great national states. The fatal weakness of Italy was not so much that the Italian states depended upon mercenaries as that they could not unite to present a common front to the invader.

Aside from their general unreliability, the mercenary soldiers were an unmitigated nuisance to friend and foe alike, and they contributed more than their share to the atmosphere of violence, brutality, and treachery that hangs over Renaissance Italy. When employed they were more dangerous to noncombatants than to their armed opponents, and when unemployed they were no better than brigands. This was especially true of the fourteenth-century *condottieri*, many of whom were foreigners from beyond the Alps. In mid-fourteenth century the "Grand Company," led by the Swabian knight, Werner of Urslingen, an unpleasant character who called himself "the enemy of God and compassion," levied blackmail on every state in central Italy. Later the same company was commanded by a renegade Knight of St. John, a Provençal known to the Italians as Fra Moriale. During the periods of truce in the Hundred Years' War, numbers of French and English soldiers flocked to Italy, including the most respectable of the fourteenth-century *condottieri*, Sir John Hawkwood, whom the Italians called Giovanni Acuto. The fifteenth-century mercenaries, on the other hand, were mostly Italian, but they were equally foreign to the cities they served, uprooted men who had lost even the local patriotism that was the Italian's only substitute for national sentiment. By that time the system was well established and the great Italian *condottieri* — Alberico de Barbiano, Facino Cane, Braccio, Gattamelata, Colleoni, Carmagnola, Piccinino, Sforza — low-born upstarts though they were, dealt on terms of near-equality with princes and played an important rôle in the complex balance-of-power politics that characterized the century. In this period, too, many of the lesser *signori* — Gonzaga, Malatesta, Montefeltro, Bentivoglio, among others — became *condottieri*.

To outline the history of all the Italian states of the fourteenth and fifteenth centuries would be impossible in anything but a work of monumental size. We shall have to limit the narrative to the five large states that by 1450 divided the greater part of Italy between them. Oddly enough, each one of these states represents a quite different kind of government. We may begin with Milan, which represents the type most common in the fourteenth century, that of the city-state ruled by a *signore* and developing into a territorial state under a hereditary prince.

From very early times, Milan played an important part in Lombard politics. Situated in the midst of rich and well-irrigated land, at the junction of the main trade routes from the coastal cities to the Alpine passes, it was one of the wealthiest and most populous cities of Italy. It was also one of the most politically disturbed. The aristocracy, who still held large estates in the good agricultural land of the *contado*, here retained a stronger position than they did in the coastal cities or the Tuscan hills. The merchants, though very prosperous, did not develop the distant commerce and the large-scale capitalist enterprise that went with it as did the Venetians and Florentines, and so were not strong enough to dominate the government. Their influence was counterbalanced, too, by a large and economically independent class of skilled

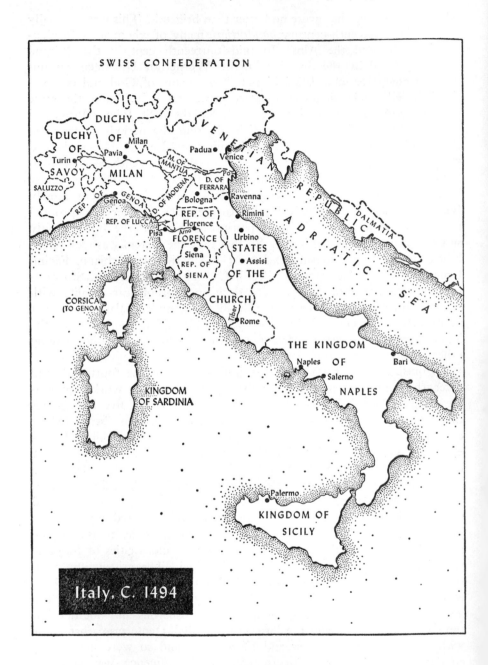

SWISS CONFEDERATION

DUCHY
OF
MILAN

DUCHY
OF
SAVOY

Milan
Pavia
Turin
SALUZZO

M. OF
MANTUA
Padua
Venice

VENETIAN REPUBLIC

Po
D. OF
FERRARA

REP. OF GENOA
Genoa
D. OF MODENA
Bologna
Ravenna

REP. OF LUCCA
Arno
Pisa
REP. OF
Florence
FLORENCE
Rimini

Siena
REP. OF
SIENA

Urbino
STATES
Assisi
OF THE
CHURCH

DALMATIA

ADRIATIC SEA

CORSICA
(TO GENOA)

Tiber
Rome

THE KINGDOM
OF
NAPLES

Naples
Salerno
Bari

KINGDOM
OF SARDINIA

Palermo
KINGDOM OF
SICILY

Italy, C. 1494

artisans. Milan's principal industry was the manufacture of weapons and armour, a highly skilled trade in which the workers could not be reduced to the position of a wage-earning proletariat as could the textile workers of Florence. In the thirteenth century each of these classes had a formal political organization of its own, and the city was further divided by strongly organized Guelf and Ghibelline parties. As happened wherever the class and party conflict was too evenly balanced, the Milanese citizens early sought relief from perpetual civic turmoil by offering the government to a dictator. From 1259 to 1277 this position was held by members of the Guelfic Della Torre family as leaders of the popular party. A counter-revolution then placed the Ghibelline Archbishop Ottone Visconti in power with the support of the *grandi*. Ten years later he laid the foundations for a hereditary *signoria* by having his great-nephew Matteo Visconti elected *capitano del popolo*. Except for a brief period when the Della Torre returned to power, the Visconti continued to rule Milan thereafter until the death of the last male member of the house in 1447.

The rise of the Visconti followed the common pattern of the north Italian *signori*. What distinguished them from the other signorial dynasties was their overwhelming success in establishing a large and strongly organized territorial state. This success they owed partly to outstanding personal ability, but still more to the wealth of Milan and the other Lombard cities they brought under their rule. At the high point of the Visconti fortunes, Giangaleazzo (1385–1402) drew from his territories an estimated annual income of 1,200,000 florins. This income was collected and accounted for in very businesslike fashion and, though Giangaleazzo spent vast sums to pay for mercenary troops, to maintain spies and diplomatic agents in every Italian state, and to stir up sedition in the states he hoped to conquer, every florin spent was a well-calculated investment. To raise the money needed to satisfy their ambition, the Visconti taxed their subjects heavily, but they generally nourished a reasonably tender regard for the goose that laid the golden eggs, avoided ruinous taxation and did much to promote the commercial and industrial prosperity of their state. There can be no doubt that Giangeleazzo understood the needs of business. He was himself closely akin to the new type of merchant capitalist in his use of a vast organization of paid agents, in his careful calculation of chances, and also in his calculated magnificence and his willingness to take large risks and make large investments in the hope of large returns. The complex series of diplomatic and military manoeuvres through which he expanded his state were all directed from his office in Pavia or Milan, where he received detailed reports from a multitude of agents and issued instructions to his generals and diplomatic representatives. "He was," wrote the Milanese historian Bernardino Corio, "most prudent and astute, of a solitary disposition . . . splendid and prodigal, sparing not his own purse nor that of his subjects, ambitious and fortunate in his undertakings above all the princes of Italy."[1]

The reign of Giangaleazzo represents not only the high point of Visconti fortunes, but also the one occasion on which it seemed possible that the northern half of Italy might be united in one strong state. At the time of his sudden death he was master of nearly all of Lombardy, the greater part of Tuscany and a number of cities in the Papal States. He had not lived long enough, however, to consolidate his conquests and his two sons, Giovanni Maria (1402–12) and Filippo Maria (1412–47) were both minors. The elder, moreover, was a vicious psychopath whose inglorious reign ended in assassination. Though most of Giangaleazzo's new acquisitions were lost and the Milanese state reduced to a shattered wreck under Giovanni Maria, Filippo Maria, who had inherited his father's talents for financial administration and devious diplomacy, succeeded in recovering control of western Lombardy. In 1423 his aggressions provoked Florence, and two years later Venice, to declare war on the expanding Milanese duchy, a war that lasted with few interruptions till his death. Both sides employed the most famous mercenaries of their day and competed for their services. In the last stages of the struggle, Filippo Maria gave his natural daughter to the great *condottiere*, Francesco Sforza, as a bribe to hold his loyalty. After the death of the otherwise childless duke, Sforza pressed a claim to the duchy in his wife's name, but the citizens of Milan disappointed him by proclaiming a republic. The Milanese, however, were no more capable of ruling themselves than they had been two centuries earlier. The Golden Ambrosian Republic was torn by party strife and it had no support from the subject cities. Still at war with Venice, it was forced to hire Sforza, and when later it tried to get rid of him he entered the city by force and in 1450 proclaimed himself Duke of Milan. Four years later the new duke was able to make peace with his enemies on terms that left him in possession of the western half of Lombardy.

The government of Venice was as nearly unique as that of Milan was typical of the city-states of northern Italy. Alone among Italian states Venice never suffered from a successful revolution, and she was largely free from the common curse of party conflict. The stability and efficiency of her republican government were the envy and despair of every contemporary political theorist. But much as they envied Venice her constitution, no other state was able to imitate it successfully, for it was the

[1] Quoted in D. Muir, *A History of Milan under the Visconti* (London, 1924), p. 124.

product of a unique geographical situation and of the peculiar character of Venetian social and economic organization. Unlike her great commercial rivals, Genoa and Pisa, the island city of Venice had no rural *contado* and hence no landholding feudal nobility to absorb. From the first she had but one powerful social class, that of the merchants who traded abroad. In Venice the merchants may not have been kings, as Browning said, but the Venetian "nobles" who ruled the city were merchants first and last, and having no land in which to invest capital they remained actively engaged in commerce generation after generation. There was thus no conflict here between old *grandi* and newly rich capitalists, such as fatally weakened the patriciate of so many Italian cities. Nor was there in Venice a class of industrial workers large enough to threaten the position of the merchant oligarchy. Finally, thanks to her isolation from the mainland, Venice was able to remain aloof from Italian politics during her formative years, and so did not become involved in the Guelf-Ghibelline feud. For all these reasons, the Venetian patricians were able to present a united front to their opponents at home and abroad, to maintain unbroken control of the government of the republic, and to use that control to promote the economic interests of their class. Under their management, the republic acquired something of the character of a gigantic joint-stock company, of which they were the stockholders and directors. To their credit it might be added that, if they profited by governmental regulation of trade and by a foreign policy devoted exclusively to commercial interests, the Venetian patricians also devoted themselves with unsparing zeal to the service of the state.

The years around 1300 marked the culmination of a long process of political evolution in Venice and the crystallization of her constitution in the form it was to retain for centuries to come. During the thirteenth century the wealth of the Venetian merchants had been vastly increased by the introduction of capitalist techniques and by the expansion of their trade in both the East and the West. In the same period the merchant class had progressively strengthened its control of the government at the expense of the *popolo* on the one hand and the *doge* on the other. In 1297 the triumphant oligarchy closed the Great Council to all but members of the two hundred-odd families represented there in the past. Since the Great Council, which was composed of some 240 members, was the source of all political authority, this meant the practical disenfranchisement of the great majority of citizens and the creation of a monopoly of power in the hands of those families that had already achieved wealth and social status. It was the Great Council that elected the Senate, the chief legislative body of the republic, and also elected, directly or indirectly, the *collegio* or cabinet, the ducal councillors and the *doge*, who made up the executive branch. The *doge*, a president elected for life, was the titular head of the state, but his authority was severely restricted in practice by his six councillors, by the members of the executive cabinet, and after 1315 by an annually elected Council of Ten, the *Dieci*. This extraordinary tribunal, a kind of Committee of Public Safety, held its meetings in secret, was empowered to deal with sedition or conspiracy, and in moments of crisis could take the direction of affairs out of the hands of the regular executive officers. It could, and on one occasion did, bring about the execution of a *doge*. Though surrounded by all the pomp befitting the head of a great state, the *doge's* principal function from this time on was to act as the personal symbol of the republic's government. Real power was vested in the Great Council, the Senate and the executive committees. Having thus steered a middle course between democracy and despotism, the Venetian oligarchy, now a closed group, remained for centuries in undisputed control. And, since the merchant fleet of the republic was owned by the state, and since the allocation of space as well as the time and destination of its sailings were determined by the Great Council and the Senate, participation in commerce as well as in politics was practically monopolized by the oligarchical families.

The century and a half following the closing of the Great Council and the institution of the *Dieci* was a crucial period in Venetian history, during which the oligarchic republic devoted its energies with single-minded purpose to the creation of a commercial empire in the Levant and a territorial state in northern Italy. The struggle for monopoly of the Levantine trade was an old one. Originally a three-cornered conflict, it was somewhat simplified by the elimination of Pisa, which was disastrously defeated by Genoa in 1284. Weakened by internal strife and a prey to the avaricious designs of the Visconti and Florence, Pisa never recovered, so that at the opening of the fourteenth century Venice and Genoa were left to dispute the eastern trade between them and to fight for commercial monopolies in the Byzantine Empire and for permanent trading posts in the islands of the Eastern Mediterranean and on the Black Sea. Naval warfare between the two great commercial republics lasted off and on, with alternating victories, until the final defeat of Genoa in 1380. The struggle had exhausted both contestants, but Venice was able to recuperate fairly quickly, thanks to her internal solidarity and the continuity of her policies. For the next half century she dominated the trade of the Eastern Mediterranean and dotted it with her colonies; but that enviable position was won at the cost of being left to face in splendid isolation the rising threat of Turkish aggression. In Genoa, meanwhile, class and party conflict, which had long weakened the republic and had more than once in the past brought it under the rule of a foreign *signore*, broke out more violently than ever. After having deposed ten *doges* in half as many years, the people of Genoa surrendered their independence to France and accepted a governor sent by Charles VI. The Genoese continued to trade, but Genoa was never again a great commercial or political power.

After her triumph in the East, Venice turned her whole attention to the conquest of a territorial state in northern Italy. This was a new policy for Venice, begun only in the second quarter of the fourteenth century, and it was fraught with dangers which the Venetian government had not yet fully realized. Until that time it had been the unique good fortune of Venice that she had no land frontier to defend and that she could therefore stand aloof from the vicious tangle of Italian politics. So long as the neighboring mainland was divided among a host of petty city-states, Venice could afford to enjoy the advantages accruing from her isolation. The growth of large states in the fourteenth century, however, constituted a deadly peril to the island republic. Venice had to import her entire food supply, most of it from the mainland. Moreover, her commercial prosperity depended on her ability to import and export by land as well as by sea. It was, therefore, a matter of vital concern to Venice to keep the routes to the Alpine passes open. Any large and powerful state on the adjacent mainland would be in a position to cut off the greater part of her food supply and wreck her trade. Should such a state form an alliance with a maritime power strong enough to blockade Venice by sea, the ruin of the republic would be complete and absolute. These were the considerations that led Venice in 1329 to abandon her traditional policy of isolationism and to join with Florence, Parma and the Visconti in a war to dismember the dangerously large state that had been built up by the della Scala lords of Verona. After nine years of fighting, Venice acquired the rich district of Treviso to the north of her, as her share of Mastino della Scala's territory. This acquisition relieved her from the threat of blockade and starvation, but it also imposed upon her for the first time the necessity of defending a territorial state from avaricious neighbors. In the following years she was drawn into repeated wars with Hungary and Austria, which resented the Venetian expansion around the head of the Adriatic, as well as with her restless neighbor in Padua, Francesco Carrara, who joined with Genoa in 1378 in an attack on Venice by land and sea that came close to destroying the republic. Venice emerged from this war with her territory intact, but in the following years had to face a more serious danger from the expanding state of Giangaleazzo Visconti.

Fear that Giangaleazzo might succeed, as he almost did, in establishing a kingdom in northern Italy reinforced in the minds of her people the conviction that Venice must expand or perish. The weakness of the Visconti state after the death of the great duke gave Venice her opportunity. In 1404 the aggressive republic seized Vicenza, Verona and Bassano from the Milanese regent and at the same time wiped out the perpetually threatening Carrara *signoria* in Padua. Turning eastward, Venice then extended her territories further around the head of the Adriatic. A long war with the Emperor Sigismund ended in 1420 with the republic in possession of the whole province of Friuli from the sea to the Alps. Meanwhile, on her western borders the Visconti state was threatening aggression once more under the able rule of Filippo Maria, who was determined to win back that part of his heritage which had been seized by Venice after his father's death. War between the two great states of northern Italy lasted from 1425 till the Peace of Lodi in 1454. The war was immensely expensive, since in campaigns waged on land Venice was forced for the first time to depend on mercenary troops. It was characteristic of the businesslike governors of Venice, however, that they insisted on getting their money's worth and refused to put up with any nonsense from their *condottieri*. When the great Carmagnola showed signs of playing a double game the *Dieci* recalled him to Venice and executed him. In the end two factors in addition to the financial drain encouraged the republic to seek a permanent peace: the renewed Turkish threat implied in the capture of Constantinople in 1453 and a shift in the foreign policy of its old ally Florence, which now under the leadership of Cosimo de' Medici supported Sforza against the too-powerful commercial republic. Besides, Venice had now acquired all the territory she really needed, having thrust her frontier westward to the river Adda, which served as a definite boundary line between her and the Duchy of Milan.

Compared with the relatively consistent development of the Visconti despotism or the Venetian oligarchy, the evolution of Florence from commune to territorial state is a story so complex as almost to defy summary. Even the most sketchy account of its history must seem disproportionately lengthy; yet we cannot dispense with it, for the cultural as well as economic achievements of this irrepressibly vital city played such a large part in the history of Renaissance Italy that we must make some attempt to understand the tumultuous political life with which these achievements were so closely related. The story may be somewhat simplified, however, if we analyse at the beginning certain tendencies which developed toward the end of the thirteenth century and which left a permanent mark on the character of the republic.

In its formative years, the Florentine commune, like most inland towns, was dominated by a patrician class, whose members were generally referred to as magnates or *grandi* and justified their position by service as mounted knights in the communal army. This class was the result of a fusion of wealthy merchant families with the turbulent nobility drawn in from the surrounding *contado*, and it displayed an odd combination of the bourgeois merchant's political shrewdness with the noble's predilection for violence and suicidal family feuds. It was also divided by a more than ordinarily violent conflict between the Guelf and Ghibelline parties. Toward the end of the struggle between the papacy and the imperial House of Hohenstaufen, the Ghibellines seized control of the city. After the triumph of Charles of Anjou and the papal forces, however, the Guelfs returned to power in 1267 with the aid of French troops and proceeded to annihilate their opponents by driving them into exile, confiscating their houses and goods and so impoverishing them that they were never able to recover. To ensure their victory, the triumphant Guelfs organized in a closely knit political club, the *Parte Guelfa*, which for more than a century was to exert an unconstitutional and generally unholy influence on the Florentine government. The Guelf Party was as predominantly aristocratic as its Ghibelline predecessor, but it wisely left the door open to the rising families of the *popolo grasso*, who were at this time increasing in wealth and numbers. In the last decades of the thirteenth century Florence entered upon a period of very rapidly expanding prosperity, and realization of the fact that the city owed much of its new prosperity to its Guelf connections, together with the fact that its chief commercial rivals in Tuscany — Pisa and Siena — were incurably Ghibelline, served to make the entire citizenry of Florence solidly and permanently Guelf. As Guelfs, the merchant-bankers of Florence secured a practical monopoly of the lucrative business of collecting papal revenue and acting as bankers for the papacy. They also secured a privileged position in the Guelfic states of Naples and France.

A further by-product of this fortunate connection was also to prove of lasting importance. The collection of papal revenue brought the Florentine merchant companies into contact with England and English wool, with the result that a great weaving industry grew up in Florence beside the already established industry of the *Calimala* guild, which finished cloth imported from northern France and the Netherlands. The economic significance of this development of large capitalist industries has been discussed in the preceding chapter. Here we need note only its political implications. In the first place, an expanding capitalist economy, which was founded upon industry as well as commerce and banking, called forth from among the *popolo* a constantly renewed group of wealthy families determined to gain political power consonant with their wealth. In the second place, the fact that they were employers of a large number of workers gave to the merchant-industrialists an economic weapon with which to reinforce their political power, while at the same time it made it necessary for them to hold political power as a means of keeping their workers in a state of subjection. Finally, the cloth industries produced a large class of poverty-stricken proletarian workers, who enjoyed neither the rights of citizenship nor the protection of guild organization, and whose burning resentment of social injustice made them a perennial menace to the bourgeois government. Fear of the violence of the wool-workers was usually sufficient to make the small shopkeepers and artisans of the craft guilds throw in their lot with the merchant capitalists, thereby assuring the dominance of the merchant oligarchy.

Before the end of the thirteenth century, then, Florence had become what she was to remain while her independence lasted: a Guelfic city ruled, though none too securely, by a merchant class. The Florentine oligarchy, however, was not a closed hereditary caste like the Venetian. Its composition was constantly changing, a fact dramatically demonstrated by one further development in the last two decades of that century. This was the adoption of a new constitution through which the rising capitalists arrogated to themselves a dominant place in the government at the expense of the older magnates. The first step was the creation in 1283 of a new executive authority for the state in the form of a committee of "priors." This was followed ten years later by the adoption of a more definitive constitution, known as the Ordinances of Justice, which with some alterations remained in force as long as the republic lasted. The new constitution was an immensely complicated structure, a triumph of perverted ingenuity, which seemed consciously designed to invite control by some minority group which could keep its unwieldy councils moving and give consistent direction to its short-term officers. The older institutions of the *podestà* and the *capitano del popolo*, each with a large council which must ratify all decisions before they became law, were retained; and to these in course of time were added various other councils and committees, for the Florentines could never resist the temptation to tinker with the constitution of the Republic. The most notable and lasting feature of the Ordinances of Justice, however, was the creation of a new corporate *signoria* composed of six (later eight) priors and a *gonfaloniere* — or banner-bearer — of justice. These collectively formed the principal governing body of the state and were elected for a term of two months from the membership of the guilds. Although this provision seemed to guarantee representation to the middle class of artisans and shopkeepers, its democratic character was in practice nullified by the fact that the seven greater guilds, the *arti maggiori*, in which the

164

merchant-industrialists and bankers were enrolled, controlled the elections and monopolized the majority of the offices, the fourteen lesser craft guilds being left only enough representation to keep them loyal to the government. The proletarian workers were, of course, excluded entirely. What is more important is that the Ordinances of Justice also disenfranchised the majority of the *grandi*. The identification of active citizenship with membership in the guilds in itself excluded many of the older families, though not all of them, since many of the magnates were merchants and were enrolled in one of the merchant guilds, usually the *Calimala*. Moreover, a later modification of the law permitted magnates to enroll in a guild without practising a trade or profession. Whether they were guild members or not, however, the majority of the magnates were debarred from the priorate by a provision that rendered ineligible all families, any single member of which had acquired the honor of knighthood within the past twenty years. In all, some hundred and fifty families were thus officially stigmatized as *grandi*.

The Ordinances of Justice represented a victory for the rising group of rich *popolani*, but like many similar political victories in Florentine history it was in part illusory. The two wealthy classes, the *popolo grasso* and the *grandi*, were too frequently interrelated by business and family ties to be clearly distinguished. Moreover, the disenfranchised *grandi* could still exert a powerful influence through the Guelf Party, in which they were strongly represented. During the early years of the fourteenth century, indeed, the magnates gained for a time complete control of the government. A violent feud had sprung up within the Guelf party between the Whites, who were moderate constitutionalists and favored acceptance of the Ordinances of Justice, and the reactionary Blacks led by the intransigent old magnate Corso Donati. In 1302 the Blacks carried through an armed revolution with the aid of French troops sent by Pope Boniface VIII. A reign of terror followed in which hundreds of White Guelfs were condemned to death or exile, among them Dante and Petrarch's father. Though they did not dare repeal the Ordinances of Justice, the Black magnates were able for years thereafter to control the elections and dictate the policy of the priors. The ranks of the *grandi*, however, had been greatly thinned by the purge, first of the Ghibellines and then of the White Guelfs. They were doomed moreover by the action of economic forces. Those of the old families which lived on inherited income were gradually impoverished and sank in the social scale. Others, like the Cerchi and Bardi, which had achieved great wealth through banking and commerce, were ruined by the disastrous bankruptcies of the first half of the fourteenth century. By mid-century their power had waned to the point where it could safely be ignored.

Meanwhile, the turbulent waters of Florentine politics were further troubled by a series of crises precipitated by wars with her commercial rivals, Pisa, Siena and Lucca. These wars were fought, after the manner of the age, by hired *condottieri* and were generally unsuccessful. On three occasions military disasters forced the Florentine people to accept the rule of a foreign *signore* in the hope of gaining more effective leadership, but on each occasion chance or a well-timed rebellion freed the city from a permanent despotism. On such occasions the restoration of the republican government presented an opportunity for reform of the constitution. On the death of their Neapolitan *signore* Charles of Calabria in 1328, a new method of choosing the priors was instituted which promised to give fairer representation to the lesser guilds. A list of those eligible was drawn up by an extraordinarily complicated process and the names placed in purses, from which a sufficient number to fill the priorate were to be drawn by lot. Once more, however, what seemed like a decisive political victory proved to be an illusion, for, by some odd distortion of the laws of probability, the names drawn were almost always those of prominent members of the merchant guilds. A more successful democratic reform followed the violent expulsion of the third *signore*, the French adventurer Walter of Brienne, in 1343. Roused to arms, the members of the craft guilds forced the merchant oligarchs to accept a new list of those eligible for office, the majority of whom were "new men" from families whose members had not hitherto held high office in the government and many of whom were from the lesser guilds. For nearly forty years they continued to play an active if not preponderant role in government. But, as always in Florentine politics, their victory was not as decisive as it appeared to be. The merchant class, though weakened by the financial panics of the forties, was still strong and was soon reinforced by the rise of new families. Moreover, it was securely entrenched in the *Parte Guelfa*. When it could not control the elections, the merchant clique was able, through the machinery of the party, to prevent undesirable candidates from accepting office by threatening to denounce them as Ghibellines. During this democratic interlude, the merchants were thus able to prevent any action that would be injurious to their interests while they awaited an opportunity to take over the government once more. That opportunity was presented by the violent revolt of the wool-workers in 1378, known as the rising of the *Ciompi*. Though all the *Ciompi* secured was the right to organize in guilds, and some representation in the priorate, the craftsmen of the older guilds regarded them with grave suspicion and feared their violence. After three years of alarms and excursions, the government of the middle and lesser guilds was so divided that the merchant group was able to carry through a counter-revolution. The new proletarian guilds were abolished, and a predominant share in the priorate was restored to the *arti maggiori*.

For the next fifty years Florence was ruled once more by a merchant oligarchy through manipulation of the apparently democratic republican government. Although the old councils of the *podestà* and the *capitano* still met, effective authority was becoming concentrated in a more informal council of prominent citizens, called a *pratica*, which was summoned by the priors to give advice whenever an important decision in matters of policy had to be made. Here the leaders of the oligarchy could express their opinion, and while the opinion thus expressed had no legislative force, it was in fact a directive and was accepted as such by the priors. The ruling clique was, however, now smaller than before, being composed of a few wealthy families under the leadership of the Albizzi who were now the most powerful family in Florence. This concentration of power lent a continuity to the government's policy that justified itself by the successful defense of the state against the threat of domination by Giangaleazzo Visconti. This was the most serious crisis in the republic's long history, and it called forth a great outburst of popular patriotism. The oligarchy also achieved the long-desired conquest of Pisa together with the remainder of Tuscany, with the exception of Siena and Lucca. With these acquisitions, Florence rose to the status of a major territorial state, on a par with Venice and Milan. The exclusiveness of the Albizzi and their friends, who had begun to display the arrogance of an established patrician class, could, however, be maintained only if justified by consistent success. According to the familiar pattern, families more recently risen to wealth resented their monopoly of power, and they found a leader in the Albizzi's wealthiest opponent, the banker, Cosimo de' Medici. An unsuccessful war against Lucca precipitated the inevitable crisis. The Albizzi paralyzed the opposition for a time by exiling Cosimo, but their power was broken. A year later the exile was recalled by popular acclaim. A government composed of Medicean partisans exiled the Albizzi in their turn, and instituted the unofficial but none the less effective reign of Cosimo de' Medici. From that moment till his death thirty years later, the unostentatious banker was the real ruler of Florence.

The revolution which inaugurated the Medici régime in 1434, and introduced a period in which generations of the Medici family left their mark upon the social and cultural as well as the political life of the city, actually made no drastic change in the constitution or the formal government of the republic. A merchant oligarchy still held control, manipulated the elections, and furnished the necessary direction and continuity to governmental policy. It is true that Cosimo de' Medici exerted a more decisive influence, especially in the conduct of foreign affairs where a consistent policy was particularly important, than had any previous political leader; but he shared the fruits of power with the members of a fairly numerous party, and left to them the actual tenure of office. He was careful also to encourage the introduction of new blood into the party and so to prevent it from becoming a closed aristocratic clique like that of the Albizzi. Finally, Cosimo spared no pains to retain the popular support that had helped him to establish his leadership. He avoided as far as possible the external attributes of power, which might have offended the democratic sentiments of the *popolo*, and he preferred to exercise his unconstitutional authority indirectly, somewhat after the manner of a modern municipal boss. Though never free from underground opposition, his rule was generally popular, and that popularity, together with the economic pressure he could bring to bear through his vast financial connections and by imposing crushing income taxes on his opponents, enabled him to dispense with the brutal terrorism that was characteristic of most despotic governments. The canny banker who for three decades held in his hands the strings of Florentine government may not have been as altruistic as his admirers have claimed, but comparison of his régime with that of any Renaissance *signore* suggests that it was not without reason that the people of Florence bestowed upon Cosimo de Medici the honorary title of *Pater Patriae*.

Milan, Venice and Florence represent three quite distinct types of government. They were alike, however, in that each had begun as an urban commune and had developed by the middle of the fifteenth century into a strongly centralized territorial state. The fourth member of the Italian state system that was taking shape in the fifteenth century had a very different history. The Papal States, or States of the Church, had formed a territorial state of a more or less feudal sort in the Middle Ages. It withstood the encroaching power of the Hohenstaufen emperors in the thirteenth century, and by the end of that century, despite the internal disorders to which all medieval states were subject, the papal sovereignty was firmly established. For the next hundred and fifty years, however, the history of the Papal States is a melancholy story of disintegration and anarchy, followed toward the end by a partial reassertion of central government. This is not the place for a discussion of the papacy during the disastrous period of the Babylonian Captivity, the Great Schism and the Conciliar Movement, since as heads of the universal Church the popes operated on a larger stage than that of Italian politics. For the present it is enough to note that the absence of the Avignonese popes from Italy for more than seventy years (1305-77) paralyzed the government of their Italian state and enabled each of their subject cities to achieve practical independence. Left to work out their own political destinies with very little interference from their papal suzerain, the cities in the Papal States followed the common pattern of the fourteenth century and for the most part accepted the rule of a local despot. In mid-century the pope's authority was reasserted with some success by Cardinal Albornoz with the aid of mercenary troops, but even that soldierly statesman could not suppress the *signori*. On the contrary he legitimized their status by conferring upon them the title of vicar in return for the payment of tribute and their formal recognition of the papal sovereignty.

During a large part of this period the popes were involved in expensive wars and diplomatic negotiations to prevent the annexation of some of their lands by the Visconti, the kings of Naples or the expanding Venetian Republic. Even Guelfic Florence waged one serious war against the pope in the years just before the *Ciompi* rising. Thanks to the popes' success in defending the integrity of their territory, the petty *signori* within it were preserved from the fate that befell the lesser lords of Lombardy who were annihilated by the expansion of the great territorial states. Until well after the middle of the fifteenth century, the States of the Church remained a happy hunting ground for those ambitious and quarrelsome lords, half prince and half *condottiere*, whose names fill so many scandalous pages of Renaissance history. After the petty tyrants had ceased to exist in Lombardy or Tuscany, there was still a Malatesta lording it in Rimini, a Bentivoglio in Bologna, a Manfredi in Faenza, a Montefeltro in Urbino, and an Ordelaffi in Forlì, not to mention the practically sovereign house of Este in Ferrara and the *condottieri*, like Braccio da Montone, Piccinino and Francesco Sforza, who carved out for themselves evanescent states in Umbria or the Marches. Even in the city of Rome, where that strange visionary Cola da Rienzi recreated the ancient Roman Republic for a few months in 1347, the people were in a more or less perpetual state of rebellion, while both in the city and the surrounding countryside the Orsini, Colonna, Gaetani and other noble families fortified their castles, defied the pope and disturbed the peace. After the end of the Great Schism and the restoration of a purely Roman papacy, however, the popes were able to begin the task of recovering their temporal sovereignty, and by 1450 they were well on the way to establishing themselves firmly as Italian princes.

To the south of the Papal States lay the Kingdom of Naples, a state in every respect different from those of the more prosperous northern half of the peninsula. A feudal kingdom, poorly endowed by nature, without commerce or industry except in the capital, and hence without communes, plagued by the lawlessness of barons and the rapacity of ecclesiastical lords, this southern part of Italy added little or nothing to the cultural achievements of the Renaissance. Its history during this period is largely the history of its rulers, whose dynastic connections with France, Aragon and Hungary lent them an importance otherwise unwarranted, and whose restless ambition made them a perpetually disturbing factor in Italian politics. A French dynasty had been established in both Naples and Sicily in 1266, when the pope called in Charles of Anjou, the younger brother of St. Louis, to rid him of the viper brood of the Hohenstaufen. The people of Sicily, however, rebelled in 1282 and transferred their allegiance to Peter III of Aragon. Thereafter the two parts of the old Norman kingdom were separated; Sicily, under a Spanish dynasty, and Naples, ruled by the French Angevins who were also closely related to the kings of Hungary. The direct Angevin line ended with Giovanna I, who died childless in 1382 after nearly forty years of spectacular misgovernment. As her heir she named Louis I, Duke of Anjou and younger brother of Charles V of France, thus furnishing the second House of Anjou and ultimately the French monarchy with a claim to Naples which, though never successfully realized, was a cause of many ills to Italy for more than a century. Louis I of Anjou failed to make good his claim, partly because he was on the wrong side of the papal schism. Charles of Durazzo, a distant cousin of the late queen, won the support of the Roman pope, Urban VI, and made himself king. After two generations, however, this cadet branch of the first House of Anjou also ended with a childless queen, Giovanna II. On her death in 1435, she named as her heir René of Anjou, grandson of Louis I. A prior bequest, however, also gave a claim to Alfonso, called the Magnanimous, King of Aragon and Sicily, who succeeded in seizing the kingdom. Although Naples and Sicily were thus reunited only during his lifetime, the Kingdom of Naples remained under a branch of the House of Aragon until the French invasion of 1494.

The middle years of the fifteenth century mark the conclusion of a definite stage in the history of the Italian states and the opening of a new era of relative stability. The Peace of Lodi, signed by Milan, Venice and Florence in 1454, ended a period of almost perpetual warfare during which these three states had become the dominant powers of northern Italy and Tuscany. The Peace was followed by the formation of a defensive league, composed at first of the three powers which had signed the peace and then extended to include the papacy and the Kingdom of Naples as well as the lesser adherents of the five major states. The league was designed to keep peace among its members and to guarantee a mutual defence against any foreign power. Though it never functioned perfectly and, indeed, threatened to break down with every shift in the precarious balance of power between the five great states, it served to furnish a framework for Italian diplomacy and to maintain a fair degree of peace for the next forty years.

B. France: the Growth of Royal Government

In France, as in Italy, the transition from the medieval to the modern state passed through its first and most decisive phase in the century and a half from 1300 to 1450. But the social and economic structure of the two countries, as well as their past political history, were very different, and the states which emerged out of medieval particularism were therefore of a different sort. France was an extremely prosperous country in the twelfth and thirteenth centuries, but her economy, unlike that of Italy, was founded principally upon agriculture, and the landholding classes retained the dominant position they had won in the early feudal period. France had, it is true, a large number of vigorous towns and cities, but their prosperity was fostered by trade with the surrounding countryside rather than by foreign commerce or export industries. The French cities could not absorb the landholding nobility as did the Italian communes, nor could they assert a comparable independence in relation to the central government. The center of gravity of medieval France was in the country, not the city, and it was the *seigneurie* which furnished the matrix in which her most characteristic institutions were cast. France was, indeed, the most thoroughly feudalized country in Europe, as Italy was the least. Yet from this restricted feudal monarchy there emerged during the next two centuries a central government which, though still feudal, was strong enough to lay the foundations of a national state, a development that in Italy was still five hundred years away.

A great many factors contributed to the rise of the French monarchy from the low estate into which it had fallen in the days of the early Capetians. The unbroken succession of the royal title from father to son for 341 years assured the hereditary status of the Capetian dynasty, while the long reigns of such forceful characters as Louis VI (1108–37), Philip Augustus (1180–1223) and the saintly Louis IX (1226–70) greatly aided the growth of royal authority. Once they had demonstrated sufficient strength to merit it, the kings could count on the support of the clergy and the bourgeoisie, who turned to them for protection from the lawless violence of the feudal nobles. They enjoyed, moreover, the imponderable prestige that clung to the royal title and the religious sanction conferred upon them by the act of consecration. The saying of St. Louis, "there is only one king in France," was not a meaningless phrase.

Nevertheless, it was mainly by exploiting their unique position at the apex of the feudal pyramid and by the exercise of recognized feudal rights and powers that the kings of the twelfth and thirteenth centuries enlarged their domain until it included more than two-thirds of the kingdom, added thereby to their military and financial resources, and created administrative and judicial institutions that needed only further development to serve as the basis of an extra-feudal government. Even St. Louis, who acted in the conviction that he was God's instrument for the enforcement of justice throughout his kingdom, was, however, still a purely feudal king, with a meticulous regard for the customary rights of his vassals, and the means he employed were those inherent in the feudal system.

At the same time, the growth of royal power within the feudal system would have been impossible had not the revival of commerce introduced into feudal society an economic element essentially alien to it: the money economy that enabled even a feudal king to mobilize wealth with which to strengthen the sinews of government and to recover some of the powers that the monarchy had been forced to surrender during the Early Middle Ages. The extent to which the king could draw upon the financial resources of the kingdom was, however, limited by the customary rights, vested interests and ways of thinking of a society shaped by the feudal system — a system originally designed to function in a relatively moneyless economy. The feudal king was expected to meet the expenses of his court, to pay administrative and judicial agents and to supplement the armed force furnished by the uncertain service of his vassals, in short, to defray all the costs of government largely from the revenues from his own lands, with the addition only of the judicial fines imposed in the royal courts, such taxes as could be levied upon the burghers in royal towns, and the occasional reliefs and aids owed by his vassals-in-chief. In an era of expanding economy even these limited sources furnished the twelfth- and thirteenth-century kings with constantly growing revenues, and hence enabled them to assert a growing practical power. But the exercise of increased authority involved greater expenditures for military force and for the maintenance of a growing machinery of government, which in turn necessitated a further increase in revenue. The result was a kind of vicious spiral that must eventually press against the ceiling imposed by the feudal system. When that occurred, as it did about the end of the thirteenth century, the kings were confronted by a fiscal dilemma. They and the ministers who basked in their reflected glory must either give up hope of any further increase in power, which they would be very loath to do, or they must break through the restriction imposed by the customary rights of the nobility and assert an extra-feudal sovereignty. With kings of the caliber of Philip the Fair and Charles V there could be little doubt as to which alternative they would choose.

In still other ways, the introduction and continued expansion of money economy served to weaken the forces of feudalism while strengthening the central government. Only the tough tensile strength of long-established custom had enabled the feudal system to absorb the alien economic factor for two centuries without losing its essential character. By the end of the thirteenth century the saturation point had been reached. So long as wealth consisted largely of land and the services of men, the feudal lord was in a very strong position. He might not be rich, but he could live off the produce of his land and command the hereditary obedience of both noble vassals and servile peasants. He was therefore independent. His thirteenth-century descendant enjoyed a much larger income, for this was a prosperous time and both produce and service could now be turned into cash; but he had also disproportionately larger expenses. He was increasingly dependent on merchants and city markets for the goods needed to maintain a raised standard of living. Commutation of services had already begun to weaken his control over his dependents. Moreover, his little world was no longer so isolated, since commerce had opened up roads and accelerated communication. All the conditions that had made possible the lord's sovereignty in his own lands were changing. In the fourteenth century, depopulation and a long agricultural depression further impoverished the landholding classes and wrought changes in the structure of agrarian society that permanently ruined all but the last vestiges of the hereditary bond between him and his tenants.

The monarchy, on the other hand, profited by a process which served both to weaken the nobility and to turn wealth into a form that could be mobilized in the service of royal government. In proportion as money replaced hereditary obligations as the essential nexus in human relations, money became the source of power. Even in the thirteenth century the kings commanded a revenue that seemed large in feudal society, and when in the following centuries they added to it by regular taxation their income, though still inadequate to their needs, was greater by far than that of any of their vassals. In the long struggle between the monarchy and the nobility — that is, between central government and the centrifugal forces of feudalism — the former commanded an increasingly potent weapon, and enjoyed moreover the support of the urban classes by whom that weapon had been forged. And that the struggle should continue was a foregone conclusion, for both king and nobles loved power. They lived for power as the miser lives for wealth.

The consolidation of royal power was a long process, begun by the feudal kings in the twelfth and thirteenth centuries and not fully completed till the age of Louis XIV, but in that long evolution the reign of Philip IV, called "the Fair" (1285–1314), marks a peculiarly decisive stage: the beginning of the transition from feudal suzerainty to national monarchy. It was as the ruler of a national state that Philip became involved in an epoch-making conflict with Pope Boniface VIII, the far-reaching results of which will be discussed later.[2] And it was his determination to assert royal authority throughout the kingdom that led him into war with Edward I, who, as Duke of Guienne, held a fief in the rich wine-growing country of southwestern France, and also with the Count of Flanders, whose territory, dotted with great commercial and industrial cities, formed almost an independent state, though it was by ancient right a fief of France. To a king who thought in terms of national monarchy these were not merely over-powerful vassals. The one was a foreign power, the other an independent prince, both holding valuable lands that belonged to France and its king. A strong foreign policy could not, however, be carried out without extending the scope of royal government within the kingdom. War with two of the richest princes in Europe was expensive, and forced the king to take the unprecedented step of levying general, non-feudal taxes on all classes. This in turn involved the king's ministers in unprecedented negotiations with local assemblies of his subjects, burghers as well as nobles and officers of the Church, thereby establishing a direct contact between central government and the people for which the feudal system made no provision. The need to gain popular support for national policies also led Philip on more than one occasion to summon general assemblies of the three Estates of the realm, thus laying the foundation for what would become the Estates General. Finally, in ways that are difficult to trace but in total effect clearly discernible, the king's ministers in this reign strengthened and tightened up all the sprawling and amorphous machinery of royal government and infused into it a new spirit.

Until about the middle of the thirteenth century, the central government of France was still composed of the king and a vaguely constituted court, the *Curia Regis*, made up of the domestic officers of the king's household and a fluctuating group of his lay and ecclesiastical vassals, to whom the king delegated administrative and judicial functions at will. It was entirely inadequate for a royal government that had begun to assume wide responsibilities. As the business to be handled by the royal court increased in volume, it became necessary to split the *Curia Regis* into more permanently organized departments with specialized functions.

2 See below, pp. 217–236.

After the reign of St. Louis, the domestic functions of the household, the *Hôtel du Roi*, were gradually separated from the governmental functions of the *Curia Regis*, while the latter were entrusted to groups of more or less permanent ministers. When a very important decision had to be made, the king might summon a fairly numerous group of his more important vassals for consultation, but the day-to-day business of government was handled by the king and a small council of trusted advisors, the *Conseil du Roi*. This was the executive branch of the government, which dealt with matters of general policy, foreign affairs, and the endless details of internal politics in a state that was still partly feudal, and in which much business had still to be carried out through personal relations with the king's vassals. By its very nature, the *Conseil* was attached to the king's person and followed him in all his peregrinations. Its membership, though fairly constant, was dependent on the king's favor and so subject to change at the king's will. Those members of the *Curia*, on the other hand, who were experts in the two most specialized functions of government — justice and finance — needed a more stable organization and a permanent location for their offices and records. By the end of the thirteenth century they had ceased to follow the court and were permanently settled in Paris. The judicial branch of the royal court thus evolved into the *Parlement* of Paris, definitively organized in 1320, with a numerous staff and definite forms of procedure. It functioned primarily as a supreme court of appeal, but it also acted as the custodian of royal law and could exercise considerable influence on royal legislation. With the passing centuries it acquired an *esprit de corps* and a sense of its own dignity with which even kings did not tamper lightly. In much the same way the members of the *Curia* who had experience in handling governmental income and expenditure formed an increasingly stable committee, which by 1304 had evolved into the *Chambre des Comptes*, permanently located in Paris.

The evolution of these specialized institutions is of crucial importance, not only because it made the royal government more efficient, but also because the great vassals and prelates, who were the normal counsellors of medieval kings, were largely replaced by a staff of career administrators and jurists. If the reign of Philip the Fair marks a turning point in the history of the French monarchy, it is chiefly because of the character and the activity of his ministers, Pierre Flotte, Guillaume de Nogaret, Enguerrand de Marigny and others less well known. Men of relatively humble birth, trained in Roman Law and the business of government, utterly devoted to the monarchy, these were the men who made and carried out royal policy. Compared with them, Philip himself is a shadowy and ambiguous figure, and French historians have never been able to determine the extent to which he was personally responsible for the sensational events of his reign. Few of his successors were so ably or so exclusively served by ministers of this type, but none dispensed with their services, and they remained the most effective champions of the monarchy against both feudal particularism and the papal claims to universal sovereignty. Guillaume de Nogaret, himself one of them, has left us a classic description of these "king's men" who permeated every department of government. "They are not nobles, but they are *chevaliers du roi:* the king has taken them for his men: from that their honor; from that their dignity. . . . They are in infinite number in the kingdom."[3] Owing everything to the monarchy, they welcomed the absolutist tendencies they found in Roman Law and resented the feudal rights and privileges that infringed on royal sovereignty. They were, in short, more royalist than the king, and they inspired the royal government with a spirit that was not only extra-feudal but anti-feudal, an attitude that was reflected on the lower levels of local government by the host of royal officials who carried the king's authority into the feudal *seigneuries* and the self-governing communes.

For all practical purposes, the king's authority in local affairs was limited to the royal domain, but it expanded as the domain expanded until by the end of the fifteenth century it included almost the whole kingdom. The principal agents of local government were the *prévôts*, who were at once judges in the royal courts, fiscal agents of the king, and his representatives in the perpetual conflict between royal and seigneurial jurisdiction. They were assisted by a throng of minor officials: clerks, collectors of customs, foresters, police officers and the like. Contemporary evidence suggests that the *prévôts* and other local officials were of rather poor quality, unamiable characters, much given to avarice and petty tyranny. This is not surprising since most of them had leased or purchased their offices and regarded them as an investment to be operated at a profit. They were nevertheless indefatigable champions of royal authority, since every extension of the king's jurisdiction magnified their own office and its profits. They were the termites who nibbled away the foundations of the feudal system and wormed their way into the administration of the communes. The ultimate decay of feudal and communal rights and immunities was, in fact, less the result of actual changes in the constitution of the state than of the ceaseless war of attrition carried on by the "infinite number" of royal officials against whom the populace complained loudly but in vain. But, though they aided the growth of royal government by destroying its local opponents, they did less to make government strong or efficient, for, having a vested interest in their

[3] Quoted in G. Dupont-Ferrier, *La formation de l'état français* (Paris, 1929), p. 94.

offices, they were largely beyond royal control. Such control as there was, the central government exercised through officers of a higher rank, called *baillis* in the north and *sénéchaux* in the south. These were men of superior caliber, appointed by the king's council and directly responsible to it. Each acted as the king's representative with full royal powers in a definitely delimited area of the domain. The division of the domain into *bailliages* and *sénéchaussées* at the end of the thirteenth century was a major step in the centralization of government, since these were purely administrative units which cut across the frontiers of the ancient fiefs and furnished the framework of an administrative hierarchy. It was, however, only partially successful. The growth of the domain by successive annexations, together with the piecemeal infringement upon seigneurial rights, militated against uniformity in local government, while the sale or leasing of offices led to an excessive proliferation of petty offices with ill-defined powers and overlapping jurisdictions. Until the Revolution swept away the Old Régime, France continued to suffer from the fact that as the medieval institutions of local government decayed they were not replaced by a uniform and efficient bureaucracy.

Both the expansion of royal authority and the resulting confusion were especially evident in the administration of justice. Until the thirteenth century, justice had been the undisputed prerogative of local authorities: lords, communes and Church courts. In that century, however, the royal government, inspired in part by the sensitive conscience of St. Louis, began to assert a competing jurisdiction, which was thereafter steadily expanded by the officers of less saintly kings. The royal courts reserved to themselves an increasingly long list of "royal cases," asserted the right to interfere when feudal courts were dilatory, and struck a fatal blow to feudal sovereignty by introducing the novel principle that all justice belongs in last resort to the king, from which it followed that anyone might appeal from the judgment of his lord to the king's courts. Appeals were encouraged by the fact that the royal courts were on the whole more just. Their procedure was based on investigation and recorded evidence rather than on the ordeal and other ancient customs, and the mechanism of appeal was facilitated by the existing administrative system. Each *prévôt* held a court which heard appeals from seigneurial jurisdiction, and from it further appeals might be carried to the court of the *bailliage* or *sénéchaussée*, and from there to the *Parlement* of Paris. Many lords retained rights of high and low justice for centuries longer, but their effective jurisdiction, together with the fees and fines which had made the seigneurial courts an important source of noble revenue, dwindled steadily.

The recovery by the royal government of a large part of the administration of justice was facilitated by the fact that it was not an expensive process. Justice not only paid for itself, but was a source of revenue. The king's acquisition of control over the armed force of the kingdom, which involved the transformation of the feudal levy into a national army, was a very different matter. For this purpose the king's customary feudal income was totally inadequate, and it could be supplemented only by levying general taxes. This, however, involved a radical departure from feudal precedent. It represented the recovery by the king of still another and vitally important function of government, the right to tax all his subjects whether they held directly from him or not, while from the point of view of the clergy, the nobles and the burghers of the self-governing communes, it represented a fatal breach in the encircling wall of customary immunities and sovereign powers that had protected them in varying degree from the intrusion of royal government. More than anything else, it was the persistent imposition of general taxes caused by the wars with England and Flanders in the years after 1294 that makes the reign of Philip the Fair a landmark in the growth of the French national state.

Such an innovation inevitably aroused much opposition. For many years, even after they had become a normal annual occurrence, general subsidies could be demanded only under the fiction that they were extraordinary aids for the defense of the realm. The royal government found legal sanction for its demands in the theory, vaguely formulated in the thirteenth century but now first put to the test, that all inhabitants of the kingdom were bound to aid the king when the realm was in danger. The various non-feudal taxes levied by Philip the Fair and his successors, mostly in the form of property, income or hearth taxes, were thus accepted as commutation of military service. They were generally assessed upon all laymen who had sufficient property to make taxation worth while, with the exception of the nobles who did military service in person. Even the clergy were taxed if they held private property, and in addition they were repeatedly forced to pay a *décime*, a tenth of their official income, for the defense of the realm. It is difficult, however, to make any valid generalization regarding royal taxes in the fourteenth century or the first half of the fifteenth, because the kings' ministers in this experimental period dreamed up new forms of taxation at frequent intervals, and also because taxes that were in theory general were seldom uniformly applied. Before collecting each successive subsidy, the kings' agents negotiated with local groups representing the clergy, nobles and burghers respectively in each administrative area, and made the best bargains they could, granting concessions where necessary, offering lords of high justice a portion of the tax collected on their lands, accepting lump sums from cities, or altering an income tax to a tax on hearths if it seemed advisable.

It is a fact of major significance for the constitutional development of France that the first consent to royal taxation came from regional assemblies, and that even after more general meetings of the Estates of the realm had granted a general subsidy, the royal government continued to negotiate in detail with assemblies of purely local scope. It was a very awkward system, involving delays that might cause serious embarrassment to a government in immediate need of money. It would have been greatly to the advantage of the royal government if it could have secured from a general assembly like the English Parliament regular and effective consent to taxes uniformly applicable to the whole kingdom. But for this France was not yet sufficiently united. Regional differences, feudal and communal particularism and class interests were too strong, while the monarchy was still too weak to weld the whole amorphous mass of France into a coherent state. At the same time, the custom of negotiating with regional groups prevented the growth of any effective check upon royal government. The concessions made to local assemblies were detailed concessions. They represented neither uniform demands nor general principles. No regional group could hope to exercise an effective influence on the policies of the national government. And the fact that members of all three Estates were accustomed to haggling with royal agents over the details of taxation in every province, *bailliage, sénéchaussée,* diocese, fief and town, goes far to explain why the Estates General permitted the control of taxation to slip out of its hands and so doomed itself to extinction. The unchecked absolutism achieved by the French monarchy at the end of the fifteenth century was thus the paradoxical result of its weakness at the beginning of the fourteenth century, as well as of the fundamental disunity of feudal France, which frustrated the attempts of the royal government to create a representative national assembly.

In the beginning at least, the Estates General, like the other similar assemblies created in nearly every Western European state at the beginning of the fourteenth century, was summoned on the king's initiative and its sole purpose was to extend royal power. Feudal kings had always summoned a Great Council of their vassals-in-chief for consultation when important decisions had to be made. It was natural, then, that kings who were beginning to exercise an extra-feudal authority should wish to summon a more widely representative body, including representatives of the townspeople with whom the king had no feudal relation. The Estates General was in essence an extra-feudal extension of the Great Council, and was composed of representatives of the three Estates of the realm, the clergy, the nobles and the bourgeoisie respectively. The first two occasions on which a king summoned representatives of the three Estates illustrate the use that might be made of such an assembly. In 1302, Philip the Fair called the Estates together for the first time to secure an expression of national support in his conflict with Boniface VIII, and in 1308 he summoned them again to present his prosecution of the Templars in the best possible light and to get from them some badly-needed moral support. Later meetings of the Estates were called at irregular intervals in moments of crisis. And since a royal crisis usually involved finance, they were commonly asked to grant a blanket consent to a royal tax, the details of which would be worked out by the government in consultation with local assemblies.

With few exceptions after the time of Philip the Fair, the meetings of the Estates General did not actually represent the whole kingdom. Usually the Estates of Languedoc and those of northern France met separately, and some meetings included still smaller areas. The Estates thus failed to serve the monarchy, as they might have done, by unifying France and giving the royal government national support. On the other hand, when in the middle decades of the fourteenth century the Estates attempted to establish an effective control of taxation and use that power to impose restraints on the monarchy, they lacked the unity necessary to maintain a consistent policy. In the disastrous years after Poitiers, when King John was a prisoner in England, the Estates of the north did succeed in carrying through something like a constitutional revolution under the leadership of the Parisian burgher, Étienne Marcel. It was a brief victory. In the next reign, Charles V (1364–80) not only recovered the powers which the monarchy had lost, but took steps to nip in the bud the growing theory that the king must ask the Estates for consent to each annual subsidy. He levied hearth and sales taxes for years at a time without calling the Estates to renew them. Thereafter the Estates General was convened less and less frequently, such consent to taxation as was necessary being obtained from local assemblies or provincial Estates. Toward the end of the Hundred Years' War, when the need for regular revenue to pay a national army had become painfully obvious and when the royal government had been strengthened by the novel prestige of victory, the Estates permitted the king to assume the permanent right to levy a direct tax, the *taille*, on all inhabitants of the kingdom except the nobles and clergy. The absolute monarchy now had no further need of the Estates General, and after 1440 it dwindled quietly into obsolescence, though provincial Estates long remained active in local affairs. As a national institution it had been doomed from the start by the preponderance of regional interests, and by the fact that it was composed of three separate parts, each voting separately and each representing an exclusive class interest. The kings used it to gain national support when it suited their purpose, but they rejected it when it threatened to limit their power. They had no inclination to exchange feudal restrictions for constitutional limitations. On the other hand, the nobles preferred to fight a losing battle to retain their individual prerogatives rather than to unite among themselves or with the other classes in an attempt to control the royal government. With the decline of feudalism, the monarchy therefore was left standing alone, the sole effective power in the state.

C. The Hundred Years' War and the Triumph of Monarchy in France

To a large extent, the growth of royal power in France was the result of political and economic forces inherent in the general character of the age and the nation, but it was also conditioned at every step by war or the threat of war. From the preliminary skirmishes between Philip the Fair and Edward I to the final expulsion of the English more than a century and a half later, war was the primary concern of the French government. It was the financial strain imposed by war that forced the monarchy to raise extra-feudal revenues and to evolve a regular fiscal system. And it was the desperate need for national defense that forced the French kings, somewhat belatedly, to transform the feudal levy into a royal army, thereby strengthening their effective power while at the same time robbing the nobles of the monopoly of military force that was the essential bulwark of feudalism. Disastrous though it was to France, the Hundred Years' War undoubtedly hastened the transition from the feudal to the monarchical state.

The war itself was the product of a feudal situation that had become an anachronism. The English king's status as vassal of the King of France for his Duchy of Guienne had caused friction even in the feudal era. It was an anomalous relation and by the end of the thirteenth century it had become intolerable to monarchs who were beginning to think in terms of national sovereignty. The kings of France would never be content until they had brought the remaining great fiefs into the royal domain, and of these the two richest were Guienne and Flanders. The English kings, on the other hand, resented the necessity of doing homage to their cousins of France, and in addition they had a powerful fiscal motive for retaining control of Guienne and for encouraging the independence of Flanders. A very large part of the English revenue in the fourteenth century came from duties on the wine trade with Bordeaux, which the English kings controlled at both ends, and from the more important export duties on wool shipped to Flanders, the profits from which depended on friendly relations with the Flemish cities. Economic interests, indeed, bound Flanders more closely to England than to France, and from the time of Edward I the English monarchs could generally count on an open or tacit alliance with the counts of Flanders or, when the count was reduced to subjection to the French monarchy, with the rebellious Flemish cities. For their part, the French kings cast covetous eyes on the only two areas in France that had a concentrated and readily taxable import-export trade. Only the preoccupation of Edward I with Wales and Scotland, and the bitter resistance of the Flemish cities to the aggressions of Philip the Fair, prevented the war begun in 1294 from becoming a decisive conflict. Peace was concluded in 1303. It continued through the troubled reign of Edward II, who married a daughter of Philip the Fair in 1308, and the difficult early years of Edward III, while Philip's three sons, the last Capetians of the direct line, followed one another in rapid succession on the French throne. It was, however, no more than a truce; and meanwhile the death of the last Capetian added one more disturbing factor to a situation that must sooner or later lead to war. As the grandson of Philip the Fair, Edward III inherited a claim to the French crown, though he was in no position to press his claim at the time and the succession passed peacefully to Philip's nephew, Philip VI of the House of Valois (1328–50). Of itself the dynastic claim was not a vital issue, but it provided Edward with a legal pretext to justify a war whenever he felt strong enough to reopen the conflict. By 1337 that time had arrived.

The Hundred Years' War can be divided conveniently into three major periods: one of fairly continuous fighting, though with frequent truces, from 1337 to 1380; a second of relative inactivity from 1380 to 1415; and a final period of English victory and ultimate defeat from 1415 to 1453.

The early years of the war demonstrated the danger to the French monarchy inherent in the independence of the great fiefs still outside the domain, for the English secured active allies in the Flemish cities and in the Duchy of Brittany, where a disputed succession had led to civil war. These same years also exposed the financial and military weakness of the French government, and demonstrated the obsolescence of feudal methods of warfare. Despite the size and wealth of their kingdom, neither Philip VI nor his successor, John II (1350–64), was able to mobilize enough military force to prevent English armies from ravaging western France almost at will. Lack of a sound strategic plan, as well as the practical lack of the siege machinery needed to take cities or the garrisons to hold them, prevented Edward from making any substantial territorial gains, except for the strategically important city of Calais, taken after a year's siege in 1347. His strategy, such as it was, seems to have been directed toward exploiting his nuisance value to the point where the French king would be willing to grant him full sovereignty over Guienne. The war thus degenerated into a series of aimless plundering raids, which achieved nothing but the destruction of the rich countryside of France, and which the French seemed unable to check. On the two occasions when the French kings were able to mobilize a large enough army and hold it together long enough to meet the English in a major pitched battle, at Crécy in 1346 and again at Poitiers in 1356, they were disastrously defeated. In both instances the French nobles, who bore the brunt of the fighting, suffered appalling losses, and at Poitiers King John himself was taken prisoner. With the king in his hands, Edward was at last able to reap the fruits of his strategy. France had suffered terribly from years of destructive war. A desperate peasant revolt, the Jacquerie, and revolutionary activity in the Estates General added to the troubles of the Dauphin Charles, who had been left to govern France without money and without an army. By 1360 he was ready to make peace on whatever terms he could get. According to the Treaty of Brétigny, arranged in that year, Charles agreed to pay a ransom of three million *écus d'or* for the captive King John, while Edward III traded his futile claim to the throne of France for possession in full sovereignty of a greatly enlarged territory in southwestern France from the Loire to the Pyrenees, together with Calais and a couple of other bridgeheads on the northern coast.

The English victories in this period of the war represented such a reversal of the apparent odds that they seemed incomprehensible to contemporaries. The solution of the problem is, nevertheless, fairly clear. The English army was a coherent force, organized, paid and equipped by the king. It could be held together for long periods, and could be trained and subjected to sufficient discipline to make it manageable on the field of battle. Such an army was expensive, and its maintenance drove Edward to some very shady financial expedients; but he was able to cut costs drastically by employing a large proportion of foot-soldiers, whose pay was much smaller than that of the mounted knights and men-at-arms. Such extensive reliance on infantry, however, might have been false economy had not the English foot-soldiers been armed with the most effective missile weapon yet seen in Europe: the deadly longbow, the use of which they had learned in the time of Edward I from their troublesome Welsh neighbors. This weapon was greatly superior to the crossbow used by continental archers, both in range and in rapidity of fire. It gave to the infantry for the first time since the birth of feudalism a place in battle equal to that of the heavily armored cavalry. The secret of English war finance, as well as of English victories, was, in fact, the unprecedented use of a balanced army of infantry and cavalry.

The French army, on the other hand, was still a feudal levy in form and spirit, even though the growing cost of armor in this period, when heavy plate was taking the place of mail, made it necessary to pay knights for the service they owed as vassals. The infantry, summoned for the occasion from the communal militia of town and village, was generally of poor quality. The best infantry in the French armies were the mercenary crossbowmen, many of them Genoese, but even these were seldom used effectively by noble commanders who shared the prejudice of their class against common-born foot-soldiers. Instead they placed their faith in the heavily armored knights and men-at-arms, who made up the bulk of the army and did most of the actual fighting. Such an army, however, was too expensive to be kept constantly under arms. As a rule, the king did not begin to mobilize an army until the campaign had started, and then the nobles with their knightly followers came in slowly and could not be held together for long. Serving for short terms, the French knights could neither be rationally organized nor disciplined, and the effect of their reckless courage was vitiated by the regional jealousies and feudal spirit of insubordination that made it impossible to control them on the field of battle. Even when present in overwhelming force, they did everything human ingenuity could devise to snatch defeat from the jaws of victory.

At both Crécy and Poitiers, the French army overtook a much smaller English force which was retreating after a plundering raid. On both occasions the English commander chose a defensible site, dismounted his relatively small force of men-at-arms to form a stable line, and trusted to his archers to break the force of an enemy charge before it reached the line. And on both occasions the French obligingly cooperated with the English tactics by making a direct frontal attack. At Crécy, the French vanguard came unexpectedly upon the English position while the rest of the army was still strung out along the route behind them. Without waiting for the main body of the army to come up, and against the king's express orders, they charged immediately and were mowed down by the English bowmen. As each successive wave of French knights arrived on the field they repeated the performance, charging with lunatic *élan* through the shattered wrecks of their own army. Those that succeeded in reaching the English line were dispatched by the men-at-arms. It was a shambles rather than a battle. At Poitiers ten years later the French king had time to plan his tactics, but the result was not very different. Arguing that the English had won at Crécy because they had dismounted their heavy cavalry, and failing to understand that the secret of the English victory was the combined use of men-at-arms with archers in a defensive position, King John dismounted most of his heavily armored horsemen and sent them lurching along on foot in successive waves against the English line. A picked body of knights, who were supposed to ride in ahead and break up the formation of the English archers, refused to wait for the dismounted force to arrive on the field and so wasted a gallant and costly charge. It was a better fought battle than Crécy, but the English line, protected by a thick thorn-hedge, held throughout the day, and as the last French charge rolled slowly up the slope toward it, the Black Prince sent a small detachment of cavalry under the Captal de Buch around the French line to attack it from the rear. This simple tactical device sealed the fate of what was left of the French army and its chivalrous king, who refused to flee even after the battle was obviously lost.

The Treaty of Brétigny, following on the capture of King John, marked the high point of English success in this period of the war, a success greater than the relative strength of the two countries warranted. With nearly a third of France nominally in his possession, Edward III was in fact dangerously over-extended. Thanks to the tactical superiority of the English army, he could send to the continent forces large enough to raid the French countryside, but he could not afford an army large enough to occupy and hold an extensive area in which the population was hostile. This was the weak point in the English strategy, and Charles V (1364–80) took full advantage of it. The first step was to organize a royal army more reliable than the feudal levy or than the mercenary companies, which both the French and English had used as auxiliary forces and which pillaged the country on their own initiative when not employed. Having secured a more regular income from continuous taxes, Charles the Wise enrolled the nobles of France in companies under royal captains and guaranteed them regular pay. The system was not entirely satisfactory and was largely abandoned during the next reign, but it enabled Charles to keep a force permanently in the field. Instead of leading the army in person, as his father had done with disastrous results, Charles gave the command to the Constable Bertrand du Guesclin, a hardened old campaigner who had risen to fame by his own achievements. Du Guesclin knew from experience the effectiveness of the English tactics and so refused to meet the opposing army in open battle. He resorted instead to guerrilla tactics; harried the enemy's line of march when they renewed their plundering raids; cut off isolated garrisons; retook cities with the aid of the disaffected populace; and so gradually reduced the area under English occupation. When both Charles and his constable died in 1380, the English had lost all but Calais and a narrow strip of coast line from Bayonne to Bordeaux.

Internal troubles in both France and England after the death of Charles V, following that of Edward III three years earlier, brought a lull in the war for a generation. The reign of the unfortunate king, Charles VI (1380–1422), was marked by misgovernment and factional strife, in the midst of which the financial and military gains of the preceding reign were largely lost. During his minority, and again after 1392 when recurrent fits of insanity rendered Charles incapable of governing, the princes of the blood fought among themselves to seize control of the government and to use its resources to further their own ambitions. Most successful of these was the king's uncle, Philip the Bold, who had been given the Duchy of Burgundy as an appanage by John II in 1364 and by marriage had added to it the Free County of Burgundy in the Holy Roman Empire, the County of Flanders, and other fiefs in northern France. During the king's fits of madness, the powerful duke used the financial and military resources of France to establish his position in the Netherlands, and to lay the foundation for the dynastic alliances that eventually brought all the rich provinces of the Low Countries into the possession of his descendants. This misuse of the government naturally aroused the resentment of the king's other uncles and of his brother, Louis, Duke of Orléans, who felt that they could misuse it to good advantage themselves. Since Louis could exert considerable influence with the king during his occasional lapses into sanity, the struggle for power between the dukes of Burgundy and Orléans was not too uneven and became increasingly bitter. It was further envenomed by personal hatred when Philip died and was succeeded by his son John the Fearless (1404–19), a hatred which culminated in the assassination of Louis of Orléans in 1407. The result of this rash act was to divide France at a time when unity was desperately needed. John the Fearless, who was beginning to act rather as the head of an independent dynasty than as a prince of France, gathered his forces in the north, while in the south the Count of Armagnac, whose daughter was married to the new Duke of Orléans, formed a party to avenge the murder. By 1411 open civil war between the Burgundian and Armagnac factions was disrupting France and reviving the lawless spirit of feudalism, as every impoverished noble seized the opportunity to fish in the troubled waters.

The civil war, following on years of misgovernment and corruption, left France a tempting prey to the young English king, Henry V (1413–22), who proclaimed himself King of France and prepared to renew the war. As Count of Flanders, John the Fearless had long followed the traditional Flemish policy of friendly relations with England, and now welcomed the aid of the invader against the Armagnac party, which had seized the mad king and gained control of the government. The French army which rallied to meet the English at Agincourt in 1415 was therefore largely an Armagnac force with little support from the Burgundian faction. It was also largely a feudal army, since the military and fiscal reforms of Charles V had been allowed to lapse. The Armagnac nobles were, in any case, feudal anachronisms who had forgotten the lessons of Crécy and Poitiers. Once more facing a smaller English army composed largely of archers, they repeated the tactics of Poitiers, stationed their own crossbowmen in the rear where they were useless, and dismounted the men-at-arms who made up the main body of the army for a massed frontal attack. But at Agincourt the mud was ankle deep and armor had grown much heavier since Poitiers. By the time they reached the English position, those of the men-at-arms who survived the sleet of arrows were almost too exhausted to lift an arm. They stood, wedged in a helpless mass, rooted in the mire, while the English archers slipped in among them with knives and mallets. The French losses were much heavier than at Poitiers, since the weight of armor and the mud made flight impossible.

Henry's battle tactics were those of Edward III, but his strategy was of a different order. His aim was not to destroy but to conquer. In place of plundering raids, he undertook the systematic conquest of Normandy, capturing castles and cities with the aid of siege artillery, which had been greatly improved since the previous period of invasion. At this point Henry would probably have been satisfied with Normandy as a permanent possession, but in 1419 the assassination of John the Fearless by the Dauphin's Armagnac supporters opened up new opportunities by bringing the murdered duke's son, Philip the Good, over to the English side in an open alliance. The Burgundians had recently gained possession of Paris and the person of the king, so that the allies between them controlled most of France north of the Loire, while the Dauphin Charles and his Armagnac followers held only parts of the center and south of France. The claim of the English king to the throne of France now seemed somewhat less preposterous. By a treaty signed at Troyes in 1420, Charles VI agreed to the marriage of his daughter Catherine to Henry, and proclaimed him his heir. The Dauphin was disowned by the king and queen in terms that gave credence to the common rumor that he was illegitimate, and Philip of Burgundy promised full support to the treaty which excluded from the succession the man whom he held responsible for the murder of his father. For two years Henry V as "heir to France" shared the government with the Duke of Burgundy. But when the helpless old king died in October 1422, it was not the victor of Agincourt who was proclaimed king in the Abbey of St. Denis, but a ten-month-old infant, Henry VI.

The death of Henry V, two months too soon for him to wear the crown of France, doomed whatever chance there was of uniting France and England permanently under one king. In any case, the chance was slim enough. Despite factional quarrels and princely ambitions, the French people, divided and weakened though they were by regional jealousies, would never accept an English king. The long war had bred in France a hatred of the foreign invader and at the same time had brought to life a new sense of French nationality. The efforts of the Duke of Bedford to conciliate the people of northern France, whom he ruled as regent for his nephew, Henry VI, met with sullen passive resistance. Charles the Dauphin still held most of the south, and had established a second capital at Bourges, which might serve as a rallying point for French loyalty. But that feckless prince, unsure of himself and surrounded by irresponsible advisers, was not a figure to inspire confidence or arouse devotion. What was needed was a forceful personality who could focus the nascent patriotism of the French people, allay their doubts concerning the Dauphin's legitimacy, and inject energy and purpose into the shiftless government of the "King of Bourges." That need was met with miraculous effect by the inspired peasant girl, Joan of Arc, who appeared at the Dauphin's court in 1429. Speaking in the name of God, whose will had been revealed to her through celestial voices, she proclaimed Charles the true king of France, rallied his army to lift the siege of the strategically important city of Orléans, and led the Dauphin through enemy territory to be consecrated and crowned at Reims. Though Joan was later captured by Burgundian forces who sold her to the English, and though Charles did nothing to save her from being condemned as a heretic and burned at the stake, the surge of national sentiment she had aroused could not be checked. In 1435 Philip the Good abandoned the losing English cause, and made peace with Charles on terms that left him free from feudal obligations for the fiefs he held in France. The Burgundian duke now held an independent principality, which included, besides the duchy and county of Burgundy, all the provinces of the Netherlands; but any future danger to France in such a powerful neighbor was for the moment compensated by his break with England. Having only the English to fight, Charles was able during the next twenty years to drive them from one city and castle after another, until in 1453 only Calais remained of all their ancient holdings on the continent.

In the last years of the war Charles VII — or the ministers who won for him the name "Charles the Well-served" — took advantage of the newly aroused national sentiment to carry through a thorough reform of the financial and military organization of the state. This was necessary to assure the triumph of the monarchy, not only over the invader, but also over the remaining forces of feudal particularism which had gained a new lease on life during the preceding half-century. The first step was to make sure of regular and permanent taxes, without the necessity of securing annual grants from the Estates. This meant little more than the recovery of the ground lost since the death of Charles V, but that little was significant. The king's right to levy taxes on his own authority was never again challenged. Normally these included the *gabelle* (a tax on salt), *aides* in the form of various taxes on the sale of merchandise, and, most important of all, a direct property tax, the *taille*, which replaced the hearth taxes of the preceding century and from which the nobles and clergy were exempt. Toward the end of the reign the *taille* amounted to 1,200,000 *livres tournois*. At the same time, Charles reorganized the administration by a series of ordinances designed to make the fiscal system more coherent and more susceptible to royal control.

Once assured of permanent income, Charles was able to undertake the urgent task of constructing an effective royal army. It was necessary first of all to get rid of the worst of the mercenary companies, whose numbers had greatly increased during the period of civil war and English conquest. These *écorcheurs* plundered friend and foe alike, and in the intervals between campaigns burned and pillaged their way through those parts of France untouched by the invasion. The next step was to impose discipline on those French and foreign mercenaries who were retained in the service. By the Ordinance of 1439, Charles revived his grandfather's regulations, limited the size of the companies, and assigned them to definite garrison duty. The Ordinances of 1445 and 1446 completed the reform. A truce with the English furnished an opportunity to disband the existing companies; but, instead of turning the whole army loose to make their own living by plunder until war began again, he re-enlisted the better elements. These, together with recruits drawn from the lesser nobility, were formed into twenty permanent companies under captains commissioned by the king. Each company consisted of a hundred "lances," the lance representing a tactical unit of six mounted men: a heavily armed man-at-arms and five lighter-armed followers. At full strength, the new companies would form a standing army of some twelve thousand mounted troops. In time of war this force was to be supplemented by a militia of trained archers, but these proved ineffective and the militia system was later abandoned. A formidable array of siege cannon and some field artillery rounded out the royal army. It was a force strong enough to defend the kingdom from external enemies and more than adequate to reduce rebellious vassals to obedience.

The end of the war found France still suffering from the effects of devastation and depopulation, but the monarchy was firmly entrenched in absolute authority, adequately endowed with revenue, and in command of a royal army that freed it from dependence on the military service of vassals. Since the Pragmatic Sanction of Bourges (1438), of which more will be said later,[4] it was also master of the French Church. Much still remained to be done. The king's control of justice was still far from complete, and state regulation of the economic life of the country had scarcely begun. Brittany and a handful of lesser fiefs still retained their feudal independence, and the principality of the dukes of Burgundy had alienated rich territories and raised a menacing rival on the northern frontier. Nevertheless, since the opening of the conflict with England the French monarchy had gained tremendously at the expense of the forces of feudalism. France had emerged from the crisis a nation, conscious of its national identity and loyal to its national king. The first stage in the transition from the feudal to the national state was completed.

D. ENGLAND: THE NEW MONARCHY AND PARLIAMENT

From the Norman conquest of England in 1066 until well into the fourteenth century, the two great states of Western Europe were closely related to one another, not only by feudal ties, but also by a language common to the nobility of both countries and by common social and cultural traditions. To a very considerable degree the evolution of the feudal monarchy in France and England followed parallel lines until the end of the thirteenth century. Thereafter the divergence of the two lines of development became more apparent, but it is important to keep in mind the fact that both monarchies grew out of the ideological and social atmosphere of feudal Christendom, and that they were subject to the action of generally similar political and economic forces. It is especially important to keep this fact in mind because it is so often forgotten, and because the structure of English feudalism, the early development of English royal government, and the eventual evolution in England of a monarchy limited by constitutional restrictions were in so many respects unique that the historian can scarcely avoid placing the greater emphasis on those elements in English history which are peculiar to it and in marked contrast to that of France.

England was, for one thing, a much smaller country than France. It

[4] See below, pp. 235–236.

was also a more united country, partly because it was smaller and hence more susceptible to centralized control, but also because English feudalism had been created by a conquering king, whereas the feudal system of France had grown up spontaneously at a time when the royal government was powerless. Neither the domain of the English king nor the fiefs of his great barons were integrated geographical areas. Both were scattered throughout the kingdom. English feudalism thus lacked the regional character that gave vitality to French particularism, and the expansion of royal authority in England did not have to wait upon the expansion of the royal domain as it did in France. Finally, the Conqueror and his successors retained and strengthened the Saxon system of shires and shire courts. These, together with their subdivisions, the hundreds and hundred courts, were administrative and judicial units deeply rooted in the life of the English people. In the courts of hundred and shire, local representatives learned to work with the king's officers, the sheriffs, or were brought into direct contact with royal justice by judges sent out from the king's court to tour the shires. Retention of these ancient Saxon courts furnished England with a connecting link between the king's government and the mass of the free population which operated largely outside the feudal system.

The early Norman and Angevin kings took full advantage of their unique opportunities. William I, Henry I and Henry II were men endowed with an extraordinary genius for government. They made the most of their position at the apex of the feudal pyramid, keeping meticulous account of the services and dues owed by their barons and other tenants-in-chief, while at the same time maintaining a firm hold on the shire administration. Even their frequent absences, due to the necessity of supervising their continental fiefs, served the growth of monarchical government by forcing the creation of relatively permanent courts within the indeterminate and fluctuating *Curia Regis* through which feudal kings normally exercised a personal rule. They were also lions of justice, intent on asserting the jurisdiction of the royal courts against their baronial and manorial competitors. By the end of the twelfth century the king's law was well on the way to becoming the common law of the land. For nearly a hundred years after the death of Henry II, royal government lacked the stimulus furnished by able and energetic kings. Richard the Lion-Hearted (1189–99) was absent during most of his reign. John Lackland (1199–1216) devoted his not inconsiderable ingenuity to exasperating his vassals and alienating the clergy. Henry III (1216–72) came to the throne as a child and as he grew up displayed a notable lack of talent for government. The feudal reaction which such weakness invited did not, however, take the form of a reassertion of independence on the part of the lords as would undoubtedly have happened in France. The Great Charter, granted by King John to meet the demands of his rebellious barons and prelates in 1215, was primarily a feudal document designed to force the king to observe his share of the feudal contract between himself and his vassals as established by custom. It did not undo the work of centralization achieved by the twelfth-century kings, though it did make clear that the king's authority was limited by law and it therefore formed a precedent of inestimable value, to which barons and people could appeal in later generations whenever there seemed any danger that the king would set himself above the law and rule arbitrarily or unjustly. Again, when the barons rebelled against Henry III and his foreign favorites in the years from 1258 to 1265, their aim was to gain control of the royal government rather than to weaken it. If royal government in the first three quarters of the thirteenth century did not fulfill the brilliant promise implied in its precocious development in the preceding century, this was nevertheless a period of considerable constitutional growth. The barons, though still entirely feudal in their point of view, gained a new sense of national solidarity by uniting in rebellion and by appealing for support to the middle classes of town and country. The principle that the king's power was limited by law and that he must in some degree consult and cooperate with representatives of the nation was established. And meanwhile the professional administrators and judges in the king's councils and courts continued to develop in more systematic form the institutions of administration, justice and finance.

The constitutional significance of the reign of Edward I (1272–1307) can be viewed in proper perspective only against this background of combined limitation and growth of royal government. Recent constitutional historians have tended to emphasize the continuity of development from the thirteenth to the fourteenth century and to see less that was novel and anti-feudal in Edward's policies than did the historians of Bishop Stubbs's generation. Yet one of the most distinguished of recent authorities refers to Edward's government as the "new monarchy" and, while doubting that Edward was consciously antagonistic to feudalism, describes his age as that of the early national monarchy which "witnessed the first tentative but unmistakable formulation of the theory and practice of the modern state."[5] Edward's reign, indeed, occupies a place in the history of the English state comparable in many ways to that of Philip the Fair in the history of the French monarchy. Similar exigencies led Edward to seek extra-feudal revenues, to tax the clergy, to oppose the excessive claims of Boniface VIII, to expand the scope of central govern-

[5] B. Wilkinson, *The Constitutional History of England, 1216–1399* (Toronto, 1948), I, 40.

ment and the jurisdiction of the royal courts, to mobilize the military force of the state, and to seek support for his policies by summoning representative assemblies for consultation and consent. Edward was intent on expanding and rounding out his kingdom, and the pressure of war as well as the need for strong government led him, as it did Philip, to acts which tended to undermine the feudal system and to infringe upon the traditional rights and privileges of the feudal nobles.

The first two decades of Edward's reign were relatively peaceful, save for one campaign in Wales, and are notable chiefly for the mass of legislation which has led historians to call him the English Justinian. Much of this legislation was simply the codification of the precedents of common law in the form of statutes, but there was also much that was new. Some statutes dealt with administrative abuses, limited the independent authority of the barons and recovered powers usurped by them in previous reigns. Others altered the laws regulating inheritance in ways that would ultimately check sub-infeudation and increase the number of the king's tenants-in-chief, thus weakening the baronial families to the advantage of the crown. Most of his statutes, however, dealt with the basic problems of criminal and civil law, and served to complete the process begun in the twelfth century by which royal law replaced feudal and manorial custom and became the common law of the land.

To an equal degree, Edward I left his mark on the judicial and administrative machinery of the state. As in France, the royal government grew out of the feudal *Curia Regis* by a process of specialization of function which was made necessary by the increasing volume of business it handled. But this process began at an earlier date than in France. As early as the reign of Henry III, the Court of Common Pleas for the trial of civil cases and the Court of Exchequer, which received and accounted for royal revenues, had acquired a separate and stable existence. To these Edward added a third, the Court of King's Bench which specialized in criminal cases. Unlike the *Parlement* of Paris, these were courts of first instance rather than of appeal. England was not so large but that important cases could be brought for hearing to Westminster. However, Edward also made the facilities of the royal courts more easily available throughout the country by sending out itinerant justices on more regular circuits and by relating the assizes they held in the quarterly sessions of the shire courts more closely to the central courts. After 1285 their decisions were reported back to the appropriate court at Westminster and had the same validity as though the case had been heard there. English justice thus acquired a centralization and uniformity combined with local availability unknown in France under the *Ancien Régime*. The royal council, which formed the permanent core of the *Curia Regis*, continued to exercise residual and appellate jurisdiction, either separately or in Parliament, though from this time on an increasingly large number of the cases not covered by common law were referred to the chancellor, who during the fourteenth century gradually evolved the separate Court of Chancery, in which decisions could be handed down on grounds of equity. Under Edward's strong hand, the council and the household offices of the Wardrobe also became much more efficient and developed into a bureaucratic administration with a professional *esprit de corps.*

During the later years of Edward's reign a series of costly wars — the conquest of Wales, the abortive conquest of Scotland and the defense of Gascony — made a strong and efficient royal government more than ever necessary, but at the same time the fiscal crises they provoked forced the king to more frequent appeals for cooperation from all the propertied classes in the state. Edward I has been traditionally regarded as the founder of the English Parliament, just as his contemporary, Philip the Fair, has been considered the creator of the Estates General. Recent scholarship, however, has tended to minimize the novelty of these institutions and to show that they evolved gradually out of the Great Council of the king's lay and ecclesiastical vassals and that their form was still extremely fluid and ill-defined. Nevertheless, the reigns of these two kings marked a crucial stage in the growth of both Parliament and the Estates General and introduced representatives of the non-noble classes as an important, though not yet essential, element. In their origins Parliament and the Estates General represent a similar stage in the evolution of the national state. The first century and a half of their history is of peculiar interest, since it demonstrates with extraordinary clarity both what was similar in the development of the two great states and the fundamental differences which in the end made one a constitutional, the other an absolute, monarchy.

From the beginning of his reign, Edward summoned Parliament more frequently than did his French contemporaries, and with increasing frequency expanded it to include two or more elected representatives from the property-owning classes in each shire and chartered town. There has been much scholarly debate concerning Edward's motives for thus establishing precedents that would eventually limit royal government. The baronial rebellion against his father's autocratic government had probably impressed upon him the wisdom of working in close cooperation with the magnates of the kingdom, but the addition of representatives of the commons to Parliament was undoubtedly intended as an extension rather than a limitation of royal power. Direct contact between the king and his non-feudal subjects was, in fact, an essential step in the transition from feudal to national monarchy here as in France. Pressing fiscal needs and the king's desire to facilitate the collection of extraordinary taxes by securing the formal consent of a larger group than the barons probably furnished the chief reason for the innovation, but Edward was no doubt also moved by a desire to secure the support of the propertied middle classes for his legislation and his national policies and to use the technique of representation as a means of establishing a more direct liaison between central and local administration. Some recent scholars have placed great emphasis upon the judicial function of Parliament as the highest court of the land. As an extension of the king's council, Parliament heard petitions and decided cases not covered by the common law courts, and this did, it is true, become an increasingly important part of parliamentary action during the fourteenth century, opening the way through "common petitions" to the initiation of legislation by the Commons. In Edward's time, however, fiscal and political problems and the enactment of statutes introduced by the royal council seem to have been uppermost in the king's mind. Representation in Parliament was as yet an obligation forced upon the knights and burghers by the king, rather than a right to be defended against royal encroachment. Edward's motives, in short, were roughly similar to those which led Philip the Fair to summon representatives of the three Estates. The vital difference between the two resulting institutions lay in the character of their component parts and also in the fact that the English Parliament was from the beginning a body of national scope, whereas the French Estates seldom represented the whole country. Parliament grew strong as a nationally representative body partly because the king was in the beginning strong enough to force representation from the whole nation.

The composition of Parliament remained fluid and uncertain through the reigns of Edward I and Edward II. At the opening session the representative knights and burghers met with the lords spiritual and temporal to hear the king's explanation of policy and requests for aid or counsel. The presence of their social superiors, however, inhibited them from participating in debate. They therefore formed the habit of withdrawing to discuss the king's requests among themselves. At first the knights and burghers seem to have met separately, but during the early years of Edward III they commonly met together in one body and so formed what came to be known as the House of Commons. Later in Edward III's reign the Commons elected a speaker who presided over their debates and reported the results to the king. By the middle of the fourteenth century, then, Parliament, though still in theory a single institution, was in practice divided into two bodies, the Lords and Commons, neither of which corresponded exactly to any one of the three Estates of France.

The House of Lords corresponded roughly to the French First and

Second Estates, but in England the lords spiritual and temporal formed a single assembly and were not in the same way considered as representing two distinct classes or estates of the realm. They were, in fact, simply the king's great vassals-in-chief, summoned by name as they had been summoned for generations to the Great Council. During the fourteenth century, however, the membership of the Lords became more definitely fixed than had been the membership of the thirteenth-century Great Council. Those lay lords who were summoned repeatedly gradually acquired a hereditary right to membership, so that the king was no longer free to summon such of his vassals as he chose. The crystallization of a hereditary peerage was further aided by the rule of primogeniture, which excluded younger sons from the succession to lands and titles. Since these younger sons and their descendants, contrary to continental usage, were technically commoners, only those peers who possessed a title and a right to a seat in the Lords were regarded as noble. At the beginning of the fourteenth century the only recognized titles were those of earl and baron, but to these Edward III added the title of duke, Richard II that of marquis, and Henry VI that of viscount. By the middle of the fifteenth century, the loosely organized baronage of the Middle Ages had thus been transformed by royal action into a hierarchical peerage in the form which it has retained with little change to the present time. In much the same way, the status of the ecclesiastical lords was more carefully defined during this period. All archbishops and bishops were summoned regularly, but the number of abbots and priors who sat in Parliament was considerably reduced. In the Parliaments of the first two Edwards representatives of the lower clergy as well as the prelates were summoned to give consent to clerical taxation, but this custom was soon abandoned. The clergy much preferred to grant subsidies and to treat with the king on matters that concerned them in their own Convocation, rather than to have Church affairs brought into Parliament. The prelates were thus able to separate their functions, sitting in Convocation as officers of the Church and in Parliament as vassals of the king. Such a distinction could, of course, never be entirely complete, but the fact that they sat with the lay lords as fellow-vassals rather than as specifically representing the interests of the Church tended to make the House of Lords a more united body than it would otherwise have been. Though occasional vague phrases suggest that people regarded the lords spiritual and temporal as in some uncertain way representing two estates of the realm, the Lords remained what it had been in the beginning: a baronial council.

The most significant difference between the English Parliament and the French Estates General is to be found, however, in the composition not of the Lords but of the Commons. The point of crucial importance is that the Commons included in one chamber representatives of both the urban bourgeoisie and the landholding gentry, the latter of whom in France would have been classed as *petite noblesse* and would have been represented in the Second Estate. The knights of the shire also represented the growing class of well-to-do free landholders of a less exalted social rank, and, at the other end of the social spectrum, the younger sons and cadet branches of the peerage. These knights and burghers, too, who united to form the House of Commons, were men who had behind them a long tradition of public responsibility and of experience in the practice of representative government. Ever since the Conquest, the English kings had made constant and increasing use of members of the knightly class, whether they were tenants-in-chief of the crown or not, in the judicial and administrative business of the shire courts. As men of substance who had knowledge of local conditions and a respected place in county society, knights were called upon by the sheriff or the itinerant justices to serve on sworn inquests and juries, to give information concerning crimes committed in the neighborhood, wrongs committed by royal officials, the ownership of disputed land, dues customarily owed to the crown, the value of property as a basis for tax assessment, or any other subject of interest to the royal government. In addition, knights of the shire were employed in all sorts of judicial and administrative business on the king's behalf, business that frequently required time-consuming investigations or trips to the royal courts at Westminster. That the burghers also had a long tradition of self-government is not so remarkable, for in some degree it was true of townsmen everywhere in Western Europe, but in feudal society this sort of "self-government at the king's command" was peculiar to England. If the summons of representatives of shire and borough to Parliament was from one point of view the extension of the Great Council to include the middle classes of the nation, it was from an equally valid point of view the centralization on a national scale of the representative government long practised in the local courts. The opinion of men so trained could not lightly be ignored. Their part in the early Parliaments was still largely passive, but the future was in their hands.

Throughout the period from the end of the thirteenth century to the middle of the fifteenth, the evolution of both royal government and Parliament was conditioned, as were the similar institutions of France, by almost perpetual warfare. War strengthened the monarchy by rallying national sentiment and by forcing the transformation of the feudal levy into a royal army, but at the same time the rising cost of war forced the king to treat constantly with Parliament, so that by the end of the Hundred Years' War Parliament was firmly entrenched behind a century and a half of precedent, in a position from which even the most autocratic kings could never evict it.

The Welsh wars of Edward I, followed by the war in Gascony and Edward's inconclusive invasions of Scotland, introduced the first stage in the transformation of the English army. Hitherto it had been composed largely of armored horsemen who were fulfilling their obligations as vassals or sub-vassals of the king. Since the Conquest the land of every vassal-in-chief of the crown had been assessed at a specific number of knights' service. In practice, however, the number of knights actually furnished on demand had been greatly diminished, and more often than not knights' service had been commuted to a money tax called "scutage." For campaigns in the Welsh hills, Edward probably needed no more knights than the feudal service would supply, but he needed them for a longer time than the customary forty days. Only a permanent force could hold the elusive Welsh mountaineers in subjection. Moreover, for fighting in hilly country foot-soldiers were as necessary and often more useful than heavy cavalry. To meet this problem, Edward introduced a new system of military organization and tactics. He asked his barons for only a small proportion of the knights' service nominally owed, but kept those knights who answered the call in the field for long campaigns by offering to pay for all service beyond the customary forty days. To supplement this small body of heavy cavalry, he drafted much larger numbers of foot-soldiers, mostly armed with the longbow, from the shire militia. In England the Saxon *fyrd*, the levy of all free men for defense of the realm, had never been allowed to die out. Edward instilled new life into the shire militia by the Statute of Winchester in 1285, which called upon all free men to supply themselves with arms in accordance with their means. And having learned from the Welsh the superb qualities of the longbow, he did everything in his power to encourage its use and to make archery the national sport of the yeoman class. From this reservoir of trained infantry, he drew the foot-soldiers he needed by sending royal "commissioners of array" to draft the requisite number of picked men from each shire. For campaigns on the English borders they served normally for three months at a time and were paid a standard wage.

The new type of army justified itself by the conquest of Wales and the success of the early campaigns in Scotland, but it vastly increased the king's need for revenue. In 1275, just before the beginning of the Welsh wars, Edward secured from Parliament consent to a permanent export duty on wool. This addition to the king's normal revenue from his estates, feudal dues and scutage, however, proved inadequate when he became involved in simultaneous wars in Wales, Scotland and France.

He was then forced to make repeated levies of a direct tax of a tenth on personal property in towns and a fifteenth on that in rural districts, and in 1294 he raised the customs duty on wool to the staggering sum of 40 shillings a pack. As these extraordinary taxes were levied in successive years, resentment mounted to the point of threatened rebellion. In the Parliament of 1297, Edward was forced to meet the demands of the disaffected barons by a formal "confirmation of the charters," that is, Magna Carta and its successors, with the addition of a guarantee that in the future no non-feudal taxes would be imposed without the consent of both Lords and Commons in Parliament. This event was of decisive importance for the evolution of the Commons as an essential part of Parliament. It made certain, at least, that they would be summoned frequently, since the king's need for extra revenue had become a chronic condition, and it gave them a bargaining power which they learned to use as a lever to pry from the monarchy further privileges and powers or the redress of specific grievances.

The reign of Edward II (1307–27) forms a kind of amorphous interlude between the reigns of the two greater Edwards, but it, too, was not without significance for the history of English government. An irresponsible athlete who left government to equally irresponsible favorites, Edward II was quite unfitted to carry on his father's aggressive foreign policy or to hold in check the barons who regarded the growth of royal power with increasing suspicion and resentment. But, as had happened in somewhat similar circumstances under Henry III, the feudal reaction took the form of an attempt on the part of the barons to control the royal government in their own interest rather than to decentralize it or weaken it in principle. The barons, however, were too exclusively concerned with the interests of their own class to retain popular support, and also too ruggedly individualistic to maintain a working control of government. The Ordinances of 1311, which placed Edward II under the tutelage of the lords, were repealed in the Parliament of 1322, and even the armed rebellion that ended the king's inglorious reign left the constitutional status of the monarchy untouched. But, if the monarchy had not been weakened, Parliament had been considerably strengthened, and the position of the Commons had been more securely established. The Statute of York, which repealed the Ordinances in 1322, contained a significant, if somewhat ambiguous, clause to the effect that all important matters touching the king or the realm should be discussed and assented to in Parliament by both Lords and Commons. Though variously interpreted, this clause seemed to establish the Commons as an essential element in Parliament, not only for grants of non-feudal taxes, but also for consideration of all important matters of state. The chief contribution of Edward II's reign to the growth of the Commons, however, was the gradual accumulation of precedent rather than any formal change in the constitution. Knights and burgesses were summoned to Parliament almost every year, and invariably when taxes were to be considered. They also began in this reign to present petitions which in fact initiated legislation. Although the Lords still took the lead, the Commons were at least present in the Parliaments that marked each crisis of this tumultuous reign, including the final tragedy of Edward's career, when he was forced to abdicate as the result of a rebellion led by his wife and son.

When Edward III (1327–77) grew old enough to take over the government into his own hands, it soon became apparent that England had once more a vigorous and warlike king. Reverting to the policy begun by his grandfather, Edward III completed the transformation of the army and organized it on the permanent basis necessary for service in long campaigns overseas. The knights and men-at-arms who followed Edward to France during the early stages of the Hundred Years' War, including those who owed military service as vassals, were paid from the beginning of the campaign, as were also the archers raised by commissions of array from the shire militia. As the war dragged on, however, the king gradually abandoned the impressment of infantry, which aroused resentment when it involved long service overseas. Instead he made contracts with barons or knights, whose military reputation would help to attract recruits, to raise companies of men-at-arms and archers at wages paid from the moment of enlistment. Like the continental *condottieri*, these captains were military entrepreneurs. They were paid by the king and in turn paid their troops and were responsible for their maintenance. With this development the last vestige of feudal organization of the army disappeared and with it the military as well as much of the political significance of the feudal barony. The contract system had its disadvantages, but it furnished the king with hardened troops for his endless campaigns, and it freed him from dependence on the service of his great vassals. Freely enlisted men who made a career of warfare, the troops raised under the new system had all the virtues of the professional soldier, but also the characteristic vices of the mercenary. For generations they were the terror of France, but in the long run England too suffered and paid a stiff price for having turned them loose upon the world. On their return home in periods of truce and at the end of the war, they formed the bands of armed retainers with which the fifteenth-century barons terrorized the countryside and engaged in rebellion and civil war.

The cost of a paid army meanwhile placed an unprecedented strain on the royal treasury, and Edward's reign was one long financial crisis. In the early period of the war he borrowed heavily from Florentine bankers and was forced into a disgraceful bankruptcy. Later he borrowed from local merchants, but government loans could be no more than a temporary expedient. Adequate income could be obtained only by national taxation, and that forced the king to treat with Parliament and to make concessions when necessary. Edward was a masterful ruler, but impetuous and generally ready to sacrifice the future for the satisfaction of his immediate desires. His relations with Parliament were on the whole peaceful, but at the cost of innumerable minor concessions and the reinforcement of the still uncertain powers of Parliament by constantly repeated precedents. The right of Commons to assent to direct taxes was now thoroughly established, but at the beginning of Edward's reign it was still uncertain whether their consent was necessary to the levy of the 40 shilling duty on wool, which Edward I had introduced and which formed an extremely important part of the king's income. A certain ambiguity in the confirmation of the Charters of 1297 made it possible for the king to levy this "maltote" or evil toll with the consent of an assembly representing the merchants only. The latter were prepared to give consent in return for certain privileges, because they could in fact divide the burden between the producers from whom they bought wool and the foreign consumers. Both Lords and Commons protested repeatedly that the consent of the wool merchants was not sufficient, since it was not they who really paid the tax, that it was a matter touching the entire community of the realm and therefore should be assented to by Lords and Commons in Parliament. The knights in Commons as well as the barons and prelates were landowners and profoundly concerned about the price of wool. They therefore worked together, and in 1340, when Edward was in especially dire need of money, they won their point and the "maltote" was included among the taxes to which Parliament must consent. For years Lords and Commons continued to agitate for the abolition of the "maltote," but eventually they came to accept it as necessary, though they could still exploit their right to consent as a means of bringing pressure to bear on the king for redress of grievances.

The long contest over the duty on wool demonstrated a growing awareness on the part of both king and Parliament of the importance of trade and of the effect of governmental policies on the economic life of the state. The fourteenth century, indeed, witnessed the first serious attempts of the English government to regulate trade on a national scale, though the attempts were still fitful and opportunistic, motivated more often by fiscal than by genuinely economic aims. The fact that England was a small country, with disproportionately valuable exports and imports which passed through a few easily supervised ports, made the taxation of trade relatively easy and served to call the attention of the government to the revenues that could be derived therefrom at an earlier date than was generally true in the continental kingdoms. But regulation instituted primarily for fiscal purposes might well have far-reaching effects upon the economic development of the country. The establishment of a compulsory wool staple by Edward II and the resulting organization of the Merchants of the Staple is a case in point, as is also the unintentional encouragement to the English weaving industry which resulted from the high export duties on wool. The *Carta Mercatoria* of Edward I, which granted foreign merchants freedom from many local tolls but obliged them to pay higher customs duties, was perhaps the clearest example of regulation designed to produce revenue even at the expense of the native merchants. As Parliament gained greater influence over governmental policy, however, the later kings were less able to ignore the interests of English commerce, and the privileges of foreign merchants were gradually limited. The economic legislation of Edward III was so frequently influenced by changes in his diplomatic relations with the Netherlands as well as by his fiscal needs that it is difficult to discern any consistent national policy. It is perhaps too early to look for evidences of a conscious mercantilist policy in the fourteenth century, but in the reign of Richard II (1377–99) the first Navigation Act (1381) and a number of statutes excluding aliens from retail trade in England seem at least to foreshadow the mercantilism of later governments.

Except for some sporadic encouragement of the weaving industry by Edward III, the national government left the regulation of industry and agriculture in this century pretty much to the traditional local authorities, but on one occasion king and Parliament undertook to regulate wages and prices on a national scale. The occasion was the desperate labor shortage caused by the Black Death and the resulting demand by laborers for wages that to the classes represented in Parliament seemed inordinate. The Statute of Laborers of 1351 attempted to force laborers in town and country to take work when it was offered at the wages customary before the great plague. The statute is notable as evidence of the growing scope of national government and of the influence of the propertied classes in Parliament, but like many more recent attempts to check inflationary pressures by legislation it was largely a failure. Its principal result was to contribute to the discontent which finally flared out in the Peasants' Revolt of 1381.

The fourteenth century was on the whole a period of steady growth in royal government. The king's council developed a greater regularity and efficiency through the work of professional administrators and jurists, while the Chancery was gradually becoming separated from the council and was evolving into an independent court of equity. At the same time the central government acquired a more direct control of local justice and administration by enlisting the services of the country gentry as agents of the crown. After 1329 members of the landholding families in each shire were commissioned as Justices of the Peace and thereafter were assigned increasingly important judicial and administrative functions. In 1388 they were required to hold court four times a year and were given jurisdiction over petty crimes. They were also required to enforce governmental regulations such as the Statute of Laborers and any other enactment that involved administration on a local scale. As the scope of governmental activity broadened in the following centuries they became the most important factors in local administration. Though serving without pay, and largely innocent of professional legal training, the Justices of the Peace were members of a class that had inherited a long tradition of public responsibility. They were royal officials, but they were not *gens du roi* as were the French bureaucrats who asserted royal authority in local affairs. They were members of families deeply rooted in the life of the shire and long accustomed to the exercise of authority. In their dual capacity as royal agents and local magnates, they formed a connecting link between central and local government that was not only generally more satisfactory but also infinitely less expensive than the continental bureaucracies.

The fourteenth century ended in a constitutional crisis, a brief experiment in absolutism followed by revolution, which left Parliament more firmly entrenched than ever. During the minority of Richard II, who succeeded his grandfather Edward III in 1377, Parliament took advantage of the king's youth to exert unprecedented control of the government, and even after Richard came of age it continued for some years to hold those powers which it had won through a century of slowly accumulated precedent. Richard, however, lacked the temperament for constitutional monarchy and was merely waiting until he felt strong enough to throw off parliamentary restraint. In 1397 he rid himself of his most dangerous opponents among the barons, and in the following year he forced Parliament to grant him the customs on wool for life, thereby freeing himself from the necessity for negotiating further grants. He then launched upon a career of arbitrary rule which, though not illegal, was still a breach with recent custom. He might easily have succeeded, since constitutional limitations upon the king's power were still vague and undefined, had he not aroused opposition by heavy taxes and by arbitrary interference with justice and local government, and had he not given the discontented elements in the state a powerful leader by driving his cousin, Henry of Lancaster, to revolt. Henry was the son of the fabulously wealthy John of Gaunt, fourth son of Edward III. Except for the infant Earl of March, who was descended from Edward's third son, he was the nearest heir to the throne. When he was exiled and his lands were confiscated by the king, he thus became the natural leader of all those who had suffered injustice at Richard's hands. In 1399 he returned to England, raised an army and forced Richard to abdicate. He then claimed the throne by the rather ambiguous right of inheritance, conquest and parliamentary confirmation.

The revolution which established Henry IV (1399–1413) and the Lancastrian dynasty lent Parliament a new prestige and opened a period of closer cooperation between Parliament and king. Though it has been argued that Parliament did not participate in the accession of Henry IV, since from the moment of Richard's abdication the Parliament he had summoned ceased to exist and a new one could not be formed until summoned by the new king, the fact remains that both the abdication of Richard and the proclamation of Henry were assented to by the lords spiritual and temporal and the representatives of the commons assembled at Westminster. And, since Henry was not the nearest heir to the throne, his title rested upon the confirmation of these representatives of the nation, whether or not they constituted a formal Parliament. It may be an anachronism to describe the Lancastrian kings as constitutional monarchs. The constitutional theories of the fifteenth century were still extremely ill-defined. There can, however, be little doubt that the dubious character of his claim to the throne forced Henry IV to depend on parliamentary support and prevented him from doing anything that would lessen its authority. His son Henry V (1413–22) was in a stronger position and by nature an imperious ruler, but his attention was absorbed during most of his reign by the war in France, and his need for financial and military support made it necessary for him to conciliate Parliament. The same necessity, reinforced by the fact that royal government was weakened, first by the king's minority and later by his incompetence, continued through the reign of Henry VI (1422–61). Parliament, and especially the Commons, was thus able to consolidate the gains made during the fourteenth century and to add to them another half-century of precedent.

It would be a distortion of reality, however, to picture the first half of the fifteenth century simply as a period of constitutional growth. The advances made by Parliament during the Lancastrian era were premature. Parliament was not yet sufficiently strong to maintain order and good government without a strong king, and its failure to do so partially discredited it. The apparent consolidation of institutions of government in this period was in fact offset by a notable increase in lawlessness and violence and by factional feuds among the aristocracy, which prepared the way for the civil wars that filled the second half of the century. This situation resulted in part from the personal weakness of Henry VI, but its fundamental cause was an unfortunate social situation produced by the long war and by the military system introduced by Edward III.

As noted above, the necessity of raising a permanent force for long campaigns overseas had forced Edward to adopt the practice of contracting with military leaders, mostly noble, for bands of volunteers. The members of these companies were paid by their patron, served under his orders and wore his uniform or "livery." During periods of truce and after the end of the war, many of these were unable or unwilling to return to civil life and continued to serve their noble employer as armed retainers. At the same time, nobles, thus supplied with the nucleus of an armed gang, used their power to organize the neighboring gentry under their leadership, offering protection and "maintenance" in any quarrel or lawsuit to those who would adopt their livery and form part of their following. This system of "livery and maintenance" furnished the greater nobles with a substitute for the vassal service they had lost, and restored something of their old feudal independence and power. The change from a feudal to a mercenary royal army, though destroying military feudalism, thus raised in its place a "bastard feudalism" that was for a time just as dangerous to royal government and public order. Though begun in the fourteenth century, this system of aristocratic gangsterism reached its height in the fifteenth, and for a large part of the century threatened to nullify the action of the royal courts. As the *Paston Letters* bear vivid witness, no man's property was safe unless he had powerful protection, and appeal to the courts might well be fatal.

The middle of the fifteenth century thus found England in a state of acute political and social crisis. It is true that the English were in many ways a more united nation than they had been in the Middle Ages. The long war, which despite ultimate defeat had been marked by an almost unbroken series of victories over a more powerful enemy, had done much to develop national consciousness in England, and had bred in Englishmen of all classes a patriotic pride in being English. If the war had made Frenchmen from all parts of France conscious that they were French, it had also made the English aristocracy conscious of the fact that they were not French, and this consciousness was powerfully reinforced by the loss of the English holdings in France at the end of the war, which finally cut the old feudal tie that had bound the two countries together. At the same time, the gradual evolution of a common English tongue tended to erase the cultural barrier that had separated the Anglo-Norman noble caste from the Anglo-Saxon commonality, while it also raised a new barrier between the former and their French cousins. Nevertheless, the transformation of all economic, political and social relations, which characterized this first stage in the transition from the feudal to the national state, had left the English people in a profoundly unsettled condition. Old institutions had disintegrated more rapidly than new ones had arisen to take their place, and it was not till the end of the fifteenth century that the period of uncertain readjustment ended with the creation of the stable Tudor state.

E. Germany: the Triumph of Particularism and the Consolidation of the Territorial States

The period we have been considering was a crucially important one for Germany, no less than for Italy, France and England. But the trend of development took a different direction from that in the two great national states. In these years, while France and England were evolving, though with some painful reverses, in the direction of national unity under strong royal governments, in Germany the forces of particularism triumphed decisively over the central government, and the construction of a national state, here as in Italy, was postponed until 1870, when it was achieved only as the result of a belated and excessive growth of nationalism and statism, the fruits of which are still apparent in the twentieth century. It is true that many of the same factors were at work in Germany as were gradually transforming the social and political structure of France and England. Except in the Hansard area in the north, urban economy developed somewhat more slowly during this period in Germany than in the other countries of Western Europe. German town life was nevertheless vigorous, and the money economy that spread from the towns served here as elsewhere to impoverish and weaken the feudal nobility, while at the same time it enabled state governments to strengthen their power by facilitating taxation and the development of paid armies. But the German governments that thus profited were not national. It was the German princes, not the emperors, who took advantage of the economic and social trend that was common to all Western Europe, and of the political situation that was peculiar to Germany, to establish territorial states that were practically independent, thereby reducing the central government to a state of innocuous desuetude and dooming the German people to centuries of political weakness and cultural provincialism.

That the development of Germany during this period was so different from that of its neighbors was largely the result of its earlier history. Never since Otto the Great founded the Holy Roman Empire in 962 had Germany been the sole concern of its rulers. Not only were Italy and later the Kingdom of Burgundy or Arles, which included all of modern France to the east of the Rhône, part of the Empire, but the imperial title carried with it vague claims to universal authority in matters temporal which brought the emperors into conflict with the spiritual rulers of the universal Church. The frequent absences of the emperors from Germany to attend to affairs in Italy, and the civil wars that accompanied the Investiture Controversy, weakened the monarchy and gave the great nobles of Germany an opportunity to establish a large degree of independence. The policy of the emperors in the twelfth century, however, was focused primarily on German interests and at the end of the century imperial government was still fairly strong. It was the complete abandonment by Frederick II of imperial interests in Germany in favor of Italy, and the resultant war of extermination waged by the popes against the House of Hohenstaufen that wrecked central government and national unity in Germany beyond repair. The long "Interregnum" (1254–73) that followed, during which various foreign princes were elected but made no attempt to rule the Empire, prolonged the anarchy that had begun in Frederick's reign and confirmed the princes in the powers they had seized. It was a period of utter chaos.

The election of a German emperor, Rudolf of Hapsburg,[6] in 1273 ended the Interregnum and gave Germany a ruler who might yet, though the chance was a slim one, have set Germany upon the path that France and England were following under Philip the Fair and Edward I. But Rudolf had been chosen largely because, as a modestly endowed Swabian count, he did not have enough land of his own to make him a menace to the independence of the princes, and the choice augured ill for the success of the revived monarchy. It was the fundamental weakness of imperial government in this period that the emperor could not levy either taxes or military service in any appreciable amount outside his own domain, and since the lands that had been attached to the crown in the twelfth century had long since been dissipated, the emperors of the fourteenth and fifteenth centuries were forced to depend almost entirely on their own hereditary estates. Under these circumstances a strong mon-

[6] Actually Rudolf was never crowned by the pope and therefore could not legally claim the title of emperor. According to medieval usage, the emperor, although entering upon all his powers from the time of his election by the German princes, was formally entitled King of the Romans until his coronation at Rome. Since there was usually a lapse of years between the election and the papal coronation, and some rulers of the Empire were prevented by circumstance from receiving the latter, it seems simpler to refer to all as emperors throughout their reigns.

archy could have been created only by the acquisition on the part of the emperors of a domain large enough to make them stronger than their princely rivals. This was the process by which the Capetian kings rose to effective national sovereignty in France. But it was not a process that could be completed in one lifetime, and its success depended on the monarchy being hereditary, so that the lands acquired by the ruling family generation after generation would remain attached to the crown. Rudolf was in fact amazingly successful in laying the foundations of a strong royal domain. He crushed his rebellious Czech vassal, Ottokar of Bohemia, and took from him the fiefs of Austria and Styria. These territories, together with his original Swabian lands, outweighed those of any other German prince. But, though they laid the foundation for the future power of the Hapsburg dynasty, they did nothing to strengthen the imperial government during the next century and a half. In the opinion of the electors, Rudolf had been too successful, and on his death in 1292 they deliberately rejected his heir and gave the crown to Adolf of Nassau who, like Rudolf himself at the time of his election, was no more than a count with a modest estate. The action of the electors on this occasion had far-reaching consequences. It reaffirmed the elective principle, and thus frustrated at a crucial time what should have been the natural development of German government in an age when hereditary monarchy was the normal form.

If the deeply rooted particularism of the electoral princes was primarily responsible for the continued weakness of the imperial government, there were other factors also which worked in the same direction. The ancient dream of empire still haunted the minds of the German rulers and at times led them to neglect the substance of national power for the shadow of a larger title. Had the German monarchs been able to cut loose from the tradition of the Empire at this point, had they frankly abandoned claims that could no longer be enforced to land outside Germany, they might yet have been able to create a unified and purely German state. Germany might at any rate have been left free to work out its own salvation. This the first two Hapsburg emperors, Rudolf and Albert I, seemed prepared to do, but they were foiled by the electors, who not only feared their power but also clung to the theory of Empire as the traditional base of the electoral system. The Empire was thus kept alive by a kind of artificial respiration, and the result was to doom German politics to perpetual interference by foreign powers whose sole interest was to stir up dissension among the princes and so prevent the growth of a strong national state. The French kings, who coveted the Kingdom of Arles, and in the early fourteenth century were encroaching steadily on the western frontiers of the Empire, missed no opportunity to embarrass the imperial government. In this they were ably seconded by the popes, who still feared and resented imperial claims in Italy which might lessen their authority in the Papal States, and who were themselves strongly influenced by French policy during the seventy years of the Babylonian Captivity.

To sow dissension in Germany was in fact pathetically easy. The princes were incurably egocentric, concerned only with defending or expanding their own rights and territories. They were moreover chronically short of cash and ready to accept bribes from any foreign power. A basic conflict of interests also fomented antagonism between the western princes who were threatened by French aggression and the more powerful dynasties, including the Hapsburgs, which had grown up in the more recently Germanized east and were more concerned with attempts to acquire the Czech or Magyar lands on their borders. It was the western electors in the Rhineland who were chiefly instrumental in defeating the Hapsburg attempt to establish a hereditary monarchy. Finally, as the imperial crown was passed by the electors from one princely dynasty to another, the emperors themselves abandoned any serious attempt to put the imperial government on a basis of permanent strength. Having no assurance of hereditary succession, having on the contrary good reason to believe that the imperial title would pass to another family in the next generation, the emperors concentrated their attention upon building up their own dynastic holdings so as to leave an enlarged territory to their heirs. They can, indeed, scarcely be blamed for refusing to exhaust the resources of their family lands in a fruitless attempt to strengthen the power of a government that would then pass to another family. The imperial government had been so denuded of practical resources, beyond what the temporary incumbent could bring to it, that it would have been a discouraging task in any case. The imperial crown did, however, carry with it one valuable prerogative which made it a prize worth paying for. The emperor could dispose of any fief of the empire that fell vacant through lack of heirs or on account of treason. These fiefs he normally bestowed upon his own heirs. A single reign might thus be enough to convert a relatively unimportant family into a powerful landed dynasty. This made the imperial title a potentially profitable investment, and candidates were willing to pay well for it, the more so since they were generally able to buy the votes of the electors with grants of powers and privileges pertaining to the imperial government, which cost the candidate's dynasty nothing. Under these circumstances the permanent beneficiaries of the imperial system were the electors, who could sell the crown over and over again and who were, therefore, heartily devoted to the elective principle.

A brief outline of German history during the first half of the four-teenth century will illustrate the way in which this situation tended to paralyse imperial government and to shift the balance of power from the emperor to the princes. Adolf of Nassau (1292–98), proved to be a stronger ruler than his sponsors had anticipated, and hence soon found himself facing a growing opposition within his own party, while in the east the late emperor's son, Albert of Austria, was bitterly hostile. When both the King of France and the pope threw their weight against Adolf, his position became untenable. He was deposed by the electors and died in battle against his successful Hapsburg rival, Albert I (1298–1308). Like his father, Albert added to the territory of the Hapsburg dynasty and labored to found a hereditary monarchy; but after his death the electors, led by the three archbishops from the Rhineland and influenced by French intrigue, once more passed over the Hapsburg heir and gave the crown to an inconspicuous West German count. The new emperor, Henry VII (1308–13) of the House of Luxemburg, raised his family to the first rank among German princes by securing the Kingdom of Bohemia for his son John, but he further weakened the imperial gov-ernment by distributing imperial rights with a lavish hand as bribes to secure the acquiescence of the princes in his dynastic ambitions. Then, having abandoned an imperial policy in Germany, Henry turned to Italy in the hope of reasserting imperial authority there and of finding in that fabulous land a new basis of power. It was a quixotic enterprise and hopelessly anachronistic. Though hailed by patriots like Dante, who hoped to see Italy restored to order under a strong ruler, and though favored at first by the pope, who hoped to use him as a counterpoise to France and Naples, Henry soon found himself bogged down in the bottomless morass of Italian politics. He was still struggling courageously, however, when he was stricken down by a fatal attack of fever. He was the last emperor to make a serious attempt to restore imperial rule in Italy.

Dynastic ambitions and foreign interference continued to frustrate the imperial government during the long and troubled reign of the next emperor, Louis IV, the Bavarian (1314–47). To begin with, his election was a disputed one, the electors having been divided between Louis and Frederick of Hapsburg, and Louis was not fully recognized in Germany until the defeat of Frederick after eight years of civil war. Throughout the remainder of his reign, Louis's energies were devoted to two ends, the acquisition of more lands for his family, the Wittelsbachs, in which he was notably successful, and a quite unsuccessful effort to secure papal recognition for his imperial title. It was his misfortune that Pope John XXII had plans of his own for Italy, which he thought might be furthered by keeping the imperial title in dispute and so preventing any renewal of imperial interference. During the civil war the pope had carefully refrained from recognizing either candidate, and he continued to refuse recognition even after the dispute had been settled by Louis's victory. In 1323 the pope made the preposterous demand that Louis surrender his imperial authority until his election had been confirmed. Louis refused and was excommunicated. The struggle lasted through the reign of three popes until the emperor's death. Louis was prepared to make large concessions, and the later popes, if left to themselves, might have been willing to compromise, but any hope of a settlement was wrecked by the French kings who dominated the foreign policies of the Avignonese popes. The result was a generation of uncertainty and instability in German politics. As the struggle continued, however, German sentiment began to rally to the cause of national independence, and in 1328 the electors, who felt that the pope's claims abrogated their own cherished rights, issued a declaration admitting the pope's right to crown the emperor-elect, but denying that the validity of the election or the powers exercised by a duly elected emperor were in any way dependent on the pope's confirmation. An imperial Diet later confirmed this declaration of the independence of the German monarchy, but since it was also a reaffirmation of the elective principle, it strengthened the position of the electors rather than that of the emperor.

The shift in the balance of power from the emperor to the electoral princes, which characterized the first half of the fourteenth century, reached its completion in the reign of Charles IV (1347–78), the second emperor of the Luxemburg line and King of Bohemia. Charles was much more interested in his hereditary Bohemian kingdom than in the Empire, and he was prepared to sacrifice imperial authority in order to secure a stable situation in Germany that would leave him free to devote himself to Bohemian affairs. The time seemed ripe for a compromise settlement of the papal-imperial problem. In the decade between Crécy and Poitiers, the French king was too deeply embroiled in the war with England to interfere. Charles was therefore able to secure full recognition of his imperial title and was crowned at Rome in 1355. In return he abandoned all claims to authority over the States of the Church, and promised not to enter them without the pope's consent. By a consistent policy of non-interference in Italy, Charles confirmed the practical separation of Italy from Germany and thereby freed imperial government at last from a commitment that had so frequently bred trouble in the past. His next step was to place the relations between the emperor and the electors on a stable basis by legalizing the *status quo*.

The Golden Bull of 1356, which was the nearest approach to a written constitution the Empire ever acquired, was designed by Charles to make the College of Electors a stabilizing force, which would prevent disputed elections and in general exert a pacifying and conservative influence on the restless German princes, lesser lords and free cities. It laid down rigid rules for the conduct of elections and guarded against dispute by limiting the right to vote to seven definitely specified electors: the three archbishops of Mainz, Cologne and Trier, the King of Bohemia, the Count Palatine of the Rhine, the Duke of Saxony and the Margrave of Brandenburg. The status of the electors was protected by declaring their territories to be indivisible and, in the case of the lay principalities, inheritable by the rule of primogeniture in the male line. They were also given what amounted to sovereign powers in their states. The whole effect of the bull, in fact, was to exalt the power of the electors, and, by guaranteeing their position, to make them a powerful conservative group, to whose interest it would be to preserve order and maintain the *status quo*. It did not change the practical situation very much at the time, but it was nevertheless a significant event. It marked the formal transfer of practical authority in Germany from the emperor to the princes.

The major theme of German history in the century following the Golden Bull was furnished by the struggle of the princes to consolidate a sovereign authority in their territorial states. There is little need to follow the history of the emperors of this period whose chief significance is that they played no significant part in German government. Charles IV was succeeded, contrary to precedent, by his son Wenceslas (1378–1400), but this revival of the hereditary principle proved abortive. Wenceslas was thoroughly incompetent; he was usually drunk and his subjects were almost always disorderly; and in 1400 he was deposed. The electors then chose Rupert of the Palatinate (1400–10), a member of the numerous Wittelsbach tribe, but holding only a part of his family's lands. He was followed by Sigismund (1410–37) brother of the inebriated Wenceslas. As King of Hungary and, after the death of Wenceslas, of Bohemia as well, Sigismund was more concerned with these non-Germanic lands than with the Empire. Thereafter the imperial crown returned, this time permanently, to the House of Hapsburg with the successive elections of Albert II (1438–39) and Frederick III (1440–93). No one, however, could have known at the time that a hereditary monarchy had in fact been established, and the Hapsburg emperors continued the exclusively dynastic policy of their predecessors. The history of Germany in this period cannot, then, be focused upon imperial government. It was the history of dozens of princely territorial states, together with a host of petty lordships and self-governing cities.

Though the Golden Bull dealt exclusively with the status of the electors, the other German princes profited in only slightly less degree. The rule that electoral territories should be inherited without division by the eldest male heir was gradually adopted by most other dynasties. Sovereign rights like those granted to the electors, too, were soon acquired by the more important princes, who then set about the task of consolidating their principalities into centralized territorial states, similar in form to the larger national states of Western Europe. In order to achieve this end, the princes had to restore order and to secure recognition of their own supreme authority everywhere within their territories. This involved whittling away the feudal privileges of their vassals and the autonomous rights of the towns. It was a task carried out under almost insuperable difficulties, and for a time it seemed more likely that the territorial principalities would follow the precedent set by the Empire and disintegrate into a new feudal anarchy. Not till the second half of the fifteenth century was the triumph of the princes fully assured.

The most dangerous opposition to the centralizing policy of the princes came from the class of "knights," who had taken full advantage of the anarchy of the late thirteenth century to assert their independence in relation to the princes, much as the princes themselves had asserted their independence in relation to the emperors. The knightly class, the *Ritterschaft*, as it developed in Germany in the thirteenth and fourteenth centuries, had no exact parallel in any other European country. It was an outgrowth of the early medieval class, peculiar to Germany, of unfree officials and armed retainers, called *ministeriales*, who served emperors and princes as administrative officers and knights. Although originally bound to their lord and subject to his will, they were granted lands and seigneurial rights, just as though they were noble vassals. During the civil wars precipitated by the Investiture Controversy in the second half of the eleventh century, the *ministeriales* rose in the social scale. Their services as knights were in great demand, and they were able to secure legal freedom and recognition as a knightly class on the fringes of the nobility. They were still, however, regarded as inferior by the old noble families, and they retained the habit of obedience which made them more reliable than the feudal vassals. Both the Hohenstaufen emperors and the princes accordingly used them as aids in suppressing the independence of the old feudal dynasties, thus advancing their social status still further and securing for them a definite place in the feudal hierarchy. At the same time, many of the old noble families were dying out or were encouraged by the favor shown to the *ministeriales* to amalgamate with them. By the end of the thirteenth century, the *ministeriales*, together with members of such declining noble families, emerged as a new aristocracy. They had now lost all trace of their servile origin, and were no longer called *ministeriales* but *Ritter* (knights). As such, they formed a distinct class of landholding lords, no longer the obedient servants of emperors or princes, but eager to assert their independent power in their fiefs. For the next two centuries they formed the most turbulent element in the German states.

In their efforts to establish their sovereign authority over the knights and the burghers of the self-governing towns, the princes were hampered by their own perpetual feuds with their neighbors. Chronic need for men and money with which to fight their interminable dynastic wars frequently forced them to surrender jurisdictional rights in order to secure the military service of the knights and the financial support of the burghers. The princes, indeed, might well have subscribed to the dictum that the lack of money is the root of all evil. All too often they were forced to alienate property to meet immediate financial needs, and the income from their lands was further depleted by the leasing of demesne at fixed rents, the commutation of labor services from their servile tenants and the continuous curse of monetary inflation. The princes were themselves largely responsible for the inflation that impoverished them, since they frequently resorted to the shortsighted policy of debasing the coinage so as to pay their debts in depreciated currency. This and other temporary expedients, such as raising loans from bankers or leasing out mining rights, merely aggravated their financial difficulties. What was obviously needed was a system of general taxation, but for this the feudal system made no provision. The princes might tax the peasants on their own personal lands, but to extend taxation further they were forced, as were the contemporary national monarchs, to negotiate with representatives of the Estates — clergy, nobles and burghers — to gain consent to extraordinary taxes.

The rugged individualism of the knights and their jealous hatred of the prosperous burghers did much to prevent common action on the part of the Estates, but if they could agree on anything it was on opposition to the prince's demand for taxation. By the end of the fourteenth century, they had learned to present a common front when necessary, and as a result the Estates had acquired a strong position in most principalities. They were ever ready to resist their lord's demands by force of arms if he encroached upon their privileges, and in many states the prince had been forced to recognize their legal right to do so. The Estates of this period, however, had not yet gained the formal organization that would guarantee them a permanent place in the constitution of the state. For the most part they were local bodies, representing only one class in a particular area, rather like the provincial Estates of France. Their native tendency toward local particularism was further intensified by the fact that the territory of many princes was composed of geographically separated units, which were grouped together or divided in varying patterns by the accidents of inheritance in each generation, so that the sense of membership in a common state developed only slowly and as a result of the growing custom of undivided inheritance. So long as the Estates retained their local character, uniting with other groups only in opposition to the prince, their policy was purely obstructive. But as the princes grew stronger during the fifteenth century and justified their demands for taxes by maintaining order, all classes were gradually won over to a reluctant recognition of the necessity of supporting the state government. In one state after another, the prince succeeded in replacing the old local Estates with a new centralized body, the *Landtag*, composed of representatives of the three Estates throughout the principality, and empowered to make grants of taxation that would be binding upon all the prince's subjects. Unlike the old autonomous local Estates, the *Landtage* met only when summoned by the prince, and though they might bargain with the princes and ask redress of grievances, they were primarily instruments of princely government. They fulfilled a function, in short, very similar to that of the earlier Parliament in England or the Estates General in France. More than any other single factor they contributed to a consolidation of central government in the territorial states of Germany, comparable to the consolidation of royal government in the great national states.

Other forces, however, were also working in the same direction during the fifteenth century. The princes were aided in the task of strengthening central government and state jurisdiction, at the expense of feudal privileges, by trained administrators and jurists who had been deeply influenced by the study of Roman Law and by the Roman conception of the state. In this, as in so many other respects, the German princes were but following the example set a century earlier by the French monarchy. The princes were aided, too, by the revolution in military technique, which accompanied the Hundred Years' War and now spread to Germany. Mercenary armies of foot-soldiers, paid out of state taxes, freed the princes from exclusive dependence on the knights for military service, and gave them a force that could be used against rebellious vassals. Artillery also gave the princes a weapon with which to destroy the castles of lawless lordlings and robber barons. Finally, the economic conditions that tended to impoverish the whole landholding class during the fourteenth and fifteenth centuries continued to weaken the position of the lesser lords, while the princes were able to improve their financial position through taxation, thus making up what they lost as landlords.

The territorial states, however, were no substitute for a strong national state as a means of maintaining either internal security or a place in relation to the other European states consonant with the potential power of the German people. While the princes were still struggling to gain power in their own states, Germany experienced a period of lawlessness unequalled since the darkest period of the Early Middle Ages. Leagues of cities and leagues of knights were organized in various parts of Germany to maintain order or, alternatively, to disturb the peace further by fighting the princes or one another. Numerous attempts were made to keep the peace by local agreements, but these *Landfrieden* had no more effect than the eleventh-century Peace of God. The prosecution of crime was left largely to voluntary organizations which administered summary justice, much after the manner of vigilantes. The most famous of these organizations, the *Veme*, for a time achieved power widespread enough to make it feared even by princes, but these secret organizations for self-help were themselves essentially lawless and subject to abuse. Once the princes had acquired control of their states, they put an end to the worst disorders within their own territories, but they could not maintain peace and order throughout Germany. For, outside the dozen or so fairly large states, there were scores of smaller ones, as well as dozens of free cities enjoying independent jurisdiction, and also innumerable tiny lordships, each of which was a practically sovereign state under a *Freiherr* who owned no superior except the emperor. In the welter of jurisdictions a criminal could easily escape justice, while many of the petty lords were themselves little better than brigands. Only a strong central government could have suppressed the robber barons and other criminals and put an end to the perpetual curse of private warfare; and only a strong central government could have given Germany the power to protect herself in the cutthroat play of international politics. But thanks to the events of the period we have been considering, a strong central government had been made impossible for centuries to come.

F. The Church and the Papacy: Crisis and Partial Recovery

The century and a half which witnessed the transformation of state governments was also a period of acute crisis in the history of the Church. In these years of uneasy adjustment to changing conditions, the government of the Church, like that of the secular states, was changing in ways that profoundly altered its character. Everywhere in Western Europe state governments were using the fiscal opportunities presented by the expansion of money economy to establish a more strongly centralized administration and to combat the jurisdictional rights and immunities, not only of the nobles and self-governing communes, but also of the clergy. At the same time, governments striving for sovereignty were forced to combat the claims of the papacy to universal authority over secular rulers. For its part, the Church, which had profited by both the particularism and the universalism that characterized the feudal era, now found itself engaged in a losing struggle to maintain the position of dominance it had won in a more favorable economic and political environment. Under these circumstances the government of the Church resorted to the means used by its secular rivals, centralized its administration, developed a more efficient bureaucracy, and by systematic taxation provided itself with the money needed to maintain a vastly expanded body of governmental and diplomatic agents, as well as the armies of mercenary soldiers which the pope, as ruler of the Papal States, now needed to protect his territory from the aggression of other Italian princes. But these means, which were eminently suited to the ends of a secular state, held hidden dangers for a religious institution and a government that owed its power to an authority not of this world. The effort to compete with the rising national and territorial states shook the fabric of the universal Church and left the papacy bereft of much of its moral authority over Christendom, for which the centralization of administrative authority within the Church was insufficient compensation. In this chapter attention will be concentrated on the institutional and political aspects of the struggle. The effect on popular piety and religious belief will be reserved for later discussion.

The fourteenth century opened with the first great Jubilee, proclaimed in the year 1300 by Pope Boniface VIII. Throngs of pilgrims came from every corner of Christendom to pour their varied coinage into the papal coffers. The authority of the Church and of the popes who were its rulers must have seemed as firmly established as in the great days of Innocent III. In the century between Innocent and Boniface, the theoretical armaments of the Church had been strengthened by the great age of scholastic philosophy and canon law. The Albigensian heresy had been crushed by the combined forces of the mendicant orders, the Papal Inquisition and Simon de Montfort's crusaders. The Hohenstaufen emperors, too, had been crushed by the pope's spiritual weapons in alliance with a French army led by Charles of Anjou. The centralization of authority in the Church had more than kept pace with the centralization of authority in the great national states, and the inevitable conflict had been postponed by the piety of the two rulers, Louis IX and Henry III, who ruled France and England respectively for the greater part of the thirteenth century. By the end of the century, however, conditions had changed in ways that shifted the balance of power between Church and state, though the nature and extent of the change might not yet be apparent. In France and England, Philip IV and Edward I were laying the foundations for a new monarchy which could no longer tolerate either the papal claims to supremacy or the clerical claims to immunity which the Church had successfully defended in the previous centuries. Against these formidable opponents the pope would have to rely on spiritual weapons that had been blunted by too frequent use for secular ends in the struggle for power against the Hohenstaufen. The position of Boniface VIII himself had been weakened by his avarice and nepotism, and by his bitter feud with a powerful Roman family, the Colonna. Despite the triumph of the Jubilee, then, the odds were against Boniface when he chose this moment to assert the immunity of the clergy from secular jurisdiction and the supremacy of the pope over secular rulers more uncompromisingly than even the most vigorous of his medieval predecessors had done.

The first and indecisive phase of the conflict between Boniface and the national monarchs had actually taken place before the Jubilee. The issue at stake was the right of secular governments, specifically the kings of France and England, to tax their clerical subjects for the defense of the realm. This was a matter of vital concern to both monarchs, since the costs of warfare on a national scale, as well as the increased expenses of government caused by the expansion of royal authority, could no longer be met without some form of general taxation, and from such taxation the clergy, who possessed great landed wealth, could scarcely be immune. On the outbreak of war between them in 1294, both Philip and Edward had levied a direct tax on clerical income. The tax was not unprecedented, but hitherto such subsidies had been levied by agreement with the papacy and usually under color of raising funds for a crusade. The new taxes posed the issue of clerical immunity to secular taxation more clearly, and Boniface replied by issuing the bull *Clericis laicos* in 1296, forbidding secular governments to levy, or clergy to pay, any subsidy or tax without papal authorization on pain of excommunication. The argument that churchmen, as subjects enjoying the protection of the state, should contribute to the defense of the realm was, however, a cogent one, and when both kings took strong practical measures to enforce their demands Boniface was forced to retreat. The following year he issued a new bull rescinding the prohibition contained in *Clericis laicos*. It was, however, no more than a truce, at least so far as Boniface and Philip the Fair were concerned. Given the intransigent character of the two protagonists, and the mutually exclusive claims of the medieval papacy and the new monarchy, it could scarcely be otherwise.

The second phase of the conflict opened on the issue of clerical immunity from the jurisdiction of secular courts. In 1301 Philip tried and condemned the Bishop of Pamiers in a royal court on a charge of treason, and demanded in somewhat peremptory terms that the pope degrade him from his office as a preliminary to his execution. However justified this action might seem from the point of view of royal sovereignty, to Boniface it was an intolerable infringement upon the rights of the Church, and with the flattering results of the Jubilee fresh in mind he was prepared to take a firm line. He demanded that the bishop be turned over to an ecclesiastical court, once more forbade the French clergy to pay subsidies or taxes to the king, and in the bull *Ausculta fili* scolded the king in vigorous terms. Further, he summoned the French prelates to a synod in Rome to consider steps for "the correction of the king." Thus challenged, Philip summoned the first meeting of the three Estates of the realm in 1302 and gained from them an expression of support for the royal cause. Boniface, however, was not deterred by this unprecedented expression of national sentiment, and a few months later issued the famous bull *Unam sanctam*, the most uncomprising statement of the superiority of the spiritual over the temporal authority made by any medieval pope. The bull recited all the familiar arguments for the papal supremacy in both spiritual and temporal matters, and ended with the flat statement that subjection to the Roman pontiff is altogether necessary to salvation for all human creatures. Once more Philip appealed to national sentiment. He charged the pope with various crimes and heresies, and secured from an assembly of French nobles and prelates approval of his demand that Boniface answer the charges before a General Council. In September 1303, Guillaume de Nogaret, the most aggressive of those legally trained ministers whom Philip had chosen as advisers, arrived in Rome to deliver the king's summons, and there secured armed support from the pope's enemies, the powerful Colonna family. He found Boniface in his native town of Anagni, seized him and held him prisoner. It was a shocking affront to the Vicar of Christ, enough to sober even his enemies, and in a few days Boniface was freed by the local populace. The shock, however, had been too much for the aged pope, who died shortly thereafter.

So far as any single event can mark the end of an era, the tragedy of Anagni symbolized the close of a period in papal history that had opened with an emperor standing barefoot before the gates of Canossa. The brief arrest of Boniface had proved nothing, but it had demonstrated the power of the national monarchy and the relative weakness of the ruler of the universal Church. The claims Boniface had asserted with such uncompromising vigor were already obsolescent. No later pope was to renew them in such absolute terms. This, at least, was guaranteed by the events of the next few years. Having struck down the pope who had challenged his sovereignty, Philip was determined to prevent a recurrence of the threat. He could not prevent the immediate election of an Italian pope; but Benedict XI, whose irenic temper and blameless character might have done much to restore the prestige of the papacy, died within the year. In the long conclave that followed, Philip's agents were able to bring enough pressure to bear to secure the election of a French prelate, the Archbishop of Bordeaux, who took the title, Clement V (1305–14). The new pope had every intention of going to Rome, but the city was in a dangerously turbulent state. Moreover, Philip was determined to keep him within range of his authority, and there were pressing problems, such as the king's continued attacks on the memory of Boniface and his trial of the Knights Templars, that called for the pope's presence in France. For several years Clement travelled about France and finally settled down in the city of Avignon on the Rhône. It was a convenient location, for Avignon was halfway between Paris and Rome on the great Franco-Italian trade route, on the borders of France, yet not a French possession. Here Clement remained, and here his successors made their home for nearly seventy years.

The long exile of the popes from the ancient capital of Christendom has been called by historians the Babylonian Captivity, by analogy with the captivity of the Jews in Babylon. The suggestion that they were held captive by the French monarchy is not entirely just, for there were other reasons for their failure to return to Rome. That city, as well as the Papal States and indeed the whole of Italy, was in a violently turbulent state during these years. On every occasion when one or other of the popes considered transferring the curia to Italy, fresh disorders discouraged the move. There was, however, reason for the suspicion that papal policy was frequently influenced by French national interests, and certainly the personnel of the curia became under Clement V, and remained throughout the whole period of the Captivity, predominantly French. All seven of the popes who ruled the Church from Avignon were French, as were also 113 of the 134 cardinals they appointed. Such a nationalization of its central government inevitably tended to weaken the medieval concept of the universality of the Church. It also served to aggravate the resentment felt by other nations, particularly the English who were at war with France, against the popes' fiscal demands or their interference in the affairs of the national churches. It is true that the papacy hitherto had been predominantly Italian. But Italy was not a national state, nor were the Italians in any political sense a nation. Moreover, Rome had been for centuries the capital, first of a universal Empire, then of the universal Church. No French papacy, resident on the banks of the Rhône, could appear to foreigners in the same degree an international power.

There were also certain practical disadvantages in the absence of the popes from Italy. It made control of the Papal States extremely difficult and at times impossible. Rome was in a perpetual state of turmoil, while nearly every city in the papal territory fell into the hands of semi-independent *signori*. The resulting loss of income from the Papal States was one reason, though not the most important, for the financial demands on the Church at large which aroused anti-papal sentiment during this period. It is doubtful if even in Rome the popes, in their capacity as Italian princes, could have kept free from participation in the wars that tore Italy and threatened the integrity of the Papal States. As it was, they were not entirely free agents, since French influence bound them more or less to the tortuous policy of the Angevin kings of Naples. Throughout the whole Avignonese period, the cost of maintaining mercenary armies in Italy formed one of the principal burdens on the papal treasury, and thus furnished a further motive for the popes' fiscal exploitation of the Church.

The fact that they were identified with France was also an embarrassment to the popes, from John XXII to Clement VI, in the last struggle between the papacy and the Empire which filled the long reign of Louis the Bavarian. While denying the doctrine of papal supremacy in matters temporal so far as it concerned their own states, the kings of France and Naples encouraged the popes to assert the claims made by the medieval papacy in relation to the moribund Empire. It was largely French interference that prevented Benedict XII from making peace with the emperor on satisfactory terms, while at the same time it stiffened the national opposition in Germany and rallied the German princes to defend the independence of the Empire. Their assertion that the election of an emperor was valid without papal confirmation severed the connection between the two universal powers, which had been a fundamental tenet of medieval political theory, and destroyed one more papal claim to supremacy over secular governments. The prolonged controversy also gave rise to theoretical attacks on the authority of the popes which bore fruit later during the period of the Great Schism and the Conciliar Movement.

The loss of papal prestige and the growing anti-papal and anti-clerical sentiment that characterized the period of the Babylonian Captivity cannot, however, be attributed principally to the identification of the papacy with French interests. To a far greater extent the criticism of the Church was caused by changes in its fiscal and administrative system, changes which had already begun in the thirteenth century, but which were carried much further by the Avignonese popes. To critical contemporaries these changes seemed the result of unbridled will to power and avarice in high places. It would be more just to see in them the almost inescapable results of the necessity faced by the Church's government of adapting to changing economic and political conditions. During the Early Middle Ages the government of the Church had been decentralized in much the same way, if not to the same degree, as that of the feudal kingdoms. Its wealth, largely in the form of land, was held by its local officers and there was little possibility of mobilizing it in the service of central government. The pope, like the contemporary kings, lived on his own income; and, lacking adequate financial resources, he could not in practice exert a direct control over local administration. This situation changed gradually with the revival of commerce and the reintroduction of money economy. Like the feudal monarchs, the popes increased their income, began to assert a more effective administrative authority, and encroached more and more upon the jurisdiction of the bishops and abbots, while at the same time, with the aid of canon law and scholastic learning, they asserted more strongly than ever their theoretical claims to supremacy. With increasing frequency the popes summoned bishops to Rome for consultation, intervened in diocesan affairs, and asserted direct authority over the religious orders and the universities. Appeals from the episcopal courts to the papal curia also multiplied steadily. By the end of the thirteenth century, the papal monarchy had progressed further than had the feudal kings in the centralization of administration and jurisdiction. It had also laid the foundations for a system of taxation that would enable it to mobilize the wealth of the Church for the maintenance of a growing bureaucracy. In the Church as in the feudal states, centralization of government and the development of a fiscal system went hand in hand, complementary parts of a single process. This process was begun by the twelfth- and thirteenth-century popes. The fourteenth-century popes, faced by the challenge of the growing power of secular governments, completed it.

One of the most significant aspects of this process, fraught with incalculable consequences, was the increasing reservation by the papacy of the right to "provide" incumbents to vacant benefices by direct appointment. Begun by Innocent III, who declared the principle that all ecclesiastical offices were at the disposal of the pope by virtue of his *plenitudo potestatis*, the practice of "reserving" benefices for papal provision grew during the thirteenth century, though it was generally applied only in individual and exceptional cases. In 1265, however, Clement IV decreed that a whole class of benefices, those falling vacant by the death of the incumbent while he was visiting the papal curia, should thereafter be reserved. Building on this foundation, the Avignonese popes vastly extended the categories of reserved benefices until they included the majority of the elective offices (the archbishoprics, bishoprics and abbacies), as well as a very large number of the lesser offices, such as those of the canons and parish rectors, which were appointive and normally at the disposal of a lay or ecclesiastical patron.

Abuses in the older system of election or appointment furnished a pretext for this extension of papal authority, but the papal provisions themselves created new and in some ways more serious abuses. All too frequently the papal nominees were foreigners, many of whom never saw the benefices to which they had been appointed, for the popes regularly used their right of provision as a means of rewarding the cardinals and the numerous officials of the curia and so reducing the expenses of the papal government. To these absentee beneficiaries were added numerous royal courtiers and governmental officials, since kings and princes, too, found it convenient to pay their favorites and servants at the expense of the Church, and the pope was usually willing, in the interest of political harmony, to accept a certain number of the candidates they nominated. Instead of preventing the intervention of secular governments in the choice of ecclesiastical officers, then, the effect of the system of papal provisions was to facilitate it by taking the benefices out of the hands of the local patrons or elective bodies. Duplication of benefices added still further to the number of absentees, since many clerics who enjoyed the favor of pope or king received more than one benefice, some of them a great many more, and could not possibly fulfill the functions of all of them. Such beneficiaries appropriated the largest part of the income from the benefice and used the remainder to pay a substitute. One result of papal provisions, then, was that in a shockingly large number of places the sheep were left without a shepherd or at the mercy of a hireling. The system, however, was too profitable, not only to the popes but also to the secular rulers, to be abandoned, no matter how strong the popular protest. In England, where antagonism to the francophile papacy aggravated the opposition, Parliament passed the Statute of Provisors in 1351 forbidding papal provisions within the kingdom, but, though reissued periodically, it was seldom enforced by the royal government.

The right of provision to benefices not only helped the popes to pay their curial officials, but also in more direct ways added to the papal income. All archbishops, bishops and abbots who received their benefices by papal provision were required to pay a number of fees and tips to the officials of the curia and a heavy "service" tax (*servitia*) to the pope and the cardinals. The *servitia* was generally fixed during the fourteenth and fifteenth centuries at one-third of the estimated annual income of the benefice. Lesser benefices to which the pope made provision were not subject to the *servitia*, but paid a similar tax, known as "annates" in the fourteenth century, though later the term was more loosely used to include all benefice taxes, including the *servitia*. The annates usually consisted of a year's income as assessed for the purpose of the papal income tax, which in practice seem to have amounted roughly to about half the gross income of the benefice. During the Avignonese period the popes also claimed the income from reserved benefices during a vacancy, that is, from the death of the incumbent until the nomination of his successor. These and other taxes on benefices are difficult to define exactly, since the practice of the popes changed from time to time, but it is clear that they were greatly extended and applied more systematically by the successive Avignonese popes. Since they were applied largely to reserved benefices, they grew with the extension of the practice of reservation and were, indeed, one of the principal reasons for that extension. Altogether they formed a large part of the popes' income, and hence were a matter of primary concern to the fiscal officers of the curia. The *servitia* alone totalled 1,123,003 gold florins in the eighteen years of the pontificate of John XXII (1316–34) or about a quarter of his total income.

In addition to the various forms of tax on reserved benefices, the popes of this period frequently imposed a direct income tax upon all the clergy for a period of from one to six years at a time. Such taxes, as well as subsidies in the form of "voluntary gifts," were first demanded for special purposes such as the Crusades or the conflict with the Hohenstaufen emperors. In the fourteenth century they were still regarded as extraordinary, but like the extraordinary taxes levied by contemporary monarchs they had in fact become almost normal. The income tax was usually a tenth of the assessed value of a cleric's income, which usually fell considerably below the amount he actually received. It brought in large sums, though the proceeds had usually to be shared with the secular rulers, who in the long run may have got more out of them than did the pope. Other sources of income included indulgences and the fees paid for dispensations from the canonical prohibition of marriage within the forbidden degrees, for the removal of canonical barriers to the holding of benefices, for the absolution of usurers, for the legitimation of bastards, and for many similar applications of the pope's plenitude of power. Fees and fines resulting from the trial of cases appealed to the papal courts also represented a profitable source of income and, as a result, such appeals were encouraged by the curia. They increased greatly in number during the fourteenth century, despite such expressions of national resentment as the Statutes of Praemunire forbidding appeals to the papal curia of cases within the jurisdiction of the royal courts, passed in 1353, 1365 and 1393 by the English Parliament.

However necessary a centralized and adequate fiscal system may have seemed to the Church's government, it could not but have many unfortunate results for the morale of the clergy and hence of the Christian community. It placed a heavy burden upon all clerics, while at the same time robbing the officers of the Church of a part of their traditional rights and revenues. If the *servitia* and annates were not paid by the beneficiary who had contracted them, they remained a permanent charge on the benefice to be paid by his successors. In cases where successive beneficiaries held office for only a short term, they might pile up to a crushing load. During the fourteenth century there were increasingly bitter complaints of the impoverishment of the clergy, a situation made all the worse by the ravages of warfare and the agricultural depression, which cut deeply into the income of ecclesiastical as well as lay landholders. To meet the demands of papal taxation from declining income, prelates were forced to increase their exactions upon their subordinates, who in turn were forced to squeeze all they could from the people under their care. The blight of fiscality thus spread from top to bottom of the Church and laid the clergy open to charges of avarice. Finally, since *servitia*, annates and the tenth were rigorously enforced by excommunication of defaulters, the faithful were frequently confronted with the scandalous sight of bishops and other high officers of the Church banned from its communion.

The great increase in the volume of business, which resulted from the centralization of Church government, necessitated a corresponding increase in the personnel of the papal curia. During the fourteenth century, the popes, particularly John XXII who possessed an unusual talent for administration, created a systematically organized bureaucracy with specialized functions. The fiscal administration became extremely efficient and developed a system of auditing and bookkeeping that might well have served as a model to any contemporary secular government. The papal court in these years took on an appearance in many ways similar to, if not more magnificent than, the royal courts. It was filled with a host of servants, chaplains, guards and petty officials, whose maintenance was a drain on the papal treasury and who also levied tips and fees from prelates, petitioners and office seekers, thereby adding to the prevalent impression of the venality of the curial officials. The cardinals, as the principal officers of the curia and counsellors of the popes, shared in the increase in wealth and power that accompanied the process of centralization. They received a share of the papal revenue and had a special fiscal administration to handle their common funds. Each cardinal maintained a princely court with a train of servants and courtiers. Since they played an important part in shaping papal policy, kings and state governments frequently exerted pressure upon the popes to nominate cardinals who could be counted upon to represent their interests in the curia. Despite such pressure, however, the number of members of the Sacred College decreased, since the cardinals themselves were strongly opposed to sharing their wealth and honors among too many beneficiaries. During the Avignonese period the number of cardinals in any conclave never exceeded twenty-six and went as low as eighteen. Many of these princes of the Church became very wealthy — one left a legacy of 150,000 gold florins — and the magnificence of their courts did much to contribute to the evil reputation of Avignon, which was widely regarded as a modern Babylon, a city of luxury and a sink of iniquity.

Deleterious as were the effects of the prolonged exile of the popes in Avignon, the situation was made infinitely worse when Pope Gregory XI finally restored the curia to Rome in 1377. The eternal city had suffered severely from the long absence of the papacy, on which its prosperity almost exclusively depended, for Rome had never developed any considerable commerce or industry beyond supplying the needs of the curia and the throngs of prelates and pilgrims who came to visit it. The cardinals, fresh from the comfort and elegance of Avignon, found it a mean, squalid city, shrunk to the size of a market town, inhabited by a turbulent populace long accustomed to faction and violence, and now determined at all costs to keep the papacy and the profits accruing from it. When Gregory died in 1378, a few months after his return, the Romans were determined to secure the election of a Roman, or at least an Italian, pope as a guarantee against the return of the curia to Avignon. The French cardinals went in fear of their lives, and with a threatening mob rioting outside the conclave, they hastily elected an Italian, Bartolomeo Prignano, Archbishop of Bari, who took the title Urban VI (1378–89). There is no evidence that the cardinals, however terrified and reluctant, did not at the time regard the election of Urban as valid, but within a few months they turned against him. Elevation to power seems to have had an unfortunate effect on Urban, bringing to the surface a latent arrogance and a tendency to violence, as well as an unsuspected antagonism to the French faction. The French cardinals accordingly withdrew from Rome, declared the election of Urban invalid because carried out under threat of force, and elected in his place one of their own number, Robert of Geneva, who took the name Clement VII (1378–94). Urban, meanwhile, had created a number of Italian cardinals who remained in Rome with him. Thus began the Great Schism of the West, which for nearly forty years divided Catholic Christendom and dealt an irreparable blow to the prestige of the papal office.

The schism aggravated all the fiscal abuses that had grown up during the preceding century, since each pope could count on income from only about half the Church. The European states were divided fairly evenly between the two obediences, in general giving their adherence to the pope at Rome or the pope at Avignon in accordance with their own political interests, for in fact the legal position of the two contestants was so evenly balanced that it was possible to adhere in good faith to either. Throughout the schism, partisanship in the papal struggle thus served to heighten the animosity already existing between many of the states. This, however, was perhaps the least of the evils resulting from the spectacle of two popes, each claiming to be the sole Vicar of Christ and each hurling anathemas at the other. Each pope, moreover, provided to benefices, with the result that the conscience of many devout Christians was seriously troubled, for no one could be certain that the sacraments on which his soul's salvation depended had been administered by a properly ordained priest. It is small wonder that the wave of anti-clerical and anti-papal sentiment, which had been rising all through the fourteenth century, now reached threatening proportions.

From the beginning of the schism all serious churchmen realized that the situation was intolerable and that the Church must somehow be reunited. But how? Despite pre-election promises and numerous gestures toward healing the schism, no pope on either side was prepared to abdicate in favor of his opponent, nor were the two colleges of cardinals willing until almost the end of the schism to imperil their own position, which was dependent upon the pope to whom they adhered. On the contrary they prolonged the schism after the death of the original contestants. The Avignonese cardinals elected Benedict XIII (1394–1417) as successor to Clement VII, while the Roman college elected successively Boniface IX (1389–1404), Innocent VII (1404–06) and Gregory XII (1406–15). In 1397 the governments of France, England and Castile made a joint appeal to both popes to abdicate simultaneously, but to no avail. The following year the French clergy with royal support attempted to force the hand of the Avignonese pope by withdrawing obedience and refusing to pay papal taxes or to accept papal provisions to French benefices. Castile and some of the German states followed suit, but the rebellion, even though backed by armed force, failed to move Benedict XIII, and in 1403 the dissident states returned to obedience. The experiment in self-government and the restoration of the elective principle in the French Church ended in disillusionment, but it served as a precedent for later assertions of the autonomy of the "Gallican" Church, which operated principally to the advantage of the monarchy, since in practice the royal government took over the powers of taxation and provision which the pope had exercised.

Force and persuasion having failed to move the rival popes, the conviction spread more and more widely among the leaders of the Church that only one solution remained: a General Council, through which the corporate body of the Church could act to heal its own wounds. There were both legal and practical difficulties in the way of this solution. According to precedent and the opinion of the canonists, a Council was valid only if summoned and presided over by the pope; but it was obvious that neither of the schismatic popes could summon a Council representing the whole Church, even if he were willing to do so, nor could any effective action be taken by a Council subservient to the pope. Almost from the beginning of the schism, however, a group of writers, mostly connected with the University of Paris, had argued that a General Council possessed authority superior to that of the pope, and that, therefore, it might act to restore unity without papal cooperation by deciding in favor of one or other of the rival popes or by deposing both. This opinion gained more adherents as other attempts to end the schism failed, while at the same time the aggravation of fiscal and other abuses which resulted from the schism created a widespread demand that the Council should act not only to restore unity but also to reform the Church "in head and members." But to put this program into effect involved a revolution in the theory and practice of Church government: denial of the divine origin of the pope's authority, rejection of the theory of papal *plenitudo potestatis,* and the substitution of a representative, constitutional Church government for the papal monarchy. Revolutionary though the conciliar theory was, however, it was not new. The basic principles had been asserted by influential anti-papal writers since the beginning of the fourteenth century. Their work, culminating in that of the conciliar theorists who wrote under the impulse of the schism, represents a body of political theory of such importance, not only for Church government but for the development of constitutional ideas everywhere, that we must pause here to trace its major outlines.

During the twelfth and thirteenth centuries, political theory had been focused principally upon the conflicting claims of papacy and empire. Partisans on both sides were agreed, however, on one fundamental principle: the unity of Christendom under two divinely ordained universal powers, the *sacerdotium* and the *imperium.* On the imperial side the theorists strove to show that the temporal authority of the emperors was independent of the papacy, being derived directly from God. It was an argument that lost much of its significance when the empire of the Hohenstaufens was destroyed, since the claims of later emperors to divinely ordained universal authority could scarcely be taken seriously, though Dante's poetic imagination could still revive for a moment the anachronistic dream. On the papal side the claims of the canon lawyers were more sweeping. Building on the vigorous but still vaguely defined assertions by Gregory VII of the sovereignty of the pope within the Church and of the superiority of the spiritual over the temporal power, the thirteenth-century canonists developed with legalistic precision the theory that the pope's authority came directly from God, while the temporal authority of secular rulers is secondary and inferior and should therefore be governed and controlled by the spiritual power, since it is the law of nature that the higher everywhere governs and controls the lower. While not denying the distinction between temporal and spiritual authority, the canonists gave to the latter jurisdiction in all matters involving the possibility of sin, which meant practically any human action. By virtue of the plenitude of power, which is his as the Vicar of Christ and successor of St. Peter, the pope was thus conceived as having ultimate jurisdiction in all matters both temporal and spiritual, to be exercised when necessary, with the pope himself the sole judge of the necessity.

It was this theory, stated in extreme form by Boniface VIII in the bull *Unam sanctam* and by the canonist Egidio Colonna in the contemporary treatise, *De ecclesiastica potestate*, that the legal advisers of Philip the Fair had to meet. The most persuasive argument, it is true, was an act of force. It was the arrest and death of Boniface and the sequel of the Babylonian Capitivity that demonstrated the impracticality of the papal claims. But there was also a good deal of theoretical writing on the royal side, from which emerged two significant ideas. In the first place, the defenders of the autonomy of the French state broke with the medieval tradition of the universality of the Empire, and claimed for the king the same powers within his kingdom as the emperor enjoyed in the Empire, a claim which opened the way for the application to the king of the dictum of Roman Law that what the emperor wills has the force of law. In the second place, the sovereignty of the pope within the Church was challenged for the first time on constitutional grounds. In the *De potestate regia et papali* (1302–03) of John of Paris and in other royalist pamphlets, the pope's authority was defined as an administrative function, which is not absolute and does not even involve *dominium* over Church property. Spiritual authority, it was argued, is vested in the Church as a whole, and if a pope misuses his power he may be deposed by a General Council or by the cardinals who elected him, just as a king may be deposed if he becomes a tyrant. It was a theory that fitted the intellectual climate of the generation that witnessed the formation of the Estates General and the English Parliament.

A second phase in the mounting attack on papal sovereignty was precipitated by the conflict between John XXII and the emperor, Louis the Bavarian. While defenders of both the papal and the imperial positions restated the familiar arguments, adding nothing but a more systematic treatment, two brilliant controversialists entered the lists rather as opponents of the papal monarchy than as defenders of the Empire, though both sought protection from the emperor and made common cause with him against the common enemy. As one of the Franciscans condemned by John XXII for heresy because of their assertion of the doctrine of apostolic poverty — a doctrine which that financial genius found peculiarly uncongenial — the great Nominalist schoolman, William of Ockham, was forced into a position where he could not but deny the pope's plenitude of power, particularly in matters of faith. His concern was to check the absolute authority of the pope, which might become a tyranny, and to defend the right of Christians to resist the pope when he erred. In essence William was applying to the pope the deeply rooted conviction of medieval people that a ruler who exercised an arbitrary power contrary to what they regarded as law, whether the law were based on revelation, natural reason or custom, was a tyrant and might be resisted by his subjects. Ultimately William placed above the pope the authority of the Scriptures as interpreted by men of sound scholarship and good will, an assertion of freedom of judgment that seems to foreshadow Luther's; but, as an immediate and practical means of limiting the pope's authority and correcting him when in error, he advocated a General Council which would represent the combined wisdom of Christendom and hence be less liable to error.

Marsiglio of Padua, the second foreigner to be drawn into the imperial-papal controversy, was an ardent champion of the autonomous authority of the secular state, though the states he seems to have had chiefly in mind were the Italian city-states rather than the Empire, and it was in the interest of the state rather than of freedom of conscience that he attacked the papal sovereignty. The *Defensor pacis* (1324), which he wrote apparently in collaboration with the Parisian Averroist, John of Jandun, was indeed more than an attack on the pope's *plenitudo potestatis*. It presented a revolutionary reversal of the rôles traditionally assigned to the spiritual and temporal powers, and would in effect have reduced the Church to the status of a department of state. Marsiglio regarded the clergy as simply one of several classes in society which performed a function necessary to the well-being of the community.

That function was merely, "to know and teach those things which, according to Scripture, it is necessary to believe, to do or to avoid, in order to obtain eternal salvation."[7] The clergy interpret divine law, transgression of which will be punished in a future life. They have no coercive authority in this world, where the only law that can be enforced by punishment is human law, which he defined as "a command of the whole body of citizens or of its prevailing part," to whom belongs final authority in the state. To this human law, enforced by the state and its courts, the clergy like other citizens are subject. Even their property is subject to the state, being in the nature of a subsidy granted them by the community for their support. As for the Church itself, it is, like the state, a community in which all authority springs from the community as a whole. It is composed of the whole body of Christians, laymen as well as clerics. The authority of the pope and the other officers of the hierarchy is, therefore, merely a delegated authority for administrative purposes and is of entirely human origin. Ultimate authority in matters of faith or doctrine, which are all that he would leave to the Church's jurisdiction, must then rest with a General Council representing the community of all believers, though the coercive power to enforce its rulings can be exercised only by the state. While paying lip service to the medieval concept of a united *Respublica Christiana*, of which all Christians are citizens, Marsiglio thus shifted effective authority to the secular states, the growing autonomy of which was already in process of destroying that unity. His theory involved a compromise with the medieval idea that there are two distinct areas of authority, spiritual and temporal, but his rejection of the superiority of the spiritual and of the divinely ordained sovereignty of the pope was nevertheless complete, too complete for acceptance in the fourteenth century. Still it furnished an arsenal of theoretical weapons for all future opponents of the papal monarchy.

The sense of intense emergency created by the Great Schism, reinforced as it was by long-standing resentment against the arbitrary exercise of the pope's fiscal and administrative powers and by a growing conviction that the much-needed reform of the Church would never be carried out by papal initiative, furnished a climate of opinion in which the radical theories of the anti-papal writers from John of Paris to Marsiglio could take on a new lease of life. It was the crisis of the schism that inspired reputable scholastic doctors like Conrad of Gelnhausen, Heinrich of Langenstein, Pierre d'Ailly and Jean Gerson to take up and develop the conciliar theory; and it was certainly the conviction that the

[7] C. W. Previté-Orton, ed., *The Defensor Pacis of Marsiglio of Padua* (Cambridge, 1928), I, vi, i.

end of the schism and the reform of the Church could be achieved in no other way that won almost universal acceptance of the theory that a General Council could if necessary force its will upon the papacy. All that remained was to find a means of summoning such a council, since neither pope could do so.

The first effort to break this impasse came from a majority of the two colleges of cardinals, with results that could only be described as unfortunate. Acting independently of either pope, they joined together to summon a General Council to meet at Pisa in 1409. There, after asserting the supreme authority of a General Council and trying the two popes *in absentia*, the Council condemned both popes as schismatics and heretics and declared them deposed. The two colleges, formally united by the Council as one body, then proceeded to elect a new pope, Alexander V. Unfortunately, neither the Roman nor the Avignonese pope would accept the Council's sentence, and both received sufficient support from politically interested states to maintain their position. The somewhat hasty action of the Council of Pisa, then, had merely aggravated the schism by adding a third pope. And when Alexander V died within a year and was succeeded by John XXIII,[8] a man of much less irreproachable character, the hope that all Europe would rally to the support of the Council's pope rapidly waned.

The failure of the Council of Pisa did not, however, discredit the Conciliar Movement. Rather it made the convening of a really ecumenical Council more imperative than ever. During the next few years the demand for a Council became more insistent, and, when the newly elected emperor, Sigismund, took the initiative, with the reluctant cooperation of John XXIII, in summoning a General Council to meet at Constance in 1414, every European state gave it support. The new Council faced three major tasks: to end the triple schism, to suppress the rapidly growing Hussite heresy in Bohemia, and to reform the Church in head and members. In the first of these it was entirely successful. It deposed John XXIII and Benedict XIII and forced the abdication of Gregory XII. Finally, in 1417, a new pope was elected, Martin V (1417–31). The unity of the Church was thus restored under a truly Roman pope, for Martin was a member of the Colonna family that had played so large a rôle, for good and ill, in the history of Rome and the papacy for many generations. The Council also took vigorous, though less successful, action for the suppression of heresy. John Hus was summoned to the Council, condemned and burned; but his Czech followers were subdued only after many years of bloody conflict, and then

---

[8] John XXIII and the Avignonese popes are regarded as anti-popes and therefore omitted from the official numbering.

only at the cost of compromise with their demands. The third item on the agenda, the reform of the Church, presented greater difficulties, and in the long run little was accomplished. Everyone recognized the need for reform, but any practical measure would inevitably infringe upon the vested interests, not only of the curia, but also of state governments and almost all members of the ecclesiastical hierarchy. Only a few minor reform measures were decreed before the election of Martin V, and thereafter the new pope was able to take advantage of the conflicting national interests in the Council to make separate agreements or concordats with each of the national groups, and thus to avoid any general decrees that would seriously limit his administrative or fiscal authority. For this Martin can scarcely be blamed, for the financial needs of the Church's government, which had been responsible for the growth of so many of the abuses against which the reformers railed, still existed and had indeed been made more exigent by the crisis through which it had just passed.

The success of the Council of Constance in healing the schism was a real triumph, but its very achievement weakened the Conciliar Movement by removing the emergency that had forced the nations of Europe into support of the conciliar theory. True, the theory still retained many staunch adherents among reforming churchmen, and it now had an officially recognized status. In a strongly worded decree the Council of Constance had declared that "a General Council constituting and representing the Catholic Church, has authority immediately from Christ, which everyone in existence, of whatever status or dignity, even of papal, is bound to obey in those things which pertain to the faith, the extirpation of the said schism and the reform of the Church in head and members."[9] Moreover, as one of its last acts in 1417, the Council provided in the decree *Frequens* for the convening of another General Council in five years, a second in seven years and thereafter one every ten years in perpetuity.

Had these decrees been put into effect, the result would have been a revolution of permanent significance in the government of the Church. But, in fact, the conciliar theory was too revolutionary, and, given the conditions prevalent in both the Church and the national states, it was utterly impracticable. The principal argument in its favor, once the schism was healed, was the need for reform, but the failure of the Council of Constance to achieve effective reform demonstrated the incapacity of an occasional Council, torn by national jealousies, to deal with deeply rooted evils that were protected by long-established vested

[9] Quoted in C. H. McIlwain, *The Growth of Political Thought in the West* (New York, 1932), p. 347.

interests. Even had it acted more strongly there was no guarantee that its decrees would have been carried out to the letter. A Council might legislate, but it could not govern. Its decrees could be put into effect only by the papal executive power, and such cooperation could scarcely be expected from popes who had no intention of surrendering either their absolute authority or the income to maintain it. On the contrary, the fifteenth-century popes without exception worked steadfastly to defeat the Conciliar Movement until it was destroyed, and Pius II was able to condemn it officially in the bull *Execrabilis* (1460).

The popes did not win their victory, however, without a struggle, and one that once more threatened the peace of the Church. Martin V was able to dissolve the thinly attended Council held at Pisa in 1423 before anything could be accomplished, but the next Council, which opened at Basel in 1431 under the newly elected pope Eugenius IV (1431–47) proved more recalcitrant. When Eugenius attempted to dissolve it almost before it had begun, the Council of Basel refused to comply, and thereafter it was constantly at loggerheads with the pope. It reasserted the supreme authority of a General Council as decreed at Constance, worked out a compromise solution of the Hussite heresy, and talked much about reform, but found that agreement on practical reforms was as difficult as it had been at Constance. In 1437 Eugenius declared it dissolved to make way for the ecumenical Council of the Greek and Roman Churches, which met in Ferrara and Florence in 1438–39 with a view to ending the ancient schism between the eastern and western branches of Christendom, and presenting a united front to the rising Turkish menace. Though only briefly successful in achieving this end, the Council of Florence redounded to the pope's credit, while the Council of Basel alienated much good will by declaring Eugenius deposed and electing in his place a layman, Amadeus VIII Duke of Savoy who took the inappropriate name, Felix V. The Council dragged out its contentious life for a decade longer, but the European states had no desire to witness a new schism, and when it lost the half-hearted support of the emperor it dwindled away to an inglorious end in 1449.

For all practical purposes, the Conciliar Movement died with the Council of Basel. It had sustained the hopes of many ardent reformers, including Nicholas of Cusa, who wrote a powerful defense of the conciliar theory as late as 1433. Nevertheless, it ran contrary to the major political currents of its time. Despite the fourteenth-century experiments with legislative assemblies, there was an inescapable drift toward centralization of government and the strengthening of monarchical power in this period when Europe was emerging from the economic and social conditions that had fostered both universalism and feudal particularism in the Middle Ages. Even in the Church a movement to establish constitutional government on the basis of a theory of popular sovereignty could scarcely appeal to monarchs who were working their way toward absolute authority, and royal control of the national churches was already sufficiently advanced so that no reform program could succeed without the support of the secular governments. The community of all believers, on which the conciliar theory rested was, indeed, fast becoming a fiction, even though unity of faith and of Church organization was to survive for a century after the Council of Constance. The significance of the Conciliar Movement, then, lies not in what it actually accomplished, but in the constitutional theories to which it gave expression and which might bear fruit when the times were more propitious.

The papal monarchy thus emerged from its long crisis with its sovereignty within the Church unimpaired, and in the following decades its administrative control of the Church was further systematized and centralized. The papacy became, in fact, the first absolute monarchy in Western Europe and the prototype of modern centralized bureaucracy. But this triumph of papal absolutism was achieved at the cost of abandoning forever the supremacy over temporal governments, claimed and in large part exercised, by the medieval papacy. Practical supremacy was in fact a lost cause before the age of the Councils, but the necessity of winning governmental support against the Conciliar Movement forced the popes to a fuller acceptance of the accomplished fact. By a series of tacit agreements or formal concordats, such as those arranged by Martin V at Constance or that by which Nicholas V won the emperor Frederick III away from the Council of Basel in 1448, they agreed to share with the secular rulers some of their rights of provision to benefices and taxation of the clergy. These were merely practical concessions. They did not touch the theory of papal sovereignty in the Church. But "they were concessions guaranteed by a bilateral agreement in the nature of a treaty, which implies two treaty-making powers . . . They were a tacit acknowledgment of the sovereignty of the national states and they mark the virtual end of the medieval theory that Christendom in its secular aspect is one great state, as in its spiritual it is a single Church."[10]

The extent to which the pope's relations with the national states had actually deteriorated was demonstrated in the most striking fashion by the attitude of the French government. Two concordats with the papacy in 1418 and 1426 left the French kings, long accustomed to preferential treatment, still unsatisfied, and in 1438 Charles VII issued the Pragmatic Sanction of Bourges as a unilateral assertion of the liberties of the Gallican

[10] McIlwain, p. 352.

Church. It deprived the pope of most of his sources of revenue in France and also of his right to provide to French benefices except for those that had been vacated at the Roman curia. Steady papal pressure later persuaded Louis XI to renounce the Pragmatic Sanction, in form if not in substance, but relations between the papacy and the French monarchy were not definitely settled until the Concordat of Bologna in 1516, and then on terms that saved the theoretical sovereignty of the popes at the expense of ceding to the king the practical control of the offices and temporalities of the Church in France.

The growing power of the national monarchies and the territorial princes was not, however, solely responsible for the reduction of the pope's status in relation to secular governments to that of one among the sovereign powers of Europe. During the period of the Captivity, the Great Schism and the Councils, the papacy had suffered an immense loss of moral prestige, which the fifteenth-century popes did little to repair. They were more concerned with recovering their fiscal and administrative powers within the Church than with restoring their spiritual authority, which indeed could have been achieved only at the cost of sacrificing their material interests. The necessity of recovering political control of Rome and the Papal States, moreover, forced the popes for a century after the end of the schism to concentrate their attention very largely on Italian politics and to treat with the other powers of Europe in their capacity as Italian princes.

VII

The Changing Social Structure

Since all history deals in one way or another with human society, it is difficult to isolate for purposes of analysis that aspect of history that may properly be termed social as distinct from economic, political, cultural and so forth. One cannot discuss economic and political developments, as was evident in the two preceding chapters, without saying a good deal about the social structure within which they operated, and on which, in turn, they exercised a constantly-shaping influence. Later chapters dealing with the general culture, intellectual activity and religious life of the age will in the same way necessarily give consideration to the reciprocal relation between these and the social milieu. Yet, though we must treat of social history under all these categories, there seems to be something lacking, something that cannot be adequately dealt with in this piecemeal fashion. It is the purpose then of this chapter to attempt, at the risk of some repetition, to furnish a general picture of the structure of society, the conditions of social life and the character of social change during the first century and a half of the period that marked the transition from medieval to modern civilization.

The First Period of Transition: 1300–1450

A. ITALY: THE CRYSTALLIZATION OF AN URBAN SOCIETY

Italy was in this period predominantly a land of cities, and it is the peculiarly urban character of Italian society that differentiates it most clearly from the other European countries. Throughout central and northern Italy, with some exceptions in the more turbulent and less prosperous areas of the Papal States, the middle and upper classes, as well as the industrial proletariat, were city dwellers. This degree of urbanization, unparalleled since the most prosperous days of the Roman Empire, was the result of a long process which was virtually complete by the end of the thirteenth century. Economic and political factors worked together during the High Middle Ages to attract or coerce the landholding nobles into the cities. In Italy, earlier than elsewhere, the precocious growth of trade and industry had forced the transition from a natural economy to one in which wealth was measured in terms of money, and that wealth was concentrated in the cities. Under the impetus furnished by embryonic forms of capitalism, commerce, industry and banking far outstripped agriculture as sources of wealth. Nobles who possessed nothing but land found themselves poor by comparison with the masters of the new economic resources. More than that, money economy acted as a solvent to all hereditary bonds between the lords and their dependents. In order to keep their workers, landholders were forced to grant freedom to their serfs and to compete with the opportunities for employment offered by urban industry. Capital to finance the introduction of more intensive cultivation of market crops was needed to make agriculture pay, and those landlords who lacked capital sooner or later lost their land. For the nobles the only hope of economic survival was to migrate to the cities and gain what share they could of moneyed wealth, either by engaging in business or marrying into merchant families. Those who failed to establish themselves in the marts of trade, like those who remained on their estates, eventually lost their land to wealthy burghers, who thus themselves became a landowning class.

Economic pressures alone, however, would probably not have so completely achieved the urbanization of the rural aristocracy. They were strongly reinforced by the political attractions and pressures exerted by the communes as they fought their way to independence of emperor and pope and at the same time extended their authority over the surrounding countryside. It was possibly a desire to share in the growing political power of the communes and to use that power to secure freedom from the authority and exactions of their overlords that first led knights and petty lords to enter the cities and lend their fighting force to the communal armies. Certainly they took a major share in the struggle of the communes for independence, and also in the conquest of the *contado*, which forced the remaining landed nobles either to enter the cities or become subject to them. Thanks to their military services, the nobles, together with the old merchant families with which they mixed to form the class of magnates or *grandi*, were able to keep political control of most of the cities until their ascendancy was challenged by the rising power of the *popolo* in the second half of the thirteenth century.[1]

Residence within the city walls did not, of course, immediately transform the feudal nobles into burghers. They built high castles of brick and stone in the city streets to serve the same purpose as the castles left behind in the *contado*. At the end of the twelfth century Florence had about a hundred such towers, some owned by single families, others by associations of allied families. From these towers the nobles issued forth to carry on bloody family feuds, to overawe the lesser populace and to keep the city in a perpetual uproar. Throughout the twelfth and thirteenth centuries, the "tower families" were the leaders of both the propapal Guelf and pro-imperial Ghibelline parties, and their innate tendency toward factional violence was largely responsible for the continuation of that struggle long after the party labels had lost their original significance. Altogether they seem to have been an unmitigated nuisance to their more peaceful fellow-citizens, and when the *popolo* became strong enough to drive them from power, as it did in Florence and many other cities toward the end of the thirteenth century, one of the first acts of the popular government was to decree the removal from the towers of their threatening upper stories and to impose especially heavy penalties on nobles who committed crimes or broke the peace.

By that time, however, the *grandi* had ceased to be nobles in any sense recognizable in the feudal age. Long residence in an urban community had imposed upon even the most intransigent of the old families a certain urbanity, and in the fourteenth century little evidence of their feudal origin remained. Even their military service ceased to be significant when mercenaries replaced the communal armies. Here and there in the country districts, particularly in the Papal States and the Kingdom of Naples, a nobility of blood still survived, but it was rapidly declining. In and around Rome the weakness of both the papal government and that of the economically backward city permitted great families like the Orsini and Colonna to act like independent feudatories of almost princely status, but they were exceptions to the rule. In general the magnate class of this period formed an essentially urban aristocracy of mixed origin, the result of a fusion of the old nobility with the early plutocracy. It was distinguished from the newly rich *popolo grasso* by a longer tenure of

---

[1] See above, pp. 149-153 and 164-165.

wealth and power, and also by a greater predilection for violence, rather than by any such obvious difference in way of life as distinguished the feudal nobles from the burghers elsewhere in Europe. Though many of the magnates were landowners, their connection with the land was no longer feudal. They handled their rural estates in the same way as did the rich merchants, as an investment to be operated on a cash basis for monetary profit. Many drew their principal income from commerce or banking or from the ownership of urban real estate which the growth of the cities had greatly increased in value. An analysis of seventy-two Florentine families who were disenfranchised as magnates by the Ordinances of Justice in 1293 furnishes significant evidence of the status of that class before their political power was broken and before the economic vicissitudes and political struggles of the fourteenth century had depleted their ranks and reduced many to poverty. Among the magnates were included most of the richest proprietors of rural estates in the surrounding countryside. More than half of the magnates owned extensive urban property, houses and shops. More than a third of them were bankers or merchants of the *Arte di Calimala*, the cloth guild. And a large number, including such powerful families as the Bardi, Cavalcanti, Cerchi, Rossi and Frescobaldi were of commercial origin, having been raised from the ranks of the *popolo* during the thirteenth century, some as recently as 1267 when Charles of Anjou had knighted a number of wealthy merchants in the hope of gaining their support for the Guelf cause by raising them to the rank of magnates. The Peruzzi, on the other hand, whose capital and international banking connections were equal to those of the Bardi, with whom their name is usually coupled, were *popolani*.

This fact reminds us that, however much the magnates might have in common with the *popolo grasso* in the way of economic status and activity, the term "magnate" carried a distinct political connotation so long at least as the republican forms of government lasted. They formed a recognized political party against whom the organized *popolo* rose in revolt in many cities around the end of the thirteenth century or the beginning of the fourteenth. The acid test for defining this kind of political nobility, aside from popular opinion, was the acceptance by any member of the family of the honor of knighthood. Where it carried the stigma of political ostracism, as it did in Florence after the Ordinances of Justice, this honor rather went out of fashion, but elsewhere it continued to be highly valued, despite the fact that it had lost most of its military significance, and contemporary writers sometimes made sport of the knightly spurs on the heels of stout bankers and businessmen. Knighthood as well as other titles of nobility flourished particularly in those states where the rule of a *signore* had levelled all parties, so that nobility lost its political significance and remained simply a mark of social prestige. Emperors, always in need of ready cash, dispensed knighthoods and other titles freely on every visit to Italy. Toward the middle of the fifteenth century princes like the Visconti offered to the old noble families the dubious attractions of a semi-royal court in compensation for the power they had taken from them. By conferring titles upon the judges and administrators who served them, the princes were also in process of creating an office-holding nobility. Even republican governments frequently conferred knighthood upon a foreign *podestà* or other officer who had served them well. Bartolus of Sassoferrato, the celebrated jurist who was himself a member of the new office-holding nobility, defined nobility in the middle of the fourteenth century as a quality conferred by a prince, i.e., by pope, emperor, lesser prince or free city. This, however, was a purely legal definition. Generally speaking, except in the surviving republics, service to the prince or long possession of a landed estate and avoidance of any base mechanical art seems to have been enough to constitute the rating of a family as noble in the popular estimation. In Venice a peculiar situation led to the ascription of nobility to all members of the ruling merchant oligarchy. In Bologna, too, where a patrician oligarchy succeeded in keeping a fairly constant control of the government, members of the four major guilds (lawyers, bankers, cloth merchants and silk merchants) were reckoned as noble, for whatever that term was worth.

The varied and somewhat ambiguous status of the Italian nobility or its equivalent during this period leads to the question of how highly nobility was valued by contemporary society, and the answer is by no means clear. On the one hand there is evidence that it did not mean very much, certainly in comparison with what it still meant in the northern countries. Humanists and other men of letters frequently ridiculed the pretentions of the knights and magnates and denied any peculiar virtue to noble blood. The numerous instances of men, including many of the despots and *condottieri*, who had risen to power without the advantage of noble ancestry, as well as the ease with which men of wealth could acquire titles, must also have done much to depreciate the practical value of nobility. On the other hand, family pride was an intensely vital sentiment in the breast of every Italian, and if his family had held wealth and social position long enough to be reckoned among the great of the land — the *grandi* — he would let no one forget it. The somewhat ludicrous scramble for titles that we meet everywhere is further evidence that the Renaissance Italian was not immune to the virus of social snobbery. This is scarcely surprising, for, whatever else upper-class Italian society may have been, it was not democratic. Moreover, the unbroken prestige of nobility in the rest of Europe must have had some influence in Italy, and would probably have had more were it not for the relative isolation enjoyed by the Italian peninsula during these years when the great states of the north were torn by war. This argument, at any rate, seems to be borne out by the notable revival of noble titles and of chivalric and courtly manners in Italy after the beginning of the foreign invasions at the end of the fifteenth century. Such a revival, indeed, had already begun in the preceding half-century, after the equilibrium established by the Peace of Lodi had enabled the princes of the surviving territorial states to turn their attention to the creation of semi-royal courts in keeping with their princely power.

As has been suggested, the distinction between the class of magnates and that next in the social scale, the rich merchants, bankers, lawyers and judges who formed the *popolo grasso*, was legally and politically fairly sharply drawn, but was otherwise somewhat nebulous. On the other hand, the distinction between the latter and the poorer members of the *popolo*, the shopkeepers and guild artisans, was not a legal one at all and represented no clearly drawn political line except where, as in Florence, a specific proportion of the offices of government was allotted to the major guilds. Yet in every other respect the rich *popolani* were much closer to the magnates and had more in common with them than they had with their humbler fellow-citizens. To lump all of the non-noble together in one class as bourgeois or middle class would be to distort the picture of Italian society beyond recognition. Wealth distinguished the merchant and banking families from the city's real middle class in more obvious and practical ways than could any title of knighthood or nobility.

Owing their position primarily to money, the *popolani grassi*, like so many of those families whose earlier acquisition of wealth now gave them status as magnates, were the products of capitalist enterprise. The techniques of capitalism made possible the rapid accumulation of wealth and its unlimited expansion through reinvestment. In this respect capitalist economy differed radically from either feudal economy, which was based upon the hereditary tenure of land, or the limited and regulated retail business of the small guildsmen. It was an economy founded upon individual enterprise and calculated risk, upon intangible resources of credit that were capable of indefinite expansion but also of sudden contraction, and it left its mark on the society that profited by it. Above all, it was a dynamic force, making society more mobile than had been possible in either the feudal or pre-capitalist urban economy. Under its impetus new families were constantly rising to wealth. But great profits could not be made without corresponding risks, and many of the wealthiest families were ruined by bankruptcy, especially during the economic crises that marked the middle years of the fourteenth century. To guard against these disastrous vicissitudes, it was a common practice among the new rich as among the older magnates to invest a part of their surplus capital in rural land or urban real estate, which though less profitable than business was also less risky, and besides had the advantage of carrying with it an aura of social respectability. Such investments, together with the opportunities furnished by partnerships and firms for inactive participation in business through the mere investment of capital, were especially attractive to the second or third generation of wealth, to the grandsons of the acquisitive entrepreneurs who had raised their families from the ranks of the middle class. These beneficiaries of inherited wealth were free to live a leisured existence, to ape the manners of the magnates or to devote themselves to the learned professions or the liberal arts. Or, if the money was not wisely invested, they might simply slip back into the class of the petty bourgeoisie, thus completing a cycle still familiar in modern society.

Much of the foregoing pattern of behavior was characteristic of a large part of the *grandi* as well as of the rich *popolani*. But there were other ways in which the development of capitalism left a peculiar psychological imprint on these entrepreneurs who acquired wealth after the commercial revolution that marked the end of the thirteenth and the beginning of the fourteenth century. During the following century and a half, the Italians perfected the techniques of business association, credit, exchange, bookkeeping and all the calculating arts that distinguish modern capitalism. The sedentary merchant or financier, who directed his far-flung enterprises by correspondence with his agents and calculated his risks with an eye on the double entries in his ledgers, replaced the older type of itinerant merchant, who travelled to the Champagne fairs or mixed trade with piracy on the high seas and fought bloody naval battles with the merchants of rival cities. The latter had much in common with the adventurous and bellicose spirit of the nobles, with whom men of his type mingled to form the magnate aristocracy of the thirteenth century communes and to take their full share in the inter-city wars and blood-thirsty factional fights that marked the century. The sedentary capitalist of the later period was by comparison less physically adventurous. The risks he took could be measured in terms of money, and the struggle for survival in a period marked by repeated economic crises bred in him a cautious regard for accurate mathematical calculation. It is significant that the members of the new plutocracy no longer fought the battles of their party or city, but left the business of fighting to the hired *condottiere*, who was himself a calculating entrepreneur. More and more, too, they left the business of government to the *signore*, to whom they paid taxes in return for the boon of civic peace. A careful "bourgeois" ethic, in short, tended to replace the freebooting spirit of the pioneers of capitalism. Yet it was an ethic quite different from that of the medieval guildsman. It expressed the attitudes of an acquisitive and competitive society, and stressed the virtues needed for survival in a capitalist economy. Many of the maxims contained in the books on domestic economy by the Florentine writers, Matteo Palmieri and Leo Battista Alberti, might indeed have struck a responsive chord in the canny soul of Benjamin Franklin.

A further effect of the growth of capitalism, of which more will be said in a later chapter, was to stimulate the spread of lay education and the development of lay culture. Business conducted by means of written instruments of credit, bookkeeping and correspondence demanded a fair amount of education of everyone participating in it, while the accumulation of liquid capital furnished a growing class with the means and leisure to cultivate the higher forms of culture. There was no radical break with the feudal and ecclesiastical traditions of the Middle Ages, but increasingly throughout the fourteenth and fifteenth centuries Italian culture was shaped by the wealthy urban laymen. Among these, of course, must be included the *signori* and their courtiers, whose spiritual kinship with the capitalist entrepreneur we have noted more than once. In a paradoxical sense the upper clergy may also be included, for the recipients of the higher ecclesiastical benefices were almost without exception recruited from the wealthy urban classes, or from among the scholars and men of letters whose talents had won them a place in cultivated society. To a very large extent they shared the lay culture of the classes from which they were drawn, and their contributions to it are frequently indistinguishable from those of the laymen. It is this common culture, more than anything else, that lends to wealthy Italian society its somewhat misleading appearance of classless homogeneity, and has led some historians to underestimate the importance of the class distinctions that still remained.

It was in any case a culture common only to the upper classes. The urban middle class — the shopkeepers and masters of the artisan guilds — were but little touched by it or by the changing social values that went with it. Most men of this class were probably able to read, for lay education was becoming increasingly common, and the participation in government of minor guildsmen chosen by lot in fourteenth-century Florence suggests a fairly widespread literacy. But they could scarcely have read many of the books that influenced the thought of the upper classes, even had they been able to do so, for in the period before the invention of printing books were shockingly expensive. Nor is there reason to believe that changing social conditions aroused in them a desire for a culture different from that which had satisfied their ancestors. The minor guildsmen, indeed, remained throughout this period a normally conservative class, instinctively opposed to change. Their economic life was bounded by the city walls. They served the local market, and they retained the forms of corporate monopoly and regulation that had been characteristic of local urban economy for centuries. Some in each generation, it is true, were able to take advantage of the opportunities furnished by a fluid economy to acquire wealth. And some gifted individuals were able to acquire the higher education or artistic training needed to raise them above the status of artisan. Many of the writers and artists who gained admittance to the cultivated society of the wealthy and powerful were sprung from the ranks of the middle class. But by the mere fact of rising from their class, these exceptional individuals left the character of the class as a whole unchanged.

The situation of the lower classes — the propertyless proletariat of the industrial cities and the rural sharecroppers or wage earners who had replaced the medieval serfs on the land — was very different from that of the guildsmen whose corporate organization gave them a privileged status. They were the products of capitalist economy as much as were the bankers and merchants, its victims rather than its beneficiaries. The urban workers in particular had none of the innate conservatism of the guild masters. They had, indeed, no old traditions to which to cling. They were a new class created by large-scale industry in the latter part of the thirteenth century. Economically enslaved and deprived of all political rights, they were filled with a smouldering resentment that threatened at any moment to break forth in violent action. But the social unrest in both city and country which was bred by the changes that accompanied the expansion of money economy and the introduction of capitalist methods was not peculiar to Italy. It was a common European phenomenon in the fourteenth century.

The contrast between the appalling poverty of the proletarian workers and the wealth of the upper classes furnishes ample proof that, however much it may have served to break down the hereditary caste barriers of the feudal age, the growth of capitalist economy had not brought a greater social equality. A homogeneous population had, in fact, never existed in the great trading cities; but by the beginning of the fourteenth century the accumulated capital that had tended to close the social gap between the *popolo grasso* and the magnates had vastly broadened the economic gap between the rich and the poor. Until fairly recent times, historians of the Renaissance paid little attention to the less fortunate members of Italian society, except perhaps to note the contrast of wealth and poverty as one of the many contrasts characteristic of the age. There is reason for this. The short and simple annals of the poor have left little material for the historian to seize upon, while the evidences of wealth, recorded in letters, portrayed in art and embodied in architecture, are still abundantly available. Further, historians of the Italian Renaissance have commonly been interested in the society of the period primarily because of the culture it produced, and that culture belonged almost exclusively to the wealthy classes. What was new in this transitional age appeared at the economic extremes of society. Both extremes must be considered, but it was the upper which set the tone for what was most characteristic in the civilization of the age.

As was natural in a society in which wealth was a primary factor in establishing status, the upper-class Italian made no attempt to hide his wealth under a bushel. Whether it was acquired by business enterprise or political power, the result was much the same. Merchant, banker, prince, prelate and *condottiere* alike flaunted for all to see the wealth that was the gauge of success. A liberal display of wealth was, indeed, necessary to maintain credit and prestige, and it was probably inspired as much by careful calculation as by open-handed prodigality. Much money was spent on the building and decoration of churches and on other pious enterprises, for thus the patron acquired credit both in this world and the next. Much went also to the patronage of art and letters, for thus, too, the patron not only satisfied his personal tastes, but also gained a double credit with his own generation and with posterity. A great deal of money was also spent to achieve more transitory effects. Public festivals of all sorts furnished opportunities for competitive display. They formed a colorful part of the life of every city throughout this period, though they did not reach their fullest elaboration till after the middle of the fifteenth century. The Renaissance Italians of all classes obviously loved a parade, and much ingenuity and taste, both good and bad, were expended on the construction of allegorical figures to be carried in procession, or floats depicting scenes from classical mythology, local history or Christian story. The city chroniclers seem never to tire of cataloguing the priceless apparel worn on such occasions by the retinues of princes, the local magnates or the members of the major guilds. Domestic festivals, marriages, christenings and so forth, were also occasions for sumptuous entertainments and ostentatious display. Contemporary descriptions of the banquets that graced such occasions suggest a volume of consumption that was, to say the least, conspicuous. Clothing, too, both male and female, but especially that of the patrician ladies, was becoming increasingly elaborate and costly. The frequency of sumptuary laws designed to limit the ruinous expense of ladies' apparel suggests both the necessity and the inefficacy of such regulations. In republican Bologna, for example, a series of edicts, from the law of 1294 forbidding the use of veils with gold thread to the comprehensive ordinances issued by the papal legate, Cardinal Bessarion, in 1453, give detailed and frequently amusing evidence of the city fathers' persistent but obviously losing battle with feminine vanity.

The impression of a somewhat vulgar display of wealth left by the accounts of public and private festivals and the futile sumptuary laws is modified, however, by other evidence which demonstrates the growing refinement of taste that characterized the social life of the wealthier classes. The town houses of the magnates were no longer fortified towers. The rich of the fourteenth and fifteenth centuries built palaces designed, as modern real estate advertisements would put it, for gracious living, with spacious airy rooms, cool shaded courts, gardens and orchards. Furniture, textiles and plate were the products of skilled artisans who had raised craftsmanship to the level of fine art. Books, pictures and statues showed a growing preoccupation with intellectual and aesthetic interests, as did the high level of conversation reported, for example, in Giovanni da Prato's famous *novella*, the *Paradiso degli Alberti*. In that charming picture of Florentine society in the late fourteenth century, as recalled by its author, perhaps with some idealization, in his later years, the scene soon shifts from the city mansion to the country villa, where Alberti and his guests could continue their learned talk in the most pleasant rural surroundings. A villa was, indeed, an indispensable adjunct to every wealthy family, and paradoxically nothing demonstrates more clearly the essentially urban character of Italian society than the prominent place the villa plays in the romances and other works reflecting the life of the period. The city was the center of the patrician's active life; the villa a refuge for his hours of ease. There he could escape not only the heat and plague that beset the city streets, but also the cares of business and the dangerous game of politics. And there, like Horace on his Sabine farm, he could enjoy for a time a sophisticated simplicity that would probably soon have lost its charms had he been exiled permanently from his city home.

While this refined society rested solidly upon a monetary foundation, it also opened its doors freely to men whose chief claim to recognition was intellectual or aesthetic achievement. This was particularly true of men of learning and letters, for the artists who worked with their hands had not yet fully emerged from the ranks of the artisans and still bore something of the stigma attached to manual labor. Among musicians the composer ranked higher than the professional performer. The company represented as guests of the merchant magnate Alberti in the *Paradiso*, for example, included the humanist chancellor of Florence, Coluccio Salutati, the Paduan physician, Marsilio di Santa Sofia, the philosopher, Biagio Pelacani, the humanist friar, Luigi Marsigli, and the blind composer, Francesco Landini, not to mention the author himself who was a noted jurist, architect and lecturer on Dante at the university of Florence. It is to be noted, too, that the ladies took their full share in the learned discussion here recorded. In this, as in other *novelle* of the period, they appear as distinct personalities, rather than as the idealized conceptions of chivalric romance. Women's place was still largely in the home, and it would be an exaggeration to say that they enjoyed equality with men. Yet there is ample evidence that they were frequently given an education like that of their brothers, and they played an increasingly active and independent rôle in social life, not only in the princely courts but also in such patrician families as the Alberti.

The place accorded by cultivated society to women as well as to men of talent argues an awareness and valuation of individual personality that goes far to justify Burckhardt's thesis that individualism was the predominant characteristic of the Italian Renaissance. Individualism, however, is a protean concept, and Burckhardt may have laid upon it a greater weight than it could bear. Certainly it was not an entirely new phenomenon, first made manifest in fourteenth-century Italy. Nevertheless, it seems altogether probable that the multiform, fluid and broadly educated society of the Italian cities should have offered opportunities and incentives for the development of individual personality far greater than had the caste-bound and corporately organized society of medieval Europe. True, the feudal age abounded in rugged individualists, but the individualism of the feudal nobles was circumscribed by the traditions and inherited status of their caste. It meant little more than the free play of ego and arrogance. With but two choices of a career, knighthood or the Church, the medieval noble had little opportunity to develop his peculiar talents or tastes. And in both clerical and burgher society, the weight of corporate solidarity was thrown heavily into the scales on the side of conformity. In the Italian cities, on the other hand, the partial disappearance during the Renaissance of hereditary caste distinctions, together with the greater variety of opportunity furnished by a complex economic, political and cultural milieu, combined to free the individual from the necessity of following an inherited pattern and enabled him to choose a career or develop tastes and interests suited to his peculiar personality.

At the same time, there were many factors in the urban society of fourteenth- and fifteenth-century Italy that not only made possible a more autonomous assertion of individual personality, but also gave it positive encouragement. Burckhardt noted particularly the incentive given to individualism by the hectic political life of the city-states, both despotic and republican. He might have found still stronger support for his argument had he been more aware of the character of the economic activity of the Italian cities. Capitalism acted as a solvent on the corporate forms of medieval urban society and furnished a powerful incentive to autonomous individual enterprise. If a new spirit of individualism characterized the upper classes of Italy in the fourteenth and fifteenth centuries, it was as clearly manifest in the calculating audacity of the entrepreneur, whose success in a highly competitive business world depended solely upon his knowledge and judgment, as it was in the self-reliance of the despot, the demagogue or the *condottiere*. Finally, it was the accumulation of surplus capital, and the opportunities afforded by capitalist techniques for passive investment, that created a class of leisured *rentiers*, who had the freedom and the means to devote their time and energies to the cultivation of any personal taste or interest. Deprived increasingly by despotism or oligarchy of an active share in political life, the members of this class were bound by no sense of responsibility. They could make of themselves what they chose, and they could develop to the fullest such gifts as they had been endowed with by nature. And for such dilettantism, the growth of a variegated lay culture offered an ever-broadening scope.

Whether the factors that thus fostered the development of autonomous personality, both in those self-reliant individuals who thrust their way to wealth and power and in those irresponsible dilettanti who raised the egocentric enjoyment of life to the level of art, also tended to breed a growing immorality remains an open question. The traditional conception of the "wicked Renaissance," it is true, applies more particularly to the period after 1450 than to the preceding century and a half; but many historians have found even in the earlier period a degree of flagrant immorality that they regarded as peculiar to Italy. There is evidence to support this opinion, but it is by no means conclusive, and much contrary evidence can be found pointing to the existence of deep piety and sound moral standards. It may be only that we are more fully informed about the Italian society of this period than about that of other countries or earlier times. The more closely modern scholars have examined the fragmentary sources of social history in any European country the more evidence they have found of violence, brutality and gross immorality. If the Renaissance Italians seem to have had a penchant for more artistically conceived crime and more highly original sin, it may be only that these nefarious activities were more fully and dramatically related by their literary contemporaries. Nevertheless, it seems inherently probable that the dislocation of political and economic life and the disintegration of traditional institutions, which characterized this transitional age in Italian history, did in fact unleash passions and weaken moral bonds. Wealth and power untrammeled by traditional sanctions might well have had that effect; and the freer play of personality that permitted the Renaissance Italians to develop a brilliant lay culture was not always a force within themselves making for righteousness.

B. The Northern Countries: the Decline of Feudal and Chivalric Society

When we turn from urban Italy to the more feudal and agrarian lands beyond the Alps, we find a social structure which, while affected by many of the factors that we have seen operating in Italy, was in one respect at least profoundly different. The northern nobles, save for rare exceptions, were not drawn into the cities and hence did not merge with the wealthy urban class. They still formed a predominantly landholding class, the distinguishing characteristics of which were noble birth and a congenital propensity to warfare and plunder. Their spheres of activity were the castle, the camp and the court. Even when attendance at a royal or princely court brought them into the capital city, they did not become part of the city's society. However desperate their need for money, they shunned the marts of trade and regarded with mingled envy and contempt the merchants and financiers, whose profitable activity they could not emulate without losing their privileged noble status. The northern nobles thus continued through the fourteenth and fifteenth centuries to live, as far as changing conditions permitted, within the traditional patterns of social life that had been established in the preceding period. They were patterns, however, that corresponded less and less closely to the realities of economic, political and military activity and were becoming increasingly artificial. Reflected in the secular literature of the period, they leave an impression of decadence, of the decay of a society clinging to forms of social behavior that have lost contact with reality. It is this impression that has led many historians to regard these centuries as the "waning of the Middle Ages."

The noble class had come into being during the early feudal era, and its primary characteristics were shaped by the brutal necessities of that rude, impoverished and lawless age. Then, under the more fortunate circumstances of the twelfth and thirteenth centuries it had acquired the graces of courtly culture and chivalrous manners, somewhat tempered by religious idealism without, however, losing the practical mastery of political power and military force that had won for it its dominant position in society. A happy combination of economic and political circumstances, indeed, operated to make these centuries of the High Middle Ages a kind of golden age for noble society. It was a period of expanding agricultural prosperity, in which the revival of commerce, the growth of cities and the resulting introduction of money into feudal economy worked to the advantage of the landholding classes, enabling them to cultivate a more refined, more leisured and more courtly social life than had been possible for their impecunious ancestors. At the same time, the growing power of central government had progressed far enough to assure a fair degree of security and stability, but not yet far enough to threaten seriously the jurisdictional powers or independent status of the feudal lords. But money economy and central government were essentially alien to feudalism, and their continued growth could not but be disastrous to feudal society, undermining the foundations of its real power and thereby sapping the vigor of its characteristic culture at the roots. By the end of the thirteenth century, the deleterious effects of these forces were becoming apparent. During the fourteenth and fifteenth centuries, they combined to deprive the nobles of a large part of the solid foundation for their claims to social superiority, though those claims were as yet unchallenged and were, indeed, asserted all the more aggressively because no longer securely grounded.

We have already seen how the continued infiltration of money economy into the manorial system tended to impoverish the landholding classes generally in France, England and Germany, and also the steps by which kings and princes, aided by monetary taxation, concentrated in their own hands political, military and jurisdictional powers that had been dispersed among the landed lords during the feudal age. The crisis through which the noble class passed in these centuries was rendered more acute by a prolonged agricultural depression, by the rising prices resulting from monetary inflation, and by the devastation and social disorder caused by wars and epidemics of unprecedented magnitude and duration. Finally, warfare on a national scale forced drastic changes in military organization and technique, which deprived the nobles of their monopoly of armed force, laid their castles open to siege by artillery, substituted royal armies for the feudal levy, and brought the heavily armored knight to the verge of obsolescence. The process by which the feudal noble was transformed into the royal courtier, and the knight into the professional soldier, was not completed in this period, but it was well begun.

Though these changes were of fundamental importance, their results were as yet scarcely visible to the eyes of contemporaries. To all outward appearances the noble class remained, and would long remain, what it had been in the Middle Ages: a hereditary aristocracy, its superiority over all commoners guaranteed by tradition, titles and vested interests, and by the hierarchical conception of the nature of society which gave its position on the upper levels of the social pyramid a kind of divine sanction. The monarchy and the bourgeoisie, the twin enemies of feudalism, might work to deprive the nobles of power, but did not deny their right to a privileged status.

The borderline between noble and non-noble was probably never as clearly drawn in practice as in theory, but it was certainly much clearer in the northern countries than in Italy. Nobility in these feudal lands was primarily a hereditary quality. On the continent all sons of a noble were noble, provided they could maintain their status by living nobly, that is, by avoiding all gainful employment in commerce, industry, finance or other bourgeois activities. This normally implied income from land or from such offices in the royal court, administration or army as were regarded as noble. In France all members of the nobility enjoyed certain privileges, such as exemption from the *taille* and other direct taxes, which sharpened the distinction between nobles and commons and made nobility a quality legally verifiable. In England the situation was somewhat different. There, only the great baronial families whose heads were entitled to a seat in the House of Lords were regarded, strictly speaking, as noble. Due to the rule of primogeniture which in England assured the inheritance of lands and titles by the eldest son or nearest heir, the younger sons of the peers and their descendants tended to lose their noble status and join the great mass of the landholding aristocracy, the knights and squires, who in France would be classed as *petite noblesse*, and who were represented in the House of Commons. These formed the class that came to be called the gentry, a class not legally noble, yet distinguished by "gentle" birth and manner of life from the urban burghers and the lower classes. As in the case of the continental nobility, gentility generally implied the means to live on income from land or from the more dignified professions and offices. The line between gentle and common was not, however, as strictly drawn as the corresponding distinction on the continent. Since the gentry did not form a legally distinct estate of the realm with special privileges, as in France, the dividing line between the gentry and the burghers was more easily crossed in both directions. Deprived by the rule of primogeniture of a share in the family estates, the younger sons of the gentry frequently entered merchant companies as apprentices or married into merchant families. Conversely, a London alderman might use the fortune made in trade to buy an estate in the country, and in course of time his descendants would be accepted by the gentry of the county, and would take their place among the Justices of the Peace. Such cases were as yet, however, exceptional. They became more common in the following period.

Despite such occasional intrusions, the English gentry, like the continental nobility, belonged to the class which had found expression for its highest aspirations in the institution and ideals of chivalry. To these they still paid more than lip service, but there was during this period a notable decline in both the ideals and practice of chivalry, as they ceased to conform to the changing conditions of the fourteenth and fifteenth centuries. The institution of chivalry had grown originally out of the circumstances of feudal warfare, and its ideals, though refined by religion and the cult of courtly love, were primarily those of the feudal warrior. As a working institution it fitted an age when wars were fought on a small scale between bands of knights who were performing the semi-voluntary service they owed as feudal vassals. The Crusades were an exception to this rule, but there the knights fought as volunteers performing the service they owed to God. In addition to the call of loyalty to his lord, the medieval knight's principal motives for fighting were natural inclination and the desire to gain personal glory. If thirst for plunder and the opportunity to hold rich prisoners for ransom was also a motive, it was less openly avowed. Plunder, of course, was generally at the expense of common folk, for whom the knights had nothing but contempt. But the actual enemies they met in the shock of hand-to-hand fighting were fellow-members of the order of chivalry. As such they were to be treated with all courtesy and generosity. No national sentiment embittered the relation between foes and, in the shifting complex of feudal politics, the enemy of today might be the friend of tomorrow. From the knights' point of view, battle was little more than an exciting sport, a sort of super-tournament, in which the individual knight had every opportunity to display his skill and valor, to win renown and do honor to his lady. So long as warfare retained its feudal character, chivalry remained a vigorous institution because it conformed to actual military practice. But the wars of the fourteenth and fifteenth centuries were of a different sort, of larger scale and longer duration, and accompanied by changes in organization and technique that made chivalry increasingly impractical.

The most obvious blow to chivalry as a method of warfare was the appearance of common-born, but well-armed, foot-soldiers on the field of battle, who proved again and again that a mixed force of archers and men-at-arms could defeat larger numbers of the best heavy cavalry in the world. But that was not the only lesson taught by the battles of Crécy, Poitiers and Agincourt and a host of lesser engagements, though the French knights were slow to learn it. It was the undisciplined spirit of feudal chivalry, the search for personal glory at all costs, that bred the inspired lunacy of French tactics at Crécy and elsewhere. Even the English knights, though better disciplined than the French, were capable of jeopardizing the success of a campaign to satisfy their chivalrous vanity. During the early stages of the war, forces on both sides frequently interrupted a campaign and turned aside from their objective to engage in pointless encounters for no other end than fun and glory. The pages of Froissart are full of such escapades. But as the war went on, fighting became too serious a business for indulgence in such lighthearted adventure. When it began to seem more important to win a nation's battles than to lose them gallantly, the spirit of feudal chivalry gradually gave way to the disciplined courage of the professional soldier. The forms of chivalry still remained, with increasing elaboration, but by the fifteenth century they were being relegated from the field of battle to the more congenial setting of tournament and court.

It was the increasingly mercenary character of warfare in this period that more than anything else created an atmosphere antagonistic to the spirit of feudal chivalry. Though never averse to plunder, the medieval knight had fought at his own expense, and so had retained a kind of amateur standing. During the fourteenth century, however, the growing disparity between falling income and the rising cost of plate armor, together with long terms of service, made pay a necessity even for nobles who owed service as vassals of the crown. After the early stages of the war, both sides depended increasingly upon mercenaries. Aside from the notorious "Free Companies" which fought wherever there was pay and in time of truce plundered the countryside, the English army was from the beginning composed of companies raised on contract by nobles or knights who acted as military entrepreneurs. Under Charles V and again toward the end of the war, the French adopted a similar system. Under these circumstances pay, plunder and ransom money became aims more and more openly avowed. Even Froissart, who does his best to place chivalry in an attractive light, has much to say about the preoccupation of knights with finance. In the early stages of the war noble prisoners were normally treated with much courtesy and were allowed to give their parole pending payment of ransom. But as time went on this chivalrous attitude toward the defeated wore thin, and we meet frequent stories of brutal treatment of noble prisoners, and even of noble ladies, in an effort to wring from them a higher ransom than they could afford.

The degree to which warfare had become a business enterprise and fighting a trade in the fourteenth century is so well illustrated by the matter-of-fact account of his career given to Froissart by a Gascon gentleman in 1388 that it is worth quoting, at least in part.

The first time I bore arms was under the Captal de Buch at the battle of Poitiers [on the English side]; by good luck I made three prisoners, who paid me . . . 4,000 francs. The following year I was in Prussia with the Count de Foix and his cousin, the Captal, under whose command I was. . . . At this time there was a truce between France and England, but the King of Navarre continued the war on his own personal quarrel with the regent of France. The Count de Foix returned to his own country, and my master and myself remained in the pay of the King of Navarre, who made a very sharp war upon France. At length a treaty was concluded, according to the terms of which it was necessary for all men-at-arms and free companies to quit the fortresses and castles held by them. Many companions, who had learned the art of war under different commanders, held councils as to what they should do, for, of course, they must live. All marched into Burgundy, upwards of 12,000 in number, and of these three or four thousand as good men-at-arms as any that could be found. . . . I was with them as a captain in many engagements, and I think we showed what we could do at the battle of Brignais, where we overpowered the Constable of France with full 2,000 lances, knights and squires. This battle, indeed, was of great advantage to the companions, who enriched themselves by good prisoners and by the towns and castles which they took in the archbishopric of Lyons. After this, by an arrangement with the pope and the cardinal, the largest number of the companions marched into Lombardy to serve the Marquis of Montferrat, who was at that time at war with the Lord of Milan; but myself and several others remained behind, having possession of many towns and upwards of sixty castles. . . . Shortly after I joined Sir John Aymeray in his intended attack upon the town and castle of Sancerre. . . . I also served in Brittany under Sir Hugh Calverley, where I made such good prisoners that they paid me 2,000 francs. I then accompanied Sir Hugh into Spain against Don Pedro, and when treaties were entered into between Don Pedro and the Prince of Wales, who wished to enter Spain, I was then in company with Sir Hugh Calverley and returned to Aquitaine with him. The war was now renewed between the King of France and the prince; it was vigorously carried on, and we had enough to do. I will tell you how I conquered the town and castle of Thurie in the Albigeois, which castle has since been worth to me about 100,000 francs. . . .[2]

And so on. The whole story is too long to recount. We may note, however, that the town was taken by no knightly exploit, but by a clever

[2] Sir John Froissart, *The Chronicles of England, France and Spain* (Everyman's Library), p. 311 ff.

ruse, the narrator and his followers entering the undefended gates disguised as women bearing water from a nearby spring.

The foregoing account illustrates a significant aspect of the disintegration of the order of chivalry, membership in which had once been aspired to as a matter of course by all who were entitled to it by birth and training. Froissart's acquaintance, after more than thirty years of apparently profitable service — if one can take the word of a Gascon at its face value — was still a squire. And the numerous instances cited in the *Chronicles* of kings or commanders offering on the eve of battle to knight all who wished to receive the honor is sufficient evidence that he had remained a squire from choice rather than necessity. A great many squires evidently felt that the honor of knighthood was no longer worth the added expense entailed in maintaining knightly estate. A squire's status was no longer a bar to service in the heavy cavalry nor even to participation in tilts and tournaments. The companies of men-at-arms are almost always referred to as including knights and squires. Not only the rising cost of plate armor for both man and horse which was required of a knight — whereas a squire could get along with less complete armor — but also the incidental expenses of knighthood, including the gold spurs and other privileged ornaments, the maintenance of a squire and servants, *largesse* and other obligations of knightly rank were making the honor too expensive for the majority of the lesser nobility. By the fifteenth century only a minority of the French nobles were knights, and in England, where that honor carried with it a number of onerous administrative and judicial services to the crown, the number was probably still smaller. The acts "in distraint of knighthood," designed in the days of Edward I to force those of the landed gentry who had the necessary property qualification to become knights, became in time a mere fiscal expedient, since most of those eligible preferred to pay a fine rather than to accept the expensive honor. The efforts of the French kings to encourage knighthood seem to have been equally abortive.

As knighthood lost much of its practical value and the exclusive privileges that had pertained to it, it became a more purely decorative honor. To this gradual change in the character of knighthood, which seems to have begun about the middle of the fourteenth century, the kings and princes contributed in two divergent ways. On the one hand, they robbed it of something of its exclusively military character by conferring it on wealthy aldermen, jurists and administrators. On the other hand, they created within the universal order of chivalry special decorative orders, such as the English Order of the Garter (1340), the French Order of the Star (1352), the magnificent Burgundian Order of the Golden Fleece (1430), and some dozen others. These orders had no other function than to enhance the prestige of the monarchy by the performance of elaborate and colorful ceremonies at court. They were highly valued, however, because of their exclusive character and as evidences of royal favor, for to acquire favor with the king was becoming a major aim in the life of those nobles fortunate enough to secure a position at court.

In this as in other respects the German knights formed an exception to the general rule. The disintegration of the Empire had left Germany without a royal court, and the courts of the territorial princes proved to be inadequate substitutes. Moreover, due to an historical development peculiar to Germany, the term "knight" had come to be applied to a distinct class of petty landholding lords, the *Ritterschaft*, a class distinguished by hereditary status and not merely by the individually acquired honor of knighthood. Always jealous of their rights, the knights, and especially those "imperial knights" who owned no superior but the emperor, were the natural enemies of the princes and the source of much lawlessness and private war. Under the pressure of falling income from land, many of them resorted to brigandage and became *Raubritter*. The term *Ritter*, which in the twelfth and thirteenth centuries had designated simply a member of the order of chivalry, had thus acquired a new connotation, and in the process had lost some of the ideal nuances connected with the concept of knighthood.

The political and social situation in Germany was, however, exceptional. Elsewhere, due to the growing power of the monarchy and increasing centralization of government, royal courts were beginning to replace the baronial courts of the feudal era as the focal centers of aristocratic society, as nobles impoverished by declining income from land sought to recoup their fortunes with the offices and pensions at the disposal of the crown. But the full development of royal courts in both England and France was interrupted and retarded by periods of feeble royal government, by rebellions and civil wars. The long insanity of Charles VI, followed by the English occupation of northern France during the early years of Charles VII, checked the natural growth of a royal court in France, as did the feeble reign of Henry VI and the Wars of the Roses in England. Neither Charles VII nor Louis XI was personally the type of *grand monarch* around whom a splendid royal court could grow. Nor were the nobles who reduced France to anarchy during the period of the Burgundian-Armagnac feuds, or those who rebelled against Louis XI in the League of the Common Weal, the stuff of whom courtiers are made. Similarly in England the transformation of the aristocracy into courtiers had to await the restoration of strong government under the first two Tudors and the destruction of the system of livery and maintenance which provided the English barons of the mid-fifteenth century with a private armed force. But what a royal court could become was already foreshadowed in the richly endowed court of the dukes of Burgundy, the wealthiest princes in the West and royal in all but name. Here in the paradoxical setting of the great Netherland cities, the forms of chivalry and of feudal society came to a last magnificent bloom. But it was a blossoming made possible by an economy and a governmental system that were essentially foreign to the conditions that had originally produced these social forms, and it had something of the artificiality of a hothouse plant, the roots of which are not deeply sunk in its native soil.

The Burgundian court enjoyed its period of greatest brilliance during the long, prosperous and relatively peaceful reign of Philip the Good (1419–67). It was, indeed, largely the creation of that vain but canny statesman and it bore the marks both of his personality and his policy. All contemporary witnesses were vastly impressed by the sumptuous entertainments he offered — and they were meant to be. The chronicles describe in endless detail the rich clothing and ornaments worn by the prince and his household and the staggering variety and quantity of food served at interminable banquets, as well as the ingenious spectacles, pantomimes, acrobatic exhibitions and allegorical tableaux that at intervals during the meal gave the guests a respite from the monotony of overeating. On one occasion a gigantic pastry was brought in containing an orchestra of twelve musicians, and when the pie was opened the musicians began to play. At the famous banquet where the duke and his courtiers took the Vow of the Pheasant to go on a crusade — a crusade, incidentally, which never took place — the duke paid for the costumes of the guests and attendants, all in matching colors. The records of the ducal treasury in the archives at Dijon bear evidence to the insane expense of all this conspicuous consumption, but there was method in the duke's madness. Lacking a royal title, but determined to play a royal rôle on the European stage, Philip advertised to the world the unrivalled financial resources that made him in fact the equal of kings. Wealth alone, however, was not enough to make a royal court. The prestige of the prince demanded that he be surrounded by formal ceremony and attended by a hierarchy of court officials at every hour of the day, all regulated by the most minute protocol. He had also to play the generous and discriminating patron of the arts. Finally, he called into his service the still unbroken prestige of nobility and chivalry, filling the court with nobles of ancient lineage from his own estates and abroad, and creating in the Golden Fleece the most magnificent of all the orders of chivalry.

Passionately addicted to all the forms of chivalry, Philip the Good spared no expense in arranging the tournaments and jousts that furnished a large part of the pageantry and entertainment of the court. This favorite sport of the medieval knights had never lost its popularity, despite the disapproval of the Church and of some of the more practical-minded rulers. But it was becoming increasingly a formalized game in proportion as it lost resemblance to actual warfare. The *melée* or sham battle fought between groups of knights, which had been the heart of the medieval tournament, was by the fifteenth century almost entirely replaced by the more carefully regulated jousts. In these stylized encounters between individual knights, clad from head to foot in full plate armor, there was little danger of the contestants being seriously injured except by accident. They must nevertheless have furnished a thrilling and colorful spectacle, as the rival knights, horse and man fully caparisoned, thundered down the lists toward one another with plumes flying and lances at rest, to the accompaniment of blaring trumpets, pounding hoofs and clanking armor. The whole spectacle was further framed in color by the costumes of the noble lords and ladies in the stands, by the pavillions of the contesting knights, by their waving pennants and all the pomp and circumstance of heraldry. Nothing could have demonstrated in more visible form the status of the noble knights as members of a superior race. Here in the well-ordered lists, these heirs to a great tradition could maintain the illusion that they were still the mainstay of the state and the sole significant force in society, and they could easily forget how other noble knights had plodded on foot through the mud at Agincourt to meet their death at the hands of base-born archers. If the allegorical trappings and ritual of such famous jousts as the "Passage of Arms of the Fountain of Tears" seem a little precious; if the fanciful emprises undertaken by knights-errant for the love of their ladies seem too consciously borrowed from literary tradition; if, in short, the whole procedure seems little more than an elaborate game for the amusement of an idle court, it was nevertheless a game that held a profound significance for the noble class and it had to be played out with the utmost solemnity. By maintaining the prestige of nobility it also served to enhance the prestige of monarchy, which was in process of reducing the nobles to the status of courtiers, and so the tournament remained a standard part of the pageantry of every royal court for another hundred years.

"Coming to the third estate, it is the estate of the good towns, of merchants and of laboring men, of whom it is not becoming to give such a long exposition as of the others, because it is hardly possible to attribute great qualities to them, as they are of a servile degree."[3] It was thus that Chastellain, the court chronicler of Philip the Good and Charles the Bold, achieved his transition from discussion of the nobility to consideration of the status of the bourgeoisie. We may follow his example without sharing

[3] Quoted in J. Huizinga, *The Waning of the Middle Ages* (London, 1948), p. 49 ff.

his prejudice, though the latter is worth noting as symptomatic of the Burgundian noble's unrealistic conception of the society he saw about him in the rich Netherlandish cities. For Chastellain, the burghers, whose wealth made the splendor of the Burgundian court possible, were simply villeins. For many modern historians they have been simply the "middle class," that middle class whose perennial rise is a commonplace of all history texts. That the bourgeois were rising during these centuries there can be no doubt, but to envisage them as making up an undifferentiated middle class is almost as unrealistic as Chastellain's prejudiced view.

Urban society had never been homogeneous, and in these transitional centuries the growth of capitalism was introducing further diversity and widening the gap between the various levels of economic and social standing. In every city larger than a market town, a group of wealthy families formed a patrician class, a clearly recognized urban aristocracy, proud of their position and ruthless in maintaining it. In the majority of cities they monopolized the offices and directed the policies of the municipal government. And, since their power and social status depended upon wealth, they displayed their wealth with an ostentation that aroused the hatred of those less well endowed, among whom were numbered not only the city's poor but also many a threadbare noble. The noble literature of the period abounds in expressions of indignation at the burghers' presumptuous display of a luxury in food, clothing, houses and furniture, which many nobles could not afford. The same attitude is reflected in the frequent royal edicts issued in the vain attempt to keep the burghers from dressing as richly as their betters or from wearing those special colors and materials that were regarded as pertaining exclusively to the nobility. It may be noted, however, that city governments in their turn promulgated similar sumptuary legislation, designed to prevent the poorer citizens from dressing above their station and aping the clothing of the rich burghers as the latter aped that of the nobles. Despite their own aspiration toward a higher social status, the patricians shared the hierarchical conception of society common to their age, and were as firmly convinced as were the nobles of the righteousness of keeping the lower classes in their place.

The patricians were, in origin at least, essentially a merchant class. It was foreign trade, supplemented in some instances by banking or large-scale industry, that created the family fortunes which raised the patriciate above the level of the shopkeepers and artisans whose retail business was limited to the local market and was necessarily on a smaller scale. But few patrician families remained actively engaged in trade for more than two or three generations. The grandchildren of the successful businessman who had founded the fortunes of the family generally preferred a more leisured or more socially desirable way of life. Income from urban real estate, from silent partnerships in business enterprise and *rentes* of various kinds enabled the heirs to commercial fortunes to live without working or, more commonly, to secure a good education and so enter the clergy or one of the profitable lay professions, of which the law attracted the largest number. Education and legal training, too, opened the way to profitable employment in the administration of city or state. Royal government, indeed, was being staffed increasingly in these years by trained men drawn from the upper bourgeoisie. Some patrician families established actual dynasties of royal jurists and administrators. In general, however, these families seldom retained their patrician status long after they had withdrawn from active commerce. They tended in later generations either to move upward into the ranks of the gentry or nobility or to drop to a lower level of wealth. The great mass of the leisured *rentiers*, lawyers, judges, doctors, royal agents and bureaucrats might still be reckoned among the upper bourgeoisie, but they could seldom compete with the great merchant families in either wealth or power. The personnel of the patrician class was thus constantly changing. New families rose to wealth, while old families deserted their class to join the nobility, or sank to a lower economic status, or simply died out. Mortality in the cities was always appallingly high, especially among children, and there is evidence that the merchant class in general during this period did not succeed in raising enough children to perpetuate itself without the infusion of new blood.

The instability of the patrician class, which resulted from this continuous turnover, may account in part for its relative failure to create a culture characteristically its own. Few families remained in the class long enough to establish a strong cultural tradition. The apparently universal aspiration of the patrician burghers toward a higher social status among the nobility and gentry must also have done much to retard the growth of a characteristically bourgeois culture. Despite pride in their own dominant position within the urban community, the patricians tended to adopt the social and cultural standards set by the nobles and to imitate as far as possible their clothing, manners and tastes. The older merchants, it is true, while sparing no expense to clothe themselves in the finest and most costly materials, generally favored sober colors and conservative styles as befitted solid businessmen. But their wives and sons had no such scruples. Contemporary accounts note that the wives of rich burghers dressed like countesses and that the *jeunesse dorée* of the cities imitated the extremest fashions of the court. Many patrician families carried imitation of the nobility to the point of adopting coats-of-arms, complete with all the customary heraldic devices.

As with the patricians, the status of the middle class of the cities was determined primarily by their economic activity and their varying degrees of wealth or poverty. In this loosely defined class were included the smaller merchants, the shopkeepers, the masters of the craft guilds and independent workers of various sorts, as well as members of the less profitable professions, such as notaries, scriveners, barber-surgeons and some few lay schoolteachers. At neither top nor bottom were the lines which divided the middle class from the patricians and the propertyless proletariat strictly drawn, nor were they in any case fixed by heredity. Throughout urban society the fortunes of individual families moved upward or downward as personal ability or circumstance dictated. Only the status of the class remained more or less constant while its personnel changed. On the whole, there was probably a greater stability in the middle segment of the urban population than in either of the extremes, for here the dynamic effects of capitalism were least apparent. Members of this class were mostly men who had some property, but not much capital for speculation or investment, nor much opportunity to make profits beyond the needs of subsistence. Concerned largely with the local market, they continued to function within the framework of economic and social organization that had been established by the regulated and monopolistic urban economy of the High Middle Ages. Guild regulations and monopolies were, if anything, more rigidly enforced than ever during the fourteenth and fifteenth centuries, and there is evidence that the guild masters were becoming more conservative and more exclusive in defense of their privileges. Certainly more and more journeymen were finding it impossible to become masters. Together with the wage earners in large industry, these formed a discontented subordinate class in the cities and contributed to the social unrest which was such a marked characteristic of this troubled period.

C. The Lower Classes and Social Unrest

The fundamental changes in economic and political organization that marked the fourteenth and fifteenth centuries had everywhere the effect of dislocating the established structure of medieval society. Some groups or classes prospered, while others declined, and within each group some individuals were able to take advantage of new conditions while others, less fortunate or less gifted, lost ground. This was a period of social unrest in all levels of society. The feudal reactions that followed the strong monarchy of Philip the Fair and Charles V in France, and the bastard feudalism created in England by the system of livery and maintenance, reflected the discontent of nobles who saw their ancient powers and privileges slipping from their grasp. The revolt of the Italian *popolo* and *popolo grasso* against the magnates who had ruled the cities, on the other hand, furnished examples of the discontent of classes that were rising in the social scale and were no longer content with a subordinate position. Social unrest might, indeed, result either from the loss of a privileged position and from economic depression or from an improvement in economic status which made men more resentful of inherited social or political disabilities. In this transitional period every class felt one or other of these motives for unrest in some degree, but at the bottom of the social scale, among the half-free peasants and the proletarian workers of the city to whom change might bring prosperity and belated freedom or starvation and economic servitude, they were felt with an intensity that broke out again and again in violent and bloody revolt.

The dynamic factors basically responsible for much of the social change and attendant social unrest were, first, the continued expansion of money economy in a rural society that had never been designed for it and, second, the growth of capitalist industry in the cities, which raised a class barrier between worker and employer that had not existed in the type of urban economy most characteristic of the Middle Ages. But the disruptive effects of these economic changes would probably not have been so great had they not been accompanied by a series of disasters — economic depressions, famines, plagues and wars — which made every crisis more acute and added immeasurably to the misery of the unfortunate.

The incalculable tragedy of the Black Death alone would have been enough to account for a great deal of social dislocation. It has been necessary to mention this great epidemic frequently in other contexts. Its social consequences, however, were such that some further account of it seems necessary here. It was apparently the first introduction into Europe of the bubonic plague. Carried from the Near East in merchant ships, it struck the seaports of southern and western Europe and southern England in 1348, spreading inland and generally northward during the two following years. After that it subsided, but did not die out. Before the end of the century, there were three or four serious returns of the plague, which caused a sufficiently high mortality to check the natural recovery of the population from the losses suffered in the first great epidemic. It is impossible to estimate with any assurance the number of those who perished. Even under the most favorable circumstances, population statistics for this period must be based on scattered, incomplete and usually unreliable evidence, but for the plague years the records are peculiarly inadequate. In many places the records normally kept by officials of parish, town or manor simply do not exist for these years because the officials themselves died. The mortality among parish priests, whose duty brought them into contact with the dying, seems to have been particularly high. Most of the contemporary accounts, written under the shock of catastrophe, are, naturally, exaggerated. Nevertheless, there is enough evidence of various kinds to justify the commonly accepted estimate that the death rate ran to at least a third and possibly a half of the total population. It is difficult to imagine the extent to which such a mortality must have broken family and social ties. It must have brought drastic changes in the circumstances of innumerable individuals, even where the condition of the social classes as a whole seemed little changed.

It is also difficult to estimate the effect of the moral shock experienced by the survivors of the plague, though it was obviously very great. There were outbursts of religious hysteria and also of irresponsible and desperate gaiety. Eccentric religious sects, such as the Flagellants, presented a serious problem to authorities of both Church and state. Religious fanaticism aroused by fear turned, as always, against the Jews, and there were terrible massacres in almost every city in Switzerland and Germany where Jewish communities existed. France and England were spared this mass murder, but probably only because the Jews had been expelled from both countries half a century earlier. The disturbed state of popular religion during this period cannot, however, be accredited in more than a temporary way to the Black Death, though the psychic shock and the death of so many of the most conscientious priests must have aggravated the spiritual ills of the age. This was a period of acute crisis in the history of the Church, during which the fiscal policies of the hierarchy aroused widespread anti-clerical feeling. Heretical or semi-heretical doctrines spread among the lower classes and gave a fanatical driving force to their demands for social justice. The Spiritual Franciscans and, in the late fourteenth century, the English Lollard preachers, seem to have added to the ferment of social unrest by their condemnation of wealth and by vague prophecies of the coming of a new age of the spirit. The socially subversive religious doctrines that spread among the illiterate masses were seldom committed to writing, and there were probably many more than our written records reveal. Behind every social disturbance of the fourteenth and fifteenth centuries, however, one can discern, if but dimly, the stirring of ideas of freedom, equality and justice founded upon the teaching of Christ, but not always in accord with the doctrines and practice of the authoritative Church.

The devastation caused by war during almost the whole of this period was a further disaster, in some places as serious in its effect on the poor as was the plague itself. Europe had never been free from war and pillage, but the wars carried on by territorial or national states with the aid of mercenary troops were on a far larger scale than those of the feudal era. Mercenary companies everywhere lived off the country, making little distinction between friendly and hostile territory, and left behind them a trail of wanton destruction. In France, especially, the systematic, wholesale devastation carried on by royal armies made the pillaging indulged in by feudal lords seem by comparison a petty retail enterprise. Large areas of France were so devastated that they had to be abandoned by what remained of their inhabitants, and the resulting group migrations of displaced persons must have added another disruptive factor to the social structure.

The expanded scale of warfare, which was one of the unfortunate results of the growth of central government in the territorial and national states, went far to counteract the benefits of stronger government, such as the promise, still but partially fulfilled, of internal peace, greater security for life and property, more even-handed justice, and freedom from the irresponsible exactions of feudal lords. Another unfortunate result was the growing burden of taxation imposed upon the people by the state. This was a new burden for all classes and was universally resented, but the noble and rich generally succeeded in avoiding the payment of anything like their fair share. For the poor, who had small margin at any time and no influence, it could be a crushing load. The workers of the city suffered under it as well as the peasants, a fact which goes far to account for the sympathetic cooperation of urban and rural workers in some of the social revolts of this period.

Barring war, taxes, plague and assorted disasters, the condition of the peasants generally improved with the breakup of the manorial system and the triumph of money economy. The improvement, however, was neither universal nor consistent, and the resulting inequalities and frustrations roused resentment both in those who found their situation deteriorating and in those who felt that it was not improving fast enough. In most places serfdom and villein services were disappearing but the process was irregular in its application and still incomplete. When so many were gaining freedom, those who still bore the stigma of bondage resented all the more bitterly the servile status that an earlier age had taken for granted. Though it did not necessarily make them richer or more secure, freedom relieved the peasants of a number of irritating and humiliating exactions and restrictions. Above all it gave them the sense of personal dignity that only free men can feel. Freedom might, and in some cases did, mean only freedom to starve, but few were willing to remain bound when their fellows were free, and once they envisaged the possibility of freedom, men everywhere were willing to pay for it or, if necessary, to fight for it. But if much of the social discontent of the peasants rose from the contrast of bondage and freedom, still more was caused by the growing disparity of economic status within the peasant class. When servile tenures were replaced by an unrestricted system of rents and wages, some peasants were able to add to their holdings by lease or purchase, while others lost the land their ancestors had held. The result was a growing rift between the rising class of free farmers who worked their land with hired labor and the landless wage earners.

The rise of the more fortunate or more industrious peasants to a position well above the average seems to have been particularly characteristic of England. The condition of the prosperous fourteenth-century yeoman farmer is well illustrated by the account of Clement Paston, the founder of a family which two generations later were wealthy landholders, lawyers and merchants.

> He was a good plain husband [man], and lived upon his land that he had in Paston, and kept thereon a plough all times in the year, and sometimes in barleysell two ploughs. The said Clement yede [went] at one plough both winter and summer, and he rode to mill on the bare horseback with his corn under him, and brought home meal again under him; and also drove his cart with divers corns to Wynterton to sell, as a good husband [man] ought to do. Also he had in Paston a five score or a six score acres of land at the most [about four times a normal villein holding], and much thereof bondland to Gemyngham Hall, with a little poor water-mill running by the river there. Other livelode nor manors had he none, nor in none other place.[4]

After the middle of the fourteenth century, numerous local peasant revolts in every Western European country attest the widespread and continuous nature of the peasants' discontent. The immediate causes, however, varied from place to place. In France, where seigneurial jurisdiction survived after serfdom had disappeared and the manorial structure had disintegrated, the lords' exaction of *corvées*, hunting rights, *banalités* (the obligation to use the lord's mill, oven and winepress) and other survivals from the age when the *seigneur* had performed all the functions of government now were the more bitterly resented because no longer justified. They continued to plague the French peasants until they were swept away by the French Revolution. During the Hundred Years' War, royal taxation added to the burden of the peasants, as did the ransoms that had to be raised to free the numerous noble prisoners taken by the English. Most serious of all, however, was the devastation caused by the war. It was a combination of these factors that led, in

[4] Quoted in G. M. Trevelyan, *Illustrated English Social History* (London, 1944), I, 15.

1357, to the wild outburst of peasant fury in the Île de France known as the Jacquerie. This was the most widespread revolt in France, but though great numbers of peasants were involved, they had neither leadership, nor organization nor positive program, and they were quickly and brutally suppressed at the cost of some 20,000 peasant lives and, it must be added, of the lives of a considerable number of noble men and women whom they had murdered. The Jacquerie, however, was a unique phenomenon in France and owes something of its notoriety to the vivid account furnished by Froissart. Most of the French peasant revolts were purely local affairs precipitated by oppression on the part of some particular lord or by some local condition.

This was true also of the numerous peasant revolts in Germany, which occurred at intervals for two hundred years before the final great Peasants' War of 1525. There, though personal serfdom was disappearing in most parts of the country, servile obligations were frequently maintained by attaching them to the land, whether it was held by bondsmen or free tenants. Moreover, the great German lords who had achieved the status of princes were now adding to the peasants' burdens by the imposition of state taxes. There as elsewhere the Church added tithes and other dues to the peasants' financial load and where, as occurred in many places in Germany, the princely landowner was an ecclesiastic, anti-clerical feeling fed the peasants' bitterness against their lord. Though on the whole the condition of the German peasants seems to have been improving in the century after the Black Death, they tended to regard the exactions from which they suffered as innovations introduced by their princes' lawyers. In the period before Luther unwittingly furnished the German peasants with a religious basis for revolt, their demand was usually for a return to the old customs, and their aim was to secure the redress of specific local grievances.

The imposition of new burdens of state taxation was also largely responsible for the most violent and prolonged of all the peasant revolts of the fourteenth century, that of western Flanders, which lasted from 1323 till 1328. In the rich country around Bruges there were large numbers of free peasant proprietors or tenants, who had grown prosperous by selling food to the great weaving cities. Their exceptionally favorable position, however, made them only the more ready to fight against any threat to their prosperity or independence. Moreover, proximity to the industrial cities had exposed them to the radical social and religious ideas current among the proletarian workers in the woollen industry. The immediate cause of the revolt was the defeat of Flanders in a war with France and the imposition on the county of a heavy indemnity, which necessitated the collection of unprecedentedly heavy taxes. The wrath of the peasants was directed primarily against the nobles, most of whom had been pro-French, and who now acted as agents of the county government in collecting the taxes. Riots against the tax collectors soon spread into a mass revolt against the noble and rich, in which the peasants were aided by the wool-workers of Bruges and Ypres. For five years the peasants and their proletarian allies waged a war of extermination against landlords and capitalists. Even the clergy were not spared. It was a war inspired by bitter hatred and accompanied by frightful atrocities on both sides. The conflagration that swept western Flanders was no flash fire ignited by the spontaneous combustion of despair, as was the Jacquerie. It was an organized political and social revolution, which aimed at winning free ownership of land for the peasants and the establishment of a rural democracy. It was finally crushed only after the massed army of the rebels had been slaughtered by the army of the King of France at the bloody battle of Cassel in 1328.

Like the revolt in Flanders, the English Peasants' Revolt of 1381 was the organized protest of a generally prosperous body of peasants and city workers against social injustice and high taxes, though it was not marked by anything like the same degree of ferocious class hatred. The fourteenth century was, on the whole, a period of prosperity and growing freedom for the English peasants. England was untouched by the direct effects of war, which so largely nullified the fruits of social progress for the rural classes on the continent. And the results of the Black Death, however tragic it may have been in human terms, worked generally to the advantage of those peasants who survived. But, though wages rose by something like fifty per cent as a result of the acute labor shortage, the attempts of the government to keep them down to their former level by enforcing the Statute of Laborers roused a continuous resentment among both rural and urban workers. And, though both villein services and villein status were rapidly disappearing, those who still bore the stigma of bondage or labored under the remnants of servile obligations were more than ever eager to be free because so many had escaped. The abolition of villeinage was one of the demands made by the peasants, but the bulk of those who took part in the revolt were already free, and among them were not a few yeoman archers back from the wars in France.

The fundamental cause of the revolt was undoubtedly a long-accumulated social discontent, but what immediately precipitated it was the heavy poll taxes imposed by the corrupt and unpopular government of the young king, Richard II, in the years 1377, 1379 and 1380. The fact that the revolt was directed as much against the government as against the landlords accounts for the relative mildness with which the rebels treated such of the gentry as fell into their hands, and also for the murder of such of the king's ministers and lawyers as they could find in London. It may also account for the ease with which they were dispersed after Richard had proclaimed himself their leader and had falsely promised to meet their demands. The dramatic story of the capture of London by the rebels and the courageous, if unscrupulous, behavior of the fifteen-year-old king have given the Peasants' Revolt a prominent place in English history. But for all its magnitude, it was quickly over, and it had no perceptible effect on the condition of the peasants and other workers. The charters of emancipation granted by the king were repealed; the Statute of Laborers was re-enforced; and villeinage continued to disappear at about the same rate as before.

The Peasants' Revolt is nevertheless interesting because it illustrates more clearly than any of the contemporary continental risings the social implications of political and religious as well as economic changes. The Statute of Laborers, which was responsible for so much of the discontent, was a law passed by Parliament at the petition of the Commons, in which were represented the gentry and the rising class of yeoman farmers, the employers of rural labor, as well as the burghers who were the employing class in the cities. It was an unprecedented use of the powers of the state to enforce regulations that in an earlier period would have been a matter of manorial custom or would have fallen within the jurisdiction of guilds and city governments. The fact that the poll taxes were the immediate precipitating cause of the revolt also illustrates the growing importance of national government for classes which hitherto had little direct relation to the state. The English peasants, in advance of their contemporaries on the continent, were already developing a sense of national policy.

They were also developing a more clearly ideological class-consciousness, which drew its inspiration from religious sources as well as from social discontent. There is ample evidence at any rate that wandering preachers — Franciscans or early followers of Wyclif — as well as many parish priests, who themselves came from the peasant class, propagated among the peasants ideas of equality and social justice based on Christian ethics, which amounted in sum to a kind of Christian socialism. A whole social ideology was contained in the popular jingle:

> "When Adam delved and Eve span,
> Who was then the gentleman?"

All contemporary accounts credit the wandering priest, John Ball, with stirring up the peasants by his inflammatory sermons. Froissart's prejudiced account of John Ball's subversive preaching may not be entirely accurate, but it catches the mood of the movement so vividly as to be worth quoting.

> Every Sunday after mass, as the people were coming out of church, this John Ball was accustomed to assemble a crowd around him in the market place and preach to them. On such occasions he would say, "My good friends, matters cannot go on well in England until all things shall be in common; when there shall be neither villeins nor lords; when the lords shall be no more masters than ourselves. How ill they behave to us! For what reason do they thus hold us in bondage? Are we not all descended from the same parents, Adam and Eve? And what can they show, or what reason can they give, why they should be more masters than ourselves? They are clothed in velvet and rich stuffs, ornamented with er-mine and other furs, while we are forced to wear poor clothing. They have wines, spices, and fine bread, while we have only rye and the refuse of straw; and when we drink, it must be water. They have handsome seats and manors, while we must brave the wind and rain in our labors in the field; and it is by our labor that they have wherewith to support their pomp. We are called slaves, and if we do not perform our service we are beaten, and we have no sovereign to whom we can complain or who would be willing to hear us. Let us go to the king and remonstrate with him; he is young and from him we may obtain a favorable answer, and if not we must ourselves seek to amend our condition."[5]

Widespread and persistent as was the social discontent of the peasants, it seldom equalled in bitterness that of the proletarian workers in the cities where there was a large export industry. There the disruptive factor was not, as in the rural manors, the shift from a natural economy to one based on money, for money economy had been characteristic of city life from the beginning. Rather it was the expansion of capital and capitalist methods of business organization from commerce into industry, which drove an ever-widening wedge between employers and workers. This was a development limited as yet almost entirely to a few great export industries. It is true that the growing tendency of guild masters to exclude poor journeymen from mastership was creating some social unrest even in those trades that served only the local market, as the appearance of journeymen guilds or *compagnonages* attests. But where there was no large capitalist industry, the social discontent in the cities seems to have been relatively mild. There is little evidence of serious trouble in Germany or France. Where there were urban insurrections, like that led by Étienne Marcel in Paris in 1357, the causes were largely po-litical, and it was the bourgeoisie rather than the workers who were chiefly involved. England had a great woollen industry, which by the middle

[5] Froissart, p. 207 f.

of the fifteenth century surpassed any of its continental competitors, but it was widely dispersed in country villages. The English cloth-workers thus had little opportunity to join forces against their employers. Moreover, they did not live in crowded and malodorous slums, and most of them had some land on which they could grow food. In the great weaving cities of Italy and Flanders, however, conditions were very different, and there the relation between employers and workers was characterized by a bitterness and violence seldom equalled in the history of social strife.

The condition of the textile-workers in the Italian city-states was particularly hopeless because the government was usually controlled by the class of wealthy merchant-industrialists who were their employers, and who used their political power to keep the workers in subjection. This was strictly true only in the republics, but in the despotic states the *signori* also issued laws in favor of the industrial entrepreneurs who brought wealth to the state. Even when a popular revolution broke for a time the control exercised by the great merchant guilds, it was only the craftsmen of the lesser guilds who profited, and they had no interest in the poor workers of the large industries. On the contrary they feared their violence and would generally side with the wealthy employers against them. Having neither property nor guild organization, the proletarian workers in the textile trades were not regarded as citizens and had, therefore, no political rights.

Conditions of labor were much the same in all the textile cities of Italy, but they can best be illustrated from the history of Florence. There the preponderant importance of the woollen industry in the fourteenth century gave the entrepreneurs of the *Arte della Lana* great political power, so that they were able to secure for their guild jurisdictional authority so extensive as to make it practically a state within the state. It had its own courts and prisons and police officers for the enforcement of its laws. It exercised complete control over all workers in the industry, fixing their wages and conditions of labor, and using the full power of the state to prevent them from forming any kind of guild or association, even for religious purposes, that might give them an opportunity for corporate action or collective bargaining. Though controlled by the *Arte*, the workers were not members. They were *sottoposti* — subjects of the guild. Entirely dependent on the *Arte* for employment, they were left to face starvation in periods of industrial depression, while the strict regulation of wages, and the competition of fresh labor imported from the countryside, prevented them from profiting very much from periods of labor shortage such as that which followed the Black Death. In many instances workers were bound not only to the guild, but also to individual masters who kept them in perpetual servitude by paying wages in advance, which then had to be worked off. By the laws of the *Arte,* no employer could hire a worker who had not fulfilled all his obligations to his current master. And any worker who showed defiance or became known as a trouble-maker could be doomed to perpetual unemployment by being blacklisted.

Under these circumstances, it is small wonder that the workers' suburbs of Florence seethed with suppressed fury, against which the government of the city had to be perpetually on its guard; for, helpless though the workers were, their very numbers made them a threat to the security of the city. Here, as elsewhere, religious ideas of a Utopian and possibly heretical character, encouraged at times by the chiliastic preaching of mystical sects like the Joachimites and by the Fraticelli — the radical left wing of the Spiritual Franciscans — added fuel to the protest against social injustice. Throughout the fourteenth century the wool-workers sought primarily the right to form a guild of their own, hoping thereby to secure not only corporate bargaining power, but also a share in the city government, such as was enjoyed by the artisans in the lesser guilds. But the combination of economic and political power arrayed against them was too strong to be broken. Even during the democratic period from 1343 to 1381, when the middle and lesser guilds were dominant, the government felt it necessary to support the employers in the great industry to which Florence owed so much of its prosperity. The briefly successful rising of the *Ciompi* in 1378 was made possible only by a political crisis in the republic. It failed for lack of effective leadership, and also because the violence of the wool-workers alienated the artisans of the lesser guilds and even their fellow-proletarians in the newly created guilds of the dyers and shirtmakers. Their former leader, the wool-comber, Michele di Lando, who had been made *Gonfaloniere* at the beginning of the revolt, turned against them and led the attack which hunted the rebels out of the city. The guild of the *Popolo Minuto* or, as it was commonly called, of the *Ciompi,* which included most of the wool-workers, was then suppressed after having been in existence for only a few weeks. The other two proletarian guilds were suppressed in the counter-revolution which re-established the merchant oligarchy three years later. During the following century the decline of the Florentine woollen industry reduced the numbers of the workers and made revolt even more impossible.

The conflict between workers and employers in the great weaving cities of Flanders was even more bitter, or at least more violent, than in Italy, and it led to a series of prolonged and bloody revolts. The class war here, however, was complicated by a number of extraneous factors. The kings of France and England interfered constantly in Flemish affairs, the former striving to reassert royal authority over the County of Flanders, the latter using control of the English wool to force the Flemish cities into alliance with them against France. Subject to pressure from both sides, the counts of Flanders, who were themselves striving to secure greater control of the rich and largely autonomous cities in the county, played a dubious and vacillating rôle. Conflicting loyalties thus added to the bitterness of the class struggle, while the frequent blockades of English wool which resulted from the vicissitudes of the Hundred Years' War caused periodic unemployment and thus aggravated the social unrest of the workers.

Until the end of the thirteenth century, the Flemish cities had been entirely dominated by a patrician oligarchy of merchant-industrialists who kept the workers in subjection. Toward the end of the century, however, the patricians felt their power slipping, and appealed for aid to the King of France. This was regarded as treason by the mass of the middle and lower classes in the cities, who were jealous of Flemish independence and had no love for the French. This situation enabled the wool-workers to establish an alliance with the Count of Flanders and with the artisans of the craft guilds to overthrow the pro-French patriciate. At Courtrai in 1302 an army composed mostly of urban workers decisively defeated the army of King Philip the Fair and slaughtered the flower of French chivalry. After their victory the weavers and fullers organized in guilds and for a time dominated the city governments. The power of the old patrician oligarchy was broken and it never recovered. The import-export trade of Flanders fell into the hands of foreigners — Italian, English and Hansard — and the woollen industry was taken over by a new class of smaller entrepreneurs. But, though they had gained the right to organize and were in a position to exert political pressure, the wool-workers soon found that they were little better off, and the resulting disillusionment added immeasurably to their bitterness. No political action could free them from economic dependence on their employers, nor guard them against the threat of periodic mass unemployment. Moreover, the craftsmen of the local guilds who had joined the wool-workers against the pro-French patricians were soon alienated by their restless violence and went over to the side of the merchant employers. The count, too, learned to fear their turbulence and allied himself with the upper classes or called in French armies to suppress them. And, as the century wore on, the growing English competition and the frequent stoppage of wool from England brought a decline in the Flemish industry which greatly aggravated all the ills from which the workers suffered.

The battle of Courtrai, then, proved not the end but the beginning of

a class war of unparalleled ferocity. The weavers and fullers of Bruges and Ypres joined the peasant rising of 1324–28 and shared in their defeat. Another civil war in 1348–49 ended in the massacre of weavers in Bruges, Ghent and Ypres and the reduction of their political powers. The weavers of the three cities rose again in 1359 and for two years held out against all opposition. There were further insurrections in 1367, 1370 and 1377 in Ypres. Finally, in 1379 the wool-workers rose in a last mass revolt against the bourgeoisie and the count. For three years civil war raged throughout Flanders until the workers were defeated in battle by the combined forces of the count and the King of France. Thereafter, the growing power of the government of the county, which from 1384 onward was in the strong hands of the dukes of Burgundy, prevented further revolts.

The following century witnessed less open social revolt than had the fourteenth, but that fact is not evidence of an improvement in the condition of the industrial proletariat in either Flanders or Italy. In both countries the "great industry" was declining so that there were not enough workers to be a serious threat. In Flanders new industries were taking the place of the old, and in these the workers lacked the organization and the tradition of revolt that had inspired the wool-workers. It may be, too, that after a century of revolt the workers were becoming adjusted to a situation that was no longer novel and that they no longer hoped to be able to change. The industrial cities of Italy and Flanders were among the chief centers of culture in Europe during these two centuries. Literature, learning, art and music flourished there in brilliant bloom under the stimulus of the patronage provided by concentrated wealth. But, in our admiration for the culture that flowered in the courts of princes and the homes of wealthy burghers, we need not forget that its economic roots were sunk in the seething misery of the workers' quarters.

VIII

Literature and Learning

The contrasting themes of continuity and innovation, which characterize the civilization of the period we are here considering, is nowhere more evident than in the history of literature and learning. Everywhere in Western Europe the old and the new were to be found together in uneasy juxtaposition, but the proportion of each in the resultant mixture varied greatly from country to country. In Italy a society very different from that which had shaped the culture of the High Middle Ages was adapting inherited traditions to new ends, so that men felt the exhilarating assurance that a new age of culture was in process of birth. In France, the classic land of medieval culture, on the other hand, the element of continuity was preponderant, for here literary and scholarly traditions were rooted in a glorious past, and the classes which had set the tone of scholastic learning and secular literature still held their dominant position. Yet here, too, the social structure was changing, and traditions that were losing touch with reality seemed tinged with decadence. In England this period saw the birth of a new literary language and, for a brief time in the second half of the fourteenth century, a brilliant flowering of English poetry unequalled until the Elizabethan age. Germany, on the other hand, was undergoing a prolonged literary depression, for there political disintegration had created a situation unfavorable to literary production of any kind.

A. The Rise of Vernacular Literature in Italy

In the generation which grew to maturity in the years around 1300 — the generation of Dante and Giotto — Italian culture came of age, and during the following two centuries Italy assumed the position of cultural leadership that France had occupied in the High Middle Ages. The new Italian culture was, above all, urban. It was very largely the product of educated laymen, whose work was designed to satisfy the taste of a wealthy and urban lay society; and its content, though still held within the framework of Christian thought, became as a result increasingly secular. It was, on the whole, an aristocratic culture, the possession of a dominant class. It left the middle class of artisans and shopkeepers relatively untouched, and it had no contact with the growing mass of the industrial proletariat. But, though aristocratic, it was neither feudal nor chivalric, for the composite upper class of the Italian cities, a class composed of merchants and bankers, landholding magnates, members of the learned professions, and government officials, was far removed from the atmosphere of the feudal courts and the chivalric society that had shaped the secular culture of the Middle Ages and that still set the tone of vernacular literature in the North. Those of its members who had secured higher education were also far removed from the academic atmosphere that had produced the most characteristic forms of medieval scholastic learning. The universities of Italy cultivated law and medicine and the secularized current of philosophy represented by Averroism rather than the theologically oriented studies which still dominated the schools of Paris and Oxford; and, after the middle of the fourteenth century, an increasing number of the Italian *literati* turned their backs on scholastic learning to devote themselves with the enthusiasm of converts to the culture inherited from pre-Christian Rome.

Although the Italians of the fourteenth century drew what inspiration they could from the medieval past and adapted medieval traditions of literature and learning to their needs, the culture of Italy in the period that began with Dante's generation seems more the beginning of something new, less the continuation and gradual transformation of older forms, than was true in the countries north of the Alps. This impression of novelty arises in part from the lack of a vigorous Italian culture in the centuries of the High Middle Ages. The dominant trends in medieval literary and aesthetic culture — vernacular epic, romance, and chivalric lyric, Gothic architecture and sculpture, secular song and polyphonic music — were all indigenous to France, and though they spread to Germany and England, they had never become fully naturalized in Italy. When the Italian contemporaries of Dante and Petrarch borrowed from the Middle Ages, they were not drawing upon a vigorous native tradition. It is difficult to explain why medieval Italy, so far in advance of the rest of Europe in its economic development, its communes seething with political and social vitality, should in almost all the higher forms of culture have lagged behind, leaving the undisputed leadership to feudal France. Perhaps it was the very precocity of its urban development which, while fitting it to be the pioneer of the increasingly urban civilization of the Renaissance, was paradoxically responsible for its relative backwardness in the Middle Ages. During the eleventh, twelfth, and thirteenth centuries, the classic age of medieval civilization, Italy was out of step with the rest of Europe. In an age when culture was predominantly feudal and ecclesiastical, the Italian communes could not contribute materially to cultural forms that were essentially alien to them. And the urban population of Italy had not yet acquired, or did not acquire until the closing years of the thirteenth century, the self-confidence and the spiritual autonomy they needed to shape a culture of their own, nor, absorbed as they were in business and politics, had they had the leisure to develop intellectual and aesthetic interests.

The most striking proof of the cultural backwardness of Italy in the age of the communes is to be found in the almost complete lack of a literature in the vernacular until the second half of the thirteenth century. When the first Italian literature appeared, the medieval French vernacular tradition was already two centuries old and had passed its peak. In Germany, too, the great age of medieval epic and lyric was drawing to a close. Medieval Italy had produced no national epic, no cycles of romance and, except for a brief period at the Sicilian court of Frederick II, no courtly lyric. Even that abortive flowering of Italian verse, fostered by the scion of Norman kings and German emperors, was an artificial growth transplanted from Provence and grafted on the stalk of the courtly Sicilian dialect. It died when the hothouse in which it grew was wrecked by the soldiers of Charles of Anjou. Until Dante's generation, the people of central and northern Italy were dependent for literary sustenance almost entirely on works composed in French or Latin. Medieval Italy had not only no literature of its own but also no literary language. The diversity of local dialects, however, can scarcely be regarded as sufficient reason for the slow growth of a vernacular literature, for it was surely no more acute than in medieval France or Germany. Perhaps the fact that the Italian dialects were closer to Latin than those of the north, that grammar schools had kept alive a knowledge of Latin among the Italian laity, and that the literature of Rome's great age formed a substitute for a national epic may have tended to prevent the medieval Italians from feeling a need for literature in their own tongue. This, at least, has frequently been suggested as an explanation, though it seems an inadequate one, for the late growth of Italian letters.

If the medieval Italian communes failed to provide future generations with a native literary tradition on which to build, they nevertheless laid the material and social foundations for the later cultural development, and these were perhaps equally important. Both the commercial and the political activity of the communes forced an unusually early development of lay education. At a time when the northern nobles and burghers alike remained contentedly illiterate, the techniques of an incipient capitalism forced literacy upon the Italian merchants and upon the agents they employed in the increasingly complex transactions of partnerships and family firms. Literacy must have been fairly widespread among the middle and upper classes of the Italian cities by the early years of the fourteenth century when Giovanni Villani reported that between eight and ten thousand boys and girls in Florence were learning to read, and that between 550 and 600 boys were taught Latin grammar and logic, the prerequisites for further study in the higher institutions of learning. Moreover, the complexities of Italian business required from an early date the assistance of a host of lawyers, notaries, and scribes, all of whom necessarily possessed considerable education. The self-governing communes, too, opened careers to educated laymen as administrators, secretaries, and jurists at a time when the governments of the northern countries still depended largely upon clerics. The learned lay professions contributed greatly to the literary development that began in Italy with Dante's generation. Finally, the commercial activity of the communes created the concentrated wealth that at the time was an absolute prerequisite to the flourishing of a secular culture. Such a culture could not thrive on ecclesiastical preferment alone, and in the period before the invention of printing — indeed for a long time thereafter — men of letters could not live by the sale of their work. The lay man of letters, therefore, must have possessed either inherited wealth or wealthy patrons. It was inherited wealth, too, that enabled the sons of successful merchants to secure a good education, to pursue the learned professions, or to devote their leisure to the cultivation of literary tastes, thus furnishing an appreciative public for the works of contemporary writers.

The last years of the thirteenth century and the first decades of the fourteenth brought a new stimulus to Italian culture, which hastened its growth and did much to determine its character. In Florence, whose citizens were to play a preponderant part in the new literary movement, a period of unprecedented prosperity set in during these years, while at the same time a political revolution assured the dominance of the class of wealthy merchants, bankers, and industrialists. Meanwhile, in the

Lombard communes the sound and fury of factional strife was being stilled beneath the dictatorship of the rising *signori*. But what these northern communes lost in civic liberty was compensated, so far as literature and the arts were concerned, by the creation of new sources of lay patronage in the courts of the *signori*, whose wealth, drawn from taxation and political power, rivalled that of the great capitalists. Self-made men themselves, the despots threw careers in government open to talent, while at the same time their vanity and the need to maintain prestige led them to gather scholars and writers to their courts. The result, however, was not, or not yet, a courtly society in the northern manner, for the *signori* were not feudal lords and their way of life was not rooted in the traditions of chivalry. The removal of the papacy from Italy in 1305, and its absence during the greater part of the fourteenth century, must also have had some effect on the growth of a secular culture by removing from Italy the most potentially fruitful source of ecclesiastical patronage. The predominantly French court of the Avignonese popes did, it is true, give patronage and encouragement to the youthful Petrarch and to some other Italians, but for the most part the support of Italian culture during this century was left to laymen. At the same time, the Avignonese papacy made a positive contribution to the development of Italian literature by bringing Petrarch and others into closer contact with the culture of Provence, the fountainhead of the stream of troubadour poetry.

It is one of the characteristics of a transitional age that social change generally precedes changes in ideas and cultural forms, for men adjust of necessity to the new situations forced upon them in practical ways by changing economic and political conditions, while still clinging to the ideological patterns and the *Weltanschauung* of the world into which they were born. We should not be surprised, therefore, to discover great segments of medieval thought and medieval literary tradition still extant in a society that had ceased to be preponderantly medieval in its economic, political, and social organization. The history of Italian culture in the century and a half after 1300 is thus largely the story of the gradual and belated adjustment of ideas and literary and aesthetic forms to the needs and interests of an increasingly unmedieval society. Nor should we be surprised that the wealth of the Italian cities did not become culturally operative until it had been in existence for several generations. Time is needed to establish a tradition of interest in the higher forms of culture among a class whose ancestors had not possessed it. Once established, however, it continued to grow, so that, even during periods of economic reversal and depression such as followed the catastrophes of the 1340's, an increasing proportion of the wealth of Italy continued to be devoted to the support of art and letters. And when the merchants, bankers, lawyers, despots, and *condottieri* of Italy had acquired a taste for culture, they were well equipped to make the most of it. Life in a calculating and fiercely competitive society had sharpened their wits, and their intellectual horizon had been broadened by travel and by correspondence through the channels of business and diplomacy with every part of the western world.

This was the kind of society into which Dante Alighieri (1265–1321) was born, just at the time when it was beginning to reach a self-conscious awareness of its cultural potentialities. There is something symbolically appropriate in the fact that Italy's first great poet was a layman, an active citizen of the great Tuscan republic which mothered so many distinguished sons, and that he spent many years under the patronage of North Italian *signori*. Except for his overpowering genius, which makes him a unique figure about whom it is impossible to generalize, Dante was in many ways the prototype of the Renaissance man of letters, and that not only in his status as a layman and a citizen who made his living by his pen. For, despite the profoundly medieval tone of his thought, he showed in his intense awareness of personality, his analytical introspection, and his concrete perception of the external world traits that were rare, though not unknown, in the Middle Ages, but were to become more frequent and more pronounced as the Renaissance progressed. Standing at the threshold of the transitional age — in the immortal words of Professor Haskins's undergraduate "with one foot in the Middle Ages, while with the other he saluted the rising star of the Renaissance" — his gigantic figure is a milestone marking the end of one period and the beginning of another.

The Florence in which Dante grew up was enjoying the first flush of the economic boom that followed the Guelf victory of 1267. He was twenty-eight when the Ordinances of Justice established a new constitution vesting power in the hands of a merchant oligarchy. Though apparently of an old Florentine family, Dante was not one of those who were disenfranchised as belonging to the magnate class. He enrolled with the qualifying appellation *poeta fiorentino*, in the guild of the physicians and apothecaries, under the provision which permitted one to enroll in a guild without actually plying a trade or profession, and so became eligible for public office. As a supporter of the constitutional party of the White Guelfs, he served as one of the priors in the year 1300 and was among those exiled under pain of death following the Black victory in 1302. He was then thirty-seven. The years of exile altered his political views and deepened his religious thought, but could not eradicate the influence of the cultivated patrician society in which he had grown to maturity beside the banks of the Arno. There he had associated with a group of young poets, including Guido Cavalcanti, scion of a powerful family of banking magnates, who were engaged in adapting the themes and poetic forms of Provençal lyric to the requirements of the Tuscan dialect and to the emotional interests of a serious-minded urban patriciate. The first significant efforts in northern Italy to write lyric poetry in the Italian *volgare* had begun in the preceding generation. Dante himself named the Bolognese philosopher and poet, Guido Guinicelli (c. 1240–76), the father of the *dolce stil nuovo*, the sweet new style. But it was in Florence and in the Tuscan dialect that the new Italian lyric poetry came into its own.

Dante and his fellow poets were fully conscious of the debt they owed to the Provençal troubadours. But the themes of courtly love, which had grown naturally in the chivalric courts of feudal France, were foreign to the manners of the Italian cities. They could not be taken over intact, as they were in the Germany of the *Ritterzeit*. They had to be transmuted in some way before they could furnish more than the most artificial stimulus to poets whose *mores* were determined by a burgher society, and who were at once more erudite and more deeply thoughtful than their chivalric predecessors in gay Provence. Guido Guinicelli had shown the way by making of love a force that inspires the gentle heart to spiritual aspiration, thus transforming the worship of the beloved into a kind of religious mysticism in which human beauty becomes a symbol of the divine. It was this philosophical and transcendental conception of love that found its fullest expression in the *Vita nuova*, Dante's account in prose and verse of the love for Beatrice which filled his life and inspired all his poetic labors. Scattered throughout the prose passages of the *Vita nuova* there are bits of curious and irrelevant learning, which remind us that Dante belonged to an age that loved the didactic and allegorical, but in their fresh delicacy the sonnets and *canzoni* rise above the conventions of his age. Here the poet looked into his own heart to record with passion and precision the most significant emotional experiences of his life. The *Vita nuova* leaves us with no clear picture of the human Beatrice, nor was it intended to, but it remains one of the great spiritual autobiographies of all time.

The strongly personal element that characterized the *Vita nuova* persists through Dante's epic description of hell, purgatory, and paradise in the *Divine Comedy*, and there, too, the ethereal figure of Beatrice reappears, now fully identified with divine beauty and truth. Even more than the transcendental love portrayed in the *Vita nuova* or the political theories of the *De monarchia*, the theological and scientific content of the *Divine Comedy* marks Dante's thought as essentially, almost anachronistically, medieval. It has been regarded by common consent as one of the two great medieval *summae*, second only to that of Aquinas. The technique of the dream vision, the frequent allegory, the Ptolemaic cosmology, the theological concepts, and the hierarchy of vices and virtues are all drawn from the common stock of medieval literature and learning, though seldom without some touch of originality in conception or treatment. But if Dante's world of ideas was largely scholastic, he was not himself in the literal sense a schoolman. However familiar he shows himself to be with the philosophical and theological systems of the Thomist school, he was still a layman and a poet. Had he been a professional schoolman, he would scarcely have chosen to clothe his *summa* in vernacular verse. Nor would so many of the vices and virtues to which he allotted their appointed places have been represented by real people, many of whom he had known in life and who, for all their function as types, retained traits of personality peculiar to themselves. Such sharply delineated and differentiated personalities had no place in the abstract world of scholastic syllogism, nor, for that matter, in the medieval allegorical poem. Even the dream world beheld in his vision has a concrete reality and a rationally articulated structure that has no precedent in the long line of medieval dream sequences. Poet and seer though he was, Dante possessed also the qualities of a Florentine burgher. Intensely conservative, he yet belonged to the urban breed that held the future of Italian culture in its hands.

With the next great Italian poet, Francesco Petrarca (1304–74), or Petrarch, we move a long step forward into the transitional period. In him the traits that foreshadow the coming age are vastly more pronounced than in Dante, while the medieval elements in his thought, though still present, are much diluted. Since Renan coined the phrase, innumerable historians have called Petrarch the first modern man. It might be more accurate to call him the first modern man of letters. He was first and last a professional writer. To his pen he owed not only a very good living, but also the friendship of princes and prelates and an international prestige such as no mere writer in the Middle Ages had ever achieved. Much of his fame depended on his Latin works, and it was as the pioneer of classical humanism that he exerted the greatest influence on his age. For the present, however, we will consider only his place in the history of Italian literature, and the evidences of a changing *Weltanschauung* reflected in his vernacular poems.

It was a coincidence of great importance for the development of the Italian literary language that Petrarch, like Dante, was a Florentine whose native dialect was Tuscan and who also travelled widely, so that his speech was not too closely bound to local usage. He was not actually born in Florence but in nearby Arezzo, his father having been driven into exile, together with Dante and other White Guelfs, two years previously. He was still young when his parents moved to Avignon, the Provençal city in which the papal court had recently settled. His father, a lawyer, intended his son to follow the same profession, and sent him to study in the law schools of Montpellier and Bologna. But Petrarch was not born to be a lawyer, and his years at the universities seem to have left little impression upon him except a hearty dislike for scholastic learning and all the learned professions. After his father's death in 1325, he returned to Avignon to take up the literary career on which his heart was set. There he mingled with the brilliant and worldly society of the papal court and won the friendship and patronage of Cardinal Colonna and other ecclesiastical dignitaries. To make himself eligible for patronage in the form of clerical preferment, he took minor orders; but he never became a priest, and his manner of life remained indistinguishable from that of a layman. He was sincerely religious, but he had no talent for asceticism. His love of this pleasant world and the fame he had won in it occasionally troubled his conscience, but he could not forsake it for long. At times he wearied of court life and of that "modern Babylon," Avignon, and sought a rather ostentatious solitude for meditation and study in the nearby valley of Vaucluse, but he always returned to the world, to travel from court to court and to bask in the adulation of his adoring public. In 1341 he was crowned poet laureate at Rome on the Capitoline hill, and for the last twenty-five years of his life he spent most of his time in Italy: in Venice where the *Signoria* lent him a palace, in Milan as the guest of the Visconti, at the court of the Carrara lords of Padua, and in travel the length and breadth of the peninsula. At last in his old age he retired to solitude once more on a little farm at Arqua, where he was cared for by his daughter Francesca, the more satisfactory of his two natural children. Citizen of the world though he was, he loved his native Italy, the home of that Roman culture he so greatly revered, and some of his finest sonnets were written in its praise.

One important event of Petrarch's life has yet to be recorded, the most important of all for his career as a poet. In 1327 the young semi-clerical dandy met a lady named Laura in a church in Avignon, and was never the same again. To her, through a long lifetime of love that found no consummation in this world, but which after her death in the great plague of '48 was rewarded by the hope of reunion in Heaven, he devoted the greater part of his vernacular sonnets and songs. Like Dante, Petrarch drew upon the treasury of Provençal lyric for inspiration; but his was a more humanly comprehensible love, and he was thus better suited to form the connecting link between the formalized medieval tradition of courtly love and the modern conception of love as a highly personal experience. His sonnets, like Horace's odes, but unlike much of the poetry inspired by chivalrous convention, express emotions capable of awakening echoes in the hearts of modern men, and they have found translators and imitators in every modern century. Petrarch's Laura is an idealized figure, as are all beloved ladies. But she is neither the feudal *grande dame* to whom the Provençal troubadour poured out his homage, nor the allegorical personification of Divine Truth whom Dante worshipped from afar. Laura was a real woman with whom the poet was for many years on intimate terms, though not as intimate as he would have liked. The plaint of the rueful lover is in the medieval tradition, but Petrarch wore his rue with a difference. As he analyses with microscopic precision every facet of the frustrated lover's emotion, he seems at times less interested in the lady than in his feeling about her, less concerned, perhaps, to sing her praises than to immortalize his own complicated state of mind. In the sonnets and throughout most of his Latin works, notably in his letters and in the confessional work he called his *Secret*, Petrarch's tireless interest in his own melancholy and distracted personality stamps his writing with a sharply etched individuality that had, with the possible exception of Abelard, no precedent in medieval literature.

It was not their content alone, however, which made Petrarch's Italian poems a seminal force in Italian and world literature. No poet since antiquity had possessed a more highly developed sense of form. Every sonnet is a work of art. Even after his major literary interests had shifted to Latin, and after the passion that burned through his early manhood had cooled with age, he continued to polish his Italian verses. Not the least part of the legacy he left to that posterity which so much occupied his thoughts was a more perfectly formed literary language and a heightened awareness of literary art.

In the early stages of the development of any literature, the evolution of a prose style tends to lag behind poetry. It is less memorable than verse and demands a reading, not a listening, public. Such a public was in existence in Italy when the vernacular literature began to emerge; but prose also seems to call for less conscious art than poetry, and so did not at first receive the same attention from those who were striving to raise literature above the level of everyday speech. Most of the prose works written before the middle of the fourteenth century were didactic in purpose, to be valued for their content rather than for their style. They included religious and moral tracts, moralizing anecdotes of the kind beloved by a burgher society, translations of moral treatises from medieval or classical Latin, flat prose versions of the French epics and romances, and historical chronicles. Of these the last are by far the most interesting to the modern reader. One in particular, the *Florentine Chronicle* of Giovanni Villani is our most precious contemporary source for the history of Florence in the last years of the thirteenth century and the first half of the fourteenth.

Giovanni Villani (1280–1348) is so typical of the class of prosperous urban laymen who were beginning to set the tone of Italian culture that he deserves somewhat closer attention than his literary talent might warrant. He also illustrates, as did his slightly older contemporary, Dante, many of the mental characteristics of the first transitional generation. His father was a well-to-do Florentine merchant, a supporter of the White Guelf party, who served, together with Dante, as one of the priors for the year 1300. In that Jubilee Year, the year to which Dante assigned his vision, young Giovanni visited Rome and there, like Gibbon four centuries later, found the inspiration for his life work.

> And being on that blessed pilgrimage in the sacred city of Rome [he wrote] and seeing its great and ancient monuments and reading the great deeds of the Romans as described by Virgil, Sallust, Lucan, Livy, Valerius, Orosius, and other masters of history. . . . I took my prompting from them although I am a disciple unworthy of such an undertaking. But in view of the fact that our city of Florence, daughter and offspring of Rome, was mounting and pursuing great purposes, while Rome was in its decline, I thought it proper to trace in this chronicle the origins of the city of Florence, so far as I have been able to recover them, and to relate the city's further development at greater length. . . . And thus in the year 1300, on my return from Rome, I began to compile this book in the name of God and the blessed John the Baptist and in honor of our city of Florence.[1]

As this quotation shows, the young merchant's son was reasonably well educated, had read the classics, and had some literary aspirations. It also suggests the deep piety and staunch civic pride bred by the communes, combined with a reverence for Rome that seems to foreshadow the enthusiasm of the later humanists. After the débacle of the White Guelf party, Giovanni travelled for a time, seeing the world, and serving as an agent for Florentine firms in Flanders and Naples. Later, he returned to his native city, made his peace with the triumphant Blacks, and began a career in commerce that brought him wealth for many years, first as a partner of the great firm of the Peruzzi and later with the Buonaccorsi, and finally financial ruin in the panic of the forties.

Villani's *Chronicle*, which begins with the Tower of Babel and ends with an unfinished account of the Black Death in which he himself

[1] *Cronica di Giovanni Villani*, VIII, 36 (ed. F. G. Dragomanni, Florence, 1844-45).

perished, presents an odd combination of medieval ideas and uncritically accepted legends with attitudes and interests that were beyond the range of the medieval chroniclers. The first part of the *Chronicle* might have been written by a medieval monk. Villani could not divorce the history of his city from the theologically oriented setting of universal history, and he saw the hand of Divine Providence working throughout its course. When his story reached the period of which he had personal knowledge, however, the shrewd realism and concrete factual sense of the experienced Florentine citizen and man of affairs came into their own. He knew the political feuds of his city and could analyse the motives of the contestants. His research took him through the streets of Florence, and he knew politics and business from the inside. Above all, he had the feeling for facts and accurate figures which the growth of capitalist enterprise was awakening in men of his class. The latter part of the *Chronicle* is replete with statistics regarding population, food consumption, cloth production, churches, schools, and public works. And, unlike the statistics that occasionally appear in medieval chronicles, they are obviously the result of careful counting and calculation. Modern research has generally confirmed their accuracy.

Interesting as Villani's work is, it is not distinguished prose. Indeed, so long as writers regarded their language simply as a medium for conveying a didactic content, they were not likely to give much attention to the refinement of style. That development came with the first serious attempts to elevate prose fiction to the level of literature, and was the work of another Florentine merchant's son, a generation younger than Villani. Giovanni Boccaccio (1313–75) undoubtedly thought of himself as a poet, and in fact he wrote great quantities of verse which might have been more highly regarded had he not suffered from comparison with his two great predecessors. During the last twenty years or so of his life he abandoned the vernacular and prided himself on his achievements as a scholar and writer of classical Latin. But he will always be remembered as the first great Italian novelist and the founder of Italian prose. Boccaccio has frequently been called the typical bourgeois, and with some reason, but there was that in him which prevented him from following the patterns of his class and enabled him to frustrate his father's persistent efforts to make a lawyer or a businessman of him. Having been apprenticed to a merchant, he was sent when still young to Naples where he spent some dozen years halfheartedly engaging in commerce and studying law, while wholeheartedly cultivating the frivolous society of the Neapolitan court. There he fell in love with a noble lady whom he called Fiammetta — she was reputedly the natural daughter of King Robert of Naples — and under her inspiration began his career as a writer.

It was inspiration, however, of a different sort from that which emanated from Beatrice or Laura. The rôle of the three ladies, indeed, symbolizes very aptly the successive stages in the descent from Dante's more than half-medieval *Divine Comedy* to Boccaccio's purely human comedy, firmly rooted as it was in the secular society of the Renaissance. There was passion in Boccaccio's feeling for his Little Flame, but there was no aura of spirituality or of chivalry about it. It may be significant that three of the books he wrote for Fiammetta were prose romances, and that, of the two narrative poems he dedicated to her, one was the story of the illicit and tragic love of Troilus for the fickle and faithless Cressida, a story not without its autobiographical implications.

Boccaccio's early prose works suffered from an excessive prolixity and were frequently overburdened with classical allusions. But they served to practise his pen, and they had some importance as prototypes of different kinds of novel, including the pastoral, which later became popular forms. It was not till his last major Italian work, the *Decamerone*, that he was able to prune and perfect his style and thus set a new standard for Italian prose. To this end the brevity imposed by the form of the short story probably helped. The *Decamerone* is in fact simply a collection of short stories, for which a gathering of ten young people in a villa outside Florence, whence they had fled to escape the ravages of the Black Death, furnished a charmingly natural setting. On each of ten days they amused themselves telling stories, as Chaucer's pilgrims did later on the road to Canterbury. The tales vary greatly in subject matter and moral tone. Some reflect on the morals and manners of the clergy; others satirize human foibles; others again seem to ridicule marital fidelity. There is no reason to believe, however, that Boccaccio had any serious moral or satirical intent. His desire was simply to amuse. Few, if any, of his stories were original; but out of anecdotes that were in the common domain he made works of art and so created a new literary genre.

The great Florentine writers of the fourteenth century had no immediate successors. Both Petrarch and Boccaccio turned in their later years from the vernacular Italian to classical Latin, and for nearly a century thereafter there was no distinguished Italian poetry and very little prose. For this remarkable hiatus in the growth of the new literature the enthusiasm of the humanists for classical Latin and Greek was largely responsible. Until past the middle of the fifteenth century, the task of reviving the ancient languages and literatures absorbed the energies of Italian men of letters, while through comparison with the polished Latinity of the ancients the vulgar tongue fell into disrepute as a literary medium. It was saved from complete oblivion only by the patriotic sentiment of the Florentines, who still revered their great writers.

Leonardo Bruni wrote Italian lives of Dante and Petrarch in 1436, and others of his circle occasionally wrote didactic works in the *volgare* for popular consumption. Except for these, however, and an occasional *novella* like Giovanni da Prato's *Paradiso degli Alberti*, Italian vernacular literature remained in eclipse until it was revived again in the generation of Lorenzo de' Medici.

B. The First Century of Italian Humanism (c. 1350–1450)

The growing preoccupation of Italian men of letters with the classics, which cut across the development of the vernacular literature, was so important an element in the culture of the Renaissance that for centuries it was regarded as its distinguishing characteristic and the primary factor in all the cultural changes of the age, including the magnificent flowering of Renaissance art. The men who brought about the revival of the classics, the humanists, were themselves responsible for the interpretation of cultural history out of which the concept of the Renaissance grew. It was their conviction that literature and art had been as it were reborn in their own time after nearly a thousand years of barbarism, and this conception of a rebirth of culture under the influence of the classics persisted through the following generations. In the eighteenth century, Voltaire still thought of this period of Italian history as characterized by "la renaissance des lettres et des beaux arts." The historians and critics who wrote under the influence of the Romantic movement in the early nineteenth century reversed the value judgments implicit in this phrase and did their best to rehabilitate the culture of the Middle Ages, but the older tradition continued. Just after the middle of the nineteenth century Georg Voigt and Jacob Burckhardt, in two books published almost simultaneously, crystallized the interpretation of humanism and the Renaissance in the form in which it was to remain for more than fifty years. Both recognized that "the revival of antiquity," as Voigt called it, was but a part of the Renaissance, but both assigned to it a place of primary importance in shaping the civilization and the spirit of the age. Early in this century a reaction against the interpretation presented by Voigt and Burckhardt set in, and since that time the whole problem of humanism and of the Renaissance has become extremely controversial. Although historians still disagree as to the relation of humanism to the Renaissance and of both to the Middle Ages, there is at least agreement that the conception of cultural history presented in crude form by the fifteenth-century humanists was absurd. The researches of the last two generations of medievalists have made it impossible to think of the Middle

Ages as a period of cultural darkness or of the Renaissance as one of sudden illumination through the revival of antiquity. The classical revival initiated by Italian humanism was, nevertheless, an important historical phenomenon and one that exerted a lasting influence on the shaping of modern culture.

One of the most important results of recent research has been to demonstrate how extensive was the influence of antique thought and classical literature on the development of medieval culture since the eleventh century. There was, we now recognize, a "Twelfth Century Renaissance," to which the term "the revival of classical antiquity" might also have been applied. But there is little evidence of continuity from the clerical humanism of the early twelfth century to the lay humanism of Italy some two hundred years later. Between the two movements fell the shadow of scholasticism, which was based upon a different part of the antique heritage. Moreover, the two types of humanism were not essentially similar, except for a common interest in classical literature. They were, in fact, as different as the ages which produced them. The Italian humanists brought to classical literature and to the whole world of antique life and thought a depth of understanding that would have been impossible to clerics whose social background was that of the feudal age.

It was Petrarch who first brought to the study of the classical Latin authors an empathetic understanding which enabled him to meet them on their own ground and commune with them as a fellow-citizen. Always intensely aware of his own personality, he was drawn to the personalities of the great writers of antiquity and turned to them for inspiration, for moral guidance as well as for models of literary form. There was a broad streak of the romantic in Petrarch's character which found satisfaction in an imaginative return to an idealized past. Under the influence of the classics he abandoned the vernacular tongue in which his great reputation as a poet had been made and turned to the ancient language. Later humanists found his classical style not entirely correct, but in his prose works at least — his familiar letters and his collection of biographies of great men, the *De viris illustribus,* among others — it was both vigorous and individual. His Latin poetry, on which he mistakenly based his hopes for immortal fame, was less successful. His long epic poem, *Africa,* which celebrated the career of the hero of the Roman Republic, Scipio Africanus, never seemed to get its feet off the ground, perhaps because Petrarch's poetic genius was essentially lyric rather than epic. His claim to the title of founder of Italian humanism rests, however, less on the example he set in his Latin works than on his new attitude toward antiquity, and on the missionary zeal with which he preached the gospel of the classics and communicated his enthusiasm to Boccaccio and others among his wide circle of acquaintances. Important as the personal influence of Petrarch was, however, the historian must look further for an answer to the question: what caused the literary world of Italy to turn for two centuries to the study and imitation of the classical Latin and Greek authors, and why at this particular stage in the development of Italian culture? Had Petrarch's empathetic feeling for the ancient writers been a mere personal idiosyncrasy it would not have aroused a similar enthusiasm among so many of his countrymen.

A much more fundamental cause of the classical revival can be found in the peculiar social development of Italy in the preceding period. The wealthy upper classes of the Italian cities had by the fourteenth century achieved sufficient cultural maturity and self-confidence to be ready to seek a culture suited to their peculiar needs. Lay education, fostered by large-scale business enterprise, was widespread among the middle and upper classes, while the concentrated wealth produced by capitalism furnished the means for patronage as well as the leisure to cultivate literature and the arts. But a society with new interests seldom creates a completely new culture. More commonly it will utilize its legacy from the past and adapt it to suit its own needs and tastes. Thus, when Italian vernacular literature began to take shape around the end of the thirteenth century and in the first half of the fourteenth, Dante and Petrarch drew upon medieval literary traditions, adapting and transforming them in the process. But neither the chivalric nor the clerical literary traditions of the Middle Ages could furnish an adequate foundation for a new urban culture. The upper-class laymen of the Italian cities had lost contact with the feudal and chivalric *mores* that had produced the secular literature of medieval France, while at the same time they lacked the professional training and special interests of the clerical schoolmen. But if medieval traditions proved inadequate the Italians had only to turn to a more distant past to find a congenial inspiration in the culture of a society very much like their own. The literature of Roman and Greek antiquity was the product of a wealthy, aristocratic, secular, and predominantly urban society, in which the citizen's life was set in the framework of a non-feudal state, a society, in short, in which the upper classes of the Italian city-states could easily imagine themselves at home. They had only to approach it in a receptive spirit to find in it a storehouse of secular knowledge and human wisdom, the whole expressed in literary forms different from and, on the whole, more perfectly finished than those inherited from the Middle Ages.

So much has been written about the humanists' preoccupation with the form of classical literature that it seems necessary to emphasize the fact that they were attracted to it by its intellectual content as well as by its aesthetic form. It was doubtless the beauty of Latin speech that first aroused the enthusiasm of Petrarch in his early youth and, poet that he was, he never ceased to revere the artistic mastery of the ancient writers. The influence of a classical sense of form was, indeed, apparent even in his Italian poetry. But as he grew older he learned to value more and more what could be learned from the thought and the varied knowledge of the ancient authors. The exigencies of their craft forced his successors to become philologists, but only the pedants among them — and let that age which is without pedants cast the first stone — ever forgot that form and content were inseparable characteristics of the literature they so greatly admired. What the humanists sought in the classics was a foundation upon which to build a culture in the broadest sense. What they found in the ancient literature was a liberal education.

The term adopted by the Renaissance scholars to denote this form of culture and education based on classical studies was *humanitas* or *studia humanitatis*. It was a term much used by Cicero and was apparently introduced into Renaissance usage in the Ciceronian sense by Leonardo Bruni in a dialogue *De studiis et litteris* written in 1401. Somewhat later the term *humanista* or humanist was applied, on the analogy with the classification of law students as jurists or canonists, to students of the humanities. The modern derivative, humanism (*Humanismus*) is a product of nineteenth-century German scholarship. Like many similar terms, it has been used in such varying senses that it seems worth while to define it carefully. Occasionally it has been used to denote mere philological classical scholarship. More frequently it has been applied to any philosophy which centers attention upon man. It has even been confused at times with an attitude that would more properly be called humanitarian. Even in antiquity some confusion as to its meaning apparently existed, since Aulus Gellius, writing in the second century A.D., felt it necessary to define the correct use of *humanitas*.

> Those who have spoken Latin and have used the language correctly [he wrote] do not give the word *humanitas* the meaning which it is commonly thought to have, namely, what the Greeks called φιλανθρωπία, signifying a kind of friendly spirit and good feeling toward all men without distinction; but they give to *humanitas* about the force of the Greek παιδεία, that is, what we call education and training in the liberal arts (*eruditionem institutionemque in bonas artes*). Those who earnestly desire and seek for these are most highly humanized. For the pursuit of that kind of knowledge, and the training given by it, have

been granted to man alone among the animals, and for that reason it is termed humanity (*humanitas*).[2]

It was in this proud sense that the Renaissance scholars used the term, with the additional limitation that for them "education and training in the liberal arts" was inseparable from the study of classical literature. As a specific historical phenomenon, humanism or the *studia humanitatis* meant a fairly well-defined group of intellectual disciplines: grammar, rhetoric, history, poetry and moral philosophy, all based upon the study of classical authors.

It is this definition of humanism as the study of both the form and the general content of classical literature that differentiates Renaissance humanism from the clerical humanism of the twelfth century, and to an even greater degree from the scholastic study of ancient Greek philosophy and science. The clerical humanists of John of Salisbury's generation were seduced by the beauty of classical Latin style and imitated it to the best of their ability. But, as devout clerics, they were suspicious of the ideas expressed in pagan writings, or were simply indifferent to their secular content; while, as products of a feudal age, they were incapable of understanding the social milieu and the ways of thinking reflected in the classical authors. The scholastic philosophers and theologians, on the other hand, who superseded the clerical humanists in the thirteenth century, were largely indifferent to classical style, but were deeply concerned with the content of certain aspects of Greek thought, though only those which could serve the technical needs of their specialized professional disciplines. Whether the scholastics were in fact closer to the living tradition of antiquity than were the men of the Renaissance, is a matter of opinion, but to call them humanists is to rob the term of all specific meaning.

Although they had their own group of disciplines, which they regarded as within their province, the Italian humanists did not form an organized academic profession. They had as yet no firmly established place in the universities, which in Italy were concerned chiefly with the professional courses in law, medicine and natural philosophy. An occasional humanist might be called to give a few lectures at a university, and several held fairly permanent posts as professors of rhetoric, fulfilling the traditional function of the earlier *dictatores* as teachers of formal composition for practical use. But, for the most part, they functioned outside the universities, as independent men of letters. As such, they formed a new class in society. Most of them were laymen, or if, like Petrarch, they had taken minor orders as a prerequisite to clerical patronage, their way

[2] *The Attic Nights of Aulus Gellius*, English translation by John C. Rolfe (Loeb Classical Library, 1927), II, 457.

of life was little affected thereby. After their work had made classical education fashionable in cultured society, some men with humanist training rose to high positions in the Church, two or three even to the highest. Some, too, had inherited wealth or combined their classical studies with such lucrative professions as the law. But the majority of the humanists remained free-lance writers and teachers, seeking a living as secretaries in the papal curia or in the chancelleries of the Italian states, as state historians, as tutors to the children of princes and wealthy citizens, or simply by soliciting patronage from princes, prelates, businessmen and *condottieri* to whom they dedicated their written works. Under the circumstances it is not surprising that some of them were guilty of flattering the rich and powerful, or that the highly competitive, uncertain and wandering life they led developed in them some unamiable qualities. Despite the high respect in which classical studies were held, the pay a humanist could claim was generally less than that accorded to a jurist or a member of the other established professions. They felt, with some justice, that they were not appreciated at their true worth, and the feeling tended to make them arrogant and assertive. Competition for patronage, too, bred professional jealousies that sometimes found expression in literary feuds replete with obscene abuse. There seems no reason, however, to believe that the humanists as a group were more immoral than any other social class. It is unfair, in any case, to judge the humanists, as Voigt and others have tended to do, by the most disreputable members of the class. A more balanced view must also take into account such men of high character and sober purpose as Coluccio Salutati, the venerable chancellor of Florence, or the inspired teacher, Vittorino da Feltre.

It is unfair, too, to judge the humanists by the disparity between what they aspired to achieve and what they actually accomplished. To reach a fair estimate of their achievement during this pioneering period, one must take into account the magnitude of their task. The restoration of all that survived of classical literature involved first of all a systematic search for manuscripts. Petrarch and Boccaccio led the hunt, and in the following generations collectors ransacked every obscure monastic library in Italy and extended the search beyond the Alps. During the Council of Constance the Florentine humanist, Poggio Bracciolini (1380–1459), combed the monasteries of Switzerland, and brought back a number of classical works unavailable in Italy, including several of Cicero's orations, a Lucretius, a complete Quintilian and nine unknown comedies of Plautus. The search was encouraged and financed by wealthy patrons who built up their libraries by buying rare manuscripts or having them copied. Nearly all the reigning princes, the Visconti, the Gonzagas, the Estensi, and such wealthy Florentine citizens as Niccolò Niccoli and

Cosimo de' Medici collected libraries which were made available to scholars. In mid-century Nicholas V founded the Vatican library, which soon became the largest public library in Europe. It is obvious, of course, that the classical authors discovered by the humanists had not been literally unknown in the Middle Ages. Medieval scholars were, in fact, fairly familiar with the principal classical authors. Still, a large number of minor works and some of major importance existed only in rare copies widely scattered and almost forgotten in decaying monastery libraries. What the humanists and their wealthy patrons did was to gather together and make available almost the whole surviving body of classical literature. When we remember that even Petrarch, who idolized Cicero, did not know the *Familiar Letters*, which Salutati discovered in 1392, we cannot doubt the importance of the collectors' work for the full understanding of antique civilization.

The collecting, copying, and diffusion of manuscripts was, however, but a part, and not the most laborious part, of the task the humanists had set for themselves. Many of the manuscripts they found were defective, having been copied by monks whose knowledge of Latin was imperfect and who were frequently careless. Poggio complained that a codex of Cicero's *Philippics*, which he had found, was so full of errors that to emend it called for divination rather than conjecture. "There is no woman [he added] so stupid or ignorant that she could not have copied more correctly."[3] To secure a faithful text it was thus necessary to compare as many copies as possible, to emend faulty readings, to weed out interpolations and reject forgeries. This in turn required a minute study of the problems of paleography, orthography, grammar, syntax and usage, all without the aid of printed texts, manuals, dictionaries and all the other aids regarded as indispensable to modern classical scholarship. In the process the humanists founded the science of critical philology. It was as yet a layman's science with little or no institutional organization, but their attitude toward it was not that of dilettanti. They brought to their task the patient and laborious devotion to minutiae which is the indispensable characteristic of the scientific scholar. When one considers the quantity of midnight oil sacrificed upon the altars of classical scholarship, the charge of frivolity so frequently brought against the humanists seems rather unfair.

As philologists the humanists were forced to develop a discriminating critical sense. Apparent in nearly all of them, it reached its fullest development in this period in the work of Lorenzo Valla (1405–57). After having been brought up in Rome, Valla led a wandering life. He taught in various cities, spent some years under the protection of Alfonso of

[3] Poggio Bracciolini, *Epistolae*, III, 17.

Naples, and finally returned to Rome to spend his last years under the patronage of Pope Nicholas V. His widely ranging critical sense, reinforced by an irrepressibly combative spirit, brought him into conflict with jurists, philosophers, monks and theologians and even for a time with the papacy. In a treatise *De voluptate* he examined in turn the ethical doctrines of Stoicism, Epicureanism and Christianity, and although he concluded that the last was superior to the other two systems, his sympathetic presentation of the Epicurean point of view shocked the serious-minded. He offended the theologians by exposing the writings attributed to Dionysius the Areopagite as spurious and by questioning the tradition that the Apostles' Creed was actually composed by the Apostles. He also combined historical with philological criticism to demonstrate that the Donation of Constantine, the document on which papal claims to territorial sovereignty in Italy were founded, was an eighth-century forgery. But, for all the diversity of his critical interests, Valla remained essentially a grammarian and philologist. His textual criticism of the New Testament, which later exerted a strong influence on Erasmus, was a work of pure scholarship without theological connotations. For the further development of humanism his most important work was the *Elegantiae linguae latinae*, a systematic survey of correct classical usage, based on an empirical study of the best classical authors. Its appearance marked a turning point in the development of humanist scholarship and literary taste. The early humanists had been eclectic in their choice of classical models, accepting as classical any pagan or Christian author prior to the seventh century A.D. Valla, with his keen critical and historical sense, distinguished between the various periods in the development of Latin, and gave his full approval only to the usage of the last century of the Roman Republic and the first century or so of the Empire. Although Valla would not have approved the exclusive Ciceronianism of some of the later humanists, his work marked a decisive step in the process which finally converted a living tongue into a dead language by selecting one moment in its historical evolution as standard and freezing it at that point.

The humanists of the first century of the movement, however, were still free from the cramping effects of a too exclusive classicism. But in their writing they did model their style on that of the ancient authors and thereby they laid themselves open to the often repeated charge that they were mere imitators, devoid of originality. The fact is simply that they wanted to write well, and they could think of no better way of doing so than to write as much like the ancient masters as possible. The method they used to achieve that end, however, led to rather more literal imitation than was altogether beneficial. It was their common practice to jot down in notebooks words, phrases, metaphors and turns of speech as well as all sorts of factual material and expressions of opinion culled from the classical authors. These they studied and committed to memory. In their own writing they drew upon this storehouse, reassembling the fragments to suit their purpose. At the worst, this method led to writing that was little more than a mosaic of borrowed phrases, overloaded with an unnecessary burden of classical allusion. At the best this detailed analysis of classical style made the writing of the humanists more correct, more flexible, simpler and more artistically integrated. One has only to turn from the rambling incoherence of a medieval chronicle to Bruni's *History of the Florentine People* to appreciate what the humanists had gained by their study of classical form, even though something of spontaneity might have been lost in the process. It was this minute study of classical authors, too, which enabled the humanists to recreate in their own minds so vivid an impression of the whole social and intellectual atmosphere of the ancient world. It must not be forgotten, either, that imitation of classical models reintroduced into literature a number of literary forms that had been neglected in the Middle Ages: the dialogue, the essay, the familiar epistle, comedy, tragedy, and the literary treatment of history, biography, moral philosophy and political theory.

Nevertheless, the fact remains that little if anything of what the Italian humanists wrote during this period has remained a living part of the world's literature; and this fact has reinforced the charge that imitation of the classics robbed them of the originality they presumably might have had if they had used their native tongue. It may be true, indeed, that the task of restoring the ancient authors and of developing a classical style absorbed the energies of the humanists and directed them into scholarly rather than creative channels. The circumstances of their employment and patronage, too, forced them to write a great deal of occasional material that could have no interest for a later age. As masters of the classical style so highly prized by contemporary taste, they were called upon to compose endless orations, eulogies and manifestos for every public occasion. But perhaps the most important reason why these writers, who were so much esteemed in their own day, have been neglected by later generations is that what they found in the classics and strove to disseminate was then new, but later became, thanks largely to their efforts, an integral part of European culture and as such seemed commonplace. It remains so in our own generation even though a classical tag no longer serves to point a moral or adorn a tale.

To have brought a fresh appreciation to classical poetry and prose, and a fuller understanding of those aspects of antique thought that medieval scholars had neglected or had failed to comprehend, was in itself an original contribution. In the classical Latin literature, which had never been deeply influenced by systematic Greek philosophy and metaphysics, the humanists found a wealth of comment on moral philosophy, ethics, history, political theory and, in general, on the problems of man seeking a pattern for the good life as individual or as citizen. For Petrarch and his successors, Cicero was not only the supreme master of eloquence; he was also the *magister vitae*, the wise man who could teach men how to live. And it added to the charm of this ancient wisdom that it was presented in literary form, not in syllogisms or *summae* or the professional jargon of the schoolmen. It was a form which appealed strongly to laymen like the humanists and their patrons, most of whom were not trained in professional philosophy or theology. Any educated man, living in a not too dissimilar society, could read and appreciate Cicero's treatises *De amicitia, De senectute* or *De officiis;* and any humanist felt himself qualified, after intensive study of the ancient authors, to write similar treatises or to discuss the problems of the good life in elegant letters or dialogues. Looking over lists of humanist writings one finds such titles as *De tyranno, De fato et fortuna, De avaritia, De re uxoria,* and many more of the same sort. That the men who purveyed the ancient wisdom to their generation were not in all instances wise men is irrelevant. Nor was it really important that most of them were not very original or systematic thinkers. The turn of phrase was frequently an echo of a classical source and the ideas were selected in an eclectic and haphazard fashion from a variety of systems. What is important is that they took from antiquity what suited the needs of their age as the scholastics had done before them. In both cases there was imitation and excessive respect for antique authority, but in both cases also the creation of something new, without which the cultural evolution of Western Europe would have been different.

One of the services which the humanists performed in their capacity as moral guides to the urban society of Italy was to erect a secular ideal of virtue and the virtuous life alongside the Christian, a lay morality alongside that of the priest and monk, an ideal not so much in conflict with Christianity as independent of it. The conceptions of the good life which they found in their classical models were based exclusively on experience in this world, the experience of thoughtful and responsible citizens. The ancient authors could speak directly to men who were trying, perhaps unconsciously, to reconcile their way of life with ideals inherited from the Middle Ages. A strong strain of Franciscan idealization of poverty ran through the piety of fourteenth-century Italy, and the medieval belief that monastic rejection of the world represented the highest form of religious life still haunted the minds of thoughtful men. It certainly haunted the troubled soul of Petrarch, and in his dilemma he turned for guidance not only to St. Augustine but also to Cicero and Seneca. In the teaching of the Stoic sages that the wise man will be indifferent to poverty or wealth, to good or evil fortune, he found an ideal of virtue that accorded well enough with the Franciscan and monastic ideals, but which still left the door open for the acceptance of wealth and honor. Among the vagrant humanists who followed him, the Stoicism they preached seems often no more than a pathetic justification of their actual poverty and the uncertainty of their lives. Stoic indifference to honors and glorification of the contemplative life of the sage was frequently distorted into a justification for the neglect of all civic or family responsibilities. But, as the humanists, and particularly the Florentine group, learned to understand Cicero more fully, they found in that noblest Roman a positive support for the active life of the citizen, and when, having recovered a knowledge of Greek, they went directly to the *Ethics* and the *Politics* of Aristotle, they found in his conception of moderate wealth as an aid to virtue an ideal more suited to the life of a mercantile society.

The ancient Greek and Roman conceptions of citizenship found a particularly responsive echo in the republic on the Arno around the turn of the century, when Florence was fighting for her liberty against the expanding despotism of Giangaleazzo Visconti. In Florence more than anywhere else the humanists were closely associated with the upper class of citizens who dominated the government of the republic. A number of them — Salutati, Bruni, Marsuppini, Poggio — held office as chancellors of the republic. Others themselves came from prominent families, or enjoyed the friendship and patronage of such wealthy citizens as the Strozzi, the Alberti, the Albizzi and the Medici, and came to share their political and social attitudes. During the struggle against the Visconti despotism the Florentine humanists gained a new appreciation of the ideals of the ancient Roman Republic, and applied them to the contemporary political scene with considerable propagandist effect. They also placed a new emphasis upon those aspects of antique thought which would give support to the bourgeois ideals of sober thrift and of responsible family and civic life and which would contribute to the education of good citizens. And these ideals of "civic humanism," as it has been called, were given a wider circulation by treatises in the vernacular such as Luigi Palmieri's *Della vita civile* and Leo Battista Alberti's *Trattato della cura della famiglia*.

Aside from their eclectic borrowings from antique moral philosophy, the humanists absorbed many ideas and attitudes simply by breathing, although at second hand, the intellectual atmosphere of the ancient world. From their reverent communion with the great poets, moralists and historians they gained a heightened awareness of individual personality, an awareness particularly marked in Petrarch, who was in this as in so many other respects the prototype of humanism. With this intensified sense of personality went a stronger desire for fame and for a secular form of personal immortality in the memory of posterity. The humanists not only yearned for immortal fame themselves, but believed it to be in their power to confer it on others through their writings, and some of them, like Francesco Filelfo, were ready to sell their pens to the highest bidder.

The humanists, it is true, were not responsible for the individualism which characterized Renaissance society — it was a natural outgrowth of the economic, social and political development of the age — but they did furnish it with models and with the authoritative sanction of antiquity. They also found in the fully developed and cultured personalities of the ancient world models for imitation more congenial to their age than the medieval ideals represented by the feudal knight or the ascetic monk. When the humanists argued, as Poggio did in the dialogue *De nobilitate*, that nobility depends solely on personal worth, they were merely applying concepts drawn from the pre-feudal society of antiquity to the post-feudal society of the Italian cities. Reverence for the sages and the great men of antiquity, too, bred in the humanists a profound sense of the dignity of man, which ran counter to the belief in man's innate depravity that was one of the persistent strains in medieval thought. It has been argued recently that St. Thomas Aquinas presented a stronger philosophical defense of human dignity and individual worth than did the humanists; and, in fact, their ideas received philosophical formulation only in a later generation in the *Oratio de hominis dignitate* (1486) of Pico della Mirandola.[4] But it is significant that the early humanists founded their concept of the dignity of man not upon man's place in a divinely ordained cosmic scheme or great chain of being, but simply upon the potentialities of man as a human being. Finally, the humanists' acceptance of the classical, pre-Christian authors as moral guides led to an emphasis upon ethical and moral conduct as ends in themselves, independent of their theological implications, which later bore such diverse fruit as, on the one hand, Machiavelli's utterly secular conception of *virtù* and, on the other, the lay piety of the northern "Christian humanists" with its Erasmian conception of religion as a matter of ethics rather than dogma, and of Christianity as the *philosophia Christi*.

The reverence of the humanists for antiquity and their efforts to find in it a pattern for life have led many historians to regard the classical revival as a revival of paganism and to blame it for the irreverence and

4 See below, pp. 516–517.

immorality, the hedonism and worldliness they found in Renaissance society. After the Romantic movement of the early nineteenth century there was long a tendency to picture the Renaissance as a peculiarly wicked age in contrast to the Christian-ascetic Middle Ages. There was certainly a good deal of immorality in Renaissance society, but there was no revolt against Christianity and very little evidence of atheism or scepticism. What there was would be found among the Averroist schoolmen rather than among the humanists. The paganism, in the strict sense of the word, to be found in humanist writings was purely a matter of literary convention. The morality they drew from antiquity was certainly not pagan in the nineteenth-century sense of the word. The humanists were in fact, like other people, more or less religious according to their individual temperaments. They were aware of no antagonism between Christian doctrine and the high-minded moral and ethical teaching they found in the ancient sages, so that they could devote themselves to their classical studies in the secure conviction that they could have all this and Heaven too. What they did introduce into the intellectual life of Renaissance Italy was not paganism but an enormously increased body of secular material and non-religious interests. Their influence greatly accelerated both the laicization and the secularization of culture, tendencies already apparent in the preceding generations and which would have developed in any case, although not so rapidly, as a result of the social changes which were transforming the medieval world. These secular interests competed with religion for the attention of lay society, but they were not in any positive way antagonistic to the Christian faith.

Recent research has established beyond doubt that many of the humanists were deeply religious, and that characteristically medieval forms of religious thought may be found in Petrarch and many of his successors. And this discovery has led some historians to regard all signs of Christian piety among the humanists as evidence of the continuation of medieval traditions and as ground for annexing the Renaissance to the Middle Ages as a kind of anticlimactic epilogue. In this connection it is sometimes necessary to point out that Christianity was not a medieval invention and that the Middle Ages have not had a monopoly of Christian faith. The fact that many humanists were pious Christians is not sufficient reason in itself for regarding them as medieval. That some characteristically medieval traits persisted in humanist thought should not be surprising, since the transition from the Middle Ages to the Renaissance was neither sudden nor complete. But the preoccupation of the humanists with antique moral philosophy and classical scholarship could not leave their religious thought entirely untouched, and it did in fact lead them with each generation further from the medieval norms. The results were not yet clearly apparent in the work of the Italian humanists of this first century of the movement, but their emphasis upon ethics rather than speculative theology and their philological interest in the works of the early Fathers, above all Valla's textual criticism of the New Testament, pointed the road along which Erasmus and the "Christian humanists" later travelled.

If the new learning, as the humanists liked to call their classical scholarship, was not antagonistic to Christianity as such, it was, however, positively antagonistic to medieval scholasticism. It was not the Christian content of scholastic thought that alienated the humanists. On the contrary it was the lack of concern with spiritual things in the so-called Averroists of the Italian universities that aroused the wrath of Petrarch and caused him to denounce them as materialists and little better than atheists. It must not be forgotten that theology never held the dominant place in the Italian universities that it did at Paris and the other northern schools. The scholastic learning with which the Italian humanists came in contact was largely concerned with law, medicine, and natural philosophy, subjects which made small appeal to the humanists who, as lay men of letters, were primarily concerned with the literary form and the ethical and moral content of classical literature. Petrarch spoke for the whole clan of the humanists when he called down a curse on all their houses: jurists, doctors of medicine, and philosophers alike. What could their knowledge contribute to the good life? Petrarch asked in his diatribe, *De suis ipsius et multorum aliorum ignorantia*, directed against the Averroists. This was one of the crucial objections of the humanists to scholasticism as they knew it. Even the systematic theology of the schoolmen, so far as they were acquainted with it, seemed inadequately concerned with the immediate ethical and moral problems of human life. A second objection was to the form of scholastic learning, which was technical, syllogistic, and expressed in Latin that fell far short of classical standards of elegance.

In rejecting scholasticism the humanists undoubtedly limited the scope of their intellectual interests. Historians of science have deplored their indifference to the natural sciences, the study of which was included under natural philosophy in the scholastic curriculum, and have tended to regard the whole period of humanist ascendance as a regrettable hiatus in the development of scientific thought. The fact may be admitted, and the explanation is simple. The humanists' interests lay elsewhere, within the circle of the *studia humanitatis*. It has also been charged that they contributed little, in this early period at least, to formal philosophy. This too may be admitted. As philosophers they were amateurs. Their philosophy was largely a matter of ethics and good sense, founded upon eclectic gleanings from antique literary sources. Its aim was simply to aid men to live well.

The difference between humanist philosophy and that of the professional schools was reflected in the work of the humanists as educators. Having rejected scholasticism, and with it the educational methods and aims of the medieval universities, the humanists were forced to construct theories of education and methods of instruction of their own. As was to be expected, they based their theories on classical models, drawing heavily upon Cicero's *De oratore* and Quintilian's *Institutio oratoris.* These works dealt primarily with the training of orators, that is, men equipped to take an active part in public affairs. Since the orator's function involved speaking well, training in literary composition was essential. But the ideal orator envisaged by Cicero and Quintilian was not merely a rhetorician, but a philosopher, a virtuous and broadly educated man; and the achievement of this ideal was the aim expressed in all the humanist treatises on education. In the civic humanist circle in Florence, education was clearly designed to produce responsible and devoted citizens. Alberti in the *Trattato della cura della famiglia* insisted on the obligation of citizens to serve the state, and Palmieri in *Della vita civile* stressed the similar educational aim of fitting men for active life in society. In the courts of Ferrara and Mantua, where the two greatest schoolmasters of the Renaissance, Guarino da Verona (1370–1460) and Vittorino da Feltre (1378–1446) founded private schools for the education of the children of princes and courtiers, the aim of education was more specifically directed toward the formation of well-rounded and harmonious personalities. Both gave due emphasis to bodily exercise as well as to book-learning. Vittorino stressed above all the duty of the schoolmaster to consider the individual personality of his pupils and to develop their potentialities to the fullest extent. It was an educational program practical only in a small aristocratic school, and the finished product it aimed at was the perfect courtier as later described by Castiglione. Despite minor differences of aim and method, however, all the humanist educators were agreed that the essential basis of education was a thorough knowledge of the Latin and Greek classics, including the writings of the early Christian Fathers. From these could be derived everything that an educated man needed to know and all, too, that was needed for the formation of his character. Except for the emphasis on classical scholarship, it was in no way a technical or professional training, although it might serve admirably as a foundation to which professional training could later be added. The great humanist schoolmasters like Guarino, Vittorino and later Federigo da Montefeltro, Duke of Urbino, could obviously reach only a small number of students directly, but their educational ideals exercised a widespread and lasting influence. Neither their curriculum nor their educational aims would have seemed strange to a nineteenth-century headmaster of Eton or Harrow.

In this program of education for life and citizenship, the study of history played an important part. The humanist educators urged the reading of the ancient historians as models of prose style, but also, as Bruni pointed out in his treatise *De studiis et litteris,* because history formed an invaluable treasury of examples of ethical, moral and political behavior from which citizens and statesmen could learn much to their advantage. More important than this rather unoriginal recognition of the pragmatic value of history, however, was the historical perspective that the humanists gained from their classical studies. The medieval world-chroniclers shared the divine view of history — a view also shared by many students. A thousand years were as a day in their sight. This, of course, does not apply to their treatment of contemporary or recent history; but, when they turned to the past, the whole history of the world since the creation flowed in one undifferentiated stream, save for the great turning point which came with the Incarnation and the founding of the Christian Church. The humanists' reverence for antiquity and contempt for medieval culture, on the other hand, forced upon them a realization of the passage of time and of the changes it had wrought, from which they developed a new periodization of history. Their interest in history began with the great age of classical civilization. As they saw it, this age had been followed by a middle age of barbarism, during which all good culture had been dead or dormant, to be revived again only in their own time. Moreover, they had learned from their classical models to think of history not as the story of mankind since the creation, but as the history of individual states. When they began to write history in the classical manner, they accordingly wrote the history of their own Italian states, usually beginning with the decline of the Roman Empire. This was, incidentally, a task for which their practical experience as chancellors and state secretaries eminently fitted them. The humanists also learned from the example of the ancient historians, as well as from their own experience, to see in history the play of human passions and political motives, rather than the inscrutable workings of Divine Providence. They thus took history out of the theologically oriented framework of world chronicle in which Augustine had placed it, and gave it a purely secular setting and content. In short, for clerical history they substituted lay history. The result was a revolution in historical thought, the beginning of modern historiography. Some critics have deplored the loss of local color which they felt resulted from the humanists' use of classical Latin in their histories, but any loss in that direction was more than compensated by the coherence and historical insight they gained from their study of the ancient masters.

The first work to demonstrate the full effect of these various factors on historical writing was that of Leonardo Bruni (1370-1444) whose *History of the Florentine People* was written while he was chancellor of the republic between the years 1437 and 1444. Here Bruni set a standard of literary style, historical criticism, and coherent organization that differentiated his work clearly from even such late medieval chronicles as that of Giovanni Villani, and made it the model followed by nearly all later humanist historians. Bruni's thought had been profoundly influenced by Aristotle's *Politics*, which he had translated, and by the political atmosphere of Florence in the period of its struggle against Visconti aggression. More than any other historian of his age he perceived the vitally important rôle of the free communes in the evolution of medieval Italy, and his conviction that political freedom was a necessary prerequisite to civic virtue and a vigorous culture led him to advance the novel theory that it was imperial despotism that was primarily responsible for the decline of Roman civilization. His rejection of the theory that the medieval empire was in fact a continuation of the Roman Empire also demonstrated the distance historical thought had travelled since Dante wrote the *De monarchia*.

The historical perspective which the humanists gained from literature and history was further reinforced by their eager study of the physical remains of the ancient civilization they so much admired, and by their desire to envisage the life of ancient Roman society as concretely as possible. Niccolò Niccoli (1363-1437), the Florentine merchant turned humanist, collected antique sculpture, coins and medals as well as manuscripts, and made them available to students. Poggio was haunted by the spectacle of grandeur and decay presented by the ruins of ancient Roman buildings and monuments and wrote a description of them in his treatise, *De varietate fortunae*. The real founder of modern archaeology, however, was the indefatigable papal secretary, Flavio Biondo of Forlì (1387-1463). With infinite labor and critical skill Biondo reconstructed the topography, monuments, manners and customs of ancient pagan and Christian Rome in two encyclopedic books: *Roma triumphans* and *Roma instaurata*. Then, enlarging the range of his research, he compiled a geographical and historical survey of Italy since ancient times under the title *Italia illustrata*. Finally, in his *History from the Decline of the Roman Empire* he furnished a factual account of Italian history from the sack of Rome by the Visigoths to his own time. This was a scholarly work, founded upon critical examination of the sources, but it lacked the literary form, the coherent organization and the historical insight of

Bruni's work. Later humanists scorned its pedestrian style, but borrowed from it freely, usually without acknowledgement.

The foregoing discussion has dealt primarily with the humanists' interest in classical Latin literature and ancient Roman civilization, for that was as yet the most important part of their recovery of the antique heritage. The first half of the fifteenth century, however, also witnessed the first decisive steps in the rediscovery of ancient Greek literature. This was in a much more literal sense a recovery of something that had been lost than was true of the revival of classical Latin. For centuries knowledge of Greek had almost disappeared in Western Europe. Despite their dependence on Aristotle and other Greek authorities, which they read in translations of uneven value, few of the medieval schoolmen could read Greek, and of Greek literature as such they knew little. Nor would they have been greatly interested had it been available. The humanists, on the other hand, were eager to recover just those parts of the Greek heritage that the schoolmen had ignored: not logic, metaphysics and science, but history, biography, poetry, drama, and works of moral philosophy. These were the aspects of Greek culture that had exerted a powerful influence on the Latin writers of the classical age, and no ardent admirer of Cicero could avoid being curious about the literature which that master of eloquence had regarded as the most perfect expression of *humanitas*.

There were, however, serious obstacles in the way of the Italian students who first desired to master Greek. They were starting from scratch. Greek manuscripts were rare in Italy, and such aids as manuals, grammars and dictionaries were practically non-existent. That Petrarch, with all his linguistic talent and enthusiasm for antiquity, never learned Greek is a measure of the difficulty involved. He treasured a manuscript of Homer, which he had acquired, but to the end it remained Greek to him. What the Italian scholars needed was a competent teacher to give them a start, and the real introduction of Greek studies into Italy can be dated from the appointment of a distinguished Byzantine scholar, Manuel Chrysoloras, to a chair in the Florentine university in 1397. At the news of his arrival scholars came from all over Italy to sit at his feet. Pier Paolo Vergerio resigned his post as professor of logic at Padua and Leonardo Bruni abandoned his legal studies to come to Florence and seize the unprecedented opportunity.

Chrysoloras lectured for only three years in Florence and for three more in Milan and Pavia, but before he returned to Constantinople in 1403 he had sown the seed which others could now cultivate. Once started, the Greek revival progressed steadily. Guarino and Filelfo followed him to Constantinople to complete their training, and returned to teach. Bruni mastered Greek sufficiently to translate a number of Greek works. Both Guarino and Vittorino gave the study of Greek an important place in the curriculum of their schools. The hunt for ancient manuscripts now included the Greek, and a number were imported from Constantinople. Thus, when an ecumenical council of the Greek and Roman churches met in Ferrara and Florence in 1438 and 1439, Italian scholars were already prepared to make the most of the opportunity to fraternize with the learned Byzantine delegates, some of whom also remained to teach after the council had ended. The fall of Constantinople to the Turks in 1453 came too late to be of decisive importance for the revival of Greek in Italy, but it did help to accelerate the movement. The refugees brought many more Greek manuscripts, and they swelled the number of Greek teachers, editors and translators, but that is all.

Although Greek studies were firmly established in Italy before 1453, the influence of Greek culture on humanist thought was as yet relatively slight. The number of Italian scholars who could read Greek well enough to be influenced by Greek style was still fairly small, and the work of translating, which spread the influence of Greek thought to a larger audience, did not get under way until the second half of the century. On the whole, it seems to have been the Greek prose writers — the historians and philosophers — who were most widely read in this period. Since Petrarch, the humanists had nourished a prejudice against the philosophical and scientific works of Aristotle, which they identified with scholasticism, but they seized upon the *Ethics* and *Politics* and the pseudo-Aristotelian *Economics* and incorporated them into their eclectic system of moral philosophy. Many of the humanists, it is true, professed a preference for Plato over Aristotle. They were charmed by his literary style and found the dialogue form of his works more to their taste than Aristotle's textbookish treatment, but the systematic study of Platonic and Neoplatonic philosophy did not begin till after the middle of the century.

C. VERNACULAR LITERATURE IN FRANCE, GERMANY AND ENGLAND

The century and a half from 1300 to 1450 was a troubled period for the countries north of the Alps, a period marked by plague and destructive warfare, by the cessation of economic growth, by the political and economic decline of the nobility, by scandal and heresy in the Church, by social revolt, and by subtle but profound changes in the character and relative status of all the social classes. It is a difficult age to characterize, since many of the most significant changes took place underneath the surface of a social order that still maintained the external forms of an earlier age. What was new in this period was often less apparent than was the decline or disintegration of medieval forms of social and cultural life. Some of the same forces were at work here as had brought about the growth of a fresh vernacular literature in Italy and had also led to the rise of classical humanism there: a steady increase in the participation of laymen and of lay patronage in the higher forms of culture; increasing lay education and an expansion of the lay reading public; and, despite much deep piety, a general trend toward secularism and realism. But in the northern countries, where medieval traditions were more deeply imbedded than in Italy, these forces failed on the whole to give new vitality to literature. With one or two notable exceptions, it was a barren and uninspiring age in literary history.

The continuation of medieval literary forms was guaranteed by the fact that the interests and tastes of the nobility and the atmosphere of the royal and princely courts set the tone for a large part of secular literature. The northern nobles, unlike the Italian, remained outside the life of the cities. A distinct social cleavage still separated them from the upper ranks of the bourgeoisie, and, of the two classes, the nobility had incomparably the greater prestige. At the same time, the social character of the noble class was changing. Economic depression impoverished the landholding classes and reduced the standard of living of the lesser nobility, while the growing power of central government was reducing the independence of the greater nobles and was gradually transforming them from feudal barons into royal courtiers. The social life of the upper crust of the nobility, and with it the literary patronage which was still largely aristocratic, became increasingly concentrated in royal and princely courts. Here the forms of feudal and chivalric culture were maintained as ornaments of the court to serve the prestige of the rising monarchy. But from these forms the reality was being slowly drained away. As the Hundred Years' War dragged on, chivalry disappeared from the field of battle and found its last refuge in the empty magnificence of tournaments and court ceremony. Its forms were more highly elaborated than ever, but they no longer corresponded to a practical way of life common to the noble class of Western Europe. And this elaboration of forms that had lost contact with reality was reflected in the literature which still followed the courtly and chivalric tradition. The court poets seemed to have no new themes for their verse, but repeated in ever more conventional form those they had inherited from medieval lyric and romance, from the dream sequences and the allegories of love.

The cult of courtly love, which formed the theme of so much of medieval lyric and romance, had flourished principally in baronial courts and could not be transplanted without loss of vitality. It was a convention that had its roots in a feudal society which found its focus in the castles of semi-independent lords. There knightly troubadours pledged a tuneful and deferential devotion to the lady of the castle, much as they pledged homage and allegiance to their feudal lord. When the focus of noble society shifted from the baronial courts to the royal court, its roots were amputated and courtly love degenerated into a conventional game. But changes in the social milieu of the nobility were not alone responsible for the altered tone of courtly love and the verse which celebrated it. Something was also due to bourgeois infiltration. Many of the writers of courtly lyrics and chronicles during the fourteenth and fifteenth centuries were bourgeois-born. Secretaries, lawyers, administrative agents of government, they were drawn into the royal courts and wrote to please the taste of the patrons they found there. They adopted the conventions of chivalric literature, but without conviction or genuine chivalric sentiment, injecting into it elements of didacticism, of prosy erudition and, at times, of plain common sense, that were essentially alien to it. The increasing volume of prose as compared to poetry in these centuries was also evidence that a reading public was replacing the listening public of the medieval courts, and this reading public included burghers as well as clerics and nobles. Prose is less memorable than poetry and so formed no part of the *jongleur's* repertoire. It had to be read. As books replaced the *jongleur* who had recited works committed to memory, there was not only more prose, but also an alarming tendency toward prolixity in both prose and verse. Much of the literature of this period rambles on and on, piling up loosely connected incidents or irrelevant details in endless succession.

The emergence of a reading public in the upper classes of the cities made the bourgeoisie for the first time a significant force in directing the currents of literary taste. As yet, however, the burghers exerted less influence on the main currents of literature than might have been expected from their increasing wealth and education. The wealthy burghers aped the clothing and manners of their social superiors — courtly literature is full of complaints that one can no longer tell a merchant from a noble or a burgher's wife from a lady — and they also read the romances and allegories of love that were popular at court. The secular book most commonly found in the libraries of patrician merchant families was that greatest of all medieval allegories of love, the *Roman de la Rose*, although its readers were probably most attracted by the voluminous second part — some eighteen thousand verses — added by Jean de Meung in the last quarter of the thirteenth century. With its ponderous and encyclopedic erudition and its unchivalrous attitude toward women, this heavy-handed sequel probably suited the bourgeois taste better than the courtly delicacy of the original allegorical romance of the garden of love, but it was widely read also in court circles. Even if the burghers had not accepted the literature designed primarily for noble consumption, they could have exerted little direct influence upon the more artistic forms of secular literature because patronage was concentrated largely in the royal or princely courts, and to these the most gifted writers naturally gravitated. Kings, princes and great nobles had not only money but also offices in government service, sinecures at court and ecclesiastical benefices at their disposal with which to reward poets and chroniclers who attracted their fancy.

Nevertheless, beginning in the thirteenth century, there was a growing body of literature that seems to have been designed primarily for a bourgeois audience or for one that may have included the provincial gentry who lived too far from the atmosphere of the royal courts to share all the interests and tastes of the great nobles. This literature had for the most part little artistic merit. It was above all didactic. A very large part of it was devoted to moral instruction or religious inspiration and reflected the lay piety that was one of the outstanding characteristics of this winter of the Church's discontent. There were also a good many instructive works dealing with practical matters and frequently set in halting rhyme. Bourgeois literature had its lighter side too, realistic and broadly humorous tales or satirical comments on the morals and manners of the nobles and the clergy. Finally, it was in bourgeois circles that vernacular drama was born, as guilds and confraternities took over the direction and acting of miracle and morality plays and so laid the foundations for the modern theatre. Undistinguished as this mass of bourgeois literature was in the main, it served to educate the rising middle class and to give it the habit of reading, until such time as it would be prepared, with the aid of printed books and the stimulus of classical humanism, to take a more decisive part in the formation of the national literatures.

What has been said about the general character of vernacular literature during this period applies more or less to all the northern countries. The literary history of each, however, was conditioned by traditions and circumstances that were in part peculiar to it. It will be necessary, therefore, to consider each of the major vernacular literatures separately, though it will be impossible here to do more than note the main lines of development and the personalities of a few of the more important authors.

During the High Middle Ages, France had been responsible for the creation and dissemination of all the major forms of vernacular literature. The courtly poets and chroniclers of the fourteenth and fifteenth centuries thus labored under the weight of a great inherited tradition, to which they could add little but the refinement and elaboration of form. Throughout this period, French literature centered in the north: in the valley of the Loire, in the Île de France, in Champagne and the French-speaking provinces of the Netherlands. Here were the royal court and the princely courts of the dukes of Burgundy, Orléans, Anjou, and Berry, and the Counts of Hainault. Southern France had never recovered from the shock of the Albigensian Crusade, but the forms of troubadour lyric had been naturalized in the dialect of northern France by the courtly *trouvères* during the thirteenth century. Together with the epics and romances, which were indigenous to the north, the lyric poetry of the *trouvères* laid the foundations for the modern French language. Thanks in large part to the centralizing influence of the royal and princely courts, the wide variety of dialect, which had characterized medieval French, gradually disappeared from written literature. As a result the French poetry and prose of this period, though still containing many archaic forms, can be read today with little difficulty, whereas that of the twelfth and thirteenth centuries demands special training.

Of the series of expert versifiers who followed one another in the courts of northern France, Guillaume de Machaut (c. 1300–71) was closest to the medieval lyric tradition which combined words and music as inseparable forms. Machaut was, indeed, a more important figure in the history of music than in that of poetry. He was born in Champagne, probably of a bourgeois family, but spent the greater part of his life in the service of kings and princes, including the blind King John of Bohemia. He was essentially a court poet and composer, although, like many musicians and men of letters, he took clerical orders and received patronage in the form of ecclesiastical preferment, ending his life as a canon of Reims. Taken by themselves, his courtly lyrics seem rather artificial, the rhymes too lush, the metrical forms of *ballade, rondeau*, and *virelai* too elaborate; but set to his music they have made a lasting place for themselves in the history of French song.

With the next French poet, Eustache Deschamps (c. 1346–c. 1406), disciple of Machaut though he was, poetry and music parted company, and the poetic inspiration of his vast production of verse (some eighty thousand lines) was considerably thinner. Deschamps was a layman who held several administrative posts in the courts of the king and the Duke of Orléans. He wrote conventional lyrics for his patrons at court, but his heart was not in the chivalric tradition. Although he wrote verses to order with indefatigable fluency, Deschamps was capable of expressing unpopular opinions with honest indignation. Particularly in his later years, when things were going badly for France after the death of

Charles V, he castigated the vices and follies of knights and courtiers in verses to which patriotic sentiment lent dignity, if not poetic inspiration.

Both the patriotic sentiment and the harsh strictures on the failings of French chivalry appeared again in the dark hours after Agincourt in the poetry and prose of Alain Chartier (c. 1385–c. 1433). But his clear perception of the bankruptcy of chivalry as a military force did not prevent him from devoting the greater part of his graceful and fluent verses to the theme of courtly love. As secretary to Charles VI and Charles VII, he was familiar with the courts of love, which formed one of the amusements of the idle courtiers, and like other poets he wrote to please his patrons. That neither he nor his patrons took the traditional themes very seriously is evident from the best known of his poems, "La Belle Dame sans Merci," with its final appeal to *dames et demoiselles* to avoid the odious example of the hardhearted lady who was impervious to her lover's plaints.

Equally conventional, if less lighthearted, were the verses of his contemporary, Christine de Pisan (c. 1364–c. 1433), the Italian-born widow of one of the secretaries of Charles VI, who made a living for herself and her children by writing love poems to order for the lords and ladies of the court. She is worth noting as probably the first professional woman writer, and because of the considerable reputation she enjoyed in her time. But that this precious bluestocking could have been regarded as a great poetess is a sad commentary on contemporary taste.

A generation later, the tradition of the courtly lyric reached its culmination in the poetry of Charles, Duke of Orléans (c. 1391–1465). Taken prisoner at Agincourt, Charles spent the next twenty-six years in captivity in England. There, and later in his château on the Loire, he whiled away the time by writing delicate and perfectly formed verses in a mood of gentle melancholy. His constant theme, "Je suis celui au coeur vêtu de noir," was scarcely vigorous enough to make great poetry, and the tradition in which he wrote was running thin. But he was at least a genuine poet, an authentic artist in verse, and no mere versifier. Charles d'Orléans stood at the end of a stream of lyric poetry which had its source in twelfth-century Provence. After him came the *grands rhétoriqueurs*, pedantic poets who wrote by rule and turned a verse by hand, and when the courtly lyric came to life again in the sixteenth century, the influence of Italy and the classics had introduced a new element and founded a new tradition. There is a poetic appropriateness in the fact that the lyric tradition to which so many French nobles had contributed in the Middle Ages should have ended with a prince of the blood royal.

French prose, while lagging behind poetry in its development, was firmly established as a literary medium during the thirteenth century by

Villehardouin's *Chronicle* and a group of prose romances. The Sire de Joinville's *Vie de St. Louis*, too, though not finished till 1309, belongs in spirit to the thirteenth century. During the following period, as the habit of reading became more widespread, prose was more and more commonly used, especially for didactic works. Few of these had literary value, but two at least deserve mention for their human interest and for the light they cast on social manners and customs. In 1371, a sober provincial knight, the Chevalier de la Tour-Landry, wrote for the instruction of his daughters a book on the behavior, manners and morals suitable for young ladies both before and after marriage. Like the sermons of the day, it was illustrated with stories or *exempla*, sometimes horrible *exempla*, which the young ladies must have found enlightening. It is a sign of the changing times that the country gentleman's attitude toward marriage and women's place in society shows little evidence of the chivalric tradition that still prevailed at court, and that his wife took a distinctly dim view of courtly love. An even more illuminating picture of home life in wealthy bourgeois circles is to be found in the book written about 1392–94 by an elderly Parisian burgher, who called himself *Le Ménagier de Paris*, for the instruction of his young wife. The *Ménagier* is much concerned with the details of cooking, supervising servants, shopping and housekeeping generally, and through it all runs the combination of piety and careful management of property that formed the distinctive character of the bourgeois class.

For the one authentic masterpiece of French prose, however, one must return to the atmosphere of the court. Jean Froissart (c. 1337–c. 1404) was a court poet whose lyrics, verse romances and allegorical dream sequences entitle him to rank with Machaut and Deschamps; but they have been so far overshadowed by his prose *Chronicle* that they have been almost forgotten. Born at the opening of the Hundred Years' War, Froissart devoted the greater part of his life to recounting the story of that long drawn out struggle, together with the contemporary conflicts in Scotland and Spain. As a native of Hainault he could view the great war from a relatively neutral position. As a young man he spent some years in England in the service of Queen Philippa, the daughter of the Count of Hainault. Later he was attached to the courts of various lords in the Netherlands and France. And at every opportunity he travelled, gathering at first hand materials for his chronicle from the men who had participated in the wars. Despite, or perhaps because of, his bourgeois origin, Froissart was inspired by a romantic love of chivalry and chivalrous deeds, and he accepted at their face value the ideals and standards of the noble class, into which he had risen as a courtier and friend of princes. It is pointless, then, to condemn him for failure to perceive the real character of the war or the basic issues involved in it. Nor, given the vivid immediacy of the stories this fourteenth-century Herodotus gleaned from oral evidence, is there any point in deploring his failure to use documentary sources or to conform to the critical standards of the modern historian. For the early part of his story he necessarily leaned heavily on the chronicle of his predecessor, Jehan le Bel, but for the events of his own mature lifetime he collected evidence from innumerable eyewitnesses. To the knights and squires whom he questioned he owed the detailed narratives that make his long and disjointed *Chronicle* a collection of masterly short stories; and, since he recounted faithfully what he was told, a great deal of the grimmer and more realistic aspects of warfare can be discerned through the chivalric haze. Without knowing it, though a glimmering awareness seems to have dawned on him in his later years, Froissart was the chronicler of declining chivalry, of knighthood no longer in flower but rapidly going to seed.

In Germany, the literary history of this period presents a dreary picture. This century and a half produced scarcely a single German writer, except for a handful of religious mystics, whose name is known to any but the specialists in the field. German literature, indeed, seems to have been caught at a low ebb between the magnificent vitality of the chivalric age — the *Ritterzeit* — which had produced Wolfram von Eschenbach, Gottfried von Strassburg, Hartmann von Aue, and Walther von der Vogelweide, to mention only the most important poets — and the growth of a patrician culture in the German cities under the influence of classical humanism toward the end of the fifteenth century. The intervening period was one of political and social turmoil in Germany. After the collapse of the medieval Empire there was no significant royal court, and the courts of the territorial princes were too small to serve as focal centers for noble culture. The class of knights was passing through a period of economic and political decline, and the burghers had not yet acquired the wealth or the cultural tradition needed to produce a vigorous literature.

For the literary history of England the fourteenth and fifteenth centuries were transitional in a double sense. They mark the crucial stage in the transition, not only from medieval to modern literary forms, but also from bilingualism, which had retarded the growth of a distinctively English literature in the High Middle Ages, to the formation of an English tongue common to all Englishmen and easily comprehensible to modern English readers. For three centuries after the Norman Conquest, England had two languages, in addition to the Latin which there, as elsewhere, was the language of the learned. During all that period, Norman-French remained the language of the ruling class, superimposed upon the native tongue of the masses of the people. As time passed, an increasing number of the middle and upper classes undoubtedly became bilingual, with the result that great numbers of French words were absorbed into the English tongue. At the same time the literary tradition of Old English was permanently broken. Being the language of the socially inferior classes, English ceased for a long time to be written, with the result that many Old English words, which a literary tradition might have preserved, dropped out of use. During this period, too, many of the highly inflected forms characteristic of a Germanic language disappeared. When English began to be written again in the thirteenth century it was already far removed from the language spoken before the Conquest. It was not till the second half of the fourteenth century, however, that English began to approach its modern form, and then only in the East Midland dialect used by Chaucer. Because of its diverse parentage, the newly formed English tongue was rich in synonyms, free in its grammatical construction and, having combined the syllabic meters of French with the accentual beat of the native tradition, capable of becoming a poetic medium of great elasticity and power.

The triumphant emergence of English as the national language in this period is evidence of a growing national consciousness, to which the long wars with France no doubt contributed. The Anglo-Norman nobility and gentry were at last beginning to think of themselves as English. Edward III was an English king in a sense that Henry Plantagenet or Richard Coeur de Lion had never been. The centralization of government which characterized the fourteenth century, and the concentration of legal and administrative as well as economic activity in the capital, must also have contributed to the growth of linguistic unity. The social barriers which had separated the Anglo-Norman aristocracy from the mass of the people were also beginning to break down. A prosperous class of merchants, who were, as Queen Elizabeth later proclaimed herself to be, "mere English," was beginning to mingle with the gentry of Norman blood. This growing administrative and social unity found visible expression in the House of Commons, where burghers sat with gently-born knights of the shire, and there in 1363 the opening address was for the first time delivered in English. French continued for a time to be the prevailing language of the royal court and, despite an Act of Parliament to the contrary in 1362, "Law French" long continued to be the technical language of lawyers. But in the later fourteenth century French was clearly ceasing to be the official language of England, and lacking official support it was rapidly dropping out of common use even among the aristocracy. Chaucer's Prioress could speak French, but only

Literature and Learning

After the scole of Stratford atte Bowe,
For French of Paris was to her unknowe.

But this was evidently regarded as an accomplishment, and not something to be taken for granted as the normal speech of a provincial lady of good family. She certainly had no trouble understanding the speech of such low-born characters as the Reeve and the Miller.

The belated emergence of an English literary language was no doubt in large part responsible for the equally belated development of English vernacular literature. For two centuries or more after the Conquest, England was, so far as literature was concerned, scarcely more than a province of France. It was also a singularly unproductive province. There, as elsewhere, literary production depended largely upon aristocratic patronage, and when the Anglo-Norman nobles read at all they read French. They could not be expected to patronize literature written in the language of the people, but at the same time their position as a socially and culturally isolated minority prevented them from making any important contribution to French literature either. The most important works written in England during the twelfth and thirteenth centuries were produced by the clergy and were in Latin. When English literature began to develop tentatively in the thirteenth century, more strongly in the fourteenth, it had therefore no native tradition on which to build. It was natural, then, that the influence of French literature, with two centuries or more of great achievement behind it, should have long remained dominant. A very large part of the works written in English during the thirteenth and fourteenth centuries was composed of translations from French or adaptations of French originals. Great numbers of metrical romances retold or imitated the material of French romance, particularly of the Arthurian cycle. The *Roman de la Rose,* too, continued to exert a profound influence here, as in its native country, and made the allegorical dream sequence an almost obligatory form. As the fourteenth century progressed, however, English writers gained in skill and confidence and began to display greater originality. After the middle of the century, the development was extremely rapid, and for the first time England produced a group of poets who could be compared with the French or German writers of the great medieval period.

Although the poets responsible for this belated flowering of Middle English were all more or less contemporaries, their work falling within the second half of the fourteenth century, they were by no means a unified group. Variations in dialect still raised a linguistic barrier between the north and west and the region around London. Moreover there appeared at this time among some of the most accomplished provincial poets an anachronistic revival of the Anglo-Saxon principle of alliterative verse, which, together with their use of obsolescent West Country dialects, not only makes them more difficult for us to read, but also makes them seem much further removed from us in time than their contemporaries in the capital. Alliteration had been the dominant feature of Anglo-Saxon or Old English poetry, combined with a strong *caesura* breaking the line into two parts, a fairly regular accented beat, and considerable freedom in the number of syllables to the line. When English poetry began to be written again after the long hiatus that followed the Conquest, alliteration had disappeared except as an occasional ornament. Until the archaic revival in the second half of the fourteenth century, English verse was constructed on a basis of meter and rhyme, principles borrowed from the French, although it still retained an accented beat and a greater elasticity in the number of syllables than French usage permitted. This was the form of prosody that was to remain characteristic of English poetry, with such changes as shifts in pronunciation required, through the age of Chaucer to modern times. The poets, for the most part anonymous, who revived alliterative verse were pursuing an archaic form which led them down a blind alley. They stood aside from the main currents of development and exercised little or no influence on later literature. They are, however, sufficiently interesting in themselves to warrant mention in even a brief survey, if only because they call attention to the conservative or backward-looking elements in this transitional age.

To one of these anonymous provincial poets, apparently a native of Lancashire, we owe four long poems, *The Pearl, Cleanness, Patience*, and *Sir Gawayne and the Grene Knight*, which are among the finest examples in all medieval literature of their respective genres. We know little or nothing about the author of these remarkable poems, and it has been suggested that the last of the four is by a different poet. The possibility of two such gifted poets appearing together in the only surviving manuscript seems, however, remote, and the poems will be considered here as the work of one man. *The Pearl* is an allegorical dream sequence, composed in stanzas which combine rhyme with alliteration. The poet had obviously read the *Roman de la Rose*, but this is no allegory of love in the conventional manner. Here the dreamer is a grief-stricken father. In his vision he finds consolation for the loss of his little daughter whom he sees, now grown to maturity, in Paradise. As in all medieval allegories, there are long stretches of didactic material, here largely theological, but there are also lyrical passages that strike a note of personal emotion rare in poems of this type. *Cleanness* and *Patience* are more purely didactic, recounting in alliterative blank verse Biblical stories illustrating the virtues of purity and submission to the will of God. The poet, who may have been a clerk in minor orders, was evidently a moralist, as were so many of his contemporaries. There is even a strong moralizing strain in *Sir Gawayne*. It is not, however, so pervasive as to spoil one of the most imaginative and artistically conceived romances in the Arthurian cycle, the only one in English that can be compared with the masterpieces of Chrétien de Troyes or Wolfram von Eschenbach. At the time when the unknown Lancashire poet was writing, the great age of romance was long since past, and Chaucer was making fun of the type in his parody romance of Sir Thopas. Romances were still being read, and written, in England, but most of them had little artistic inspiration. They were as a rule formless and incoherent, burdened with endless detail, and metrically monotonous. The appearance at this late date of so forceful and original a work as *Sir Gawayne* is, therefore, all the more remarkable. Although it may have been based on some French romance since lost, the version of the Gawayne story told here is unique in surviving literature. It is unique, too, in the degree to which it welds into a coherent entity the aspirations of romantic chivalry and the irrationality and subconscious depth of Celtic mythology. Appearing when it did, it seems as anachronistic in spirit as it was consciously archaic in form and vocabulary.

Equally remarkable, although in a very different way, is the *Vision of William concerning Piers the Plowman*, commonly ascribed to William Langland (c. 1332–1400). Whether all of this long and disjointed allegorical dream sequence, which consists of eleven loosely connected visions, was written by one man and, if so, whether the author was William Langland or another poet by the same name are questions that have been the subject of much scholarly debate, but need not concern us here. Internal evidence suggests that the author was a West Country-man, probably from Shropshire, a poverty-stricken clerk in minor orders with a wife and daughter to support, who spent a large part of his life in London. What is beyond doubt is that the poem expresses a deeply felt concern for the sufferings of the poor and a passionate conviction of the need for moral reform in Church and society that raise it far above the level of the ordinary didactic treatise. In poetic quality its alliterative blank verse falls below the standard set by the author of *The Pearl*, but any poetic lack is compensated by the author's earnestness and by his capacity for making his allegorical abstractions — Falsehood, Gluttony, and the like — seem concrete personalities, depicted in realistic action. In any case it is not its artistic form that makes *Piers Plowman* one of the most significant of medieval poems. Rather it is the fact that nowhere else, except perhaps in the *Canterbury Tales*, and then without the compassion and moral indignation that inspired Langland, can one find so comprehensive a picture of late fourteenth-century society or so vigorous an expression of the religious and social unrest that filled England on the eve of the Peasants' Revolt and the Wyclifite heresy. Yet, for all his idealization of honest labor in the figure of the Plowman and his bitter arraignment of the clergy, Langland was neither revolutionary nor heretical. His thought, despite his awareness of the evils caused by the changing times, was solidly medieval. He was a reformer, but a conservative reformer. He would not alter the social structure, which he believed to be divinely ordained. Indeed, he seems to have felt that it was the disintegration of the social order which he observed going on about him that was responsible for many of the evils of the time. The cure lay in moral regeneration within the existing framework of society. If each man would do his Christian duty in the position in which God had seen fit to place him, all would yet be well.

Turning from Langland and the *Pearl* poet to Chaucer, we enter a different world and one in which we can find ourselves more comfortably at home. It is difficult, indeed, to remember that Chaucer was the contemporary of the author of *Piers Plowman* or the still more thoroughly medieval poet who wrote *The Pearl* and *Sir Gawayne*. The relative modernity of Chaucer may be accounted for in part by the fact that the East Midland dialect in which he wrote was the direct ancestor of modern English. His immense prestige helped to establish it as the national literary language, but it was also the dialect of the capital, the court, and the two university towns, and here French and English influence met and mingled on more equal terms than was possible in the more isolated West Country. What is more striking about Chaucer, however, is the quality of his mind, which seems closer akin to Shakespeare than to the authors of the *Roman de la Rose*. He is in somewhat the same sense as Dante a transitional figure, between the medieval and the modern. His materials were mostly drawn from the common stock of medieval literary tradition, but his characters emerge from the conventional setting of allegory and dream sequence as clear-cut, fully rounded personalities, no longer types but characterized by individual peculiarity and idiosyncrasy. Above all, like Dante, he saw the world from the vantage point of the urban layman who could use both the clerical and the chivalric traditions inherited from the Middle Ages, but was not wholly committed to either.

The circumstances of Chaucer's life gave him extraordinarily broad and varied opportunities to observe all classes of society at home and abroad, and to profit by the inspiration and example of contemporary trends in continental literature. He was born in Thames Street in London about 1340. His father was a prosperous wine merchant, and as a boy Chaucer must have known the busy life of the London streets and the docks where sailors from Bordeaux and Bruges unloaded the wines that were his father's stock in trade. When still young he was attached to the court as a page, and before he was twenty he had served with the royal army in France, had been captured and ransomed. By 1367 he was receiving a pension as a yeoman in the king's household and had married one of the queen's ladies in waiting. For the rest of his life he moved freely in the society of the court, making the acquaintance of the courtiers and their ladies, the foreign noblemen and the French poets, like Froissart, who were drawn to that brilliant center of international culture. Between 1370 and 1380 his experience was broadened by a series of diplomatic missions in the king's service to France, to Flanders and, most important of all, to Italy, which he visited twice in 1372 and 1378, on the latter occasion on royal business to the court of Bernabò Visconti, lord of Milan. Despite his familiarity with royal and princely courts, Chaucer never identified himself completely with courtly society, nor lost the common touch. From 1374 to 1386 he held the post of Controller of the Customs and Subsidies on Wool in the port of London, an office which kept him in daily contact with the commercial world of the wharves into which he had been born. In these years he occupied a little house over the city gate at Aldgate. For a time after 1386 he lived as a country gentleman in Kent, was made a Justice of the Peace and represented the county in Parliament as a Knight of the Shire. In 1389 he returned to the king's service as Clerk of the King's Works, in which capacity he supervised a number of royal buildings and was responsible for hiring workmen, buying materials, and directing building and repair operations. In 1391 he resigned his clerkship, but he continued to hold important administrative posts until almost the time of his death in 1400.

It was this varied experience that gave Chaucer his intimate knowledge of men and women in all ranks of society and developed his novelist's eye for what was both characteristic of the type and peculiar to the individual. But experience alone would not have made him a poet nor, in that difficult birth-hour of the English tongue, a master of English rhyme, meter and poetic diction. Much reading and years of study and experimentation were needed before in middle age he found his mature style. In these years the models he chose to imitate were the *Roman de la Rose* and the courtly lyrics of Machaut, Deschamps, and Froissart. Ignoring completely the contemporary current of alliterative English verse, he adapted the French forms of versification and naturalized them permanently on English soil. The influence of French metrical forms remained with him throughout his life, but after the 1370's his contact with Renaissance Italy freed him from too close adherence to the narrow conventions of the French courtly tradition. He knew the *Divine Comedy* and some, at least, of Petrarch's sonnets, but of the three great Florentines, it was the bourgeois storyteller, Boccaccio, whom he found most congenial. Oddly enough, he seems not to have known the prose *Decamerone*, but he found inspiration for the development of his own peculiar gifts in the narrative poems, particularly the *Filostrato* from which he borrowed the plot for his greatest single poem, *Troylus and Cryseyde*. He knew many of the Latin classics, too, and frequent borrowings from Virgil, Ovid and others indicate the range of his poetic debts.

Like Shakespeare, who borrowed most of his plots, Chaucer could borrow right and left and still display the highest kind of originality. Whatever he borrowed he transmuted through the alchemy of his genius into something rich and strange. *Troylus and Cryseyde*, in the depth and subtlety of its psychological analysis of the star-crossed lovers, is a very different thing from the rather banal story told by Boccaccio. Under Chaucer's hand Troylus ceases to be merely the conventional lover, and the faithless Cryseyde develops into as complex a character as ever graced a modern psychological novel. Even the ineffable busybody, Pandarus, becomes a completely original creation. In *The Hous of Fame* and *The Parlement of Foules*, both written after his Italian journeys, he returned to the allegorical dream vision so dear to medieval tradition, but introduced into both poems a vivid realism in characterization and an inextinguishably comic spirit that were entirely his own. The loquacious eagle, who carried Chaucer in his claws in the vision of *The Hous of Fame*, is, indeed, one of the great comic characters of English poetry.

Only at the end of his life did Chaucer declare his complete independence of foreign models and create a work that was entirely original in conception and rooted in English soil. The scheme of the *Canterbury Tales*, a group of stories told by members of a social group, was not new, although Chaucer seems not to have known any of the earlier models, including the *Decamerone*. But the idea of using for his social framework a group of pilgrims, who represented a cross section of English society, was not only original but happily conceived. In the general prologue, and in the separate prologues which introduce each tale, Chaucer had an opportunity to portray the whole range of English society, lay and clerical, gentle and common, each typical of his trade, order or rank, yet each a distinct, fully rounded personality. Where Langland, who had also surveyed English society, saw his characters in the glass of allegory darkly, Chaucer saw them face to face. All that he had learned from a lifetime of eager observation of his fellow-men went into these vivid sketches of the Miller and the Carpenter, the Friar and the Pardoner, the Prioress and the Wife of Bath, the Merchant and the Man of Law, the Squire and the Knight, and all the other varied characters who rode to Canterbury under the genial supervision of Harry Bailly, the host of the Tabard Inn. Everything he had learned, too, from his French, Italian, and Latin sources and from years of practice in writing English verse went into the tales they told. The tales, indeed, are as varied as the characters who tell them, and as complete a reflection of the life and thought of the age. Here are romances, fairy tales, beast fables, saints' lives, stories borrowed from French, Italian, and classical authors, and intermixed with them the crude yet invariably comic tales of such lewd fellows of the baser sort as the Reeve and the Miller. "Here," as Dryden remarked, "is God's plenty."

No account of Chaucer's contemporaries would be complete without mention of John Gower (c. 1330–c. 1408), although his once great reputation has suffered, perhaps unduly, from the fact that his work is much less appealing than that of Chaucer to modern standards of taste. He was a Kentish gentleman of means, well educated and familiar with both the capital and the royal court. Like so many of the writers of this period he was a layman, but of a strongly religious and moral bent. He was conservative in his social views and in his adherence to conventional literary forms. His first major poem, the *Mirrour de l'Omme*, was written in French and dealt at interminable length with the struggle of virtues and vices for the soul of man. This was followed by an equally lengthy Latin poem, aptly entitled *Vox Clamantis*, which castigated the evils of English society in the dark days after the Peasants' Revolt of 1381, much in the manner of William Langland. Only late in life did he turn to the use of his native tongue, which by that time was replacing French at the royal court, in the *Confessio Amantis*, a poem of some 34,000 lines consisting of more than a hundred stories of passionate love, set in a didactic and allegorical framework. The stories, borrowed from classical, Biblical, and medieval sources, were recounted in fluent and regular English verse, which demonstrate a high degree of technical skill. Modern critics find him humorless and irritatingly didactic, but both his stories and his moralizing digressions were very much to the taste of the fifteenth-century reading public. He was very widely read, and he may have contributed almost as much as Chaucer to making the East Midland dialect the literary language of England.

Compared with Chaucer's generation, the fifteenth century seems peculiarly uninspired in its literary production. Chaucer's towering figure cast a long shadow and fastened the blight of imitation upon generations of "Chaucerians." Increasing lay education was in this century adding to the numbers of the reading public, and literary taste was less exclusively dictated by the court. The fact that literature was now mostly designed to be read rather than listened to had the effect of encouraging the writing of prose and of incredibly lengthy and prosaic poems. The two principal English successors of Chaucer, John Lydgate (c. 1370–c. 1450) and Thomas Hoccleve (c. 1368–c. 1450), the former a monk of Bury St. Edmunds, the latter a layman and clerk of the Privy Seal, were both more notable for the quantity than for the quality of their verses, and only the blunted taste of an uncritical age could have compared either to Chaucer or Gower.

If the prolixity and didacticism of so much fifteenth-century poetry and prose reflected the growth of reading habits among the gentry and the merchant class, the miracle and morality plays marked the emergence of the middle class of urban craftsmen as a cultural force. In England, as in France and Germany, the fourteenth and fifteenth centuries witnessed the birth of popular drama. Dramatic interludes had been introduced into the liturgy of the Church as early as the tenth century, especially at Christmas and Easter. In the course of time, these dramatic bits had grown until they could no longer be contained in the liturgical framework, and they had to be moved out of the church into the churchyard. Finally, with growing popularity, they were removed from the precincts of the church altogether to the streets and market places, and from the supervision of the clergy to that of the guilds. Religious drama thus fell into lay hands and was progressively secularized. The miracle plays were essentially episodic, growing by accretion of episodes from the Old and New Testament, until in the larger towns whole cycles evolved covering the Biblical story from the Creation to the Day of Judgment. Normally each episode was assigned to a particular guild, which supplied the players and bore the expense. We know little of the anonymous authors of these early plays, except that they were not men of distinguished poetic or dramatic talent. The plays that have survived, however, show a robust sense of realism and flashes of rude humor which mark them as precursors, however primitive, of the full-grown secular drama of the Elizabethan age.

D. Late Scholastic Philosophy and Science

In the countries north of the Alps learning, like literature, seems during the period from 1300 to 1450 largely a continuation of medieval tradition, yet with certain novel elements that mark it as characteristic of this changing age. Philosophy, theology and science remained for the most part a clerical monopoly, the concern of a professional class of schoolmen in the universities. The classical humanism which had created a new form of lay learning in Italy had as yet scarcely touched the north. At Paris and Oxford scholars continued to debate the basic problems that had dominated scholastic thought during the preceding two centuries, but the great age of synthesis was past. The fourteenth century opened with a period of brilliant, although largely destructive and critical, speculation and the founding of the last great schools of medieval philosophy, those connected with the names of Duns Scotus and William of Ockham. But what was essentially new in these systems was worked out before mid-century, and thereafter the adherents of the various schools — Thomist, Scotist, Averroist, Ockhamist — continued to repeat and define with endless logical subtlety the positions of the great masters, but without adding anything of importance to the established systems. As a result, scholasticism tended to fall into disrepute among educated laymen as well as among the most spiritually minded clerics. It no longer attracted the best minds, which found satisfaction for their intellectual curiosity and spiritual aspirations elsewhere.

The task which had occupied the schoolmen in the twelfth and thirteenth centuries had been to absorb Greek philosophy, as represented primarily by Aristotle and his Arabic commentators, and to reconcile it with the Christian faith. In the third quarter of the thirteenth century that reconciliation was achieved, so far as it ever could be achieved, in the work of St. Thomas Aquinas. But though the gigantic synthesis he erected, in which reason and revelation each was assigned its due place, was to remain an enduring edifice, it was not immediately accepted as authoritative. The Latin Averroists continued to teach pure Aristotelian philosophy, as embodied in the commentary of Averroës, and to keep philosophy and theology in separate intellectual compartments, paying what seems at times no more than lip service to the latter. On the other hand, those schoolmen who felt that Aristotelian rationalism was imperilling the primacy of faith, gathered their forces not only against the Averroists but also against the elements of Aristotelianism in the Thomist system. In 1277 the archbishops of Paris and Canterbury simultaneously condemned the teaching of the Averroists and included in their condemnation some propositions drawn from the works of St. Thomas. This condemnation marked a turning point in the history of medieval philosophy. It did not, it is true, destroy Averroism, nor did it prevent the adherents of Aquinas, especially those of his own Dominican order, from teaching his doctrine. But it did alter the intellectual atmosphere of the French and English universities for a time. During the next two generations the most influential teachers at Paris and Oxford directed a concerted attack upon the synthesis of reason and revelation, philosophy and theology that had been achieved in the previous century. In particular they subjected to searching criticism all attempts to demonstrate by natural reason the truth of the basic doctrines of the Christian faith and also those aspects of the Aristotelian system that seemed to curtail the omnipotence of God by making the world-order a necessary product of the Divine Nature.

The first step, though only a partial one, in this direction was taken by a Franciscan of Scottish birth who taught at Oxford and Paris around the turn of the century and whose dialectical skill won for him the title of the Subtle Doctor. John Duns Scotus (c. 1266–1308) belongs both chronologically and in the character of his philosophy more to the thirteenth than to the fourteenth century. He was a Realist and his intricate system of thought was, on the whole, more constructive than destructive. In the controversies which divided the schools during the next two centuries his adherents were classified with those of Aquinas as followers of the *via antiqua*, the old way, as opposed to the Ockhamists who arrogated to themselves the distinction of following the *via moderna*. There were, however, elements in his characteristically Franciscan thought which opened the way to the Nominalism and the divorce between reason and faith which characterized the following generation.

One such element was his novel conception of the principle of individuality. As a Realist he asserted the real existence of universal essences common to all members of a given genus or species. All men, he argued, share a common human nature, and the essence of that human nature, which the intellect can comprehend by a process of abstraction, is a universal. But there is also in each individual man, something which is peculiar to him alone. Thus there is a human essence common to both Socrates and Plato, which characterizes them as men and distinguishes them from other animals. But Socrates and Plato each possesses individual characteristics peculiar to him alone, an individuality which distinguishes them from one another; and this individuality is a real entity, as real as the universal essence common to all men. Scotus called this individual entity *haecceitas* (thisness), as distinct from the universal *quidditas* (whatness). The distinction may convey little meaning to the modern mind untrained in medieval metaphysics. It conveyed little to the mind of Erasmus. Yet it was an important contribution to the great debate that had occupied the intellect of Western Europe for two centuries. It marked the beginning of a shift in emphasis from preoccupation with universal essences to concern with individual things.

A second element in the philosophy of Duns Scotus that was to echo through the following centuries was his exalted conception of the absolute freedom and omnipotence of God. By asserting that God's will is not bound by any necessity, but is absolutely free and spontaneous, Scotus decreased the area of what could be proven by natural reason to be necessary attributes of the Divine Being, and thereby drove a wedge between philosophy and theology. The thought of Scotus sometimes seems ambiguous, at least to the modern mind prevented by mental fatigue from following all the involutions of his logic, and various conclusions could be drawn from different parts of his system. His successors picked up certain aspects of his teaching and rejected others. William of Ockham carried the two elements mentioned above, which represent only a part of the vast range of his thought, far beyond anything Scotus would have allowed, while at the same time attacking the Scotist system as a whole.

The revolutionary thinker who broke radically with the thirteenth-century synthesis and founded the *via moderna* was, like Scotus, an Oxford-trained Franciscan. William of Ockham was born some time between 1290 and 1300. He studied and taught at Oxford until 1324, when he was summoned to the papal court at Avignon to answer charges of teaching erroneous doctrines. While there he joined with the leaders of the Spiritual Franciscans in defending the doctrine of apostolic poverty which had been condemned by Pope John XXII. In 1328 Ockham, together with the General of the Franciscan Order, Michael of Cesena, and other Spirituals, fled from Avignon and took refuge with the emperor, Louis the Bavarian. Ockham's active partisan support of the emperor in his quarrel with the papacy has been noted in an earlier chapter. The political theories he developed in the course of his defense of the rights of both Church and state against papal absolutism were an important contribution to medieval political thought, and they played a significant rôle in the development of the Conciliar Movement, but they had only an indirect relation to his philosophy and need not be considered here. He was then writing less as a formal philosopher than as an excommunicated rebel denying the pope's power to make him give up a doctrine dear to his Franciscan soul. All that can be said for the connection between the philosopher and the political theorist is that the same keenly analytical mind operated in both and, perhaps, that the Nominalist frame of mind was more apt than the Realist to envisage the Church as the community of all believers and to defend individual freedom against corporate authority.[5] His stormy career ended in 1349 when, like so many others, he fell a victim to the Black Death.

William of Ockham was a revolutionary figure in the history of

[5] See above, pp. 71–72 and 230.

scholastic philosophy not so much because his ideas were new — many of them were in fact drawn from earlier systems — as because he pressed his ideas to their ultimate conclusion with remorseless logic. Formal logic, based on Aristotle but developed in his own fashion, was the weapon he used to attack the rationalism of his predecessors. He was uncompromising in his rejection of all forms of Realism, both that of the Augustinian Platonists and the more moderate Aristotelian Realism of Aquinas and Scotus. Ockham's genius was analytical rather than synthetic. He used with a surgeon's precision the so-called "razor" of logic — the principle that it is futile to postulate more entities when it is possible to work with fewer — to shear away everything that seemed irrelevant or that could not be demonstrated as necessary in the systems he attacked. And when he had finished, little remained of the systems of philosophy which had furnished a rational basis for theology. Yet, while denying the possibility of proving by rational demonstration the existence of God, the immortality of the soul, or any other article of Christian faith, Ockham was not a sceptic or an agnostic. On the contrary, he was a Franciscan theologian who believed profoundly in the truth revealed in the Scriptures and who was deeply suspicious of any system of thought that would substitute reason for faith, even in part, or that would circumscribe the omnipotence of God. His aim was to free faith and Divinity from the bondage of reason and necessity.

The basis of Ockham's attack on the Realists was a theory of knowledge combined with a theory of being radically different from theirs. The Augustinian Platonists had believed that the intellect can perceive the immutable forms or ideas, which exist in the mind of God, directly by the aid of divine illumination, without necessary reference to sensible things. Aquinas and the moderate Aristotelian Realists had asserted that all knowledge arises from apprehension of particular things through the senses, but that what is known is not the individual object but rather the essence or nature of the object, which is universal. It is the intelligible species, abstracted and made general by the intellect. In contrast to both these positions, Ockham maintained that real knowledge comes only from direct and immediate intuition of individual existent things. We can know only individual objects with certainty. Further, Ockham asserted that only individual things actually exist, and that if a thing exists it must be individual. The genera and species, the essences and natures, all the universals of the Realists can have no real existence, for if they did exist they would be individual and so could not exist in a number of different things. Moreover, if they did exist we could not know them since they cannot be perceived by direct intuition. The universals, in short, are merely names or terms — whence the designation of his philosophy as Nominalist or Terminalist. They are convenient mental signs standing for a group of individual things which have certain observed similarities, and which can therefore be classified under one term for purposes of argument and as a means of ordering thought. The Realists, Ockham declared, confuse words with things. By postulating the existence of universals they simply clutter up thought with a number of unnecessary entities. Here the razor descended.

Ockham did not deny that we actually think in generalities or universal concepts. We can form a concept of man, based on direct intuition of a number of individual men, and that concept can be used in a logical proposition. But Ockham was careful to distinguish between "terms of first intention" which stand for things and "terms of second intention" which stand for concepts. Nor does Ockham deny that from argument based on such concepts we can demonstrate certain truths as probable, but they cannot be demonstrated as certain. We can show that a given thing or event is the probable cause of another thing or event which we find generally associated with it. But we have no intuitive experience of the causal relation and therefore no evident knowledge that the relation is one of cause and effect. Thus from the existence of one thing we cannot argue the existence of another thing as its necessary cause, nor can we posit the existence of an essence or nature as the cause of a given action. In short we know only individual things, not the relation between them. One result of this line of reasoning was the rejection of the proof of God's existence as the first cause in an infinite chain of causation. Another result was the refutation of the Platonic notion that the world-order is determined by the immutable Ideas which St. Augustine posited as existing in the mind of God. We cannot argue from the existence of general concepts in the human mind the existence of their prototypes in the mind of God. Finally, Ockham argued that we cannot demonstrate the fact that the world-order is in any sense necessary. The fact that God created the world as He did does not imply that He could not have created it otherwise, and in this assertion Ockham included the moral order as well as the physical order. All things are contingent upon God's inscrutable will. Thus we cannot argue from the nature of created things to the nature of God. God must remain unknowable, for we have no direct intuition of His being, no natural intuition of the Divine Essence.

It is obvious that this comprehensive and fundamental denial of the rational basis of theology might lead to scepticism; and in fact it did so among some of Ockham's disciples. But that was not his intention, nor was it the result among the majority of those who were influenced by his thought. The effect was rather to shift the emphasis from reason to faith.

Scepticism about the powers of reason bred a more profound reliance on simple faith and a tendency toward mysticism, both, as we shall see, evident in the movement of lay piety known as the *Devotio Moderna*.[6] But, if Ockhamism led to greater emphasis upon faith, it also reduced the intellectual content of theology by divorcing it entirely from philosophy, and so contributed to the discrediting of scholastic learning. Too many of Ockham's disciples occupied themselves with attacks on other systems, with logic-chopping and nice verbal distinctions which offered no real sustenance to either soul or intellect. Small wonder that many of the spiritually minded turned from the arid disputations of the schools to find inspiration in the simple and unintellectual ideal of the Christian life represented by the *Imitatio Christi* of Thomas à Kempis. Finally, Ockham's destruction of the medieval synthesis of philosophy and theology, his sole reliance upon faith, and his insistence upon both the omnipotent will of God and the isolated existence of the individual soul opened the way for Luther's radical break with Catholicism and for Calvin's doctrine of predestination.

The foregoing discussion of Ockham's philosophy has emphasized its theological implications, for these were in fact Ockham's primary concern. His theory of knowledge and his conception of the nature of reality, however, also had an important influence on the development of late scholastic science. His insistence that only direct intuition of individual things furnishes evident truth, and his rejection of all *a priori* arguments, undoubtedly stimulated the empirical side of scientific thought. It also tended to shake confidence in the Aristotelian system of qualitative physics, in which the causative factors are qualities inherent in things as their essence or nature. In the Aristotelian system, in other words, all things act in accordance with their nature which determines how they will act; but "nature," in this sense, is simply the universal essence in operation as the quality causing action of a given sort. Ockham's denial of the real existence of universals, therefore, implied a rejection of the nature of things as a causative factor. Ockham himself was only incidentally interested in natural science, but most of the men who advanced scientific speculation in the universities of Oxford and Paris during the fourteenth century were adherents of the Nominalist *via moderna*, even though they might not accept all the implications of Ockham's philosophy.

Ockham cannot, however, be regarded as the sole founder of the empirical approach to scientific theory. A number of his predecessors in the thirteenth century — Robert Grosseteste, Albertus Magnus, and Roger Bacon among others — had pointed to the necessity of observation and experiment. Of these Grosseteste (c. 1175–1253), Bishop of

[6] See below, pp. 347–352.

Lincoln, was perhaps the most original thinker. His theory begins with the observation of individual phenomena, regarded as the effects of some cause. Thus, he argued, when we observe the same thing happening in a number of instances we can form an hypothesis concerning its cause. But this hypothesis must then be checked by experiment under varied conditions before it can be accepted as true. This result is achieved by assuming the hypothesis to be true and then deducing from it what must be the necessary effect. If experiment shows that the effect does not in fact follow, the hypothesis must be abandoned. The basic assumption here is the regularity or uniformity of nature, so that what happens in all or most observed instances may be accepted as a natural and necessary sequence of cause and effect. Grosseteste's theory, however, involved no departure from the Aristotelian system. For him, as a Realist, the cause always was an essence or nature, i.e., a universal. As such it is a general principle prior to the particular, and the particular can be deduced from it by *a priori* reasoning as a necessary effect. Ockham, too, accepted the regularity of nature in practice, although reserving in theory God's power to change it by an arbitrary act of will. But he departed radically from the traditional systems in denying the reality of the universals as causative factors and hence the evident truth of all causal relations. For him a regular sequence of events is simply that and nothing more. We know the natural order only by observing what it in fact is in particular instances. We cannot explain it. Ockham thus injected an element of scepticism into scientific thought by casting doubt on the ready-made proofs furnished by the Aristotelian system. This scepticism, however, did not discourage scientific thought, but served rather to free it from bondage to the closed system of Aristotelian physics and to reinforce the empirical approach by discouraging *a priori* reasoning. The result was a good deal of uninhibited speculation about matter and space, about the possibility of a void, of the infinity of the universe and of the plurality of worlds.

From all this speculation one theory emerged which was to prove of basic importance for the later development of both terrestrial and celestial physics. This was a theory of motion developed by Parisian Ockhamists during the fourteenth century which played a decisive rôle in the eventual disintegration of the Aristotelian system. According to Aristotle and his medieval commentators the natural state of all things is one of rest; and the only form of natural motion is that by which objects seek to find rest by rejoining their natural element, that is, the element in which their essence exists in pure form. Thus heavy objects in which the element of earth predominates are drawn by a disposition inherent in their nature toward the earth. Conversely, fire has an inherent disposition to move upward toward the sphere of fire which surrounds the sphere of air. All other motion is violent motion and can be accounted for only by the continuous application of a moving force. Once the force is removed the moving object will immediately come to rest or fall in natural motion towards the earth. This theory obviously presented difficulties in relation to the motion of projectiles. When, for example, a stone is thrown or an arrow leaves the bowstring it continues to move although the moving force is no longer in contact with it. This difficulty Aristotle met by supposing that the initial motion set up a disturbance in the air which continued in waves of decreasing intensity, carrying the projectile along until it gradually died out and the projectile fell to the ground. Ockham rejected this theory on various quite sensible empirical grounds, but at the same time would not admit that the bow imparts to the arrow a special quality of motion as an entity separate from the arrow itself. All we can know about motion by direct intuition is that a body can be observed to move. Here he seems to be approaching the theory of inertia by arguing that a thing moves simply because it is in motion.

Ockham's theory did not satisfy the fourteenth-century physicists and, indeed, he himself did not develop it. But his rejection of the Aristotelian theory did open the way for a theory of motion which was to hold its own until the seventeenth century. Jean Buridan (c. 1300–c. 1358), a professor at the University of Paris, seems to have been principally responsible for originating the theory that the motive force imparts "impetus" to the object moved, which impetus would keep it moving at a uniform velocity indefinitely if it were not checked or diverted by the interference of external forces. Thus the bowstring imparts impetus to the arrow which keeps the arrow in motion until it is gradually reduced by air resistance and the downward pull of gravity. The theory was also used to explain the acceleration of falling bodies, which Aristotle had accounted for by arguing that heavy bodies rush the more eagerly toward the earth the nearer they approach their natural element. The new theory assumed that an original impetus was imparted to the falling body by the force of gravity and that this impetus was constantly reinforced by the steady pull of gravity adding further increments of impetus. The adherents of the theory of impetus seemed not quite sure how to define it in current philosophical terms. Was it a substance or an accident? They evidently felt, however, that it was something distinct from the moving body and imparted to it by the moving force, a position which Ockham's rigid Nominalism would not admit. Yet impetus was something quite different from the Aristotelian disposition inherent in the nature of things. According to Buridan, impetus could be measured by the quantity of matter in a body multiplied by its velocity. The theory of impetus thus had the advantage not only of according well enough with the observable facts, but also of substituting measurable forces for unmeasurable inherent qualities.

The destructive effect upon the Aristotelian system of the theory of impetus becomes clearer when it is applied, as it was by several of the Parisian Ockhamists, to the motion of the heavenly bodies. Aristotle had been forced to assume that the sun, the planets, and the fixed stars are kept in motion by the continuous and immediate pressure of some moving force. This in turn led to the assumption that the planets are imbedded in crystalline spheres which are moved by Intelligences, i.e., spiritual forces which in Christian thought might be assimilated to the hierarchy of the angels. Buridan perceived that the theory of impetus made the Intelligences unnecessary. God could simply have imparted to the spheres their initial impetus which, there being no air resistance or other diversional force in the heavens, would continue undiminished to eternity. That this theory implied a mechanistic universe in which God was simply an initial cause Buridan was well aware, and he strove to justify it on Biblical grounds.

> One does not find in the Bible that there are Intelligences charged to communicate to the celestial spheres their proper motions [he wrote]; it is permissible then to show that it is not necessary to suppose the existence of such Intelligences. One could say, in fact, that God, when he created the Universe, set each of the celestial spheres in motion as it pleased him, impressing on each of them an impetus which has moved it ever since. God had therefore no longer to move these spheres, except in exerting a general influence similar to that by which he gives his concurrence to all phenomena. Thus he could rest on the seventh day from the work he had achieved, confiding to created things their mutual causes and effects.[7]

A generation later Nicole Oresme (died 1382) gave a more vivid form to Buridan's statement by comparing the celestial universe to a mechanical clock, which God had set going and then left to run by itself.

In the same work, *Le Livre du ciel et du monde* (1377), in which he compared the universe to a clock, Oresme also proposed the hypothesis that the earth rotates on its axis while the rest of the universe remains motionless. The movement of the earth he accounted for by Buridan's theory of an impetus imparted to it on the analogy of a spinning top. In defending this hypothesis he also met many of the objections later brought against the Copernican theory. His motionless universe, however, did not account for the changing relation of the planets to one

[7] Quoted in A. C. Crombie, *Augustine to Galileo, The History of Science, A.D. 400–1650* (London, 1952), p. 253.

another and so could not satisfy the astronomers, and, in the end, Oresme himself preferred not to accept it. All he was saying, in fact, is that when one thing moves in relation to another it is impossible to tell which is moving. There is no evidence that Copernicus was influenced by Oresme or even knew of his work, which had not been published. But that Oresme could consider the hypothesis seriously is evidence of the degree to which the Aristotelian cosmos had come unstuck under the influence of Ockhamist metaphysics and the theory of impetus.

There can be no doubt that the development of modern science was in some degree foreshadowed by the scientific speculation of the Parisian Ockhamists and of their predecessors at Oxford and Paris in the thirteenth century. The extent to which their work contributed directly to the later developments, however, remains uncertain. There seems to be adequate evidence that the theory of impetus was taught right through the period from Buridan to Galileo. But the full implications of the theory were only dimly realized in the fourteenth century, and before the end of the century the scientific movement had died out in the northern schools, leaving a hiatus between fourteenth-century speculation and that of the sixteenth and seventeenth centuries. Much of the later scientific thought originated not in Paris but in Padua and the other Italian universities, or outside the uinversities entirely. The work of the early Parisian Ockhamists, indeed, seems in retrospect a brilliant promise without fulfillment. The late scholastics remained, like their predecessors, primarily theologians, metaphysicians and logicians. Ockham, himself, cared little about natural science as such. And even the most brilliant of his successors were more concerned with radical speculation than with the actual observation and experiment that would have placed their empirical hypotheses on a solid foundation of fact. The tendency of the Nominalists toward an excessive preoccupation with logic, too, distracted their attention from productive scientific investigation. Despite the empiricism inherent in Nominalist philosophy, the Ockhamists continued, almost as much as did the adherents of the *via antiqua*, to live in a world of abstractions. And in such an intellectual atmosphere the sciences concerned with concrete, measurable reality could not take deep root.

The situation in the Italian universities was somewhat different. There the lay element was stronger and the tone of thought more secular. Until nearly the end of the thirteenth century the universities of Bologna, Padua, and Salerno had been concerned primarily with the study and teaching of law and medicine. Aristotelian philosophy occupied only a small place in their curricula until after the middle of the century, when it was introduced in relation to the study of medicine. Only after the beginning of the fourteenth century did natural philosophy take an independent and firmly established place in Padua and the other Italian universities, and then as an importation from Paris in the form of Averroism, just at the time when the Averroist school of integral Aristotelianism was losing ground in the north under the impact of the condemnation of 1277 and the subsequent Ockhamist onslaught. Natural philosophy was thus a fairly new study in Italy in the fourteenth century, and it was free from the theological affiliations which could not be escaped in Paris or Oxford. It was also relatively free from the paralyzing effect of a great inherited tradition and from the internecine quarrels between the schools which tended to sterilize scholastic thought in the north. The Italian universities, especially the medical schools of Padua and Salerno, absorbed the Terminalist logic and the principles of inductive science already worked out at Oxford, but they were relatively little affected by the revolt against Aristotle which was rife in Paris in mid-century. The generally lay tone of the Italian schools, as well as their practical concern with medicine and their Averroist tendency to treat natural philosophy as an autonomous subject with its own brand of truth, should have created an atmosphere favorable to the advance of science, and to a certain extent it did. But the full fruit was borne only in the age of Galileo and Harvey. In the meantime, faithful adherence to the closed system of Aristotle, as expounded by Averroës, retarded advance, for at this stage in the development of the physical sciences the next important step could come only from a fundamental break with the Aristotelian cosmology and qualitative physics.

The most original and independent philosopher in the hundred years following the death of Ockham and Buridan was never a member of a university faculty and, though university-trained, he owed as much to non-scholastic as to scholastic traditions. Nicholas of Cusa (1401–64) is a baffling figure who cannot be fitted neatly into any recognized pattern. He has been regarded as the last of the medieval or the first of the modern philosophers, or simply as a transitional thinker. It is perhaps nearer the truth to regard him as *sui generis*. He does not properly belong to this section, but he would be rather more out of place in any other context. Born in Germany, Nicholas received his early education at Deventer where the Brethren of the Common Life introduced him to the strain of Rhineland mysticism and the *Devotio Moderna*. After a year at Heidelberg, where he was exposed to Ockhamist philosophy, he went to Padua and spent six years there studying canon law, mathematics and astronomy. There, too, he felt the full impact of early humanism. He learned Greek as well as classical Latin and acquired a lasting admiration for the critical spirit of Lorenzo Valla. Ordained priest in 1426, he returned to Germany, but his continuous activity in the affairs of the Church frequently brought him back to Italy. He took part in the Council of Basel, but later became an ardent supporter of the papacy. He was created cardinal in 1448, and Bishop of Brixen in 1450. As Papal Legate in Germany in 1451–52, he labored to strengthen ecclesiastical discipline and to reform religious life and clerical morality. His numerous treatises were thus written during such leisure as the life of a busy prelate afforded.

The philosophy of Nicholas of Cusa was at once broadly eclectic and highly personal. The influence of humanism is evident in his distrust of syllogistic logic and in his tendency to use the dialogue form rather than the scholastic method of systematic exposition. At the same time, his primary concern was with the metaphysical problems that had occupied the scholastics for the past three or four hundred years, to which he added the kind of scientific speculation introduced by the fourteenth-century Parisian Ockhamists. He was profoundly influenced by Neo-platonic mysticism, being especially devoted to the works attributed to Dionysius the Areopagite and his ninth century commentator, John Scotus Erigena. The speculative mysticism, verging on pantheism, of Meister Eckhart also attracted him, and he seemed frequently to be echoing Eckhart's bold antinomies.[8] The Ockhamists had taught him to reject Aristotle and the rational synthesis of Thomas Aquinas, but he could not accept the Nominalist position, and he was repelled by the agnosticism of the Ockhamists and their divorce of theology from philosophy. What his metaphysical system seems to attempt is a new synthesis that would restore the union of philosophy and theology.

Nicholas was in agreement with Ockham in his belief that knowledge of God and His relation to the created universe cannot be achieved by pure reason. Such knowledge is at best approximate. But, he asserted, a superior form of knowledge can be attained by the intellect, which he distinguished as a higher mental activity freed from bondage to the principle of contradiction which governs formal logic. Whereas reason asserts that nothing can have at the same time contradictory or inconsistent qualities, the intellect can comprehend God as the synthesis of oppositions (*coincidentia oppositorum*). In the absolutely infinite being of God all the distinctions and oppositions to be found in finite creatures are transcended and united. Although the intellect, when illuminated by Divine Grace, can grasp this concept, the manner in which this union takes place surpasses our finite knowledge. We must, therefore, in a sense remain in a state of ignorance about the nature of God; but once we fully realize God's infinity and transcendence, we may hope to attain a learned ignorance, *docta ignorantia*, which is superior to the

[8] See below, pp. 344–345.

knowledge that can be reached through reason. What is thus apprehended, however, transcends the powers of language as it transcends reason, and it can be expressed only by symbols or analogies. Nicholas himself frequently resorted to the use of mathematical concepts or geometrical figures to express his meaning. It is not always clear to the unilluminated mind or to one unlearnedly ignorant of mathematics.

The doctrine of the coincidence of opposites in God, and the corollary doctrine that all the multiplicity of created things in their distinctive individuality are emanations of the Divine Being, led Nicholas to make assertions that have a distinctly pantheistic flavor, and he was accused of renewing the pantheistic errors of Eckhart. God, he asserted, contains all distinct and finite things in His infinite unity. Thus all things are in God. Conversely, since He is the cause of all the diversity of created things, He is immanent in all things. Nicholas was firm, however, in his rejection of the charge of pantheism. God and the universe are not identical. The universe is a concrete and imperfect reflection of God, just as each individual thing is an imperfect reflection of the universe. Of all created things man, the microcosm, most perfectly mirrors the universe, containing in himself all levels of the Platonic hierarchy of being, from matter through organic and animal life to spiritual rationality. He is also thereby the counterpart of the identity of opposites which is the Divine Nature. Since he unites in himself only the levels of created existence, however, man is but an imperfect mirror of Divinity. Only in Christ in whom were united human and divine nature, the created and the uncreated, is the coincidence of opposites perfectly reflected. He is thus the essential link between man and God.

When he turned to scientific speculation, Nicholas followed in general along the lines suggested by Buridan, Oresme and the other Parisian Ockhamists. He was at one with them in his critical attitude toward Aristotelian physics, and he accepted their theories of impetus, the acceleration of falling bodies and the flight of projectiles. He also followed Oresme, and incidentally some ancient Greek astronomers, in maintaining that each star constitutes a world with its own force of gravity capable of holding its parts together. He also asserted, more daringly, that each star is inhabited as the earth is. He went further than Oresme, however, in suggesting not only that the earth moves, but that it is not the center of the universe. The universe, he argued, while not spatially infinite, is unbounded. It has no circumference and therefore can have no center. Since the earth is not the center of the universe it cannot be without motion, he asserted in the treatise *De docta ignorantia*. Nicholas cannot, however, be regarded as in any real sense a forerunner of Copernicus. His ideas, in so far as they were novel, were intuitions unsupported by evidence and based on abstract mathematics rather than observation.

It is difficult to estimate the extent of the influence Nicholas exerted on later thinkers. His mathematical speculations stimulated Leonardo da Vinci, and his metaphysics and cosmology served as a starting point for the pantheistic philosophy of Giordano Bruno. But mathematics and science were peripheral to his major interest, which was to construct a theocentric metaphysic that would demonstrate more satisfactorily than any preceding system the truths of the Christian faith. His philosophy was, however, too incoherent, too largely based on mystical intuitions, to achieve that end. He founded no school. The professional theologians ignored him, and where there is evidence of his influence on religious thought it is usually among men like Lefèvre d'Étaples who had already been attracted to Neoplatonic mysticism.

I X

Popular Piety, Mysticism and Heresy

The changes which occurred in the economic, social and cultural conditions of Western Europe during the fourteenth century and the first half of the fifteenth were inevitably accompanied by significant changes in the religious life of the age. This was moreover a peculiarly troubled period in the history of the Church. The story of the long crisis which lasted through the period of the Babylonian Captivity and the Great Schism has already been told. The history of the papacy and of the internal vicissitudes of the Church as it adjusted to changing economic and political conditions, however, tells us little about the people's faith in these years that tried men's souls, nor about the quality of popular piety and religious aspiration. That is the subject of the present chapter. It is a problem that cannot be treated, of course, without reference to the Church, the institution which still furnished the framework of religious life; but much of the most vital religious experience of this period was to a large extent independent of the official leadership of the ecclesiastical hierarchy or was even in opposition to it, an opposition that in some instances led deeply pious men beyond the frontiers of orthodoxy into the lonely wilderness of heretical speculation.

A. The General Tone of Religious Life:
Symptoms of Decline

Throughout this critical period the doctrinal beliefs of the orthodox majority remained largely unchanged. The piety and religious practices of ordinary folk, too, remained pretty much what they had been. Most of what was said about medieval popular religion in an earlier chapter would apply equally well to this period, with some alterations of nuance. But it is the nuances that are important. What concerns us here is the changing barometric pressure of the religious atmosphere, and this is something that we can feel, but that is very difficult to measure with any degree of assurance. What evidence we have is confusing and often contradictory. Much of what the contemporary satirists and reforming preachers tell us must be discounted well below its face value, since it is of the essence of satire to exaggerate, and it has always been the custom of reformers to paint their picture in the darkest colors. Indeed the very volume of denunciation of contemporary religious life to be found in sermons, in the propaganda of the Conciliar Movement, and in such reflections upon the social scene as Langland's *Piers Plowman* or Gower's *Vox Clamantis* may indicate the survival of strong religious feeling quite as much as the prevalence of the sins to which it calls attention. This century and a half produced its quota of saints and more than its fair share of mystics; and, as we shall see, there were in many places evidences of a strong revival of lay piety. Nevertheless, the impression one receives from the contemporary evidence is that as Western Europe struggled through a century of plague and warfare, social unrest, crises in the internal organization of the Church, and the scandals of the Great Schism, the prevailing tone of religious life was less healthy than it had been, and that the level of spirituality among both the clergy and the rank and file of lay folk was at a low ebb.

Historians used to ascribe so many of the changes that occurred in this period to the shock of the Black Death and its later recurrences that we are now, in reaction, perhaps too prone to underestimate its effect. Yet it is inconceivable that the death of a third of the population within a few months could have been other than a traumatic experience which would leave its mark on the spiritual life of the survivors. Huizinga has called attention to the obsession with death and the physical corruption of the body which runs through so much of the literature and art of the fourteenth and fifteenth centuries and also to what he has called "the extreme saturation of the religious atmosphere."[1] To what extent

[1] J. Huizinga, *The Waning of the Middle Ages* (London, 1924), Chapters XI and XII.

the more morbid and hysterical tendencies in the religious life of the people, for which he furnishes ample evidence, were the results of the great plague cannot, of course, be determined, but one feels that it must have been at least in part responsible for them. The appalling loss of life among the clergy, as among all other classes, must also have left the Church sadly understaffed at a time when popular piety was being subjected to strain from a great many directions. The social unrest among both the peasants who were emerging from the manorial system and the proletarian workers in the cities who were the victims of a growing capitalism frequently bred religious ideas that were obscurely heretical or, at least, challenging to the authority of the Church and subversive of the social order. Among all classes there was much criticism of the wealth of the clergy, and evidence of a strong anti-clerical bias resulting from the manifest abuses, mostly financial in origin, in the administration of the Church. This anti-clerical feeling was normally accompanied by unshaken faith in the efficacy of the priesthood, but it must have created a certain tension in the religious sentiment of the people. The wandering friars still drew great crowds to hear their sermons, but the emotions stirred by these masters of the preacher's art were not incompatible with a materialistic conception of the means of salvation, and they may have been rather an indication of religious instability than of spiritual vitality.

At their best the popular sermons aroused in their hearers a more vivid realization of Christ's Passion, which found increasing expression in the art of the period, but preachers also amused their audiences and held their attention with literal-minded stories tending to encourage the common man's natural inclination to transfer adoration from the spiritual entity to the concrete symbol. Stories of the miracle-working powers of the saints, and still more of their relics, tended to make men forget that the saints work by intercession rather than in their own right. Picture and story made the saints all too familiar, all too human, so that, while occupying a larger place than ever in popular imagination, they lost something of the spiritual aura which true veneration requires. The proliferation of doubtful relics, too, inflated the spiritual currency of the age and cheapened one of the most vital elements in popular religion. Never had the trade in relics flourished so profitably, as the record of such royal collections as that of Louis XI indicates and as, on a lower level, does Chaucer's Pardoner with his sack full of "pigges bones." There seems also to have been a marked increase in the popularity of pilgrimages to the more famous shrines, to which pilgrims were attracted by the promise of indulgences as commutation of penance either in this world or in purgatory. Some devout people, like Thomas à Kempis, were beginning to question the virtue of pilgrimages, and moralists suggested that many pilgrims went solely for the pleasures of the trip as a modern tourist might. We may recall that it was the Wife of Bath who, of all Chaucer's pilgrims, was the most persistently addicted to these excursions. It is difficult to reconstruct or assess the feelings of the average man of this period when he called upon the name of a saint or sought contact with his relics; but the ease with which the whole system later fell in many parts of Europe before the onslaughts of the Protestant reformers suggests that quantity had somehow vitiated quality. Within the Catholic Church, of course, the veneration of saints survived; but the Counter-Reformation pruned away much of the luxuriant growth which had threatened to sap its vitality.

If the spiritual level of the masses was declining during the fourteenth and fifteenth centuries, the hierarchy of the Church itself must be held in part responsible. The preoccupation of the papal curia with fiscal concerns spread downward through all ranks of the clergy, laying upon them a burden of clerical taxation which they were forced to pass on to the people under their care. The growing practice of selling indulgences and pardons, and of exacting payment for masses, also tended to introduce a financial element into the process of salvation and to encourage ordinary men to take a rather mechanical view of the services of the Church. That danger might have been averted by the preaching and moral influence of a devoted and spiritually minded priesthood; but the Church in this period of crisis was ill-equipped to produce such priests in great numbers. For one thing, a great many parishes were left in the care of poorly paid and poorly trained vicars, who were hired as substitutes by absentee rectors or by monastic foundations which had appropriated the rectorship of the parish and its accompanying tithes. The growth of papal provisions to benefices in the fourteenth century enormously increased the number of parishes thus served by starveling vicars, since administrators and others with influence in the papal or royal courts were frequently given the income from parishes, sometimes several parishes, which they had no intention of serving personally. There is evidence, too, that episcopal supervision of the parish clergy was not as regular or as strict as it had been, nor were the bishops themselves, under the system of papal provision, generally of as high quality. Relaxation of episcopal supervision must have been particularly unfortunate in this century of plague, warfare and social tensions when priests of high character were more than ever needed. Here again we must beware of taking the strictures of the reformers and satirists too seriously. There were doubtless many priests who possessed all the fine qualities of Chaucer's gentle and conscientious Parson. The weight of the evidence, however, seems strongly on the side of a general deterioration among the rank and file of the secular clergy.

In the towns, at least, the inadequacies of the parish priests might be compensated for in many ways by the activity of the mendicant friars, whose numbers had grown enormously by the fourteenth century, so that they swarmed, as Chaucer put it, "as thikke as motes in the sonne-beem." Of the four great orders of friars — Franciscans, Dominicans, Augustinians and Carmelites — the first two were by far the most numerous and important. Each of these two great orders had a special character, an imprint left by the spirit and purpose of its founder. In the course of time, however, the differences between them had become much less marked, although they never disappeared entirely. In the early years of the fourteenth century, the Franciscan order was torn by a conflict, of which more will be said later,[2] between the Spirituals, who clung fanatically to the rule of absolute poverty, and the Conventuals, who were prepared to accept corporate property. The former were condemned by Pope John XXII and suppressed, though a few continued in resistance as a kind of spiritual underground movement. The Franciscans of this period, at least until the reform movement introduced in the fifteenth century by the group known as Observants, had thus come to accept a relaxed form of the rule of poverty, one more nearly in accord with that of the Dominicans. In the case of the Franciscans, however, the ownership of property implied a disparity between ideal and practice which must have had a demoralizing effect. It is, at any rate, evidence that the first enthusiasm had left the order, and that the spirit of St. Francis had been institutionalized and brought into accord with the spiritual potentialities of ordinary men. The friars still did important work as preachers at a time when the parish priests too often neglected the pulpit. They had churches of their own everywhere, constructed along new architectural lines as preaching churches, and around them had grown up numbers of confraternities of lay men and women, of which the Franciscan Third Order was the most widespread. For all that, it is clear that the mendicant orders, and especially the Franciscans, were no longer the vitalizing force in popular religion that they had been in the first century of their existence — or that they would be again — and in the second half of the fourteenth century a wave of criticism arose against them.

The activity of the friars as preachers and confessors inevitably aroused the animosity of the parish priests who felt their rights infringed upon and their income reduced accordingly. Professional jealousy, however, does not account for the great mass of criticism and scurrilous comment in the literature of this period. Boccaccio could evidently count

[2] See below, pp. 356–358.

on a favorable reception for his stories of rascally friars. The portraits of the typical friar presented by three Englishmen of widely divergent character and aims — Langland, Wyclif, and Chaucer — is equally damning, and they agree with one another in almost every detail. Langland and Wyclif, it is true, were in their different ways reformers and filled with moral indignation. But one cannot accuse Chaucer of reforming zeal. His good-humored tolerance bears the stamp of truth. Aside from the fact that the friars were thrown into competition with the parish priests and were thus tempted to use every art to attract audiences to their churches and penitents to their confessionals, the mendicant life placed temptations in the way of the friars which must have been difficult for the rank and file to withstand at a time when the enthusiasm of the order was at a low ebb. This seems to have been particularly true at this time of the Franciscans who, with notable exceptions, were in general less well educated than the Dominicans and whose convents were less closely disciplined. They were accused of being sturdy beggars who wheedled dainty food from housewives, thrust themselves into the homes of the well-to-do, extracted gifts from unprotected widows and from the dying, interfered in family affairs, haunted taverns, and generally stirred up trouble in the parishes. Such a blanket indictment is undoubtedly unfair, but it is evidence at least that a good many people were beginning to regard the friars as unmitigated nuisances.

As demands for reform in the Church grew in volume toward the end of the fourteenth century, the monks, too, came in for their share of criticism, although it was seldom as bitter as that directed against the friars. The burden of complaint was that the monks lived well off the income from their lands while neglecting their spiritual duties; that they were worldly, indolent, and avaricious; and that, in general, they had little odor of sanctity about them. Again we must allow for the exaggeration of reformers and satirists. Yet, in the long history of alternating relaxation and reform, which had characterized monasticism from its early days, this seems to have been on the whole a period of relaxation with few efforts at reform. Certainly the great age of medieval monasticism had passed. Spiritual stagnation was accompanied in many places by material decline. Many of the smaller monasteries and nunneries were loaded with debts and in sad financial straits. Even the larger and more prosperous houses must have found their income from land shrinking in this period of general economic depression for the landholding classes. In France, too, the monasteries suffered severely from the devastation of the Hundred Years' War. The effect of diminished monastic income on the individual monk, however, was in most places compensated by a corresponding decrease in the number of monks among whom the endowment had to be shared. For the decline in the number of monks the competition of the various orders of friars was in part responsible. A more effective cause, however, was probably a waning enthusiasm for the monastic life, which no longer attracted so many of the devout. There is also evidence that many monasteries, faced with shrinking income, voluntarily restricted the number of novices whom they would accept.

A notable symptom of decline in the spirit of monasticism was the growth of what has been called the wage system within the monasteries, and with it a general disintegration of the common life. According to canon law and immemorial custom the monks were forbidden private property and were to be supplied with their needs from the common funds. The first breach in this system came with the payment to the monks of clothes money instead of an issue of clothes from the communal store. By the fourteenth century this had become normal, although Church officials, and especially the bishops in their visitations, were still fighting a rear-guard action against it. During the course of the fourteenth and fifteenth centuries payments of cash to the monks for other purposes became increasingly common. In addition there were cash presents at specific times or dividends from the monastic income. Gifts to the monastery in the expectation of prayers for the soul of the donor, too, now frequently took the form of money to be distributed among the monks. As a result of these various sources of income, the monk might have, in addition to his board and keep, a fairly considerable amount of pocket money, and might be in a position to leave a substantial sum in his will. At the same time, it was becoming more common for at least the older monks to have a private apartment where they ate and slept instead of sharing the common refectory and dormitory. It is difficult to see how such developments could have been avoided at a time when every institution was in process of adjusting to a money economy, particularly since the monks, like other landlords, were ceasing to farm their lands directly and were renting them out for cash. But however inevitable the process, it introduced into the monastic life an essentially alien and demoralizing element.

B. Lay Piety and Mysticism

The symptoms of decline in the traditional forms of religious life, while too evident to be ignored, represent only one aspect of a complex situation. The widespread agitation for reform of the Church which accompanied the Conciliar Movement is sufficient proof that there was still much vital religious sentiment, and that the ills which beset the Church were by no means mortal. There was also in this period, particularly in Germany and the Netherlands, a rising tide of lay piety which grew up more or less outside the official ecclesiastical orbit, and which was in part a reaction against the formalism that characterized so much of contemporary religion. The distinguishing traits of this movement were an almost exclusive emphasis upon personal morality and the inner life of the spirit. For the most part it was concentrated in towns, where lay education was spreading and creating a new reading public for books of devotion. Even before the invention of printing, there was a growing volume of vernacular works in prose and verse designed to give moral instruction and to stimulate personal piety. Most of this inspirational literature in England and France, however, followed traditional lines. What distinguished the lay piety of Germany and the Netherlands was a new note of mysticism introduced during the fourteenth century by Dominican preachers in the Rhineland and later spreading to the Netherlands. In the fifteenth century the movement originated by the German mystics and transformed by their Dutch successors grew into a great revival of popular piety to which its adherents gave the name *Devotio Moderna*.

Something has already been said about the strain of mysticism which ran like a brightly colored thread through medieval religion. The mysticism discussed there was largely monastic. The cloister and the hermitage offered the ideal setting for the contemplative life, and to them the medieval mystics naturally gravitated. St. Francis was in this respect exceptional, and something of his personal mystical experience of union with Christ, on which the stigmata set its visible seal, carried over into his preaching and that of his early followers. By the fourteenth century, however, the element of mysticism was dying out among the Franciscans or had drifted into heretical speculation among the Spirituals who, as we shall see, were infected by the apocalyptic doctrines of Joachim of Flora. The German Dominican mystics of the fourteenth century were like St. Francis in taking mysticism out of the cloister and making it a force to inspire popular piety, but there the resemblance ended. Their mysticism was of a different sort, marked by the traditional traits of their order. It had a highly intellectual content of speculation and theory, and was firmly set in a framework of scholastic philosophy.

The founder of this school of German mysticism, Meister Eckhart (1260–1327), was a highly trained scholastic philosopher and theologian. Like most Dominicans he was an adherent of the Thomist system, but he stressed more strongly than Aquinas had done the Neoplatonic elements which had been introduced into Christian thought by St. Augustine. He was also strongly influenced by the works of the pseudo-

Dionysius the Areopagite. From him Eckhart took the Neoplatonic idea that the universe is an emanation from the Divine Being, and that all creatures proceed from God and return to God, a doctrine difficult to keep free from pantheistic implications. The purely speculative or scholastic side of Eckhart's mysticism is very difficult for the modern mind to grasp, and it need not concern us here, except to note that it aroused uneasiness in the official guardians of orthodoxy. A year before his death he was charged with heresy by the Archbishop of Cologne and summoned to trial. As a Dominican, Eckhart refused to recognize the local jurisdiction of the archbishop and appealed to the papal curia. His case was therefore removed to Avignon, but he died before a decision had been reached. The final result was the condemnation by Pope John XXII in 1329 of twenty-eight propositions taken from Eckhart's writings as dangerous or heretical. Eckhart was certainly not a conscious heretic, and his work taken as a whole seems orthodox enough. But his efforts to express both the utter transcendence of God and His immanence in the soul led him to use paradoxical expressions which, when taken out of context, might well have alarmed conventional theologians.

It was not his Latin writings, filled as they were with metaphysical speculation, which made Eckhart a force in the spiritual life of the German people. Rather it was his ability as a popular preacher to translate his ideas into the vernacular and to present them in terms within the comprehension of untrained minds. In his sermons and popular tracts he created the German vocabulary he needed to express his thought, and so became one of the formative influences on the development of German prose. Many of his surviving sermons were preached to nuns in the Dominican convents under his care, who copied them down and so were responsible for their preservation. But he also preached to large audiences of lay folk, while excerpts from his sermons were frequently included in books of devotion and so reached a still larger public. What Eckhart sought in his own experience was the soul's union with God, and he strove in his sermons to persuade his hearers that that such a union was possible to those who earnestly desired it and were prepared to abandon all else in order to achieve it. He taught that there is an "apex of the soul" or a "spark" in the innermost recesses of the soul in which union with God may take place through Divine Grace. Of this he spoke with an assurance born of personal mystical experience, and the force of his intense conviction kindled a flame in many of his hearers. In the following generation numerous mixed groups of lay men and women, clerics, and religious formed loosely organized associations for mutual aid in the cultivation of the inner life of the spirit. The name by which these groups were commonly known was "the Friends of God."

Eckhart's influence might not have been so effective or so far-reaching if it had not been carried on into the next generation by two of his disciples, Johann Tauler (c. 1300–61) and Heinrich Suso (c. 1295–1366), both of them Dominican friars. It was Tauler who was chiefly responsible for giving German mysticism its practical direction as an inspiration to piety. His sermons were largely free from speculation — homely, simple, and easy to understand. His theme was still the union of the soul with God, but he talked more about the preparation of the soul for the mystical experience by love of God and one's neighbors and by forgetfulness of self. In his hands mysticism became something that could inspire men and women, themselves perhaps incapable of the true mystical experience, to live better lives and achieve a more spiritual piety. For all his emphasis on the practical expression of piety in daily life, Tauler was a genuine mystic. Avoiding the lofty intellectual speculation of Eckhart on the one hand, and the visionary ecstasy of Suso on the other, he represents what was sanest and healthiest in the movement. Tauler was primarily a preacher, speaking directly to the souls of men. Suso's influence, on the other hand, was exerted largely through his writings. He was a poet and a master of German style. His books, the best known of which were *The Little Book of Truth* and *The Little Book of Eternal Wisdom*, were widely read in lay circles and among the religious. The basic doctrines are Eckhart's, but Suso's passionate meditation upon the sufferings of Christ made his mysticism more clearly Christocentric. By placing the Incarnation firmly in the forefront of his thought, he infused a human warmth into Eckhart's chilly theism, and at the same time guarded against the pantheistic implications which might be drawn from Eckhart's intellectual doctrine of the union of the soul with the Divine Essence.

As the influence of these Dominican preachers spread through the Rhineland it evoked a great volume of anonymous devotional literature in the German language. A typical example is *The Book of the Poor in Spirit* by a Friend of God, a systematic exposition of mystical theology as taught by Tauler and the other leaders of the movement. Until recently it was thought to be written by Tauler himself, but it was apparently the work of one of his disciples. Less systematic but more inspired was the little collection of anonymous writings to which the name *Theologia Germanica* was later given. For centuries this remained a popular book of devotion, to be surpassed only by *The Imitation of Christ*. Of it Luther said that it had taught him more about man and God than any book except the Bible and the works of St. Augustine. The result of this movement was undoubtedly to deepen the religious life of both lay folk and religious who came in contact with it. At the same time, the speculative side of German mysticism could give rise to strange and unorthodox notions among the uneducated once it spread beyond the control of soundly trained preachers. There is evidence that Eckhart's paradoxical utterances served as a stimulus to the obscure heresies that, as we shall see, throve among the poorer urban classes. After the passing of Tauler's generation the mystical movement in the Rhineland lost the firm and orthodox guidance it needed to keep it healthy. Before the end of the fourteenth century the flame of German mysticism was dying out. The Friends of God as a group had almost disappeared. And what remained of speculative mysticism tended to assume more eccentric forms. Early in the following century, Jean Gerson, the reforming Chancellor of the University of Paris and himself a devotee of the inner life, felt it necessary to warn against the dangers of false mysticism.

Just as German mysticism was declining, a closely related yet fundamentally different movement began in the Netherlands, which was to exert a more far-reaching and longer lasting effect on the lay piety of the pre-Reformation era. It undoubtedly owed much of its original inspiration to the German Dominicans and the Friends of God, but it was relatively little affected by the speculative side of their thought. The only one of the Netherland mystics who seems to have been directly influenced by Eckhart's esoteric doctrines was the Fleming, Jan Ruysbroeck (1293–1381), whose writings Gerson later regarded with considerable alarm. It was probably through him that the influence of German mysticism was passed on to the founders of the movement known as the *Devotio Moderna*. Gerard Groote, at any rate, who was the real founder of that movement, visited Ruysbroeck in his hermitage at Groenendael and was much impressed by him. But it was the impact of Ruysbroeck's personality rather than his abstract doctrines that kindled Groote's enthusiasm and confirmed his determination to cultivate the mystical life.

Gerard Groote (1340–84) was born in the Dutch town of Deventer in the valley of the Yssel, a branch of the lower Rhine. Inherited wealth enabled him to study philosophy, canon law and medicine at Paris, where he took his M.A., and to pursue his studies further at Prague and Cologne. As a young man he was already famous as a scholar, but gave no evidence of more than normal interest in religion. The turning point in his life came in his mid-thirties when he experienced a profound religious conversion. It was at this time that he visited Jan Ruysbroeck seeking inspiration and guidance. Thereafter he spent two years or more in a Carthusian monastery leading a life of contemplation, until finally, in 1379, he felt prepared to go forth and preach the Gospel. He was as yet a layman, and he never did become a priest. He was, however, ordained a deacon in 1380, and was licensed to preach by the Bishop of Utrecht. For the next three years he travelled all over Holland as an itinerant evangelist, drawing great crowds to hear his sermons. The doctrine he preached was simple and easily comprehensible, for, despite his own scholastic training, he had no patience with abstruse speculation. The endless disputes of the schoolmen now seemed to him merely a waste of time. The essence of religion, he taught, is spiritual communion with God through Christ. As a true mystic, he urged men to cultivate the inner life of the soul, for the kingdom of heaven is within us. But his teaching had also a strong moral content. To achieve communion with God men must transform their lives, free themselves from sin, and carry their inner religious experience into the practical activities of daily life. He called upon his hearers to repent, to nurse the spark of divinity which lies dormant in each man's soul, to imitate the life of Christ, and to show their love of God by loving their neighbors.

Groote's success as a preacher, as well as his forceful comments on the indolence and worldliness of many clerics, aroused the animosity of both the secular clergy and the mendicant orders. As a result of their complaints, his license to preach was revoked in 1383, and he returned to Deventer where a little group of disciples gathered about him. Several of these lived in the vicarage of one of Groote's earliest followers, Florentius Radewijns, making their living by copying manuscripts. It was this little group who formed the association known as the Brethren of the Common Life shortly after Groote's death in 1384.

From this small beginning a movement grew which spread throughout the Netherlands and into Germany. In the following years houses of the Brethren were founded in one city after another, while similar houses for women spread with equal rapidity. The Brethren and the Sisters of the Common Life were not regular religious orders, nor were they for some time recognized by the authorities of the Church. Although regulated by self-imposed rules, they were not bound by formal monastic vows. Unlike the mendicant orders they were entirely self-supporting, but the money they earned was pooled in a common fund from which they all drew the simple necessities of life, any surplus being expended in works of charity. Groote had urged the copying of manuscripts, not only as a means of making a living, but also as a way of making books of devotion more plentifully available to pious folk. He had also been actively interested in the religious education of boys, and a tradition of educational activity remained with the Brethren. Jan Cele, one of Groote's closest friends, became rector of the city school at Zwolle, and instituted reforms there that soon made it famous. In Deventer the Brethren never had a school of their own, but the cathedral school was so much under their influence as to be considered theirs, and the dormitories they established for poor boys drew many students. In many other cities in both the Netherlands and Germany the Brethren either founded schools or offered their services to those already existing, and in many places they founded dormitories for poor boys or used their influence to find them lodging in pious homes.

The animosity of the secular clergy and the mendicant orders, which had forced Groote to cease preaching, followed the Brethren for many years. For more than a generation they had to struggle for their existence. Groote himself had foreseen that the little group which was already contemplating the adoption of the Common Life would meet opposition and possibly persecution, and on his deathbed he advised those of his disciples who felt drawn to the monastic life to enter a recognized monastic order. They could thus regularize their own status and also be in a position to offer protection to the Brethren who preferred to remain in the world. Accordingly in 1386 a group of the Brethren from Deventer founded a monastery of the Augustinian Order of Canons Regular at Windesheim. There they continued to live in the spirit of Groote's teaching, writing and copying books of devotion and so reinforcing the work of the Brethren. As the fame of their piety spread, numbers of other monasteries, new and old, joined them and adopted their rule, thus forming the Windesheim Congregation. Through this Congregation the movement begun by Groote and his followers at Deventer became the inspiration for the most widespread and effective reform of monastic life in the fifteenth century. Some idea of its extent may be gained from the fact that by 1464 the Congregation included some eighty-two priories scattered through the Netherlands and Germany. For many years the various houses of the Brethren and the monasteries of the Windesheim Congregation remained in close contact, bound together by their common adherence to the spirit of the *Devotio Moderna,* but in course of time the two organizations tended to drift apart. It was difficult to retain the original close relations between monks who had chosen the secluded contemplative life and the Brethren who remained active as teachers and workers in the world. The contribution of the Windesheimers to the spread of the New Devotion was very great in the first half of the fifteenth century, but thereafter the movement exerted its most vital influence through the schools in which the Brethren of the Common Life were active and in which sound teaching was combined with religious instruction and inspiration. From these schools emerged some of the most influential religious leaders and humanists of the century before the beginning of the Protestant Reformation. It was through the influence of their pupils, men like Nicholas of Cusa, Jan Standonck, and Erasmus, that the ideals of the *Devotio Moderna* were disseminated over a far larger

area than could have been reached directly by either the Brethren themselves or the Windesheim monks.

It has been said that the best way to understand the spirit and teaching of the *Devotio Moderna* is to read *The Imitation of Christ*. Certainly it is the most convenient way, for that little classic of Christian devotion has retained its phenomenal popularity throughout the centuries and is still widely read and easily available in every European tongue. There has been much debate over the authorship of this guidebook to the Christian life, but it seems fairly certain that it was compiled early in the fifteenth century by Thomas à Kempis (1380–1471), a monk of the Windesheim Congregation, who had been educated under the influence of the Brethren in the school at Deventer. It may be that Thomas à Kempis based his work on the notebooks left by Gerard Groote, whose biography he wrote and whom he greatly admired. The spirit of the book is, at any rate, in entire accord with Groote's teaching and with other less well-known books produced by adherents to the *Devotio Moderna*.

One striking characteristic of the *Imitation*, and of most of the other devotional manuals which issued from the houses of the Brethren or the Windesheim monasteries, is an almost complete lack of concern with dogma and systematic theology. In all of this literature there is little attempt to relate piety to doctrine, and hence little that is specifically Catholic. The *Imitation*, in fact, has through the ages continued to give inspiration equally to Christians of all denominations. A second characteristic of the *Devotio Moderna*, which goes far to explain the first, is its strong ethical and moral orientation. The aim of its exponents, like that of all other mystics, was to achieve the inner union with God which transcends the bounds of the human intellect. But this close communion with God is possible only to the pure in heart. It is not to be won by intellectual speculation. Hence the primary concern of the truly devout person is to so live that his conscience remains pure and undefiled. Compared to a good life, the learning of the schools is relatively unimportant. A few quotations from the *Imitation* will illustrate the pervasive nature of this theme.

> What will it profit thee to dispute profoundly of the Trinity, if thou be void of humility, and art thereby displeasing to the Trinity?
> Surely high words do not make a man holy and just; but a virtuous life maketh him dear to God.
> I had rather feel compunction than understand the definition thereof.
> Surely, an humble husbandman that serveth God is better than a proud philosopher that neglecting himself laboreth to understand the course of the heavens.
> If I understood all things in the world, and were not in charity, what

would that help me in the sight of God, who will judge me according to my deeds?

Truly, at the day of judgment we shall not be examined what we have read, but what we have done; not how well we have spoken, but how religiously we have lived.

There is a great difference between the knowledge of an illuminated and devout man and the knowledge of a learned and studious clerk.

The author makes it clear that he does not intend to condemn learning, provided it is within the bounds of orthodoxy, "but a good conscience and a virtuous life is always to be preferred before it." At the same time, he evidently felt that learning carried to excess could be dangerous to the soul, for in one place he admonishes: "Cease from an inordinate desire of knowing, for therein is much distraction and deceit."

This rejection of formal theology and philosophy as superfluous may be in part a reaction against the sterility of fifteenth-century scholasticism, and particularly against the destructive tendenices of the Ockhamist school; but its roots went deeper than that. What the followers of the *Devotio Moderna* sought was guidance for the Christian life, and this they found more clearly and simply set forth in the Gospels and the Acts of the Apostles, which presented models for imitation that even the unlearned could comprehend. The Brethren of the Common Life and the Windesheim monks regarded the copying and dissemination of manuscripts of the Bible, including translations into the vernacular, as one of their most important tasks. Bible reading formed part of the daily routine of the Brethren, and on Sundays and holidays outsiders were invited to listen to the reading and discussion of a passage from the Scriptures. Exposition of the Bible, too, played an important part in the curriculum of the schools which were reformed under their influence. The *Imitation* is remarkable both for the number of Biblical quotations it contains and for the lack of references to any other source. That its author regarded the reading of the Scriptures as an absolute essential is evident in the chapter in which he couples it with Holy Communion as the two things necessary to the faithful soul.

> For I perceive two things to be very particularly necessary for me in this life, without which this miserable life would be insupportable to me.
>
> Whilst I am detained in the prison of this body, I acknowledge myself to stand in need of two things, namely, food and light.
>
> Unto me then thus weak and helpless Thou hast given Thy sacred body for the refreshment both of my soul and body; and Thy word Thou hast set as a lamp unto my feet.

If the ethical strain in the *Devotio Moderna*, with its emphasis on personal piety and the good life, tended to reduce formal theology to a position of secondary importance, the mystical strain, with its emphasis on the inner life of the spirit and direct communion with God, tended in much the same way to minimize the importance of the intermediary agencies provided by the Church. Except for the fine fourth chapter "Concerning the Sacrament," the *Imitation* has practically nothing to say about the services of the Church. And even the sacrament of the Eucharist, which is the only sacrament considered here, seems rather a necessary food for the spirit than a means of salvation. In their intense preoccupation with the inner life, the writers of this school tended to regard visible symbols and formal acts as mere externals without value unless accompanied by strong internal feeling. "If we esteem our progress in religious life to consist only in some exterior observances, our devotion will quickly come to an end." This is a note that we will meet again in Erasmus and the Christian humanists of a later generation,[3] and with it a reminiscent emphasis upon reading of the Scriptures coupled with contempt for scholastic theology.

In all the writings of the *Devotio Moderna* there was no questioning of the orthodox beliefs or practices of the Church, but there was a fundamental shift in emphasis, and therein lay a threat to ecclesiastical authority and a subtle criticism of the institutionalized religion of the day. The Brethren of the Common Life were not heretics. They were simply humble Christians who sought in contemplation and in imitation of the life of Christ a closer communion with God. Yet the movement contained elements dangerous to the Church, especially as it spread beyond the confines of the cloisters and the houses of the Brethren to literate lay men and women who found themselves dissatisfied with the spiritual sustenance offered by the contemporary clergy. The radical shift in emphasis it involved represented a movement away from the sacramental-sacerdotal aspects of medieval religion, on which the authority of the official Church over the lay world was basically founded. Despite the strongly ascetic and otherworldly strains in the *Devotio Moderna*, and its close affiliation with monasticism, it was in essence a personalization of piety and its ultimate effect a laicization of religion.

There were mystics in other countries as well in this troubled period, men and women who found in the inner life a refuge and the fulfillment of their spiritual aspirations. Many of them helped through writing, preaching, and personal influence to stimulate the devotion of lay folk and religious. But they worked for the most part as isolated individuals, and they founded no popular movement comparable to that of the German

[3] See below, pp. 545, 549–552.

Friends of God or the Netherlandish *Devotio Moderna*. The fourteenth century saw what has been called the flowering of English mysticism, illuminated by the names of Richard Rolle, Walter Hilton and Juliana of Norwich. These, together with the anonymous author of *The Cloud of Unknowing*, were all solitary contemplatives. The numerous manuscript copies of their works in monastic libraries testify to their popularity among the religious, and today they are treasured by students of English literature, but there is little evidence of their impact upon society at large. Very different was the rôle played by two remarkable women, St. Birgitta of Sweden (1303–73) and St. Catherine of Siena (1347–80), both of whom drew from their own intense mystical experience the strength to combat the corruption they saw at the papal court and throughout the Church. Both, too, used their great personal prestige, perhaps with decisive effect, to bring about the return of the papacy from Avignon to Rome. A generation later the great French mystic, Jean Gerson (1363–1429), became one of the most effective leaders of the Conciliar Movement which succeeded in healing the Great Schism. Like St. Catherine and St. Birgitta, he combined the cultivation of the inner life with public activity as a practical reformer. He was also a schoolman, Chancellor of the University of Paris, and a vigilant defender of orthodox belief, much concerned lest unregulated mysticism lead astray the feet of the unwary. The mystical theology he taught in the Paris schools was traditional, moderate, and discreet. His influence undoubtedly helped to counteract some of the more negative effects of the Ockhamist Nominalism then dominant at Paris, and the continued popularity of his works throughout the fifteenth century indicates that they brought comfort to many troubled souls. He was not, however, a sufficiently original thinker to found a new movement, and he was rather too academic to exert much influence upon contemporary lay society.

C. Heretical Deviations

Despite much variation in the quality of religious thought and feeling, most of the people of Western Europe retained throughout this period an unshaken faith in the fundamental dogmas of the Catholic Church and, despite much discontent, remained obedient to its authority. No picture of the two centuries before the Protestant Reformation would be complete, however, without some account of the innumerable minor heretical deviations that proliferated in the crowded workers' quarters of the industrial cities, as well as of the Wyclifite and Hussite heresies which issued from the universities of Oxford and Prague. Just how many heretics there were in this period it is impossible to estimate. Most of the heretical groups were undoubtedly small; but, taken all together, they made up a sectarian movement comparable in many respects to the post-Reformation Anabaptists. Both before and after the Reformation, the sects represented a particular type of lay piety, individualistic and anti-hierarchical, fanatically attached to some specific doctrine and, for the most part, characterized by an austere morality.

The motive force behind nearly all the heresies of this period was revulsion against the worldliness, avarice and immorality of many of the clergy, combined with resentment aroused by the wealth and fiscal practices of the Church. Such sentiments did not, of course, necessarily or in most cases lead to heresy. Demands for reform and passionate denunciations of the clergy filled the air in the fourteenth and fifteenth centuries, voiced by writers and preachers of unimpeachable orthodoxy. To many earnest churchmen, as well as to many devout laymen, the wealth of the Church seemed the most insurmountable obstacle to reform. The immense success of the mendicant orders in the thirteenth century had been largely due to their voluntary poverty. The Spiritual Franciscans, too, had idealized poverty as the way of life sanctified by the example of Christ and the Apostles, and thereby reinforced the widespread belief that true holiness could be achieved only by renouncing all material possessions. It must not be forgotten that this was a period of economic crisis, in which the spread of money economy and the growth of capitalism were causing a radical dislocation of the social structure. William Langland was not alone in feeling that the times were out of joint and that the love of money was the root of all evil. When in his vision he saw all men, laymen and clergy alike, serving Lady Meade, i.e., illicit gain, he turned for guidance to the poor plowman who thus became the embodiment of the Christian ideal. When this idealization of poverty was combined with a burning sense of social injustice, it is not surprising that some men were driven into rebellion against a Church whose wealth was in such glaring contrast both to their own poverty and to the apostolic way of life.

Social discontent and anti-clerical sentiment, however, were not in themselves sufficient to found a heretical sect. Some doctrine was needed to justify rebellion and to free men from dependence upon the clergy for the administration of the sacraments. The Waldenses or Poor Men of Lyons, who were still one of the most numerous of the heretical sects in the fourteenth century, found their original inspiration in a literal reading of the New Testament. Peter Waldo and his early followers, who founded the sect in the late twelfth century, had been laymen who simply followed Christ's command to His disciples to go forth in complete poverty to preach the Gospel. Only when they were forbidden to preach were they forced into heresy and schism. Their doctrine continued to be a simple evangelical Christianity, but colored by an increasingly anti-sacerdotal bias. They denounced the vices of the clergy and compared the contemporary Church unfavorably with the simplicity and poverty of the Apostles. Denying the validity of sacraments administered by an immoral priest, they made apostolic life rather than ordination the prerequisite of priestly power, and so felt justified in appointing priests of their own, or even in asserting that any pious layman might preach and administer the sacraments. Some apparently went so far as to deny the doctrine of transubstantiation altogether. Lack of centralized organization made it difficult for them to maintain uniformity of belief, and in the fourteenth century some groups shared the aberrations of more eccentric sects. In general, however, the Waldenses continued to be men and women of simple faith and pious life, heretical only in their denial of the authority of the hierarchical Church and of the exclusive power of the priesthood to interpret the Scriptures and administer the sacraments.

Another group of heretical sects, apparently quite numerous and wide-spread in the fourteenth century, drew their justification for revolt against the Church from speculative mysticism of a pantheistic type. These sects went by various names. Contemporary documents refer to them, often indiscriminately, as Brethren of the Free Spirit, Beghards, or Turlu-pins. As the condemnation of Meister Eckhart showed, it was possible for even well-trained orthodox theologians to be led by radical mysticism into the expression of opinions that savored of pantheism. It is not surprising, then, that semi-literate zealots and misguided *illuminati* should carry the logic of Neoplatonic mysticism to the point where it not only ceased to be Christian, but also became subversive of all ecclesiastical and social order. Starting with a pantheistic belief in the immanence of God in everything, they taught that it is possible in this life to achieve perfect union with God, and that those who achieved this state of perfection are thereafter incapable of sin. For the perfected, the sacraments, the penitential system and all the services of the Church are meaningless. As free spirits, they are no longer bound to obey any ecclesiastical or civil authority or even to observe the moral law; for, being one with God, whatever they do is holy. Most of the Brethren of the Free Spirit seem to have been in fact austere ascetics, but their doctrine could easily become a justification for immoral excess. Despite their condemnation by the Council of Vienne in 1311 and the continued efforts of the Inquisition, sects of this type persisted throughout the fourteenth century and did much to discredit mysticism and to cast suspicion upon even such perfectly orthodox mystics as the Brethren of the Common Life.

Heretical tendencies in this period also found encouragement in the apocalyptic prophecies of Abbot Joachim of Flora (1132–1202). Similar prophetic speculations concerning the coming of the millennium have been common in Christian history, but those of the Calabrian abbot were more radical than most in their implications, and they exerted an extraordinary influence on religious thought for more than two centuries. In his rather obscure mystical writings, based on an elaborate comparison of the Old and New Testaments and a too literal reading of the Book of Revelation, Joachim outlined a scheme of world history, dividing it into three ages. The first, that of God the Father, was the age of the Old Testament, an age of obedience to the law; the second, that of God the Son, was the age of the New Testament, an age of faith; the third, which he foresaw as coming in the near future, would be the age of the Holy Spirit, when men would perceive truth by direct mystical intuition. By an elaborate system of numerical calculations, Joachim dated the opening of the new age at the year 1260. It would last a thousand years, to be followed by the end of the world and the Last Judgment. But first there must come a period of martyrdom and dreadful suffering for the Church under the rule of Antichrist. The age of the Spirit would be introduced by a new mendicant order, which would replace the ecclesiastical hierarchy of the age of the New Testament. In this age of direct illumination, there would be no need for the sacraments or the authority of the Church. Revolutionary as Joachim's prophecies were, their heretical implications seem not to have been fully realized until his writings were published in 1254 by a young Franciscan, Gherardo da Borgo San Donnino, under the title *The Eternal Gospel,* together with commentaries that exaggerated their heretical elements. According to Gherardo, the "Eternal Gospel" of Joachim was to supersede the New Testament as the New Testament had superseded the Old. The radical interpretations added by Gherardo were officially condemned in 1256, and many people were disillusioned when the millennium failed to arrive on schedule in 1260. Nevertheless, Joachimite ideas continued to fascinate many speculative minds, including Dante's, and to stimulate the imagination of various mystical and anti-sacerdotal sects.

The Joachimite prophecies appealed with special force to the Spiritual Franciscans, whose devotion to the ideal of absolute poverty finally drove them into rebellion and heresy, and who quite naturally identified themselves with the mendicant order of contemplatives which, according to Joachim, was to reign in the age of the Spirit. With the institutionalization of the Franciscan ideal, the rule of absolute poverty had proved to be impractical for the majority of the friars, and in 1279 a compromise solution of the problem was given papal sanction in the bull *Exiit qui seminat* of Nicholas III. Property given to the Franciscans was not to be owned by them, but was to be held in trust by the papacy for the use of the order. To the Spirituals this seemed a mere legal quibble, and their refusal to accept the papal ruling forced them into rebellion against both their superiors in the order and the hierarchy of the Church. Forgetting in their devotion to the ideal of poverty that charity is also a virtue, they were loud in their denunciation of the wealth of the Church and the vices of the clergy. In Italy and southern France, where they were most numerous, the Spirituals gained popular support among the lower classes in the towns, and added fuel to the anti-clerical and anti-papal sentiments that were already all too strong. By the opening years of the fourteenth century the situation had become so alarming as to call for drastic action on the part of the Church government, a task for which Pope John XXII was peculiarly suited. In a bull of 1317 he excommunicated all those Franciscan zealots who would not submit to the authority of their superiors and accept the official ruling on poverty. Some twenty-four of the Spirituals were arrested and imprisoned, and four of the most stubborn were burned as heretics. The remainder either submitted or escaped to carry on increasingly radical agitation among the poorer townsfolk.

Having suppressed or expelled the intransigent zealots, the Franciscan order enjoyed a short period of tranquillity until a second storm broke. The Franciscans had long taken pride in the belief that their rule of poverty was founded upon the example of Christ and the Apostles. Even the Conventuals, who had accepted a compromise with the strict ideal, asserted the exclusive claim of their order to imitation of the apostolic way of life, a claim not unnaturally resented by the secular clergy and the other religious orders. It implied, indeed, not only pretentions to peculiar sanctity on the part of the Franciscans, but also a criticism of the wealth of the clergy and the papacy which played into the hands of the anti-clerical heretics. In 1321 the debate over this issue was reopened by the action of a Dominican inquisitor who condemned a Provençal enthusiast for declaring that Christ and the Apostles had possessed nothing either individually or in common. A Franciscan judge who was present declared this to be no heresy but an accepted article of faith, guaranteed by the bull *Exiit qui seminat* of 1279, in which Nicholas III had also forbidden any further discussion of the matter. At this point John XXII forced the issue by refusing to hold property in trust for the use of the order, thus leaving the Franciscans no legal alternative but to give up either their theoretical poverty or their actual property. This singularly effective step John followed up by declaring, in the bull *Cum inter non-nullos* (1322), that it was heretical to assert that Christ and the Apostles

357

had not owned the goods, such as food and clothing, which they used. Meanwhile the General Chapter of the order had reasserted the doctrine of apostolic poverty, and the general of the order, Michael of Cesena, continued to defy the pope's authority. Finally, in 1328, Michael fled to the court of Louis the Bavarian, taking with him, among others, the brilliant young Nominalist philosopher, William of Ockham. The story of Ockham's long polemic against the papal monarchy has been told elsewhere. It was, in the long run, perhaps the most important result of the controversy. But another result was that a number of less illustrious friars also seceded from the order, and went to swell the number of those ragged zealots who continued for more than a century to agitate against the papacy and to stir up anti-clerical feeling among the socially underprivileged classes.

Although the Inquisition usually made a distinction between enthusiasts of the Spiritual type and the more doctrinally motivated followers of Michael of Cesena, the two groups tended to merge and were generally lumped together under the name of Fraticelli. This term was also used loosely to designate other heretical groups who may or may not have been directly influenced by the dissident friars. It is impossible to estimate the number of those who were led into rebellion and heresy by the teaching of the Fraticelli. The Inquisition records show 113 burned as heretics in Provence between 1318 and 1350. Thereafter they seem to have been chiefly active in Italy, although persecution apparently drove some north to merge with the Waldenses or the Brethren of the Free Spirit. In the preaching and writing of the Fraticelli, Joachimite doctrines played a large part. The prophecies of the Abbot of Flora gave them the comforting assurance that the time of martyrdom would pass with the dawning of the millenium. Meanwhile, they believed that the Spirit had already departed from the visible Church, and they unhesitatingly cast John XXII in the role of Antichrist. The more extreme taught that all members of the clergy since John's reign were heretical and, in characteristic sectarian fashion, they regarded themselves as the sole representatives of the true Church. The whole history of the Fraticelli is obscure, for they were essentially an underground movement. There seems no doubt, however, that they found their most receptive audience among the industrial proletariat, nor that their defiance of authority and their inflammatory condemnation of wealth poured oil upon the flames of social unrest. The fact that the Fraticelli were reported to have been especially active in Florence around 1378, the year of the *Ciompi* revolt, can scarcely be altogether coincidental.

Heretical tendencies also throve in the numerous semi-religious confraternities of men and women, who sought to imitate the apostolic way of life without taking the perpetual vows of the regular religious orders. These groups represented a movement of lay piety which spread throughout Western Europe in the thirteenth and fourteenth centuries and was not in itself, or necessarily, heretical or even anti-clerical. The religious motive behind the movement was primarily the desire of pious lay folk to put into practice the apostolic ideals of chastity, poverty and manual labor. By working with their hands and sharing their goods in common, these pious brotherhoods found a means of embracing poverty without resorting to mendicancy. Normally their rules provided for regular religious observances, and they usually wore some form of distinctive garb. They occupied, in short, an anomalous position, halfway between the lay and religious modes of life, without the steadying influence of centralized organization or an established rule. It was a position which left them peculiarly susceptible to heretical notions, the more so since most of them were recruited from the poor and semi-literate classes of the towns, among whom a sense of social injustice had bred strong anti-clerical sentiments. Their history, like that of the Fraticelli, is obscure, but they represented an element in the religious life of the fourteenth century too important to be entirely ignored.

The male confraternities, known as Beghards in Germany and the Netherlands and by other names elsewhere, seem to have been especially open to heretical tendencies. Those of southern France, indeed, became so closely associated with the dissident Spiritual Franciscans that they fell under suspicion and were suppressed as heretics by the Inquisition. Among them, as among the Fraticelli, Joachimite prophecies combined with excessive devotion to poverty to drive them into reaction against the contemporary Church. In Germany and the Netherlands, the Beghards seem rather to have been identified with the Brethren of the Free Spirit, and shared their condemnation by the Council of Vienne. From that time on, the term Beghard became almost synonymous with heretic in contemporary usage, thus doing a grave injustice to many perfectly orthodox groups. In Germany, too, the movement was further discredited by vagrant Beghards who made a public nuisance of themselves by begging as well as by spreading heretical doctrines. By the end of the fourteenth century the Beghards had almost disappeared, the orthodox among them having been for the most part absorbed into the Third Order of St. Francis.

Much more numerous in the Netherlands and Germany were the feminine counterparts of the Beghards, the Beguines. Economic and social forces combined with religious motives to make this form of semi-religious organization more attractive to women than to men. Medieval society made little provision for unmarried women. Ladies of noble birth, whether maid or widow, who could not make a suitable marriage or who preferred a life of chastity and religious devotion, might find refuge in the nunneries, but these were usually closed to their social inferiors. For women of the middle and lower classes, houses of the Beguines served as substitutes. There they could find security, satisfaction for their desire to lead a devout life, and at the same time an opportunity to make a respectable living by engaging in spinning, lace-making or some other light craft, pooling their earnings in the common fund. In the great textile centers of the Netherlands, some quite large communities were formed, with a number of houses forming a single *béguinage*. These could be kept under close ecclesiastical supervision. In some of the smaller communities, too, Dominican friars undertook the spiritual guidance of the inmates and guarded against the introduction of heretical notions. Since the Beguines did not form a recognized religious order, however, it was difficult to maintain adequate supervision, while their location in cities and their close connections with the working classes left them open to heretical infiltration. By the opening years of the fourteenth century, the prevalence of unregulated mysticism and heretical doctrines among the Beguines aroused serious concern in the hierarchy, and at the Council of Vienne they were condemned along with the Beghards. Thereafter the Beguines, including many who were perfectly orthodox, suffered sporadic persecution until, in 1374, Pope Gregory XI gave official sanction to communities of proven orthodoxy and under ecclesiastical supervision. The movement thus survived, free from the taint of heresy, but devoid also of much of its original religious fervor.

Until the last quarter of the fourteenth century England had remained remarkably free from the taint of heresy. So little, indeed, had the Church to fear there that no legal machinery had been set up for imposing the death penalty. Yet in few places was there more general discontent with prevailing conditions in the Church or more urgent demands for reform. In England, too, the long war with France bred a growing nationalism which aggravated resentment against the fiscal demands of the French popes at Avignon, and against the practice of papal provisions to English benefices. Englishmen also suspected that some of the money sent to Avignon was used to finance the war against them. The growing anti-papal sentiment of Lords and Commons found expression in the Statutes of Provisors and Praemunire and in the rejection by the Parliament of 1366 of the pope's claims to the tribute promised by King John as a vassal of the papacy. The second half of the fourteenth century, moreover, was filled with social unrest and a rising tide of resentment of the poor against the rich landowners, including the monks and higher clergy, a resentment which finally culminated in the Peasants' Revolt of

1381 and the murder of Archbishop Sudbury by the rebels. Here, as on the continent, social unrest tended to assume religious connotations and to find expression in anti-clericalism. At the same time, the growing number of books of devotion in the vernacular gave evidence of a strong strain of piety among the middle and upper classes. But lay piety could develop along independent lines, and the spread of literacy among the laity might open the way for the dissemination of ideas dangerous to the Church. For many reasons, then, England seemed ripe to receive the subversive ideas which Wyclif began to proclaim at Oxford in the last years of the Babylonian Captivity and the first years of the Great Schism.

Until he was drawn into the royal service, John Wyclif (c.1330–84) had enjoyed a successful, but in no way abnormal, career as a scholastic philosopher, a popular teacher and an ornament of the Oxford schools. His mind had been formed amidst the interminable and frequently acrimonious debates which characterized fourteenth-century scholasticism. Nowhere, indeed, was the conflict between the schools more bitter than in Oxford, where the radical speculations of Duns Scotus and William of Ockham had originated, and where their adherents still fought with one another and with the champions of extreme Realism, among whom Wyclif was one of the most distinguished. The metaphysical basis of Wyclif's theological doctrines was already laid before he began his career as an active agitator, and doubtless he already shared the common conviction of the need for reform in the Church; but it is doubtful that he would ever have developed his ideas beyond the range of conventional scholastic debate, much less beyond the bounds of orthodoxy, had he not been called into royal service at a time when the current of anti-clerical and anti-papal feeling was running strongly and the times seemed ripe for action. Thereafter national sentiment combined with the heat of controversy and the awakening of conscience, which resulted from his experience with the realities of the world outside the academic halls, to transform the scholastic philosopher into the practical reformer and the radical theologian.

The fortunes of England were at a low ebb in the early 1370's when Wyclif began to receive royal patronage. Edward III was sinking into senile depravity; the Black Prince was ill and dying; and in France the English armies were steadily losing ground under the persistent pressure of Bertrand du Guesclin's companies. Money was desperately needed to carry on the war, and in their need Parliament and the royal council cast covetous eyes on the wealth of the Church. In 1371 the Convocation of the Clergy was forced under protest to grant a subsidy of unprecedented size. Even this seemed insufficient to the anti-clerical hotheads, and voices were raised in Parliament to suggest that in a national emergency part of the temporal possessions of the clergy, which had originally been given to them by lay benefactors, might be confiscated for the common good. In the following year, Gregory XI demanded a subsidy of twenty thousand pounds from the English clergy to finance his wars in Italy. Anti-papal sentiment rose to fever pitch, and the government forbade the collection of the tax pending negotiations with the pope. When at about this time Wyclif began to take an interest in politics, therefore, relations between England and the papacy had reached a state of crisis in which it might have seemed possible that the government would undertake the partial disendowment of the Church, free it in some degree from papal control, and, at the same time, rid it of abuses against which reformers had long fulminated in vain. This, at least, was the impression Wyclif apparently received from the climate of opinion in the capital, an impression possibly exaggerated by wishful thinking and by his lack of political experience.

Although Wyclif was one of the ambassadors sent to Bruges in 1374 to negotiate with papal envoys over the matter of papal taxes and provisions to benefices, the services the royal council expected of him were those of a propagandist rather than a minister of the crown. Except for an occasional call to preach in London churches in support of the government's anti-clerical policies, what was required of him was chiefly written propaganda. After the conclusion of the mission to Bruges he therefore returned to Oxford and began the composition of two massive treatises *On Divine Dominion* and *On Civil Dominion*. His argument in these lengthy and rambling works, filled as they are with scholastic definitions and distinctions and an odd mixture of theological and feudal concepts, is difficult to follow, but the general purport is clear enough. Dominion, that is, lordship over all things, belongs to God alone; and all human dominion, including ownership of property, is held immediately from God in return for service. It follows, then, that the sinner who, by virtue of sin, is delinquent in his service to God forfeits his right to all lordship. In short, human dominion is never absolute, but is always contingent upon Grace. Logically this involved denial of rights of government or property to all men, lay or clerical, who were not in a state of Grace. But Wyclif seems to have been principally concerned with the application of his doctrine of dominion to the authority and temporal possessions of the clergy and the ecclesiastical hierarchy, up to and including the pope. Since dominion is founded solely upon Grace, he argued, the pope's authority is not absolute, but is contingent upon his personal character. Similarly the possessions of all ranks of the clergy are contingent upon their beneficiaries being in a state of Grace, and, if any cleric habitually lives in mortal sin or fails to perform his spiritual function, the secular government should deprive him of his endowment. This, at least, was the part of his argument that attracted the most attention, not only in England, but also at Avignon.

There was, it is true, little that was strictly original about Wyclif's doctrine of dominion. Much of it was in fact taken from arguments advanced by FitzRalph, Archbishop of Armagh, earlier in the century in the heat of the Franciscan controversy over apostolic poverty. Still earlier, Egidius Romanus had used the theory that all dominion comes from God through His vicar the pope to justify the pope's plenitude of power. What was novel and revolutionary was that Wyclif turned the doctrine against the papacy and the whole body of the clergy. It is not surprising, therefore, that in 1377, as soon as Wyclif's work was brought to his attention, Gregory XI condemned eighteen propositions taken from that part of the treatise *On Civil Dominion* which dealt with the authority and temporal possessions of the Church. At the same time he issued bulls demanding Wyclif's arrest and imprisonment, a demand which offended English national sentiment, since it seemed an encroachment upon episcopal jurisdiction and also seemed to threaten the establishment of a papal inquisition in England.

Before the papal bulls could reach England, Edward III had died and the crown had passed to his ten-year-old grandson, Richard II. During the new king's minority, government was carried on by a faction-ridden Council of Regency, in which one of the principal figures was Edward's fourth son, John of Gaunt, Duke of Lancaster, who had already acted as Wyclif's protector. Given the anti-clerical bias of Gaunt and the Council and the general temper of the country, the English bishops evidently felt it inexpedient to take strong action against Wyclif, and the death of Gregory XI early in 1378 removed for the time any threat of further action from the papacy. Wyclif was thus left free to continue his writing and teaching at Oxford, with all his doubts concerning the authority of the papacy vastly magnified by the opening of the Great Schism.

He was now prepared to reject papal authority more strongly, while ascribing more unqualified power to the secular government. In two characteristically lengthy and disjointed treatises *On the Church* and *On the Office of King* he reached conclusions in many respects reminiscent of those enunciated earlier in the century by Marsiglio of Padua and William of Ockham, although the road by which he reached them was different. He asserted the superior authority of the secular government in all things temporal, including clerical patronage and ecclesiastical property, and once more called upon the monarchy to disendow the clergy and so restore their spiritual character. Kings, he argued, are the vicars of God and so should be obeyed. As for the Church, he agreed with both Marsiglio and Ockham in denying that it is composed of the clergy only, but where they defined it as the community of all believers, Wyclif, whose theology had been profoundly influenced by the pre-destinarian theories developed at Oxford a generation earlier by Thomas Bradwardine, defined the Church as composed solely of those predestined to salvation, among whom the pope and the other members of the hierarchy might or might not be included. With this idea he reinforced his earlier doctrine of dominion founded on Grace, denying plenitude of power to a pope who might be "foreknown" to be damned, and making the efficacy of the sacraments dependent upon the personal character of the priest or bishop. As a corollary of the doctrine of predestination he also declared salvation to be independent of the services of the Church, rejected the validity of indulgences, and denied the power of pope or priest either to excommunicate the righteous or to absolve those who were not worthy in God's sight.

Wyclif had been forced to glorify the monarchy through recognition of the fact that only the secular government could carry out the disendowment which he regarded as the prerequisite to reform of the Church, but his theological radicalism had now carried him further than his sponsors in the royal council were prepared to follow. It is doubtful, indeed, if the king's ministers ever considered the disendowment of the Church as more than a counter to be used in bargaining with the papacy. The royal government had profited too greatly by the opportunity to pay its ministers with ecclesiastical benefices to consider disendowment seriously. Before the end of 1378 even the anti-clericals in the royal council had apparently decided that Wyclif was becoming more of a liability than an asset, and when, in the following year, he began to question the accepted doctrine regarding the Eucharist they washed their hands of him.

The basis of Wyclif's Eucharistic doctrine was purely metaphysical and was implicit in the extreme Realism of his earlier philosophical writings; but hitherto he had not pressed the logic of his argument to the point of challenging the dogma of transubstantiation. That he now rejected the possibility of the total annihilation of the substance of bread and wine, and asserted that it still persisted in the elements of the sacrament after consecration, is evidence of a growing radicalism in his thought. He did not at any time deny the Real Presence of Christ in the elements of the sacrament, but attempted to show by a variety of meta-physical arguments, which finally approached fairly closely to Luther's later doctrine of consubstantiation, that it was a spiritual rather than a formal or substantial presence.

> The truth and faith of the Church [he wrote] is that as Christ is at once God and man, so the sacrament is at once the body of Christ and bread — bread and wine naturally, the body and blood sacramentally.[4]

Finally, he insisted that the words of the priest are not the cause but "make the occasion only" of the sacramental presence of Christ in the Eucharist. The enunciation of his Eucharistic doctrine ended any hope Wyclif might have had of winning the support of the upper classes. Even those who shared his conviction of the need for disendowment and reform were not willing to follow him into open heresy. Moreover, the Peasants' Revolt of 1381 led to a general reaction in the direction of conservatism and to a climate of opinion unfavorable to radical speculation. Courtenay, the newly elected Archbishop of Canterbury, was accordingly able in 1382 to secure the condemnation of a number of Wyclif's conclusions and then to expel him and his followers from Oxford. Oddly enough, Wyclif was not himself mentioned in the condemnation, and he was allowed to retire to his rectory at Lutterworth, one of the three livings he had held successively as an absentee rector during his career at Oxford. There he remained undisturbed until his death in 1384.

During these last years at Lutterworth Wyclif continued to write with feverish energy, partially paralyzed though he was by the effect of a stroke. In treatise after treatise he poured forth vitriolic attacks on papacy and priesthood, monks and friars. The test he now applied to every aspect of the Church's government, beliefs and practices was conformity with the literal sense of the Bible which, he declared, alone contained the law of God. This was not a new idea with him, but it was developed more radically now that he was removed from the arena of scholastic debate. While fully aware of the allegorical interpretation of the Bible, and prone to use it himself on occasion, he proclaimed its literal sense to be its true meaning and that sense to be so clear and plain that it could be understood by laymen and even by the unlettered.

> The New Testament [he wrote] is of full authority, and open to the understanding of simple men as to the points that be most needful to salvation. . . . [and again] No man is so rude a scholar but that he might learn the words of the Gospel according to his simplicity.[5]

[4] Quoted in H. B. Workman, *John Wyclif, A Study of the English Medieval Church* (Oxford, 1926), II, 38.
[5] *Ibid.*, II, 151.

If all men could understand the Gospel, then, it should be made available to all as the one sure and authoritative guide. This, of course, necessitated translation into the vernacular, for few laymen and, possibly, no very large number of priests were sufficiently learned to read the Latin of the Vulgate. Recent research has minimized the share of Wyclif in the translation of the Bible associated with his name, if indeed any part of it was his own work; but he certainly inspired it and may have supervised it in part. It was to prove the most potent instrument for the propagation of his teaching.

The translation of the Bible, however, was not the only example of the use of the vernacular by Wyclif's disciples as a means of spreading their doctrine among the laity. In the years following their expulsion from Oxford they poured forth a flood of English treatises and sermons, some of them translations or paraphrases of Wyclif's writings. Several of the Oxford group, as well as other "poor priests," also travelled through the country as missionaries spreading their doctrine by word of mouth. Most of the academic "Lollards," as the adherents of Wyclif's heresy came to be called, however, recanted under threat of persecution, and, after the passage of the statute *De haeretico comburendo* in 1401 imposing the death penalty on heretics, Lollardy lost most of its adherents among the propertied classes. The later history of the Lollards is uncertain, since after having been driven underground they left little record of their activities, except when individual members of the sect were seized and brought to trial. It is therefore impossible to estimate their numbers, or to say with certainty whether the movement persisted into the sixteenth century to form a link between the teaching of Wyclif and the Protestant Reformation. What does seem clear is that only where it found support in social discontent — among the artisans and craftsmen — did it make a lasting impression. It seems clear, too, that after the defection of the Oxford group had cut its intellectual roots, and in proportion as it won adherents from the working classes, Lollardy drifted further away from the specific teaching of Wyclif and approached more nearly to the type of anti-clerical and anti-sacerdotal heresy common among the working classes on the continent. Much of Wyclif's doctrine was, indeed, too firmly rooted in scholastic metaphysic to appeal directly to the unlettered, while his appeal to the literal sense of the Scriptures must have been largely frustrated by the mechanical difficulty of multiplying copies of the vernacular Bible without the aid of printing. At the same time, his program for reform of the Church was too sweeping and too negative to win wide acceptance among the politically influential classes. Neither the government nor the majority of the people were ready, despite much discontent, to jettison the established Church, nor were they ready to embrace an heretical doctrine of the Eucharist on the strength of a metaphysical argument.

Wyclif's doctrine produced more vigorous and lasting fruit when transplanted to the distant soil of Bohemia. Earlier in the century Charles IV (1346–73), who was much more interested in his hereditary kingdom of Bohemia than in the Holy Roman Empire, had made Prague an active center of international culture, and with the founding of the University of Prague that city became the educational capital of central Europe. Charles had also done much to free both the Bohemian state and the Bohemian Church from German domination, and so gave encouragement to the growth of Czech national consciousness. The reform movement begun in the latter part of the fourteenth century by a series of popular preachers thus coincided with a wave of rising nationalism. At this crucial juncture Bohemia was brought into close relations with England by the marriage of Anne of Bohemia, the sister of King Wenceslas, to Richard II. Among the Czechs who followed in her train were a number of students who studied at English universities and returned with copies of Wyclif's philosophical and theological works. About 1401 Jerome of Prague brought back the *Dialogus* and *Trialogus*, the two most important theological works of Wyclif's last years; but others of his works had been current among the masters of the University of Prague for some time before that. They evidently found their most favorable reception amongst the Czechs at the university, who were as yet outnumbered by the Germans and other foreigners. In 1403, at any rate, when propositions taken from Wyclif's works were condemned by the faculty, it was over the protest of the majority of the Czech masters. The reception of Wyclif's teaching, however, was not the original cause, but rather a contributing factor of the movement which swept Bohemia into heresy and schism, a movement which owed its strength to a combination of Czech nationalism, revulsion against the growing scandals of the Great Schism, the prevailing demand for reform in the Church and, finally, the personal leadership and eventual martyrdom of John Hus.

The personality of Hus (1370–1415) was very different from that of Wyclif, despite the fact that both began their careers as scholastic philosophers and scored their first successes in an academic environment. Hus was above all a popular preacher, and in 1402, a year after his ordination to the priesthood, his appointment to the pulpit of the Bethlehem Chapel gave him the perfect opportunity to exercise his talents. This chapel, which had recently been founded and endowed for the preaching of sermons in the Czech language, soon became the most vital center of religious life in Prague. There Hus preached to crowds of laymen sermons noted for their clarity and simplicity and for the directness of their appeal to the emotions of his audience. Many of his sermons were directed against the vices of the undisciplined and simoniacal clergy, and voiced demands for reform very similar to those expressed by Wyclif. Whether he ever accepted Wyclif's doctrine of the Eucharist is doubtful — he denied it to the end — but he did adopt the greater part of Wyclif's teaching concerning the nature of the Church, including the assertion that the Church is the community of those predestined to salvation, and he defended Wyclif in the debates at the university. It was inevitable, then, that the clergy whose animosity he had aroused by his denunciation of their vices should brand him as a Wyclifite and use the condemnation of Wyclif as a weapon against him. On those grounds the Archbishop of Prague excommunicated Hus in 1409, and attempted to prevent him from preaching in the Bethlehem Chapel. The following year the archbishop also commanded all of Wyclif's books that could be found to be burnt in public. By this time the Bohemian clergy were sharply divided into two parties, one led by Hus and supported by King Wenceslas and the people of Prague, the other led by the archbishop and supported by the anti-pope John XXIII. Relations between the two parties were further strained when in 1412 the pope proclaimed an indulgence to raise money for his war with the King of Naples. Hus vigorously assailed the traffic in indulgences and declared them to be useless, and in reply the pope excommunicated him and laid an interdict on the city of Prague so long as Hus remained within it. Out of consideration for his fellow citizens Hus then left Prague, and spent the next two years wandering through Bohemia, preaching and writing, and thereby gaining a wider following than he might have secured had he remained in the capital.

Such was the situation in 1414 when the Council of Constance convened with a view to ending the Great Schism, reforming the Church "in head and members," and suppressing heresy. The settlement of the controversy over Hus was bound to have an important place on the agenda, if only because Emperor Sigismund, who had taken the initiative in summoning the Council, was heir to his childless brother Wenceslas and was concerned to free Bohemia of heresy before he inherited it. Even before the Council met, Sigismund urged Hus to go to Constance to defend his position before the Council, and to that end guaranteed him a safe conduct. There was, however, little hope that Hus could win the Council over to his views and, perhaps, still less that he himself would compromise. The Council, which early in its proceedings condemned all of Wyclif's works and ordered his bones to be exhumed and cast out of consecrated ground, was not likely to look favorably upon anyone tainted with his doctrines. And Hus proclaimed his adherence to too many of Wyclif's doctrines to pass unscathed. His trial ended in his condemnation as a confirmed heretic, and he was turned over to the secular arm to be burnt — a sentence carried out by that same branch of the secular arm that had furnished him with a safe conduct. A year later Jerome of Prague, who had accompanied the master to Constance, suffered the same fate.

Far from ending the trouble in Bohemia, the death of Hus was the signal for a national rising of the Czech people against the authority of the Church. For a time the influence of the tolerant King Wenceslas prevented violent action, but on his death in 1419 both the Catholic Church and the Hussites resorted to arms, the former to crush the heresy, the latter to defend their beliefs and their national independence. Repeatedly in the following years the pope preached a crusade, and Sigismund, who now claimed the Bohemian throne, rallied the armed force of the Empire. To meet the assault the Bohemians raised an army, the most effective part of which was composed of artisans and peasants recruited from the most fanatical wing of the Hussite movement and commanded by Jan Zizka, an old soldier of remarkable military genius. Time and again in the years between 1420 and 1431, the Hussites defeated and drove out the larger armies of the crusaders and carried the war beyond their own frontiers. Even after Zizka's death in 1424, the tactics he had taught his followers, based on the use of a circle of farm wagons which could serve as a mobile unit of defense or attack, made the Hussite army invincible. So impossible did it seem to crush the heretics by force that when the Council of Basel met in 1431 many of the hierarchy were prepared to make some gestures toward reconciliation.

Meanwhile, though still united against the invaders, the Hussites were becoming increasingly divided among themselves by radical variations in belief and practice. The moderate party, representing the bulk of the middle and upper classes and the majority of the masters of the university, clung fairly closely to the doctrines actually taught by Hus. So far as they could, they maintained a normal ecclesiastical organization. As the continued struggle demanded some clear-cut issue on which they could agree to hold the line, they came to attach a particular importance to the right of the laity to receive communion in both kinds, that is, both the wine, which the Catholic Church reserved for the priest, and the bread. It was this doctrine, which Hus had enunciated, but to which he had not attached paramount importance, that gave them the name of Utraquists. Basically it was an assertion of the equality of all believers, and as such derogatory to the status of the clergy, but it was not as clearly heretical as was Wyclif's denial of transubstantiation. The tenacity with which even the most moderate Utraquists clung to the right to receive the cup, however, suggests that it had become a symbol, the abandonment of which would mean total surrender.

Almost from the beginning of the Hussite revolt, more radical doctrines spread among the poorer classes, and the unity of the movement was threatened by sectarian deviations. The most important of the radical groups were the Taborites, so called from their concentration in the southern Bohemian town of Tábor. It was from these that Zizka recruited the fanatical core of his formidable army. Among the Taborites the most extreme doctrines of Wyclif, which Hus himself had rejected, found full acceptance and were put into consistent practice. With the inexorable logic of the semi-literate, they rejected every belief or practice of the Church which they could not find literally commanded in the New Testament. They recognized no sacraments except baptism and communion, and interpreted the latter in the most radical Wyclifite sense. They denied the existence of purgatory, and hence the validity of indulgences and of prayers or Masses for the dead. They also condemned the veneration of saints and relics, and in their iconoclastic enthusiasm destroyed the pictures and statues in the churches. Finally, they broke completely with the ecclesiastical tradition of the Church by electing their own priests and bishops, who were also reduced to a status little different from that of laymen. These extreme anti-sacerdotal tendencies, though stemming largely from Wyclif's most radical utterances, were probably reinforced by the influence of Waldensian and other heretical groups long established in southern Bohemia. Some splinter groups seem also to have been impregnated with the doctrines of the Brethren of the Free Spirit which even the radical Taborites regarded with horror. What might be called the left wing of the Hussite movement, in short, was developing a pattern of beliefs and attitudes not unlike that of other sectarian movements both before and after the Reformation.

As the gap between the more conservative Utraquists and the radical sectarians widened, the former became more ready to negotiate a reconciliation with the Church if an acceptable compromise could be found. The calling of the Council of Basel offered an opportunity, and after two years of negotiation the Utraquists made their peace with the Church on the basis of a limited recognition of communion in both kinds. The agreement, however, was totally unacceptable to the radicals, whose army had been largely responsible for the victories that had forced the Council to negotiate, but which, after years of fighting and plundering, was becoming a public nuisance. Once the formal reconciliation was accomplished, Catholic and Utraquist nobles united to crush the Taborite army. Scarcely had the Utraquists restored peace in Bohemia by eliminating the armed force of the Taborites than they were forced once more by the intransigent attitude of pope and Council into a breach with the Catholic Church. The agreement reached in 1434 had, in fact, never been fully satisfactory to either party. The papacy regarded it as a temporary concession, whereas the Utraquists regarded it as merely a preliminary to further negotiation. When it became evident that the papacy would be content with nothing but complete submission, the Utraquists once more went their own way until, with the outbreak of the Reformation, they were absorbed into the newly founded Protestant churches.

X

Art and Music

The periodization we have followed thus far applies only imperfectly
to the history of art and music. The difficulty arises not merely from the
fact that large elements of medieval tradition run parallel to, or interact
with, the new developments that occurred in the years around 1300, or
that changes occurred at different times in the various arts and in different
countries — this was true also of other aspects of European civilization —
but also from the fact that a second period or stage of development seems
to open up in the early years of the fifteenth century and continue well
into its third quarter. A further difficulty arises from the lack of agreement among art historians as to terminology. In Italian art the two di-
visions I have mentioned correspond to Vasari's first and second *maniera*,
and are commonly termed Late Gothic and Early Renaissance respectively. There is fairly general agreement that a new period in northern
art and in music opened with the early fifteenth century, but less agreement as to what it should be called. Most art historians hesitate to use
the term Renaissance for northern art until nearly the end of the fifteenth century, while historians of music are inclined to term the fourteenth century Late Medieval and the whole of the fifteenth century
Early Renaissance.

Whatever terms we use, comparison of the works produced at the beginning and end of the period will demonstrate that a profound change was taking place in all the arts. There was a vast increase both in quantity and in technical proficiency. There were also subtler, but equally decisive, changes in spirit and content. In the most general way this period was characterized by an increasingly secular tone in both art and music, despite the continued preponderance of religious themes and subject matter, and by increasing dependence on lay patronage. Partly as a result of lay patronage the hierarchy of the arts was reversed. Whereas in the High Middle Ages architecture had been the dominant art, with sculpture dependent upon it and painting relatively insignificant, painting now takes pride of place, followed by sculpture and with architecture, caught between decadent Gothic and an incipient Renaissance style, sinking to third place in historical and aesthetic interest. Finally, it is in this period that art and music ceased to be generally anonymous. We are entering an age of known masters, identifiable not only by name, but by a distinctive personal style. The historian can now sprinkle his pages with names familiar to most of his readers. He can write with the comforting assurance which only names and dates can give him, but at the same time he will find it more difficult to generalize, to characterize the dominant trends, or to avoid the danger of substituting for a history of art and music a mere collection of biographical sketches.

A. ART AND ARCHITECTURE IN ITALY

The conviction so frequently expressed by Italian writers during the Renaissance period — and raised to the status of orthodox dogma by Vasari — that art was reborn in Giotto's generation, was not without justification in view of the relative backwardness of Italian art prior to the end of the thirteenth century. During the two centuries of the High Middle Ages, Italy was largely outside the sphere of influence of Gothic architecture and art. As a result, Byzantine and Romanesque traditions continued to dominate Italian art long after they had passed the most creative stage of their development. At the same time, freedom from Gothic influence helped to prepare the way for a precocious revival of painting by preventing it from being relegated to the minor art of book illumination. Italian architects never eliminated the wall space from their buildings as did Gothic builders, and so the need for mural paintings as wall decoration continued, nor were painted altarpieces abandoned in favor of the sculpture that served to decorate every feature of the Gothic church. Mosaic, the most characteristic form of Byzantine decoration, was dying out in Italy in the thirteenth century, although still practised

373

in Venice; but there was also a well-established tradition of Byzantine fresco and panel painting. The evolution away from the flat two-dimensional and rigid forms of Byzantine painting — the *maniera greca*, as Vasari called it — which took place in the fourteenth century thus did not result from the introduction of new media, but rather from a new way of viewing external reality.

The techniques involved in mural and panel painting differed from one another and presented different problems, with results that went far to determine the development of Italian painting. Murals throughout our period were executed by a fresco process, which consisted of the application of pigments mixed with water to a freshly prepared layer of wet plaster composed of mixed lime and sand. The colors then sank into the plaster, solidifying as the plaster dried. Although some colors might be added later to the dry plaster, the true fresco had to be completed before the plaster dried, and it could not be retouched. The painter had to work rapidly and do only as much at a time as could be completed in one day. The fresco technique thus encouraged the depiction of monumental figures with a minimum of detail. Panel painting, on the other hand, was executed in tempera on a dry ground, the pigments, until the introduction of oils in the fifteenth century, being mixed with a binder of white of egg or egg-yolk. The colors were then applied to a wooden panel, the surface of which had been prepared by adding a ground of plaster of Paris mixed with glue, and allowed to dry. Not only were panel paintings, which were usually designed to serve as altarpieces or as domestic furniture, smaller in scale, but the medium permitted finer and more detailed work than was feasible in wall painting. There was thus a closer relation between panel painting and book illumination, which opened the way for an interchange of influences between Italian painting and northern illumination during the fourteenth century. Since most Italian artists, however, were employed on frescos as well as panels, they were generally less given to the depiction of microscopic detail than were the Flemish panel painters, whose technique grew directly out of the illuminator's art.

The remarkable advances in Italian painting in the fourteenth and fifteenth centuries were due in part simply to the successive contributions of a series of exceptionally talented painters — to that inexplicable and unpredictable quality which is the artist's personality. But art also develops to a certain extent by a kind of inner logic from generation to generation, as artists adopt what they want or are able to assimilate from the work of their predecessors. The artist thus, in a sense, inherits the tools of his craft; but what he chooses to do with them depends not only upon his own personality but also upon the wishes and tastes of his patrons. Now patrons cannot produce art, but they can produce a demand which the artist must satisfy if he is to be successful; and the character of patronage in this period was very different from that which had financed and directed the art of the High Middle Ages.

We should not be misled by the fact that the vast majority of Italian paintings were still religious in subject matter. With some exceptions, notably the commissions placed by the Franciscan and Dominican orders, patronage was passing from the hands of ecclesiastics to those of wealthy laymen. To an increasing degree art thus came to reflect the taste and religious sensibility or worldly interests of wealthy citizens and princely courts. The influence of lay patronage seems particularly clear in the Tuscan republics, which fostered the most significant developments of Trecento and early Quattrocento art. There the greater guilds took upon themselves responsibility for financing and directing the decoration of churches; municipal governments commissioned paintings for public buildings; and nearly every wealthy family ordered frescos and altarpieces for their private chapels. Many family chapels were attached to Franciscan or Dominican churches, which thus gradually acquired a collection of paintings by the outstanding artists of the day. Lay confraternities, organized under the influence of the friars, added to this stock for the decoration of their own chapels. Nor was the use of painting confined to churches and public buildings. Panel painting freed art from dependence on architecture. A panel painting could be commissioned independently or become an article of commerce. As the fourteenth century progressed there was a growing demand for such paintings, still mostly religious, for the homes of the wealthy — a demand which expanded still more rapidly in the following century as portraits and secular scenes were added, the latter being particularly in demand for the elaborately decorated *cassoni*, or chests, which formed part of the furniture of every wealthy home.

Not all the prodigious quantity of painting which the growth of lay patronage called forth was, naturally, of the first order. The majority of painters were, no doubt, simply skilled craftsmen, and even the most accomplished artists were generally enrolled in guilds and trained as apprentices in the workshop of a master. The freedom with which painters travelled from city to city to fulfill commissions, however, indicates that guild regulations were not unduly restrictive. Almost without exception the painters were recruited from the lower middle class — the class of the artisans — for painting was still regarded as a manual occupation and, as such, unsuitable for the upper classes. Nevertheless, the growing refinement of taste among patrons, and the resultant competition for the services of the best painters, was gradually elevating the artist to a status superior to that of the mere artisan. Competition for their services also encouraged painters to develop a personal style, and so fostered original-ity. Giotto's contemporary fame was as exceptional as his genius, but many lesser painters were in demand by patrons who valued the individual characteristics of their style. The workshop system, in which the master taught and worked with his apprentices and assistants, guaranteed a certain continuity of tradition from master to pupil, while at the same time leaving the master himself free to develop his own style and to imprint his personality on the products of his shop. The concept of the artist as genius was as yet only vaguely foreshadowed — it belongs to the High Renaissance — but there is evidence that the artist as an unusually gifted individual was emerging from the anonymous mass of skilled artisans. Before the end of the fourteenth century Filippo Villani included biographical notices of several artists in his book, *The Famous Citizens of the City of Florence*. Artists, too, were generally included in the comments on the rebirth of culture which occur so frequently in fifteenth-century writing, and, after Brunelleschi had reduced perspective to a mathematical science and Ghiberti, Alberti and others had written tractates on the theory of painting, art acquired something of the intellectual stature of the learned professions.

It is easier to document the effect of lay patronage on the volume of art produced, and on the social status of the artists, than to determine the ways in which the taste and interests of patrons conditioned the form, content and tone of art. Yet it is difficult to escape the conclusion that the growing tendency of painting to represent human figures and natural objects as faithfully as possible reflected the interests and mentality of the class which was now furnishing the principal patronage for art, and which shaped the climate of opinion in which the artist himself grew up. It is worth noting that what Villani specifically admired in Giotto's painting was its close resemblance to nature, so that his figures seemed to live and breathe. Laymen, no matter how well educated, were not professionally trained to think in abstractions, and there was little in the practical experience of successful businessmen that would fit them to appreciate Byzantine painting with its innate tendency to de-materialize nature and reduce the human figure to a symbol. On the contrary, the exigencies of business encouraged a sober and concrete view of things as they are, as they can be seen, touched and measured.

The growing naturalism of Trecento and Quattrocento painting, however, did not so much materialize as humanize art. Italian society was deeply pious, but the quality of its piety was different from that which had inspired Byzantine or High Gothic art. The most powerful force in the religious life of Italy in this period was the preaching of the mendicant friars, and especially of the Franciscans. Addressing themselves directly to lay audiences, the friars dwelt lovingly on the human story of the Holy Family, and aroused emotions of adoration and tenderness focused on the Incarnate Christ and His Virgin Mother, emotions in which abstract dogma had little part. The piety inspired by Franciscan preaching was essentially a lay piety; it could find no satisfaction in art that expressed only the hieratic and the transcendental. What the pious laymen asked of religious painting was that the objects of adoration should be presented as credible human beings, moving in a comprehensible space. Under the influence of this type of religious sensibility, cult images, such as the Virgin and Child, lost their impersonal rigidity and melted into human warmth, so that the "Madonna Enthroned" was frequently replaced by the "Madonna of Humility," a mother seated on the ground or on a pillow, holding a baby in her arms. Narrative paintings, illustrating the lives of the Holy Family or the saints, were enriched with genre-like details drawn from the Apocryphal Gospels and the *Golden Legend*. New iconographical themes, such as the story of Joachim and Anna, the Virgin's parents, added variety and drama to pictorial art, and challenged the skill of the artist to portray them with convincing realism.

The new tendencies in Italian art made their appearance, less as a gradual evolution than by a sudden leap, in the work of one great artist. Giotto (c.1266–1336) occupies a position in the history of painting comparable to that of his contemporary, Dante, in the history of Italian literature. In their different media, each presented a fundamentally new vision of a universe peopled by fully realized human beings. Of the two, Giotto marks a more decisive break with the past, for in him Franciscan piety and the layman's view of the world and man was unmixed with the scholastic intellectualism that made the *Divine Comedy* in its totality a kind of *Summa Theologica*. Something he undoubtedly owed to his predecessors, to Gothic modelling and to Byzantine perspective; but his fully rounded figures, moving naturally in a space conceived in depth, were essentially new. His naturalism did not depend on realistic detail, as in Gothic art, but on a realistic composition of the entire scene, in the relation of the figures to one another and to the space they inhabit.

At his best, Giotto was a narrative painter. In his most important works — the frescos painted successively in the church of Assisi, the Scrovegni chapel in Padua and the Peruzzi chapel in Florence — he told stories from the legend of St. Francis and the lives of the Holy Family. Art critics are still debating how much of the Assisi frescos can actually be attributed to the youthful Giotto, but those in Padua and Florence are undoubted products of his mature genius. The stories he painted there present human beings in dramatic action. The composition in each is emotionally unified by the moral relation of the figures to one another, a relation made explicit by expressive gesture. This effect could not have been achieved had not Giotto possessed an unprecedented ability to see nature in the round, and had his figures not been visually presented as solid bodies naturally related to one another in space. His men and women, drawn in simple lines without irrelevant detail to distract the eye, stand firmly planted on the ground. They have volume and weight, and one feels that one could walk around them. At the same time they move, and the suggestion of movement is intensified by contrast with the completely immobile figures to be found in many of the scenes. They are, in a sense, idealized figures, for Giotto has eliminated everything but the essential, yet it is not an idealized humanity that they represent. They are of this world, a world of concrete reality, but a world also conceived in terms of moral values and human emotions. We can enter into that world, as we cannot enter into that of Byzantine or Gothic painting, however much we may admire these for their mastery of line and color.

The impression created by Giotto's painting was so overwhelming that his Florentine followers could do little more than attempt to imitate his treatment of figures, space and perspective. Some of them were first-rate craftsmen — Maso di Banco could handle perspective more accurately than Giotto — but they could not equal the intuitive authenticity of his vision of the moral and physical world. After mid-century the Giottesque manner was wearing thin with repetition, while, at the same time, a changing moral and social atmosphere after the Black Death brought a partial revival of the hieratic and symbolic elements of thirteenth-century art. Nevertheless, Giotto's cataclysmic advance in the direction of naturalism was never completely lost. For Italian painting it represented a point of no return. Even those painters who, like the Sienese of the first half of the fourteenth century, were closer to Byzantine and Gothic tradition, could never again represent their world in two dimensions.

The difference in cultural tone between Florence and Siena, so near to one another and so superficially similar, is an unsolvable enigma, as, indeed, is the overwhelming pre-eminence of Florence in all branches of intellectual and aesthetic activity throughout the fourteenth and fifteenth centuries. Whatever its cause, the difference between the cultural atmosphere of the two Tuscan republics can be seen in the contrast between Giotto and Maso on the one hand and Duccio (c.1278–1319) and Simone Martini (c.1285–1344) on the other. Duccio did not so much break with Byzantine tradition as refine it and endow it with grace and movement. Simone Martini's paintings have the aristocratic, rather stylized refinement of Gothic illuminations, but his figures, if lacking the majestic simplicity of Giotto's, are nevertheless convincingly rounded; their gestures are natural and they are set in a more fully realized space than the illuminators had yet achieved. What was most characteristic of Sienese painting in the early fourteenth century was visual beauty of line and color, an air of elegance and luxury and a richness of detail that seems calculated to appeal to a courtly and aristocratic rather than a bourgeois taste.

It is not surprising, then, that when the northern illuminators, who worked for patrons in the princely courts, began to note the advances made by Italian painting they should be more directly influenced by the decorative art of Simone Martini and the Sienese than by Giotto and the Florentines. Close commercial relations between Italy and the Netherlands kept a constant flow of influence running between these two poles of economic and artistic activity, and in the fourteenth century the current ran mostly northward. By the end of the century the amalgamation of the Italian treatment of figures and space with Gothic detail and stylized elegance had produced a sumptuous, decorative and aristocratic type of painting, which art critics have called the International Style or International Gothic. In the opening years of the following century a returning current introduced it into Italy in the magic dream-world of Pisanello and in the lavish ornament, the rich brocades and brilliant colors of Gentile da Fabriano's "Adoration of the Magi."

The work of Pisanello (c.1395–1455) and Gentile da Fabriano (c.1370–1427) belongs chronologically to the first half of the fifteenth century; but it does not strike the characteristic note of early Quattrocento painting. It was, indeed, already anachronistic and, despite the employment of Gentile to decorate the family chapel of the Strozzi, it was essentially alien to the Florentine tradition that was to dominate the art of the century in Italy. The artist whose work gave new direction to the painting of the fifteenth century was of a very different sort. Masaccio (1401–28) died too young to have left a large body of work, but the frescos he painted in the family chapel of the Brancacci were alone enough to establish his position in the very first rank of Renaissance artists.

Masaccio has been called Giotto reborn, and the resemblance of his art to that of his great predecessor is, in fact, too obvious to be ignored. At the same time, the difference between them is almost equally striking. If Masaccio put Florentine painting back on the road along which Giotto had directed it, and from which it had wandered under Sienese and Gothic influences, he did not begin at the point where Giotto had left it, but a long distance further on the way. Giotto's use of perspective had been fumbling and intuitive; Masaccio could profit by Brunelleschi's recent discovery of the optical laws of linear perspective. He could profit also by the sculptor Donatello's studies of human anatomy, and, in general, by the changed intellectual atmosphere introduced by classical humanism. His nobly proportioned figures have the volume and weight — the "tactile values" — of Giotto's; but they are more individualized, and the bodies underneath the clothing are fully articulated so that they move more freely. Masaccio's paintings have none of that fussy preoccupation with realistic detail that characterized the International Gothic — in this respect, too, he resembled Giotto — but they have a comprehensive realism in the relation of figures to one another and to landscape and architecture that went far beyond anything achieved by the Giottesque or Gothic painters. The medieval artists' subjective view of the world, which made the size of their figures proportionate to their importance in the picture, still lingered as a vestigial remnant in Giotto. With Masaccio, perspective and proportion obey objective laws. Masaccio's world, like Giotto's, is homocentric, and it has often been said that he represents the humanist tendency to make man the measure of all things. In a sense this is true, but in a more literal sense it is also true that he cut man down to size and placed him in his proportionate relation to a real world. If he makes man the measure of all things it is only because of man's moral grandeur, which he could depict with all of Giotto's sure grasp of the essential and the significant.

The general direction taken by Italian painting in the half-century after Masaccio was toward an increasing naturalism and a scientific concern for the correct representation of anatomy, chiaroscuro, perspective and space. This was a period of scientific observation and experimentation, which brought notable advances in technical proficiency. If at times technical proficiency became an end in itself, and the desire to represent objects exactly led to an indiscriminate representation of details not essential to the picture, this phase was, nevertheless, a necessary prelude to the flowering of the classical art of the High Renaissance, while, at the same time, it produced a number of paintings without which the world would be appreciably poorer. One need not accept all of Berenson's depreciation of the artistic achievement of the Quattrocento naturalists to agree with his conclusion that "their efforts to reproduce objects as they are, their studies in anatomy and perspective, made it inevitable that when another great genius did arise, he would be a Leonardo or a Michelangelo, and not a Giotto."[1]

The majority of paintings during this period were still devoted to religious subjects, but the drive toward naturalism tended to water down the spiritual significance of the scenes portrayed. There were, of course, exceptions. The limpid spirituality of Fra Angelico (1387–1455) transcends the naturalistic technique he shared with his generation. It is diffi-

---

[1] B. Berenson, *Italian Painters of the Renaissance* (London, 1952), p. 54.

cult, on the other hand, to discover any spiritual element in the "Saint John in the Desert" of Domenico Veneziano (d. 1461), where a vigorous young nude figure seems caught in the act of undressing in the midst of a bare landscape of rocks and mountain peaks. There is rather more in his "Annunciation," but it seems primarily designed as an exercise in linear perspective which is saved from aridity only by its uncluttered clarity and the supple grace of the angel and the Annunciata. The paintings of Fra Lippo Lippi, too, are chiefly notable for his acute observation of the surface of things, for all the bland piety of his Madonnas and the robust charm of his healthy children. With Paolo Uccello (1397–1475), obsession with the problems of perspective and foreshortening dominates everything else. There is emotional force, on the other hand, in the brutal realism of Andrea del Castagno (c. 1420–57), which raises his art to a level of significance above that of mere naturalism.

If naturalism, in so far as it became an end in itself, was a doubtful asset to religious art, it was, on the other hand, of inestimable value to the art of portraiture, for which there was a new and increasing demand during the fifteenth century. Portraits were rare in the High Middle Ages, and when they did appear in painting there was no apparent attempt to reproduce an authentic likeness. In the fourteenth century, portraits of the donors began to be introduced into religious pictures, thereby combining piety with ostentation, and this practice became more common in the following century. The increasing demand for portraits in the fifteenth century, both as details of a religious painting and as independent panels for domestic use, was in part an evidence of that awareness of personality and of desire for immortality this side of the grave that Burckhardt noted as a characteristic of Renaissance society; but it was also in part created by the growing proficiency of the artists in naturalistic representation, which enabled them to perpetuate the features of a donor, ill-favored though they sometimes were, in all their individual peculiarity. In one respect, however, the Italian portraits of this period seem more formal and give a less vivid impression of personality than those painted during the fifteenth century in the Netherlands. Almost all are in full profile. There may have been iconographical reasons for this in portraits of donors introduced into religious pictures, but in the independent bust-portraits the predilection for full profile may possibly be explained by the influence of the medallists who, in turn, were influenced by the example of antique coins and medals. Whatever the reason, profile portraits continued to appear, though no longer exclusively, to the end of the century and beyond.

The independent portrait introduced a purely secular element into painting which, together with such secular subjects as Uccello's hunting and battle scenes, tended to break down the exclusively religious tradition of pictorial art. At the same time, naturalistic representation of expensive clothing, jewels and furniture, designed to proclaim the wealth of the donor, introduced a somewhat secular air into religious paintings themselves. All of these tendencies, which reflected the taste of a wealthy, cultivated and worldly society, became increasingly evident in the second half of the century. After mid-century, too, the number of accomplished painters who arose to meet the growing demand, and the sheer volume of painting, in northern Italy as well as Tuscany, increased enormously, thereby adding to the difficulties of the historian who would attempt a brief summary of the art of the period.

Italian sculpture, while not as prolific as painting, followed somewhat similar lines of development during this period. The two arts were, indeed, closely related. The artists of the Italian Renaissance were a remarkably versatile group, and many of the leading sculptors also practised painting. New tendencies in the one art were thus the more easily transferred to the other. Moreover, both developed under the same kind of patronage. Italian architecture did not lend itself to the densely sculptured façades of the northern Gothic, and the Italian sculptors were not to the same degree forced to carry out a scholastically determined iconographical program. While still employed principally for the decoration of churches, they were most frequently commissioned by lay patrons, guilds or corporations. The guilds of Florence made themselves responsible for the statues of their patron saints on Or San Michele, and the *Arte di Calimala* supervised the construction of the great bronze doors of the Baptistery. By far the most frequent use made of sculpture in Italy was for articles of church furniture: pulpits, altarpieces, tabernacles, tombs and fonts. These were individually commissioned, and the smaller pieces were produced in the artist's own workshop. As a result, the Italian sculptors were under less pressure than the northern Gothic carvers to fit their work into a uniformly planned ensemble. They were freer to create an individual style, and this hastened their emergence from the anonymous mass of skilled craftsmen.

In sculpture, as in painting, Byzantine and Romanesque traditions had lasted undisturbed in Italy until the second half of the thirteenth century. But from then on sculpture was more directly influenced than was painting by both antique and Gothic models. The influence of Roman antiquity on Renaissance painting was necessarily indirect, since hardly any examples of ancient painting survived. Examples of Roman and Hellenistic sculpture, on the other hand, were fairly numerous and became available in larger numbers as the humanist enthusiasm for antiquity led to the disinterring of all the relics of ancient art that could be found.

Before the end of the thirteenth century Nicola Pisano (c. 1220–78) introduced figures copied directly from Roman sarcophagi into the scenes carved in relief on the pulpits he constructed for churches in Pisa and Siena. Classical sculpture was not, however, the only model available. Gothic sculpture in the thirteenth century was much more highly developed than Gothic painting and exerted a correspondingly greater influence when it began to penetrate Italy around the turn of the century. Nicola's son, Giovanni Pisano (c.1250–c.1320), broke away from his father's premature and too literal imitation of the antique and approached more nearly to the fluent lines and restless movement of the French Gothic. The scenes he carved in high relief on the two great pulpits in Pistoia and Pisa have, however, an emotional intensity and dramatic action seldom achieved by Gothic sculpture. At the same time his full-length Madonna in the Scrovegni Chapel in Padua — fit companion for Giotto's frescos — has the dignity of a Roman matron and an expression of grave foreboding that contrasts sharply with the pert elegance of the contemporary Gothic Madonna in the choir of Notre Dame in Paris. One is reminded that when Gothic sculpture began to influence Italian art it was already sinking into a decadent mannerism at home. In Italy this tendency of the Late Gothic was counteracted by the sobering example of classical antiquity.

The virtuosity of Giovanni Pisano's high-relief style continued to influence Italian sculpture throughout the fourteenth century; but meanwhile a tendency of a quite different kind resulted from Giotto's revolutionary introduction of three-dimensionality into painting. From this point onward sculptors in relief strove increasingly for pictorial effects, their figures no longer crowded on top of one another in the manner of the antique sarcophagus or the Gothic tympanum, as with Nicola and Giovanni Pisano, but grouped in a natural relation to one another. The influence of the master painter is clear in the reliefs executed by Andrea Pisano (c.1270–1348) on the first pair of bronze doors for the Florentine Baptistry and on the campanile of the Duomo which Giotto had himself designed. It is still more evident in the beautifully simplified relief of the "Second Annunciation" which Orcagna (c.1308–c.68), himself a painter, carved for the tabernacle of Or San Michele. Here the Giottesque figures of the angel and the Virgin to whom he announces her approaching death are set within a small room that gives a convincing suggestion of spatial depth. In the first half of the following century the advances made by painters in the use of correct perspective and in the organization of figures, landscape and architecture in a naturalistically conceived space were reflected in the low reliefs of Jacopo della Quercia (1374–38) and in the two pairs of bronze doors for the Baptistery on which

Lorenzo Ghiberti (1378–1455) spent most of his mature life. In the first pair the pictorial effect was somewhat diminished by the quatrefoil frames of the twenty-eight panels, which Ghiberti felt forced to adopt to make his doors match those designed by Andrea Pisano a century earlier; but in the second pair, begun in 1427, he abandoned Andrea's scheme and set ten large panels in square frames. Seldom in the history of sculpture has relief seemed so nearly a picture in bronze. Despite Ghiberti's skillful use of the new techniques that were revolutionizing painting in his generation, however, he stands rather at the end than the beginning of a stylistic tradition. The suave grace and flowing lines of his figures and drapery seem more closely akin to the last manifestations of the International Gothic than to the frescos which Masaccio had just finished in the Brancacci Chapel.

It is Donatello (1386–1466) who occupies the position in the history of sculpture that Masaccio holds in painting. Breaking with the remnants of Gothic tradition, he combined an unprecedented fidelity to nature with the moral grandeur of antique art. Yet, great as was his reverence for antique sculpture, which he studied on a visit to Rome with his friend Brunelleschi, he was no mere imitator. Few artists of any age have created with such inexhaustible originality, and what he learned from antiquity he transmuted into something entirely his own and, in its nervous energy, essentially unclassical. Donatello was one of the most prolific of Renaissance artists, and in the course of a long lifetime he produced almost every possible kind of sculpture. In his narrative reliefs he heightened the pictorial effect by abandoning the physical recession of high relief and by creating the illusion of spatial depth through the use of an elaborate architectural setting in strict linear perspective projected on a low relief plane. He broke new ground by giving to marble statues designed to stand in a niche, like the magnificent St. Mark he carved for the *Arte dei Linaiuoli* on the façade of Or San Michele, a sense of movement that freed them from dependence on the architectural structure. Later he completed the emancipation of sculpture with his bronze David, the first free-standing nude figure since antiquity, and the great equestrian statue of the *condottiere*, Gattamelata, in Padua. No artist of this generation made so close a study of anatomy, and through his work sculpture repaid its debt to painting by sharpening the painters' observation of the human figure.

It is further proof of the highly developed individuality of the Italian artists that, despite the great influence of Donatello, the sculptors of the mid-fifteenth century cannot fairly be classified as his followers. One could not, for example, mistake the sculpture of Bernardo Rossellino (1404–64), with its classical restraint, or that of Desiderio da Settignano (c.1430–64), with its infinite delicacy, for the work of Donatello.

In the case of Luca della Robbia (1400–82) the personal style was the more marked in that, while also working in marble, he invented a new technique of glazing terracotta and did most of his work in that medium. Enamelled terracotta served a unique aesthetic purpose by adding a note of color to architectural settings that might otherwise have seemed cold. It was a technique that in the facile hands of Luca's nephew, Andrea della Robbia, tended to degenerate into pretty sentimentality, but no such fault can be found with the boldly modelled figures of the elder artist who, of all the Italians of that generation, ranks closest to Donatello.

In conclusion, two new developments in the sculpture of the mid-fifteenth century must be mentioned: the portrait bust and the monumental tomb. Both reflected the desire of Renaissance men to perpetuate their fame and to leave a memento of their personalities to posterity. We have already noted the vogue of painted portraits. The portrait bust served the same purpose, but was more directly influenced by the surviving examples of Roman and Hellenistic portrait sculpture. The almost excessive realism of antique busts had undoubtedly inspired Donatello's statues of saints and prophets, but there is no proof that he attempted explicit portraiture except in the equestrian statue of Gattamelata. The earliest surviving Renaissance portrait bust is that of Piero de' Medici carved by Mino da Fiesole (1453). Thereafter such busts, frequently clad in Roman togas or antique armor, became increasingly common. Portraiture, although generally of a more idealized sort, was also a feature of the elaborately constructed tombs, set in a pesudo-classical architectural framework, which now began to fill the churches and chapels of Italy. So clearly do these monuments reflect concepts inspired by the revival of antiquity that they have frequently been referred to as humanist tombs, and it is fitting that one of the earliest and most impressive was that erected in Santa Croce in honor of the great Florentine humanist, Leonardo Bruni. It was the work of Bernardo Rossellino and it served as a model for many later tombs. Browning's bishop obviously had such monuments in mind when he ordered his tomb in St. Praxed's church.

Compared to the magnificent achievements in Italian painting from Giotto to Masaccio, and in sculpture from the Pisanos to Donatello, the architecture of this period is relatively undistinguished. Not that there was not a good deal of building. Communal pride in the republics, and the vanity of princes in the despotic states, alike found expression in the construction of churches and public buildings; while private wealth, especially toward the end of the period, was increasingly displayed by the building of great town houses or *palazzi*. But fourteenth-century Italy developed no consistent style comparable to the northern Gothic, and many of the larger buildings suffered from changes of plan during the process of construction. Church architecture was still a mixture of Romanesque and Byzantine with later Gothic elements, varied according to the personal taste of architects or patrons. It was only in the first half of the fifteenth century, and then only in Florence, that something like a distinctively Renaissance style began to appear, largely as a result of Brunelleschi's intensive study of the monuments of classical antiquity.

Filippo Brunelleschi (1377–1446) was one of that versatile breed of Florentine artists who could turn their hand to any art. He was trained originally as a goldsmith and sculptor, and he abandoned sculpture only after his sample design for the bronze doors of the Baptistery was rejected in favor of Ghiberti's in the famous competition of 1401. Later his scientific bent led to his discovery of the optical laws of linear perspective, thereby contributing an invaluable aid to the development of painting and sculptural relief. In the meantime, as Vasari tells the story, he left Florence in a huff when his model panel for the bronze doors was rejected, and went to Rome with his young friend Donatello to study the ancient monuments there. When he returned to Florence it was as an architect, his mind filled with memories of antique Roman pillars and ornaments, eager to adapt the principles of classical architecture to buildings intended for more modern purposes. The fact that he was called upon to design churches and *palazzi* rather than temples or theatres fortunately prevented Brunelleschi from too literal imitation of the antique. In some instances, for example the great dome he designed as the crowning feature of the cathedral of Santa Maria del Fiore, he was forced to adapt his plans to a structure already begun, in this case more than a hundred years earlier. The dome was an engineering *tour de force* and remained a model of dome construction, but it could not make the cathedral a classical building. In the churches of San Lorenzo and Santo Spirito, too, he was forced to adapt elements of the Roman basilica to the traditional cruciform ground plan of the medieval church. Classical inspiration is more clearly evident in some of his smaller buildings, for example the chapel he designed for the Pazzi family or the loggia of the Ospedale degli Innocenti. The airy grace of the latter, however, which makes it one of the loveliest of Renaissance buildings, owes more to Brunelleschi's personal genius than to any antique model.

The originality that resulted from the adaptation of classical principles to buildings for which there was no antique precedent is equally evident in the massive façade of the *palazzo* Brunelleschi designed about 1435 for Luca Pitti, one of Florence's wealthiest citizens. Unfortunately it was not completed in accordance with Brunelleschi's plans, and it is not as perfect an example of the new type of town house as the slightly more

GIOTTO, LAMENT OVER THE DEAD CHRIST.

SCROVEGNI CHAPEL, PADUA

9

DOMENICO VENEZIANO, ST. JOHN IN THE DESERT.

NATIONAL GALLERY, WASHINGTON

DOMENICO VENEZIANO, ANNUNCIATION.

FITZWILLIAM MUSEUM, CAMBRIDGE

PRINTED IN WEST GERMANY

SIMONE MARTINI, ANNUNCIATION.

UFFIZI, FLORENCE

12

13

GHIBERTI. STORY OF JACOB AND ESAU.

BAPTISTERY, FLORENCE

DONATELLO, DAVID.

MUSEO NAZIONALE, FLORENCE

15

modest structure built for Cosimo de' Medici some five years earlier by Michelozzo Michelozzi (c. 1396–1472). Vasari tells us that Cosimo preferred Michelozzo's design to Brunelleschi's more grandiose conception which might excite the jealousy of his fellow citizens, but the resultant building was modest only in the most relative sense. It stands today in its simple grandeur a fitting symbol of the wealth and solid power of the banker who won for himself the title of *Pater Patriae*. With the appearance of the Florentine *palazzo*, later imitated throughout Italy, domestic architecture for the first time took its place beside the ecclesiastical as building in the grand manner.

B. Art and Architecture in the North

The general impression created by northern art in the fourteenth century is quite different from that made by the contemporary Italian scene. Whereas Italian painting and sculpture, emerging from a period of conservative and undistinguished activity, seem to take on new life and a new direction, the art of the North grew out of the vitally creative age of the High Gothic and by contrast has an air of elegant decadence. In architecture the synthesis of form and function began to degenerate into the refined but less structurally sound tendencies of the Flamboyant and Perpendicular styles. Sculpture lost spiritual force in the pursuit of a refinement tending toward prettiness or a detailed realism. Painting, it is true, did not in the same way suffer by contrast with past achievement, but it remained till the end of the fourteenth century a minor art and shared the general tendency toward refined triviality. Nevertheless it was in painting chiefly that the new artistic impulses originating in Trecento Italy exerted an invigorating influence on northern art, and prepared the way for the magnificent flowering of Netherlandish painting in the following century.

It was in painting, too, that lay patronage first began to replace that of the Church. Lay patrons did not take over the control and direction of church decoration as they so frequently did in the Italian cities, but this fact did not affect the patronage of painting, since it had been almost entirely divorced from architecture. The structure of the Gothic church left little or no place for mural paintings and even painted altarpieces remained rare until the fifteenth century. Painting, therefore, was for the most part confined to book illumination. This was in origin a monastic art, but it was dying out in the monasteries as the vitality of the old Benedictine foundations began to decline. As early as the thirteenth century lay craftsmen were beginning to take the lead in illumination, and in the following century the most handsomely decorated books were executed by lay painters for lay patrons. The character of lay patronage in the North was, however, different from that in Italy. It was centered chiefly in royal and princely courts. The princes of the House of Valois and the great nobles who frequented the royal court were the patrons whose taste set the tone of northern illumination. Such wealthy burghers as could afford illuminated books aped the taste of their social superiors, and so did little to influence the style of the illuminators' workshops. Despite the general impoverishment of the French nobility, the fashions of the court in this period were marked by fantastic extravagance. Princes and great nobles collected illuminated books much as they collected jewels, ivories and other *objets d'art* which could be carried with them in their itinerary from one château to another. As the history of literature in the fourteenth century demonstrates, the northern upper classes were beginning to form a reading public. The illuminators were thus called upon to illustrate a wide variety of books: secular works such as romances, chronicles, collections of poetry and translations from the classics or the contemporary Italian writers, as well as books of devotion, the ever-popular *Golden Legend*, psalters and breviaries. Most popular of all were the "Books of Hours," designed for private devotion. Combining piety with conspicuous consumption these called forth the finest products of the illuminators' art.

Throughout the fourteenth century the Île de France continued to be the most fruitful center of northern art, as it had been in the High Gothic age. Paris, with its royal court, attracted artists from all the surrounding area, and furnished employment for a number of illuminators' workshops. Here in the 1320's Jean Pucelle introduced into the miniatures, scattered throughout the text or stretched across the bottom of the pages, something of the modelling and perspective of Duccio and the other Sienese painters, and opened the way toward a less linear and two-dimensional style. He also enclosed his pages with a dense decorative border of branching leaves and flowers, interspersed with tiny and exquisitely natural birds, butterflies and animals. Fine as his drawing and coloring were, however, his miniatures were still subordinate to the manuscript page and too tiny to permit of a full development of figures or space. Still, they were admirably suited to the taste of patrons who appreciated elegant and decorative art, and they remained the model to be followed, though with an increasing tendency toward trivial mannerism, until the last quarter of the century.

When a further notable advance in Parisian painting occurred in the last years of the fourteenth century, it was due to the work of Flemish immigrants, who brought with them a more naturalistic tradition and a fresh infusion of Italianate treatment of volume and space. Minatures now freed themselves from dependence on the manuscript text and became practically independent pictures. Landscapes portrayed in depth and figures in the round, a combination of Sienese line and color and a touch of Giottesque volume, together with the indigenous Gothic obsession with naturalistic detail and an aristocratic predilection for rich clothing and armor — these were the characteristic ingredients of what we have already noted as the International Style. In the North its principal exponents were illuminators rather than panel painters, the most distinguished being the anonymous master who created the sumptuous *Heures du Maréchal de Boucicaut,* and the Limbourg brothers, whose *Très Riches Heures du Duc de Berry,* begun in 1413, contains the best-known and loved of all the illuminations of the International Style.

The jewel-like perfection of these Books of Hours is proof that they were collectors' items, designed for a luxury-loving clientele that could be satisfied only with what was costly, and they were valued as much for their exquisite workmanship as for their intrinsic beauty. The taste of a courtly aristocracy, feverishly exaggerating the symbols of status as it felt its hold on the realities of power slipping, is also reflected in the stylized artificiality which prevented the paintings of this school from being entirely naturalistic representations of a real world. Where the real world does appear, as in the peasant scenes in the calendar pictures of the *Très Riches Heures,* it is in marked contrast to the scenes depicting the lords and ladies. The peasants are portrayed with an earthy solidity that is almost Giottesque, but the courtly figures retain the insubstantiality and elongated elegance of Gothic linearity. At the same time, even the peasant scenes, despite their genre-like naturalism, seem designed to suit the sensibilities of a self-conscious and sophisticated aristocracy. They are overcast with an idyllic atmosphere that dilutes the harsh realities of poverty, cold and labor.

The great age of the Paris illuminators passed with the decimation of the French nobility at Agincourt and the further disruption of courtly patronage which resulted from the English invasion. The death of the Duke of Berry in 1416 deprived the Parisian workshops of their most munificent patron, and after the assassination of John the Fearless in 1419, the new Burgundian duke, Philip the Good, retired to the Netherlands. For the next half-century or more the rich Netherland cities and the Burgundian court were the chief centers of northern art. The most talented Flemish painters were no longer drawn to Paris as they had been in the preceding generation. They now remained at home to enjoy the patronage, not only of the ducal court, but also of wealthy patricians and ecclesiastics in the most economically advanced and cosmopolitan cities north of the Alps. There, the aristocratic influence of the court was tempered by a more sober and pious bourgeois tradition that helped to free painters from the elegant mannerism of the International Style, while still leaving them ample opportunity to display their virtuosity in the depiction of material wealth. After the second decade of the fifteenth century, with the van Eycks and other Flemish painters, a new and distinctively Netherlandish style of panel painting emerged from the International Gothic, as in the same generation a new and distinctively Italian style emerged with Masaccio and his contemporaries.

The new styles which appeared simultaneously in Italy and the Netherlands respectively had certain characteristics in common. In both, an immense advance in naturalism was achieved by the use of correct perspective and a more effective use of light and shadow to model figures and endow them with volume and tangible solidity. In both, the escape from two-dimensional linearity was at last complete. The two national styles were, nevertheless, markedly different, and, except for some interchange of technical procedure, they exerted relatively little influence on one another. What current of influence there was, indeed, seems in the fifteenth century to have run mostly from north to south.

The difference between Italian and Netherlandish painting in this period may be best illustrated, perhaps, by a comparison of the two painters who, each in his own way, most fully expressed what was characteristic of their respective national styles. It is significant that Masaccio was a fresco painter, whereas Jan van Eyck (c. 1380–1441) painted nothing larger than a panel and apparently, as the recently discovered illuminations in the *Très Belles Heures de Notre Dame* now in Turin and Milan seem to indicate, began his career as a miniaturist. Where Masaccio achieved his naturalistic effects primarily by means of sound articulation of the human figures, expressive gestures, the relation of the figures to one another in space and the composition of the whole scene, van Eyck's naturalism consisted of infinitely minute detail, each object lovingly portrayed in its individual particularity. His vision of objects in the foreground is microscopic and is frequently balanced by an equally minute telescopic view of tiny figures in distant landscapes seen through a window. Yet, despite his meticulous depiction of the infinitely small, van Eyck's paintings are more than enlarged minatures. His figures have a monumental quality unprecedented in the International Gothic, and they stand solidly and freely in a fully realized space. His compositions, too, have the power to transcend detail, so that the eye takes in the whole picture at a glance, the details merging into a general impression of richness. For all the accuracy of his vision, however, van Eyck's figures lack the anatomical articulation of Masaccio's, and they seldom move. His perspective, too, was the product of an empirical workshop tradition rather than of a mathematical theory. It may not be an exaggeration to say that where the Florentine artists were scientists, the Flemings were craftsmen, but with a craftsmanship raised to the level of virtuosity and sometimes of genius.

It was for his mastery of his craft that Jan van Eyck was praised by his contemporaries and hailed by later generations as the founder of Flemish painting. It takes nothing from his greatness that he must now share that honor with the vigorous and prolific painter commonly known as the Master of Flémalle, as well as with his own older brother, Hubert van Eyck, who, after having been relegated to the realm of legend by art historians, has now been restored to existence and re-accredited with a share in the magnificent Ghent altarpiece. Nor can Jan any longer be regarded as the inventor of oil painting. Oil had been used, though rarely, as a medium for binding pigment long before the fifteenth century. On the other hand, the technique which the van Eycks perfected was not oil painting as we understand it today, but consisted rather of a process by which pictures were built up in successive strata by applying layers of a translucent oil paint over an opaque ground of tempera. Whether the process was entirely new or not, the use made of it by the van Eycks and their contemporaries was revolutionary. It gave their work an unprecedented depth and luminosity, and enabled them to combine the body of a tempera painting with the minute detail of a book illlumination.

The great Flemings exploited the potentialities of this technique to the full, not only in the realistic depiction of furs, jewels, costly fabrics and carved furniture, but with equal effect in the painting of portraits. Jan van Eyck, the Master of Flémalle, and Roger van der Weyden may, indeed, be regarded as opening a new era in portrait painting. The large number of surviving independent portraits, as well as portraits of donors introduced into the wings or central scenes of altarpieces, indicate that there was a growing demand from nobles, wealthy citizens and ecclesiastics, which the Flemish painters' mastery of detailed verisimilitude both stimulated and satisfied. Unlike the contemporary Italian portrait painters, the Netherlanders generally presented their subjects in three-quarter face or full face. The result, heightened by their mastery of detail, was to give their portraits a more immediate impression of the sitter's personality. There is about nearly all the Netherlandish portraits a sense of intimacy such as was seldom achieved by even the greatest Italians. A similar intimacy characterizes the paintings of domestic interiors, like that which forms the setting for van Eyck's double portrait of Giovanni Arnolfini and his wife, which seem to draw the onlooker into the scene.

Like the Nominalist philosophers, the Netherlandish artists saw reality in the individual person or thing in all its peculiarity, with little of that striving toward the ideal essence which in Italian art so frequently raises a barrier of abstraction between the viewer and the thing portrayed.

There is rather less naïve delight in the individual phenomena of the visible world in the painting of Roger van der Weyden (c. 1400–64), van Eyck's most serious rival among the early Netherlandish painters. On the other hand, there is a greater emotional intensity in his religious paintings and a rhythmic movement that is quite different from the static serenity of van Eyck's Madonnas and formally posed donors. In "The Descent from the Cross" in the Prado all the figures move and express intense emotion. The heightened religious sensibility of the Netherlands in the period of the *Devotio Moderna* is evident in Roger's predilection for scenes from the Passion, and even in the Columba altarpiece "Adoration of the Magi" — in which, incidentally, Charles the Bold appears as one of the three kings — a tiny crucifix hangs above the head of the wistful Madonna, symbolizing a sad foreknowledge of things to come.

It is futile to attempt here to characterize the works of all the artists who, as heirs to the founders whom we have mentioned, carried on the tradition of Netherlandish painting into the second half of the fifteenth century. The mid-century brought no break in that tradition, but only variants resulting from differences in the personalities of the painters. On the whole, however, there was less difference of style among the Netherlandish painters, perhaps because of the strong workshop tradition, than we find among the contemporary Italians. Petrus Christus (c. 1410–72) is obviously a disciple of van Eyck, although his paintings are plainer, simpler and more homely. Hugo van der Goes (1440–82) was an altogether more original and vigorous painter. In his passionate and disturbed personality there was an inner tension that led to his vain search for peace in the monastic life and to ultimate madness. It is reflected in the dramatic gestures, the contrasting lights and shadows and the heightened emotionalism of his religious pictures. In Hans Memling (c. 1430–94), on the other hand, there is no tension. His serene, receptive spirit and his superb technical proficiency enabled him to absorb all that the art of van Eyck and van der Weyden could teach him; but his work is derivative rather than original, that of a great disciple rather than a great master. He was at his best as a portrait painter, the most popular of his generation, and here, at least, he could compete on an even footing with either of his great predecessors. Memling does not quite mark the end of the characteristic fifteenth-century Netherlandish style — Gerard David (1460–1523) carried it on into the following century — but before his death that style had begun to disintegrate and new currents from Italy were once more beginning to exert an influence on northern painting.

One may doubt whether the term Late Gothic is an adequate designation for the magnificent era of Netherlandish painting introduced by the van Eycks and the Master of Flémalle; but one can have no such hesitation about its applicability to the architecture and sculpture of France and the surrounding countries during the fourteenth century and the first half of the fifteenth. The great age of cathedral building had passed its peak, and both architects and sculptors were beginning to work for royal or wealthy lay patrons as well as for ecclesiastics, constructing and decorating private chapels, palaces and public buildings. Throughout the period the basic structural techniques of Gothic architecture continued to be used, but with an increasing tendency toward elaboration and refinement. In England the single transverse ribs of the High Gothic vault were replaced by multiple ribs forming a complex geometric pattern, finally culminating in the peculiarly English phenomenon of the fan vault. English architecture, too, increasingly emphasized vertical lines and light construction, although the full development of the Perpendicular style, the last and purely national phase of English Gothic, did not come until after the middle of the fifteenth century. In France a similar tendency away from simple structural lines toward overwrought decoration can be seen in the curvilinear complexity of the Flamboyant style. German architecture as yet showed few characteristically national peculiarities, in general following the lead of France as it had done since the spread of Gothic forms from the Île de France in the preceding century.

In sculpture, too, the French Gothic style enjoyed an international vogue, its development in many respects paralleling that of contemporary painting. Throughout the fourteenth century French sculpture was characterized by an increasing naturalism, qualified by an equal striving after aristocratic elegance, which could at times degenerate into trivial mannerism. The beginning of the descent from the classic simplicity of the High Gothic can, indeed, be observed as early as the middle of the thirteenth century. The Virgin on the central support of the north portal of Notre Dame of Paris, carved about 1255, is a very human young woman, with little of the hieratic majesty of the Virgin enthroned on the twelfth-century western portal, but still retaining a matronly dignity. The "Vierge dorée" of Amiens, a decade or so later, is a lovely aristocrat whose tilted head and hipshot pose emphasize her delicate femininity. In the fourteenth-century Virgin of the choir of Notre Dame this pose is exaggerated to the point of artificiality, and the fastidious features, thin lips and plucked eyebrows give little suggestion of either the virgin or the mother. A similar mixture of naturalism and affectation can be observed in the group of hilariously Foolish Virgins on the Cathedral of Strasbourg.

Toward the end of the fourteenth century a more vigorous sculptural style, more serious and touched with the earthy Netherlandish realism, was introduced by a group of sculptors working in Dijon, the capital of the old Burgundian duchy. The Madonna carved by the Flemish Jean de Marville (died 1389), "ymagier et varlet de chambre" of Duke Philip the Bold, for the portal of the Chartreuse of Champmol has the hipshot pose and cascading draperies of the fourteenth-century cathedral Madonnas, but the earnest, almost tragic face has little in common with the Paris model. In the following generation the great Dutch sculptor, Claus Sluter (died 1406), continued the work on the Chartreuse and on the elaborate tomb of Philip the Bold with its quaintly realistic circle of mourners. His masterpiece, the most impressive sculpture north of the Alps, was the so-called "Well of Moses," originally designed as a pedestal for a crucifixion standing in a fountain in the cloister of Champmol. Only the pedestal remains, around which are grouped the majestic figures of Moses, David and four prophets. Despite the powerful carving of these figures, however, they represent no such break with medieval tradition as occurred in Quattrocento Italy under the influence of classical antiquity. In the generation when Donatello was absorbed in the study of human anatomy, the northern sculptors were still hiding the body under masses of drapery. The period when Dijon was a vital center of art was brief, since the dukes who were its patrons soon moved their court to the Netherlands, but the Burgundian style continued to influence northern sculpture to the end of the century.

Claus Sluter was the most famous northern sculptor of his day, but he was not the only one who enjoyed a considerable reputation. The age had passed when the personality of the sculptor was lost in the anonymity of the masons' lodge. To an increasing degree sculpture was being freed from dependence on architecture, and it was now more commonly produced in the artists' own workshops than in the lodges attached to building operations. Even the statues intended for placement in niches on cathedral portals or façades were now mostly shop work and, as a result, lacked the close integration with the building that had been characteristic of the High Gothic. Independent statues of the Virgin, crucifixes and *pietàs*, now produced in much greater numbers and frequently for lay patrons, as well as sculptured altar screens and pieces of church furniture, were invariably shop work, specially commissioned for a specific purpose.

This was also true of the numerous effigies on tombs, the principal means by which sculpture met the growing demand for portraiture which is so evident in the painting of the fifteenth century.

C. Music: the *Ars Nova* and the Early Renaissance

The thirteenth century, as we have seen, was a period of vigorous experimentation in musical composition, characterized by the invention of the rhythmic modes, the introduction of the polytextual motet and successively more complex forms of mensural notation. Theory, as always, lagged behind practice, but by the opening years of the following century the cumulative effect of innovation was such that it could no longer be ignored, and theorists were beginning to talk about a new school of composition. Among these the most influential was Philippe de Vitry (1291–1361) who about the year 1320 undertook to expound, codify and give theoretical sanction to the novel elements in current practice in a treatise to which he gave the proud title, *Ars Nova*. Poet, composer and musical theorist, officer of the royal household and eventually Bishop of Meaux, de Vitry enjoyed an international reputation. His treatise evidently carried a good deal of authority and was instrumental in shaping the musical idiom of France for the next two or three generations. Modern historians of music have recognized, and perhaps exaggerated, his influence by adopting the term "*ars nova*" to designate the prevailing style of the fourteenth century.

Actually the *ars nova* was less new than the title of de Vitry's work suggests. It was, in fact, an outgrowth of the Gothic polyphony of the preceding century, but rationalized, refined and held within more prescribed limits. Like the majority of composers since Perotinus, the practitioners of the *ars nova* in France were obsessed with the problems of rhythm and by the effort to differentiate the voices in a polyphonic composition by making each rhythmically independent. Aside from a greatly improved system of mensural notation, de Vitry's principal contribution was the authoritative sanction he gave to the use of "imperfect" or duple time. Although common enough in recent usage, it was now for the first time placed on a basis of theoretical equality with "perfect" or triple time, which had hitherto alone been recognized as legitimate. De Vitry was also largely responsible for the popularity of a rhythmic device which became one of the distinguishing characteristics of the French *ars nova*. This device, known as "isorhythm," consisted of the repetition, either in the tenor alone or in all voices, of rhythmic patterns longer and more complex than the rhythmic modes of the age of Perotinus. These repeated patterns, although quite independent of the melody, lent a certain degree of structural unity to motets and other polyphonic compositions in which the voice lines, composed consecutively rather than simultaneously, had otherwise little more than a roughly contrapuntal relation to one another.

Despite the fairly general acceptance of the new tendencies by composers and theorists, there were conservatives who viewed the innovations of the new school with alarm, particularly when they were applied to church music. There could, indeed, be no doubt that music was moving further and further away from the authorized forms of liturgical chant. There was a danger that the polytextual motet, with three or four different texts sung simultaneously, would obliterate the sense of the liturgy, while such rhythmic extravagances as the hocket — a rapid alternation of notes and rests — could not but produce a restless effect out of keeping with the spirit of church music. Pope John XXII voiced the sentiments of the conservatives in a strongly-worded bull in 1324–25 condemning the innovators and all their perfidious ways.

> Certain disciples of the new school [he declared], much occupying themselves with the measured dividing of the *tempora*, display their prolation in notes which are new to us, preferring to devise methods of their own rather than to continue singing in the old way; the music therefore of the divine offices is now performed with semibreves and minims, and with these notes of small value every composition is pestered. Moreover, they truncate the melodies with hoquets, they deprave them with discants, sometimes even they stuff them with upper parts (*triplis et motetis*) made out of secular songs. . . . Their voices are incessantly running to and fro, intoxicating the ear, not soothing it. . . . As a consequence of all this, devotion, the true end of worship, is little thought of. . . .[2]

The aged pope's disapproval of contemporary music failed to check its development, but it may have had the effect of encouraging composers to turn from sacred to secular subjects to which the pope's anathema did not apply. The growth of lay patronage in the Italian cities and in the royal and princely courts of the North was, however, probably an even more effective inducement to lure composers away from the traditional liturgical themes. Whatever the cause, there was at any rate a decided shift during the fourteenth century in the volume of production from sacred to secular music. Secular motets set to vernacular words became increasingly common and were rivalled in popularity by songs in the *trouvère* tradition which were now commonly given a polyphonic set-

[2] Quoted in H. E. Wooldridge, *The Oxford History of Music* (2nd Ed., London, 1929), I, 294 f.

ting. Monody had lasted longer in secular song than in liturgical music however, and in the various song forms of the fourteenth century the words were still frequently sung by a solo voice while the remaining voices were performed as an instrumental accompaniment.

The trend toward secular court music and the popularity of polyphonically accompanied song is especially evident in the work of the composer who, more than any other, seems the very personification of the French *ars nova*. We have already met Guillaume de Machaut (c. 1300–71) in his capacity as a court poet whose verses, refined and elegant though they were, shared the artificial conventionality characteristic of so much French poetry in this period. It was his music that brought them to life, and the immense popularity of his songs is attested by the large number of surviving manuscripts. Of the 140 compositions that have come down to us, only seven were religious; and of the remainder all but seventeen motets were songs in various forms — *ballades, rondeaux* and *virelais* — mostly for accompanied solo voice.

Among Machaut's few liturgical works, at least one was of major importance: the great Mass, popularly called the Mass of Notre Dame which, according to an apparently ill-founded tradition, was said to have been composed for the coronation of Charles V in 1364. Aside from its intrinsic merit, Machaut's Mass is noteworthy as the first known instance of a complete setting of the Ordinary of the Mass by a single composer. Arranged for four voices, the greater part of the Mass is in motet style, with a Gregorian chant as a *cantus firmus* in the tenor. The principal exceptions are the Gloria and the Credo, which are in *conductus* style, all voices moving together note against note, a style eminently suitable to their length and to the character of the text. Unique in its century, Machaut's Mass is also the supreme achievement of the French *ars nova*. It is, in fact, a kind of *summa* of the musical style of the age, employing as it does in its various movements almost all the musical devices, including instrumental accompaniment, current in the fourteenth century. It continued to be performed for more than two hundred years, and it has enjoyed a renewed popularity in our own generation.

The Italian *ars nova*, which flourished vigorously from about 1325 to 1425, shared many of the characteristics of the contemporary French style, but was nevertheless a largely independent movement. Italian composers were less influenced than the French by the polytextual motet which had dominated French music in the late thirteenth century, and they freed themselves almost completely from dependence on a *cantus firmus* borrowed from a pre-existing melody. In so far as they were indebted to earlier musical forms, they owed most to the *conductus*, in which all parts were newly composed and moved in the same rhythm, and to the Provençal troubadour song with its free melodic voice line and frequent melismatic passages. In general, the Italian composers of the fourteenth century were more interested in melody than in rhythm, and so avoided the somewhat arid intellectuality of the French motet style. Their music was preponderantly secular, written for the despotic courts and for the cultured upper classes of the cities. The literary as well as musical tastes of cultivated Italian society found expression in the madrigal — usually a setting of serious poetry, but otherwise having little in common with its sixteenth-century successor — which depended almost entirely on melody for its effect. In this form "imitation" — the repetition of a melodic phrase in another voice — was used as a unifying device much more frequently than was customary in the French *ars nova*. Most of the madrigals seem to have been written around mid-century, and were replaced in popularity toward the end of the century by the *ballata*, which bore a close resemblance to the French *virelai* and may be evidence of a growing French influence. This was the form most frequently used by Francesco Landini (1325–97), the blind Florentine organist, who was the most prolific as well as the most talented Italian composer of the century and a master of smoothly flowing melodic song.

After Landini's death the independent Italian style lost its vigor, and for more than a hundred years thereafter Italy produced little distinguished native music. In France, too, the characteristic style of the *ars nova* was petering out around the turn of the century in an artificial rhythmic complexity that threatened melodic invention with complete atrophy. In the years after Agincourt the center of musical as well as artistic production moved from the Île de France northward to the Burgundian court in the Netherlands. There a new style began to develop in the 1420's which for a century thereafter dominated the music of Western Europe. In many of its forms the music of the great Netherlandish composers was an outgrowth of earlier French traditions, but it owed much of its melodic and harmonic characteristics to English influences introduced into northern France by the English occupation after Agincourt.

During the fourteenth century English music had developed an idiom of its own, very little influenced by the French preoccupation with rhythmic complexity. The English composers had a stronger feeling for sonority and preferred to keep their rhythms simple, the various parts moving together in step, so that they frequently achieved the sonorous effect of vertically conceived chords, in contrast to the French practice of keeping the parts as clearly distinct as possible by giving each its own rhythm. The sonority of English music was enhanced by a tendency, in its origins peculiar to the English idiom, to employ ${}^6_3$ chords and other triads and, in general, to place thirds and sixths on a par with fourths and fifths, the traditional "perfect" consonances, as both melodic and harmonic intervals. Other peculiarities of English musical usage, which made their appearance around the turn of the century, were a freer treatment of the *cantus firmus* borrowed from a pre-existing melody, now frequently ornamented and placed in the middle or top voice, and, finally, the *cantus firmus* Mass. Complete compositions of the Ordinary of the Mass had not been unknown on the continent in the fourteenth century, although Machaut's Mass is the only one certainly composed by one man. The original contribution of the English composers in the early years of the fifteenth century was the use of the same *cantus firmus* throughout all movements as a unifying device. The structural unity thus achieved appealed to continental as well as English composers, and after the first quarter of the fifteenth century the *cantus firmus* Mass became, and for a hundred years or more remained, one of the most important forms of musical composition.

The flowering of English music in the early fifteenth century was the work of a group of talented composers, but the introduction of English stylistic elements into continental practice was largely due to the influence of one man. John Dunstable (c. 1390–1453) was one of the two or three most distinguished composers of his generation, even more famous on the continent than in his native land, and he so far overshadowed his fellow-countrymen that their contribution has been unduly neglected. He was attached as court musician to the Duke of Bedford and apparently spent some years in France during the time (1422–35) when the duke was acting as regent for his young nephew, Henry VI. His works, some sixty of which survive, cover a wide range of form and content and represent the culmination of the peculiarly English musical idiom to which he gave its definitive stamp. His influence on the two leading contemporary Netherlandish composers — Dufay and Binchois — was recognized by fifteenth-century writers, and it was through them that elements of English style passed into the main stream of European music.

Guillaume Dufay (c. 1400–74) occupies a place in the history of music comparable to that of Jan van Eyck in the history of painting. Both of these great Netherlanders, in their different media, turned away from the artificiality and preciosity that had characterized music and art alike around the turn of the century to pursue a new ideal of naturalness and simplicity in works conceived on a grander scale and with an expanded tonal range. Trained as a choir boy in Cambrai, Dufay later became a canon of the cathedral there and maintained an intermittent connection with it for the rest of his life. For many years, however, he travelled in

France and Italy in the service of the pope and of various princes. His unrivalled fame gained him liberal patronage wherever he went, and the varied interests of his patrons led him to compose music for both church and court in almost every contemporary musical form. His travels also served to broaden his experience by bringing him into contact with Italian as well as French and English styles.

It is in his liturgical music that Dufay shows the influence of Dunstable and the English idiom most clearly. The relatively high proportion of church music among his compositions may in itself owe something to English influence, although it may merely have reflected a tendency common to his generation. As composers freed themselves from the artificialities of the late *ars nova*, they recovered a feeling for the melodic beauty of Gregorian chant, although generally as something to be paraphrased and elaborated. At the same time, they found in the fully composed Ordinary of the Mass an opportunity for musical composition in the grand manner. The revived interest in sacred music may also have resulted in part from the rising tide of piety that accompanied the spread of the Netherlandish *Devotio Moderna*. Whatever the cause, it is clear that the balance which in the fourteenth century had shifted in the direction of secular music was now swinging back. Dufay himself composed at least eight complete Masses, as well as a number of independent sections of the Ordinary and numerous sacred motets and settings of office hymns. The last five of his complete Masses are of the *cantus firmus* type already developed by English composers. In some instances the *cantus firmus* was borrowed from a Gregorian chant, but in others he used snatches of secular song. The most famous example of the latter practice, which later became very common, is the Mass "Se la face ay pale," in which he used as the *cantus* a melody borrowed from one of his own *ballades*. A quite different use of a pre-existing melody appears in several of Dufay's office hymns, in which a stanza of traditional Gregorian chant is followed by one in which the melody is paraphrased and elaborated in the upper voice of a polyphonic setting. In these, and still more commonly in the Magnificats he wrote in each of the eight ecclesiastical modes, Dufay made frequent use of the harmonic device known as *fauxbourdon*, that is, in modern terminology, a succession of $^6_3$ chords, or triads in the first inversion. Although *fauxbourdon* was apparently an invention of continental composers of Dufay's generation, it was clearly influenced by the English fondness for $^6_3$ chords and was, in fact, scarcely more than an adaptation of the earlier English descant, differing from it only in that the melody was in the top rather than the bottom voice. Although it was used sparingly by Dufay and his contemporaries, *fauxbourdon* was an important step in the direction of a more sonorous harmonic texture.

Dufay remained more completely within the French musical tradition in his secular motets and *chansons*. Both the texts and the music of his *rondeaux, ballades* and *virelais* follow the conventions of *trouvère* song, but with a more simple and melodic quality than was common in the French *ars nova* and which he may have derived in part from his acquaintance with the Italian music of the preceding generation gained during his long sojourn in Italy. In his secular as well as liturgical works Dufay expanded the tonal range at both ends, with the result that the voice lines no longer crossed so frequently, but were differentiated by pitch and timbre rather than, as in the French *ars nova*, by rhythm. Freed from the artificialities of the late *ars nova*, Dufay's *chansons* are charming and eminently singable. In this respect he had only one rival in his generation, Gilles Binchois (c. 1400–60). Unlike Dufay, Binchois was known almost exclusively for his secular *chansons*. Born in Flanders, Binchois was for some thirty years connected with the Burgundian court, and his settings of poems by Christine de Pisan, Alain Chartier and Charles d'Orléans are distillations of the chivalric atmosphere of the court presided over by Duke Philip the Good.

THE BROTHERS LIMBOURG, APRIL,
FROM THE TRÈS RICHES HEURES DU DUC DE BERRY.

MUSÉE CONDÉ, CHANTILLY

JAN VAN EYCK, MADONNA OF CHANCELLOR ROLIN.

LOUVRE, PARIS

*ROGER VAN DER WEYDEN, ADORATION OF THE MAGI,
FROM THE COLUMBA ALTARPIECE.*

ALTE PINAKOTHEK, MUNICH

19

JAN VAN EYCK, GIOVANNI ARNOLFINI AND BRIDE.

NATIONAL GALLERY, LONDON

HUGO VAN DER GOES, NATIVITY,
FROM THE PORTINARI ALTARPIECE.

UFFIZI, FLORENCE

21

THE MASTER OF FLÉMALLE, PORTRAIT OF A GENTLEMAN.

NATIONAL GALLERY, LONDON

VIRGIN OF THE CHOIR OF NOTRE-DAME.

CATHEDRAL OF NOTRE-DAME, PARIS

HANS MEMLING, THE MYSTICAL MARRIAGE OF ST. CATHERINE.

HÔPITAL ST. JEAN, BRUGES

The Second Period of Transition

(c. 1450–c. 1520)

X I

The Reorientation of Christian Europe:
Contraction in the East and Expansion
to the West

The shift in the center of gravity of Western Europe from the Mediterranean to the Atlantic, which characterized the period following the middle of the fifteenth century, was, as we shall see, evident in the spheres of economic, political and cultural activity. This shift was in large part the result of a natural evolution within the countries of Western Christendom, an evolution which had its roots in the preceding period. But it was also accompanied by changes in the geographical horizons of Catholic Europe, which accelerated its reorientation toward the West, although they did not become fully effective until after the end of the period under consideration here. The conquest of Constantinople by the Turks, the opening of a new ocean route to India, and the discovery of the New World in the western hemisphere have a symbolical significance out of proportion to their real importance for contemporaneous history. In a dramatic way they mark the end of one era and the beginning of another. For this reason it seems suitable to begin our study of the second stage in the transition from medieval to modern civilization with the two movements which these events symbolize: the shrinkage of the eastern frontiers of Christendom and the expansion of the European horizon by exploration and discovery. At the same time we must avoid the temptation to exaggerate the influence of these movements upon the thought and actions of men to whom these events were current news, the significance of which they could but dimly apprehend. Only in retrospect was it possible for men to perceive that Europe had reached a turning point in her history, or that the discoveries made by Portuguese and Spanish navigators would in the long run prove more important than the extinction of the old Roman Empire in the East.

A. THE EXPANSION OF THE OTTOMAN EMPIRE

The eastern horizon of medieval Christian Europe had in fact begun to contract long before the old Byzantine capital fell before the advancing Turks. The eastward drive of European merchants and crusaders had reached its limits around the turn of the twelfth century. The final extinction of the Crusaders' kingdom in Syria in the last decade of the thirteenth century marked one stage in the ebb tide of European domination in the Levant. Meanwhile, for a generation or two before the end of that century, European travellers, seeking trade or the salvation of souls, and encouraged by the relative peace established by the Tartar Empire of the great khans, had penetrated the land mass of central Asia and opened up to Christian Europe a fleeting glimpse of the distant land of Cathay. But, early in the following century, the anarchy which accompanied the gradual disintegration of the Khanate of the Golden Horde closed that window to the Far East. Then in mid-century the Ottoman Turks, already established in Asia Minor, crossed the straits to Gallipoli and began the conquest of the Balkan states. In 1356 the sultan established his capital on European soil at Adrianople. From there the Turks pushed their conquests westward through Macedonia and northward through Bulgaria to the Danube. By the end of the fourteenth century, Constantinople and a little land around it were all that remained of the Byzantine Empire. For a time after the turn of the century the Ottoman advance was checked by the meteoric irruption of the great Mongol conqueror, Tamerlaine, but in the 1430's they were pressing westward into Greece and were threatening the Adriatic coast. Still Constantinople held out, thanks to her superbly defensible site. In a desperate effort to gain help from the West the emperor, John Palaeologus, negotiated a reunion of the Greek and Roman churches at the Council of Florence in 1439, but the union was no sooner consummated than it was broken by the intransigence of the Greek zealots. Thereafter the days of the Byzantine Empire were numbered.

When in 1453 Sultan Mohammed II rode into Constantinople through a breach in her once impregnable walls, and on the same day ordered the transformation of Justinian's great church, the Hagia Sophia, into a Mohammedan mosque, he was but writing *finis* to a story the outcome of which was already determined. Yet few events in the history of the world have made so powerful an impression upon the imagination of both contemporaries and later generations. Mohammed II, himself, seems to have felt the epoch-making quality of the event, as he mused before the emperor's palace on the transitory nature of human greatness. Later historians, too, were impressed by the symbolical character of the fall of Constantinople as the final episode in the decline and fall of the Roman Empire, and used it as the point at which to draw a line between the Middle Ages and modern times. Seizing upon the cataclysmic event as an easy answer to the problem of causation, they also ascribed to it the initial impetus to the classical Renaissance in Italy and the great age of exploration and discovery. It is now recognized that the capture of the Byzantine capital did not alter the practical situation in any such drastic way. The Greek refugees came to Italy too late to do more than assist a classical revival already reaching its peak. As Voltaire remarked, the Greeks could teach the Italians nothing but Greek, and, one might add, even for that they were no longer essential. Nor was the fall of Constantinople responsible for the desire of the European peoples to find a new route to the East. The Ottoman Empire did not extend across the major trade routes to India until after the Portuguese sea route had rendered them obsolete. Even the Italian trade with Constantinople was not ruined, although the Italian merchants lost many of their special privileges there. The Greek Orthodox Church also survived, the sultan having declared himself its protector as successor to the Roman emperors. In many ways the Ottoman Empire simply replaced the dying Byzantine Empire. Yet it would be a mistake, as great as that of the historians who exaggerated the significance of the event, to underestimate the importance of the fact that the new empire was not only a non-Christian state, but also one which possessed a potential capacity for aggression and expansion which the Byzantine Empire had not shown since the days of Justinian.

The reign of Mohammed II (1451–81) demonstrated the menacing vitality of the Ottoman state. A great statesman, perhaps the most gifted of his generation, an efficient administrator and organizer, as well as a conqueror, Mohammed devoted his energies for thirty years to the task of consolidating and rounding out his empire. One after another he overran the remaining Balkan states south of the Danube: Serbia in 1459; Bosnia in 1463–64; the Venetian-held Morea (the Peloponnesus of antiquity) in 1458–60; and before the end of his reign he was firmly established on the coast of the Adriatic. Meanwhile he had seized the islands of the Aegean: Thasos, Imbros, Samothrace and Lesbos. Venice fought courageously to hold her possessions in the Aegean, but the war which lasted from 1463 to 1479 ended in a humiliating peace and the loss of her commercially important colony on the island of Negroponte. To the eastward Mohammed extended his conquests around the Black Sea, wiping out the remaining Genoese colonies there. To the south he completed the subjugation of Asia Minor by conquering the troublesome principality of Karaman. Within the empire, Mohammed developed a unique military and administrative system, which not only strengthened the state but also guaranteed the despotic powers of the sultan. Boys, most of whom were levied as tribute from the conquered Christians, were given intensive military training and indoctrinated with fanatical loyalty to the sultan. These formed the élite infantry corps, the janizaries, who were the shock troops of the Ottoman army. A much smaller number of especially promising children were also selected to be trained in the palace school for administrative posts. The result of this system was a disciplined military force and a highly trained body of administrative officials wholeheartedly devoted to the service of the sultan and the state.

The death of Mohammed II gave Catholic Europe a breathing spell and an opportunity, largely wasted, to strengthen its defenses against further Ottoman aggression. The new sultan, Bayazid (1481–1512), was immediately involved in civil war with his brother Djem, and was forced to abandon the siege of Rhodes, the island outpost of Christendom in the Aegean held by the Knights Hospitalers of St. John. He was also forced to abandon the foothold in southern Italy which his father had won by the capture of Otranto. Even after Djem was defeated he still remained a threat to the sultan, for, having taken refuge with the Knights of St. John who later turned him over to the pope, he was still a potential claimant to the throne and might be made the spearhead of a Christian attack on Bayazid. Pope Innocent VIII and his successor, Alexander VI, however, used this valuable asset only to extort from the sultan an annual payment for their services in keeping Djem out of circulation. After the death of Djem in 1495, Bayazid felt free to take stronger action, and in a war with Venice (1499–1503) seized nearly all the republic's remaining strongholds in the Morea. Further Ottoman advance to the west, however, was checked by the sultan's preoccupation with disturbances in Asia Minor.

Throughout the following reign, that of Selim I (1512–20), Ottoman expansion was directed against the Moslem states of the Middle East, thus relieving once more the pressure on Christian Europe. In the opening years of his reign Selim invaded Persia, defeated the shah in 1514, and annexed a large part of northern Mesopotamia. Having thus secured his eastern frontier, Selim then turned southward to invade the territory of the Egyptian Mamelukes, which extended north through Syria to the borders of Asia Minor. The Mameluke army, which had degenerated through years of unrestrained license, was no match for the Ottoman janizaries, nor were the subject peoples of Syria and Egypt eager to support the extortionate Mameluke government. In two campaigns, in 1516 and 1517, Selim overran Syria and Egypt, thus extending the Ottoman Empire in a great semicircle around the whole eastern end of the Mediterranean. By this time the Ottoman Empire had also become a sea power, with the largest and most efficient navy in the Mediterranean. The stage was now set for the double-pronged drive to the west under the next sultan, Suleiman the Magnificent, which carried the Turks through Hungary to the gates of Vienna and through North Africa to the Atlantic.

B. The Sea Road to the Indies and the Founding of the Portuguese Empire

While the eastern frontiers of Christendom were shrinking, in the West maritime explorers were opening up horizons far more distant. Both movements had begun before 1450, but it was in the seventy years following that the decisive events occurred which turned the face of Europe from the inland sea to the open ocean. The two movements were not unrelated, but the incentive to find a water route to the riches of the fabulous East was present before the rise of the Ottoman threat. The expansion of the Turkish Empire, indeed, came too late to be a decisive factor in the search for a new route to India. Despite the galling necessity of sharing the profits of the eastern trade with Arab middlemen, the Italian merchant states were well enough content with the existing situation. At any rate, superbly equipped as they were for the task, they contributed little but the services of individual navigators to the exploration of the Ocean Sea. It was not, then, any threat to the long-established eastern trade so much as the desire of the states along the Atlantic seaboard to break the Italian monopoly that formed the most compelling motive for the explorations of the fifteenth century. But systematic exploration could scarcely begin until the governments of those states had acquired the political power and the financial means to direct such expensive and hazardous enterprises, as well as the awareness of the national economic interest needed to spur them to take the initiative, an awareness which the Italian merchant states had long possessed. Explorations such as those which opened up the sea road to India and led to the discovery of a new world would, indeed, have been beyond the powers, psychological as well as material, of a feudal state.

The monarchies of the western states, it is true, had begun to surmount the handicaps imposed by the feudal system for some time before they began to take any interest in exploration. The economic recession which followed the middle of the fourteenth century, however, created an unfavorable atmosphere for expansion. Moreover, France and England were preoccupied with the Hundred Years' War and its aftermath until nearly the end of the fifteenth century, while Spain was divided among rival kingdoms until the marriage of Ferdinand and Isabella, and thereafter their Catholic Majesties were primarily concerned with the conquest of the Moorish kingdom of Granada until 1492. It was thus left to Portugal, a small but strongly governed country, strategically placed at the southwestern tip of Europe, to take the lead, and that it did so was largely due to the persistent driving energy of a dedicated prince. These considerations may help to explain the fact that the explorations did not begin in a serious and consistent fashion at an earlier date, although nearly all the other prerequisite conditions had been present for a century or more.

Almost all the pertinent geographical knowledge on which the fifteenth-century explorers had to depend had been available to Western Europeans since the twelfth or thirteenth century, as had been also the essential navigational instruments: the compass, the astrolabe, and the quadrant. Ancient Greek cosmographers had demonstrated the spherical shape of the earth and had estimated its size with varying accuracy. Their findings, with much additional knowledge and speculation, were then gathered together in the early years of the Christian era in Strabo's *Geography* and a century and a half later in Ptolemy's encyclopedic work by the same name. In this form the ancient Greek knowledge of geography was handed on to generations of Arabic scholars who translated, annotated and expanded the works of Strabo and Ptolemy before they were introduced into Western Europe in the great revival of learning which characterized the twelfth and thirteenth centuries. Among medieval scholars Ptolemy enjoyed an immense authority, comparable to that of Aristotle in philosophy and physics or of Hippocrates and Galen in medicine. For the practical concerns of geographers and navigators it was of no importance that he placed the earth erroneously at the center of the universe. But his authority also helped to keep alive certain errors which did have a considerable effect upon the course of exploration. Of these the most important was his adoption of Strabo's estimate of the circumference of the earth at 18,000 miles in place of the nearly accurate estimate of 25,000 miles made by Eratosthenes in the third century B.C. At the same time he extended the land mass of Asia some 2,500 miles too far to the east, a combination of errors that gave unwarranted encouragement to Columbus. A further error of a more discouraging sort was his assertion that the Indian Ocean was an inland sea, surrounded on the south by a *terra incognita* which connected Africa with the eastern borders of Asia.

During the Middle Ages Arabian merchants traded down the eastern coast of Africa as far as Zanzibar, and mapped the western coast of India. Both Moslem and Christian pilots, too, had charted the coast line of the Mediterranean with great accuracy. The most important medieval additions to geographical knowledge, however, were made by travellers overland. In the early thirteenth century the great Mongol conqueror Gengis Khan founded a vast empire stretching from the Dnieper to Peking and thereby opened up central Asia to European explorers. In mid-century two Franciscan missionaries, Giovanni de Plano Carpini and Guillaume de Rubruquis, the former sent by Pope Innocent IV, the latter by King Louis IX, penetrated Asia as far as the court of the Great Khan at Karakorum and returned to write books describing what they had seen. And before the end of the century Marco Polo had returned from his wanderings to make the most important contribution to geographical knowledge since antiquity.

Marco Polo's famous book is not a travel book in the ordinary sense of the word. It is strangely objective and impersonal. The actual story is passed over briefly in stark outline, and we learn almost nothing about the adventures encountered by the Polos in their journeying. In a few pages we are told how the elder Polos, the brothers Niccolò and Maffeo, travelled to the court of Kublai Khan and returned in 1269 as ambassadors of the khan, armed with a golden tablet as a guarantee of safe conduct and with a letter to the pope. Two years later they set out again, this time taking with them Niccolò's young son Marco. After three and a half years on the road they came once more to the court of the Mongol ruler. There Marco entered the service of the Great Khan, and for seventeen years travelled on official missions to almost every part of the khan's great empire. Finally, eager to return home, the Polos found an opportunity to travel as escorts of a royal princess affianced to a Persian prince. This journey they made by sea, sailing down the coast of China, through the straits between Sumatra and Singapore to India, and thence to the Persian Gulf and so overland to the Mediterranean. In all this we learn little directly about the character of the two brothers or young Marco, except that he was a gifted linguist who learned several Asiatic languages and that he was a keen and practised observer. This latter fact, however, is important enough to deserve emphasis, for it accounts for much of the value of his book. Marco soon noticed that the khan was always disappointed when his agents on their return from a mission failed to tell him of the distant parts of his empire they had visited.

> And [the book tells us], as he knew all the sovereign's ways, like a sensible man he always took much pains to gather knowledge of anything that would be likely to interest him, and then on his return to court he would relate everything in regular order, and thus the emperor came to hold him in great love and favor. And for this reason also he would employ him the oftener on the most weighty and most distant of his missions.[1]

When, years later, he dictated his systematic description of the lands and the people he had visited in the khan's empire and on his homeward voyage, this long training stood him in good stead. Modern travellers, the first Europeans to follow in his footsteps through central Asia, have borne out the accuracy of his observations. His own contemporaries did him less justice. Unlike most medieval travellers' tales which were accepted with undue credulity, Marco's account was received with unwarranted scepticism. His description of the vast riches of the East led the Venetians to nickname him Marco Millioni. But even if he was not fully believed, his story made a profound impression upon the imagination of the European peoples. And no one could take from the Polos the credit of having been the first Europeans to sail the Pacific and of having demonstrated once for all that the Indian Ocean was not an inland sea.

Within a generation or so the road the Polos had travelled to China was rendered impracticable by civil disturbances in the Tartar Empire, and the profits that might be gained by establishing direct contact with the fabulous East remained an unattainable dream for two centuries longer. The man who, more than anyone else, was responsible for the ultimate attainment of that goal was, however, in all probability not primarily concerned with finding a new route to India. The Portuguese prince, Dom Henrique, whom historians have called Henry the Navigator (1394–1460), was a scholarly ascetic, endowed from early youth with a keen curiosity about the nature of the earth, combined with fanatical religious zeal. But it was the mystery of Africa rather than the Far East that aroused him to action and dominated his life. In 1415 he had participated in the conquest of the Moorish stronghold of Ceuta on the

[1] G. E. Parks, ed., *The Book of Ser Marco Polo* (New York, 1929), p. 14.

African coast across from Gibraltar. There he learned of the overland trade in gold and ivory carried on by the Moors across the Sahara to Guinea and Timbuktu. From that time he devoted all his energies and the wealth furnished by the crusading Order of Christ, of which he was Grand Master, to the task of reaching the lands below the Sahara by sea. His motives were strangely mixed: intellectual curiosity, the crusader's dream of outflanking the Moslem states of North Africa, the pious hope of bringing Christianity to the heathen, and a very practical desire to add to the territory and wealth of Portugal by discovering new areas for trade and colonization. Realizing that successful exploration of the unknown Atlantic must be systematic and scientifically directed, he established a school for navigators and a headquarters for the direction of expeditions at Sagres on Cape St. Vincent. There he gathered scholars of all kinds, map-makers, theoretical geographers and practical navigators, and with their aid sifted, compared and codified the information brought back by the captains whom he dispatched each year with orders to sail ever further and further south.

Here we cannot follow the course of discovery step by step. The first step, the breaking of the psychological barrier presented by Cape Bojador which tradition had set as the terminal point of navigable ocean, was perhaps the most important. Before Henry died in 1460 his men had discovered and colonized the Azores and the Madeiras, and had pushed down the African coast well beyond Cape Verde. Meanwhile, a profitable trade in gold, ivory, slaves and precious woods had been established along the coast of Guinea, and the island groups had become valuable economic assets. The most important results of Henry's work, however, were the improvements in shipbuilding and instruments of navigation, and the experience gained by his captains in sailing their sturdy little *caravels* for long distances out of sight of land. As the work of exploration continued, the hope of opening up a sea route to India grew on Henry, and he left it as a legacy to the future rulers of Portugal.

Royal preoccupation with war and other problems slowed up the progress of exploration for two decades after Henry's death, but when John II succeeded to the throne in 1481 systematic efforts were once more renewed. By 1483 Portuguese sailors had reached the Congo. Then, in 1488, Bartholomeu Dias sailed around the Cape of Good Hope and established the latitude of the southern tip of Africa. The last uncertainty had been removed and the sea road to India was now open. Vasco da Gama's epoch-making voyage with a fleet of four ships followed in 1497 after years of preparation. To avoid the dangers of coastal sailing, da Gama set a course southwestward from Cape Verde and swung around in a great semicircle to the Cape, thereby securing the most advantageous winds. Luck or genius, and the courage to sail out of sight of land for ninety-six days, had put him on the course followed by sailing ships until the present century. Having rounded the Cape, he felt his way up the African coast to Melinda and then struck northeastward across the Indian Ocean, finally dropping anchor off Calicut on the Malabar coast of India in May, 1498.

The brilliant success of da Gama's voyage was partially marred by his failure to establish friendly relations with the ruler of Calicut, partly as a result of the jealous intrigues of the Arab merchants who resented the intrusion of the European interloper into their preserves, but also partly because of his own intransigent arrogance. He found, too, that the goods he had brought for trade were of too poor quality to bring good prices in India. Still the spices, fine fabrics and precious stones he brought back were conclusive proof of the profits to be gained by tapping the eastern trade at the source, and the following year King Manoel the Fortunate, who had come to the throne in 1495, sent out a larger expedition of thirteen ships under the command of Pedro Alvares Cabral. Following the course set by da Gama, Cabral steered southwestward from the Cape Verde Islands, but swinging further to the west touched upon the coast of Brazil and claimed it for his king. Between Brazil and the Cape the fleet ran into violent storms during which Bartholomeu Dias went down with his ship, as did the captains of three other vessels. Arrived in Calicut, Cabral found its ruler still unfriendly, and some forty of his men were massacred by an Arab-led mob. He was able to trade profitably, however, at Cochin and Cannamore, and returned to Lisbon with cargoes which brought a net profit of more than one hundred per cent for the voyage, despite the loss of five ships of the original fleet.

The experience of da Gama and Cabral convinced the Portuguese government that trade in the East would have to be backed by force — force sufficient to sweep the Moslem traders from the Arabian Sea and to extort trading privileges from the native princes. The task might well have seemed beyond the powers of a small and distant country, but there were elements in the situation which gave the Portuguese a fair hope of success. The Malabar coast was cut off from the interior of India by the mountain range of the Western Ghats, and was divided into a number of petty principalities which were always jealous of one another and frequently at war. These principalities owed their prosperity to the fact that they were the principal exchange centers of the eastern trade. To their harbors came pepper from the interior and, more important, the spices, Chinese silks, Indian cottons, gems and ivory from further east; and here these precious cargoes were picked up by Arab traders who carried them to the Red Sea or the Persian Gulf and thence overland to the Mediterranean. Mutual animosity could be counted on to prevent the native princes from uniting against the Europeans, and economic necessity would force them to trade with the newcomers if there was no one else to buy their goods. The first essential step for the Portuguese, then, was to eliminate their Moslem competitors. That they were completely successful within a decade of their first appearance in eastern waters was largely due to the superior quality of their ships and cannon. The Arab ships were designed only to sail before the monsoon winds, which alternated direction with the seasons and assured them a fair wind back and forth across the Arabian Sea. They were no match for the Portuguese *caravels*, which were designed to sail in all weathers and rigged to tack against the wind. The Arab boats were also too frail to ship cannon or to withstand the firepower of the Portuguese guns. After a naval battle in 1509, in which a large Arab fleet was destroyed with no loss to the Portuguese, the Moslem traders gave up the contest and abandoned the Indian trade.

Meanwhile, the Portuguese were establishing strongholds on land to serve as centers for permanent trade and also as naval bases from which to maintain their control of the eastern seas. King Manoel was now envisaging the creation of a commercial empire in the East under royal government, and in 1505 he appointed a viceroy to act as his representative there. Dom Francesco d'Almeida, the first viceroy, laid the foundations by building forts at Cochin and Cannamore and destroying the Arab fleet. It was his successor, however, Affonso d'Albuquerque, viceroy from 1509 to 1515, who was the real architect of Portugal's oriental empire. Realizing that the Portuguese needed a city of their own in the East to serve as a capital and base of operations, Albuquerque seized the city of Goa with its magnificent harbor on the Malabar coast. He also succeeded in blocking the Persian Gulf by the conquest of Ormuz. Not content with domination of the Malabar coast, Albuquerque then struck eastward and in 1511 seized Malacca and with it control of the narrow strait between the Malay Peninsula and the island of Sumatra, the main trade route for goods brought westward from China and the spice islands of the East Indies. From there in the next few years the Portuguese spread out to seize the rich spice-bearing islands of the Moluccas and to fortify strategic bases in the Malay Archipelago. Meanwhile, the erection of a strong fortress at Colombo on the island of Ceylon had given them practical control of the shipping in the Bay of Bengal and the Coromandel coast of India.

The little kingdom of Portugal lacked the manpower to conquer extensive territory or to colonize on a large scale. What the Portuguese aimed at — and achieved — was a purely maritime empire resting on strategically located naval bases from which, with their heavier ships and guns, they could control the shipping of the Indian Ocean. The trade in spices was a royal monopoly and all the most valuable cargoes were reserved for Portuguese ships, native merchants being allowed to trade in other commodities only under license and all ships sailing without an official pass being liable to seizure. In this far-flung network of naval bases lay both the strength and the weakness of the Portuguese empire. For a century or more it enabled a tiny European kingdom to hold the golden East in fee; but it was always inadequately manned and the isolated bases were dangerously open to attack. The high mortality rate during the long sea voyage from Portugal was a constant drain on the nation's human resources, and the impossibility of sending out Portuguese women to the East led to mixed marriages with native women, with results unfortunate for the morale of the few resident Portuguese on whom the survival of the empire depended. When, in the seventeenth century, nations endowed with equal maritime skill and a healthier economy invaded the East, the Portuguese empire crumbled. Meanwhile they enjoyed their brief and bloody hour of dominion and sudden wealth. To the Portuguese pioneers must forever go the honor of having solved the mystery of Africa and of having opened the sea road for European trade with the Far East, but also the more dubious honor of having founded the European commerce in Negro slaves and of having established the precedent for European imperialism in India and the East Indies.

C. SPANISH EXPLORATION AND COLONIZATION IN THE NEW WORLD

While Portuguese explorers were still feeling their way down the African coast, which stretched discouragingly further and further before them, theoretical geographers and practical navigators were assessing the possibility of finding a shorter and more direct route to India or Cathay by sailing westward across the open ocean which, as far as they could know, alone separated Western Europe from the east coast of Asia. Several attempts to find such a route, indeed, were made by Portuguese and other navigators, including more than one by English seamen out of Bristol, before Dias rounded the Cape. In all probability, however, these early explorers to the west aimed primarily at discovering the mythical islands with which tradition, dating back to antiquity, dotted the ocean beyond the Azores and which might serve as further stepping stones to the distant shore. Given the information — and misinformation — handed down in Ptolemy's authoritative work and in that of his medieval commentators, the western route seemed perfectly practical, provided the distances were not too great; and until Dias demonstrated that Africa could be circumnavigated there was no assurance that any other route was possible. On the other hand, it presented far greater psychological hazards than did the exploration of the African coast. The most important hazard, of course, was the question of distance, which the impossibility of determining longitude with certainty rendered dangerously conjectural. Then, too, the Portuguese exploration of Africa was a gradual process, extending the area of the known step by step, and, moreover, paying its way by trade — a consideration of some practical importance. The discovery of land beyond the Ocean Sea to the west, on the contrary, would have to be achieved in one decisive leap into the unknown — a leap that might well carry the explorer beyond the point of no return. It was the supreme distinction of Columbus that he was prepared to make that leap, to sail on westward till he found land. He, too, hoped to find islands on the way, but unlike his predecessors he was determined that he would not risk missing his objective by wasting time looking for them.

Christopher Columbus (1451–1506) had left his native Genoa as a young man, and he had had some years of seafaring before he settled in Lisbon in 1477 to make his living as a cartographer and to dream, in that hotbed of explorer's tales, of the enterprise that became the ruling passion of his life. In him, as with many of the explorers, religious fervor and missionary zeal were combined with greed and intellectual curiosity, but he had also a touch of mysticism and an almost unique conviction that his divinely appointed enterprise could not fail. He found encouragement in Ptolemy, but even Ptolemy's erroneous reckoning placed the coast of Asia a perilously long way to the west. Marco Polo served him even better, for that intrepid traveller, to whom the journey overland must have seemed long indeed, had placed the coast of China still further east and had also reckoned the distance to the golden isle of Cipangu (Japan) as some fifteen hundred miles, surely no great distance from Europe. Finally, his incurable optimism led Columbus to accept the most favorable estimate of the length of a degree of longitude to be found in any medieval geographer, a good ten per cent less than Ptolemy's already shrunken figure. As early as 1484 he presented his plan to King John of Portugal and asked for ships to sail westward to Japan or India. The king was sufficiently impressed to refer the matter to a committee of experts, who detected the flaws in Columbus's reckoning and rejected the proposal as impractical. Soon after, any remaining hope that he might interest the Portuguese government in his enterprise was lost when Dias rounded Africa and opened an assured way to the East. But by that time

Columbus had left Portugal for Spain. Here, too, the scientists were doubtful, but the most insuperable obstacle he encountered was the preoccupation of Ferdinand and Isabella with the conquest of Granada. It was only after that last Moslem stronghold in Spain had fallen in January of 1492 that Isabella, perhaps drawn to Columbus by her perception in him of a sense of dedication not unlike her own, promised him the support he needed and the honors he demanded as the price of success.

The story of Columbus's voyage of 1492–93 is too well known to need retelling. Compared to many other exploring voyages, the trip over was short and amazingly easy. On this and on his three later voyages he proved himself a magnificent dead-reckoning navigator, although his occasional efforts to find his latitude by celestial observation were always distressingly wide of the mark. He had, moreover, the luck or good judgment to sail southwest to the Canaries before taking off, and so reached the latitude of the northeast trade winds, and on his return trip he struck far enough north to take advantage of the prevailing westerlies, which same winds might have defeated him on the outward voyage had he tried to sail westward on the latitude of Spain. He returned strong in the conviction that he had discovered islands off the coast of Asia, although he had found no spices, little gold and no inhabitants but naked Caribs, who showed no evidence of the highly developed civilization known to exist in the Far East. The assurance that he had indeed found a route to the Indies, however, led Ferdinand and Isabella to seek a guarantee of legal possession of the new-found lands from the Spanish pope, Alexander VI, who issued bulls granting Spain all lands found west of a line one hundred leagues beyond the Azores, and leaving to Portugal all newly discovered land east of that line. This seemed to the Portuguese to cramp their activity unduly, and in the following year, 1494, they reached an agreement with Spain, guaranteed by the Treaty of Tordisellas, which shifted the line of demarcation 270 leagues further west, a fortunate move since it later enabled them to claim Brazil as within their sphere.

The high hopes raised by Columbus's first discovery were soon followed by disappointment and disillusion. Although the Admiral himself clung stubbornly to the conviction that he had found land near India, further exploration of the Caribbean islands and the adjacent mainland made it increasingly clear that a continent stood in the way. During the next decade or two explorers probed the coast line from Florida to Brazil, but found no breakthrough that would open the way to India. In 1513 Vasco Nunez de Balboa worked his way with incredible hardship across the Isthmus from Darien, and found that a great ocean did exist, separated by only a narrow strip of land from the Atlantic. But still no way had been found to reach it by water. And in that same year the Portuguese reached and conquered the Moluccas, the richest prize in the East. It was not only the dwindling hope of reaching India, however, that drove countless adventurers to their death on the fever-ridden coast and in the steaming jungles of Central America. The lure of gold was as powerful an incentive, although no great quantity was found until, in 1519, Hernando Cortes fought his way to the uplands of Mexico and launched the conquest of the Aztec kingdom of Montezuma.

The conquest of Mexico opened a new era of expansion, but meanwhile the work of colonization had already begun in the islands and at some places on the mainland, and the foundations of a Spanish empire in the New World had already been laid. From the beginning it differed radically from the Portuguese empire in the East. The primitive natives of the Caribbean, and even the more highly developed peoples of the interior of Yucatan and Mexico, offered few opportunities for profitable trade. The only possible sources of wealth in these western Indies were gold and silver mines, pearl fisheries, and the rich soil warmed by a tropical sun. To exploit these a maritime empire founded on a few naval bases was not enough. What was required was conquest, colonization, and the enslavement of the native population to furnish the necessary labor — a process justified, as the Portuguese slave trade in Africa had been, by the conversion to Christianity of such hapless heathen as survived. Beginning with Hispaniola, where Columbus proved that his ability to govern a colony was not equal to his talent as a navigator, the Spaniards settled one after another of the islands and partitioned the natives among them to work the land and the mines. The colonization of Jamaica was begun in 1509, that of Cuba in 1511, and of Puerto Rico in 1512, while in 1509 the first settlement on the mainland was begun at Darien. The growth of Spain's vast mainland empire, however, belongs to a period beyond the chronological scope of the present volume, as does also that of the Portuguese in Brazil.

The first stages of discovery, conquest and colonization were largely the work of independent adventurers, the greedy, savage and indomitable *conquistadores* who fought the Indians, the climate and one another to find wealth that few of them lived long to enjoy. Most of them had secured some form of commission from the Spanish crown and the promise of extensive rights in the lands they conquered. But the Spanish monarchs, who were in process of establishing absolute government in Castile at the expense of the feudal nobles, the great military orders and the privileged towns, had no intention of letting the government of their nascent empire in the New World slip out of their hands or become adulterated by a kind of bastard feudalism. No sooner was the work of conquest completed, and settlement begun, than the royal government asserted its rights and appointed royal ministers, judges and financial officers to supersede the *conquistadores*. As early as 1503 the *Casa de la Contratacion* was established at Seville to regulate trade with the new colonies, and a committee of the Council of Castile — later made an independent Council of the Indies — was given responsibility for direct control of all colonial government. Even the hereditary right of the discoverer's son, Diego Colón, to the title of viceroy, though officially recognized, was not permitted to interfere in any serious way with the absolute authority of the crown. And hand in hand with the authority of the monarchy, in the New World as in the old, went that of the Spanish Church, zealous to convert the heathen, doing its best to protect the natives from a too brutal exploitation, but intolerant of any deviations from orthodoxy. Between them, crown and Church achieved to a remarkable degree the transplantation of Spanish culture to the New World and made the new Spain, so far as distance and varying conditions permitted, an extension of the old.

While Spain was thus laying the foundations of a colonial empire, the extent and value of which could as yet be but dimly foreseen, the work of exploration went on. By the end of the second decade of the new century it had been demonstrated that there was no water way through the Isthmus to the great sea of which Balboa had caught a tantalizing glimpse in 1513. Still the hope of finding a western route to the Indies, unclaimed by the Portuguese, died hard. There remained still the possibility that South America could be circumnavigated as Africa had been, and that the distance from the southern tip to the Spice Islands might prove less than that from the Cape of Good Hope. The still-unchallenged authority of Ptolemy lent credence to this assumption, and the eternal uncertainty about longitude also made it seem possible that the Moluccas actually lay within the Spanish zone if the line of demarcation fixed by the Treaty of Tordisellas were extended through the poles to the other side of the world. The young King Charles and his advisers were thus ready to lend a sympathetic ear to Magellan's request for a fleet with which to duplicate the achievements of Dias and da Gama, but in the opposite direction and under the Spanish flag.

Ferdinand Magellan was a Portuguese nobleman, who had already spent years in the East under Almeida and Albuquerque before he left Portugal in disgust at the ingratitude with which King Manoel had rewarded his services, and sought his fortune in Spain. Like Columbus and other explorers who sold their services to a foreign government, he was a man obsessed with an idea, and he had the ability to inspire others to share his conviction. He was, at any rate, able to persuade the Spanish government to give him five ships with provisions for two years, and in September, 1519, he set sail for the coast of South America. By the time the southern winter forced him to lay up in the port of St. Julien he had passed the forty-ninth parallel. During the winter he lost one of his ships on a reconnaissance and he had serious trouble with some of his crew. In the spring he sailed on, probing every inlet till he finally found the straits that still bear his name. There, while he was still feeling his way through the shoal water of the narrow straits, the crew of his largest ship, the *San Antonio*, which carried the greater part of his stores, mutinied and sailed back to Spain. Despite the argument of some of his men that having discovered the straits was enough, Magellan pressed on with his three remaining ships. By sheer bad luck he missed all the islands that dot the South Pacific, and sailed for ninety-eight days without sight of land till he hit the Ladrones, with those of his crew who had survived sick with scurvy and half-dead from starvation. From there a week's sail took him to the Philippines, which he claimed for Spain, and which proved to be the only advantage the Spanish monarchy gained from his voyage. There, too, for Magellan the voyage ended. He was killed in a brush with hostile natives. His crew, scarcely enough of them left to man two ships and deprived of leadership, blundered on to the Moluccas, where one of the ships was forced to surrender to the Portuguese. The remaining ship somehow managed to find its way home and finally, with no more than a fragment of its crew still alive, dropped anchor in Seville harbor in September, 1522.

Magellan's heroic voyage proved both that there was a southwest passage to the East and that under sixteenth-century sailing conditions it was impractical. Above all, it demonstrated the immense breadth of the Pacific, hitherto unsuspected. It did not, however, preclude the possibility that a northeastward slant of the coast of Asia might bring it closer to northern Europe, and that somewhere beyond the range of Spanish exploration there might be a northwest passage to Cathay. As early as 1496, Giovanni Caboto, a Genoese-born Venetian citizen known to the English as John Cabot, sold Henry VII the idea of sailing west to Cathay, and sold it cheap since Bristol merchants bore the cost of the voyage, which took place the following year. Cabot found land on the south shore of Newfoundland or Cape Breton Island and returned. A second voyage in 1498 accomplished little more, nor did that reputedly made by his son Sebastian Cabot in 1509. Nothing that they found on those cold and barren coasts excited the cupidity of Europeans, and the real pressure to find a northwest passage did not come till after Magellan's pioneer voyage to the south. The year after the return of the pitiful remnant of Magellan's fleet, Francis I sent out the Florentine Giovanni da Verrazano to seek the northern passage. Verrazano probed the eastern coast line of North America from New Jersey to Maine, but found no channel to the Pacific nor anything worth claiming for France. Except for these early abortive attempts, the story of westward exploration and resultant colonization by the nations of northern Europe belongs to a period well outside the limits of our present study. The story of the first great age of exploration and the expansion of the European horizon is the story primarily of the Portuguese and Spanish pioneers.

XII

The Shifting Economic Fortunes
of the European States

By the middle of the fifteenth century Western Europe was emerging from the long depression complicated by incessant warfare and intermittent plague which had weighed upon its economy for more than a hundred years. In some countries the upward trend probably began earlier, but for France the conclusion of the Hundred Years' War in mid-century was a decisive factor in opening the way to a general recovery, while the pacification of Italy by the Peace of Lodi in 1454 acted in the same way as a stimulus to Italian economic life. There is evidence, too, despite the uncertainty of vital statistics which make the demographer's task a form of speculative enterprise, that the population of Western Europe as a whole was increasing after having remained relatively static or, at best, having grown very slowly since the Black Death. While, however, economic recovery and an increase in the volume of production and exchange seem to have been fairly general, there were marked differences in the relative rate of economic growth in the various countries or regions. The techniques of capitalism were being employed more commonly in the old commercial and industrial centers and were spreading to less advanced regions, but there were no notable developments in the form or methods of capitalist enterprise. The interest of this period for the economic historian, therefore, does not center upon the development of capitalist forms of commercial and industrial organization, banking, credit and exchange as was the case in the preceding period, but rather upon the shifting economic fortunes of the European states. Variations in the rate of growth or of decline, not only from country to country, but from region to region or city to city, and from one branch of commerce or industry to another, make generalizations hazardous, but it seems clear that the most significant development was a decline in the economic importance of Italy in relation to the countries to the north and west. This period, in fact, witnessed the beginning of that shift in the center of gravity of European economy from the Mediterranean to the Atlantic states which became much more decisive after 1520 and which, on the economic level, marks one of the most distinct differences between medieval and modern Europe.

A. The Indian Summer of Italian Economy

Since we are concerned here primarily with changes in the volume of production and exchange rather than with the form and spirit of capitalist enterprise, our analysis must be quantitative rather than qualitative. And it is quantitative analysis which presents the most serious difficulties, since statistics for even this relatively late period are distressingly few and uncertain. In attempting to estimate the expansion or contraction of economic activity, the historian is here forced to rely upon general impressions derived in part from scattered and frequently unrelated statistical information, in part from contemporary estimates which are more likely to be colored by subjective reactions than by objective data, or upon *a priori* reasoning based upon changes in the general picture of world trade. Taking all the available data together, the impression emerges that Italy experienced in this period an upward trend in prosperity — an increase in absolute wealth — but that changes in the international situation prevented her economy from expanding as rapidly as did that of her rivals, and so gradually deprived her of the hegemony she had enjoyed during the preceding centuries. In order to arrive at some sort of balance we must consider first the factors limiting or contracting Italian economy, and then the compensating factors favoring its growth. In the following sections we will consider the relatively more rapid expansion of southern Germany and the countries facing the Atlantic.

The position held by the Italians in the Levant had been deteriorating for more than a century before the Turkish conquest of Constantinople signalled the end of their privileged position in the lands of the old Byzantine Empire. So long as the great Mongolian Empire of the khans remained intact, the Venetian and Genoese colonies on the Black Sea were the terminal points of a trade route that ran overland all the way to Peking; but after the breakup of that empire by about 1340 the overland trade from China practically ceased. The Genoese colonies at Kaffa and Tana and the other Italian posts on the Black Sea still did a flourishing trade with southern Russia and Persia for more than a century longer, but under conditions made increasingly precarious by the anarchy which characterized the governments of those regions. From the middle of the fourteenth century the steady expansion of the Turkish Empire was a growing threat to the Venetian and Genoese colonies in the Aegean Islands, on the coast of the Black Sea and on the mainland of Greece. It was a threat, however, rather to their territorial possessions than to their trade, although that also necessarily suffered. The Ottoman Turks were primarily conquerors rather than trade rivals. Even after the fall of Constantinople and the Turkish conquest of the Aegean islands, the Italian merchants continued to trade with the conquered territory; but they had lost their privileged position and were forced to pay for the right to trade. The Venetians did not accept this humiliating situation without a struggle. From 1463 to 1479 they waged a war against the Turk, during the course of which they lost the rich island of Negroponte in the Aegean. Meanwhile, in 1475, the Italian colonies at Kaffa and Tana on the Black Sea had also been wiped out.

The Turkish conquests undoubtedly decreased both the volume and the profits of Italian trade with Constantinople, the Aegean and the Black Sea; but they did not materially affect the more important commerce in Far Eastern products, since the two major trade routes through Syria to the Persian Gulf and through Egypt to the Red Sea were still outside the range of Turkish expansion. The Italian spice trade, in fact, continued to increase in volume until the end of the fifteenth century, despite customs duties imposed by the Mameluke sultans that more than doubled the price. Alexandria and Beirut swarmed with Venetian and Florentine merchants, and were visited annually by the Venetian galley fleets which, in the last years of the century, normally brought back some three and a half million pounds of spices a year. Then came the blow that cut Italian spice imports to perhaps a quarter of their former volume and eventually reduced this staple of medieval Italian trade to negligible proportions. The effect of the Portuguese invasion of the Indian Ocean was felt in the Levant a year before the first large shipments of pepper and other spices reached Lisbon in 1503. By 1509 there were no longer sufficient quantities of spices to pay the high cost of galley freight, and the annual sailing of the Venetian galley fleets to England and Flanders was suspended. When the Ottoman Turks overran Syria and Egypt in 1516 and 1517 the Eastern trade was already lost. Only later, when the Portuguese hold on the Indian Ocean began to weaken, was there some recovery.

While Italian trade in the Levant was thus losing ground, Italian commerce, industry and finance were also being forced to meet rising competition from the north and west. The Venetian trade route north to southern Germany was still heavily travelled, but more and more of the goods were being carried by merchants from Augsburg and Nürnberg. Toward the end of the fifteenth century the rise of the great South German banking firms also offered the first serious challenge to the supremacy of the Italians in international finance. As the century wore on, the growing woollen cloth industry in England used up more and more of the English wool, leaving little for the moribund Italian industry. In both England and France, too, protectionist legislation was beginning to restrict the activity of foreign merchants to the disadvantage of the Italians. France had emerged from the Hundred Years' War, and the later conflicts with the Burgundian dukes, with a strong central government which displayed its powers, not only in attempts to regulate the national economy, but, more disastrously for the Italians, in the invasions of Italy which began in 1494 and continued to disrupt Italian economic life during the remainder of this period.

While not underestimating the losses enumerated above, we must also note on the credit side of the ledger evidences of gain which outweighed the debits and still left Italy with a favorable balance, despite the deterioration of her position in relation to other countries. All contemporary comments indicate that Italy was still fabulously rich. Certainly her wealth impressed the greedy invaders from France and Spain. Italian merchants were still active in every center of trade in Europe, using their inherited skill to combat the growing difficulties placed in their way. And the Italians still dominated the Mediterranean trade, which, with the general expansion of European economy, continued to increase in volume despite the shrinkage of some markets in the Levant. As has been indicated, the spice trade flourished with undiminished vigor until the end of the fifteenth century, but it was only a part, if a very valuable part, of the trade which the Italians carried on, not only with the Levant but also with North Africa, Spain and southern France. Syrian cotton, alum and dyestuffs, wine from Crete, African and Spanish wool, oil and salt, cloth and other articles of Italian manufacture, these were but a few of the staple commodities carried, not in the expensive galleys but in the large round sailing ships which a revolutionary improvement in rigging around the middle of the century had made safer and more manageable. They continued to bring solid profits to the Italian merchants throughout the sixteenth century. Florentine merchants had taken an increasingly active part in this sea-borne trade since the early years of the fifteenth century. After the conquest of Pisa in 1406 gave them a port, the Florentines constructed a merchant marine of their own and were no longer entirely dependent on foreign shipping. The largest share of the Mediterranean commerce, however, still belonged to the Venetians. The time had not yet come when Venice spent what Venice earned.

The manufacture and finishing of fine woollen cloth, which had been Italy's largest industry, was in this period dying of starvation for lack of English wool, but its place was taken by a growing silk industry which was no longer dependent on raw silk from the East, since silkworms were now being cultivated in Sicily and many parts of Italy. In this period Italy had something like a monopoly of the manufacture of silk and other such costly fabrics as cloth of gold; although Louis XI, who reckoned that France was paying the Italians half a million gold crowns a year for these luxury cloths, introduced the silk industry into France in 1467, and later kings protected the infant industry by banning the importation of foreign fabrics. A further substitute for the old woollen industry was also found in the manufacture of lighter and cheaper cloths made from Spanish and North African wool. Shipbuilding was still a large industry in Italy, although the supply of suitable timber was running short in the Venetian hinterland. Other industries, too, were still thriving, especially those devoted to the production of luxury goods, such as Venetian glass and mirrors, tooled leather goods and objects of art — fields in which Italian skill and taste were still unrivalled. Milanese armor still led the European markets although the raw material had to be imported from northern mines. Italy, in fact, had few mineral resources and hence could not profit by the improved mining techniques that were enriching other countries.

There was, however, one notable exception. The discovery of rich deposits of fine alum at Tolfa in the Papal States in 1462 brought the papal treasury an annual income of 100,000 ducats in royalties, and added to the fortunes of the Medici and other financiers who held shares in the *Societas Aluminum*, the company organized to handle production and sale. Alum was an indispensable ingredient in the dyeing of cloth, being used to set the colors, and as the only other large source of supply was in Turkish territory in Asia Minor, whence it could be imported only at excessive cost, the *Societas Aluminum* was obviously on to a good thing, especially as the pope felt justified in pronouncing ecclesiastical censures on any one using the infidel alum instead of his own more sanctified product. The alum works at Tolfa soon became one of the largest mining operations in Europe, employing more than 800 workers.

The Italian bankers no longer held the near monopoly of international finance that they had enjoyed for so long, but they still played an immensely important part in the handling of bills of exchange, in financial services to popes, kings and princes, and as traders and bankers in every great commercial center of Europe. Florentine and other Tuscan bankers monopolized papal finance and enjoyed especially favorable relations with the kings of France and Naples. Accumulated capital and a tradition of knowledge and skill in the techniques of international finance enabled the Italian bankers to hold their own long after Italy had ceased to be a serious competitor in other fields of economic activity. Genoa, in particular, remained one of the great centers of international finance until the seventeenth century.

In the period we are here considering, however, the Florentines were still the most important Italian bankers. The fame of the Medici banking house has tended to overshadow its numerous Florentine rivals — the Pazzi, Strozzi, Frescobaldi and Gualterotti, among others — and the spectacular decline and ultimate collapse of the Medici firm toward the end of the fifteenth century has tended to create an exaggerated impression of the general decline of Italian banking. For this reason, and also because the Medici have most commonly been considered from other points of view, it is worth while considering the history of their bank in some detail from its height under Cosimo *Pater Patriae* to its bankruptcy under his grandson. In its best days the House of Medici was undoubtedly the greatest banking house in Europe. It had branches in Venice, Milan and Rome and beyond the Alps in Avignon, Bruges, London and Lyons, all of which were engaged in commerce in commodities as well as in banking and exchange operations. Where the Medici had no branch of their own they had correspondents who would act as their agents in handling bills of exchange. Cosimo and other members of the family also had a controlling interest in three industrial enterprises, two of which manufactured woollen cloth, the other silk. Except for a brief interruption in the reign of Sixtus IV, when the pope quarrelled with the Medici and transferred his business to the rival firm of the Pazzi, the Medici were the principal bankers for the papacy. Through their network of branches and agencies papal income from all parts of Europe was transferred to Rome, and from them many a prelate raised the loan needed to pay the fees for his consecration. It was papal favor, too, that gave the Medici a controlling share in the company which exploited the alum mines at Tolfa. From all these services to the papacy the Medici received a handsome profit, not to mention cardinal's hats for two members of the family, both of whom were elevated to the chair of Peter after the banking house on which their fortune had been built had ceased to exist.

The organization of these multifarious enterprises was of a kind more common in the fifteenth century than it had been in the day of such early family firms as the Bardi and Peruzzi. In firms of the latter type there was only one body of capital, in which members of the family and some trusted outsiders held shares. The firm owned and operated all the branch houses, which were managed by salaried factors. The Medici enterprises, on the other hand, were organized as a group of interlocking but legally distinct partnerships. The home bank, and the various industrial enterprises in Florence and the branches in other cities, each formed a distinct partnership in which the resident manager held shares, but in which members of the Medici family retained a controlling interest. In 1458 Cosimo de' Medici was the senior partner in eleven such partnerships. As head of the family he had the ultimate authority, but even so energetic and methodical an executive as Cosimo could not manage in detail the activity of even the home office and the local cloth-manufacturing companies, to say nothing of branch houses as far distant as London and Bruges. He could only outline general policy, select able and trustworthy men as managing partners, and keep a watchful eye on their general conduct of the business. This Cosimo did with notable success. His son Piero, plagued as he was with gout, was less efficient, but he was sufficiently conservative to avoid excessive risks. Under the magnificent Lorenzo, however, the managers of both the home office and the branches abroad were left a much freer hand. Lorenzo's other interests, both as *de facto* ruler of Florence and as patron of art and letters, were too divergent and absorbing for him to give much consistent attention to business. One after another, his branch managers got into trouble through carelessness or over-optimism. During the lifetime of Cosimo the managers of the Bruges branch were under strict orders not to extend credit to princes, but after 1471 Lorenzo's managing partner at Bruges, Tommaso Portinari, was permitted to make large loans to Charles the Bold and later to the duke's son-in-law, Maximilian of Hapsburg, who was notoriously the most unreliable debtor in Europe. These loans, together with the extravagance of Portinari, who lived like a noble at the court of the Burgundian dukes, contributed to the collapse of the Bruges branch in 1478. In the same year the London branch was also dissolved, with losses of more than fifty thousand florins written off. Here, too, loans to the government were a contributing factor, but in this case they were an unavoidable risk, being the price paid to Edward IV for licenses to export wool. Other branches had also been liquidated or were in bad shape when the expulsion of the Medici from Florence in 1494, and the confiscation of their property in the city, brought their whole financial edifice crashing to the ground.

The carelessness or bad judgment of the branch managers was not, however, the sole cause of the débacle. Francesco Sassetti, who acted as manager of the home bank and general manager of all the Medici enterprises for Lorenzo, seems to have suffered from the same faults. Then, too, under Lorenzo profits were withdrawn to maintain his princely status instead of being plowed back into the business as they had been under Cosimo's more canny management. Lorenzo's position as ruler of Florence also forced him at times to make policy decisions for diplomatic rather than purely economic reasons. A still more serious danger arose from the fact that the Medici business was carried on to an increasing degree with money deposited with the bank and on which it had to pay interest. As the proportion of the firm's capital held by the family declined through losses, withdrawals or declining earnings, the firm became increasingly vulnerable to any crisis that might shake its prestige and cause a run on the bank by the depositors. Moreover these deposits had to be repaid in gold at a time when the price of gold in relation to the silver coinage used in everyday transactions was rising steadily, more than twenty per cent between 1475 and 1495. Before the final crash the solvency of the bank had become so precarious that Lorenzo was forced to bolster it with money appropriated from the *Monte delle Dote*, a mutual fund for the payment of dowries.

B. The Rise of South German Capitalism in Commerce, Industry, Mining, and Finance

One of the most notable events in the economic history of the second half of the fifteenth century and the early decades of the sixteenth was the rise of a group of South German firms, mostly from Augsburg and Nürnberg, to a position of European importance, rivalling if not surpassing the Italians in the fields of international commerce and finance. Behind this period of sudden growth lay several generations of slower development in trade and industry. As the overland routes through eastern France declined in importance, more of the Venetian inland trade shifted to the route which ran north through the Brenner Pass to Augsburg, Nürnberg and Leipzig, and thence to Lübeck and the other Hanseatic cities on the Baltic. The Venetians, who cared little for overland trade, left this route largely to merchants of the inland cities, and by the fifteenth century it was monopolized by the South Germans, who now had their own establishment in Venice, the *Fondaco dei Tedeschi*. It was here that they learned the techniques of capitalist organization and finance which enabled them to take full advantage of the opportunities that were opening up to them after the middle of the fifteenth century. Nürnberg, too, had capitalized upon her central position to build up her trade, not only to north and south, but also to east and west. At a time when Lübeck and the Hanse towns were clinging to an exclusive monopoly, Nürnberg opened her markets freely to foreign merchants and became in the fifteenth century the focal center of a trade that radiated in all directions through central and southern Germany and the neighboring Slavic lands to the east. Meanwhile a growing textile industry — the manufacture of linen cloth and the mixture of cotton and linen known as fustian — added to the fortunes of the merchants who controlled the trade and put out the materials to the weavers, much after the fashion of the earlier Flemish and Italian capitalists.

It was the revival of mining in central Europe, together with the consequent growth of the metal industries and the metal trade, however, which was primarily responsible for the rapid development of large-scale capitalist enterprise in the South German cities after the middle of the fifteenth century. Medieval mining, which had produced an expanding volume of silver, copper, tin, iron and other ores during the twelfth and thirteenth centuries, had been mostly surface mining, carried on by small groups of independent miners who worked shallow pits or caves. This medieval mining boom slackened off early in the fourteenth century, as the available surface veins of ore began to be worked out. The general economic recession which set in after the middle of the century also probably had a depressing effect on the industry. At any rate, there seems to have been a decided slump in mining for more than a hundred years until a new boom began in the second half of the fifteenth century. The revival affected nearly all the old mining districts, but was most intensive in the silver and copper mining areas of eastern and southern Germany, the Tyrol, Bohemia and Hungary. The general economic recovery of the late fifteenth century undoubtedly helped to stimulate this renewed activity, but the decisive factor in increasing production was the introduction of improved methods of draining the mines and supporting the walls, so that shafts could be sunk to much deeper levels, thereby opening up new and rich veins of ore. Pumps driven by horsepower were employed where necessary. More frequently, where the mine was on a hillside, long adits were bored out from the side of the shafts to the surface of the slope below the level of the pits, thus providing drainage. At the same time, new methods of extracting ore and working the metals increased profits and encouraged investment. One of the most important

431

of these was the discovery about 1451 of a method of extracting silver from argentiferous copper ore, which not only vastly increased the quantity of available silver, but also cheapened the production of copper. Meanwhile, the demand for copper was also stimulated by the discovery in the Tyrol and elsewhere of large deposits of calamine, the ore of zinc, the metal which, alloyed with copper, produces brass.

The labor required to sink deep shafts and construct drainage adits, as well as the installation of pumping and hoisting machinery, demanded a large initial outlay of capital before returns could be expected, and this capital was provided for the most part by merchants who were drawn by the profits of the metal trade to invest in shares in the mining companies or to lend the requisite funds on mortgage. Without the capital already accumulated as a result of trade and industry in the South German cities, indeed, the mining boom of the second half of the fifteenth century would probably not have taken place. Mining was becoming too expensive for the small independent miners. Only large companies, holding extensive concessions from the prince or lord who claimed regalian rights, could afford the necessary investment. The independent working miners were thus of necessity replaced by capitalist entrepreneurs on the one hand, and on the other by large numbers of wage-earning workers who were entirely dependent on the mine owners for employment. Here, as earlier in the large textile industries, the introduction of capital brought with it the growth of an industrial proletariat. In 1525 Charles V estimated, probably without exaggeration, that there were more than a hundred thousand workers in the mines and metalworking plants of the Holy Roman Empire.

A similar development of capitalist enterprise, accompanied by the appearance of an industrial proletariat, took place in the various extractive and metalworking industries as a result of the expanding production of the South German mines. This was a period of marked technological advance in all the processes of smelting ore and of casting, rolling and forging metal. Water power was extensively used for crushing ore and to operate the bellows of forges and blast furnaces. Even where new methods were not invented, larger and more expensive installations were required to handle the growing volume of production. The establishments set up to perform the complicated process of extracting silver and copper from copper ore, and to prepare the metals for the market, in some cases involved a larger concentration of capital and labor than could be found in any single mining operation or, possibly, in any other private enterprise in Europe. Inevitably these industries fell under the control of merchant companies, which not only possessed the requisite capital but were also engaged in the metal trade, buying up ore or producing it in mines they themselves owned and selling the metal and metal wares in foreign markets. Great quantities of silver and copper were exported south to Venice or north to the Baltic coast and thence by sea to Antwerp. In these years, too, the manufactured copper, brass and iron wares of Nürnberg sold in every market of Europe.

The subsidiary metallurgical industries, which were concentrated in cities, often at a distance from the mines, were largely free from governmental control. The princes who claimed regalian rights over the precious metals which were found on their lands, on the other hand, maintained an increasingly close regulation of actual mining operations, sometimes themselves financing the work or participating in the mining companies. In any case, the German princes claimed the right to buy up the product of mines on their land at a price well below the market, or claimed a share of the ore as royalties. Perennially in need of money as they were, the princes profited by this situation to raise loans from merchant-industrialists, to whom they mortgaged the product of their mines or farmed out their regalian rights for a term of years as guarantee for the loan. The larger merchant companies were thus drawn into the hazardous but profitable sphere of state finance, and were almost forced to develop the moneylending and banking side of their activities. At the same time, such concessions gave the commercial companies a guarantee of large stocks of metals for export, and this encouraged them to open branches in the principal markets of Italy, the Netherlands, France and Spain. Once established, such a network of branches abroad also enabled them to engage in exchange operations, as the Italian merchant-bankers had done before them. By the end of the fifteenth century, the largest Augsburg and Nürnberg firms had adopted all the techniques of their Italian predecessors, and were beginning to replace them as the dominant powers in international finance. It was money from Augsburg that helped to finance the first Portuguese ventures to India.

Except for their predominant interest in mining, the metal industries and the trade in metals, the great South German firms added little that was new in the way of capitalist organization or technique. They were family firms of varying, but already familiar, types. Some admitted outsiders to partnership; others kept the shares within the family circle and maintained a highly centralized direction. All of them, like the earlier Italian firms, expanded their working capital by taking money on deposit. Like the Italian firms, too, they continued to trade in commodities of all kinds, even after banking and exchange operations had become a major preoccupation. Of these South German firms the most famous was that of the Fuggers. Partly as a result of their political connections and the preservation of their records, which makes possible a close study of their activities, their importance has been somewhat exaggerated in relation to such rival firms as Welser, Hochstetter, Meuting and Paumgartner. Nevertheless, at the height of their fortunes the Fuggers did occupy an almost unique place in European finance, comparable to that of the Medici a generation earlier, and hence deserve the special attention they have been accorded.

Compared with the Welsers and some of the other patrician families of Augsburg, the Fuggers were parvenus. The founder of the family fortunes, Hans Fugger, was a linen weaver who migrated to Augsburg about 1380 and began to combine trade with weaving. His sons expanded the commercial side of the family business, importing from Venice spices, silk and woollen cloth and the raw cotton used in the manufacture of fustian. They were prosperous businessmen, but by no means the wealthiest citizens of Augsburg. It was only in the third generation that the firm founded by the three brothers, Ulrich, Georg and Jakob, rose to great wealth and outstripped all its rivals. Of the three, Jakob, although much the youngest — he was born in 1457 — had by the 1480's become the acknowledged leader. The other brothers were capable businessmen, but it was Jakob whose broad vision and combined caution and daring were largely responsible for their phenomenal success. After the death of Georg in 1506 and Ulrich in 1510, Jakob admitted their sons to partnership, having none of his own, but he kept the control of all the activities of the firm in his own autocratic hands until his death in 1525. As a young man Jakob had served his apprenticeship in the *Fondaco dei Tedeschi* in Venice, where he had mastered the art of accounting and where, too, he may have absorbed something of the capitalistic spirit of that great commercial city. In the latter respect, however, there was probably little that Venice could teach the man who was called by his contemporaries Jakob the Rich and who in his old age, when urged to give up speculation and enjoy his great wealth in peace, replied that "he had no intention of doing so, but wished to make a profit as long as he could."[1]

The rise of the Fugger firm followed much the same course, in its early days at least, as that of the other Augsburg houses. While continuing the old trade with Venice in spices and textiles, Jakob and his brothers shifted their interest more and more to mining and the metal industries, exporting silver and copper to Venice and Antwerp, spreading a network of branches across Europe, and engaging in even larger banking and exchange operations. A series of loans to Duke Sigmund of the Tyrol, which were guaranteed by concessions of the duke's royalties

[1] Quoted in J. Strieder, *Jacob Fugger the Rich, Merchant and Banker of Augsburg, 1459–1525* (New York, 1931), p. 12.

in the mines on his land, gave the Fuggers a large share in the Tyrolese silver and copper trade from 1487 onward. These loans and the corresponding concessions were later continued by Sigmund's heir, Emperor Maximilian I. The firm's largest investment in mining and metal-working, however, was not in the Tyrol but in Hungary, which was opened to German exploitation after the Peace of Pressburg in 1491. There the Fuggers held a practical monopoly of the rich silver and copper mines and engaged in cartel agreements to keep the prices high. After the election of Maximilian the firm's connection with the House of Hapsburg became increasingly close. Throughout the whole of the impecunious emperor's reign the Fuggers were his principal bankers, financing his harebrained schemes and securing ample concessions in return. The high point of the firm's services to the House of Hapsburg, however, came after Maximilian's death, when Jakob Fugger financed the election of Charles V by lending him more than a half a million gold gulden with which to bribe the Electors. It was this dramatic display of wealth, with its incalculable political consequences, which more than anything else established the reputation of Jakob Fugger as the greatest financier of his age.

Meanwhile, the Fuggers had also established close relations with the papacy, and after the fall of the Medici bank in 1494 they took over a large part of the papal banking. Their unrivalled influence with the emperor and other German princes put them in a favorable position to take over the transference of papal income from Germany to Rome. Among other sources of papal income, the Fuggers were active in the collection and transfer of the funds raised from indulgences. They also made loans to archbishops, bishops and other prelates to enable them to pay the dues they owed to the papacy. They were popularly regarded as having been responsible for the accumulation of two bishoprics and the Archbishopric of Mainz by that ambitious young pluralist, Albrecht of Brandenburg, and were also supposed to have exerted an illegitimate influence on the appointment of other prelates.

The great age of the South German firms did not last long. By the middle of the sixteenth century the flow of silver from the New World broke the boom in European silver mining and cut the roots from which the German firms had drawn their basic strength. As the century wore on they shifted their financial operations more and more to Antwerp and Spain, speculating on the Antwerp *Bourse* and lending money, that would never be repaid, to the Spanish crown. After the collapse of Antwerp as a financial center in 1576 those firms that remained in business went rapidly downhill, and the bankruptcy of the Spanish government toward the end of the century completed their ruin. While it lasted, however, the wealth of Augsburg and Nürnberg furnished the material setting for an age of flourishing culture, the high period of the German Renaissance. During the lifetime of Jakob Fugger these two cities produced a brilliant group of artists, humanists and scholars: the painters Albrecht Dürer, Hans Burgkmair and the elder Holbein; the sculptors Adam Kraft, Veit Stoss and Peter Vischer; the humanists Konrad Peutinger and Willibald Pirckheimer; the Nürnberg chronicler Hartmann Schedel and the geographer Martin Behaim; and, product of a vigorous local tradition, the Meistersinger and poet Hans Sachs. Constant commercial intercourse with Italy opened these cities to the influence of the Italian Renaissance, and there is ample evidence that the fellow-citizens of Jakob Fugger who served their apprenticeship in Italy learned there more than the art of accounting. The wealthy patrician families who provided the patronage for art and letters in Augsburg and Nürnberg, however, were not themselves the heirs of a long cultural tradition as were the Medici and their other Italian contemporaries, nor was the cultural life of these cities concentrated in princely courts. For all its brilliant achievements, the culture of the South German cities could not rival that of Italy in the High Renaissance.

C. Rise and Decline in the Maritime States of the North and West

While the South German cities were enjoying their meteoric rise to great wealth, an increased volume of production and exchange was bringing a less spectacular, but more enduring, prosperity to the states along the Atlantic and North Sea coasts. For this the general recovery which characterized the late fifteenth and early sixteenth century was in large part responsible; but commercial and industrial growth was also fostered by the economic policies of royal and princely governments, by increasing mastery of the techniques of capitalist enterprise and, finally, by the first commercial fruits of the great age of exploration. Not all trading centers of the north and west, however, profited equally by the new currents. Some of the older cities, too strongly bound to the methods that had brought wealth in the past, declined in relative importance, while newer cities took advantage of the new opportunities. Political factors as well as new trade routes worked to the advantage of some states more than others. It will be necessary, therefore, to survey the various states and note the course of development in each.

The Netherlands, which had been brought under the strong government of the Burgundian dukes before the middle of the fifteenth century,

The Netherlands at the End of the Fifteenth Century

NORTH

SEA

ZUYDER ZEE

COUNTY OF HOLLAND

Amsterdam

B. OF UTRECHT

DUCHY OF GELDERLAND

Rotterdam

C. OF ZEELAND

DUCHY OF BRABANT

Antwerp

Bruges

Ghent

Scheldt

Ypres

Louvain

D. OF LIÈGE

Maas

D. OF LIMBURG

COUNTY OF FLANDERS

Brussels

Lille

COUNTY OF ARTOIS

COUNTY OF HAINAULT

C. OF NAMUR

Liège

Arras

B. OF CAMBRAI

BISHOPRIC OF LIÈGE

Rhine

DUCHY OF LUXEMBURG

FRANCE

437

were still prosperous on the whole and still formed the most important center of economic activity in northern Europe. But within the Netherlands radical changes were taking place, the most striking of which was the decline of Bruges and the corresponding rise of Antwerp to a dominant position in international trade and finance. Even before the final decline set in, the ancient woollen industry of Bruges, and with it that of the other old Flemish cities, was ruined by the stubborn refusal of the guilds to alter their methods and to find a substitute for the failing supply of English wool. At the same time, the attempt on the part of Bruges to fight the rival English industry by prohibiting the import of English cloth resulted only in forcing the English Merchant Adventurers to establish themselves in Antwerp and to transfer to that city the bulk of English trade with the continent. The refusal of Bruges to permit foreigners to trade except through the intermediary agency of native hosts also encouraged merchants to seek the freer atmosphere of the rival city. The Hanseatic merchants, themselves becoming increasingly conservative and bound by traditional ties to Bruges, clung longest to their *kontor* there, but even they were forced before the end of the fifteenth century to abandon the dying city. Finally, any hope that Bruges might recover her lost leadership was permanently wrecked by the silting in of the Zwyn, which was gradually cutting Bruges off from her outlet to the sea and in the sixteenth century left her landlocked.

The rapid rise of Antwerp to a position of even greater importance than that enjoyed by Bruges in the preceding period was not, however, solely due to her greater freedom from obsolete restrictions upon trade and industry. Other factors, including the governmental policies of the Burgundian dukes and their Hapsburg successors, worked to her advantage. The ducal government, jealous of its authority and concerned with the prosperity of the whole state, was naturally inimical to the special privileges and exclusive monopolies of the old Flemish towns and inclined to favor the newer and less independent Brabantine city. Moreover, since most of the trade of the Netherlands was not in the hands of natives but was brought to them by foreigners, the dukes were eager to attract as many foreign merchants as possible and so declared Antwerp an open port. Finally, the rebellion of Bruges against Maximilian of Hapsburg, who had become regent for his young son in 1482 after the death of Mary of Burgundy, led him to encourage merchants in every possible way to transfer their business from Bruges to Antwerp. During Maximilian's regency the great South German firms, Meuting, Hochstetter, Fugger and Welser, one after another opened branches in Antwerp and made it the principal market for copper and silver in Western Europe. Hapsburg diplomacy, too, was instrumental in making Antwerp the northern staple for the sale of alum from the Papal States, and it may also have helped to make Antwerp the principal center for the distribution of spices brought by the Portuguese, under royal monopoly, from India. Meanwhile, new and thriving industries were growing up in the hinterland of Antwerp in Brabant and northern Flanders: the most important being the manufacture of linen cloth, tapestries and light cloth woven from Spanish wool. These industries were carried on largely in rural districts, villages and small towns and were mostly controlled by Antwerp capitalists who put out the material to the workers and who were hampered by no guild restrictions. The concentration of so much business in Antwerp attracted not only merchants but also money and credit, with the result that by the end of the fifteenth century Antwerp was fast becoming the financial capital of Europe and had already replaced Bruges as the center of northern banking and exchange. At the *Bourse*, built in 1485, merchants and financiers from every country in Europe traded in commodities, in future shipments, and in bills of exchange. Here, in the first modern stock exchange, fortunes were won and lost in speculative buying and selling, and fluctuations in the market caused tremors in the countinghouses of Augsburg, Genoa and Lisbon.

A second important development within the Netherlands was the rise of Dutch commerce and industry. Holland and the neighboring Dutch-speaking provinces had lagged far behind Flanders and Brabant until the fifteenth century; by mid-century, however, they had developed a vigorous cloth-making industry. Shipbuilding, too, was becoming important, and Dutch merchant ships were beginning to penetrate the Baltic. They appeared there first as carriers of Hanseatic merchandise, but soon Dutch merchants themselves were trading within the old Hanseatic preserve. It was significant for the future development of Holland that her commerce was not, like that of the southern Netherlands, a passive trade. The Dutch did not wait for trade to come to their ports, but went seeking it on the high seas. At the same time, Dutch fishermen were cultivating the herring fisheries of the North Sea, which were becoming a more important source of supply as the old Hanseatic fisheries in the Baltic began to fail. The great age of Dutch commerce was yet to come, but by 1520 Amsterdam had become one of the busiest ports in northern Europe, and the Dutch challenge to the other maritime nations could no longer be ignored.

The rise of Holland as a commercial power coincided with the decline of the Hanseatic League, and was at least partly responsible for it. Dutch penetration of the Hanseatic monopoly in the Baltic began so gradually that the Hansards were scarcely aware of the threat until it had assumed dangerous proportions. In the early fifteenth century the

League was more concerned with English competition, since the English merchants had the backing of king and Parliament and could demand free access to the eastern Baltic ports in exchange for the special privileges enjoyed by the Hansards in London. The disruption caused by the Wars of the Roses, however, prevented the English government from pursuing any consistent policy in mid-century, and the English merchants lost the foothold they had gained in the Prussian ports. Then in 1474, thanks to the aid the League gave to Edward IV in the time of his greatest need, the Hanseatic privileges in London were reaffirmed without corresponding concessions to the English merchants in the Baltic. For the rest of the century the Hanseatic position in London was secure, while the English stayed out of the Baltic. Nevertheless, Hanseatic trade had passed its peak, and the League was clearly beginning to disintegrate. Lübeck, the conservative leader of the League, could no longer count on the support of Danzig and the other Prussian ports, nor upon Cologne and the West German members. In the face of rising competition and changing conditions the old cities of the League could only try to enforce more rigidly than ever the regulations that had brought them success in the past. The misguided loyalty of Lübeck to Bruges was symbolical of her inability to adjust to the era of freer capitalism represented by Antwerp and Amsterdam.

For English commerce and industry the fifteenth century was a period of alternating depression and recovery. An upward trend in the second quarter of the century was broken by the disturbance caused by the Wars of the Roses. A new period of expansion began only in the last two decades of the century, stimulated by the restoration of peace under Henry VII, by his commercial treaties with the Netherlands and Spain, and by the Navigation Acts designed to foster the development of English shipping. The manufacture of woollen cloth was still England's principal industry, and the export of cloth now far exceeded that of raw wool. The Merchants of the Staple still exported wool to Calais, but their trade had shrunk, while that of the Merchant Adventurers, who exported cloth to Antwerp and traded in other commodities there, was growing steadily. After the monopoly conferred upon the Merchant Adventurers by Act of Parliament in 1494, indeed, they handled the great bulk of English trade with the continent, except for that directed toward the Baltic which was still a Hanseatic monopoly. English trade was still largely a regulated trade, and was concentrated increasingly in London. The woollen industry, on the other hand, escaped almost entirely from either city or governmental regulation. It was a rural industry, carried on in country villages by local clothiers who put out the wool to spinners and weavers living in their own homes and raising at least a part of their food on their own land. Wool was woven in many parts of England, but the need for water power to operate fulling mills was leading to an increasing concentration in the hilly country to the west of England and in Yorkshire.

The economic recovery of France during this period seemed all the more striking in contrast to the long devastation and disruption of all economic activity caused by the Hundred Years' War. France was a naturally rich country, but her prosperity depended upon agriculture, inter-regional trade and small industries rather than upon distant commerce and large-scale industry, so that capitalism developed slowly here. The career of Jacques Coeur, the fabulous merchant who, in the last years of the Hundred Years' War, made a huge fortune by combining commerce in the Mediterranean with supplying the army and the royal court, operating the royal mint, and serving Charles VII in the double capacity of moneylender and finance minister, was altogether unique. Italian firms still held a near monopoly of French banking and finance, although the South German houses were becoming increasingly active in Lyons around the turn of the century. But, if French commerce and industry produced few great capitalist enterprises, the total volume of both internal and external trade was growing steadily after the restoration of peace. The royal government labored to restore roads and, wherever possible, to abolish the innumerable tolls which added to the cost of transporting goods. As the currents of trade shifted from the Mediterranean to the Atlantic, the southern French ports entered upon a slow decline, but Bordeaux, now recovered from the English, and the other western seaports profited by the new opportunities for Atlantic trade.

Of all the countries on the Atlantic seaboard, however, it was Portugal which in this period profited most directly from the new ocean trade routes. The early explorations directed by Henry the Navigator opened up the Madeiras, the Azores and the Cape Verde Islands to Portuguese colonization. From these islands the Portuguese imported sugar, wine, timber and cattle. From the west coast of Africa, too, they imported gold dust, slaves and ivory. The value of these goods was considerable, but was far surpassed by the spices and other oriental wares brought back from India by the Portuguese fleets after the turn of the century. The new trade route had been opened up under the direction of the royal government, and from the first it claimed a monopoly of the trade in pepper and other spices. Part of the profit, however, went to Genoese financiers and to the Welsers and other South German firms who had helped finance the voyages. The secondary profit arising from the distribution of the spices throughout Europe also went almost entirely to foreign merchants. The Portuguese government, eager for a quick profit, made no attempt to handle the European end of the spice trade. Lisbon was, in fact, poorly situated to act as a distributing center, and most of the cargoes from India were shipped on to Antwerp, to the great profit of that city and of the merchants who frequented it. The wealth from the East thus enriched the Portuguese government, but did less than it might have done to stimulate Portuguese commerce and industry.

At the beginning of the sixteenth century Spain stood on the threshold of a period of unprecedented wealth, but the influx of gold and silver from the New World did not begin in earnest until after the conquest of Mexico by Cortes in 1521, and that of Peru by Pizarro a decade later. It thus lies beyond the chronological scope of this book. Considerable quantities of gold, though not of silver, were, it is true, mined in Hispaniola and Jamaica before Cortes looted the hoarded treasures of Montezuma and called attention to the much greater resources of the mainland. From the beginning of the century sufficient gold was brought back to make the fifth claimed by the crown a substantial addition to the royal treasury, and also to give the first impetus to that rise in prices which continued at an accelerated pace throughout the century and which historians have called the price revolution. Colonization of the islands of the Caribbean, too, had already begun to furnish the basis for a moderately profitable trade. By 1503, at any rate, commerce with the colonies was sufficiently important to justify the establishment of a special institution to regulate it, the *Casa de la Contratacion*. Still, what Spain got from her transatlantic colonies in the three decades after 1492 probably did little more than pay for the cost of discovery and colonization and compensate for the losses resulting from the expulsion of the Moors from Spain after the fall of Granada. Spain at the end of our period was a land rich in promise, but the fulfillment of the promise still lay in the future.

Both the Portuguese penetration of the Far East and the Spanish colonization in the New World were carried out under governmental direction, and they presented unusually clear-cut opportunities for the maintenance of royal regulation and control. Both governments strove to exclude foreigners from their overseas preserves and to regulate colonial trade with a view primarily to enriching the mother country and its rulers. Within the European states royal regulation of industry and trade faced greater difficulties, but there is evidence in the economic legislation of the Western European monarchies, especially of England and France, of a kind of precocious mercantilism in this period, although the economic policies of royal governments were frequently dictated as much by diplomatic, political or fiscal interests as by purely economic aims. Whatever their motives, the increasingly frequent efforts of the kings of England and France and other European states to encourage native industry, to protect their merchants by excluding foreign competition or by negotiating trade treaties, to build up their merchant marine and so to regulate foreign trade as to create a favorable balance, all show a growing awareness on the part of royal governments of their responsibility for what publicists were beginning to call the common weal. Debates in Parliament and such popular pamphlets as the *Libelle of Englyshe Polycye* also indicate the growth of an economic nationalism more fully developed in theory than the limitations of administrative machinery made possible in practice.

In essence the system later known as mercantilism was simply the protective and regulative economic policy of the medieval cities transferred to the larger area of the national state. It was a natural accompaniment of the growth of central government at the expense of feudal and urban particularism, and, at the same time, it reflected in the economic sphere the breakup of medieval Christendom into potentially hostile national units, which was one of the most striking characteristics of this period. But before the mercantilist system of regulation and control on a national scale could be put into practice effectively — or as effectively as was ever possible — it was necessary to abolish many ancient local privileges, to do away with the innumerable tolls that impeded internal trade, and to create an administrative machinery capable of carrying out the directives of the central government. The monarchs of this period, still preoccupied with the problem of consolidating their political power within the state and of defending their dynastic interests, could make no more than occasional gestures in the direction of enforcing a national economic policy. Nor were those efforts always well-advised. Still, ineffective as it frequently was, the activity of royal governments was now a factor to be taken into consideration in assessing the changing economic fortunes of the European states.

XIII

The Consolidation of the Territorial and National States and the Wars in Italy

A long tradition of historical periodization has established the year 1453 as a turning point in European history. Few historians, it is true, would now ascribe to the fall of Constantinople the cataclysmic significance accorded to it by an older historical school. Yet, when we remember that the Hundred Years' War was finally concluded in the same year, and that a long period of warfare in Italy ended in the following year with the Peace of Lodi, we may well regard the years around the middle of the century as marking the end of an era in political history. The period which it brought to a close had witnessed the first stage in the transition from the medieval to the modern state in Western Europe; from commune to territorial state in Italy, and from feudal to monarchical state in France and England, and to territorial principality in Germany and the Netherlands. The next four decades were relatively free from major wars, and were characterized by an upward trend in economic activity after a century or more of stagnation or recession. The balance of both economic and political power was shifting to the disadvantage of Italy, as the rulers of the larger European states took advantage of the breathing space to consolidate their territory and to establish their government on a more secure foundation. In this second stage in the transition to the modern state, dynastic interests predominated over all others, for feudalism had ceased to form an adequate framework for political life, and national consciousness was not yet strong enough to replace it. All the cohesive forces in the state in this period — and for many decades to come — were concentrated upon the person of the prince, and the interests of the state were subordinated to, or were regarded as identical with, those of the ruling dynasty. It was around the person of the prince that the European states consolidated their territories and centralized their governments in the decades of relative international stability after 1453, and it was dynastic claims that precipitated a new era of international warfare after 1494.

A. ITALY FROM THE PEACE OF LODI TO THE FIRST FRENCH INVASION (1454–94): THE ERA OF EQUILIBRIUM

The Peace of Lodi marked the conclusion of a long period of almost uninterrupted warfare, during which Milan, Venice and Florence had expanded to form territorial states, while successive popes had struggled to prevent their aggressive neighbors from annexing parts of the Papal States, and the ambitions of the kings of Naples had injected an unpredictable element into every Italian crisis. It also introduced a new era of relatively stable equilibrium, marred, indeed, by numerous brush-fire wars, but by no great conflagration for forty years. There were now five large territorial states in the Italian peninsula, and a similar number of smaller states more or less dependent on their more powerful neighbors. In the north, the Duchy of Milan and the Republic of Venice divided Lombardy between them, except for the little buffer state of Mantua under the *condottieri* marquises of the House of Gonzaga. Further south, Florence had established a territorial state in Tuscany, weak in military force, but a power in international finance. Its wealth, combined with the diplomatic skill of three generations of the Medici family, won for it a place in the state system of Italy out of proportion to its real power. Compared to it the other two surviving Tuscan republics, Siena and Lucca, were insignificant as factors in the balance of power. Surrounding Tuscany on three sides, the Papal States stretched eastward from Rome across central Italy, then northward along the Adriatic and inland to the north of Tuscany. Only the territories of the House of Este — Modena, Reggio and Ferrara, the last a feudatory of the papacy —

separated the Papal States from the two aggressive northern powers, Milan and Venice. The fifth large state, the Kingdom of Naples, occupied the remainder of the peninsula to the south.

Following the Peace of Lodi the five major states made an unprecedented effort to establish a stable state system in Italy. In 1455 they formed a league, into which the lesser states were later drawn. The signatories of the pact pledged themselves to come to the aid of any one of them threatened by aggression from a foreign power or from any other member of the league. The aim of the league was to establish a political equilibrium in Italy, which would maintain the territorial *status quo* and prevent suicidal warfare. A pious hope was also expressed that the Italian states might thus be freed to take part in a crusade against the Turks; but in this respect the league was a complete failure. Although Venice later fought gallantly to preserve her colonial empire in the Levant, the Italian states were no more ready than those of the rest of Europe to sacrifice their immediate interests in common action against the infidel for the protection of Christendom. In the less openly avowed — and perhaps never very clearly conceived — purpose of presenting a solid front in face of a possible French invasion or a reassertion of the imperial claims in Italy, the state system thus established was more successful. The conclusion of the Hundred Years' War made the threat of French intervention a more real menace than it had been, and for the next forty years it hung like a cloud over the northern horizon until the storm finally broke in 1494. A French invasion might at any time be directed against the Kingdom of Naples, where the second Angevin dynasty still asserted its claim to the throne against the usurping House of Aragon. The French kings were always ready, when convenient, to support their cousins' claims, and when, in 1481, the Angevin claim reverted with the extinction of the family to the French crown their interest became more direct. At the same time, a French invasion might equally well be directed against Milan, where the dukes of Orléans maintained a hereditary claim to the duchy through their ancestress, Valentina Visconti, only daughter of Giangaleazzo. After the death of Filippo Maria in 1447, they were the nearest legitimate descendants of the Visconti line. That these dynastic claims were not pressed sooner was doubtless due primarily to the fact that Charles VII and Louis XI were preoccupied with the problem of consolidating their government at home, but also in part because the equilibrium of the Italian states gave them little encouragement to invade. Some at least of the Italian statesmen of this era — Francesco Sforza and Cosimo de' Medici, for example, and above all Lorenzo de' Medici — realized that French conquest of any Italian state would threaten the liberty of all, and, further, that any serious disturbance of the balance of power in Italy would open the way to French intervention, since any state left isolated against its enemies would inevitably call in the foreigner to redress the balance.

The formation of the league does, indeed, seem to indicate a certain awareness of a community of interest among the Italian states. The appearance of Italian solidarity, however, was largely illusory. The Italian League was designed less to present a united front against foreign invasion than to prevent any one Italian power from rising to a position of hegemony in the peninsula. This was the danger that the Italian statesmen, mindful of the spectacular conquests of Giangaleazzo Visconti and the ambitious designs of Venice and the kings of Naples, were anxious to guard against. Weary of war, they desired only to maintain the *status quo*, except when it could be broken to their own advantage, and their only common bond was their recognition of the fact that the conquest of any one state by another threatened the liberty of all. Even this, however, was not strong enough to prevent them from seizing any immediate advantage that presented itself. The Italian League was thus in no sense a step in the direction of Italian unity, but rather a guarantee that unity would not be forced upon Italy by the expansion of any one state to national proportions. The league, as a formal entity, did not last long; but the political equilibrium was maintained, despite temporary shifts in the balance, until the French invasions. In general Venice and Milan offset one another in the north, Naples and the papacy in the south. Milan and Naples, whose spheres of influence did not conflict, generally remained on friendly terms. Florence, jealous of Venetian commercial rivalry and suspicious of any strengthening of papal power in the States of the Church which surrounded Tuscany on three sides, generally threw in her lot with Naples and Milan, thus forming a kind of triple alliance, which was broken on only one nearly disastrous occasion and which served as a steadying element in the uncertain equilibrium of Italy.

Until his death in 1465, Francesco Sforza worked consistently to maintain the balance of power in Italy in close association with Cosimo de' Medici. The old *condottiere* needed a period of peace to establish his new dynasty in the Duchy of Milan. His only aggressive act was to add Genoa to his domain. The ancient commercial republic had for years been torn by civil strife and in 1458 sought internal peace by placing itself under the sovereignty of France. The French governor, Jean d'Anjou, however, used his position simply as a base from which to press his family's claims against Naples, and was driven out by a popular rebellion in 1461. After a further period of anarchy, the Genoese accepted Sforza as their lord, and Louis XI, busy with affairs at home, legalized the accomplished fact by bestowing Genoa on Sforza as a fief. Under the Sforza dynasty the Milanese duchy entered on a new era of prosperity. The introduction of rice-growing together with irrigation from the newly constructed Martesana canal brought a revival of agriculture, while the growing silk industry added to the prosperity of the cities. The Sforza dukes were able to draw an immense income from their territory in the form of taxes without goading their people to revolt, and they used that income to strengthen the governmental machinery of the state and to make Milan a leading center of Renaissance culture.

The ducal government was so firmly established by the time of Francesco's death that it survived through a decade of misrule under his son, Galeazzo Maria, who had all the vices but few of the virtues of the Renaissance despot. Even his assassination in 1476 did not lead to a popular rising against the dynasty. Instead his young son, Giangaleazzo, aged eight, was allowed to succeed peacefully to the duchy under the regency of his mother and of Cicco Simonetta, the most trusted counsellor of the two preceding dukes. The chief danger to the new régime came not from the people but from a faction of malcontent nobles led by a brother of the late duke, Ludovico Sforza, called "Il Moro." After three years of turmoil Ludovico succeeded in ousting the duchess and Simonetta with Neapolitan aid, and established himself as regent and effective ruler of Milan. Under his rule Milan reached the height of its economic and cultural flowering, but Il Moro's position became increasingly precarious after the young duke came of age. To make matters worse, Il Moro made the mistake of marrying Giangaleazzo to Isabella of Aragon, a grand-daughter of King Ferrante of Naples, in the hope that it would help to cement the traditional Neapolitan-Milanese alliance. To his chagrin he found the young duchess and her Neapolitan kinfolk intriguing to oust him from the regency and to restore the government to the titular duke. They had every reason to feel confident that they could manage that feeble and indolent young man and take the government into their own hands. Had Lorenzo de' Medici lived a little longer his influence might just possibly have prevented a breach in the triple alliance on which the equilibrium of Italy depended, but after his death in 1492 his son, Piero, abandoned the traditional policy of his house and supported the Neapolitan claims. Il Moro thus found himself without allies, and called in France to redress the balance, thereby opening the floodgates of invasion and sealing the doom of Italian liberty. The young King Charles VIII may have needed little encouragement to press his claims to the throne of Naples, but Il Moro must bear the responsibility for presenting the occasion for the long-delayed catastrophe.

The history of the Venetian Republic in these years may be summarized more briefly. Although the conquest of a mainland state in the eastern half of Lombardy and around the head of the Adriatic had made Venice one of the great Italian powers, her energies were directed primarily toward defending her commercial and colonial empire in the Levant. During the long war against the Turks, 1463–79, her rôle in Italian politics was largely a passive one. The acquisitive instincts of her ruling oligarchy, however, made her a constant threat to her neighbors on the Adriatic. The stability and efficiency of her government aroused admiration and envy in the other Italian states, while the ruthlessness of her diplomacy and her tendency to play a lone hand also aroused universal fear and distrust. It was fear of Venice as much as anything else that held the triple alliance of Milan, Florence and Naples together.

To a very large extent the history of Florence in this period is the story of its unofficial ruling family, the Medici. Cosimo *Pater Patriae* had been one of the principal architects of the Peace of Lodi and the Italian League and, fully aware of the military weakness of the republic, he labored for the remaining decade of his life to preserve the balance of power on which the security of his state clearly depended. Florence was now entering on a period of rising prosperity. The decline of her woollen industry was at least partially compensated by a vigorous growth in the manufacture of fine silk fabrics, and after 1453 Florentine merchants were beginning to replace the Venetians in trade with Constantinople and to rival them in Alexandria. Having secured a seaport by the conquest of Pisa during the Albizzi régime, Florence was becoming a power in the maritime commerce of the Mediterranean. Peace and prosperity tended to make the Florentine people content with Medici leadership, but at the same time the greater sense of security left envious members of the plutocracy free to conspire against the Medici dictatorship in the hope of replacing it with a dictatorship of their own. Shortly after the Peace of Lodi and again during the reign of Cosimo's gout-ridden son, Piero (1464–69), attempts were made to break the Medici hold on the government by restoring the old system of election by lot. In both instances the Medici weathered the storm and succeeded in re-establishing the system which Cosimo had introduced of having the names of the *gonfaloniere* and priors selected by hand from the purses by a carefully screened committee of *accopiatori*. So long as the Medici could control the elections through the *accopiatori*, their unconstitutional control of the government was reasonably secure.

The peaceful accession to power of Piero's twenty-year-old son, Lorenzo, in 1469, is proof that the lordship of the Medici was both firmly established and generally popular. From the beginning Lorenzo displayed, despite his youth, a political virtuosity more flamboyant, if no less astute, than that of his grandfather. Gifted with great personal charm, a generous and discriminating patron of art and letters, and himself a poet of considerable talent, Lorenzo identified himself with all the cultural aspirations of his city, and inspired a warmer loyalty than did either of his predecessors. "Il Magnifico," as the Florentines called him for lack of a more formal title, was also more clearly the prince. With his marriage to Clarice Orsini, he entered the circle of the great noble families of Italy, and in his diplomatic negotiations with other powers he acted as the actual ruler of his state. Much of his power, indeed, depended upon the recognition by the Florentine people of the fact that, in the precarious balance of Italian power politics, the republic needed a prince, *de facto* if not *de jure*, to represent her interests. This function Lorenzo fulfilled with, on the whole, remarkable success.

The only serious crisis of his reign was precipitated by the ambitious designs of Pope Sixtus IV, who in 1474 secured the lordship of Imola for his nephew Girolamo Riario. It was clear that the pope intended, not merely to found a dynastic state for his family in the Romagna, but also to use it as a base for the assertion of papal authority in that always half-independent part of the Papal States. The Florentine people had long considered the neighboring Romagna as within their sphere of influence, and they regarded any strengthening of papal authority there as a threat to their own frontiers. Venice and Milan, too, were close enough to the northern borders of the Papal States to fear the growth of a strong power there. Under these circumstances, Lorenzo abandoned the old triple alliance and formed a new one with Milan and Venice. This move not only upset the traditional balance of power, forcing the papacy and Naples into a balancing alliance, but also made Sixtus implacably hostile to Lorenzo. Rome now became the rallying point for all Lorenzo's enemies, including some members of the Florentine patriciate who were jealous of the Medici. In this superheated atmosphere Girolamo Riario and Francesco Pazzi, the Roman representative of one of the oldest Florentine banking houses, hatched a plot to assassinate Lorenzo and his brother, Giuliano, and to seize the government of Florence. Later they were joined by a personal enemy of Lorenzo, Francesco Salviati, Archbishop of Pisa, and other malcontents. The plot was put into effect on a Sunday in 1478; the scene, the cathedral of Florence; the time, the celebration of High Mass; the signal for the assault, the ringing of the sacring bell at the elevation of the Host. The choice of such a time and place was dictated by the difficulty of getting the two brothers together in a vulnerable position at any other time, but it was nevertheless ill-advised. At the last moment the mercenary who had been hired to assassinate Lorenzo objected to the sacrilege, and had to be replaced by two priests who bungled the job. Pazzi himself struck down Giuliano and stabbed him to death, but Lorenzo, although wounded, escaped. Meanwhile, the archbishop, whose share in the execution of the plot was to raise a popular revolt, occupy the *Palazzo Pubblico* and seize the government, found the people solidly loyal to the Medici. Together with such others of the conspirators as could be found, he was seized by the angry mob and hanged from the windows of the *Palazzo*.

The immediate effect of the Pazzi conspiracy was to entrench Lorenzo more firmly than ever in the affections of his people. Had the plot succeeded it would not have meant the restoration of republican liberty, but merely the replacing of the Medici domination by the Pazzi faction in alliance with a foreign power. Lorenzo's danger, however, did not end with the extermination of the conspirators. Sixtus IV now took up the attack. He excommunicated Lorenzo, and laid an interdict on Tuscany in punishment for the execution of the archbishop, and followed this by open war against Florence in alliance with the King of Naples. Lorenzo's allies, Milan and Venice, honored their pact with him in principle; but Milan was paralyzed by the recent death of Galeazzo Maria Sforza and the struggle of Il Moro for the regency, while Venice was fully absorbed in her war with the Turks. By the end of 1479 the situation of Florence, threatened by papal and Neapolitan troops, was desperate. At this point Lorenzo resorted to a bold stroke of diplomacy. Convinced that it was not really to the advantage of Naples to upset the Italian balance of power by strengthening the Papal States at the expense of Florence, he set out for Naples in December to present his argument in person to King Ferrante. To the Florentines he seemed to be walking into the lions' den, and he was certainly staking much, perhaps his life, on a gambler's chance. The way had been prepared for him, however, by Ludovico Il Moro, who had just been established as regent of Milan with Neapolitan aid, and Ferrante was weary of fighting the pope's battles. After two months of negotiation, Ferrante signed a treaty of peace with Florence, which was followed by a renewal of the old triple alliance. The situation was once more normal, and so it remained till after Lorenzo's death. When, in 1482, Venice and the pope united in an attack on Ferrara, the triple alliance stood firm in opposition and maintained the *status quo*.

During the last decade of his life, Lorenzo consolidated his position in Florence and established more firmly the status of his family as a princely house. The marriage of two of his daughters to scions of wealthy Florentine families strengthened his position at home, while the marriage of his heir, Piero, to an Orsini and of his third daughter to Franceschetto Cybo, son of Pope Innocent VIII, secured further recognition for his dynasty abroad. His close family alliance with Innocent also enabled him to plant his younger son, Giovanni (later Pope Leo X) in the College of Cardinals at the uncanonical age of seventeen. Meanwhile, Lorenzo had taken advantage of the prestige he gained by his dramatic Neapolitan venture to secure a constitutional base for his hold on the Florentine government. Immediately after his return from Naples, he instigated the creation of a new Council of Seventy, composed of picked Medicean supporters, who were to serve for life and fill vacancies by co-optation. This new council took over the powers of the older councils, nominated the *gonfaloniere* and priors, and through subcommittees directly controlled foreign and military affairs, finance and trade. Il Magnifico was still not a titular prince, but his control of the Seventy and the sweeping powers granted to them gave him an almost absolute authority. In these last years his most serious troubles were financial. Among Lorenzo's many talents that of business management was not conspicuous. The Medici bank was failing, while his expenses as the uncrowned prince of Florence were rising. Since a large part of his expenses were incurred in the public interest and in what was in everything but name a public capacity, Lorenzo felt justified in supplementing his income from the public funds. Just how and to what extent he did so is not entirely clear, but since no question of his right to an official income would have arisen had he been a titular prince, the Florentine people who accepted his rule and profited by his diplomatic skill had little reason to grumble.

As the relations of Florence with the papacy have indicated, the States of the Church formed throughout this period an essential ingredient in the political equilibrium of Italy, and the history of the papacy itself is inextricably bound up with that of the other Italian powers. After their final triumph over the Conciliar Movement in mid-century, the popes were able to restore the theory of papal monarchy within the Church and to centralize still further their fiscal and administrative bureaucracy. But this was achieved at the cost of concordats or agreements with the secular states of Europe, in which the papacy negotiated as one of the European powers and thereby sacrificed something of its claim to universal authority. Having thus adjusted their relations with the major secular states, the popes of the second half of the fifteenth century concentrated their attention on the political problems arising from their position as Italian princes. The political history of the papacy in this period may therefore be more conveniently treated as part of the history of Italy than, as in the previous period, in the wider context of international affairs.

As rulers of a territorial state the popes had to deal with two major problems. First of all they had to defend their territory from the nibbling aggression of the other powers around their poorly defended frontiers. It was this need that drew the popes into the balance-of-power system of Italian politics and gave them an interest, to which their own acquisitiveness sometimes blinded them, in maintaining the territorial *status quo*. In the second place, they had still to transform their semi-feudal suzerainty into an effective monarchy. In this respect, the Papal States had lagged behind the other territorial states of Italy, with the possible exception of the Kingdom of Naples. During the fourteenth and early fifteenth centuries, indeed, the popes had been able to maintain their nominal authority only by recognizing the existence of the numerous petty lordships and free communes that had sprung up throughout their states. By the middle of the fifteenth century, the pope's authority was fairly well established in Rome and the surrounding area on the western seaboard, although even there the great Colonna, Orsini and Savelli clans still retained much of their old feudal independence, fought one another and on occasion gave active aid to the pope's enemies. Further eastward in Umbria and across the Apennines in the Marches of Ancona, the semi-autonomous communes and lordships were mostly too small to cause serious trouble. In the Romagna, on the other hand, a number of well-established princely dynasties were strong enough to defy the pope on occasion, and at any time paid him little more than lip service. This was the northeastern section of the Papal States, lying between Tuscany and the Adriatic, and parts of it were regarded as within their sphere of influence by Florence, Milan and Venice. The latter, indeed, had seized and held Ravenna. Compared to the Tuscan and Lombard states the papal territories were mostly poor, with little commerce or industry. The popes were able to draw considerable income from the alum mines discovered at Tolfa after the middle of the century, but the weakness of their government prevented the collection of taxes in sufficient quantity to meet the cost of the mercenary troops that would have been needed to establish their authority more firmly.

Still a third problem absorbed much of the attention of every pope after the middle of the century. Like the other princes of their age they were much concerned with the aggrandizement of their families. But, since their own office could not be made hereditary, the best they could do was to use the papal authority while they had it to enrich their relatives by conferring high ecclesiastical offices upon them, by placing their nephews in the College of Cardinals or in principalities in the Papal States, or by arranging marriages for them with the princely houses of Italy. To this end they frequently sacrificed the long-term interests of the papal monarchy. It is true that establishing a nephew in one of the semi-independent lordships in the Romagna or arranging a marriage alliance with one of the other Italian powers might immediately strengthen the pope's position at home and abroad; but any advantage to the papacy passed with the death of the pope, and the next pope was left with a heritage of his predecessors' greedy *nepoti*. One of the most pernicious effects of this unbridled nepotism was that it packed the College of Cardinals with an accumulation of papal nephews. At the same time, their deep involvement in Italian politics forced the popes for diplomatic reasons to nominate to the cardinalate one or two members of every princely house in Italy as well as of the great Roman noble families. It was generally found expedient, too, to nominate representatives of the republics of Venice and Florence and of each of the great European states. The college thus became an essentially diplomatic body, its members primarily concerned with their dynastic or national interests. It should not be surprising, then, that the popes elected from this body were men more concerned with politics and family ambition than with the spiritual leadership of Christendom.

A genuine effort to lead Europe in a crusade against the Turks lent dignity to the pontificate of the first two popes who took office after the fall of Constantinople, although both were also much interested in the advancement of their families and left nephews in the College of Cardinals. During a brief reign Calixtus III (1455–58), a Spaniard of the Borgia family, labored to organize a crusade, and himself drew heavily on the papal resources to build a fleet for action in the Aegean. His successor, Pius II (1458–64), carried on the work with invincible optimism, hoping against all probability that the Italian states and the European sovereigns could be moved to sacrifice their particular interests and to abandon their mutual animosities in common action against the advancing infidel. As a preliminary step Pius summoned the kings and princes of Europe to a congress at Mantua in 1459. The attendance at the congress was disappointingly small. The great powers were slow to send representatives, and when these did arrive they were reluctant to make binding promises or had not been empowered to do so. Nevertheless the pope, persuaded by his own eloquence that the princes would respond, issued a bull calling for a crusade and for the collection of a tenth of their income from the clergy and of one-thirtieth from the laity throughout the Church. Three years passed in delays and evasions, while the tithe collected with much grumbling was largely diverted to the treasuries of the states, and the fleet constructed for the crusade became involved in an Angevin-Neapolitan war. Finally, Pius made a last desperate appeal to the crusaders to meet at Ancona in 1464, and himself promised to lead them. Ill and prematurely aged though he was, the pope journeyed across the Apennines in the summer heat, only to find at Ancona no more than a few bands of poorly equipped and mutinous soldiers. The fleet promised by Venice finally arrived, but the dying pope had lost hope. Two days later he was dead and the crusade died with him.

Thereafter pope after pope made halfhearted gestures toward organizing a crusade, but with no practical result. The crusading ardor of the Middle Ages could not be revived, nor could the sense of Christian unity that had made the great crusades possible be restored at this late date. The pope was no longer the effective leader of a united Catholic Christendom; national interests had replaced consciousness of membership in the *Respublica Christiana;* and the rulers of the European states, however much they might deplore the Turkish conquests, had more immediate and pressing concerns at home. If the fall of Constantinople symbolized the end of an era, so, too, did the fiasco at Ancona.

Pius II has always attracted more attention from historians than the tragic futility of his pontificate seems to warrant. The reason, no doubt, is that his many-sided personality seems to typify to an unusual degree much that was ambiguous in the intellectual and spiritual atmosphere of this transitional age. As Aeneas Silvius Piccolomini, he had already won for himself an international reputation before he took holy orders at the age of forty and began his rapid rise in the hierarchy. He was widely known as a poet, humanist, novelist and historian, but also as a supple diplomat and eloquent orator, who had served in turn the Council of Basel and the Emperor Frederick III. Few men of his age had a broader or more intimate knowledge of the entire European scene. Yet, for all his experience and his clear-sighted analysis of political reality, he failed to recognize the fact of the disintegration of Christendom into a congeries of national entities and sovereign states. Just as he clung to the anachronistic hope of uniting Europe in a crusade, so he retained a thoroughly medieval concept of the Empire as a universal state. His concept of the papacy was also at least partly anachronistic. He addressed the Congress of Mantua as though he were still the recognized head of a united Christendom; and at the conclusion of the council he issued the bull *Execrabilis* reasserting the theory of papal supremacy and denouncing as an abominable error the practice of appealing from a pope to a future General Council. Yet, while asserting the universality of the Church and the papacy, he was deeply absorbed in Italian politics, and in his capacity as an Italian prince he frittered away a large part of his pontificate in conflict with his rebellious subject, the terrible Sigismondo Malatesta, lord of Rimini, or in futile negotiations with the other Italian powers. Despite the European range of his experience, he remained an Italian. If there was in his policy any conflict between the head of the universal Church and the Italian prince, he seemed unaware of it, just as he was unaware of any conflict between the Pius and the Aeneas in his own character. Perhaps, after all, the clue to the personality of this clever and versatile man is simply the essential frivolity, the naïve vanity and infinite capacity for self-deception that are evident on every page of his own account of his pontificate, the *Commentaries,* which form one of the most revealing autobiographies of this period.

The next pontificate, that of Paul II (1464–71), a Venetian nephew of Eugenius IV, was relatively uneventful; but with the accession of Sixtus IV (1471–84) the papacy became the storm center of Italian politics for more than a decade. More completely than any of his predecessors, Sixtus functioned as an Italian prince, incidentally transforming the curia into a princely court, a center of scandalous luxury, if also of discriminating patronage of art. Two ruling ambitions dominated his pontificate: to strengthen the temporal power of the papacy within the Papal States and in relation to the other Italian powers and to establish his numerous relatives in positions of wealth and power. These two ambitions he strove to co-ordinate by making systematic nepotism an instrument for the aggrandizement of the papal monarchy. Five of his nephews and one grand-nephew were made cardinals, of whom one, Giuliano della Rovere, remained for three decades a power in papal politics and was eventually elected pope as Julius II. His lay nephews he used to form marriage alliances with reigning houses and to found dynasties. Two nephews married into the royal family of Naples, thereby winning King Ferrante for a time away from the triple alliance; a third married a natural daughter of the Duke of Milan and still another the heiress of the Duke of Urbino. For his favorite lay nephew, Girolamo Riario, Sixtus procured the lordship of Imola as a center from which to expand papal authority in the Romagna. The story of the Pazzi conspiracy and the war with Florence which resulted from this move has already been told. In 1481 Girolamo added Forlì to his domain, and in the following year his further ambitions drew the pope and Venice into a war to dismember Ferrara. When the triple alliance rallied to the support of Ferrara, the pope switched sides in the hope of wresting Ravenna and Cervia from Venice. Meanwhile the turbulent old pope was waging a violent feud against the Colonna family in a vain effort to rid Rome of their disturbing influence. In none of his grand designs was Sixtus successful, but he came close enough to success to demonstrate the potential strength of the papacy as a factor in Italian politics. That potential remained in abeyance during the undistinguished pontificate of his successor, Innocent VIII (1484–92), but was revived thereafter with greater effect by Alexander VI.

To the south of the Papal States, the Kingdom of Naples remained what it had been for generations, a poverty-stricken and unruly feudal state. Under Alfonso of Aragon the royal government was established somewhat more firmly, but the great barons were still rebellious and resentful of domination by a foreign dynasty. During the long reign of Alfonso's illegitimate son, Ferrante (1458–94), who was weakened by the fact that his kingdom was now separated from Sicily and Aragon, the barons were more than once in open rebellion in alliance either with the Angevin claimant to the throne or with the pope. Relations between the kings of Naples and the popes were always subject to strain because of the ancient papal claim to overlordship over the kingdom, which they still regarded as a vassal state. Naples was also traditionally hostile to Venice because of the republic's efforts to establish her hegemony in the Adriatic. During most of this period, then, Naples remained a partner in the triple alliance with Florence and Milan, until the break with Ludovico Il Moro and Ferrante's death in 1494 combined to precipitate the first French invasion.

B. The Great European States and their Dynasties: the Era of Consolidation and Centralization

While the Italian states were enjoying a period of stability and equilibrium, elsewhere in Europe developments were taking place which came close to completing the transition from feudalism to absolute monarchy and, at the same time, created a new balance of power in Europe which overshadowed the smaller state system of Italy and menaced its very existence. The most general characteristics of this period were, first, the centralization of government and the consolidation of territory under absolute monarchies and, second, a realignment of the European states as the result of dynastic marriages and the reassertion of dynastic claims. In all the countries except Spain, which now emerged for the first time as a European power, the developments of this period were largely the continuation of processes already begun and described in an earlier chapter. We may, therefore, review their history somewhat more briefly, concentrating attention on changing conditions, while at the same time noting the political events and personalities, without which the history of the age would be incomplete.

France

The transformation of France from a feudal to a monarchical state was a long, slow process, which was alternately accelerated and retarded by the events of the Hundred Years' War and by the factional strife which filled the reign of the hapless King Charles VI and the early years of Charles VII. At the end of the war, the monarchy had freed itself from any effective constitutional limitation upon its authority; it had gained the right to impose taxes without the consent of the Estates General; and it had at its disposal a formidable standing army. France had been devastated and desperately impoverished by the war. Its people were weary of war, and all except the great feudatories and their followers, who had exploited the prevailing anarchy to their own advantage, looked to the king to restore order. The monarchy was still ill-provided with actual means to enforce its authority, but it had asserted its control of the fiscal and military resources of the kingdom, and it was the only power in France capable of governing. France, moreover, had gained a new national solidarity with the expulsion of the English. For the first time in nearly four hundred years no part of France except the city of Calais was under the jurisdiction of a foreign king. The last stages of the war, too, illuminated by the flaming spirit of the Maid of Orléans, had bred in Frenchmen a new sense of national identity, incomplete though it still was.

Nevertheless, France was still not a united state, nor was the authority of the royal government coterminous with the national frontiers, which were also considerably more restricted than those of modern France. The royal domain, the territory directly under the authority of the crown, included in 1453 only about half the kingdom. Outside it were the great fiefs in the hands of ancient feudal families and the appanages of cadet branches of the Capetian house — Anjou, Orléans, Bourbon and Burgundy. In most of these fiefs the king had already established his right to collect taxes, and royal officers were normally able to exercise a limited but growing jurisdiction. Brittany, however, was practically independent, owing only the most formal allegiance to the crown. The Duchy of Burgundy and the other French fiefs held by the Burgundian dukes were even further removed from royal control. The most important task now facing the French monarchy was thus the consolidation of the kingdom by the incorporation of these outstanding fiefs and appanages into the territory subject to the central government, and the achievement of that task, almost complete by the end of the century, marks the second stage in the evolution from medieval to modern France.

The struggle to subdue the independent and rebellious feudatories occupied most of the reign of Louis XI (1461–83). In many ways this strange and enigmatic king was well equipped by nature for the rôle he had to play. He had great native shrewdness, reinforced by indefatigable energy, and uninhibited by moral scruples of any kind. He had also an unequalled knowledge of his country and its people, a firm grasp on present reality and a clear vision of the future of the monarchy. At the same time, he showed glaring defects of character that more than once came close to ruining his chances of success. He was suspicious, treacherous, cruel and vindictive, extravagant and miserly by turns, and his love of deception for its own sake sometimes led him to spin a web of intrigue so tangled as to defeat its own ends. He offended the nobles by his meanness and his contempt for chivalric pageantry, while at the same time he aroused resentment among the bourgeoisie by the high taxes needed to finance his foreign policy. His vindictiveness and his tyrannical methods antagonized all his most powerful vassals as well as the princes of the blood, and in 1465 they formed a coalition, known as the League of the Common Weal, in open revolt against him. Had the League been able to secure support from the bourgeoisie and the lesser nobles the revolt might have been successful. As it was, Louis was forced to make concessions to the leaders of the League, including the Duke of Burgundy, to end the civil war. Even then disorder among the nobles of the outlying fiefs continued for many years, while the king concentrated his attention on the recovery of the Burgundian domains within the French frontiers.

When Louis came to the throne, the aged Duke Philip the Good ruled an independent principality which included the Duchy of Burgundy and the Counties of Flanders and Artois, for which he no longer did homage to the King of France, as well as the County of Burgundy, Luxemburg and the Netherland provinces which lay within the Holy Roman Empire. The "Grand Duke of the West," the richest prince in Christendom, was in fact a king in all but name, and his court, the most brilliant in Europe, overshadowed that of the king in Paris. At the very beginning of his reign Louis won a temporary advantage by persuading Philip to sell him the strategically important Somme towns, which had been ceded to Philip in 1435 as part of the price for his abandoning the English alliance. The high taxes needed to raise the large sum required for the purchase, however, helped to precipitate the War of the Common Weal, and Louis had to surrender the towns again as the price demanded by Philip's son, Charles the Bold, for abandoning the League. Louis never forgave Charles for his defeat, and when that rash and ambitious prince succeeded his father in 1467 war between them was inevitable, although it was a war fought on the king's part more by diplomacy and intrigue than by military force. Louis took full advantage of the duke's ambitious designs to ring him around with enemies. Charles was determined to form a solid middle kingdom between France and the Empire by seizing Alsace and Lorraine, and thus linking the Duchy and County of Burgundy with Luxemburg and the Netherlands. His conquest of these upper Rhineland territories alarmed the Swiss Confederation, and gave Louis the opportunity to use the formidable Swiss infantry against his enemy. Although he had signed a formal truce with Charles in 1475, Louis poured money into the Swiss cantons, furnished the Duke of Lorraine with funds to hire mercenary troops, and so set the stage for the defeat and death of Charles at Nancy in 1477.

The death of Charles the Bold left the Burgundian state leaderless for the moment and exhausted by the war. His daughter and heiress, Mary, sought aid by marrying Maximilian of Hapsburg, the son of the Emperor Frederick III, but even with his help she was unable to defend all her possessions. Louis now pressed the war with all his forces, and it was only after the death of Mary in 1482 that the war came to an end, with both sides exhausted. The Treaty of Arras signed in that year by Louis and Maximilian, who was acting as regent for his infant son, Philip, gave Louis Picardy and the Somme towns and, most important of all, the Duchy of Burgundy, which was now incorporated into the royal domain.

Meanwhile, in the periods of truce in his war with Burgundy, Louis had succeeded in subduing his rebellious feudatories. The Armagnac lands were confiscated and broken up. The princes of the blood were reduced to the position of docile pensioners, and in 1481, with the death of the last member of the direct line of the House of Anjou, the Angevin appanage, together with Provence and the Angevin claims to the Kingdom of Naples, reverted to the crown. Brittany, however, retained its independence, and the task of absorbing it into the domains of the crown was left to Louis's successor.

When Charles VIII (1483–98) came to the throne he was only thirteen years old, a feeble child who showed little evidence of having inherited any of his father's qualities, good or bad. His older sister, Anne of Beaujeu, however, a forceful woman whom Louis had regarded as the least foolish of a foolish sex, acted as regent until Charles was full-grown and guided the government through the troubled years of the king's minority. As might have been expected, the great nobles took advantage of the death of the terrible old king to break into rebellion, led by Francis, Duke of Brittany. The old Celtic duchy with a language of its own had never become fully French. The Breton dukes had always regarded themselves as sovereign in their own duchy. They admitted no royal officers into their domain; their subjects paid no royal taxes; and they followed a completely independent foreign policy. The size, military strength and strategic position of Brittany made it, when in alliance with foreign powers, a real menace to the security of France, and the regent accordingly devoted all her energies to subduing it. After a long and costly war she finally forced Francis to accept a humiliating peace treaty in 1488. But after the duke's death the same year, a new danger arose. The duchy was inherited by his daughter Anne, who at once accepted an offer of marriage from Maximilian. Such a marriage alliance, uniting Brittany with the Netherlands under the House of Hapsburg, would have been a disaster for France, offsetting the recovery of Burgundy. Anne of Beaujeu acted promptly. Invading Brittany with a large army in 1491, she forced the Duchess Anne to renounce her betrothal to Maxmilian and instead to marry Charles VIII. Brittany was thus at last brought under the French crown, and the consolidation of France was almost complete.

The acquisition of Brittany and the suppression of the rebellious nobles left Charles VIII undisputed master of France, and free to undertake the grandiose designs that appealed to his romantic soul and feeble intellect. He was free also from the restraining influence of his overpowering sister, who now resigned the regency and retired to her husband's Duchy of Bourbon. Thus left with absolute authority over a great national state, with a formidable standing army and a large income from taxes at his disposal, the young king was all too ready to listen to the ambassadors of Ludovico Il Moro of Milan and the greedy courtiers who encouraged him to assert his inherited claim to the Kingdom of Naples. To secure the neutrality of the other powers, Charles paid a pension to Henry VII of England, ceded Roussillon to Ferdinand of Aragon and surrendered his claims to Franche-Comté and Artois to Maximilian. Then, in 1494, he set out upon the first of those invasions of Italy which were to cost France so much and bring her so little in return through the next half-century.

The reigns of Louis XI and Charles VIII witnessed not only the territorial consolidation of France and the extension of royal authority to all parts of the realm, but also a steady, if less spectacular, growth in all the organs of royal government, and this growth continued at an accelerated pace under Louis XII (1498–1515) and Francis I (1515–47). There were few radical changes in the structure of government. Rather there was a continuation of an evolutionary process begun in the preceding centuries. The institutions of central government were elaborated and made more efficient, while local government was brought more directly under the control of the absolute monarchy. The administration of justice and the fiscal system were reformed by royal ordinances, and were made more systematic and more highly centralized. Above all, there was a notable increase in the number and the activity of royal officers throughout the kingdom. These greedy and aggressive officials of the crown were the instruments through which the absolute monarchy undermined feudal privileges, seigneurial jurisdictions and the autonomy of the towns.

Yet despite the triumph of centralization over particularism which the royal government achieved during this period, it did not succeed in imposing uniformity upon the laws and institutions of France. Many local variations of custom and jurisdiction, as well as inequalities in the weight of taxation and methods of collection, survived as a result of the piecemeal absorption of the various fiefs into the royal domain. In general the rising monarchy was content to assert its authority over local institutions of law and government without destroying them or replacing them with a uniform system. What the monarchy did achieve was to bring the government of the communes directly under the control of royal officers and to break the independent jurisdiction of the nobles. No longer able to rebel successfully, and stripped of the greater part of their authority over their dependents, the great nobles became courtiers and pensioners of the crown, finding in the pageantry and etiquette of the royal court a compensation for the loss of real power. The lesser nobility, too, impoverished by agricultural depression and the necessity of facing rising prices with a fixed income, sought careers in the royal army and took the king's pay.

Along with the nobility and the towns, the clergy and the Church fell increasingly under the control of the triumphant monarchy. The Conciliar Movement, more strongly entrenched in France than elsewhere, had undermined the theory of papal supremacy and had left a legacy in the form of Gallicanism, that is, a loosely defined theory of the administrative autonomy of the French Church, which the monarchy could pervert to its own uses. When the Council of Basel failed to reassert the conciliar theory successfully or to reform the Church, Charles VII had formulated the liberties of the Gallican Church in the Pragmatic Sanction of Bourges, which, among other limitations upon papal jurisdiction in France, denied the right of the papacy to tax the French clergy and, by reasserting the canonical rule of free election, denied also the right of papal provision to French benefices. While papal authority in France was being thus undermined, generations of royal ministers, nurtured on the principles of Roman Law, had been asserting the king's absolute sovereignty over all subjects and all institutions in France. From the point of view of the royal government, then, Gallicanism was scarcely more than a means of asserting the autonomy of the French Church in relation to the papacy, but not in relation to the monarchy. In practice, the Pragmatic Sanction did not, in fact, secure freedom of election or clerical immunity from taxation. In one way or another, by political pressure on the electors or, during periods of reconciliation with the papacy, by securing papal provision of royal candidates, the kings of this period exercised a *de facto* power of nomination to all important benefices in the French Church, and in the same devious fashion they also diverted the greater part of the taxation of the French Church into the royal treasury. Nomination of royal ministers to bishoprics tightened the alliance between the French hierarchy and the monarchy, while the kings also used abbeys *en commende* and other benefices to subsidize the scions of noble families and so render the nobility more dependent upon the crown. At times when they needed papal support for their diplomacy, the French kings were prepared to make concessions in theory but not in practice, and when at last in 1516 the Pragmatic Sanction was replaced by the Concordat of Bologna between Francis I and Leo X, the monarchy retained by agreement the control of the national Church which it had usurped in the preceding century.

In the towns the royal officers asserted an increasing authority not only over the communal government but also over the regulation of commerce and industry. Following its general policy of transforming existing local institutions into instruments of royal authority, the central government did not abolish the guilds and corporations, but was content to bring them under the control of royal officials. Further, where no guilds existed the government created new ones, and so extinguished the last traces of free industry. The government was, however, more successful in imposing regulation upon the economic life of France than in using its power to stimulate recovery after the terrible devastation of the late war. Its efforts at enforcing a mercantilist policy were sporadic and often misguided, and in the long run they probably did more to stifle than to encourage industry. Louis XI, whose bourgeois turn of mind made him unusually aware of the economic needs of the country, did, it is true, succeed in introducing the silk industry into France, and also did much to improve communications, encourage the growth of fairs, and remove toll barriers to internal trade. But his successors were more concerned with political than with economic problems, and, despite their efforts to impose uniformity, local variations in weights and measures, coinage, tolls and taxes still remained to hamper the free circulation of trade within the country. The rapid increase in general prosperity, which characterized the last years of the fifteenth century and the first decades of the sixteenth, owed less to royal regulation than to the re-establishment of order and security, which was the most important achievement of the monarchy.

SPAIN

In Spain the process of centralization and consolidation, which characterized the political history of this period, began later than in France, but once begun, it progressed more rapidly. It can scarcely be said to have begun, indeed, until after the union of the crowns of Aragon and Castile under Ferdinand and Isabella in 1479. Yet, when their joint reign ended, with the death of Isabella in 1504 followed by that of Ferdinand in 1516, Spain was well on the way to becoming, in fact if not yet in constitutional theory, a national state under an absolute monarchy — a state, moreover, destined to become in the sixteenth century the most powerful in Europe. Like the French monarchs of the fifteenth century, the Spanish rulers had to combat the turbulence of the nobles, the remnants of feudal particularism, and papal interference in the national Church. They had to restore order, recoup the royal finances and strengthen the machinery of central government. But, in addition, they had also to cope with conditions that were peculiar to the Spanish peninsula. Anarchy, such as that which flared up in France during the Burgundian-Armagnac feud and in England during the Wars of the Roses, had been chronic in Castile for more than two hundred years. The consolidation of Spain, moreover, involved no mere absorption of outstanding fiefs into the royal domain, but the union of a group of disparate kingdoms, each with its own traditions and institutions. It also involved the absorption or expulsion of two racial and religious minorities: the Moslem Moors and the Jews.

Since Spain remained almost completely isolated from the rest of Europe until the closing years of the fifteenth century, and since the Spanish kingdoms showed few signs of that early stage in the transition from the medieval to the modern state which characterized the period from 1300 to 1450, it did not seem necessary to consider Spain in the chapter dealing with the political developments of that period. Before discussing the rise of absolute monarchy under Ferdinand and Isabella, the unification of Spain and its emergence as a European power, we must therefore pause to review briefly the historical evolution which determined the conditions with which their Catholic Majesties had to deal.

The central theme in the history of medieval Spain is the long crusade against the Moslems who had occupied the peninsula in the opening years of the eighth century, and the circumstances of the reconquest left their mark on the Christian kingdoms that grew up in the wake of the receding Moslem tide. As the reconquest spread slowly southward, the frontier counties tended to become independent, breaking away from the parent state to form separate kingdoms. The nobles and the crusading orders who spearheaded the reconquest were rewarded with huge grants of land, over which, in the absence of strong central government, they acquired sovereign powers. Bred in a tradition of perpetual guerrilla warfare, the nobles also fought one another and their kings as fiercely as they fought the Moor. Finally, when the reconquest came to a halt in the middle years of the thirteenth century, with only the small kingdom of Granada left in Moslem hands, even such unifying effect as the crusade had had was removed, and both the nobles and the monarchs were left free to quarrel among themselves. The next two hundred years were filled with rebellion, civil war and war between the states. Of these, Castile was by far the largest, occupying the central plateau, and flanked by the Kingdom of Portugal to the west and three Aragonese kingdoms to the east. In the north the little Kingdom of Navarre straddled the Pyrenees, while Moslem Granada occupied the southern tip of the peninsula.

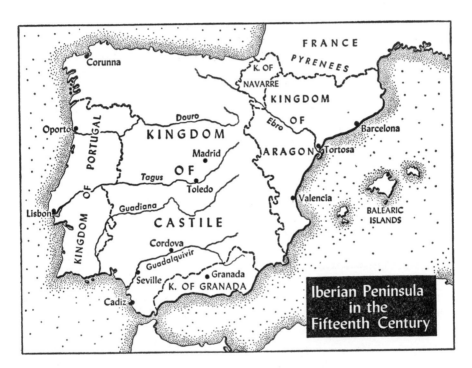

Iberian Peninsula in the Fifteenth Century

Castile was in many ways the most backward of the Spanish states, but its size and central location made it the heart of the national state that grew out of the union of the crowns of Aragon and Castile and the later conquest of Granada and Navarre. It had borne the brunt of the long crusade against the Moors, and it was deeply divided by the separatism or regionalism that resulted from the circumstances of the reconquest. It was itself formed by the union of two kingdoms — Castile and Leon — under one crown, and a long succession of weak kings had prevented the monarchy from controlling the anarchic nobles and crusading orders. It was the chronic anarchy of Castile, indeed, which checked the completion of the reconquest for more than two hundred years, since only Castile shared a common frontier with Granada after the middle of the thirteenth century and the other states then lost interest in conquering a territory that would inevitably be absorbed into Castile. Virtually land-locked as it was by the states that cut it off from the sea along most of the eastern, western and southern coasts, Castile was more isolated than the other kingdoms and had little foreign trade. Nor did the barren uplands of the central plateau support a vigorous agriculture, although they did furnish grazing grounds for the great migratory flocks of merino sheep. Despite the poverty of the country and the lack of foreign trade, however, the long guerilla warfare had encouraged the building of walled towns, and these had been granted many privileges and a large degree of self-government by the monarchs who hoped for their aid against the rebellious nobles. The townspeople were represented as a third estate in the Castilian *Cortes*, an institution similar to the French Estates General, but founded half a century earlier and possessing somewhat greater authority than its French counterpart, including a more clearly recognized right to give consent to any taxation beyond that due to the crown by royal prerogative. Since the clergy and the nobles claimed exemption from direct taxation, however, the struggle against royal exactions was left to the third estate, which could scarcely carry it on successfully against a strong monarchy.

The kingdoms which Ferdinand of Aragon brought into the union presented a marked contrast in almost every respect to that inherited by his wife. Although much smaller than Castile, the territory of the Aragonese crown was divided into three kingdoms — Aragon, Catalonia and Valencia — each with its own peculiar traditions, its own Cortes and other governmental institutions. In addition, Ferdinand inherited a territorial empire in the Mediterranean, including the Balearic Islands and the kingdoms of Sicily and Sardinia. Aragon itself was an inland state with a strongly entrenched landholding aristocracy. The feudal system was more tightly organized in Aragon than in Castile, and the Aragonese nobles showed a greater ability to cooperate in the defense of their liberties. They dominated the Cortes, which in Aragon was divided into four estates, two of them noble. Thus, while there was less anarchy in Aragon and the authority of the crown was therefore more effective, there were more firmly established limitations to absolutism than in Castile. In contrast to Aragon, Catalonia was a seaboard state, centering around the prosperous commercial city of Barcelona, whose maritime trade rivalled that of the great Italian seaports. In culture as well as in economic interests, Catalonia was quite distinct from Aragon. Its language was not Spanish, but was derived originally from southern France and was closely akin to Provençal. The Catalans were a seafaring people, and it was largely through Catalan influence that the Aragonese dynasty acquired its commercial and territorial empire in the Mediterranean. The third of the mainland kingdoms, Valencia, was less important. It had been conquered from the Moors only in the middle of the thirteenth century, and was thereafter settled by Aragonese nobles and Catalan burghers, while retaining a large Moorish population.

The problem of unifying their various kingdoms was one of the most difficult that Ferdinand and Isabella had to solve, and they were able to do no more than lay the foundation upon which their Hapsburg descendants could build. They made, in fact, no attempt to merge the institutions or the administrative machinery of Castile and the Aragonese states. They did, however, achieve a very considerable uniformity of policy, and they pooled the military resources of the two crowns for the conquest of Granada and to press Ferdinand's dynastic claims to the kingdoms of Naples and Navarre. In internal affairs, the two monarchs concentrated their attention primarily on the organization of a strong central government in Castile. This was not only the most important of the territories brought together by the union of the crowns, but the one which presented the most favorable opportunities for the extension of royal power. The chronic anarchy which had nullified royal authority under a succession of feeble rulers had, at the same time, prevented the development of effective constitutional guarantees against absolutism. The deeply ingrained particularism of the Castilian nobles prevented them from uniting in opposition to the crown, so that all that was needed was a strong, consistent policy to reduce them to subjection. From the beginning of their reign, the two monarchs set to work systematically to destroy castles built without royal permission, to resume lands and privileges illegally usurped, to punish the lawlessness of the nobles and to deprive them of the most important offices in the government, which were given to trained lawyers of humble birth who would be wholly at the service of the monarchy. In compensation, the nobles were allowed to retain their traditional titles and honorary offices, and were encouraged to regard the royal court as the source of honors. The proud Castilian grandees and hidalgos were intractable material to work with, but, like their French contemporaries, they were gradually being transformed into courtiers. At the same time, the great crusading orders were brought under the control of the crown by the expedient of making Ferdinand Grand Master of each, so that their wealth and power could be used in the service of the monarchy.

In their struggle with the nobles, the monarchs could generally count on the support of the townspeople, and in the early years of their reign they received valuable assistance from the Cortes. Once firmly established, however, they began to regard the Cortes as a check upon their authority and thereafter summoned it less and less frequently, usually limiting the summons to the third estate who alone were concerned with taxation. By the end of the reign the power of the Cortes had declined almost to the vanishing point. In the same way, they used the *Hermandad*, an organization founded by the towns for the suppression of crime, until the royal administration of justice was strong enough to cope with lawlessness, and then disbanded it. Meanwhile, their Catholic Majesties were reorganizing the royal councils into an efficient bureaucracy, capable of exercising an effective control of every aspect of the nation's life. They introduced few new taxes, but by reforming the system of collection and by ensuring honest administration they were able to add immensely to the resources of the crown. During the thirty years of Isabella's reign, the revenues of Castile increased at least thirtyfold. The most important source of revenue was the *alcabala*, a ten per cent tax on commercial transactions and one which, in the long run, proved disastrous to Spanish economy. Before the end of the reign of Isabella the treasury of Castile was also beginning to receive its first installments of the newly discovered wealth of the Indies. Thereafter, the center of gravity in Spain shifted decidedly from the eastern kingdoms to Castile, as the importance of Barcelona declined with the general relative decline of Mediterranean commerce, and as the growth of the Spanish overseas empire extended the authority of the Castilian crown to the New World.

Not content with taming the nobles and reducing the autonomy of the towns, Ferdinand and Isabella also took vigorous steps to gain control of the national Church. This was, indeed, an essential step in the establishment of absolute monarchy, and despite their undoubted devotion to the Catholic faith, the two monarchs had no more inclination to tolerate papal interference in their territory than had the contemporary rulers of France. In 1482 they challenged the papal right of provision to Spanish benefices and secured from Pope Sixtus IV permission to nominate the incumbents of all the most important ecclesiastical offices in their kingdoms. This right they later extended in practice to the lesser benefices as well. Having gained control of the hierarchy, their Catholic Majesties imposed a definitely national character upon the Spanish Church and made it an instrument for the extension of royal power. Both in old Spain and in the New World the clergy became the most devoted supporters of the absolute monarchy. In justice it must be added that the monarchs used their authority to institute a much-needed reform. Aided by Isabella's chief minister, the able but inflexible Cardinal Ximenes, they restored discipline and punished immorality among both regulars and seculars, raised standards of clerical education, and in general so elevated the moral and spiritual quality of the Spanish priesthood that there was little left for the Counter-Reformation to achieve.

A similar combination of religious zeal and desire for national unity also led their Catholic Majesties to impose religious uniformity upon their states by a ruthless campaign for the extermination of heresy and infidelity. The Spanish kingdoms had inherited from their Moslem past a large and prosperous Jewish as well as Moorish population, and for some time after the reconquest both had been treated with considerable tolerance because of their undoubted economic value to the Christian states. Growing persecution during the century before the accession of Ferdinand and Isabella, however, had forced formal conversion on the majority of the Jews, and it was to these *conversos* or doubtful converts that the two monarchs first turned their attention. Their first step was to petition the pope in 1478 to introduce the Inquisition into the Spanish kingdoms under royal control. There it worked with terrible efficiency under officers nominated by the crown and backed by the full power of the secular arm. It had, however, no authority over professed Jews. To rid Spain of these Ferdinand and Isabella seized upon the moment of religious exaltation following the conquest of Granada in 1492 to decree the expulsion of all professed Jews from their realms. At the same time, the conquered Moors were offered very generous terms, and these were observed until 1499, when the implacable Cardinal Ximenes was placed in authority over Granada. Thereafter a campaign of systematic terrorism forced many Moors to accept conversion, thereby falling under the jurisdiction of the Inquisition. Then, in 1502, urged on by Ximenes, Isabella decreed the expulsion of all professed Moslems from her kingdom, into which Granada had been absorbed. The expulsion of the Jews and Moors undoubtedly contributed to the unification of Spain, but at the cost of losing a large number of highly skilled merchants and artisans, a price Spain could ill afford to pay. The immense powers vested in the Inquisition and its subservience to the crown also made it an effective instrument for the extension of royal authority as well as for enforcing unity of belief, but for this, too, Spain paid a high price in the loss of intellectual freedom.

Finally, as the ultimate prerequisite to making the united Spanish kingdoms a European power, Ferdinand and Isabella undertook to reorganize their armed forces, and replaced the undisciplined feudal levies they had inherited by a national army, which for a century and a half remained the most formidable in Europe. The long campaign against Granada, which occupied the early years of their reign, furnished the opportunity to create a royal army and to experiment with new tactical formations, and these were later developed to greater efficiency by such brilliant commanders as Gonzalo de Córdoba, the "Great Captain" of the Italian wars. The rugged uplands of Castile and Aragon bred men with great powers of endurance, who had a long fighting tradition and who needed only the discipline of a paid and permanently organized army to turn them into first class professional soldiers. The heart of the new Spanish army was formed by the infantry regiments, composed partly of pike-men and partly of men armed with short sword and javelin, and supported by smaller detachments armed with arquebuses, the most effective hand firearms of the period. All were furnished with light helmets and body armor. Formed in hollow squares with the pikes on the outside, they were almost invulnerable to cavalry attack, while the combination of weapons and the firepower of the arquebusiers made them a more flexible unit than the massed columns of pikes used by the mercenary Swiss and the German *Landsknechte*, who formed the only other good infantry forces available at this time. The Spanish cavalry, mostly light horsemen, were less numerous and less effective. The artillery, on the other hand, formed an increasingly important arm as commanders learned how to use it in the field to best advantage.

It was this army, together with his own remarkable diplomatic skill, which enabled Ferdinand to play a decisive rôle in the international complications precipitated by the French invasions of Italy. Throughout the joint reigns of their Catholic Majesties, foreign affairs were left almost entirely in the hands of Ferdinand, partly because of his natural predilection for diplomacy, but also because it was his dynastic claims to Naples and Navarre that drew Spain into the international scene.

ENGLAND

In the second half of the fifteenth century, England passed through a crisis which for a time almost paralyzed royal government, but which in the long run prepared the way for the creation of a more absolute monarchy and a more highly centralized state. There was here, however, no serious problem of territorial consolidation, such as marked the national growth of France and Spain. Nor was it necessary to extend the jurisdiction of royal government at the expense of local institutions or feudal rights and privileges. That had already been achieved. There was, however, a desperate need to restore the effective authority of the central government in practice, and to combat the bastard feudalism that had developed in the closing years of the war in France and now threatened to disintegrate the state. The crying need of this period in England was for what Sir John Fortescue called "good governance," and good governance could be restored only by a strong monarchy, a monarchy freed both from control by baronial magnates and from undue parliamentary limitations upon its authority. The constitutional development of the Lancastrian era had been premature. What England needed at this point was not a stronger Parliament, but a stronger monarchy, and this she acquired only after three decades of dynastic bickering and civil war had demonstrated the necessity for it. Like France and Spain, England in this period was moving through anarchy toward absolutism. But what made the English development unique was that the movement toward absolutism stopped short of completion. In the Tudor state which emerged from the crisis, England acquired a monarchy sufficiently absolute for all practical purposes without destroying Parliament or altering materially the legal basis of government.

The end of the Hundred Years' War freed England from her long involvement in war on the continent, but it did not bring her peace. As has already been explained, the creation of a mercenary army for service in France left England a dangerous heritage of lawlessness and disorder. Through the system of livery and maintenance, the English barons terrorized the countryside and intimidated royal officials and the courts of justice. The long minority of Henry VI (1422–61) greatly weakened the government, and even after the feeble and saintly king grew up he proved utterly unable to control his own council or to enforce order in the kingdom. The royal finances were in a desperate state. Parliament, as well as the royal council, was dominated by baronial cliques. The king's government was discredited by defeat in France and by lack of effective administration. In 1450 popular discontent broke out in a serious rebellion in the south of England led by one Jack Cade. Within a few months after the cessation of hostilities in France in 1453 the king suddenly fell into the first of those fits of insanity which incapacitated him periodically for the rest of his life. This, together with the belated birth of an heir shortly thereafter, precipitated a conflict within the royal family which soon added civil war to the prevailing anarchy.

The dynastic conflict brought on by the madness of the king and the birth of his son, Prince Edward, had been long in the making. Edward III had left too many descendants for the peace of England. During the minority of Henry VI the royal council had been torn by a bitter feud between the king's uncle, Humphrey, Duke of Gloucester, and a faction led by his great-uncle, Cardinal Henry Beaufort, an illegitimate son of John of Gaunt, the fourth son of Edward III and founder of the Lancastrian line. When Henry came of age and began to misgovern in his own right, the Beaufort faction gained the ascendancy in the council.

After the death of both the Cardinal and Duke Humphrey in 1447, the Beaufort clique, now led by Edmund Beaufort, Duke of Somerset, continued to control the government and exploit it in their own interests. The baronial opposition to the Beauforts was now led by Richard, Duke of York, who was descended on his father's side from Edmund of York, the fifth son of Edward III, and on his mother's side from Edward's third son, Lionel, Duke of Clarence. So long as the king was childless, Richard of York was heir presumptive to the throne. The birth of Henry's son was, therefore, a shock to his hopes. Nevertheless, he recognized the infant prince as heir, and satisfied himself by claiming the regency during the king's illness. The queen, Margaret of Anjou, however, feared that his ambition might yet become a threat to her son, and when in the following year the king relapsed for a time into sanity she persuaded him to exclude York from the council and restore Somerset to control of the government. Faced by the queen's implacable enmity in addition to the long-standing hatred of the Beaufort clan, Richard raised his followers in self-defense, thus beginning the first of those civil wars which are known as the Wars of the Roses, from the tradition that the white rose was the badge of York, the red rose that of the reigning Lancastrian dynasty.

The story of the civil wars is a dreary tale of treachery and pointless violence, savagely fought battles and even more savage executions, full of sound and fury, but signifying very little. The fortunes of York and Lancaster rose and fell with bewildering rapidity, triumph alternating with defeat. In 1460 Richard of York was defeated and killed, but in the following year his son, Edward, won a decisive victory and was crowned in London as Edward IV, while Queen Margaret fled with her son and the helpless old king to Scotland. The Yorkist triumph, however, failed to bring peace. Lancastrian opposition continued in the north, and soon Edward faced a new danger from the growing enmity of his cousin, the powerful Earl of Warwick, who had helped him to win the crown. In 1470 Warwick openly espoused the Lancastrian cause and raised a revolt which drove Edward into exile and placed Henry VI once more on the throne. It was a brief restoration. The following year Edward returned with aid from his brother-in-law, Charles the Bold of Burgundy. Warwick the King-maker was defeated and slain in the bloody battle of Barnet, and in a second battle at Tewkesbury the indomitable Queen Margaret was captured and her son killed. The execution of Somerset and other rebel leaders and the murder of the helpless old king in the Tower completed the Yorkist triumph. For the next twelve years (1471–83) Edward IV ruled firmly and made a promising start on the all-important task of restoring order, ably aided by his brother Richard, Duke of Gloucester. That task, however, was no more than well begun when Edward's early death left the throne to his twelve-year-old son, Edward V, and thereby precipitated the last tragic phase of the civil wars.

In the struggle for the regency which followed the death of Edward IV, Richard of Gloucester was forced by circumstances and by motives that can no longer be clearly discerned along the road that led to ruin for himself and his dynasty. Opposed to him were the queen, Elizabeth Woodville, and her numerous kin who hoped to exploit the king's minority to their own advantage. At first Richard was content to secure control of the government as regent with the title of Protector; but within the year, while still laying plans for the young king's coronation, he suddenly reversed his position. Declaring his nephews illegitimate on the ground of recently discovered evidence that Edward IV had been first betrothed to a Lady Eleanor Butler, which, if true, would have rendered his later marriage to the queen invalid according to strict canon law, Richard asserted his own claim to the throne and was crowned as Richard III (1483–85). Such a usurpation was not unprecedented in fifteenth-century England, and most Englishmen were probably willing to accept a strong king rather than face the dangers of a minority. A series of executions rid Richard of the Woodvilles, and a rebellion led by the Duke of Buckingham, still another descendant of Edward III, fizzled out. But Richard was not yet secure, for a rumour was spreading that he had murdered his nephews in the Tower, and in Brittany Henry Tudor was preparing with French aid to assert his own dubious claim to the throne. It was a very dubious claim indeed, traced through his mother Margaret Beaufort to the illegitimate progeny of John of Gaunt, but with the aid of French troops and Richard's growing unpopularity it was enough. In August, 1485 he landed with a French army at Milford Haven. A few days later Richard was killed fighting courageously on Bosworth Field, and Henry Tudor was King of England.

The Wars of the Roses had been fought for no constitutional principle, no conflict of class interest, for no reason, indeed, that could lend them dignity. The participants most deeply involved were the turbulent nobles, backed by their henchmen among the gentry who were attached to them by livery and maintenance. For them the civil wars were simply an opportunity to carry on their personal feuds and indulge their taste for violence and plunder. The burghers and many of the gentry remained more or less neutral, carrying on their businesses or managing their estates as best they could, and hoping for the day when a strong government would restore peace and order. Trade and industry as well as agriculture undoubtedly suffered during the first few years of the wars, but the relative peace of the last decade of the reign of Edward IV brought about a considerable revival. On the whole, the Wars of the

Roses caused no more than a temporary delay in the economic expansion which England shared with the rest of Europe in the second half of the fifteenth century. But they did have two important results, which hastened the transition from the medieval to the modern English state. Three decades of intermittent warfare, confiscations and executions decimated the ranks of the baronage and left few of the old noble families extant and in possession of their lands. And these three decades had also bred in the English people a fear of civil war and a desire for strong government which, together with the extinction of so many over-mighty subjects, was the surest guarantee of the survival of the new Tudor dynasty, and one which compensated it for the lack of a clear hereditary title.

The accession of Henry VII (1485–1509) has customarily been regarded as the beginning of modern English history. Yet his government instituted no radical departure from precedent and certainly did not shock the constitutional sense of contemporary Englishmen. What he did was pretty much what Edward IV had done in the last decade of his reign, but he did it more efficiently and over a longer period of time. Like Henry IV a century earlier, he owed his royal title in part to parliamentary confirmation of the accomplished fact of conquest, and hence he could not deny its authority. But wholesale confiscations and resumptions of alienated lands had restored the solvency of the crown, and Henry's shrewd financial sense enabled him to add to his income in a variety of ways without asking much in the way of direct taxes from Parliament. Since he was to a large extent financially independent of Parliament, and since his policies were on the whole beneficial to the burghers and country gentry who formed the body of the Commons, he was able to manage his Parliaments and to use them as instruments for the strengthening of royal government. The crown still possessed very large areas of undisputed authority. Henry made no unprecedented claims for the royal prerogative, but he exercised it with unprecedented effectiveness. It is thus the fact of strong government rather than any novel constitutional principle that makes his reign a turning point in English history. It was the great achievement of Henry VII that he survived the turbulent backwash left by the civil wars, and that he planted his dubious dynasty so firmly upon the throne that it too survived as long as an heir remained. And in doing so he gave England order and stable government for the first time in nearly a hundred years.

Had he not restored order, indeed, Henry's dynasty would not have survived. To prevent the return of civil war it was necessary to suppress the remaining lawless barons and to deprive them of the irresponsible military power they had acquired through the system of livery and maintenance. This Henry achieved largely through the instrumentality of the

Court of the Star Chamber, which was the royal council acting in its judicial capacity, and which could not be intimidated as could the local courts by the barons and their armed retinues. Once the power of the barons was broken, the policing of the shires and the administration of justice on the local level could be left to the sheriffs and the Justices of the Peace. The powers of the latter, men drawn from the county gentry whose interest it was to restore order, Henry increased by successive acts of Parliament, while at the same time keeping them under close surveillance by the central government. In the words of a statute of 1489, it was Henry's intention "that the king's subjects might live in surety under his peace in their bodies and goods," and his efforts to achieve that end won the loyalty of the solid middle classes in town and country upon whose support the stability of his government depended.

Next to order at home, Henry needed peace abroad and recognition of his dynasty by the great foreign powers. Refusing to be drawn into the confused conflicts of continental politics, he established a cordial entente with England's ancient enemy, France. He secured a formal treaty of friendship with the Hapsburg prince, Philip, who had inherited the Burgundian Netherlands, a treaty which assured English merchants of favorable treatment in their most important foreign market. Finally, he established his dynasty as the equal of the greatest European houses by negotiating a marriage for his eldest son, Arthur, with Catherine of Aragon, daughter of Ferdinand and Isabella. This alliance with the powerful Spanish dynasty Henry regarded as so important that, when Arthur died within a few months after the marriage, Henry secured a papal dispensation for the remarriage of the widowed Catherine to his second son Prince Henry, with results that no one could at that time have foreseen.

When Henry VII died he left to his heir a greatly strengthened monarchy, a kingdom ordered and at peace, a well-filled treasury and a prosperous people. Keenly aware of the power of money, Henry had not only amassed a fortune unequalled by any king in Europe, but had also taken care to feed the geese that laid the golden eggs. His diplomacy had enabled him to avoid the ruinous expenses of war, while at the same time it had fostered the prosperity of English merchants by securing favorable conditions for the expansion of English trade. He had maintained a sufficient magnificence at court to furnish a suitable setting for the royal majesty, but he had been careful to get his money's worth and had lived well within his income. His successor, the flamboyant and self-willed young King Henry VIII (1509–47), reversed most of these cautious policies. Though equally avaricious, the new king had none of his father's passion for sound economy. He yearned for martial glory, and became involved in pointless and profitless wars on the continent which, together with the reckless extravagance of his court, soon emptied the treasury and made it necessary for him to make increasing demands upon the purses of his people. The reign of Henry VIII brought profound changes in royal administration and in the relation of Church and state, but those changes fall mostly outside the chronological scope of this book. Here we have to deal only with his first decade.

What need be said about the early years of Henry's reign concerns his all-powerful minister, Cardinal Wolsey, rather than the king. A relatively obscure ecclesiastic when Henry came to the throne, Wolsey soon gained the confidence of the young king and dominated the royal council. Before long he was regarded as the real ruler of England and he may have himself forgotten that he held his power only at the king's pleasure. As chief minister of the crown, chancellor, Archbishop of York, cardinal and papal legate, Wolsey united in his own person the authority of the monarchy, the law and the papacy in England. He was the architect of Henry's opportunistic foreign policy, which accomplished little of lasting value, but for a time gave his master the pleasing illusion that he was the arbiter of Europe. At home, as legate and chancellor, he dominated both Church and state, and he taught Henry how authority over both might be united to create a monarchy more absolute than England had ever known. He taught him, too, how authority over the *Ecclesia Anglicana* might be made to yield profit as well as power. When the authority he held at the king's pleasure was suddenly stripped from him, he left these lessons as a legacy to the master he had served with such zeal and who in the end had left him naked to his enemies.

GERMANY AND THE HOUSE OF HAPSBURG

The political evolution of Germany in the fourteenth and fifteenth centuries followed a course in one respect radically different from that of France, Spain or England. There was in Germany no movement toward national consolidation, and in the Empire no growth of centralized government. On the contrary, the events of this period merely confirmed the fact of the disintegration of the Empire and postponed the unification of Germany for centuries. The general tendency toward centralization of government and the strengthening of monarchical authority, which characterized the evolution of the other European countries, operated in Germany only within the individual principalities. Here, as elsewhere, the anarchy which accompanied the death throes of feudalism opened the way for the emergence of the modern monarchical state by rallying all but the most lawless elements of the population to the support of the only kind of government that could enforce order. But the destiny of

Germany for the next four hundred years was determined by the fact that what emerged from this transitional period was not one national state but a number of territorial states. Little more need be said about the growth of these states after 1450, except that the tendencies already noted continued at an accelerated pace, under the leadership of princes who had grasped the new principles of state government, and who used concepts drawn from Roman Law to bolster their authority and the financial means furnished by general taxation to strengthen their military power and the administrative machinery of their states. Such princes were Albrecht the Wise of Upper Bavaria (1467–1508), Ludwig of Lower Bavaria (1450–79), Albrecht Achilles of Brandenburg (1471–86) and Magnus of Mecklenburg (1477–1503). In the general history of Europe these princes do not loom large, but they and others like them laid the foundations of autonomous states which lasted till the nineteenth century.

While the princes of Germany were thus consolidating their authority in their territorial states, the imperial title, for what it was worth, returned to the Hapsburg dynasty with the election of Albert II (1438–39), followed by that of Frederick III (1440–93). Through most of Frederick's long reign the fortunes of the House of Hapsburg were at a low ebb. Hungary and Bohemia, which had been inherited through his wife by Albert II, were lost to the Hapsburg dynasty after his death. The Swiss Confederation, now a practically independent state with a strong military force, was nibbling away at Hapsburg territory. The imperial title added little to Frederick's actual power, since he could neither raise taxes nor an army outside his hereditary lands, and even there was frequently threatened by rebellion. Part of the Hapsburg lands, too, had been bequeathed to other branches of the family. Only at the very end of his reign were all the Hapsburg territories united and restored to obedience. Frederick's otherwise inglorious reign did, however, mark the first step upon the road that within three generations was to make the Hapsburg dynasty the dominant power in Europe. In the crisis that followed the death of Charles the Bold of Burgundy in 1477, his daughter, Mary, sought to gain aid for the defense of her lands against Louis XI by marrying Frederick's son, Maximilian. It was an event of far-reaching importance, for it brought to the House of Hapsburg the principality of the Burgundian dukes: Franche-Comté, Luxemburg and the rich commercial and industrial provinces of the Netherlands.

From this time on, the Hapsburgs held lands on both the eastern and western frontiers of Germany. The imperial title now acquired a new importance for them, as the only means of tying their widely separated possessions together. At the same time they were preoccupied for years to come with the defense of these peripheral lands against the rising threat

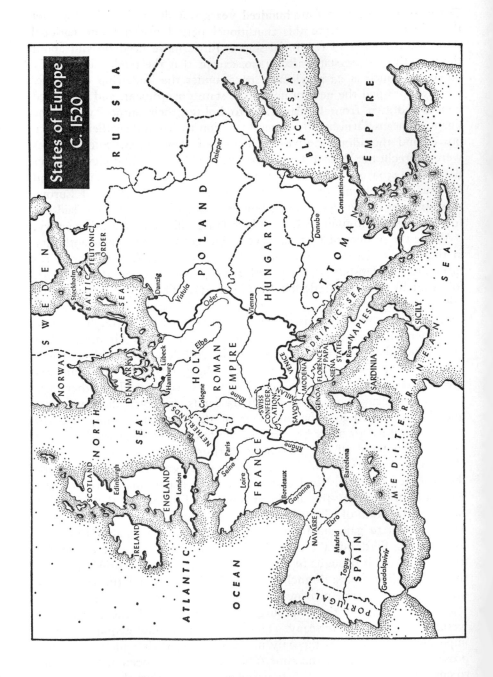

States of Europe
C. 1520

BLACK SEA

OTTOMAN EMPIRE

Constantinople

SWEDEN

NORWAY

BALTIC SEA

TEUTONIC ORDER

Stockholm

Danzig

Dnieper

POLAND

HUNGARY

Vistula

Oder

Vienna

Danube

DENMARK

Lübeck

Hamburg

HOLY ROMAN EMPIRE

Elbe

Cologne

Rhine

ADRIATIC SEA

VENICE

MODENA

FLORENCE

PAPAL STATES

Rome

NAPLES

SICILY

SARDINIA

MEDITERRANEAN SEA

NORTH SEA

SCOTLAND

Edinburgh

NETHERLANDS

SWISS CONFEDERATION

MILAN

SAVOY

GENOA

SIENA

ENGLAND

London

Paris

Seine

FRANCE

Loire

Rhône

Bordeaux

Garonne

Barcelona

IRELAND

ATLANTIC OCEAN

NAVARRE

Ebro

Madrid

Tagus

SPAIN

Guadalquivir

PORTUGAL

of the Turks to the east and French aggression to the west, and thus became involved in foreign wars and international diplomacy which bore little relation to the national interests of Germany. When Maximilian (1493–1519) succeeded his father as emperor, there seemed for a time a possibility that he might do something to restore imperial power in Germany. He was a gallant, knightly figure, talented and popular, and many Germans who yearned for a government strong enough to maintain order and to restore the Empire to its place in European affairs looked hopefully to him for leadership. But, for all his varied talents, Maximilian was hopelessly unrealistic and incurably a Hapsburg. The numerous attempts made during his reign to reform the imperial government came to nothing, while Maximilian wasted his resources in fruitless foreign wars for the aggrandizement of his dynasty. Both at home and abroad his reign was marred by almost unrelieved frustration and failure.

Nevertheless, the fortunes of the House of Hapsburg continued to soar as the result of a series of marriage alliances and fortuitously advantageous births and deaths. The death of Mary of Burgundy five years after her marriage to Maximilian left her Burgundian lands to their son Philip with Maximilian as regent. Declared of age in 1493, Philip became the independent prince of the Netherlands, and as heir to Maximilian he was in a position to seek alliance with the greatest European dynasties. In 1496 he married Joanna, daughter of Ferdinand and Isabella, who became, after the death of her brother, the heiress presumptive to the two Spanish crowns. Since the two kingdoms had never been formally united into one state, when Isabella died in 1504 Castile passed to her daughter and was claimed by Philip in his wife's name. Two years later he himself died, leaving his Burgundian lands and his Spanish claims to his six-year-old son Charles, Joanna having meanwhile been incapacitated by insanity. While Charles was growing up his grandfathers took over the government of his inherited states, Ferdinand as regent of Castile, Maximilian as regent of the Netherlands. But on Ferdinand's death in 1516 Charles came into the full sovereignty of all the possessions of the Spanish crowns: the two kingdoms of Spain, the Aragonese kingdoms of Sardinia, Sicily and Naples and the Castilian empire founded by the Spanish *conquistadores* in the New World. Finally, on Maximilian's death in 1519, Charles inherited the Hapsburg lands in Germany — the duchies of Austria, Styria, Carinthia, and Carniola and the County of Tyrol — and was elected emperor as Charles V.

With this vast collection of hereditary lands and the still imposing, if somewhat unsubstantial, sovereignty conferred upon him by the imperial election, Charles found himself at nineteen ruler of more than half of Western Europe. The result was to upset the existing balance of power and to precipitate half a century of international conflict, the story of which lies beyond the scope of the present work. It is enough here to note that the center of gravity of his personal empire, if one may use that term to include all his possessions, lay in his hereditary lands rather than in imperial Germany. It was essentially a dynastic empire, brought together by the fortunes of dynastic inheritance, and it was held together by no common bond except the person of the ruling prince.

C. The Wars in Italy (1494–1520)

Having traced the history of the greater European states and their ruling dynasties to about 1520, we must now turn back to 1494 and the beginning of the wars in Italy in which nearly all the European powers became directly or indirectly involved. During the forty years between the Peace of Lodi and the first French invasion Italy, as we have seen, had enjoyed a rare interval of relative peace, founded upon the rather shaky equilibrium maintained by the five major Italian states. Italy had also enjoyed in those years an immunity from foreign interference, for which the maintenance of the balance of power in the peninsula was only in part responsible. To a greater extent Italy owed its security during those years to the fact that the most potentially threatening foreign powers were otherwise occupied. The French monarchy was engaged, first in the effort to restore order after the Hundred Years' War, then in the struggle for the annexation of Burgundy and Brittany to the royal domain. The Aragonese monarchy, already in possession of Sicily and with a possible acquisitive interest in Naples, was also preoccupied with affairs nearer home. Not till the union of Aragon and Castile under Ferdinand and Isabella was Spain a strong enough power to compete with France for the domination of Italy, and even then their Catholic Majesties were not free to engage in foreign wars until the conquest of Granada had been completed in 1492.

By the opening years of the last decade of the century France, too, was free to engage in wars of conquest, and the young king, Charles VIII, was nourishing his dynastic claims to the Kingdom of Naples. Meanwhile, the equilibrium of the Italian states was being violently disturbed by the growing antagonism between the ruling family of Naples and the Milanese regent, Ludovico Sforza, Il Moro. The aged King Ferrante realized clearly enough the danger of upsetting the balance of power, but his death in January, 1494 left the kingdom to his son Alfonso, the chief instigator of the movement against Il Moro. When the new king secured the support of Pope Alexander VI in addition to that of Piero de' Medici, the Milanese regent was left isolated. In desperation he turned to Charles VIII for aid, urging him to assert his claims to the Kingdom of Naples. Perhaps Ludovico hoped to use the threat of a foreign invasion that might never materialize, as other Italian statesmen had done before him. If so, he was mistaken. This time the invading army came, and Ludovico was forced to open the gates of Italy to it.

The army which the young French king led down into Italy in the late summer of 1494 was the most formidable force that the peninsula had ever seen. It numbered in all some 30,000 effective troops with an additional swarm of non-combattants and camp followers. Its hard core was formed by the heavily armored men-at-arms of the companies of cavalry recruited from the nobility of France. Like their feudal ancestors, they were trained to warfare from their youth, but services in the royal army had made them professional soldiers endowed with virtues of discipline and loyalty which feudal armies had seldom possessed. For infantry the French depended principally on the incomparable Swiss mercenaries. These well-drilled and disciplined mountaineers had developed a new tactical formation, which for more than a generation made them the most formidable infantry in Europe and an indispensable part of the various armies fighting in Italy. Armed with enormously long pikes and drawn up in deep columns, they could hold off cavalry attacks or, when charging in close formation, they could run over opposing infantry with the devastating effect of a steam roller. Like all mercenaries, they were undependable when their pay was in arrears, but once engaged in battle they fought with inflexible courage. Finally, the French armed force was augmented by a train of artillery, the largest and finest then in existence. Against such a force, the smaller and less well-balanced armies of the Italian *condottieri* could not hope to stand. These were doubtless less ineffective than Machiavelli's famous denunciation would suggest, but the Italian mercenaries lacked the *élan* of the noble French *gendarmerie*, and they were inadequately supported by either infantry or artillery. The greatest military weakness of Italy, however, was political in origin. It sprang from the inability of the Italian states to unite and to pool their resources in close cooperation against a foreign enemy.

The story of the first French invasion of Italy can be told very briefly. From first to last it was a triumphal march — little more than a military parade. Having been speeded on his way through Lombardy by Ludovico Sforza, Charles entered Tuscany. There he was met by Piero de' Medici in a panic, who surrendered to him the principal fortresses of the Florentine state, including the city of Pisa for which Florence had fought so long. This was more than even the pro-French party in Florence was willing to condone, and Piero was driven out by a popular uprising. The republic then made peace with Charles and formed an alliance with him in the hope of regaining Pisa. In Rome the feeble resistance presented by Alexander VI collapsed before a blow was struck, and Charles entered the papal city, as he had entered Florence, riding at the head of his troops with lance at rest. In the Kingdom of Naples, too, resistance faded away before the advancing army. King Alfonso abdicated in favor of his son Ferrantino and fled. On February 22, 1495, Charles entered the city of Naples, and within a few days the whole kingdom was in his hands.

The prize so easily won was almost as quickly lost. The greed of the king's French favorites and the arrogance and brutality of the French soldiers soon alienated the Neapolitans of all classes. Meanwhile, the spectacular demonstration of France's military power aroused apprehension among Italian statesmen everywhere and made them willing at last to bury their mutual animosities for a moment to unite against the aggressor. The lead in negotiating a league against the French was taken by Ferdinand of Aragon. As King of Sicily he was alarmed at the occupation of the southern part of the peninsula by French forces. Moreover, he had a somewhat ambiguous dynastic interest in restoring his dispossessed cousin to the Neapolitan throne, since he would prove an easier prey than the French for future conquest. The League of Venice which he helped to organize included, besides Ferdinand himself, Alexander VI, who feared a strong French army in the neighboring kingdom; the Republic of Venice, which viewed with alarm French control of the lower Adriatic; Ludovico Il Moro, who had no more need of the French alliance since the opportune death of his nephew and who feared the Orléanist claims to his duchy; and, finally, the Emperor Maximilian, who was attracted to interference in Italy by his dynastic interest in Trieste and Fiume as well as by the invincible optimism that always made his reach exceed his grasp. The inclusion of two foreign powers in the league was a prophetic omen. Italy was losing control of its own destiny. With his line of communication thus threatened, Charles hurried north with the bulk of his army, and, after a bitter battle with the forces of the league at Fornova, escaped through the Alpine passes to France. Thereafter the expulsion from Naples of the remaining French army of occupation was only a matter of time. By 1496 the Spanish troops under Gonzalo de Córdoba had restored King Ferrantino to his capital. The storm that had swept Italy had passed, having apparently made little change in the *status quo*.

Nevertheless, Italy was not what it had been before 1494. The French invasion had demonstrated the ease with which a great power might win land in Italy. If it had also shown that land so won might be difficult to hold and of little real value to the conqueror, that was not the lesson the European monarchs chose to learn. The fact remained that Italian isolation had been broken beyond repair. French troops had blazed a trail the length of the peninsula; Spanish troops had effected the reconquest of Naples; and only his chronic lack of financial resources had prevented Maximilian from asserting dynastic and imperial claims in the north. Having tasted blood, the eagles were gathering over Italy.

Meanwhile, one Italian state had been profoundly changed by the effect of the invasion. The surrender of the Florentine strongholds to Charles had not only led to the expulsion of the Medici; it had also left the republic sadly weakened. The loss of Pisa, which had not been restored before the French retreat, was a bitter blow to Florentine pride as well as to the seaborne trade of the republic, which depended on the Pisan port. After the expulsion of the Medici, the republic had been restored with a broadened democratic base; but for the next four years its policies were dominated by the Dominican friar, Girolamo Savonarola. During the years immediately preceding the French invasion, this fiery preacher had gained a fanatical following by his denunciation of the vices of princes, clergy and people, and by his prophecies of disaster if they did not repent of their sins. The death of Lorenzo, whom Savonarola had denounced as a tyrant, and the coming of Charles in the guise of the sword of God seemed to bear out the friar's prophecies and added immensely to his prestige. Riding the wave of religious enthusiasm which he had aroused, Savonarola used his dominant influence with the new republican government to secure laws designed to enforce a moral regeneration of Florence and, meanwhile, continued from the pulpit to call the people to repentance, to denounce worldliness of all kinds, and to demand the reform of the Church in head and members. His attacks upon the immorality of the papal curia soon led to his being forbidden to preach, but the prohibition served only to increase the violence of his denunciations. In 1497 he was excommunicated, but still remained defiant and challenged the validity of excommunication by a pope whom he held to be no true instrument of God. Meanwhile the opposition to him was gaining strength, as the old oligarchical families and those who found his moral legislation too stringent united against him. Once his prestige began to decline the end came quickly. The republican government, which was falling increasingly into the hands of the aristocratic faction, was not prepared to risk an interdict and to fight the pope indefinitely in his behalf. He was arrested and in May, 1498, condemned to death and burned.

In that same spring Charles VIII died, leaving the throne to his cousin, the Duke of Orléans. The new king, Louis XII (1498–1515), began immediately to plan an invasion of Italy, but this time directed primarily against Milan, to which he had an hereditary claim as the grandson of Valentina Visconti, daughter of the great Giangaleazzo, and hence sole legitimate heir to the old Visconti line of the dukes of Milan. His first step was to secure the alliance or neutrality of the members of the league which had driven Charles out of Italy. A treaty with Ferdinand of Aragon, in which Louis apparently gave some assurance that he had no immediate designs on Naples, secured the neutrality of Spain. Venice was won over by the promise of Cremona and other territory to be annexed from the conquered duchy of Milan. Louis then secured the support of Alexander VI by conferring on his son Cesare Borgia the Duchy of Valentinois and by promising him aid in the conquest of the Romagna. Maximilian was engaged in a war with the Swiss, which resulted in the Confederation winning its independence, and he could safely be ignored. Ludovico Sforza was thus, for the second time in his career, left without an ally. In 1499 the French troops swept through the Milanese. Ludovico fled, but returned with Swiss reinforcements the following year only to be captured when his Swiss mercenaries refused to fight their fellow-countrymen in the French army. He spent the rest of his life in a French prison.

Having conquered the Duchy of Milan, Louis XII turned his attention to Naples. The experience of Charles's abortive conquest of the southern kingdom had demonstrated the impracticability of conquering Naples against the opposition of the Spanish army stationed in Sicily. Louis therefore began negotiations with Ferdinand and, on the argument that half a loaf was better than no bread, offered to share the conquest with him. The result was a perfidious treaty, for which the ground had probably been laid in the previous treaty of 1498, by which Ferdinand agreed to abandon his cousin's cause and join Louis in conquering and partitioning the Neapolitan kingdom. Caught between the French and Spanish forces the King of Naples was helpless. By 1502 the entire kingdom was in the hands of the allies. Almost immediately, however, the victors began to quarrel over the division of their ill-gotten gains. The Spanish army under the "Great Captain," Gonzalo da Córdoba, crushed the French opposition in two desperately fought battles in 1503, and by the beginning of the following year the French were forced to abandon Naples, leaving the conquered kingdom to Ferdinand. These events created a new balance of power in Italy, resting upon French occupation of Milan and Spanish occupation of Naples, with Venice and the papacy the only remaining Italian powers whose weight in the balance need be considered, since Florence, enfeebled and still struggling to recapture Pisa, had become little more than a vassal state of France.

While France and Spain were thus establishing themselves in Italy,

Pope Alexander VI was chiefly concerned with the subjugation of the semi-independent lordships in the Romagna. This was a necessary step toward the restoration of effective papal monarchy in the States of the Church, but Alexander was motivated less by concern for papal authority than by ambition for his own family. Cesare Borgia, his favorite since the assassination of his elder son, the Duke of Gandia, was to be the beneficiary as well as the instrument of conquest, replacing the petty despotisms of the Romagna with one large state under his rule. The first part of this plan was carried out successfully with French aid. Cesare drove out one after another of the Romagnole *signori*, but before he could establish himself in the conquered territory his father's death in 1503 deprived him of papal support. Any possibility that he might retain some of the fruits of his victories then disappeared with the election to the papacy of the bitterest enemy of the House of Borgia, Cardinal Giuliano della Rovere, who took the title Julius II (1503–13).

Cesare Borgia's reconquest of the Romagna now furnished a starting point from which the new pope was able to carry on, putting into effect a process of consolidation and centralization in the States of the Church analogous to that carried out in the preceding half-century by the monarchs of the great European states. Julius II had all the brutal driving energy of his uncle, the terrible Sixtus IV, but he was less interested in the advancement of his family and was sincerely devoted to the cause of restoring to the papacy full authority over all the lands that had ever belonged to it. Having cleared the way by pacifying the Orsini and Colonna factions in and around Rome, the old warrior-pope led his troops against the Baglioni of Perugia and the Bentivoglio of Bologna in 1506 and brought these cities under direct papal government. His next objective was to recover the cities in the northern Romagna — Ravenna, Cervia, Rimini, Faenza, Forlì — which had been seized by Venice after Cesare's downfall. The acquisitive republic had taken advantage of the general disruption of the *status quo* in Italy to expand her territory at the expense, not only of the Papal States, but also of the Hapsburg dynasty, the Duchy of Milan, the Kingdom of Naples and the small neighboring states of Mantua and Ferrara. All of these states were but waiting for a suitable opportunity for revenge, so that Julius II had little difficulty in finding the allies he needed to wage war on the powerful republic. In the winter of 1508–09, the League of Cambrai was formed with the object of conquering and partitioning all the Venetian territories except the city itself. Each member of the league, which included the pope, Emperor Maximilian, Louis XII as Duke of Milan, Ferdinand of Aragon as King of Naples, the Duke of Ferrara and the Marquis of Mantua, was to recover the territory he had lost, while Louis and Maximilian were to divide the remaining Venetian territories between them. The war opened with a crushing defeat of the Venetian army at the hands of a superior French force at Agnadello. Following up their victory, the French occupied the area assigned to them at Cambrai, while Maximilian occupied Verona, Vicenza and other cities in the Venetian territory and besieged Padua. Meanwhile, Julius recovered the Romagnole cities and Ferdinand the Apulian ports which Venice had occupied. This was the darkest hour in Venetian history, but in 1510 the republic was saved by an unexpected reprieve. Julius II negotiated a separate peace, and thereafter set himself to the task of breaking up the League of Cambrai and forming a new league against the French.

The reasons for the pope's sudden reversal are clear enough. The league had been too successful. Once he had recovered the Romagnole cities and forced the Venetians to abandon their annoying independence in matters of Church government, he had no desire to see the great republic crushed. It was the only independent Italian state strong enough to maintain the balance against France. And France could be a more dangerous neighbor to the Papal States than the republic had been. The "liberation of Italy from the barbarians," which Julius now proclaimed as his aim, could, however, be accomplished only by the aid of other barbarians. Julius therefore began to play upon the jealousies and antagonisms among the allies who had formed the League of Cambrai, and by the end of 1511 had succeeded in forming a new Holy League, dedicated to the expulsion of the French from Italy. Beside the papacy and Venice, it included Ferdinand of Aragon, Emperor Maximilian, the Swiss Confederation and Henry VIII of England. Despite a brilliant victory over the forces of the League in the hard-fought battle of Ravenna, the French were unable to hold their own against so many enemies and before the end of 1512 withdrew from Italy. The abandoned Duchy of Milan was then restored to Massimiliano Sforza, Il Moro's son, under the protection of the Swiss.

The expulsion of the French brought about a drastic change in the government of Florence, a reversal of the revolution that had followed the first French invasion. The republic, under the leadership of Piero Soderini, who had been made *gonfaloniere* for life in 1502, had remained faithful to the French alliance and now suffered the consequences. Despite the formation of a militia force, organized by Machiavelli as a means of freeing the state from dependence on mercenaries, the republic was no match for a league that had driven the French out of Italy. Machiavelli's militia had justified its existence by the reconquest of Pisa in 1509, but it now broke before the assault of the veteran Spanish troops. The result was the restoration of the Medici. Cardinal Giovanni, his younger brother Giuliano and his nephew Lorenzo entered the city as private citizens, but at the head of four hundred lances. Two days later the system of government which had existed under Lorenzo the Magnificent was restored with the cardinal in full control. The following year Cardinal Giovanni was elected pope as Leo X (1513-21), and thereafter the Medici lordship had the full backing of papal power and prestige, with young Lorenzo acting as the family's representative in control of the Florentine government.

A second by-product of the victory of the League was the conquest of Navarre by Ferdinand of Aragon and its absorption into the growing Spanish state. Navarre was a small and poor kingdom, but it had a considerable strategic importance because of its command of the passes through the Pyrenees. Its king, Jean d'Albret, had acquired the throne by marriage to the heiress, Catherine de Foix, but his title was disputed by a collateral branch of the House of Foix. Both families were French and had large estates in France, but in the early years of the century Louis XII had favored the Foix claims and so had driven Jean d'Albret into an uneasy alliance with Ferdinand. This situation was reversed by the death of the rival claimant, Gaston de Foix, the brilliant young general who had commanded the French army at Ravenna and died there at the moment of victory. Ferdinand, who had married Gaston's sister, Germaine de Foix, after the death of Isabella, now pressed the claim he had thus acquired, and Jean d'Albret was forced to fall back upon an alliance with France. Louis XII, weakened though he was by his recent defeat in Italy, was bound to resist Ferdinand's designs on Navarre which would place the Pyrenean passes in Spanish hands. Unwilling to fight his way through the mountains of Navarre against French resistance, Ferdinand concocted an ingenious scheme to immobilize the French army while he overran the mountain kingdom. His young English son-in-law, Henry VIII, had already joined the Holy League and was eager to gain glory by recouping the English losses in the Hundred Years' War. He was thus easily persuaded to join with Ferdinand in a proposed invasion of France, with Guienne as his share in the spoils of victory. Henry accordingly dispatched an army which landed at Fuenterrabia on the border between Spain and France. There it remained inactive, but serving the purpose of preventing the French from sending aid to Navarre while Ferdinand completed his conquest of the kingdom. It then became apparent that Ferdinand had no intention of joining in an invasion of France, and the English army, mutinous and decimated by disease, was forced to return to England in disgrace.

The remaining years of Louis XII gave Italy a brief respite from invasion, but his death in 1515 left the throne to his ambitious young cousin,

Francis I (1515–47), who immediately led a French army along the familiar road into the Milanese duchy. The Holy League had been weakened by the withdrawal of Henry VIII, who had made peace with France in 1514, and of the Venetian Republic, which had been forced by Maximilian's continued aggression into seeking an alliance with France. It had also been weakened by the death of Julius II. The new pope, Leo X, still adhered to the League, but he lacked the driving energy of his predecessor. The most serious opposition to the French advance came from the Swiss, who had established a protectorate over the Duchy of Milan. At Marignano the French and Swiss armies clashed in one of the most decisive battles of the Italian wars. For the first time the Swiss columns of pikes went down to defeat before the combined force of the French heavy cavalry, artillery and mercenary German and Gascon foot-soldiers. Thereafter the Swiss withdrew from Milan, leaving the French in possession of the duchy, and the Confederation never again played an independent part in international affairs. The Swiss still fought as mercenaries, but changes in the art of war were robbing them of the tactical superiority they had enjoyed so long. In the future, victory would go most commonly to armies in which horse, foot and artillery were equally balanced and in which the pike was more adequately supported by firearms. And such an army could be put into the field and maintained only by a great state with ample financial resources.

The French recovery of Milan was followed by another brief period of relative peace in Italy until the outbreak of hostilities in 1521 between Francis I and the young Emperor Charles V, who had inherited the Kingdom of Naples and was prepared to press imperial claims to northern Italy. In the meantime, Francis took advantage of his Italian triumph to negotiate the Concordat of Bologna with Pope Leo X, in which he traded the shadow of the Gallican liberties asserted in the Pragmatic Sanction for the substance of royal control of ecclesiastical benefices in France. The peace in Italy was, however, no more than a truce, made possible in part by the death of Ferdinand in 1516 and the resultant temporary paralysis of Spanish foreign policy. But that event, followed by the death of Maximilian and the election of Charles V in 1519, created a new balance of power in Europe, of which the balance of power in Italy was but a part. The greater part of Western Europe was now divided between two great dynasties: the House of Valois in France, represented by Francis I, and surrounding France on all sides the vast possessions of the House of Hapsburg, represented by Charles V. In the conflict between these powerful rulers, one firmly established in southern Italy, the other in the north, the Italian states were helpless pawns, and the almost certain result was the domination of the peninsula by one foreign power or the other.

XIV

Continuity and Innovation in the Social Scene

There are fewer cogent reasons in social than in political history for regarding the middle of the fifteenth century as marking a turning point and the opening of a new period. It is natural that this should be so, for specific events may have an immediate effect on political history whereas social change occurs gradually as men adjust slowly to altered conditions. The general direction of social evolution in the years between 1450 and 1520, indeed, remained very similar to that which had characterized the preceding period. European society was still changing, but on the whole it was moving along lines already established. Nevertheless, the impact of political events together with certain alterations in the economic and cultural environment, did in some respects give a new direction to the evolution of the social classes and altered the tone of social life. We may take the element of continuity more or less for granted, and concentrate attention on what was new or different, if only by virtue of the acceleration of tendencies already apparent. This was the period in which the royal and princely courts came fully into their own as the focal centers of aristocratic society; while in Italy, if not yet in the north, the culture of the High Renaissance lent to courtly society an air of refinement and cultivated taste, and made of the courtier the prototype of the modern concept of the gentleman.

A. THE REFINEMENT OF SOCIAL LIFE AND THE GROWTH OF A COURTLY SOCIETY IN ITALY

The urbanization of the nobility of central and northern Italy, and its resultant fusion with merchant families to form a relatively fluid upper class — a class dependent for status more upon wealth and culture than upon birth — had been completed long before 1450. In the process descendants of the old nobility had gradually lost the distinctive *mores* of a hereditary feudal aristocracy. They had become, in fact, indistinguishable in their manner of life from those whose ancestors had risen from the ranks of the *popolo* by way of business or politics or the learned professions. The composition of this urban upper class was constantly shifting as new families rose to wealth and old families died out or fell upon hard times, so that by the middle of the fifteenth century the proportion of genuinely noble blood in its veins must have been rather small. During the fourteenth century and a large part of the fifteenth the very concept of nobility seemed to be disappearing or, at least, becoming very difficult to define. As the fifteenth century wore to a close, however, the social pendulum seemed to be swinging backward. Upper-class Italy remained urban, but the tone of its social life was becoming increasingly aristocratic. This was particularly apparent in the princely states, where a courtly society was in process of formation around the person of the prince; but in the great republics, too, and even in the provincial cities, the manners of the upper class were becoming more refined, more formal, more in keeping with the ideals of a courtly aristocracy than of the prosperous and cultivated but still soberly responsible class of merchants and citizens that had dominated republican life in the earlier period. The change was here largely a matter of nuance, but it foreshadowed the future development of Italian society. The Medici family was obviously exceptional, but the progressive development from Cosimo *Pater Patriae*, through Lorenzo the Magnificent to the Grand Dukes of Tuscany is symbolical of a trend in the evolution of upper-class Italian society from the fifteenth to the sixteenth century.

The political framework within which this social evolution took place was shaped first of all by the stabilization of Italian politics after the Peace of Lodi (1454). During the next forty years there were few dynastic changes in the despotic states, and their rulers were no longer mere *signori*, but princes. The House of Sforza was firmly established in Milan, that of Este in Ferrara, that of Gonzaga in Mantua, and, *mutatis mutandis*, that of the Medici in Florence. In the Papal States the Montefeltro dukes held a small but princely court in Urbino as did the Malatesta in Rimini, while the papal court itself became one of the most splendid in Europe under popes who were more prince than pontiff. The decades of stability afforded the Italian princes the opportunity to consolidate their position as sovereign rulers. Like the rulers of the larger ultramontane states, they surrounded themselves with noble courtiers and demonstrated their sovereign powers by conferring titles of nobility on the officials and diplomats who served them. Although smaller in scale than those of the northern monarchs, their courts were equally elegant and a good deal more cultured. They not only acted as a magnet to attract the intellectual and social élite of Italy, but they set a standard of refined and aristocratic manners which exercised a growing influence on the *mores* of the upper class everywhere. In the republics a princely court, was, of course, impracticable, although the circle of Lorenzo de' Medici formed a reasonable approximation. Moreover the era of Medici domination tended in subtle ways to undermine the sense of civic responsibility among the Florentine patriciate and to encourage the cultivation of manners more befitting an aristocratic leisured class. The Venetian aristocracy was always unique — half merchant, half noble — and it seemed peculiarly resistant to change. Yet even in that formidable oligarchy the noble element seemed to be gaining ground in the fifteenth century, since Venice had become a territorial state with subject cities whose government required the services of an officeholding nobility.

The French invasion in 1494 ended Italy's all too brief period of stability and introduced a new era of almost perpetual invasion and eventual foreign domination. As successive waves of French and Spanish soldiers swept over Italy, the Italians of the upper classes were brought into constant contact with noblemen whose manners and ideals, or, at any rate, whose prejudices still bore the stamp of feudalism and chivalry. Much has been said about the refining influence which Italian culture and social grace exerted upon these foreign barbarians; but in exchange the invaders communicated to the Italian aristocrats something of their own concept of nobility as a hereditary caste and of the manners befitting a nobleman. As the century wore on the manners of the Spanish nobles, proud and rigidly punctilious, increasingly influenced the social tone of the Italian courts.

Meanwhile, economic as well as political conditions encouraged the transformation of the Italian urban patriciate into a courtly aristocracy. Italy was prosperous in this period as a result of the general upward trend of European economy, but the sphere of its activity was becoming increasingly circumscribed and its position in relation to the rest of Western Europe was deteriorating. The upper classes were losing something of the aggressive and acquisitive spirit that had characterized the early capitalists, and even the more bourgeois virtues of thrift and sobriety were disappearing. There was now a more pronounced tendency to invest inherited wealth in land and to enjoy the fruits of passive investment. To the scions of the old wealthy families money was something to be spent rather than made. Consumption, indeed, had never been so conspicuous as on the eve of the invasions, so that the invaders gained an impression of wealth in Italy greater than actually existed. The Italian aristocracy was not yet barred from participation in business as were the French and Spanish nobility, but the countinghouse was ceasing to be its spiritual home.

Finally, Italy was experiencing in this period the full flowering of that many-sided culture which we identify with the Renaissance, and it acted as a powerful incentive toward the refinement of social life. By the middle of the fifteenth century, humanism had passed its formative period and its fruits now became the common possession of most men — and many women — of the upper classes. Not only was some knowledge of the classics regarded as a necessary part of a gentleman's education, but a large part of classical literature had been translated and made available in the vernacular. The example of the ancients set a standard of civilized behaviour which the cultivated Italians eagerly strove to emulate. At the same time, humanism, while itself an aristocratic movement in the sense of being a culture for the élite, served as a partial counterbalance to the growing cult of nobility. It helped to maintain the tradition that for entry into the best society culture and talent were as necessary as noble birth and that without them inherited nobility was not enough. Artists, poets and scholars were thus enabled to take their place beside titled courtiers and to make the courts centers of culture as well as of good breeding. Such a society might be vicious but it would not be boorish.

Despite the moderating influence of humanism, however, the growth of the princely courts enhanced the value of titles of nobility and of noble birth. It also led to a revived interest in tournaments and the trappings of chivalry. In Ferrara the young ladies of the House of Este sponsored a romantic revival of the medieval *chansons de geste* and encouraged Boiardo to retell the story of Roland. The resulting poem, however, merely served to demonstrate the vast gap which separated the urban Italian courts from the society that had produced the feudal epics and chivalrous romances. The princely courts which were emerging in Italy toward the end of the fifteenth century represented a new social ideal, which owed more to the evolution of a native tradition of culture and urbanity than to any foreign influence. It also reflected a political situation that was uniquely Italian.

Social Developments

The new ideal of courtly society found its most effective expression in a remarkable book, *The Courtier* (*Il Cortegiano*) by Count Baldassare Castiglione, published in 1528 but written some years earlier. Castiglione (1478–1529) was himself an accomplished courtier and diplomat, who came close to embodying the ideal he here presented to the world. Born of a noble Mantuan family and on his mother's side related to the princely family of Gonzaga, he had been taught Latin by Giorgio Merula and Greek by Demetrios Chalcondylas during his youth in Milan, where he also frequented the court of Ludovico Il Moro, at that time the cultural center of northern Italy. Later, he served in turn Gianfrancesco Gonzaga, Marquis of Mantua, Guidobaldo da Montefeltro, Duke of Urbino, and his successor Francesco Maria della Rovere, the nephew of Pope Julius II. He was sent on at least one diplomatic mission to England and spent some years at the papal court of Leo X. For the last five years of his life he was ambassador for the unfortunate Clement VII at the court of Charles V in Spain. When Castiglione put the finishing touches to his masterpiece not long before his death, he had had a lifetime of experience in the most polished courts of Europe; but he still found the most perfect model of a courtly society in the little ducal court of Urbino, where he had spent his happiest years in the service of Duke Guidobaldo and his duchess, Elisabetta Gonzaga.

Although the primary purpose of *The Courtier* was to describe the attributes and behavior of the perfect courtier — and incidentally of the court lady, to whom most of Book III is devoted — it also presents a vivid portrait of the ideal court, a nostalgic reconstruction of that of Urbino about the year 1507. Urbino, small though it was, had been made a center of humanist culture and courtly manners by the previous duke, Federigo da Montefeltro. That scholarly *condottiere*, who had been trained in youth by the great humanist schoolmaster Vittorino da Feltre, had for thirty years spent the money he made as a mercenary captain on the maintenance of a well-appointed court and the collection of one of the finest libraries in Italy. Now, a generation later, the tradition of culture, upright morality and good manners which he had established was carried on in the gracious circle presided over by the Duchess Elisabetta. As in the *Paradiso degli Alberti*, which portrayed upper-class Florentine society a century earlier, the interlocutors in *The Courtier* are a rather mixed lot. Literature, learning and the arts are again represented, and the ladies take an active part in the conversation, but the large proportion of men of noble or princely family among those present marks the difference between the ducal court and the patrician society of republican Florence. There is also in Castiglione's dialogue a lighter tone, an easier give and take; and the didactic passages are frequently interrupted by laughter and a good-natured jest. The participants in the dialogue are well-educated and familiar with the classics, but they wear their learning lightly. The influence of humanism is evident in the frequent appeal to the example of the ancients, but also in the moral standards implied in the portrayal of the perfect courtier. It is an essentially lay morality that we find here, independent of Christianity and with no tinge of medieval asceticism or *contemptus mundi*. Like the orator in Cicero's *De oratore*, Castiglione's courtier should be a good and upright man, a man of integrity; but these qualities are presented as necessary attributes of the perfect courtier rather than as virtues tending to the soul's salvation. There are three future cardinals in the group, but they have the good taste not to introduce an extraneous religious note into a conversation which, for all its serious purpose, was designed for the polite amusement of a cultivated court.

Since Castiglione's characters are engaged in constructing the picture of an ideal courtier, they take for granted that he will not only be a man of unimpeachable character, but also be blessed with a handsome appearance, natural grace, numerous talents and noble birth. This last qualification, it is true, is disputed, not by one of the common-born members of the group, but by young Count Gaspare Pallavicino, who argues eloquently that nobility of birth does not seem essential to a courtier.

> I quite agree [he replies to Count Ludovico da Canossa, who would have the courtier nobly born and of gentle race] with what you say as to the good fortune of those endowed from birth with advantages of mind and body: but this is seen as well among the humbly born as among the nobly born, since nature has no such subtle distinctions as these; and often, as I said, the highest gifts are found among the most obscure. Therefore, since this nobility of birth is won neither by talent nor by strength nor by craft, and is rather the merit of our predecessors than our own, it seems to me too extravagant to maintain that if our Courtier's parents be humbly born, all his good qualities are spoiled, and that all those other qualifications that you mentioned do not avail to raise him to the summit of perfection; I mean talent, beauty of feature, comeliness of person, and that grace which makes him always charming to everyone at first sight.[1]

But Count Ludovico has the last word. There is an intrinsic value in hereditary nobility "it being reasonable that good should beget good"; pride of ancestry is an incentive to great deeds; and, finally, it has practical advantages and so should be attributed to the perfect courtier, "as

[1] B. Castiglione, *The Book of the Courtier*, trans. L. E. Opdycke (New York, 1929), I, 15, p. 23 f.

well for many other reasons as for universal opinion, which is at once disposed in favor of noble birth."

Then follows a long list of the accomplishments which the courtier should possess. First of all, he should be proficient in the use of arms and in all bodily exercises befitting a gentleman, such as riding, jousting and playing tennis. "The principal and true profession of the Courtier," Count Ludovico declares, "ought to be that of arms; which I would have him follow actively above all else, and be known among others as bold and strong, and loyal to whomsoever he serves."[2] But the military and bodily exercises, which were all that was required of the medieval knight, were not enough for the Renaissance courtier. He should also have a liberal education and be "more than passably accomplished in letters, at least in those studies that are called the humanities, and conversant not only with the Latin language but with the Greek. . . . Let him be well versed in the poets, and not less in the orators and historians, and also proficient in writing verse and prose, especially in this vulgar tongue of ours."[3] Count Ludovico, who carries the argument in the first book, is proudly aware that such accomplishments are not common to the nobility outside of Italy. "Besides goodness," he declares, "I think that letters are for everyone the true and principal ornament of the mind; although the French recognize only the nobility of arms and esteem all else as nought. Thus they not only fail to prize but they abhor letters and hold all men of letters most base, and think they speak very basely of any man when they call him a clerk."[4] Proceeding with the list of necessary accomplishments, the count will not be "content with the courtier unless he be also a musician and unless, besides understanding and being able to read notes, he can play upon diverse instruments."[5] Finally he would have him able to draw and paint, even though this art "may seem to savor of the artisan and little to befit a gentleman."[6] But, since the courtier is, above all, a gentleman, he should in the exercise of these accomplishments preserve his amateur standing. He should do all things easily and without apparent effort, but also without professional finish. This applies to games as well as to more serious accomplishments. Castiglione, speaking through Messer Federico Fregoso, has no objection to the courtier playing games such as dice and cards, provided he does not spend too much time on them or play only for money, but he strongly advises against chess, "since whoever would excel in the game of chess must spend much time on it, and give it as much study as if he would learn some noble science . . . and yet in the end with all his pains he has learned nothing but a game."[7] One is reminded of the

---

[2] *Ibid.*, I, 17, p. 25.
[5] *Ibid.*, I, 47, p. 62.
[3] *Ibid.*, I, 44, p. 58.
[6] *Ibid.*, I, 49, p. 64.
[4] *Ibid.*, I, 42, p. 56.
[7] *Ibid.*, II, 31, p. 106.

later English dictum that to play billiards well is the mark of a gentleman; to play too well is the mark of a misspent youth.

Aside from the native endowments and cultivated achievements of the courtier, Castiglione gives a good deal of attention to the problem of how he should behave. Perhaps it is enough to say that he should behave like a gentleman, in very much the modern sense of the word. Many of his ideals of conduct undoubtedly had their origin in medieval chivalry, but the nuances are more modern than medieval. A certain standard of conduct is required of him, not because he is a knight — knighthood is never expressly mentioned — but because he is a gentleman. Chivalry in the broadest and most ideal sense of the word characterizes the courtier's conduct towards the ladies, but of the chivalric cult of *l'amour courtois* there is not a trace. At the same time, there are frequent bits of pragmatic counsel which remind us that Castiglione is concerned, not only with the conduct befitting a gentleman, but also with that which will serve to advance a courtier who has his way to make in the world. There is much sage advice about the importance of making a good impression and of securing favorable advance publicity when travelling to a new court. The courtier should be modest about his accomplishments, but not to the extent of hiding his light under a bushel. He should, at any rate, so arrange the bushel that his light will inadvertently shine through.

> If our courtier excels in anything besides arms, [Messer Federico advises] I would have him get profit and esteem from it in fine fashion; and I would have him so discreet and sensible as to be able with skill and address to attract men to see and hear that wherein he thinks he excels, always appearing not to do it from ostentation, but by chance and at others' request rather than by his own wish. And in everything he has to do or say, let him if possible come ready and prepared, yet appearing to act impromptu throughout.[8]

Finally, it is the first duty of the courtier to serve his prince and win his favor. As Messer Federico puts it, "I would have the courtier strive, with all the thoughts and forces of his mind, to love and almost to adore the prince whom he serves, above every other thing, and mould his wishes, habits and all his ways to the prince's liking."[9] But he should not do this as a flatterer, nor merely to secure his own advancement, but so that he may be in a position to offer good counsel and have it accepted. With the growth of absolute monarchies, the problem of good counsel was one that concerned serious political thinkers everywhere in Europe. But Castiglione's courtier, like Machiavelli's prince, was the

[8] *Ibid.,* II, 38, p. 114.   [9] *Ibid.,* II, 18, p. 91.

product of a kind of state that existed only in Italy. The Italian courtier's devotion to his prince was not rooted in patriotism, nor did he owe him an hereditary loyalty. He was free to leave his service provided only that he did not do so when the prince was at war or in adversity. With this exception, the ideal here presented could be adopted by gentlemen and courtiers throughout Europe; and the number of editions, in Italian and in translation, published during the next two or three hundred years suggests that it was thus universally accepted. There is, indeed, good reason to regard *The Courtier* as one of the most influential books written in the sixteenth century.

B. The Reconstruction of the Aristocracy in the Northern and Western States

As in Italy, some of the most significant changes in the tone and organization of society elsewhere in Europe occurred among the upper classes. In France, England and Spain the final emergence of a strong centralized government under absolute monarchs — the Tudor monarchy was a partial exception, but absolute enough for all practical purposes — had deprived the nobles of the last vestige of their feudal independence. This completed a process begun in France and England some two hundred years earlier, but interrupted and impeded by civil wars, by periods of feeble royal government and, in England, by the bastard feudalism of the age of livery and maintenance. In Spain it was a newer development, scarcely begun until the union of the Spanish crowns under the firm rule of Ferdinand and Isabella. The aristocracy survived the loss of the greater part of its political and jurisdictional powers with all its claims to social status and privilege still intact; but its character and, to some extent, its composition were changing. The nature and direction of change differed in each of the countries, but the salient facts were: first a greater dependence upon the monarchy for wealth, power and honor, which caused ambitious nobles and gentlemen to regard the royal court as the source from which all blessings flowed, and second the reconstruction of the aristocracy by recruitment from the ranks of the gentry and upper bourgeoisie.

In France economic as well as political forces operated to thin the ranks of the old nobility and to reduce the survivors to dependence on the monarchy. As we have seen the landholding class was faced with a declining real income during the greater part of the fourteenth and fifteenth centuries, while at the same time the expense of maintaining noble status was rising. Under these circumstances many *seigneurs* were unable to hold their lands and dropped out of the noble class. Others of the *petite noblesse* lived on in a state of genteel poverty on their country estates or took service in the ranks of the élite cavalry companies. The more fortunate, who could afford the expense of maintaining a suitable appearance at court, sought aid from the king in the hope of recouping their depleted finances. For many of them the hope was realized, since the king found it expedient to grant them sinecures at court, offices in the army, nomination to the more lucrative benefices in the Church, or pensions as a means of securing their subordination to the monarchy. The cost of this system of poor relief for the nobility was considerable and imposed a heavy drain on the royal treasury, but as the cost of transforming potentially troublesome nobles into subservient courtiers it was probably worth it. At the same time, it served the additional purpose of enhancing the prestige of the monarchy by surrounding the king's person with the scions of the most ancient lineages in France.

Thanks to the royal service and royal bounty, many of the old fighting nobility — the *noblesse d'épée* — survived the crisis. Some were also aided by the handsome *dot* that accompanied marriage with the daughter of a wealthy and socially aspiring bourgeois, thus reviving the family fortunes by a welcome infusion of capital. But the continued existence of a numerous noble class, which lasted till the revolution, was also assured by recruitment from below, as a growing number of members of the upper bourgeoisie, especially of those who had gained wealth through service in the royal government or the judiciary, entered the ranks of the nobility by the process of ennoblement. There were various ways in which a wealthy bourgeois could edge his way into the nobility. He might purchase a noble estate or fief, takes its name and live nobly, that is, perform such duties as were required of the nobility and abstain from engaging in business or other common pursuits. In time he, or rather his descendants, might be tacitly accepted as noble and share the privileges of that class, including exemption from the *taille*. Royal officers, however, periodically investigated the claims of such bogus nobles and fined those who could not validate their claims. The safest and most common practice was to acquire, at a price, letters of ennoblement from the king, who might also grant nobility as a reward for services to the government. Since many of those thus ennobled were judges in the royal courts, members of the *Parlement* of Paris or holders of administrative or financial offices in the royal government, a new *noblesse de robe* took its place beside the old *noblesse d'épée*, or, if not quite beside it, only a step or two to the rear. This introduction into the nobility of new recruits endowed with money, legal training and business sense, which became more frequent in the following centuries, not only assured the survival of a large noble class, but also altered to some extent the character of the French aristocracy. At the same time it served to check the rise of the bourgeoisie in the social scale and as a political force by removing from it its most wealthy and influential members. For, once ennobled, the ex-bourgeois cut himself off as completely as possible from the class into which he had been born, and claimed all the perquisites and privileges of the class into which he had thrust his way.

If the nobility of France was only very partially and gradually reconstituted by the intrusion of the *anoblis*, the English peerage was almost entirely replaced during these years. The old nobility, a much smaller group than in France because it did not include the gentry, was decimated by the mortality and confiscations of the Wars of the Roses, followed by the execution of certain over-mighty subjects by the first two Tudor kings. Henry VII and Henry VIII were thus able to repopulate the House of Lords with peers of their own creation and entirely devoted to the new dynasty. These new peers lacked the independent spirit of the old baronage, and their interests were very similar to those of the gentry from which class they had been raised by royal favor. With the disappearance of so many of the old baronial families and the recovery of royal authority, the gentry became more than ever the mainstays of government and the arbiters of social life in the counties, acting as lords-lieutenant or deputy lieutenants of the shires, as sheriffs and as Justices of the Peace. They also formed a vital connecting link between the aristocracy and the wealthy burghers, frequently sitting as borough representatives in the House of Commons. Deprived by the rule of primogeniture of a share in the family estates, the younger sons of the gentry frequently migrated to the city to seek their fortunes in the legal profession, in government service or in trade. When one speaks of the rise of the middle class in this period — as historians constantly do — it is well to remember the close interrelation of the two classes of burghers and gentry in England where the dividing line between the bourgeoisie and the aristocracy was not as clearly defined as in France, and passage from one class to the other was correspondingly easier.

The position of the English gentry was in other respects different from that of the petty nobility of France. Their services as county officials and Justices of the Peace bound them closely to the monarchy and bred in them a sense of responsibility and service to the state. They were also losing something of their military tradition. The Tudor monarchs had no standing army and there were fewer opportunities for a gentleman to make a career of arms. With the restoration of royal authority, too, life in the country was safer and more peaceful. The new manor houses that were built in the Tudor era were not designed as fortresses but as homes.

On the whole, the English gentry seem to have been more prosperous than their French equivalents, partly because of the growing demand for wool and partly because many family fortunes were reinforced by wealth derived from royal service, the law or trade. They also seem to have been more wedded to country life, more content to find prestige and status in the life of the county.

In both countries, however, the royal court was becoming more than ever a magnet to attract to itself the ambitious and greedy — the great families who claimed a place near the king as their right, and the impoverished scions of lesser families who hoped to make their fortunes by gaining the monarch's favor. Both the French and English courts acquired a new magnificence at the turn of the century. In France the expenditure for the upkeep of the court and the innumerable sinecure offices and pensions to favorites grew rapidly under Charles VIII. They were somewhat curtailed by the more economical Louis XII, but expanded to unprecedented proportions under the open-handed Francis I, who liked to think of himself as the first gentleman of France, and regarded parsimony as no fit attribute for a gentleman. In England, Henry VII, who had as keen an appreciation of the value of money as any merchant, kept a tight hold on expenditure, but he nevertheless understood the importance of maintaining a court befitting the majesty of a king, especially of a king whose dynasty was none too securely established. His son shared his conviction of the importance of giving monarchy a suitable setting, but he had none of his father's natural tendency toward economy. His accession opened an era of unprecedented extravagance.

The royal courts of the opening years of the sixteenth century were different in many ways from the smaller princely courts of Italy. The French court, in particular, was more exclusively noble. Although much of the practical work of government was carried on by trained officials drawn from the upper bourgeoisie, the honorary offices, of which there were an incredible number, were reserved for the aristocracy. These offices were not only lucrative, but carried great social prestige and afforded opportunities to attract the attention of the king, the source of all honor and advancement. At the same time, a vestige of the feudal tradition still lingered on to give these courts a distinctive character. On the one hand, the French and English courtiers owed a deeper allegiance to their king than did the professional Italian courtier to his prince; on the other hand, despite the increasing formality of court etiquette, the heads of great families were not yet prepared to accord monarchy the subservient reverence demanded a century and a half later of the courtiers of the Sun King. In character as well as in time, the courts of this period stood midway between the chivalric and semi-feudal courts of the fourteenth and early fifteenth centuries and the fully developed royal court of the seventeenth. The formal aspect of chivalry still played a part in court pageant and ceremony, but the obsession with it which had characterized the Burgundian court of Philip the Good was a thing of the past. When Francis I had himself knighted by the Chevalier Bayard on the field of Pavia, it was an anachronistic gesture. And the immense personal prestige enjoyed by Bayard, the knight without fear and without reproach, was in part due to the fact that he was himself an anachronism.

The northern courts could not yet compete in refinement of manners and breadth of culture with the Italian courts as depicted by Castiglione. To the Italians the northern invaders still seemed somewhat barbarous. Yet there were signs of a growing interest in letters and learning, which would bear fruit later in the century. Both Francis I and Henry VIII were well educated and took a sympathetic interest in men of letters, although Henry proved less liberal in his patronage than Erasmus and other scholars had hoped. It was not so much royal patronage, however, as a change in the attitude of the aristocracy that marks the difference between the court in the sixteenth century and that of the preceding period. There were still plenty of nobles in France who justified Castiglione's gibe that they thought they spoke very basely of a man when they called him a clerk; but there is also evidence that an increasing number of young gentlemen in both France and England were being sent to the universities or were being initiated into book-learning by private tutors. The fact is that the growing complexity of government in the kind of state that had developed by the sixteenth century demanded education of the governing class. If the nobles were to hold their place as counsellors of the king and as his ambassadors abroad, and not leave all these posts to men of the middle class, they would need more than the conventional training in good manners and the use of arms, which had been all that was required of their ancestors. The case for book-learning on the part of the aristocracy was put very clearly and at an unusually early date in a letter written in 1465 by Jean de Lannoy, a great noble of the Netherlands and a knight of the Golden Fleece, for the future guidance of his young son. After outlining a program of education, first at home under a tutor and then at the universities of Louvain, Cologne or Paris, de Lannoy came to the heart of the matter.

> Those who have learned and retained much, [he wrote] and who have the greatest desire to learn and know, attain great good, honor and riches. . . . This has often caused me deep displeasure, not for envy of them, but because of my simplicity and slight knowledge and because

I was never put to school. I therefore know and can know nothing. I realize that this chance is for me lost and gone, never to be recovered, for I do not see or expect any remedy as to Latin or other studies. No day passes that I do not regret this, and especially when I find myself in the council of the king or of the Duke of Burgundy, and I know not nor dare not to speak my opinion after the learned, eloquent legists and *ystoryens* who have spoken before me. For I do not know the order or manner of speaking and can say nothing but "Master John or Master Peter has spoken well, and I am of his opinion." Whence I have often felt deep shame and humiliation in my heart.[10]

Nobles with such appreciation of book-learning were rare in the fifteenth century. Philippe de Commines found few at the court of Louis XI. But the need for education on the part of the nobles and gentry as members of the governing class was urged repeatedly in the following century, nowhere more cogently than by that very sensible English gentleman, Sir John Elyot, in his *Boke named the Gouvernour* (1531).

It is difficult to determine how much of the changing attitude of the nobility and gentry toward formal education was due to the spread of humanism and the example of the cultured Italian courts, but these were certainly not without influence. The wars which began in 1494 brought the French aristocracy into direct contact with Italy at the height of its Renaissance, and, although soldiers are notoriously impervious to the culture of the lands they invade, something of what they found there must have brushed off onto the northern nobles. It is not without reason that French literary historians normally date their national Renaissance from the wars in Italy or the reign of Francis I. Meanwhile, too, classical humanism was being naturalized in the northern lands, and was beginning to provide both the aristocracy and the bourgeoisie with a body of literary material in which the traditional themes of medieval chivalric literature played no part. The active protagonists of the new learning were for the most part of the educated middle class, many of them members of the learned professions; but Lord Mountjoy, who was tutored by Erasmus in the last years of the fifteenth century, was not the only young aristocrat to secure a classical education as a preliminary to a career at court.

In Germany, the lack of effective central government prevented the growth of a royal court capable of drawing to itself the nobility of the land or of setting a standard of culture and refined manners. Emperor Maximilian was himself a cultivated person, interested in the new learning and a patron of art and music. He had, moreover, the personal

---

[10] Quoted in J. H. Hexter, "The Education of the Aristocracy in the Renaissance," *The Journal of Modern History*, XXII (1950), p. 14.

charm and chivalric aura that could have made him a suitable focal point for a brilliant court. But his court, whether in Brussels or Vienna, was no more than provincial in scope, and he was chronically inpecunious. If the mass of the German nobility frequented a court, it was that of their territorial prince, and these tiny provincial courts remained largely immune to the new currents of taste and culture. There were exceptions like Albrecht of Brandenburg, Archbishop of Mainz, and Ulrich von Hutten, the knight turned humanist and poet. But contemporary evidence indicates that the German nobility were on the whole uncultivated boors, more noted for heavy drinking and gross gluttony than for intellectual eminence.

The growth of strong royal government in Spain during the last years of the fifteenth century and the first of the sixteenth was rapidly transforming the character of the Spanish nobility, until recently the most turbulent in Europe. The great nobles, who had large landed estates, were gradually shorn of their independent authority and drawn to court, while the lesser nobles, the *hidalgos*, found employment in the royal administration or the army and became devoted supporters of the monarchy. After Spain became involved in the wars in Italy, the Spanish aristocracy, like the French, were exposed to the influence of the Italian courts, although the strong religious sentiment and rigid orthodoxy characteristic of the Spaniards of that period tended to immunize them from the more secular aspects of Renaissance culture. They were also distinguished, as Castiglione observed, by a certain gravity and reserve, less volatile and free in their manners than the French, as befitted the proudest aristocracy in Europe.

When we turn from the aristocracy to the non-noble population of the cities, that amorphous group often lumped together under the rubric "middle class," there seems little to add to our earlier comments. They were still a far from homogeneous class, a great differentiation of wealth and status dividing the merchant capitalists and members of the learned professions from the rank and file of shopkeepers and guild masters. With rising prosperity and an increasing volume of production and exchange the population of the cities was growing in numbers and wealth, and hence in political influence. But, as we have seen, the growth of that influence was minimized by the desertion of the wealthiest and most influential families, who were able to fulfill their social aspirations by joining the ranks of the nobility or gentry. The time had not yet come when the French bourgeoisie would try to destroy the privileges of the nobility. As yet their highest ambition was to find a place for themselves among the privileged. And the two means of achieving that end were wealth and education. The classical humanism spreading from Italy found the most fertile soil for its growth among the upper ranks of the bourgeoisie. Like the Italian patricians a century or more earlier, they found in it a culture more to their taste than either the scholasticism which still dominated the universities, or the chivalric poetry and romance which had hitherto constituted the greater part of available secular literature.

C. Social Unrest on the Eve of the Reformation

The seventy years between the end of the Hundred Years' War and the beginning of the Protestant Reformation were on the whole less disturbed by social unrest and open revolt of the underprivileged than was the preceding period. The first stage in the disruption of the medieval social pattern by the intrusion of capitalism into industry and of money economy into the manorial system was now past. Moreover, social tensions, although still present everywhere, were somewhat minimized by a general economic recovery after a century or more of stagnation or recession. On the other hand, an increase in the population, which was beginning to recover the losses due to the Black Death and other calamities of the fourteenth century, was depriving laborers of the bargaining power they had enjoyed during the period when labor, particularly on the land, was scarce. Rising prices, the first impact of the price revolution of the sixteenth century, also worked to the disadvantage of hired labor, as wages tended to lag behind the rising cost of living. Nevertheless, in most of the Western European countries what social unrest there was seems to have been kept well under control and to have left few marks on the history of the period. In England and Germany, however, special circumstances bred a social tension in the years just before the Reformation, which deserves closer examination.

The disruption of the manorial system in England had been practically completed before the middle of the fifteenth century. With the passing of labor services and demesne farming, landlords were left dependent upon the income they received as rents from the tenants on their estates, without even the seigneurial dues which the French nobility retained as a legacy from their feudal past. Conversely, the tenants, freed from servitude and manorial jurisdiction, owed their landlord no more than the cash rent they paid for the use of their land. Those of the tenants who held their land in hereditary tenure by copyhold — and could prove it — were fairly secure in its possession, paying a fixed rent in money of decreasing value. But many tenants held their land on leases for life or a term of years, and it was to the interest of the landlords to increase their number wherever possible. These tenants were in a more precarious position, since landlords, themselves faced by the rising cost of living, strove to increase their income by exacting fines for the renewal of a lease or by raising the rent when the lease fell due. Under these circumstances many small tenants lost their land, while more prosperous or efficient tenants seized the opportunity to add to their holdings. The result was a growing disparity among the rural classes. On the one hand, a growing class of yeoman farmers acquired enough land to lay the foundations of a family fortune which might enable their descendants to enter the learned professions or even eventually to move up into the ranks of the gentry. On the other hand, a much larger number became landless wage earners, or, where there was an oversupply of labor, were forced to take to the roads as vagabonds. All of these factors, including increased population and monetary inflation, created an atmosphere of unrest in rural England, the basic causes of which were not understood and which tended to focus attention on one evil practice which all men could understand.

The enclosure of land by permanent hedges or fences to form privately operated fields was nothing new. It had been going on ever since the manorial system, with its open fields and commons, had begun to break up. In many cases enclosure was to the advantage of the tenants rather than otherwise. When the scattered strips in the open fields were thrown together to form individual holdings, the result was more economical and productive farming. The enclosure of waste or forest for cultivation also provided more land for more workers. But, when landlords enclosed for their own use commons on which the villagers had pastured their livestock, the tenants bitterly resented this infringement upon their immemorial rights. The enclosures which caused the greatest furor, however, were those resulting from the conversion of arable land into pasturage for sheep. The English woollen industry was expanding in these years and the price of wool was rising. It might then be quite profitable to enclose a number of small peasant holdings, and perhaps some common, and turn them into pasture. The result was not only to deprive the peasant families of their land, but also to leave them without employment, since a couple of shepherds could care for the sheep on an acreage that would have needed the labor of some forty men to cultivate.

Recent research has demonstrated that only a small proportion of the arable land, mostly in the Midlands, was actually converted to pasture. It was not enclosure alone that was responsible for the number of vagabonds and "sturdy beggars" who gave so much concern to the government and to serious observers of the contemporary scene. But the significance of the enclosure movement must be judged less by the actual extent of the evil than by the degree to which it affected public opinion; and there is ample evidence in the efforts of Parliament to control it by legislation and in the outcry of preachers and pamphleteers that it was regarded as a serious menace to English society. Thomas More was echoing a commonly held opinion when, in the first book of the *Utopia*, he had his traveller, Raphael Hythloday, ascribe the great number of thieves and vagabonds to be found in England to "the increase of pastures, . . . by which your sheep, which are naturally mild, and easily kept in order, may be said now to devour men, and unpeople not only villages but towns; for wherever it is found that the sheep of any soil yield a softer and richer wool than ordinary, there the nobility and gentry, and even those holy men the abbots, not content with the old rents which their farms yielded, . . . enclose grounds that they may lodge their sheep in them." The enclosure movement was but a symptom of a more general disturbance of the social and economic structure of England, but it served to crystallize a sense of social injustice, and, as so often in the past, social unrest tended to take an anti-clerical direction. It would be easy to persuade land-hungry men that the idle monks had no right to the fat acres they still possessed.

In Germany, too, the years preceding the Reformation were marked by a growing unrest on the part of the peasants. The discontent, which centered in the older parts of Germany to the south and the west, was directed less against the landlords as such than against the princes of the territorial states, including many bishops and abbots who claimed sovereign powers over their lands. These territorial princes were beginning to find in their political and judicial authority a means of compensating for the decline in their income from land by imposing direct and indirect taxes, fines and obligations of various kinds upon the peasants. With the aid of jurists trained in Roman Law they were also introducing new legal concepts and procedures, which were unfamiliar to the peasants and which tended to give the prince a more absolute authority than medieval custom had allowed. The peasants complained, too, that the princes were using their double power as sovereigns and landlords to revive obsolete servile obligations and to limit the peasants' use of commons, forests and waste land, depriving them of their customary rights to pasture their livestock on the commons and to hunt and fish in the forests and streams.

Throughout the fifteenth century and the first quarter of the sixteenth there were numerous peasant revolts on the lands of individual lords or princes. What the peasants demanded in these instances was the rectification of specific grievances, which they regarded as innovations, and the restoration of the old customs. But, since in each instance both the old customs and the new grievances were in their specific form peculiar to the individual territory, these local revolts could not spread into a more general rebellion. They were, however, sufficiently numerous to indicate a general and chronic state of unrest.

Meanwhile, a second and potentially more dangerous form of revolutionary agitation was spreading among the peasants and to some extent also among the poorer classes in the towns in the generation or two before the Reformation. The watchword of this movement was not the restoration of the old law, but of God's law — not *das alte Recht*, but *das Göttliche Recht*. Combining a passionate sense of social injustice with a literal and unhistorical interpretation of the Bible, peasant agitators wandered through the country stirring up the peasants to demand a complete reorganization of society, the overthrow of lords and princes, the disendowment of the clergy, the abolition of serfdom and of all taxes, manorial dues and clerical tithes, in short, of all those evidences of social inequality which could not be justified by specific Biblical authority and hence were contrary to God's law. God, they argued, had made all men free and had created land, water and wood for the free use of all. Many of these revolutionary ideas, including the strong anticlerical bias that characterized the movement, had their origin in the semi-heretical sects which had spread among the underprivileged classes in the fourteenth and fifteenth centuries. They may also have owed something to the radical left wing of the Hussite movement in Bohemia.

In the opening years of the sixteenth century, the specific grievances of the peasants who had been demanding the restoration of the old customs were united with the more radical appeal to divine law in a movement which spread rapidly through southern and western Germany and which took as the symbol of revolt the peasants' bound shoe (*Bundschuh*). The combination of religious fanaticism with social discontent not only gave the new movement a greater driving force, but also freed it from restriction to an individual territory or lordship, since the *Göttliche Recht* to which it appealed was universal. Unlike the earlier spontaneous local revolts, too, this was an organized movement, led by agitators who in one area after another enlisted the peasants as sworn members of a secret league or conspiracy. In the Bishopric of Speyer in 1502, in the Breisgau in 1513 and again in the upper Rhineland in 1517, *Bundschuh* revolts were fully organized and the date for the rising set; but in each case the conspiracy was betrayed to the authorities and was crushed before the signal for revolt could be given. So far as immediate practical results were concerned, the *Bundschuh* movement was a failure. But the fusion of revolutionary social and religious ideas it represented formed a combustible mixture, which any spark might ignite into a general conflagration. That spark was contributed by Luther's defiance of authority, by such aspects of his doctrine as trickled down to the peasants, and by the wide diffusion of the New Testament in his German translation. The result was the great Peasants' War of 1525.

XV

Literature and Learning

In the history of literature and learning the period from the middle of the fifteenth century through the second decade of the sixteenth was in many respects different from that which preceded it. It witnessed the culmination and decline of Italian humanism, the revival of Neoplatonic philosophy and of vernacular literature in Italy, the spread of classical humanism across the Alps and the evolution in the northern countries of a program of religious and educational reform under the aegis of Christian humanism. The Italians were still the schoolmasters of Europe, but the center of gravity of intellectual life was shifting to the north.

An additional reason for regarding the middle years of the fifteenth century as marking a turning point in the history of European culture was the introduction of printing with movable type by Johann Gutenberg of Mainz in the years around 1450. Few events, perhaps not even the discovery of the New World half a century later, can be regarded as so truly epoch-making. The effect of the printed word on the evolution of modern civilization has been of incalculable magnitude. The period we are here considering experienced only its initial impact, but even in its infancy printing had begun to exert a shaping influence on learning and literary taste. It added a new dimension to scholarship and it altered in fundamental ways the relation of the author to his public. By making books available in quantity and at a reasonable price, so that men of modest means could buy more books than even princes had been able to afford, printing vastly expanded the reading public. Many of the books published to meet the growing demand were of the traditional types, but there was now a growing tendency to write learned works in the vernacular, especially in Italy, or to translate the classics into the national tongue so as to reach a wider audience. Most important of all in this period, printing enabled scholars to make the Latin and Greek classics available in carefully edited editions. Without it the rapid spread of humanism in northern Europe would scarcely have been possible, nor would the humanists have been able to reach an international audience for their own work, thereby welding all of Western Europe, if only for a moment, into a single commonwealth of letters.

A. Humanism and Philosophy in Italy

The 1450's saw the passing of the great generation of classical scholars whose work had very nearly completed the major achievements of Italian humanism. Bruni and Vittorino da Feltre were already dead; Valla died in 1457, Poggio in 1459, Guarino in 1460, Flavio Biondo in 1463. The two popes who brought humanism into the Vatican, Nicholas V and Pius II, died in 1455 and 1464 respectively. In the following decades a new generation reaped the fruits of their predecessors' labors, but added less that was essentially new. The scholars of this generation had learned good classical Latin and sound philological method in youth, and they were also able to profit by the services of the Greek refugees, who fled from Constantinople after 1453 bearing with them Greek manuscripts and prepared to make a living as teachers and translators. These refugees did not introduce Greek studies into Italy, since that had been done half a century earlier. But they did help to make Greek literature and philosophy more easily accessible. By the turn of the century, too, the printing press was beginning to make both the Latin and Greek classics still more easily available in good scholarly editions. A knowledge of the two ancient languages, or at least a fair command of Latin, could now be taken for granted among educated people, while the substance of antique thought was still more widely diffused through translations.

Building upon what had already been achieved, the humanists of the second half of the fifteenth century and the opening decades of the sixteenth were able to concentrate their attention upon the refinement of classical scholarship and upon writing fluent and correct classical Latin and Greek in both prose and verse. On the whole they were less concerned with the recovery of antique thought than their predecessors had been; but they gave more attention to poetry, lecturing in the universities on the works of the Latin and Greek poets, emending texts and preparing annotated editions for the press. Cicero was still the idol of the humanists, but the emphasis was shifting from the content to the form of his work. Among some of the successors of Lorenzo Valla, concern for correct Latinity led to a narrow and pedantic Ciceronianism, prose writers refusing to use any word or usage not sanctioned by the master; but such exclusive imitation of Cicero was condemned by the most broadly cultivated of the humanists until after the end of the century. At the same time, the tendency toward pedantic purism in the use of Latin was balanced by a relaxation of the exclusive preoccupation with the ancient languages which had characterized the first half of the century. Scholars who did not have to strive so hard to acquire a mastery of the ancient tongues now felt free to turn their attention in part to the vernacular and to contribute to the revival of literature in the national language.

The most distinguished representative of the mature and refined Italian humanism of this period was Angelo Poliziano (1454–94), whose international fame as scholar and man of letters is attested by the fact that English usage has anglicized his name as Politian, a compliment usually reserved for antique authors. Poliziano's command of the two ancient languages, as well as his poetic talent, were demonstrated at a remarkably early age. When he was no more than sixteen he had translated four books of the *Iliad* into Latin verse. This precocious achievement brought him to the attention of Lorenzo de' Medici, who took him into his household as secretary and, later, as tutor to his sons. In 1480 he was made professor of Greek and Latin literature in the *Studio*, the Florentine university, and there until his death at the age of forty he lectured regularly on Homer and Virgil and other Greek and Latin authors. At once poet and scholar, he brought to his classical scholarship a poet's imagination and to his poetry a classicist's command of vocabulary and form. He wrote poetry in Latin, Greek and Italian, all with equal facility. It was not all, perhaps, great poetry. Much of it bears the marks of having been written to order for some special occasion. But no poet of his generation handled the poetic forms of all three languages with more ease and grace or with a more faultless taste. Poliziano's great contemporary reputation, however, rested more upon his scholarship than his poetry. His systematic textual criticism brought to perfection the method introduced a generation earlier by Lorenzo Valla; and his *Miscellanea*, a collection of philological and critical material drawn from his lectures, did for his generation what Valla's *Elegantiae* had done for the previous one.

As both scholar and writer Poliziano, like many of his contemporaries, seemed primarily interested in perfection of literary form. He loved the formal beauty of the classics and strove to reproduce it in his own writings. The method still in use was that worked out by the humanists of the first half of the century: the collection and memorizing of words, phrases, metaphors and turns of speech culled from the ancient authors. Poliziano's aim was to imitate classical style as accurately as possible, but his conception of imitation was not a servile copying. Like the best Latin writers of his generation — the Neapolitan Giovanni Pontano (1426–1503) and the Venetian aristocrat Ermolao Barbaro (1453–93) for example — he refused to be bound by exclusive adherence to Ciceronian forms. His prose style was eclectic and thereby achieved spontaneity. It was the fruit of a vast erudition and a minute study of the whole range of classical literature; but he had so mastered this material as to have made it part of himself, so that he could write a Latin at once classical and altogether his own. But he and his contemporaries were almost the last Italian humanists to enjoy such freedom. The time was coming when arbiters of taste, like Browning's bishop ordering his tomb in Saint Praxed's church, would scorn Ulpian and demand "choice Latin, picked phrase, Tully's every word." Already younger men, like Paolo Cortese (1465–1510), were scandalized by Poliziano's stylistic liberties and criticized him severely for his departure from Ciceronian usage. For the next generation of Italians the immense authority of Pietro Bembo (1470–1547) was decisive and gave the victory to the Ciceronians, although in the North Erasmus still defended the freedom claimed by Poliziano.

The triumph of exclusive Ciceronianism was, however, but one aspect of the decline of Italian humanism. By 1520 its task had been accomplished. Not only had nearly the whole range of classical Latin and Greek literature been studied and absorbed, but the greater part of it had been printed in scholarly editions. The moral and ethical content of antique thought, which the early humanists had adopted as the acme of human wisdom and as a guide to the good life in this world, had by this time become widely diffused through the upper classes of Italian society. The demand of the broader reading public which had been created by the printed book was already calling forth translations of the classics into the vernacular, while more and more serious prose as well as poetry was being written in the national tongue. Thus while the Latin writing of the humanists became increasingly bound by a narrow and sterile pedantry, the intensive study of antique thought and form, which was the great contribution of the humanists of the fourteenth and fifteenth centuries, bore fruit in a revived Italian literature. The classics would long remain the essential basis of a liberal education, but literary Latin, having been frozen by pedantic adherence to one stage in its historical development, was ceasing to be a living language. The humanists had killed the thing they loved.

The humanists' self-appointed task of drawing from ancient literature the materials from which to construct a secular morality and a lay ethic that would meet the needs of their society was, as we have seen, pretty well completed by the 1450's, but it was only after that date that humanism began to exert a shaping influence on formal philosophy. Several factors combined to prevent any fruitful intercourse between humanism and philosophy before the second half of the century. In the first place, despite the beginning of Greek studies around 1400, the thought of the early humanists was shaped almost entirely by Latin literature. And in the major fields of formal or speculative philosophy the Latin writers could give them little more than unsystematic echoes of Greek thought. In the second place, as lay men of letters the humanists were not attracted by formal philosophy — logic, metaphysics and natural philosophy — as currently represented in the professional faculties of the Italian universities. They were, in fact, repelled by it. They found its form uncouth and its content abstract and impersonal, offering little of the human wisdom they found so attractively, if unsystematically, presented in Cicero's treatises. The early humanists, in short, neither contributed to philosophy nor were touched by it simply because they were not philosophers at all. Thus humanism and a vigorous tradition of scholastic philosophy continued as parallel streams in Italian thought for more than a century, with the humanists worshipping at the shrine of Cicero while the schoolmen continued to sit at the feet of Aristotle.

The marriage of humanism and philosophy, when it finally came in the last three or four decades of the fifteenth century, was a belated by-product of the revival of Greek studies. The Council of Ferrara-Florence (1438–39), which brought so many learned Greeks to Italy, not only stimulated the already growing interest in Greek literature, but also aroused among the Italian humanists a new interest in Platonic and Neoplatonic philosophy. Among the Byzantine scholars who came to the council several, including the aged Gemistus Pletho and Bessarion, who remained to become a cardinal in the Roman Church, were ardent defenders of Platonic philosophy with Neoplatonic trimmings in opposition to the Aristotelians. They found a receptive audience in the Italian humanists who, since Petrarch, had asserted a preference for Plato over Aristotle, whom they identified with scholasticism, without knowing very much about either. The Platonic dialogues appealed to the humanists by their literary elegance, their imaginative insights and their essential spirituality, which contrasted with the technical terminology and materialistic naturalism of the Averroist school of Aristotelian natural philosophy dominant

513

in the universities. In the teaching of Socrates they found an ethic not too far removed from that of Christ, and to an even greater extent they found in the writings of the Neoplatonists a religious aspiration easily reconcilable with Christian doctrine. In this discovery there was little that was really new. St. Augustine had been strongly influenced by Plato, and a persistent strain of Platonism ran through the Augustinian tradition of the Middle Ages, while generations of medieval mystics had drawn inspiration from the Pseudo-Dionysius and other late Neoplatonic writers. But in Italy the Platonic tradition had been thrust into the background by the scholastic cult of Aristotle, so that the Platonic and Neoplatonic writings now made available came as a revelation. Left to themselves, however, the literary humanists, unsystematic and eclectic thinkers, would probably not have gathered more than a few vague ideas from this mass of material. Nicholas of Cusa, writing in mid-century, used Neoplatonic concepts freely in the construction of his metaphysical system, but his esoteric doctrine of the coincidence of opposites in the Divine Unity found few followers. The important rôle played by the Platonic revival in the second half of the century was largely due to one man who combined humanistic interests with scholastic training and who devoted his life to the study and elucidation of Plato and his successors.

Marsilio Ficino (1433–99) was still a fairly young man when his interest in philosophy attracted the attention of Cosimo de' Medici. That aged Maecenas had become a convert to Platonic philosophy under the influence of Gemistus Pletho, and he now conceived the idea of founding a native school of Platonic studies. In 1462 he gave young Ficino a villa near Careggi, a library of Greek manuscripts and a life endowment. Faithful to his trust, Ficino spent the remainder of his life studying, translating, expounding and publishing the works of Plato and the Neoplatonists and making his villa a center of philosophical discussion frequented by all the intelligentsia of Florence: Lorenzo de' Medici, Bernardo Rucellai and other members of patrician families, the humanists Poliziano and Cristoforo Landino, Leo Battista Alberti and the poet Girolamo Benivieni, among others. As his fame spread, Ficino also attracted scholars from other parts of Italy and from lands beyond the Alps. The Platonic Academy, or Florentine Academy, as Ficino's circle of friends and students was later called, had no formal organization, nor was Ficino a systematic teacher. This was, indeed, part of the secret of his wide influence. What Ficino achieved, among other things, was to take philosophy out of the schools and to make it available to the cultivated but unacademic society of Italy.

Despite strong humanistic leanings, Ficino did not share the general humanist aversion to scholasticism as such, nor was he inimical to Aristotle. He owed a good deal, indeed, to the philosophical tradition of the schools. But he was drawn to Plato rather than Aristotle by the strain of religious mysticism which ran through the Platonic tradition and which he hoped might serve as a source of spiritual renewal to Christian piety. His two most important original works, *De religione Christiana* and *Theologia platonica*, both published in 1474, were attempts to fuse Christianity and Platonism in a single system. In the Platonic tradition Ficino found a philosophical basis for the conviction that it is in the nature of man to find his highest good in the knowledge and enjoyment of God, who is infinite beauty, truth and goodness. From this he deduced a proof of the immortality of the individual soul, which had been denied by the naturalistic teaching of the Averroists. Since mortal man can rise only imperfectly and briefly to the vision of God, it followed, so he argued, that man's end must be achieved in an after-life. It was not as closely reasoned a proof as that offered by Aquinas, but it held a strong appeal to men who were not trained metaphysicians but who were happy to have a philosophical basis for their religious aspiration.

A second doctrine which held a similar appeal was the theory of love which Ficino elaborated in his Commentary on the *Symposium* and which he later translated as *Il libro dell' amore*. Here he taught that all love is a desire for beauty, and all beauty is a reflection of the beauty of God. Love may, then, be awakened by the physical beauty of a loved person, but thence love may ascend through a series of increasingly intellectualized and spiritualized stages to the ultimate stage of love of the perfect and infinite beauty of God. A doctrine which thus justified and spiritualized sensual love could not but appeal to a courtly society more intellectually cultivated than that of the Middle Ages, and it had a wide and pervasive influence on secular literature for the next hundred years. A lengthy exposition of this theory was placed in the mouth of Pietro Bembo in the closing pages of Castiglione's *The Courtier*, and echoes of it can still be found in Spenser.

Finally, Ficino found in Platonism and still more in the teaching of the Neoplatonists — Plotinus, Proclus and the Pseudo-Dionysius the Areopagite — a conception of man's place in the universe which furnished a philosophical basis for the humanists' conviction of the dignity of man. Man is not only a microcosm, an epitome of the macrocosm of the universe; he also occupies a central place in the great chain of being which ascends from the lowest form of physical matter to the purest spirit which is God. He is thus the ontological link between the material and the spiritual. This doctrine, which focused attention on man, together with his theory of love, goes far to explain Ficino's following among humanists, men of letters and courtly dilettanti, and lent his teaching an importance that might not have been justified on strictly philosophical grounds. But if Ficino's Neoplatonism appealed most strongly to men who were not professional philosophers, his great translation of the complete works of Plato (1463–82) and of the leading Neoplatonists was, at least, a solid contribution and a milestone in the history of philosophy. The religious content of his philosophy, which was in many ways in harmony with the elements of undogmatic lay piety and mysticism inherent in the northern *Devotio Moderna,* also exerted an inspiring influence on such leaders of northern Christian humanism as Colet, Lefèvre and Erasmus.

Of the members of the Florentine Academy only one other, Giovanni Pico, Count of Mirandola (1463–94), was primarily a philosopher. In his brief career this brilliant young scion of a princely family was unable to develop his ideas into anything approaching a system, yet he enjoyed a contemporary reputation that seems out of proportion to his actual achievement. He had, indeed, set himself an impossible task, that of reconciling not only Christianity and Platonism, but also Aristotelianism, the mystical lore of the Hebrew Cabbala, some elements of Arabic philosophy, as well as fragments of Pythagorean and Zoroastrian learning. In his eclectic borrowing Pico resembled the early humanists who took from ancient literature anything that suited their purpose, but to mere eclecticism he added a positive syncretism founded upon a conviction of the unity of truth. All philosophies, he held, contain numerous errors, but also specific and demonstrable truths which are aspects of a single truth. He brought to his study an amazing linguistic range, including not only Greek and Latin, but also Hebrew and Arabic, and a vast if somewhat disorganized erudition. At the age of twenty-four he drew up nine hundred theses which he was prepared to defend in debate. Some of his theses, however, were condemned as heretical by a papal commission and the debate was forbidden, while Pico was forced to flee for a time from Italy. The oration which he had prepared as an introduction to these theses was also suppressed and was published only after his death under the title: *Oration on the Dignity of Man.* Brief as it was, it was one of his most important works. Only the first part of the *Oration* actually corresponds to the title, but it was the part that had the widest repercussions. Here Pico went beyond the position taken by Ficino. Man is not merely the microcosm and the link in the great chain of being between the material and the spiritual. He is master of his own fate. Alone of creatures he is absolutely free. He can make of himself what he wills.

He can descend to the level of the beasts or rise to the level of the divine. He is thus in a sense emancipated from the hierarchy of being. In this magnificent conception the vague yet pervasive notions of the dignity of man which had dominated the cultural ideals of the humanists were given their loftiest expression in the framework of a philosophical system. The remainder of the *Oration*, which outlines the argument of the theses and stresses the basic concept of the unity of truth, was founded upon too wide a range of undigested esoteric learning to have much impact upon philosophical thought. His teaching did, however, bear unexpected fruit in Germany, for it was through his inspiration that Johann Reuchlin undertook the study of Hebrew and became enamoured of cabbalistic learning, thus introducing Hebrew studies into northern humanism.

Although Italian humanism found its most congenial philosophical counterpart in Neoplatonism, its ideals were also beginning to influence the currents of Aristotelian philosophy in the old universities. In their capacity as philologists the humanists served Aristotelians as well as Platonists by preparing scholarly translations or editions of the Greek texts of the ancient philosophers and their Greek commentators. Before the end of the fifteenth century the best of the latter, Alexander of Aphrodisias, had begun to replace Averroës as the prime authority on Aristotle, and a new generation of Aristotelians had arisen who could go directly to the sources and who could think in Greek words. It is significant that in 1497 a chair was established for the teaching of Aristotle in Greek. Nor was this the only difference between the new school of Aristotelians and their predecessors, the Latin Averroists. Bred in an intellectual atmosphere impregnated with humanist ideals, the new generation turned from the impersonality of Averroist natural philosophy to a consideration of divinity and immortality in relation to the individual soul, and focused attention on man and his destiny. One of the prime tenets of the Averroists was that the intellect, which is common to all men, is alone immortal. The individual soul, which participates in it, lives after death only as a part of this single, eternal and immutable intellect of mankind. It followed that, according to the principles of natural philosophy, there is no personal immortality and hence no rewards or punishments in a future life. It was against this doctrine that Petrarch and the early humanists and, later, Ficino and the Platonists rebelled, not only in the interest of the Christian faith, but also because of their conviction of the worth of individual personality. And it was against this impersonal conception of the soul that some humanistically oriented Aristotelians now rebelled, but with quite different results.

The philosopher who in this period most effectively combined Aristotelian naturalism with humanist concern for individual man was Pietro Pomponazzi of Mantua (1462–1524). As a student at Padua and later as professor of philosophy at Padua, Ferrara and Bologna, Pomponazzi worked within the academic tradition. He was trained originally as a Thomist; then, under the influence of Averroist teaching, he abandoned the Thomist argument for the immortality of the soul. But he did not, at the same time, accept the Averroist doctrine of the unity of the intellect. His solution of the problem which concerned so many thinkers of his age was finally crystallized in a treatise *On the Immortality of the Soul*, published in 1516, and in an *Apologia*, written in answer to his critics two years later. Following Aquinas, he asserted that the intellect or soul is the true essence or "substantial form" of man, but he denied the Thomist belief that it is separable from the body and, therefore, capable of immortality. The soul can rise above mere bodily function to grasp universal and abstract truths, and hence participates in a kind of relative immortality; but it cannot function without the body and hence is essentially and absolutely mortal. It is born with the body and dies with it. Immortality he would hold as an article of faith — this is the saving formula used by Italian Aristotelians for two hundred years — but he would not teach it as a philosopher, since it was contrary to natural reason. To the argument that immortality was a necessary sanction to ethical conduct he opposed a purely naturalistic morality that was largely Stoic in origin. Virtue is its own reward and vice its own punishment. Hence rewards or punishments after death are not only unnecessary, but actually minimize virtue by making it not an end in itself but subject to hope or fear of an eternal judgment. In his different way, Pomponazzi, like Pico, was declaring the dignity and autonomy of man. And in a more positive way than the humanists had dreamed of he was asserting the rights of a purely secular ethic, independent of Christian dogma.

The Renaissance was admittedly not one of the great productive periods in the history of philosophy or science; but it was not as sterile as has sometimes been thought. If the humanists were not philosophers in the strict sense of the word — much less scientists — they nevertheless profoundly altered current attitudes toward man, his morality and his place in the universe; and in their capacity as classical philologists they served both philosophy and science by making available the whole range of antique thought in scholarly editions. The Florentine Neoplatonists reinforced the humanist *Weltanschauung* and gave spiritual inspiration to religious thinkers who were in revolt against scholasticism, besides providing secular literature with an ennobling theory of love. Meanwhile, the living Aristotelianism of the Italian schools furnished a bridge between the natural philosophy of the thirteenth century and the scientific rationalism of the age of Galileo and Descartes.

B. The Revival of Italian Vernacular Literature

The most convincing proof that the task of Italian humanism had been practically completed by the second half of the fifteenth century is the fact that the literary world of Italy was beginning to return to the national language after more than a century of neglect. The men who now turned to writing vernacular poetry and prose were almost without exception trained in the classics, and they were prepared to utilize the lessons they had learned from antiquity for the construction of a truly national literature. They brought to their task an urbane *humanitas*, leavened by familiar intercourse with the ancients, a spiritualizing tincture of Neoplatonism and, above all, a sense of form. The vernacular poetry of this period, like that in Greek and Latin, was in general more notable for elegance of form than for depth of feeling or intellectual content, but it suited the taste of a cultivated patrician or courtly society, at once refined and frivolous.

As might have been expected, the first evidence of a revival of the vernacular appeared in Florence. The founders of Italian literature in the fourteenth century had been Florentine. They had given the Tuscan tongue a prestige unequalled among the dialects of Italy, and it was on this foundation that the new generation of Italian writers built. It is true that Florentines had also been in the vanguard of the humanist movement and that the city on the Arno had been the most active center of the new learning. But civic patriotism had there prevented the utter extinction of the *volgare* even at the height of militant classicism. In the period of intensified republican feeling that followed the Visconti threat to Florentine independence in the early years of the fifteenth century, the *volgare* found defenders among patriotic citizens like Giovanni da Prato, the author of the *Paradiso degli Alberti*. And, though the classicists' prejudice against the vulgar tongue was still strong, such civic-minded humanists as Leonardo Bruni were aware of the value of the native literary tradition. Bruni himself wrote the *Lives of Dante and Petrarch* (1436) in Italian, and his friends Alberti and Palmieri resorted to it for their books on domestic economy and civil life, both written in the 1430's. It was not till a later generation, however, that the cultivated circle which gravitated about Lorenzo de' Medici began to place Italian on an equal footing with Greek and Latin as a medium for *belles lettres* in poetry as well as in prose. The surviving classicism of that generation took the form, not of contempt for the vernacular, but of a belief that Italian could rise by imitation to a level with classical Latin, just as the latter had in its time risen by imitation to a level with Greek. The humanist Cristoforo Landino (1424–98), when lecturing on Dante and Petrarch in the Florentine *Studio*, reminded his audience that the founders of Italian literature had been familiar with Latin poetry and eloquence and asserted flatly: "Let no one believe that he could express himself eloquently, nay even tolerably, in the *volgare* without previous genuine and perfect familiarity with Latin letters."[1]

There was no doubt a certain amount of patriotism involved in the revival of the native Florentine tongue by Lorenzo and his circle; but defense of the *volgare* was no longer identified with concern for the tradition of republican liberty, as it had been earlier in the century. The members of Lorenzo's household wrote Italian poetry for their amusement and because, secure in their knowledge of the classics, they could afford to do so. Il Magnifico, the heart of that versatile group, was himself a poet, who, despite a sound classical training, preferred to use Italian; and his example did more than any scholarly defense could have done to make the vernacular respectable. Lorenzo's poetry was that of a talented dilettante, the by-product of a busy life; but at its best it had a charm and vitality that has earned it a secure place in the history of Italian literature. If his verse generally lacked emotional depth, it reflected the wide range of interest, the intellectual energy and the *élan vital* that brought him to his death, a burned-out ruin, at forty-three. He wrote Petrarchan sonnets, love lyrics in a variety of forms, carnival songs, religious *laude*, Neoplatonic dialogues in verse, the charming pastoral idyll of the shepherd Corinto and his lass, descriptions of country life, a mythological poem in the manner of Ovid's *Metamorphoses* of the nymph Ambra pursued by a river god, and a religious play or *sacra rappresentazione* for which Heinrich Isaak supplied the music.

Taken together, Lorenzo's poems leave one wondering how much they tell us of their author and what manner of man he was. Many of them were probably written simply because he wanted to write poetry; but at times purely personal emotions filter through the conventional forms. They show a genuine love of natural beauty, of flowers and the Tuscan countryside; a vivid love of life with melancholy overtones; and a deep, if intermittent, religious sentiment. He is best remembered today for his carnival songs, some of them ribald, which demonstrate his conscious

[1] Quoted in H. Baron, *The Crisis of the Early Italian Renaissance* (Princeton, 1955), I, 312.

identification with the people he ruled. One theme recurs frequently, at its best in the *Song of Bacchus* written for a carnival procession:

> Quant' è bella giovanezza,
> che si fugge tuttavia!
> Chi vuol esser lieto, sia:
> di doman non c'è certezza —[2]

It appears again in the closing line of the *Corinto*:

> Cogli la rosa, o ninfa, or che è il bel tempo.

"Gather the rose, nymph, while it is time." It is a mood that was to echo through European literature for generations. It has been regarded as the theme song of the Renaissance. But, while recognizing this as a characteristic note, can we discount the sincerity of the Neoplatonic mysticism and religious aspiration of Lorenzo's *laude*, as in the lines:

> O Dio, o somne bene, or come fai,
> che te sol cerco e non ti truovo mai?[3]

Il Magnifico was not a simple person, nor was this a simple age.

With the Maecenas and uncrowned prince of Florence thus devoting himself to poetry in the vulgar tongue, it was a foregone conclusion that others would follow suit, most notable among them his protégé, the humanist Poliziano. A more skillful versifier than Lorenzo, Poliziano had a light touch and exquisite taste; but beyond graceful rephrasings of the "Gather ye rosebuds" theme his Italian lyrics had little to say. By far the greatest poet of Lorenzo's circle was still a struggling young artist whose poetic gifts, nurtured on admiration for Dante and encouraged by the example of Lorenzo and Poliziano, developed only later in life. Michelangelo Buonarroti was only seventeen when his patron died. His long life carried him far beyond the chronological limits of this book, and his greatest lyrics, especially those written to Vittoria Colonna, belong to the period after 1520. In spirit he was more akin to Dante than to Lorenzo and his friends, but it was to his youthful experience in the Medici household that he owed the abiding interest in Neoplatonic philosophy and the ideal of Platonic love that continued to inspire his verse to the end of his life.

Such high seriousness, however, was rare in the generation after Lo-

---

[2] "Fair is youth, forever fleeting! Let who will be merry, be so: there is no certainty of tomorrow."

[3] "Oh God, oh supreme good, why dost Thou so ordain that I seek Thee only, and yet find Thee never?"

renzo. The more common tendency in the years when Medici patronage shifted from Florence to the Rome of Leo X and Clement VII was an increasingly puristic and empty Petrarchism, which paralleled the exclusive Ciceronianism of the later humanists. And in both of these tendencies, the dominant figure was Pietro Bembo. Venetian-born though he was, Bembo adopted the Tuscan of the great fourteenth-century triumvirate in much the same spirit as he did the Latin of Cicero, and his vast authority as an arbiter of taste, crowned eventually with a cardinal's hat, set the seal upon Tuscan as the literary language of Italy. But imitation and purism were not fatal to the modern tongue as they were to the ancient. Italian was a living language and could survive, in the long run enriched rather than stultified by a period of intensive concentration upon form.

Lyric poetry, crystallized in the form of the Petrarchan sonnet, seems the most characteristic expression of the native Italian genius, but in this period of revived vernacular literature it was almost overshadowed by another genre, one new to Italian *belles lettres*. This was the romantic and sophisticated recreation of medieval French epic for the amusement of a cultured society far removed from the feudal environment in which the epic tales had originated, a society which, nevertheless, was in superficial ways modelling itself upon the royal and princely courts of the greater states beyond the Alps. The medieval epics were, it is true, not unknown to Italy; but they had appeared there late in a humble and unpolished form for strictly popular consumption. During the fourteenth century stories drawn at random from the Charlemagne cycle had been rudely adapted in Italian verse by anonymous street-singers, who would gather a crowd at a corner of the city square and sing a canto at a time for such small change as the crowd would toss to them. It was thus that the paladins and paynims of the *chansons de geste* — among them the Roland of the *Chanson de Roland* and the Renaud de Montauban of the *Quatre Fils Aymon*, italianized as Orlando and Rinaldo — all mixed together and with various extraneous trimmings entered the consciousness of the Italian people. From this fund of popular story, already at one remove from the original, the poets of the Italian courts now drew the material for a new kind of epic poem.

The pioneer in introducing the street-singers' tales to polite society was — we have learned to expect this — a Florentine and a member of Lorenzo de' Medici's familiar circle. Luigi Pulci (1432–84) was the devoted buffoon of the Medici household, jovial, irreverent and laughter-loving, yet with the jester's traditional undertone of melancholy. Perpetually debt-ridden and lacking the classical education common to that group, Pulci sang for his supper and repaid his patron's kindness by furnishing amusement for him and his guests. Of his contributions to this worthy cause the most important was a retelling in verse of the popular epic *Orlando*, which he produced a bit at a time over a period of some fifteen years before finally committing it to print in 1478 under the title *Morgante*. Then five years later he added a sequel telling of Charlemagne's invasion of Spain and the battle in the pass of Roncesvalles, the material this time drawn from another popular *cantare*, the *Spagna in rima*. To this augmented work he gave the title *Il Morgante maggiore*.

It is significant for Pulci's treatment of the story that the titular hero is no longer Orlando but the giant Morgante who was conquered and converted by Orlando and thereafter became his faithful squire. Morgante was one of the *dramatis personae* of the original street-singers' version; but Pulci gave him a much more important and more comic rôle. He also furnished him with a companion, the stunted giant Margutte, a thorough rascal who boasted seventy mortal sins and but one virtue: that he had never betrayed a friend. A second interpolated character was the devil Astarotte, who was summoned from hell by the magician Malagigi to transport Rinaldo by magic arts from Egypt to the pass of Roncesvalles. This amiable fiend became Rinaldo's guide, philosopher and friend, whiling away the journey with learned disquisitions on theology and Platonic philosophy. The Rabelaisian giants and the courteous and erudite fiend are pure Pulci. The rest of the story, especially the final scene at Roncesvalles, is nearer the earnest simplicity of the street-singer, but even when he seemed most serious Pulci's comic spirit would break through. It was a saving grace. His audience had no doubt a certain romantic interest in tales of chivalry. The patrician society that surrounded the Medici was becoming more consciously courtly — as witness the elaborate tournaments held by Lorenzo and his brother Giuliano. But it was the comic rather than the courtly elements in Pulci's poem that probably appealed most to the sophisticated group around Lorenzo's dinner table. His off-beat reproduction of the street-singers' tale must, indeed, have appealed to them in much the same way as did Lorenzo's carnival songs or Poliziano's polished versions of peasant folk songs. Secure in their own intellectual and social superiority, they could affect a popular simplicity and be amused by a vulgarity garnished with wit, no longer naïve but transformed into art.

If the cultivated patriciate of Florence thus required Pulci's Rabelaisian touch to make the chivalric epic palatable, the more genuinely courtly society of Ferrara could take it straight. Nowhere in northern Italy had the feudal spirit survived as strongly as in the domain of the ancient House of Este. The Este dukes were proud of their nine-hundred-years-old name, and there was no democratic or bourgeois nonsense about them. They shared the humanist learning and artistic connoisseurship common to their class, but they were also *condottieri* and their court had a distinctly military flavor. The ladies of the House of Este, too, were both erudite and romantically interested in tales of chivalry. It was to please the taste of this aristocratic and at least superficially chivalric court that Matteo Maria Boiardo, Count of Scandiano (1441–94), wove together materials drawn from both the popular Italian version of the Charlemagne cycle and the Arthurian romances, superimposing the themes of romantic love, enchantment and knight-errantry upon the bare bones of the Roland epic to produce a new composite: the *Orlando innamorato*, Roland at last in love. Like Pulci, Boiardo added a character entirely of his own invention, but this time it is the fair Angelica, daughter of the King of Cathay. She causes all the paladins at Charlemagne's court to fall in love with her and then flees, hotly pursued by Orlando and Rinaldo. Angelica inadvertently drinks of a magic fountain which causes her to fall in love with Rinaldo who, meanwhile, has drunk from a neighboring fountain which turns his love to hate. Thereafter the story wanders from land to land, with innumerable side plots. Orlando, faint but pursuing, forgets his duty to the emperor. Eventually Angelica and Rinaldo drink once more of the magic fountains and their position is reversed. Boiardo meant no burlesque of chivalry. He simply revelled in the improbable world of Arthurian fantasy and knight-errantry.

Boiardo left his story incomplete, but a generation later Lodovico Ariosto (1474–1533) furnished a sequel, *Orlando furioso*, which so far overshadowed Boiardo's work as almost to consign it to oblivion for generations. Ariosto was not only a more gifted poet than his predecessor, but, Ferrarese though he was, he wrote in the Tuscan dialect that had become the literary language of Italy and so found a wider and more lasting audience. His treatment of the Orlando story, too, with its undertone of irony, held a greater appeal for contemporaries and for later generations still further removed from the chivalric tradition. Yet his story is on the face of it a continuation of Boiardo's. Still the star-crossed lovers pursue one another through enchanted landscapes; but now Angelica falls in love with a young Saracen and Orlando goes raving mad. In the end Orlando's lost wits are restored to him by Astolfo, the globe-trotting English knight, who travels to the moon to find them. A sadder and a wiser man, disillusioned with love, Orlando then returns to his duty and to fight with the emperor against the infidel. There was little of either the epic or the chivalric spirit in Ariosto's urbane poem, but there was infinite art and an inexhaustible fund of formal beauty.

Between the lines of Boiardo's and Ariosto's poems we can discern the features of the cultivated and courtly ladies and gentlemen for whom they were written. We meet them face to face in Castiglione's *The Courtier,* not, it is true, in the court of Ferrara, but in the very similar if somewhat more humanistic court of the *condottieri* dukes of Urbino. The picture of the courtier and the court there presented has been discussed in a previous chapter. We need note here only that Castiglione's book was not only the most perfect expression of the aristocratic social ideal of its age; it was also a landmark in the revival of Italian vernacular prose.

C. History and Political Theory in the Italian Vernacular

Further evidence of the emancipation of Italy from exclusive devotion to classical Latin as a literary medium is to be found in the increasing use of Italian for such learned subjects as history and political theory. The generation that lived through the chaotic period of foreign invasion, perpetual warfare and shifting diplomatic alignments which followed the first French invasion had its attention forcibly directed toward politics and war, and the more thoughtful turned to history to seek answers to their problems. This was especially true of the Florentines, who had witnessed the expulsion of the Medici in 1494, the restoration of the republic and its desperate attempt to maintain its independence, and, finally, its collapse when the Medici were restored to power with the aid of foreign arms in 1512. The following years saw the appearance of a new school of Florentine writers of history and political theory. They wrote in the national language, but they were trained in the humanist tradition. Like the earlier humanists, they owed much of the literary form, method and historical perspective of their work to study and imitation of the ancient historians, but the experience of their generation had given them a more profound appreciation of the importance of military force and power politics than the humanists had possessed. Of the writers who thus combined lessons learned from the study of antiquity with the results of their own disillusioned observations, the most important were Niccolò Machiavelli and Francesco Guicciardini.

Niccolò Machiavelli (1469–1527) began his literary career only in middle age after he had been deprived of office and forced into retirement by the return of the Medici to Florence in 1512. During the preceding fourteen years he had served the republic in the arduous post of secretary to the Council of Ten, the elective committee in charge of foreign affairs, diplomacy and war. In that capacity he had travelled on numerous missions as envoy or observer, had written lengthy reports to the Ten, had taken a leading part in organizing a Florentine militia to replace the mercenaries whom he despised, and, in general, had enjoyed unusual opportunities to observe the political, diplomatic and military life of Italy during those turbulent years. That he had indeed enjoyed these opportunities there can be no doubt, for politics were the breath of life to him. In enforced retirement he continued to think about politics, and set himself the task of formulating and putting into writing his own observations, reinforced by ardent study of ancient and modern history, concerning the means by which states might be established and preserved in strength and stability. In the year following his retirement he began work on what was to be his most comprehensive discussion of the problems facing states and the methods of dealing with them, the *Discourses on the First Ten Books of Livy*. Then, in the fall of 1513, he broke off that project to write the book by which he has always been best known, *The Prince*.

It is unfortunate for Machiavelli's reputation that he has been judged largely by the latter work, for it is in this little book that the maxims of ruthless power politics and statecraft at its most crafty, which are commonly designated as Machiavellian, appear most nakedly. It was dedicated to the Medici princes, no doubt partly in the hope that it might lead to its author being restored to office and the active political life he loved, and it bears the marks of having been written for a special occasion. The *Discourses*, a much longer discussion of themes suggested by Livy's history of the Roman Republic, shows clearly a preference for a republican form of government when possible and a concern for the welfare of the citizens that is more in keeping with Machiavelli's long and devoted service to the Florentine Republic. Yet even here he admitted that when a state has become corrupt, as he believed Florence and the other Italian states to be, it could be saved only by a strong prince, and such a prince must let no consideration of private morality stand in the way of his success. The *Discourses* have a less shocking impact than *The Prince*, but many of its maxims seem to spring from much the same conception of statecraft. A great deal of the interminable scholarly debate over the interpretation of Machiavelli's work, indeed, has focused on the question of whether the two books merely present different aspects of a coherent political philosophy, or whether they express two different points of view and, if so, which most truly represents their author's real opinions.

It is natural that Machiavelli's numerous detractors should concentrate attention on *The Prince*, but so have many of his most ardent defenders. In Germany in the nineteenth century and in Italy since the *Risorgimento*, in particular, Machiavelli has been hailed as a prophet of national unification, and the eloquent last chapter of *The Prince*, with its passionate appeal to the Medici to rally Italy and free it from the barbarians, has been cited as proof that his work was motivated by a patriotic desire to see Italy free and united — at any cost. From this point of view it was possible to excuse his exposition of the means by which a prince might seize power at the expense of his subjects' liberty, on the ground that under the existing circumstances government by a prince was the only possible form of government for Florence, and that only a strong prince, capable of expanding his state, could make Florence the nucleus of a united Italian movement to drive out the foreigner. In the same way it was possible to excuse Machiavelli's arguments for the necessity of force, cruelty, treachery and fraud as instruments of successful government on the ground that they were justified by *raison d'état*, the necessity of state which knows no moral laws. Scholars afflicted with the Hegelian doctrine of the state went still further and argued that only through the identification of citizens with a strong state could a corrupt Italy be morally regenerated. Machiavelli thus became, in Francesco de Sanctis's phrase, the "Luther of Italy."[4] Other defenders, somewhat less enthusiastic, have regarded Machiavelli as a detached and objective political scientist, a sort of late nineteenth-century Positivist, concerned only with the observation and analysis of political reality.

Whatever the purpose of Machiavelli's work, one fact seems clear: it was a product of its time and place. At any rate, it seems unlikely that either *The Prince* or the *Discourses* could have been written much earlier or elsewhere. Before so radical a break with traditional political theory was possible several developments were necessary. In the first place, states of the kind which most absorbed Machiavelli's attention — autonomous republics or principalities lacking the assurance of hereditary succession and the legal and constitutional supports characteristic of the national monarchies — had made their appearance only in Italy, and that fairly recently. Elsewhere absolute monarchy was evolving gradually out of feudalism. Only in Italy had the breakdown of medieval forms of government opened the way for the creation of the state as a work of art, to be maintained by calculated statecraft. It is significant that in *The Prince* and in many places in the *Discourses* Machiavelli's maxims are directed toward the problems of the "new prince" who in one way or another has seized power. This was a familiar Italian phenomenon. The state he envisages, too, is one beset by actual or potential enemies within and without, and subject to rapid changes of fortune, a situation familiar to Italy in the fourteenth and fifteenth centuries and one intensified by the foreign invasions since 1494. In the second place, Machiavelli's thought was profoundly influenced by the cult of antiquity and the interest in secular history which conditioned the intellectual atmosphere of

[4] F. de Sanctis, *History of Italian Literature* (New York, 1931), I, 463 ff.

his generation. Throughout the *Discourses* he based his arguments constantly on the policy of the Roman Republic and other ancient states, reinforced by examples chosen from more modern history. In *The Prince*, where he is dealing with a more specifically Italian situation, he cites modern events more frequently, but references to antiquity are still numerous. Like the humanists, he sought to recover the wisdom of the ancients, not, however, in their favorite fields of literature, ethics and moral philosophy, but in that of practical politics, a field in which he felt that the lessons to be learned from antiquity had been unduly neglected. Assuming, as did both the humanists and their ancient models, that human nature is unchanging, he believed that what could be learned from ancient history was equally applicable to his own time.

What emerged from Machiavelli's writings was not a systematic political theory — not, indeed, a political theory at all in the strict sense of the word. Rather it was a collection of maxims for successful political and military action under a variety of circumstances. He was not concerned with the theory of sovereignty, nor with the rights of citizens, nor with the constitutional basis of law. Still less was he concerned, as were other writers on the subject of the rule of princes from Thomas Aquinas to Erasmus, with the problem of how in a moral sense a prince *should* rule. On this point he was quite explicit: "For there is such a difference between the way men live and the way they ought to live [he wrote in the fifteenth chapter of *The Prince*] that anybody who abandons what is for what ought to be will learn something that will ruin rather than preserve him. . . . Hence, if a prince wishes to maintain himself, he must learn how to be not good and to use that ability or not as is required." Machiavelli, in fact, asks only how a prince *can* rule, how states *can* be preserved and made strong, and this attitude pervades both *The Prince* and the *Discourses*. The answers he finds are based on an acute analysis of events in the immediate or distant past, but they are presented with a dogmatic certainty that seems at times naïve. If a government follows his maxims it cannot fail — unless, of course, Fortune intervenes, and even then the ruler armed with his rules of conduct and with *virtù* has a fair chance of circumventing that fickle goddess. We may admit the sincerity of Machiavelli's patriotism, yet still find it difficult to escape the conclusion that his primary concern was with political expediency — that, in fact, he was fascinated by the game of politics. The stable government and public-spirited citizenry that he envisages as the end product of his maxims have a Utopian quality, but his most sharply delineated prescriptions are directed toward short-term advantages. The political techniques he advocates were, indeed, largely those which had been actually practised by Italian governments, although not always as intelligently as he could have wished, for the past two centuries, and which were in part responsible for the corruption and political weakness he observed in contemporary Italy. The rules for successful government which he regarded as universally applicable were in reality shaped by conditions that were peculiar to his age and nation.

It would be a mistake to read into Machiavelli's political theories, as has often been done, concepts of the state which came into existence only in the nineteenth century. Yet there can be no doubt that his preoccupation with the secular state as the sole means by which in this wicked world men can achieve security of life and property marks a break with traditional political theory. Concentrating attention on the question of how states can be made strong, he excluded from consideration the preconceptions of Christian theology and morality as irrelevant, thereby affirming by implication the autonomy of politics, as the humanists, though in less radical fashion, had affirmed the autonomy of secular ethics and morals. It is perhaps unfair to say that Machiavelli was indifferent to morality or religion. He recognized that they were essential to the health and stability of the state as instruments to be promoted and used by a wise government. In the *Discourses*, I, 11, he wrote: "As the observance of divine worship is the cause of the greatness of a state, so the contempt of it is the cause of its ruin. For where the fear of God is wanting, either the state must needs be ruined or it must be maintained by the fear of some prince, supplying the defect." There is genuine moral indignation in his condemnation of the corruption of contemporary society and the Church. The conception of human nature, too, which is fundamental to his political theories, was based on a moral judgment. He believed — and this is possibly an unconscious inheritance from one persistent strain in medieval religious thought — that men are essentially selfish and prone to evil unless coerced by superior force. The government of any state must, he believed, operate on that assumption if it is to escape ruin. If all men were good, the rulers of states might abide by the laws of private morality; but in a world of wicked men this is impractical. It is not that Machiavelli says "evil be thou my good." He never condones immorality or unethical conduct in private individuals. It is simply that in the limited area of practical politics, which it was his unique contribution to isolate, actions are judged solely by their results, and ethical and moral considerations have nothing to do with the case. What he requires of the rulers of states is not virtue in the normal Christian — or Stoic — sense of the word, but *virtù*, that is, the quality of effective excellence that enabled men to achieve great things, even, when necessary, by evil means.

Two further works round out Machiavelli's contribution to the fields of politics and history. In *The Art of War,* published in 1521, he developed the theory, already announced in his earlier works, that mercenaries are useless and that only a state defended by its own citizens can hope to be secure. This was one of the principal lessons he had learned from his study of the Roman Republic, and was, at the same time, his final justification for the attempt to raise a Florentine militia, which had been one of his major concerns during his years in office. Then, in his last years, he was commissioned by the University of Florence, at the behest of Cardinal Giulio de' Medici, to write the *History of Florence.* After a lifetime of using history to demonstrate his political theories, he now had the opportunity to use his political experience and speculation to elucidate the history of his native state. The results were only partially satisfactory. His approach to history was fundamentally unhistorical. What really interested him were the general rules for political conduct which could be illustrated by historical examples, rather than the unique historical event in itself. Large sections of the *History* were plagiarized from the earlier works of Flavio Biondo, Villani and others, with little evidence of more mature political interpretation; and when occasionally a given turn of events seemed to illustrate one of his favorite maxims he was not above altering the facts to make them fit more perfectly. Nevertheless, the *History,* if to a lesser degree than his earlier works, bears the imprint of a vigorous and original mentality. The unfailing verve of Machiavelli's literary style, his broad grasp of the whole course of Florentine history and his ability to sort out the tangled threads of internal politics raises his narrative well above the level of those earlier historians from whom he borrowed with little acknowledgement.

If Machiavelli was a political theorist first and an historian second, the reverse was true of Francesco Guicciardini (1483–1540), although he shared many of his older friend's assumptions concerning men and politics. Guicciardini entered the service of the Florentine government just at the moment when Machiavelli was forced to leave it. Thereafter he served the Medici in various important governmental and diplomatic posts until almost the end of his life. His experience with Italian politics left him cynical and disillusioned, and it was in that mood that in his last years he wrote the *History of Italy* covering the disastrous years from 1492 to 1534. More realistic than Machiavelli, he rejected his friend's belief that from the study of history it was possible to formulate general rules for political action that would be universally valid. He thought Machiavelli's maxims too rigid, too dogmatic. Each historical situation is unique and must be dealt with on its own merits. Guicciardini was at his best in analyzing individual political and diplomatic situations, disentangling all the knotted threads and laying bare the motives of the persons involved. The motives he found were generally of a low sort, rooted in egotism and love of honor and power, for such were the only motives that his experience had taught him to know or recognize. For all his apparent realism, it was thus a somewhat warped picture of contemporary Italian politics that he presented, and one which exerted a lasting influence on the historical judgment of the Renaissance. The *History of Italy* was, none the less, a masterpiece of its kind and the first successful attempt to expand the scope of history beyond a single state to include the whole of Italy together with its foreign invaders.

D. THE RISE OF NORTHERN HUMANISM

In the countries north of the Alps, humanism, or the new learning as its devotees liked to call it, came late. A few scholars there were in the first half of the fifteenth century — the English prince, Humphrey, Duke of Gloucester, the German cardinal, Nicholas of Cusa and the French chancellor, Jean de Montreuil, for example — who had felt the stimulus of Italian humanism; but they were isolated figures who founded no school. It was not till the second half of the fifteenth century that the new learning began to strike roots in the northern lands, and it scarcely began to bear fruit until the last decade. Then for a generation it flourished with a vigor and originality of thought surpassing that of the contemporary protagonists of Italian humanism.

There were many reasons why the medieval cultural traditions lasted longer in the north and why the new learning, like the spring, came slowly up this way. As we have seen, there was no such fusion of the nobility with the wealthy merchant class as had taken place in the Italian cities. Despite declining independence and power, the feudal nobles of the north retained their social prestige and their privileged status as a distinct hereditary caste. They clung to the cultural forms traditionally associated with their class all the more tenaciously as their real power declined, and their literary taste continued to set the tone of vernacular *belles lettres* through most of the fourteenth and fifteenth centuries. The urban bourgeoisie, for their part, could not by themselves produce a vernacular literature capable of competing with the chivalric forms, reinforced as these were by the patronage of the royal and princely courts. The wealthier burghers, who aped the manners of the nobles, accepted the literary tastes of their betters and read the same romances and chivalric lyrics. The writing which more directly reflected the interests of the middle class, and also of the provincial gentry who were out of touch with court life, was generally unaesthetic, didactic in purpose and pedestrian in style. At the same time, and for much the same social reasons, higher education was left more exclusively to the universities than in Italy, and in the northern universities scholastic philosophy and theology continued to form the dominant interest of the faculties until well into the sixteenth century. The naturalization of classical humanism in the lands beyond the Alps was thus delayed and inhibited by the continued domination, for more than a century and a half longer than in Italy, of both vernacular literature and higher learning by cultural traditions peculiar to the nobility and the clergy — traditions which had taken shape in the feudal era and which were utterly alien to the spirit of classical antiquity.

Despite these inhibiting conditions, however, there were factors operating in northern society and culture which created an atmosphere increasingly favorable to the reception of the new learning. Here, as in Italy at an earlier date, the rise of capitalism and of new forms of state government, both of which demanded the services of literate and professionally trained personnel and stimulated lay education and hence lay participation in culture, set the stage for the appearance of new forms of literature and learning. At the same time, the decay of feudalism as a political structure and of chivalry as a social ideal was sapping the roots of the medieval vernacular literary tradition. It was kept alive for a time in the courts of France and Burgundy, but only by artificial respiration. By the second half of the fifteenth century all vitality had been drained out of it and only the formal husks remained. Even before that time, the chivalric tradition had ceased to inspire German poetry, nor could it leaven the lumpishness of post-Chaucerian English verse. A similar fate had also befallen the scholasticism still firmly entrenched in the universities. The three great schools of scholastic philosophy and theology — Thomist, Scotist and Ockhamist — had reached their fullest development before the middle of the fourteenth century. Their followers could add little but an increasingly empty refinement of subtle distinctions and logical niceties. Lacking the vigorous tradition of Averroist natural philosophy which still flourished in Padua and Bologna, what intellectual energy remained in the northern schools was expended on the bitter feuds between the followers of the *via antiqua* (the Thomists and Scotists) and the Ockhamist *via moderna*. For a time enthusiasm for the Conciliar Movement had infused new life into the Paris faculties, but it passed with the failure of the councils and was further diminished by the dangers and uncertainties that beset Paris in the last stages of the Hundred Years' War. The simultaneous decline of chivalric literature and scholastic learning thus created a cultural vacuum into which the new learning was drawn, slowly at first, then in an irresistible flood.

Literature and Learning

Given the conditions that were beginning to prevail in the north and west of Europe by the end of the fifteenth century, it is possible that a revival of interest in the literature and thought of antiquity might have occurred there spontaneously. The people of the northern countries, it is true, could not look back across the Middle Ages to classical antiquity and recognize in it, to the same degree as did the citizens of the Italian city-states, a social and political structure in many ways similar to their own. Classical civilization, therefore, could not serve them to the same extent as a model, nor could they feel that Roman antiquity represented the great age of their own national past. On the other hand, the bankruptcy of medieval chivalric and scholastic traditions was more complete than it had been in the age of Petrarch and the need for a new stimulus at least as great. Whether or not a spontaneous "revival of antiquity" might have occurred in the north is, however, an irrelevant question. The fact is that by the time the northern people were ready to absorb the classical heritage the achievement of Italian humanism was almost completed and the results were there for the taking. Italian scholars helped to introduce the new learning to the north. The art of printing made the works of the Italian humanists, as well as their editions of the classical texts, easily available to northern scholars, and nearly every leading figure in the northern movement at some time visited Italy to further his education. Finally, the Italian wars which began before the end of the fifteenth century brought countless French and Spanish nobles into contact with a brilliant culture in which humanism played an important part, and, if few of them became classical scholars, many were at least impressed by the prestige of the classics in the cultured Italian courts and lost something of their contempt for book-learning as something fit only for clerics.

If northern humanism was in a sense an importation from Italy, it was not, however, a mere copy of the Italian model. Grafted on the stalk of different national cultures, it developed along different lines. The influence of classical culture did not permeate the middle and upper classes in the north as fully as it did in Italy, nor did the wisdom of the ancients to the same degree serve as a model for a secular ethic and a guide to civic life. Among some of the northern humanists the new learning meant no more than philological scholarship and the cultivation of classical poetry and eloquence. The more thoughtful turned to Christian as well as classical antiquity, added Biblical to classical scholarship, and found in the combination of the two the inspiration for a far-reaching program of social, educational and religious reform. This "Christian humanism," most perfectly exemplified in the work of Erasmus, was the most significant aspect of the northern movement, and as such will be reserved for special discussion in the following section. Meanwhile we must trace the spread of humanism through the northern countries and note its more general characteristics.

The pioneers of northern humanism were mostly wandering scholars who gained in Italy a taste for the classics, Greek as well as Latin, and returned to teach and to spread the gospel of the new learning. They were not as a rule productive scholars. Their influence was personal, and we know more about them from the reputation they enjoyed than from their written works. In Germany, where the new learning appeared somewhat earlier than in France or England, the man who made the greatest impression on his contemporaries was the Frisian, Rudolf Agricola (1444–85). A man of commanding presence, musician and artist as well as scholar, Agricola excited the admiration of the Italians among whom he studied for ten years before returning to the north, finally to end his days at Heidelberg, where he aroused an interest in classical studies both at the court and the university. After his return from Italy he had also spent some time in the Netherlands, and there exerted a significant influence on the schools of the Brethren of the Common Life, in which many of the humanists of the next generation gained their early training. Among those who learned both classical Latin and Greek from him, one of the most influential was Alexander Hegius, who became headmaster of the school at Deventer in Holland from 1483 to 1498. Under his guidance the Deventer school became the most famous center of secondary education in the north with a reputed attendance of some two thousand boys. Here, and at the other schools associated with the Brethren, boys received a sound basic training in the classics combined with religious instruction in the spirit of the *Devotio Moderna*, a combination which left its mark on the thought of Erasmus and many of the other Christian humanists.

As the reception of Agricola at Heidelberg indicates, the German universities were not at first inhospitable to the new learning. A few humanists found their way into the Arts faculties, and their classical scholarship was welcomed by many of the theologians, particularly among the followers of the *via antiqua*, as an aid to the study of divinity. The older universities of Paris, Oxford and Cambridge were somewhat more conservative. Some Greek instruction by Italian or Greek immigrants was available in the University of Paris from the late 1450's, and in the 1490's Greek was introduced to Oxford by William Grocyn, an English scholar who had studied in Italy with Poliziano and Chalcondylas. In the last two decades of the century, too, a little group of humanists gathered in the University of Paris under the leadership of Robert Gaguin (1433–1501). A distinguished diplomat and professor of law as well as an enthusiastic Ciceronian, Gaguin lent his great prestige to the furtherance of the new learning and was hailed by the younger generation as the father of French humanism. This humanist infiltration, however, left the structure of scholastic learning almost untouched until after the turn of the century. The humanists who entered the Arts faculties were themselves deeply religious men who had at first no thought of challenging the traditional methods of philosophy and theology. The schoolmen who formed the controlling body of the universities, for their part, were too deeply involved in the controversies between the *via antiqua* and the *via moderna* to pay much attention to the newcomers or to regard them as a menace to traditional instruction. What difficulties the humanists encountered arose chiefly from the exigencies of the university budget, as has been the case with more recent educational innovations. The available funds were already allocated to the older disciplines and the humanists had to struggle for adequate salaries. So long as they confined their teaching to instruction in the classical languages, that is, to grammar, poetry and rhetoric, there was no serious conflict between the proponents of the new learning and their more conservative colleagues. Only later, when the reforming humanists began to infringe upon the theologians' preserves and to demand a radical change in the method and aims of theological study did the normal inter-departmental friction develop into a bitter feud.

Outside the universities the new learning found its earliest support in the cities, among the patrician merchants, civic officials, members of the learned professions and some of the higher clergy. In the Netherlands, the Rhineland and South Germany, the spread of humanism was facilitated by the close commercial contact between these areas and Italy. Germany had no royal court to keep alive the chivalric literary tradition and nowhere in the north was the cultural void left by the decline of that tradition felt more keenly. The fragmentation of the Empire had also left the imperial cities practically independent, and independence had bred in the governing patrician class of these cities a self-confidence that prepared them to accept the new humanist culture. Augsburg and Nürnberg, rising to unprecedented wealth in the second half of the fifteenth century, early became centers of lay humanism, as to a lesser degree did the Rhenish cities of Strasbourg and Basel with their great printing houses. The French cities on the whole presented a less favorable atmosphere. Paris was largely dominated by the royal court and the university with their divergent cultural traditions. The new learning did, however, find independent patronage among the small but influential élite of royal officials, advocates, judges and ministers of finance who formed the rising class of *noblesse de robe*. Of the provincial cities, only Lyons, the great center of international trade, became an active center of classical studies and of the publication of books devoted to the humanities. In England only in London did a humanist circle form under the influence of Colet, More and Linacre.

Finally, by 1520, the new learning was beginning to find patrons and adherents in the royal and princely courts. The new type of international diplomacy required the services of men who could write treaties or manifestoes or represent their governments on public occasions without offending the growing taste for classical Latinity. Everywhere humanists were finding employment in the chancelleries, not only of the great national monarchies, but also of the smaller German principalities. The time when courtiers would regard a classical education as necessary had not yet come, but a taste for the classics was becoming fashionable, and it was an asset to be able to turn a Latin verse or epigram and to embellish an oration with a Latin or Greek tag. The influence of the Italian courtly ideal, as expressed in Castiglione's *The Courtier*, worked strongly in that direction as the century went on. Moreover Henry VIII, Francis I and Emperor Maximilian were all favorable to the new classical culture and helped to make it popular at their courts.

Northern humanism, like its Italian prototype, was a complex movement containing within itself many different types of *Weltanschauung*. The cult of the classic languages was the one common bond which united the humanists and welded them into a self-conscious class, international in scope. Many of the humanists displayed strong national sentiments, but humanism itself was cosmopolitan. Nearly all the humanists were widely travelled men, and wherever they went Latin served them as a means of communication. When they wrote, they wrote Latin, and the printing press gave their works an international circulation. They also corresponded with scholars of other countries and rallied in mutual defense when attacked by the conservative schoolmen. Many of them latinized or hellenized their names, with results more startling than in Italy where a Latin ending tacked onto an Italian name made relatively little difference. Thus Lefèvre d'Étaples became Faber Stapulensis, Johannes Jäger became Crotus Rubianus and Conrad Mut became Mutianus Rufus, while Johannes Heussgen and Philipp Schwarzert hellenized their names as Oecolampadius and Melanchthon respectively.

Pure philological scholarship formed a large part of northern as of Italian humanism, although the northern late-comers did not have to serve the long apprenticeship that had been necessary for the Italian pioneers, since these had already laid the groundwork. Many of the humanists were simply teachers of the classical languages and literatures. Others were active in preparing translations or scholarly editions of the classics for the printing press. Had Erasmus never done anything else, his services in this direction would have earned him a distinguished place in the history of classical scholarship; and in the French jurist, Guillaume Budé (1468-1540), and the English physician, Thomas Linacre (1460-1524), the north could boast scholars in both Latin and Greek as competent as any Italian after Poliziano. The north, too, had its scholarly printers, the Frobens and Amerbachs of Basel, Sebastian Gryphius of Lyons, Henri Estienne and Josse Badius of Paris, and Thierry Martens of Louvain, who were worthy rivals of the Venetian Aldus.

Thanks to the availability of printed books and the foundation already laid by Italian scholars, the study of Greek spread almost as rapidly as that of classical Latin through the northern countries. Until the opening years of the sixteenth century it was still regarded as necessary to visit Italy to gain a thorough training in Greek, but most of the leading northern humanists had at least a fair knowledge of the second ancient language. What is rather more surprising is the widespread interest in Hebrew, an interest proportionately greater in the north than in Italy and largely due, as we shall see, to the greater prevalence of Biblical scholarship. The most distinguished Hebraist of the turn of the century was the German Doctor of Law, Johann Reuchlin (1455–1522). He was already an accomplished Latin and Greek scholar before he visited Italy and became interested in the Hebrew language and literature. He was particularly fascinated by the mystical lore of the Hebrew Cabbala to which he was introduced under the influence of Pico della Mirandola. Returning to Germany, he continued his studies and in 1506 published the *Rudiments of the Hebrew Language*, the first Hebrew grammar written by a Christian and designed for students who were not raised in the Hebrew tradition. This book which opened the way to Hebrew studies in Christian schools was one of the most important works produced by northern humanism. Reuchlin's later studies of the Cabbala enjoyed a *succès d'estime* among the humanists, but they were too esoteric and generally woolly-minded to gain many followers. More important were his application of Hebrew philology to Old Testament exegesis and his defense of Hebrew learning which brought him into conflict with the conservative theologians; but this part of his activity — and, indeed, the revival of Hebrew in general — belongs more properly to the story of the reform program of Christian humanism than to that of pure scholarship.

Important as were their scholarly activities, it was the humanists' ability to write classical prose and verse that won them patronage at court and in wealthy patrician society, and it was their command of classical elegance that drew men of widely different backgrounds together in a kind of mutual admiration society. It was his style even more than his scholarship or his serious thought that won for Erasmus international recognition as the prince of the humanists. Wherever groups of humanists were found they exchanged verses and familiar epistles in the Ciceronian manner, many of them intended for publication. Erfurt had a little group of "poets" centering around Mutianus Rufus. Most active in organizing the German humanists was the wandering poet, Conrad Celtis (1459–1508), who founded literary societies in the Rhineland and later in Vienna. Except when inspired by zeal for social and religious reform, the writing of the humanists was generally undistinguished and made no lasting contribution to the world's great literature. It was no less important for that. Under the tutelage of the humanists the northern countries served an apprenticeship in literary form which in the following generations bore fruit in the vernacular literatures. At the same time, as apostles of the classics and through their services as scholars, publicists and educators, they introduced into the common domain of European culture a great body of secular literature that was not specifically noble or clerical or bourgeois, but was designed to appeal to all educated people. The age when the best sellers were written in classical Latin was a brief one in the north, scarcely more than a generation; but when it had passed the vernacular literatures were revitalized. Other factors must be taken into account, but the difference between the formless and pedestrian drivel of the fifteenth century and the literary world of Montaigne and the Pléiade, of Drayton and Jonson, Marlow and Shakespeare is in part, at least, the measure of the humanist contribution to the formation of modern literature.

The humanists were themselves aware, perhaps unduly, that they were the harbingers of a new day. They shared the attitude of their Italian predecessors toward the literary culture of the Middle Ages, which they regarded as a period of deplorable barbarism between the great age of classical antiquity and their own day of the revival of good letters. This sense of belonging to an age of renewal or rebirth lent to their writing a note of optimism that had been generally lacking in the literature of the preceding century. At the same time, their devoted study of the distant world of antiquity gave them a sense of the past and with that an historical perspective which was one of the important contributions of humanism to modern thought. In this respect, too, they were but following in the footsteps of the Italians, and when they turned to writing history they adopted, so far as their different national situations would permit, the literary form, the secular tone and the concepts of the nature and use of history already established by Bruni, Biondo and the other Italian historians.

The Italian example was also responsible for the patronage of historians by monarchs who wanted comparable histories of their states. Henry VII and Louis XII went to Italy directly and commissioned Italian humanists, Polydor Vergil and Paulo Emilio respectively, to write their national histories. The unification of the national states around their ruling dynasties made it possible to apply the Italian concepts of state history without much change. The result was a secular history, which removed the national history from the framework of world chronicle and divested it of much legendary material.

The situation in Germany was radically different and the humanist historians there, while adopting the literary form of Bruni and the antiquarian research of Biondo, could not so completely escape from the tradition of the medieval chronicle. The ramshackle structure of the Empire furnished no satisfactory focus for a state history, while the individual territorial states were too small and too inextricably involved in the shifting fortunes of feudal politics. Yet, despite its lack of a foundation in political reality, German nationalism was a powerful force in the humanist generation, such as Germany was not to see again until the Romantic movement. The nationalism of the German humanists had, indeed, much in common with that of the later romantics, in that it expressed a sense of cultural rather than political unity and sprang in large part from resentment of the inferior rôle in international affairs which lack of political unity had forced upon their country. An equally strong motive was resentment of Italian claims to cultural superiority. In reply to the Italians, who called them barbarians, the German historians developed the theme of the unique place of the German people in world history. With the aid of Tacitus, whose *Germania* Celtis published, they were able to establish the antiquity of the German people as the *Urvolk* of Europe. They turned the destruction of the Roman Empire by the German barbarians into a source of national pride, and in the transference of the imperial title to the German rulers — the *translatio imperii ad Teutonicos* — with all the claims to universal authority that it implied, they found balm for their wounded spirits. This conception of the divinely ordained function of the Empire bound Aventinus, Nauclerus, Trithemius and the other German historians to the medieval tradition of the world chronicle and the Four Monarchies, and it prevented them from producing realistic state histories comparable to those of the Italians from Bruni to Machiavelli. The patriotic sentiment they helped to inspire did, however, play a significant rôle in the cultural development of their country and was not without influence on the course of the Protestant Reformation, as was evidenced by the adherence to the Lutheran revolt of Ulrich von Hutten, the most nationalistic and least spiritual of the German humanists.

E. CHRISTIAN HUMANISM AND THE ERASMIAN REFORM PROGRAM

The term "Christian humanism," commonly applied to the religiously oriented humanism of the north which found its fullest expression in the work of Erasmus, is a useful one. It denotes one distinct aspect of the general humanist movement; but it requires some careful definition and qualification. It should not be understood to imply that the Italian humanists, for example, were not Christian, still less that they were in any real sense of the word pagan. While varying in the depth and intensity of their personal piety, they were almost without exception faithful sons of the Church. Nevertheless, the Italian humanists in general tended to keep their classical studies and their religion in more or less separate compartments, not in conflict but independent of one another. The pioneers of northern humanism, too, as well as those later devotees of the new learning in the north who are not included among the Christian humanists, were nearly all deeply religious men. Their orthodoxy was unquestioned, and they accepted the religious practices of their day as they found them. What distinguished the Christian humanists was the fusion of classical humanism with evangelical piety, out of which they evolved a positive program for social and religious reform and for the reorientation of both popular piety and theological studies. It was this positive program that made Christian humanism a revolutionary movement, one which helped to prepare the way for a Reformation that its principal protagonists neither desired nor could accept.

Both the driving force and the peculiar quality of the religious thought of the Christian humanists were in large part an inheritance from the combination of lay piety with mysticism and zeal for the reform of the Church, which had been endemic in the northern countries for two centuries and which was most fully formulated in the movement known as the *Devotio Moderna.* The essential characteristics of this movement, as we have seen, were concern for the direct relation of the individual soul to God and the reflection of that relation in personal conduct. While entirely orthodox, it tended to bypass the formal mediatory ministrations of the official Church and to ignore the dogmatic speculations of scholastic theology. Its finest expression was the *Imitation of Christ.* Similar tendencies were also widely spread among less orthodox groups of the sectarian type like the Beguines, the Lollards and the Brethren of the Free

Spirit, as well as among such exponents of orthodox mysticism as the Parisian, Jean Gerson. In almost all its forms the rising tide of popular piety in the north found its principal inspiration in the New Testament, in the Gospel story and in the example of the Apostles.

Different as it was from the predominantly secular tone of Italian humanism, this northern religious tradition shared with it certain qualities which made the fusion of the two possible. In both there was a primary emphasis on ethics rather than dogma, on moral philosophy rather than formal theology or metaphysics. Both were essentially lay movements in the sense of being largely independent of either ecclesiastical authority or the professional learning of the schools. So far as either movement could amalgamate with philosophy, it was with Neoplatonic mysticism rather than with the rational Aristotelianism of the Thomist school or the logical Terminalism of the late Ockhamists. Finally, in both movements the fundamental characteristic was a return to the ancient sources and an attempt to model life upon their example. All that was needed to bring the two movements together was to apply to the sources of Christianity the historical perspective and the techniques of philological and historical criticism already developed in relation to classical literature. The first partial step in that direction had already been taken by Lorenzo Valla in his *Annotations on the New Testament*. Full realization of the way in which the humanist approach might clarify the meaning of early Christianity and point the way to reform of contemporary life, however, came only around the turn of the century with the work of Lefèvre, Reuchlin, Colet and, finally, Erasmus. In their hands the new learning became the handmaid of theology, as scholastic philosophy had been for the medieval theologians.

Despite the common attitudes and aims that make it possible to regard the Christian humanists as a distinct group, they differed in many of the nuances of their thought, and they represented different varieties of religious experience. The contribution of each of the leaders of the movement must, therefore, be considered separately.

The wide variety of influences which contributed to the formation of Christian humanism is particularly evident in the career of Jacques Lefèvre d'Étaples (1450?–1536), who for three decades after his return from his first visit to Italy in 1491–92 was the acknowledged leader of the reforming humanists at the University of Paris. Lefèvre had been a professor of philosophy for years before he went to Italy. There he learned to interpret the works of Aristotle in their historical setting and with the aid of the original Greek texts. After his return he published nearly the whole body of Aristotle's works in good translations, together with a commentary designed simply to elucidate the literal meaning of the text and to explain each part in relation to the system as a whole. The strong strain of mysticism in Lefèvre, which demonstrated his kinship with Gerson and the earlier northern mystics, also found new nourishment in the teaching of the Florentine Neoplatonists. From Ficino and Pico he learned not only to reconcile Aristotle and Plato with Christianity, but to go beyond the Aristotelian investigation of the visible world to the invisible and transcendental, as illuminated in the esoteric works of the early Neoplatonists. In 1494 he published Ficino's translation of the *Hermetic Books* attributed to Hermes Trismegistus, a storehouse of the occult wisdom of ancient Egypt. He also published Traversari's translation of the works traditionally ascribed to Dionysius the Areopagite, the source of much medieval mysticism. Meanwhile, he had become fascinated by the teaching of the medieval mystics Ramon Lull and Richard of Saint-Victor, and was profoundly influenced by the mystical speculation of Nicholas of Cusa, all of whose works he published. In 1510 he visited Germany, where he was entertained by the Brethren of the Common Life in Cologne and there gained a closer acquaintance with the practical mysticism of Gerard Groote, Thomas à Kempis and other leaders of the *Devotio Moderna*.

Lefèvre's devotion to Aristotle, whom, despite his own tendency toward mysticism, he continued to regard as the best guide to understanding of the visible world, was rare among the humanists; but his historical and philological approach to Aristotle, his preoccupation with the exact meaning of the text, his rejection of medieval scholastic commentaries and his impatience with dialectical quibbling over isolated texts were all in the humanist tradition. He entered the main stream of Christian humanism, however, only when he carried over his long war against scholastic commentaries and his efforts to restore the true sense of the original texts from his study of Aristotle to that of the Bible. In 1509 he made a start in that direction by publishing four early Latin translations of the Psalms, together with a fifth in which he strove to reconcile variants in these by referring to the original Hebrew. A more important contribution was his edition of St. Paul's Epistles in 1512. Here he presented in parallel columns the Vulgate version and his own translation from the Greek, followed by a commentary. His corrections of the Vulgate were neither daring nor always well-founded, but his commentary, like those in which he had already revolutionized the teaching of Aristotle, represented a radical innovation. Here he ignored the traditional scholastic apparatus and explained the thought of St. Paul in simple terms, endeavoring to seize the Apostle's intention and to enter into communion with his spirit.

There was more of the mystic than of the dogmatic theologian in

Lefèvre's interpretation of St. Paul. He came close to the doctrine of justification by faith later asserted by Luther, yet without developing it into a dogmatic system. As a disciple of the mystics he insisted above all on the spirit without which works are vain. Hence, while not rejecting fasts, pilgrimages, the veneration of relics, or other formal observances, he condemned those who regarded them as having a virtue in themselves. Finally, he asserted, as Erasmus was soon to do in the prefaces to his edition of the Greek New Testament, and Luther not long thereafter, that the Scriptures contained all that we need for salvation. "Let us therefore cling to Christ alone and the apostolic doctrine." In his aims and methods Lefèvre was in many ways close kin to Erasmus, but the temper of their souls was different. Lefèvre's conceptions of the nature of fallen man and the necessity of Grace was closer to Luther's, and he was soon to travel further along the road to the Reformation. He found much to admire in Luther's early works, and in his *Commentaries on the Four Evangels* (1522) he asserted the doctrine of justification by faith without his earlier qualifications, and he explicitly denied the efficacy of the sacraments *ex opere operato*. The following year he followed Luther's example, and incidentally put into effect Erasmus's hope that the Scriptures would be made available to all men, by translating the New Testament and later the Old Testament as well into French. Meanwhile, the opposition of the theologians forced him to leave Paris. For several years he worked with the Bishop of Meaux, Guillaume Briçonnet, to restore the ideals of the primitive church in his diocese. He was now commonly regarded as the leader of the Reform in France, and only the protection extended by Briçonnet and later by Marguerite de Navarre saved him from persecution. Yet he was never a doctrinaire Lutheran, nor was he willing to break with the ancient Church, which he still hoped might be reformed from within. To the end he remained a mystic, largely indifferent to dogma, finding in the Gospels the inspiration for a religion of pure spirit.

We have followed Lefèvre's career beyond the point where the Reformation cut across the Christian humanist program. We must return now to Germany where, in the years immediately preceding the appearance of Luther, a bitter controversy broke out between the adherents of the new learning and the conservative theologians. It began in 1509 when a converted Jew named Pfefferkorn, backed by the Dominicans of Cologne, secured an imperial mandate empowering him to seize and burn Hebrew books belonging to the Jewish community in Frankfurt. These books, it was argued, served merely to confirm the Jews in their beliefs. It is doubtful whether Maximilian himself had anything to do with issuing the mandate. When protests reached him he suspended it, and requested an opinion from several theological faculties as well as from some private scholars. Among the latter the most important was Johann Reuchlin, who, as we have seen, had been active in introducing Hebrew learning into Germany. Alone among those consulted, his opinion was unfavorable to Pfefferkorn's scheme. A large part of Hebrew literature, including the Cabbala, to which he himself had devoted much study, the Talmud and the rabbinical glosses and commentaries on the Bible, he declared to be valuable for Christian theology. The remainder was mostly harmless and, in any case, beyond the jurisdiction of inquisitors since the Jews were not heretics, never having been Christian. Pfefferkorn replied with a violent personal attack on Reuchlin, to which he responded in no more courteous spirit. The Faculty of Theology of Cologne then took up the attack on Reuchlin and a war of pamphlets ensued. Before long everybody got into the act. The humanists almost to a man rallied to Reuchlin's defense, while the theological faculties of Mainz, Louvain and Paris joined in condemning him. Finally, in 1513, the inquisitor of Cologne summoned Reuchlin to trial for heresy. The trial, shifted from court to court and eventually transferred to Rome, dragged on for six years and ended, although rather inconclusively, in Reuchlin's favor.

As the controversy progressed it soon became apparent that the real issue at stake was not the burning of the Hebrew books, which as a matter of fact ceased, but the defense of the new learning against the scholastic conservatives. The significance of the Reuchlin affair was that it brought the latent hostility between the humanists and the conservative schoolmen into the open and aligned the former in the rôle of the children of light in battle array against the obscurantists of the theological faculties. What broke the uneasy truce that had hitherto existed between the two factions was the claim made by Reuchlin and his fellow Christian humanists that the Bible should be studied in its original languages and that Hebrew as well as Greek was an essential prerequisite to the interpretation of the Scriptures, and hence to theology. It was the demand for a return to the sources that rallied the humanists to Reuchlin's side, as it was the corollary rejection of scholastic glosses and the traditional theological arguments based on the Latin text that accounted for the bitterness of his opponents, many of whom, moreover, had small Greek and less Hebrew and no desire to learn either. The fact that Reuchlin was not a theologian but a mere layman and grammarian made his meddling with the text of the Bible all the more intolerable, nor did it help that his Biblical studies were purely philological and that he drew from them no such unsettling theological conclusions as did Lefèvre. The conflict between the new and the old methods was probably inevitable, but it was made much more bitter by the acrimonious and frequently scurrilous tone of the controversialists on both sides. On the whole, the humanists had the best of the literary exchange. At least they were funnier. The *Letters of Obscure Men,* an anonymous lampoon, probably written by Crotus Rubianus and Ulrich von Hutten, purporting to be a collection of admiring letters addressed to Reuchlin's enemies by ignorant and dissolute monks and priests, was a triumph of hilarious satire. More than any other humanist attack it served to fix upon the theologians the stigma of barbarism.

Meanwhile, in England a small but influential group of Christian humanists had grown up under the leadership of John Colet (c.1466–1519) who, after some years of teaching at Oxford, became Dean of St. Paul's in London in 1504. Unlike Reuchlin, Colet was not primarily a humanist. He was not a distinguished classical scholar, and his puritanical rejection of the world and his insistence on the depravity of fallen man did not fit the normal humanist pattern. Spiritually he was closer akin to Lefèvre, having like him brought back from Italy an interest in Neoplatonic mysticism and a particular devotion to the works ascribed to Dionysius the Areopagite. Unlike Lefèvre, however, he had no scholarly knowledge of Greek and he had nothing but contempt for rational theology. He wrote little. His influence was exerted almost entirely through lectures and sermons and through personal intercourse with his friends. In his sermons he preached a simple evangelical piety that had much in common with the continental *Devotio Moderna,* and his impatience with empty formalism caused him to denounce many contemporary religious practices in terms that led to his being suspected of Lollardy. It was his personality, the ascetic purity of his life and his flaming religious zeal that made him the spiritual guide of Thomas More, Erasmus and his other humanist friends; but his most significant contribution to the program of Christian humanism was his method of Biblical exegesis.

Years before Lefèvre turned from the elucidation of Aristotelian texts to the critical study of St. Paul, Colet had introduced the literary and historical method of interpretation in the public lectures on St. Paul's Epistles which he began in Oxford in 1496, shortly after his return from Italy. For centuries scholastic theologians had treated the Biblical texts as isolated units to be interpreted in the traditional four senses or to be used as propositions from which to deduce logical arguments supporting points of speculative theology, all with little concern for their context. Colet broke with the tradition completely. He was not interested in proving points of doctrine, but in trying to understand St. Paul's meaning. To achieve this end he related the Epistles to their historical setting, to the personality of St. Paul and to the situation of the little groups of primitive Christians to whom they were addressed. At the same time, as a literary critic Colet recognized that St. Paul's frequent metaphors as well as his choice and arrangement of subject matter must be understood in the context of the rhetorical structure of the entire epistle and the practical purpose the Apostle hoped to achieve. The clarity and vividness with which St. Paul's message, read in this fashion, emerged from the text were a revelation to a generation of listeners already repelled by the sterility of decadent scholasticism. A few years later the infinitely broader erudition and sounder philological scholarship of Erasmus was to gain for this method international recognition.

Before turning to Erasmus, however, something must be said about another member of Colet's circle who also helped to shape the thought of the great Dutch humanist. Thomas More (1478–1535) was much more a humanist and man of letters than the ascetic Dean of St. Paul's, and, despite a secret hankering for the ascetic life, he loved the world that Colet despised. He was a brilliant scholar, familiar with Greek as well as classical Latin, a successful lawyer and highly respected judge, member of Parliament at twenty-six and Under-Sheriff of London at thirty-two, later a distinguished diplomat and royal official. His contribution to humanism, however, belongs to the early part of his life before royal service and religious controversies claimed his time. We are here not concerned to follow him through the years of his growing favor with Henry VIII, his chancellorship and his final martyrdom. More remained all his life an affectionate and loyal friend to Erasmus, but it was in the years between their first meeting and the publication of the *Utopia* in 1516 that they were most intimately associated. Erasmus made his last brief visit to England in 1517 and already the obligations of the king's service were closing around More.

What distinguished More from the other leading Christian humanists was the breadth of his practical experience and his clear perception of the social and political ills of his day. These were the qualities that, together with his wit and literary talent, made the *Utopia* one of the few humanist works to gain a permanent place in the world's literature. The book was begun in Antwerp in 1515 when More was engaged in an embassy to Prince Charles, later the emperor. There, as the introductory pages tell us, he was introduced by Erasmus's friend, Pierre Gilles, to an ancient mariner named Raphael Hythloday, who had travelled much to the far places of the earth and had lived for five years in the hitherto unknown land of Utopia. The second part of the book, written while More was still in Antwerp, is a detailed and circumstantial account of that ideal commonwealth, in which all men are equal, all labored and shared their goods in common, so that there was no place for pride, greed or sloth —

the besetting sins of European society — and no incentive for any to seize wealth and power or to oppress their fellow men. The first part, with the probable exception of the introduction, was added the following year after More's return to England. It consists of a dialogue in which More, Gilles, and Hythloday discuss the evils of contemporary society and the problem, much on More's mind at the moment, of the duty of enlightened men to offer their services and counsel to princes. Here More condemns such economic practices as the enclosure of common land for sheep pasturage, unjust laws like the death penalty for petty larceny, oppressive taxation and needless wars of conquest, and concludes with Hythloday's eloquent argument "that as long as there is any property and while money is the standard of all things, I cannot think that a nation can be governed either justly or happily."

The meaning of More's *Utopia*, like that of Machiavelli's *Prince*, has been variously interpreted. More has been hailed, on the one hand, as a proto-Socialist centuries ahead of his age and, on the other, as a conservative medieval Catholic opposed to the new phenomena of commercial capitalism and absolute monarchy. Both views fail to see More and his work in the context of his own age and the group to which he belonged. A more percipient judgment, offered by a recent student of the *Utopia*, is that "the Utopian Discourse is the production of a Christian humanist uniquely endowed with a statesman's eye and mind, a broad worldly experience, and a conscience of unusual sensitivity, who saw sin and especially the sin of pride as the cancer of the commonwealth."[5] It is a criticism of contemporary society based on Christian principles combined with the ethical wisdom of the ancients, and it is at the same time a literary *tour de force*, a description which might apply equally well to Erasmus's *Praise of Folly*. Some of the confusion regarding the meaning of *Utopia* arises from the unwarranted assumption that it expresses fully More's views on all the subjects that interested him. Its meaning has also been obscured by the fact that the satire is double-edged. The Utopians are not Christian. Their commonwealth, therefore, is founded upon natural reason, unenlightened by Christian revelation, and upon those virtues — wisdom, temperance, justice and fortitude — which even the pagans may possess. It was the contrast between a society without benefit of Christianity and the prevailing condition of Christian Europe that gave point to More's satire; but at the same time the necessity of maintaining his fiction prevented him from expressing his views on such questions as religious practice, toleration and the status of the clergy in a specifically Christian community. His discussion of Utopian religion remained, therefore, necessarily somewhat ambiguous.

[5] J. H. Hexter, *More's Utopia: The Biography of an Idea* (Princeton, 1952), p. 78.

As the foregoing account of its leaders indicates, Christian humanism originated more or less independently in the various northern countries. It was welded into an international movement by Erasmus of Rotterdam (1466 or 69–1536). At the height of his career, in the decade immediately preceding the outbreak of the Lutheran Reformation, Erasmus was universally hailed as prince of the humanists, and he became for a time the recognized leader of all who hoped for the reform of Church and society by the peaceful means of enlightened education and a return to the spirit of evangelical Christianity. He was, himself, completely cosmopolitan, a citizen of Europe. His native Holland was too small to give him a sense of nationality, and he lived for years in Paris, Italy, England, Basel and Louvain. He travelled constantly, at home everywhere and nowhere. Few men have had as widely scattered a circle of friends and acquaintances; but what made it possible for him to dominate the literary world of Europe, as no more than one or two writers have done since, was his classical scholarship and his unrivalled command of Latin style. Erasmus was fortunate in that he lived in an age, the last of its kind, when Latin was still the most popular vehicle for literature. His books needed no translator to make them best sellers throughout the length and breadth of Western Europe. At once scholar and popularizer, leavening his most serious thought with wit and tempering his reforming zeal with common sense, he appealed to a wide variety of readers. In his works the two traditions of classical humanism and evangelical lay piety were blended in perfect harmony; but the resulting amalgam, in the form stamped upon it by the unique quality of his mind and personality, was an essentially original creation. It made a powerful impact on his own age and it has continued to appeal to like-minded men of all creeds in the generations since.

Erasmus was introduced to the two traditions that were to shape his thought early in life, in the school of the Brethren of the Common Life at Deventer. There the spirit of Gerard Groote and the *Devotio Moderna* still lingered, and there, too, the young Erasmus secured the foundation of his classical education and felt the stimulating influence of Alexander Hegius. He had further opportunity to study the classics in the monastery of the Augustinian Canons Regular at Steyn into which he was drawn by force of circumstance as a penniless orphan. The six years or so he spent as a monk at Steyn were doubtless not as unpleasant nor as unprofitable as he afterwards remembered them. He evidently had access to a wide range of classical authors, as well as to the works of the leading Italian humanists. Among the latter Valla's *Elegantiae* aroused his particular enthusiasm and helped to shape his style. But Erasmus had no real vocation for the monastic life. He longed for wider horizons and

548

seized the first opportunity to leave the monastery, never to return. Having secured permission to go to Paris to study theology, he enrolled in the strictly conservative College of Montaigu, but remained only long enough to acquire a lasting distaste for scholasticism. Then followed four or five years of struggling existence as a tutor and literary hack. These years made him an accomplished Latin scholar and stylist, but he was drifting with no clear purpose. The turning point in his life came in 1499, when one of his pupils, Lord Mountjoy, took him to England with him for a visit. There he met Colet and More.

Erasmus was at least thirty, and possibly two or three years older, when he met the two Englishmen who were to enrich and give direction to his life. Of the two, More was closest to his heart, but it was Colet who awakened his dormant religious sense and set before him the task that was to occupy much of his time and energy for the rest of his life, that of editing and publishing the New Testament and the works of the earliest Fathers. Much as he admired Colet, Erasmus could not share his asceticism or his mysticism; but Colet's evangelical piety, his emphasis on the spirit and his impatience with both dogma and ceremonial observance were close enough to the tradition of the *Devotio Moderna* to strike a responsive chord, while his historical and literary method of interpreting the Scriptures pointed a way to theological studies that appealed to the humanist in Erasmus. The humanist, however, could not be content, as Colet was, with interpretation based on the Latin text of the Vulgate. He must have the original Greek, the very words of Christ and the Apostles, and for this he was not yet prepared. He therefore returned to Paris and for the next six years labored, amidst further wanderings and under conditions of nagging penury, to perfect his knowledge of Greek. While he was thus engaged his purpose was strengthened and given more precise direction by the discovery of a manuscript of Lorenzo Valla's *Annotations on the New Testament*, which he edited and published in 1505.

Meanwhile, Erasmus had not forgotten that scholarship was only half of the program of Christian humanism. In 1503 he published the *Enchiridion Militis Christiani* (the *Handbook or Weapon of a Christian Knight* — the word *Enchiridion* carries both meanings). Here he presented a practical guide to piety, addressed to a layman, and expressing more explicitly than in any of his other works his conception of the essential meaning of Christianity. Throughout the little book, the influence of Colet and the *Devotio Moderna* is clearly manifest. True piety is a matter of the spirit, not of formal observances, and it must find expression in the conduct of daily life. Erasmus says little about theological doctrine or the ministrations of the Church, much about the "philosophy

549

of Christ" and Christian conduct. The *Enchiridion* never achieves the intensity of feeling of the *Imitatio Christi*, but it belongs to the same family.

For years lack of means prevented Erasmus from going to Italy to imbibe Greek scholarship at the source. When the opportunity came in 1506 he had progressed so far that there was little the Italians could teach him. Still, the Italian visit served to ripen his thought, and the cordial welcome he received from scholars there gave him a confidence he had hitherto lacked. The most fruitful part of his stay in Italy was the year he spent in Venice in close collaboration with the group of Greek and Latin scholars which gathered around the great printing house of Aldus Manutius. At the Aldine press Erasmus brought out a greatly enlarged edition of the *Adages*, already published in Paris. This work, with its more than three thousand proverbs or sayings culled from the Latin and Greek classics, immediately established his reputation as one of the greatest living scholars. Later he reissued augmented versions at intervals, and before his death more than sixty editions had been published. The book owed its popularity in large part to its practical usefulness. It made available, with explanation and comment, a vast storehouse of those classical tags which contemporary taste felt to be a necessary adornment of literature or public oratory. At the same time, the commentaries on the *Adages* served Erasmus as a vehicle for criticism of those aspects of contemporary life in Church and society which he felt to be contrary to the spirit of Christ. Written in a racy style, mingling erudite discussion of the classics with anecdotes and pointed observations on the contemporary scene, the commentaries were read by people whom he could not otherwise have reached. Erasmus was learning to sweeten the pill and to conceal his propaganda for reform under the pleasant guise of entertainment.

Back in England again in 1509 he was busy for several years working on the text of the New Testament and lecturing on Greek at Cambridge. The first fruit of his renewed contact with his English friends, however, was not a work of erudition but the gossamer fantasy and double-edged irony of the *Moriae Encomium*, the *Praise of Folly*. In this little book, written in More's house while he was resting from his trip from Italy, Erasmus directed the shafts of his wit at many of those evils — or follies — in the social, political and religious life of his age that More was to satirize a few years later in the *Utopia*. Here Folly, a cheerful and amiable goddess, extols her own services to mankind and praises her followers, among whom a prominent place is given to warring and worldly popes and prelates, schoolmen vain of their empty knowledge, and monks who think that precise performance of formal observances will atone for a dissolute life. His victims might squirm, but there was very little they could do about it, for after all it was Folly speaking. The tone is different, but the message is the same as in the *Enchiridion*.

A more daring attack on what Erasmus felt to be profoundly unchristian in the secularized papacy also emerged from this visit to England. Shortly after the death of Julius II in 1513 he wrote the *Dialogue of Julius excluded from Heaven*. In it the old warrior-pope, whom he had seen march in triumphal procession with his troops through a breach in the walls of Bologna, was depicted standing before the gate of Heaven, trying in vain to show St. Peter any good reason why he should be admitted. The author makes no attempt to refute the arguments of the canonists for papal supremacy. The biting point of the satire emerges simply from the historical perspective which places St. Peter in the context of the Gospel story and underlines the contrast between him and his latest successor. There was too much dynamite in the dialogue for Erasmus to admit its authorship, and it was not published until 1517. He was immediately suspected, but was able to talk himself out of serious trouble, though not without a certain amount of equivocation.[6]

By 1516 Erasmus was at last ready to carry out the task he had begun years before under Colet's inspiration. In that year his edition of the Greek New Testament, together with new Latin translation and notes, appeared from Froben's press in Basel. The Erasmian New Testament was greeted with a storm of mingled applause and indignation. Humanists everywhere, as well as many churchmen, hailed it with enthusiasm, but the conservative scholastic theologians were aghast. The Reuchlin controversy, still raging in Germany, was sufficient indication of what their attitude would be toward any meddling with the Vulgate text or assumption that the original text was necessary. Now Erasmus had not only presented the original Greek to the public, but in his translation and notes had indicated for those who could not read Greek the places where it varied from the accepted Latin version. Finally, in the preface, which he called *Paraclesis*, addressed to the pious reader, he challenged the exclusive right of the theologians to read and interpret the Sacred Scriptures.

> I dissent most vehemently [he wrote] from those who would not have the divine Scriptures read by the unlearned, translated into the vulgar tongue, as though Christ taught in such an involved fashion that he would be but barely understood by a few theologians, as though the

[6] The Erasmian authorship of the *Julius Exclusus* has been challenged by C. Stange, *Erasmus und Julius II, Eine Legende* (Berlin, 1937). For the arguments, which I still find convincing, for ascribing the dialogue to Erasmus, see my edition of the *Erasmi Opuscula* (The Hague, 1933), p. 41 ff.

safeguard of the Christian religion lay only in its being unknown. . . . I would desire that all little women (*omnes mulierculae*) should read the Evangel, should read the Pauline epistles. And would that these might be translated in all languages, so that they might be read and known, not only by Scots and Irishmen, but even by Turks and Saracens. . . . Would that from these the ploughman might sing at the plow, and that with something from these the weaver might keep time to his loom; would that with stories from these the traveller might while away the tedium of his voyage.[7]

As if all this were not enough to disturb the theological faculties, Erasmus returned to the attack with a long essay on "The Method of Attaining to True Theology," inserted in the second edition of the New Testament in 1519. In it he challenged the validity of the theological studies of the past four hundred years and proposed a radically different curriculum in their place. At the basis of his disagreement with the traditional theologians lay a fundamentally different conception of what was "true theology," a conception that owed much to the *Devotio Moderna* and to Colet, and one that he had himself been developing ever since the *Enchiridion*. True theology, for Erasmus, was simply the philosophy of Christ as clearly expressed in the New Testament. From this premise, he launched a double-barrelled attack on the methods of traditional theology: first, a rejection of dialectic as the principal tool of learning and the substitution for it of philology and history, and, second, the rejection of all medieval glosses and commentaries and the substitution for them of direct study of the scriptural texts as they were originally written. The first requirement for the training of theologians, he argued, should be a thorough knowledge of the three ancient languages, the second a general training in the humane disciplines, especially history, grammar and rhetoric. As for dialectic and the learned systems of the Thomists and Scotists, they might better be ignored. They merely tended to obscure the meaning of the sacred Scriptures. It is no wonder that the theologians were annoyed, and when he attempted to put his theories into practice by persuading a wealthy friend to found a college for the study of the three ancient languages under his direction at Louvain he was subjected to bitter personal attack.

The years immediately following the publication of the New Testament marked the high point of Erasmus's career, but he had still much work to do. In 1519 he returned to the technique of concealed propaganda for reform in the *Familiar Colloquies*, which he continued to reissue in enlarged editions at intervals for the next fourteen years. These dialogues had been begun years earlier as examples of conversational

[7] H. Holborn, ed., *Erasmus: ausgewählte Werke* (Munich, 1933), p. 143.

Latin for the boys he was tutoring, and, indeed, the published *Colloquies* continued to serve this pedagogical purpose for generations. Erasmus now realized, however, that they gave him the perfect opportunity to express his views on all the subjects nearest to his heart. At the same time, he was careful not to overload them with serious matter. Like the *Praise of Folly*, they were read for entertainment, and they have shared with it a lasting popularity. In his last years, too, he continued to edit and publish scholarly editions of the classics and the Church Fathers and to write textbooks for school use. He also wrote *Paraphrases* on the books of the New Testament. Despite the literary and scholarly activity that lasted through pain and illness almost to the day of his death, these last years were somewhat anti-climactic. His quiet voice was blanketed by the storm of controversy Luther had raised, and as Christendom split into warring factions he found himself increasingly isolated. In 1521 the animosity of the theologians drove him out of Louvain. The next eight years he spent in Basel, close to Froben's printing establishment. Then, when Basel became Protestant, he retired to the little Catholic town of Freiburg in the Breisgau, and there he remained till his final illness drove him back to his friends in Basel.

Erasmus's refusal to take a strong stand either for or against Luther was misunderstood and resented by partisans on both sides of the religious controversy that was disrupting the unity of Christendom. He was accused of cowardice, vacillation and duplicity, and the charge has been echoed by many historians, Protestant and Catholic alike, ever since. The misunderstanding arose from the fact that Luther did seem to be following in the humanist's footsteps in his demand for reform of abuses in the Church, in his condemnation of reliance on formal observances and the mere mechanics of salvation, in his rejection of scholastic theology and in his dependence on the direct literal sense of the Scriptures. Erasmus, himself, at first shared this view, though alarmed by Luther's violence and apprehensive of the tumult that might ensue. He and Luther had the same enemies, and Erasmus for some time regarded the attacks on Luther as an extension of the obscurantists' war on the new learning. During the crucial months before the Diet of Worms he used all his influence to protect Luther from being condemned without a fair trial. It is not remarkable, then, that both Catholic and Protestant partisans agreed with the view summarized in the epigram: "Erasmus laid the egg that Luther hatched."

Those who have envisaged Erasmus as a sort of lost leader of the Reformation who lacked the courage of his convictions have failed to perceive the fundamental difference between the whole conception of the nature of God and man held by the Christian humanist and the Reformer. For one thing, Erasmus could never accept Luther's doctrine of predestination and the bondage of the will, and, when he finally agreed to write something against Luther, it was this basic doctrine that he chose to combat in the *Diatribe on the Free Will* (1524). Luther replied more in anger than in sorrow and the breach between the two was thereafter irreparable. Erasmus's critics have also tended to concentrate attention on his negative criticism of the contemporary religious scene and to ignore the positive aspects of his reform program and what he really hoped to achieve for the betterment of Christendom. It might, perhaps, be more just to alter the famous epigram to read, "Erasmus laid the egg that Luther broke." For, in fact, the dogmatic controversy which the Reformer aroused, and the schism in the Church which resulted from it, wrecked all hope of the kind of revitalization of undogmatic Christian piety through enlightened education and return to the pure "philosophy of Christ" to which Erasmus remained faithful to the end. The isolated position he maintained in his last years was due neither to vacillation nor to cowardice, but to his firm adherence, against pressure and blandishments from both camps, to the position he had taken before Luther's appearance on the scene, and to the cause to which he had given his life's work. The road on which he had set his feet led neither to Wittenberg nor to Rome. At the same time, it never led him away from the universal Church he had so long labored to reform from within.

XVI

Art and Music

The second half of the fifteenth century witnessed the last phase in that development of the fine arts that we identify with the Italian Quattrocento and the great age of Netherlandish painting. There was no significant turning point in the years around 1450, but a new period opened toward the end of the century when Italy entered upon the High Renaissance, as historians of art have agreed to designate the period from the last decade of the fifteenth century through the first two or three decades of the sixteenth. In these years, too, Italianate influences began to alter the style of northern art, and to reverse the current of influence which in the preceding half century had run from the Netherlands to Italy as Italian painters gradually adopted the superior technical processes of the great Flemish artists. In the history of music this period also represented a culmination of a period of growth, the last great age of Netherlandish dominance. No single year can be taken as marking the end of an era; but the death of Leonardo da Vinci in 1519, of Raphael in 1520, of Heinrich Isaak in 1517 and Josquin des Prez in 1521 justifies us in closing our study at about that point, with the feeling that to go further would mean writing another and different story.

The Second Period of Transition: 1450–1520

A. ART AND ARCHITECTURE IN ITALY

A brief account of Italian art during this period is a difficult, if not impossible task, because of the large number of distinguished artists — more numerous than any other time or place could boast — with whom one should deal. Certain common tendencies may be discerned, but such was the force of personality even in those artists who were not of the very first rank that no general characterization will do justice to their individual styles. As for the giants of the High Renaissance, one can do little more than repeat the superlatives heaped upon them by generations of critics and historians. Moreover, one can no longer simplify the story by concentrating attention upon the two Tuscan republics. Florence, it is true, was still the most productive center until the turn of the century, but one can no longer ignore the Umbrian towns, the northern courts of Ferrara and Milan, or the great commercial republic on the lagoons with its university city of Padua. After 1500, too, Rome became for a brief time the magnet that drew artists from all parts of Italy, and, when her golden age ended with the sack of the city in 1527, Venice carried on the tradition of Renaissance painting for another half century.

The artists of this period enjoyed as their birthright a level of technical proficiency for which they had to thank the remarkable progress made during the preceding century and a half. They were also given encouragement and material support by patrons who had themselves inherited a long tradition of culture that had refined their taste and intensified their aesthetic appreciation. Italy may not have been as prosperous in the age of the Medici as in that of the Bardi and Peruzzi, and the High Renaissance reached its peak in the midst of the disasters that followed upon the foreign invasions; but neither economic stagnation nor the tumult of war could offset the effect of generations of education in the appreciation of art, which seems to have made almost every wealthy citizen and every prince and pope a patron. That there was still ample wealth to support art is obvious from the results, and if much of it was inherited wealth rather than the product of a vigorously expanding economy, it was for that reason the more likely to be spent on those things that gave pleasure to the mind and the senses. The growth of territorial states and the stabilization of the political scene after the Peace of Lodi had also placed unprecedented wealth based on taxation in the hands of a few Italian princes, including the popes, and made their courts centers of munificent patronage. The patrons of this era were less exclusively concerned with the decoration of churches and chapels. Art no longer needed the justification of serving piety — although there was still, of course, much religious art — but could be valued for its own sake. To an increasing degree patronage now came from connoisseurs who collected works of art for their own enjoyment, and thus paintings and pieces of sculpture found their way into princely courts, private *palazzi* and the villas of wealthy citizens. Under such patronage the proportion of secular subject matter notably increased. Portraiture flourished as never before and, as might be expected in an age steeped in veneration for antiquity, scenes inspired by classical mythology began to rival those drawn from the Scriptures or the *Golden Legend*.

A substratum of scientific naturalism continued to run through Florentine painting till nearly the end of the fifteenth century. There were still technical problems to be solved, and these attracted men of a scientific bent of mind who could find little outlet for their scientific interests elsewhere. This was not a distinguished period in the history of the natural sciences, which were still dominated by the abstract logic and qualitative concepts of Aristotelian physics. The artists, however, although many of them were literate and sufficiently educated to consort familiarly with members of the intelligentsia, were not university-trained and so were free to exercise their native scientific curiosity in concrete and practical empiricism. Many of them practised more than one art, turning their hand to painting, sculpture or architecture as the occasion demanded, and this versatile activity broadened their scientific knowledge. Painters had learned correct perspective — the great technical discovery of the first half of the century — from an architect, and the practice of architecture continued to develop among painters that knowledge of mathematics and geometry which all the theorists of the age, from Alberti and Piero della Francesca to Leonardo, regarded as essential to their craft. In much the same way, the practice of sculpture heightened the painters' interest in the study of anatomy, which during the second half of the fifteenth century laid the foundations for the easy mastery of the human figure achieved by the painters of the High Renaissance.

The value of scientific anatomical study is especially apparent in depiction of the nude, and it was in this period, in fact, that the nude figure for the first time since classical antiquity became in its own right a subject for art. The growing prevalence of the nude in Italian painting cannot, however, be accounted for simply by the artists' scientific interest in anatomy. It also represented the culmination of the long effort, which had begun with Giotto, to express in painting the tactile values of the fully rounded, three-dimensional figure. At the same time, and in a more fundamental way, the appearance of the nude in art reflected a changing attitude toward the body, as ascetic distrust of the flesh lost its hold on an increasingly mundane society, and the theologians' conviction of

557

human depravity was replaced by the humanists' concept of the dignity of man. The change was apparent earlier in the century in the sculpture of Donatello, but was now reinforced by the Neoplatonic doctrine of human beauty as that which awakens the soul to contemplation of successively more spiritualized forms of beauty, leading ultimately to recognition of the absolute beauty of Divine Truth. This was a concept that found its fullest expression in Michelangelo's exclusive preoccupation with the nude.

Of the two artists whose workshops were the busiest in Florence, Andrea del Verrocchio (1435–88) and Domenico Ghirlandaio (1449–94), little need be said here, except that both were superb craftsmen in the naturalistic tradition, who passed on a heritage of technical proficiency to artists greater than themselves. Verrocchio was more outstanding as a sculptor than as a painter, and we will return to him, but his painting of landscape backgrounds showed an unusual sensitivity to atmospheric effects which bore fruit in his pupil Leonardo. Michelangelo owed less to Ghirlandaio, in whose workshop he studied for a time, but he may have profited by exposure to a thoroughly sound, if uninspired, technique. An air of prosy literal-mindedness hangs over this generation of scientific naturalists, who had lost the religious inspiration that had infused the soul of Fra Angelico and who had not yet found the classical ideal of the next generation. The one note of pure lyric poetry was struck by a painter who cared little for the problems of correct anatomy and perspective that concerned his fellow artists, but was more gifted than any in his ability to convey an impression of fluid movement. Sandro Botticelli (1444–1510) brought to pagan and Christian themes alike a dreamy subjective charm and a feeling for delicately modulated line that place him at the opposite end of the spectrum from Giotto and Masaccio. At the behest of the Medici he painted the "Birth of Venus," but his Venus has the same virginal purity and wistful sadness and, incidentally, much the same features as his Madonnas. Later, he fell under the spell of Savonarola and turned his back on pagan subjects; but it is not his religious sensitivity so much as the flowing rhythm of his linear design that makes his art seem a revival of the late Gothic tradition.

The true successor to Masaccio in this generation was Florentine only by virtue of having worked and studied there in his youth. Piero della Francesca (c.1416–92) was born and spent most of his life in the little provincial Umbrian town of Borgo San Sepolcro, although he left it frequently to work in Arezzo, Urbino, Ferrara, Rimini and elsewhere. He did not return to Florence, yet the four or five years he spent there, working with Domenico Veneziano, studying Masaccio's frescos in the Brancacci Chapel, and learning the science of perspective from Brunelleschi and Alberti, left a permanent impress on his art and thought. He shared to the full the scientific interest of the Florentines. He was fascinated by the mathematical and geometrical problems of proportion and perspective, and in his last years he abandoned painting to study mathematics and to write a book *De perspettiva pingendi*. We may not share his Platonic faith in mathematical proportion as a symbol of divine harmony, but the underlying sense of order it imposed upon his paintings, together with their cool ashen color and the impersonal serenity of his monumental figures, have a strong appeal for our generation, so that he has become one of the most highly respected of Quattrocento painters. These same qualities, on the other hand, led to his being neglected by nineteenth-century critics who were seduced by the Pre-Raphaelite grace of Botticelli or the academic competence of Ghirlandaio. Piero could be a great narrative painter, as his frescos illustrating the Legend of the True Cross at Arezzo demonstrate, but he was never a mere illustrator. He was not interested in the decorative detail, the rich brocades and carved furniture that filled the work of more fashionable painters. Nothing irrelevant was allowed to detract from the essential significance of his solidly constructed figures or from the masterly organization of the spatial relationships between the component parts of his pictures.

Piero's feeling for space made him one of the few effective landscape painters of Quattrocento Italy, for in this respect the Italians lagged behind the great Netherlanders. In pure space composition, however, he was surpassed by two other Umbrian painters of very different character, Pietro Perugino (c.1445–1523) and Bernardino Pinturicchio (1454–1513). The ability to create the impression of infinite uncluttered space, whether in a city square or in the open fields, space that draws the viewer into its depths and in which he can breathe freely, seems to have been the peculiar gift of the Umbrian painters. Without that gift Perugino would have been no more than a gently attractive painter of more sweetness than force, and Pinturicchio scarcely more than a fashionable illustrator; with it they merit the place they have continued to hold in popular esteem through all the shifts in critical taste.

To find a painter as austere and as far removed from the prevailing taste of the age as Piero della Francesca we must look northward to the university town of Padua, where Andrea Mantegna (1431–1506) grew up among humanists and scholars steeped in reverence for Roman antiquity. Of all the Italian painters, he was the most directly influenced by the antique, by the desire to reproduce literally the external appearance of ancient Rome. His paintings, even of religious subjects, are filled with Roman buildings, Roman armor, costumes and ornaments, and figures which have the monumental dignity of Roman senators and centurians.

But it is not his romantic idealization of ancient Rome that makes Mantegna the most important painter of his day in northern Italy. Rather it is his mastery of three-dimensional form, of foreshortening and perspective, and the uncompromising vigor of his design. There are no soft Umbrian landscapes here, but sterile, sun-baked rocks. Indeed rocks seem to have held a peculiar fascination for him, and he painted them with the scientific accuracy of a geologist.

As the fifteenth century drew to a close, overshadowed by the threat of foreign invasion that was soon to become a terrible reality, Italian painting seemed to have lost the driving force that had achieved so much technical progress in less than a hundred years. The decade prior to the second French invasion of 1498 saw the death of Pollaiuolo, Verrocchio, Ghirlandaio and Piero della Francesca. Botticelli and Mantegna had passed their peak, and the most popular painters left in central Italy were such decorative illustrators as Perugino, Pinturicchio and Filippino Lippi, who were covering walls with impeccable but uninspired frescos. The Florentine Leonardo had been working for the past sixteen years at the court of Ludovico Il Moro in Milan, but he seems less a representative of the waning Quattrocento than a harbinger of things to come. For, in fact, the turn of the century proved to be not the end of a period of progress, but the beginning of a brief era of more glorious achievement: the High Renaissance. It is easy to see why this period is regarded as the climax of Renaissance art, but it is difficult to characterize it. If we leave aside for the moment the Venetian colorists, the art of the High Renaissance consists essentially of the work of three great figures, Leonardo, Raphael and Michelangelo, each so different in personality and style as to make any generalization inapplicable. Yet all three have this in common, that in their different ways they represent the final fulfillment of the long process of evolution that had begun with Giotto two centuries earlier, and that fulfillment having been reached, they could have imitators but not successors. Moreover, each used the technical mastery of pictorial representation inherited from the Quattrocento to create ideal forms. In this sense, as well as in the perfection of harmony and balance, theirs was a classic art.

The eldest of the triumvirate of the High Renaissance, Leonardo da Vinci (1452–1519), would occupy a prominent place in the history of his age if he had never finished a picture — and, as a matter of fact, he finished very few. He was not merely versatile, as other Florentine artists were; his talents and his insatiable curiosity were almost encyclopedic in range. He was at once painter, sculptor, musician, engineer, inventor and empirical scientist; his mind was occupied with so many projects that few bore practical fruit, and the greater part of his intense mental activity is known to us only through the notebooks he left, filled with exquisite drawings illustrating his observations of nature, his scientific theories and his mechanical inventions. For all his multifarious activities, however, he regarded himself as primarily a painter, and it is as such that we are here concerned with him. His largest painting, the "Last Supper," which because of his experiment with a new fresco technique is unfortunately in bad condition, is nevertheless masterly in the grouping of figures, the sense of movement and the expressive gestures that clearly delineate the character of each participant. In all of these respects, as well as in the chiaroscuro, it seems the fulfillment of all that Masaccio had attempted in "The Tribute Money." His use of chiaroscuro — or rather of that characteristic blending and softening of light tones into dark, known as *sfumato,* which was his peculiar contribution — is still more evident in the "Virgin of the Rocks," where the play of light rippling over the surfaces and blending into shadow at the edges lends a touch of mystery foreign to the bright linearity of the Quattrocento. Here, too, the atmospheric treatment brings a new element of aerial perspective to the depiction of distant landscape.

Unlike Leonardo, Raphael Sanzio (1483–1520) was a prolific painter, who worked with apparently effortless ease. He was, indeed, the painter *par excellence* of the Renaissance, in whom the technical achievements of the age culminated in something as near perfection as has ever lain within the grasp of human endeavor. From his Umbrian childhood and his early training in the workshop of Perugino, Raphael acquired a feeling for space composition, which remained one of his most striking attributes, and as a young man he visited Florence, there to absorb, without imitating, what could be learned from Leonardo and Michelangelo. It was Raphael's almost unique talent to be able to learn from the most diverse examples and to coordinate all that he learned into a synthesis unmistakably stamped with the imprint of his own serene personality, his own vision of beauty and his own infallible sense for harmonious and integrated composition. His innumerable Madonnas set a standard of feminine beauty that has lasted through the centuries, and in his large frescos on the walls of the Signatura in the Vatican, notably the "School of Athens" and the "Disputa," he created the most magnificent group compositions of the age, incidentally determining for all time our pictorial conception of ancient Greece. By the time Raphael reached maturity, Rome had replaced Florence as the focal center of Italian art, and most of his important work was done in the service of the popes Julius II and Leo X. His career was as brief as it was brilliant. Loaded with honors and commissions, and appointed chief architect of St. Peter's on the death of Bramante in 1514, he was already being forced to turn over much of the actual execution of his paintings to students and assistants, when he died at the age of thirty-seven.

Michelangelo Buonarroti (1475–1564), the third of the giants of the High Renaissance, was older than Raphael, but survived him by forty-four years, so that a large part of his life falls beyond the chronological boundaries of this study. Here we can deal only with his first and relatively brief period of activity as a painter. By natural tendency he was a sculptor rather than a painter, and his painting showed the sculptor's vision. Unlike the painter-sculptors of the Early Renaissance whose reliefs seemed to be carved paintings, Michelangelo's frescos have the effect of painted sculpture. The three-dimensional volume of his titanic figures and their freedom from all unessential detail place him in the line that leads from Giotto through Masaccio and Piero della Francesca, but he ignored completely their other great achievement, the grouping of figures in space. Only one subject for art really interested him: the human body, preferably nude. One feels that if he had been free to choose he would never have painted anything but male nudes, whose muscular bodies expressed the tension and sense of shackled power he felt in his own soul. Even when he painted the Holy Family the background was incongruously filled with nude figures. No painter has ever endowed the human figure with such sculptured plasticity, and to this end he sacrificed everything that the past two centuries had achieved in the pictorial representation of the visible world in its totality. His isolated figures have an uncompromising clarity that is at the opposite extreme from Leonardo's atmospheric *sfumato*, and he never attempted to place them in a fully realized setting. Beauty there is in his painting, but it is not the mysterious beauty of Leonardo or the ideal beauty of Raphael. It is the beauty of fearful symmetry, to which his contemporaries applied the term, *terribilità*. Almost the whole of Michelangelo's career as a painter until he was past sixty was compressed into one gigantic undertaking: the frescos on the ceiling of the Sistine Chapel which he painted for Julius II from 1508 to 1511. In one incredible sustained effort, he filled this vast vault, measuring fifty-four by one hundred and thirty-four feet, with a thronging mass of figures, enough to have occupied any other painter for a lifetime. Then, as though weary of painting, he abandoned it for the next twenty-five years.

There were other competent Italian artists in those wonderful opening years of the sixteenth century — Fra Bartolommeo and Andrea del Sarto among others — who would be more highly regarded had they not been overshadowed, and overawed, by the giants of their age. Even before the death of Leonardo and Raphael, and half a century before the death of Michelangelo, the perfection of their respective achievements had blocked

BOTTICELLI, PRIMAVERA.

UFFIZI, FLORENCE

PIERO DELLA FRANCESCA, MADONNA AND CHILD WITH SAINTS.

BRERA, MILAN

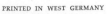

MANTEGNA, AGONY IN THE GARDEN.

NATIONAL GALLERY, LONDON

27

LEONARDO DA VINCI, VIRGIN OF THE ROCKS.

LOUVRE, PARIS

RAPHAEL, THE SCHOOL OF ATHENS.

VATICAN, ROME

PRINTED IN WEST GERMANY

MICHELANGELO, HOLY FAMILY.

UFFIZI, FLORENCE

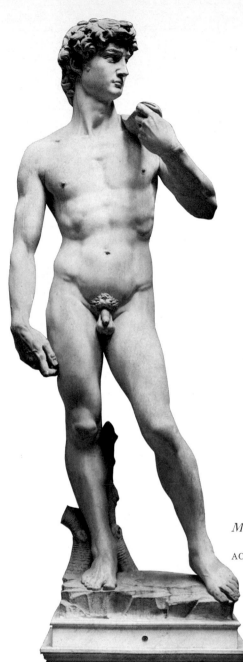

MICHELANGELO, DAVID.

ACCADEMIA DELLE BELLE ARTI, FLORENCE

PRINTED IN WEST GERMANY

31

GIORGIONE, FÊTE CHAMPÊTRE.

LOUVRE, PARIS

the way to further progress and imposed upon their followers the blight of imitation. Having passed its peak, the High Renaissance declined rapidly into Mannerism, while at the same time its questing spirit was throttled by the oppressive hand of the Counter-Reformation. One part of Italy alone escaped this double blight. Venice, culturally as well as politically a world in itself, rich, proud and autonomous, came late to painting, but when she did it was to develop a style characteristically her own and one that survived in full vigor for half a century after the decline had set in elsewhere in Italy.

Venice had never shared the intellectual interests of the other great Italian republic. Her merchant oligarchy, protected by the most stable and ruthlessly efficient political system in Italy, remained generation after generation devoted to the service of business and the state, with little time to spare for scholarship or intellectual curiosity. At the same time, wealth and assured position bred among the Venetian patricians a sensuous love of luxury, which was intensified in the late fifteenth and sixteenth centuries as failing commerce left them freer from the cares of business, but still rich enough to indulge their hedonistic tastes. These tastes found their fullest aesthetic satisfaction in painting and, more specifically, in painting that relied primarily upon light and color rather than on the clear delineation of form that characterized Florentine art. Unlike the versatile Florentine masters, the Venetian painters were nothing but painters. With their intense interest in color, they adopted oil painting earlier — from about 1475 — and more completely than did the central Italians. Around the turn of the century, they also began using canvas rather than wooden panels for the easel pictures that were greatly in demand for the decoration of private *palazzi*. For these paintings intended for private consumption, the taste of patrons more and more frequently dictated secular subjects. There was also, of course, a continuing demand for altarpieces, for, however mundane, the Venetians were still orthodox and never neglected the public forms of piety. Secular subjects appeared again, however, in the murals and large canvases commissioned by the state government and the guilds for the decoration of public buildings. Many of these depicted the colorful pageants that formed so large a part of the life of a city devoted, as was no other city in Italy, to the glorification of the state. Pageantry, indeed, long continued to be a characteristic element in Venetian art, not only with such sixteenth-century painters as Veronese (1528–88), but two centuries later with Canaletto and Guardi.

The master who in the second half of the fifteenth century gave Venetian painting the direction it was to follow for more than a hundred years was Giovanni Bellini (c.1430–1516). He came of an artistic family.

Both his father and his brother Gentile were painters, and his sister was married to Andrea Mantegna. In his early years Giovanni was dominated by his brother-in-law's stark genius; but as he grew older he worked away from the hard linear structure of Mantegna toward a vision of reality in terms of light and color. Where the Florentines of the Quattrocento had used color as something added to design, Bellini finally achieved a style in which design was expressed through color. This way of viewing the world, but not his deep religious sentiment, he passed on to the two pupils who developed it to its fullest extent: Giorgione and Titian.

Giorgione da Castelfranco (1477–1510) died too early to leave a large body of painting, but those he completed are the most perfect expressions of a mood and a painterly vision that was peculiarly Venetian. The mood is idyllic, Arcadian, and had little or no religious connotation. It was most evident in those of his paintings, like the "Tempest" and the "Fête Champêtre," in which the figures blend into the landscape and have no particular significance in themselves. The art of landscape painting had not yet progressed to the point where it could do without human figures; but by painting the figures into the landscape and by the use of an aerial perspective that suggested depth by making distant objects less distinct, Giorgione achieved an atmospheric unity unequalled by any of his predecessors or contemporaries, except, perhaps, Leonardo. But whereas Leonardo made his human figures central to the picture, Giorgione frequently opened up his compositions by placing them at the sides, so that the viewer looks through a gap or over the heads of the group to the hazy distance.

The harmony of light and color, which in Giorgione has the lyric delicacy of chamber music, swelled into full orchestration with Titian (c.1477–1576). Although he was about the same age as Giorgione, Titian began to develop as a painter only after his companion's death. He had still, however, sixty-six years of working life left and, as in the case of that other immortal, Michelangelo, a large part of his achievement belongs to a period later than we are concerned with here. While still under the spell of his brilliant friend, he caught something of Giorgione's poetic quality in such paintings as "The Ages of Man" in which, as in Giorgione's "Tempest," the figures are grouped at the sides and we look through the gap into deep atmospheric landscape. This was not, however, Titian's prevailing mood. As he grew older his paintings acquired a monumental nobility and his use of color became more impressionistic. But we cannot follow him through his long and incredibly productive career, nor can we consider the other younger Venetian painters, Tintoretto and Veronese, who carried on the tradition of Venetian color and pageantry, untouched by the Counter-Reformation and almost untouched by Mannerism, until nearly the end of the century.

A large part of Titian's immense reputation was gained as a portrait painter. The demand for portraits increased enormously during the sixteenth century, but it had already been growing steadily during the fifteenth. More and more frequently portraits of donors or of friends of the patron or the painter, and occasionally self-portraits of the painter himself, crept into frescos and altarpieces. With the increasing demand for easel paintings, however, the independent portrait became the normal method of perpetuating the features of popes, cardinals, princes and doges, as well as of scholars, men of letters and, indeed, anyone who could afford to have his portrait painted. Toward the end of the fifteenth century the profile portrait began to be replaced by the full or three-quarter face pose, which had been customary in the Netherlands throughout the century, but which had hitherto been rare in Italy. The gain in characterization and impact resulting from this change can be seen by comparing Gentile Bellini's profile portraits of several doges with his brother Giovanni's magnificent full-face portrait of the Doge Leonardo Loredano. By their very nature, formal portraits imposed certain restraints upon the artist and limited the range of composition. There was little opportunity for exploiting space composition or movement, two of the problems that interested painters in this period, but the first of these could be introduced at least partially by the expedient of setting the portrait against a background of landscape. By its necessary concentration on the individual, too, the portrait ran counter to the tendency of classical art to present ideal forms rather than particular things. But such was the demand for portraits that only Michelangelo, steeped as he was in Neoplatonism and uncompromising in his idealism, was able to resist it; although Leonardo came close to doing so, finishing only one or two portraits, and then only when his own artistic sense rather than the demand of patrons was the motivating force.

Sculpture continued to play a secondary rôle among the arts in Italy during the second half of the fifteenth century, as it had done during the earlier period. There were advances in technical proficiency, but methods and subject matter remained pretty much the same. One new form, however, did appear after mid-century: the bronze statuette, of which the "Hercules and Antaeus," of Antonio Pollaiuolo (1429–89), is one of the finest examples. Such statuettes had been very popular in antiquity, and they now made a similar appeal to connoisseurs who made a practice of collecting objects of art for their private delectation. In general, the sculptors of the late fifteenth century maintained a fairly high level of competence, but the generation following the death of Donatello, Bernardo Rossellino and Desiderio da Settignano in the mid-sixties produced only one really outstanding master: Verrocchio, whose activity as a painter we have already noted. Working in both marble and bronze, Verrocchio is the only sculptor of his generation who can be compared with Donatello. Two of his most effective pieces, indeed, seemed specifically designed to challenge comparison with the similar works of his great predecessor — the bronze David, now in the Museo Nazionale in Florence, and the equestrian statue of the *condottiere*, Colleoni, in Venice. The latter is one of the finest of all equestrian statues, more dramatic and more perfectly finished than Donatello's Gattamelata.

In sculpture as in painting the turn of the century brought the fulfillment of the High Renaissance, and in this age Michelangelo stands alone, dwarfing all others by the magnitude of his achievement. Marble was ever the medium he found most congenial, although he was constantly distracted by other activities and left less finished work than might have been expected of his long career. His work, too, was frequently interrupted or frustrated by quarrels with his patrons, caused partly by his own intractable personality and partly by their unwillingness to finance his grandiose projects as they were originally planned. Some of his best work was accomplished in the years before he was summoned to Rome by Julius II in 1505. Among these are the Pietà in St. Peter's and the Madonna and Child now in Bruges. To this period also belongs the colossal David, quite different in conception from the earlier Davids of Donatello and Verrocchio, in which Michelangelo's love of the muscular nude figure found its most perfect expression. In Rome he began work on the ill-fated tomb of Julius II, responsibility for which haunted him for the next forty years. From the beginning his work on it was constantly interrupted. In 1507 he was commissioned to do a more than life-sized bronze statue of the warrior-pope in Bologna to commemorate Julius's conquest of the city. On this statue, which incidentally was melted down a few years later by the rebellious Bolognese and the bronze used to cast cannon, he worked for some sixteen months. Scarcely had he finished when he was recalled to Rome by his imperious patron and set to work on the frescos of the Sistine Chapel. Again work on the tomb was interrupted by the death of Julius and by new demands from his successor, Leo X, among them a commission for the tombs of Giuliano and Lorenzo de' Medici on which Michelangelo began work in 1524. Meanwhile, the heirs of Pope Julius had forced a drastic reduction in the plan for his tomb, and, as finally completed, it represented only a fraction of the original design. Only the gigantic seated figure of Moses remained to suggest the scale on which Michelangelo had intended to work.

Michelangelo's sculpture, even more than his painting, cast a spell over his successors. Feeling that they could not surpass him, they could only imitate, and, in doing so, they exaggerated the elements of his style which only his genius had kept in balance.

Much of Michelangelo's time and energy in his later years was taken up with architectural projects. In 1546 he was appointed architect of St. Peter's, a post which Raphael had also held during the last six years of his life. While restoring the main outlines of Bramante's plan, Michelangelo altered it in detail and redesigned the dome, thus leaving his mark on the finished building. In the Renaissance, as in no other period, architecture was regarded simply as one of the arts, to which any artist might turn his hand regardless of previous training. It will be recalled that two of the most successful architects of the early fifteenth century, Brunelleschi and Michelozzo, had begun their careers as sculptors. The early training of the most famous architect of the High Renaissance, Donato Bramante (1444–1514), was equally irrelevant to his later career. He had been trained as a painter in his native Urbino, but later abandoned painting to devote himself entirely to architecture, first in Milan and finally, from 1499, in Rome. There under the patronage of the popes and the influence of the remnants of Roman architecture, he developed the nearest approach to a classical style achieved by any architect of that age. The necessity of adapting his designs to contemporary purposes fortunately prevented too direct imitation, but he was remarkably successful, not only in his use of classical columns and ornaments, but still more in catching the spirit of classical architecture. The harmonious proportions and severe restraint that characterized his buildings during his stay in Rome is especially evident in the small circular Tempietto, the little temple he erected in the cloister of San Pietro in Montorio. Had St. Peter's been constructed in accordance with his original plans, we might have had a grander example of his style and, perhaps, a more perfect building than finally resulted from the alterations imposed upon it by a long series of architects extending into the Baroque era. In architecture, as in the other arts, the classical moment did not last long. It outlived Bramante who, if not as original an architect as Brunelleschi, was more closely attuned to the classical spirit, but it was already passing when Michelangelo took over the direction of St. Peter's.

B. THE FINE ARTS IN THE NORTH

The tradition of Netherlandish painting founded by the van Eycks and the master of Flémalle continued to dominate art in northern Europe until almost the end of the fifteenth century. Here, as in Italy, the mid-century marked no break in artistic development. Toward the end of the century, however, new tendencies began to make their appearance. The Netherlandish monopoly was broken and, although Gerard David (died 1523) still carried on in a dying Bruges the tradition of Eyckian craftsmanship, among most other northern artists alien influences or personal idiosyncrasy marked their work as different from that of the preceding period. Change was both gradual and unevenly distributed, yet with the artists to be considered in this chapter, particularly the group of German painters born in the 1470's, one feels that northern art was entering a new era.

It was, however, a confused period and one that defies satisfactory generalization. Changing economic, political, cultural and religious conditions all contributed to the divergent tendencies that become apparent. In the Netherlands the center of both economic and artistic activity was shifting from Bruges and the old Flemish cities with their strongly established traditions to the freer and more cosmopolitan city of Antwerp or to the rising commercial towns of the northern Dutch provinces. Brussels was still the seat of the ducal court and an important center of patronage, but the court itself was losing its Burgundian atmosphere under the Hapsburg Maximilian and was more open to foreign influences. Meanwhile, the phenomenal rise of South German capitalism was paralleled by a corresponding growth of artistic and cultural life in Nürnberg and Augsburg, while in Basel and the Rhineland cities the development of the printing industry was opening new opportunities for German artists to find employment as engravers.

Toward the end of the century humanism was crossing the Alps to awaken new cultural interests in northern Europe and open the way for other Italian influences. The artists we are here considering were the contemporaries of Erasmus, Reuchlin and Lefèvre. Like them, many of the artists visited Italy, but, like them too, what they brought back took a different form from the Italian prototype. National artistic traditions were as yet too strong to be immediately or radically altered by contact with a foreign culture. Moreover, the vitality of religious unrest in the northern countries, the movement of lay piety and mysticism, and the persistent demand for reform, all tended to create a cultural atmosphere in the north different from that of Italy, and to prevent both artists and humanists from absorbing completely the spirit of the Italian Renaissance. It was among the artists of the Netherlands and Germany that the partial amalgamation of Italian and northern traditions occurred earliest, although still not universally. France was as yet less affected. When Italian art came to France it came directly through the importation of Italian art and artists to the court of Francis I, but that Italian invasion, which marked the beginning of the French Renaissance, did not occur until after the period included in this study.

Of all the northern countries, the Netherlands had long been the most closely related to Italy through constant commercial intercourse. Throughout the fifteenth century there was a numerous and wealthy settlement of Italian merchants and bankers at Bruges, some of whom, like Giovanni Arnolfini, had their portraits painted by Flemish artists. Through them, too, Netherlandish paintings, like the Portinari altarpiece painted by Hugo van der Goes for a partner of the Medici bank, found their way to Italy and were much admired. But while Netherlandish technique exerted some influence on Quattrocento Italian painting, the northern artists for their part remained curiously untouched by the characteristic elements of Italian art until nearly the end of the century. Despite their unparalleled technical proficiency, the Netherlandish artists lacked the intellectual vigor that drove the Italians, and especially the Florentines, to master one pictorial problem after another. They showed no interest in the mathematical and anatomical studies that absorbed the attention of the scientifically minded Florentines, nor were they capable of assimilating the element of monumental simplicity that ran from Giotto through Masaccio and Piero della Francesca to culminate in the idealized classical figures of Michelangelo. Nothing, indeed, could be further from their own unquenchable delight in portraying all the *minutiae* of the visible world. When Netherlandish artists did begin to seek inspiration in Italian art around the turn of the century, it was no doubt partly because the humanists had aroused their interest in transalpine culture, but rather more because their native tradition of minute craftsmanship had run its course, leaving little room for further progress in that direction. It was as though the decline of the Eyckian tradition had created a vacuum that must in some way be filled.

Among the artists who visited Italy in these years we need mention only Quentin Massys (1466–1530), Jan Gossaert, called Mabuse (c.1478–1533), Lucas van Leyden (1494–1533) and Bernaert van Orley (c.1493–1541). They went seeking stimulus, but no more than their predecessors were they capable of assimilating the full spirit of the Italian Renaissance. What they brought back was scarcely more than the superficial mannerisms and décor of Italian art. They painted the traditional scenes, but with more accurate perspective, and filled them with Roman pillars, arches, medallions and naked *putti*. The most distinguished member of this group, Massys, was also the one most firmly rooted in native tradition, yet one has only to compare him with his contemporary, Gerard David, to see how far he had departed from it. Like so many northern artists,

Massys was a masterly portrait painter, as witness his portrait of Erasmus painted in Antwerp, and in this field, indeed, the northerners could learn little from the Italians. Mabuse was a more literal copier of Italian themes, including a nude "Neptune and Amphitrite" that strikes an alien note in northern art, but no one could mistake his paintings for Italian work. These men were respectable painters, good craftsmen, but the impression they leave of a foreign element imperfectly assimilated has led some art historians to feel that the influence of Italian art on that of the north at this time was unfortunate. It is also possible, however, that had they been men of greater genius they might have profited more by contact with Italy without losing their own originality.

In one Netherlander of this generation, at least, originality was uninhibited by Italian influences or, for that matter, by any other artistic tradition. The private world of Hieronymus Bosch (c.1450–1516) is an isolated phenomenon in the history of pictorial iconography. His technical procedure, too, was his own, and it bears no relation, except in the extreme precision of minute detail, to the norm of Netherlandish painting. So far as his paintings, filled as they are with surrealist monstrosities and touches of grisly humor, can be decoded, they suggest a moralistic and satirical intent and the workings of a superheated religious imagination. Bosch was born and spent most of his life in the little Dutch town of 's Hertogenbosch, which was one of the centers of activity of the Brethren of the Common Life, but it is not their quiet piety that is reflected in his paintings. He seems rather more in tune with the eccentric sectarian movements to be found in northern Europe both before and after the Reformation. On the other hand, there is evidence that he aroused no suspicion of heresy in his own small home town, and his works were later collected eagerly by that pillar of orthodoxy, Philip II. We may agree with Erwin Panofsky that "like Philip II, himself, he may have been a case for psychoanalysis, but not for the Inquisition."[1] But we may at the same time feel that in his paintings we catch a glimpse of the darker and more disturbed side of religious life in this troubled age, translated into visual images by an artist of genius.

Further evidence of the heightened religious emotionalism to be found in the generation preceding the Reformation can be seen in the few surviving works of one of the greatest German painters, Matthias Grünewald (c.1475–1528). By far his most impressive work is the great Isenheim altarpiece, painted between 1513 and 1515. Here on the outside of the wings the Crucifixion is portrayed with a brutal realism that raises religious emotion to the height of hysteria. On the inside of the altarpiece when the wings were opened are the strongly contrasting panels of the

[1] E. Panofsky, *Early Netherlandish Painting* (Cambridge, Mass., 1958), p. 357.

Virgin and Child with an angel orchestra, flanked on either side by the Annunciation and the Resurrection, the whole an ecstatic vision in brilliant color. In its violent expressionism, Grünewald's paintings are at the furthest removed from the serene harmony of the pictures that Raphael was painting at just that time in Rome.

Grünewald represents a purely German artistic tradition at the peak of its power and technical skill. His more famous contemporary, Albrecht Dürer (1471–1528), on the other hand, absorbed what he could from Italian art without, however, losing his essentially northern character. His native city of Nürnberg had at this time close commercial relations with Venice and was experiencing an economic boom with the growth of commercial, mining and finance capitalism. It was also one of the early centers of humanism in Germany, and Dürer numbered among his closest friends the patrician humanist, Willibald Pirkheimer. Dürer's earliest contact with Italy came in his youthful wander years and was renewed later during a lengthy stay in Venice from 1505 to 1507. There he met and admired the aged Giovanni Bellini, but Dürer, a superb draughtsman with more talent for line than color, wisely did not attempt to imitate the Venetian's painterly technique. More than any northern painter, however, he was able to assimilate the monumental nobility of Italian art and to adopt more than its superficial mannerisms. Above all, he shared the intellectual vigor and scientific interests of the great Italians. He studied anatomy and was fascinated by the mathematical problems of proportion and perspective. Like Piero della Francesca, he devoted much of his time in his last years to writing treatises on the mathematical basis of painting, and before his death published *The Art of Measurement* and *The Doctrine of Proportion.*

Dürer seems akin to the Italians too in his self-awareness and his feeling for personality. Not only did he sign almost all his work with his monograph, usually adding the date and sometimes a more specific account of the circumstances, but at intervals throughout his life he painted self-portraits marking the stages of his growth. He was also careful to record the story of his family and to preserve his own notebooks and the diary of his trip through the Netherlands in 1520–21. No other northern painter of this period has left so complete a record of himself. The same awareness of personality is evident in the innumerable portrait paintings, drawings and sketches he left depicting a wide variety of people. In these there is a depth of psychological insight unequalled on either side of the Alps. These portraits, too, reflect his own profound moral earnestness and his concern for the inner life of the spirit. He was much impressed by the spiritual piety of Erasmus's *Enchiridion*, and though he never became a Protestant, he admired Luther and shared his hopes for reform. At the same time he had an almost pantheistic love of nature and an appreciative eye for all things both great and small. He was one of the first artists to paint landscapes for their own sake without the intrusion of human figures, and also one of the first to paint independent pictures of flowers, grass or small animals.

One of the most prolific artists of his age, Dürer worked in almost every known pictorial medium: oils, tempera and water colors, and he left innumerable drawings in pen, pencil, charcoal and silver point. His great international reputation, however, rested primarily on his woodcuts and copper engravings. The technique of making prints from woodcuts and engravings was a by-product of the printing industry, and it was already well established when Dürer learned the craft as an apprentice of Michael Wolgemut in Nürnberg and later in the workshop of Martin Schongauer in Alsace. Nevertheless, he was one of the first major artists to devote himself seriously to supplying prints for the press. The pre-eminence of line and drawing in the engraver's art suited his talent, and he labored all his life to improve his engraving technique and even experimented with the newer technique of etching. Through his prints, individual copies of which were fairly cheap, thousands of people who would never have seen his paintings became familiar with his art and might even own a copy of such masterpieces as "The Knight, Death and the Devil," "St. Jerome in his Cell" or the great series of illustrations of the Apocalypse and the Passion.

Two other German painters, almost exactly of an age with Dürer and Grünewald, give evidence of the vitality of German art in this generation. Hans Burgkmair of Augsburg (1473–1531) was frequently associated with Dürer in the service of Emperor Maximilian I, and like him was influenced by the Italian Renaissance. Lucas Cranach the Elder (1472–1553) also worked for Maximilian in his youth, painting religious scenes and portraits showing a strong influence of Italian grace and color. In 1504 he entered the service of Frederick the Wise and remained in Wittenberg until his death nearly half a century later. In his long life, Cranach experienced the first impact on German art of both the Italian Renaissance and the Lutheran Reformation. He was a close friend of Luther, whose portrait he painted, and in his later years he abandoned the traditional themes of religious art, which were frowned upon by Protestant opinion as idolatrous.

The same restriction of the iconographical field confined the last great German artist of this period almost exclusively to portrait painting. Hans Holbein the Younger (1497–1543) was, like Dürer, a South German, but a generation younger. His mature work lies beyond the scope of this book, but no account of the art of the German Renaissance would be complete without him. Born in Augsburg, he travelled to Basel, where he made woodcuts for Froben's press, and thence to England, where he executed a memorable series of portraits of Henry VIII and a host of contemporary English figures, portraits in which Italian and northern traditions blended to form a kind of new international style. More rugged than those of Massys, less penetrating than Dürer's, Holbein's portraits nevertheless leave a vivid impression of their subject's personality, which still shapes our mental image of the leading figures in the England of Henry VIII.

When we turn from painting to sculpture and architecture, we find less evidence of transition to what can properly be called a Renaissance style until after 1520. In all the northern countries the late Gothic tradition of sculpture continued, with an increasing drift in the direction of naturalism and a more general divorce of sculpture from architecture. The art of sculpture had already died out almost completely in the masons' lodges, and the sculpture of this period is nearly all shop-work, most of it of a fairly routine kind, but with here and there works of genuine artistic merit. A few regional centers in France developed a local tradition of skill. Tours was one of the most distinguished of these. There Michel Colombe (c.1430–1512) carved graceful, lifelike statues and reliefs, and trained assistants who carried on the local tradition until the intrusion of Italian forms in the reign of Francis I. In Germany, too, there were regional types, differing from one another, but all apparently very little influenced by Italian or classical models. One of the most active centers was Nürnberg, then at the height of its prosperity and renowned for its metal work. The metal-workers' skill in casting is evident in the fine bronze statues of Peter Vischer (1460–1529), notably the King Arthur executed for Maximilian in Innsbruck. Something of the metal-worker's style, too, was carried over into stone carving by Adam Kraft (c.1450–1509) in the great tabernacle in the Lorenzkirche, a soaring spire of lace-work in stone sixty-five feet high, which was regarded as one of the most spectacular achievements of the age.

The most characteristic and distinctive German sculpture of this period, however, was in neither metal nor stone but in wood. In Nürnberg Veit Stoss (c.1438–1533) carved in wood the great Annunciation, unique of its kind, in the Lorenzkirche, as well as numerous other pieces. Of all the German sculptors in wood the most uniformly attractive was Tilman Riemenschneider (1468–1531), who spent most of his working life in Würzburg. His style is highly individual and unmistakably his own. For all their lifelike naturalness, his figures are not literal-mindedly realistic, but are as idealized as Raphael's Madonnas. His Madonnas and the beautiful statue of St. Elizabeth in Nürnberg, all of which bear a strong family resemblance, are sweet-faced and pensive and have about them an air of gentle melancholy. The suave lines and smooth surfaces of his work are not characteristic of the wood-carver's technique and remind us that he also worked in stone and bronze. In North Germany almost all the sculpture of this period was in wood, and here the rugged realism that seems most suited to the medium reached its full development. One of the finest examples of this peculiarly German style is the magnificent oak altarpiece carved by Hans Brüggemann for the cathedral in Schleswig (1515–21), which contains scores of highly individualized figures, each a study in realistic characterization.

In architecture as in sculpture native traditions continued to develop as yet largely untouched by the Italian Renaissance. The great age of cathedral building in France and Germany was past, but in England the rising prosperity that followed the restoration of internal peace in the last decades of the fifteenth century brought renewed building activity marked by the full development of the Perpendicular style, the peculiarly English form of Late Gothic. Henry VII's Chapel in Westminster Abbey, St. George's Chapel, Windsor, and the Lady Chapel of Gloucester Cathedral, among others, are superb examples of Perpendicular Gothic with its intricately ribbed vaulting. It was in this period that the two great universities acquired many of their finest buildings, including King's College Chapel, Cambridge. It was in this period, too, that were built those vast cathedral-like churches which today tower above small moribund villages as mementos of both the piety and the prosperity of the men who made their fortunes from wool. With the coming of the Reformation there was a slump in church building, but also a notable development of domestic architecture, as Tudor manor houses began to replace the castles of a more turbulent age. In France, too, the growth of royal power, reinforced by cannon which made castle walls obsolete, led to the building of *châteaux* designed for pleasant living rather than defense, but this style of architecture was only beginning in the reign of Francis I.

C. Music

In the preface to his *Book of the Art of Counterpoint*, written in 1477, the Netherlandish musical theorist Johannes Tinctoris celebrated the great advances made in the composition of music during the middle half of the fifteenth century.

> Although it seems beyond belief [he wrote], there does not exist a single piece of music, not composed within the last forty years, that is regarded by the learned as worth hearing. Yet at this present time, not to mention

innumerable singers of the most beautiful diction, there flourish, whether by the effect of some celestial influence or by the force of assiduous practice, countless composers, among them Jean Ockeghem, Jean Regis, Antoine Busnoys, Firmin Caron and Guillaume Faugues, who glory in having studied this divine art under John Dunstable, Gilles Binchoys and Guillaume Dufay, recently deceased. Nearly all the works of these men exhale such sweetness that in my opinion they are to be considered suitable, not only for men and heroes, but even for the immortal gods.[2]

Had Tinctoris written forty years later he might have added the names of a still more brilliant galaxy of composers: Jacob Obrecht, Heinrich Isaak, Alexander Agricola, Loyset Compère, Pierre de la Rue, Antoine Brumel, Gaspar van Weerbecke and, greatest of them all, Josquin des Prez. He might also have noted with justifiable pride that all the composers on his list, with the exception of the English Dunstable, were like himself born in the Low Countries.

The domination of European music by Netherlandish composers for a hundred years (c. 1420–c. 1520) — years of crucial importance for the evolution of polyphony — is one of the most remarkable phenomena in musical history. The court of the dukes of Burgundy and the rich commercial and industrial cities provided liberal patronage for music as for art, but that alone would not account for the concentration of musical talent in the Netherlands and the adjacent portions of northern France. There was liberal patronage elsewhere, and, in fact, many of the Netherlanders spent a large part of their active career abroad, seeking employment in Florence, Ferrara, Milan or Rome, at the royal courts of France and Spain or the imperial court of the Hapsburgs. In the case of the greatest, one must take into consideration the unpredictable quality of personal genius, but that there were so many competent composers may be in part due to the personal influence of such recognized masters as Dufay, Ockeghem, Obrecht and Josquin, who established a distinct musical tradition, for, no matter how far they wandered, the Netherlanders clung to their native tradition and maintained a strong *esprit de corps*.

Much of the general competence of the Netherland musicians, both as singers and as composers, may also have been the result of the training they received in the cathedral choirs of Antwerp, Cambrai and other cities. The character of cathedral and church choirs in the Netherlands was changing radically during the fifteenth century. As early as 1410 the cathedral chapter in Antwerp secured the right to divert the income from a number of prebends to pay the salaries of professional singers who

[2] Quoted in O. Strunk, *Source Readings in Music History* (New York, 1950), p. 199.

were not necessarily clerics. By 1480 the number of salaried singers had risen to sixty-three, to whom must be added a professional organist. There was also an endowed choir school for the education and musical training of the boys who sang the soprano parts. The size of the Antwerp cathedral choir was unusual, as might be expected from the richest city in the Netherlands, but other cities had similar establishments on a smaller scale and each formed a practical training school for performers and composers. Biographical information about the early years of many of the Netherlandish composers is lacking, but we know that Dufay was trained as a choir boy at Cambrai and that later, after years abroad, he returned to Cambrai as a canon and as supervisor of the choir. Ockeghem as a young man was a chorister at Antwerp. Josquin des Prez received his early training as a choir boy at St. Quentin. Obrecht, too, was undoubtedly trained in church choirs, though we know of him only as choir master in various Netherland churches, including Utrecht, where Erasmus is said to have been one of the choir boys under his care. When professional choirs began to be established in Italy and in the royal courts of France and Spain the choristers trained in the Netherlands were in great demand. There were a number of them in the papal choir, which by 1483 had twenty-four paid singers.

The fact that so many of the leading Netherlandish composers were connected with church choirs at home or abroad was one reason, in addition to those noted in an earlier chapter,[3] for the increasing proportion of sacred music they produced during the fifteenth century and the early years of the sixteenth. The *cantus firmus* Mass, which had originated with Dunstable and his English contemporaries and had been introduced into the Netherlands by Dufay, continued to be a favorite musical form. As the century progressed, however, the treatment of the *cantus firmus* became freer, and eventually, though it was still frequently practised, it ceased to be regarded as an essential method of binding together the settings of the various parts of the Ordinary of the Mass. As composers began to free themselves from dependence on a borrowed *cantus firmus* in motets as well as Masses they employed the technique of imitation more consistently as a unifying device, the same musical theme being introduced in one voice after another, thus creating a complex yet unified contrapuntal structure. At the same time, there is evidence of a growing feeling for harmony, marked by the occasional use of a chordal construction vertically conceived.

The origins of harmonic composition may be traced back to the *fauxbourdon* of Dufay's generation; but it also owed something to the influence of Italian music with which the northern composers were

---

[3] See above, p. 400.

brought into contact during their lengthy sojourns in the south. The fifteenth century was on the whole a sterile period in Italian music. It produced not a single composer of the first rank. The native love of song, however, found expression in various popular or semi-popular forms: religious *laude*, secular carnival songs and half-popular, half-courtly *frottole*. The term *frottola* in the strict sense applies to a specific form of strophic poem set to music, but it was also used generically to denote a number of other poetic forms mostly designed to be sung to the accompaniment of the lute or other musical instruments. Neither the poetry nor the music of the majority of the *frottole* was distinguished, but they took on a courtly polish under the patronage of Isabella d'Este at Mantua and spread from there to the courts of Ferrara and Urbino. Unlike the polyphonic *chansons* of the north, their rhythms were simple and direct, with the melody in the upper voice, supported by block-chords in four-part harmony. Alien though the *frottole* were to the northern musical tradition they inevitably exerted some influence on the Netherlanders who brought home with them a stronger feeling for harmonic composition as a result of their contact with Italian song.

Both the systematic use of imitation in strict counterpoint which was the primary characteristic of Netherlandish music in the late fifteenth century, and the occasional introduction of chordal harmony, demanded a closer relation between the voices and led to a radical change in the method of composition. Hitherto the normal method had been to com-pose the voices one after another. Theorists had recommended writing the tenor first when composing a motet, and the upper voice which carried the melody when composing a *chanson*. By the end of the fif-teenth century, however, composers had begun to think of all parts simultaneously, not successively but in constant relation to one another, even though the character of contrapuntal polyphony remained essen-tially linear. The result was a much more closely integrated web of sound and a more even balance between the voices. There was at the same time a radical change in the method of performance. Whereas earlier poly-phonic vocal music had been performed by soloists, true choral poly-phony began to appear in the second quarter of the fifteenth century and gradually developed into the fully realized *a capella* style of the genera-tion of Josquin des Prez. Such choral singing of complex polyphonic compositions would, of course, have been impossible without highly trained choirs, and its development was at once cause and effect of the growth in quantity and quality of the professional singers employed in the cathedral choirs and in the chapels of kings and princes.

The relation between the rise of the professional choir and the growth of choral polyphony is further attested by the fact that the latter de-

577

veloped first in church music. Until the choral style was carried over into secular music toward the end of the fifteenth century, *chansons* continued to be composed for solo voice accompanied by instruments. They also continued to be bound by the fixed forms of *trouvère* song until Josquin introduced the through-composed polyphonic *chanson*. Together with the secular motets, *chansons* were court music or were designed for the delectation of a wealthy and cultured patrician class. While still performed by gifted amateurs, like Castiglione's perfect courtier, the growing complexity of polyphonic song increasingly called for highly trained and therefore professional performers, both vocal and instrumental. Thus, just as the cathedral choir raised the level of sacred music by the employment of professional choristers, so the princely courts raised the standard of secular music by fostering the virtuoso performer. Behind the *chansons* of this period lay a wealth of popular song on which composers drew freely for their themes, but in their hands the popular song was transformed into the art song, which demanded more of the performer than the natural untrained ear or voice.

The Netherlandish composers of the fifteenth century can be fairly clearly divided into three generations, each with one dominant figure among a number of gifted contemporaries. The first generation, that of Dufay, has been treated in an earlier chapter. Of the second generation, which came to maturity around the middle of the century, the leading figure was Johannes Ockeghem (c. 1420–c. 1495). Although only some twenty years younger than Dufay, on whose style his own was to a large extent founded, Ockeghem's music marked a step further away from such elements of the Gothic *ars nova* as still remained in the work of the older master. His contemporaries, at any rate, regarded him as the founder of a new style. His career took him away from his native Hainault for most of his mature life. From 1452 until his death he was employed in the service of three successive kings of France: Charles VII, Louis XI and Charles VIII. Nevertheless he continued to be revered as their leader by the rising group of Netherlandish composers, and on his death several of the younger generation wrote laments in his honor. The lamentation written by Guillaume Crétin calls the roll of more than a dozen composers recently deceased, beginning with Dufay, who are represented as welcoming Ockeghem to their company in the afterworld, while the magnificent *Déploration de Johannes Ockeghem* of Josquin des Prez calls on his surviving disciples, Josquin, Brumel, La Rue and Compère, to weep for the death of their good father.

Like Dufay, Ockeghem was primarily a composer of church music, and he was at his best in his numerous Masses, some with a borrowed *cantus firmus*, others freely composed. He also wrote a number of religious

HIERONYMUS BOSCH, THE GARDEN OF EARTHLY DELIGHT.

PRADO, MADRID

QUENTIN MASSYS, THE BANKER AND HIS WIFE.

LOUVRE, PARIS

34

ALBRECHT DÜRER, SELF-PORTRAIT.

LOUVRE, PARIS

35

MATTHIAS GRÜNEWALD, THE CRUCIFIXION,
FROM THE ISENHEIM ALTARPIECE.

MUSÉE D'UNTERLINDEN, COLMAR

MATTHIAS GRÜNEWALD, VIRGIN ADORED BY ANGELS,
FROM THE ISENHEIM ALTARPIECE.

MUSÉE D'UNTERLINDEN, COLMAR

HANS HOLBEIN THE YOUNGER, CECILY HERON.

ROYAL COLLECTION, WINDSOR CASTLE, COPYRIGHT RESERVED

ST. GEORGE'S CHAPEL, WINDSOR.

ALBRECHT DÜRER, ADORATION OF THE MAGI.

UFFIZI, FLORENCE

motets. In all of them, despite the variety of form which reflects Ockeghem's experimental spirit and technical virtuosity, the predominant quality is melodic. Sustained melody characterizes all the voices, but, although he evidently followed the traditional practice of linear composition, the closely interwoven texture is proof that he was also thinking of all parts as elements of an integrated whole. While more sparing than some of his contemporaries in the use of imitation, he maintained a continuous polyphonic flow by frequently overlapping the beginning of a phrase in one voice with the conclusion of the preceding phrase in another. His effort to maintain the melodic quality of all voices led him to keep them apart with few crossings, and this, in turn, forced him to extend the tonal range even further than had been done by Dufay, especially toward the bass, and to fill in the sonority by using four rather than three voices, a practice which thereafter became normal procedure.

Secular music was never a major preoccupation with Ockeghem, but he nevertheless left some twenty *chansons*. Fine as these are, especially the lovely *Petite camusette* and *L'autre d'antan*, they are more traditional than his Masses and motets, although in them, too, the voices cross less frequently than in the *chansons* of the preceding century. As a writer of secular court music he was surpassed by Antoine Busnois (d. 1492), who stood in much the same relation to him as had Binchois to Dufay. Although he held several church posts, including that of choir master of St. Sauveur at Bruges, Busnois was primarily a court poet and musician, having been for some years in the service of Charles the Bold. In his graceful and elegant *chansons*, of which between sixty and seventy that are certainly his survive, he extended the tonal range downward, as did Ockeghem, but his use of imitation was much more consistent and so helped to prepare for the pervading imitation of the following generation.

The third generation of Netherlandish composers, most of whom were born around the year 1450, marked the full flowering of the Netherlandish polyphonic tradition. With their passing, in the years between 1505 and 1521, passed also the domination of European music by the masters from the Low Countries. Of that brilliant group, of which we can here consider only the most outstanding members, by far the greatest was Josquin des Prez (c. 1450–1521). Born in Hainault and trained in cathedral choirs, Josquin, like many of his countrymen, spent a large part of his mature life abroad. For about twenty-five years, from 1474, he was in Italy, employed as singer and composer by Cardinal Sforza in Milan, then in the choir of the Papal Chapel at Rome and in the service of Ercole d'Este, Duke of Ferrara. A memento of his employment at the court of Ferrara survives in the form of a letter addressed to the duke by his secretary advising him to engage Isaak instead of Josquin because Isaak "is able to get on with his colleagues better and composes new pieces more quickly," and adding: "It is true that Josquin composes better, but he does it when it suits him and not when one wishes him to."[4] The duke evidently ignored the advice. Later Josquin was for some years director of the royal chapel of Louis XII. After the king's death he returned to the Netherlands and spent his last years in Brussels and Condé. Numerous encomiums by contemporaries, including Luther and Castiglione, attest the superlative reputation he enjoyed in his own day, and time has not dimmed its radiance. More than one recent historian of music has declared Josquin to be one of the greatest composers of all time.[5]

The diversity of Josquin's style makes it difficult to characterize. He utilized almost all the forms currently in vogue, but he also adapted and enriched musical forms that were already becoming archaic. At times his style seems consciously conservative; at other times he is radically progressive, a harbinger of things to come. One striking characteristic of his work — and one which marks him as a forerunner of much sixteenth century music — is its expressive quality. The close adaptation of the music to the mood of the text is especially evident in the motets, which some critics regard as his finest compositions. While still at times employing a borrowed *cantus firmus* in his Masses and motets, Josquin frequently broke free from dependence on that traditional device — just as in his *chansons* he broke free from the fixed forms of *rondeau, virelai* and the like — and relied upon pervading imitation to bind together the polyphonic structure. At the same time, he was capable of breaking the flow of contrapuntal polyphony to write phrases of purely chordal harmony which demonstrate a quite modern feeling for tonality. He was above all a singers' composer, at his best when writing for choral performance. He may, indeed, be regarded as the principal founder of the *a capella* style of the sixteenth century.

Only one of Josquin's contemporaries could rival his versatility. Heinrich Isaak (c. 1450–1517) was a truly international figure, a prolific and tuneful composer who wrote Italian, French and German songs, as well as motets and Masses, including an unprecedented polyphonic setting of the Propers for the entire Church year. He seemed equally at home in Florence, where he taught the sons of Lorenzo de' Medici and was organist of Santa Maria del Fiore, and in Innsbruck and Vienna in the service of Maximilian I. The fact that he wrote music to French, Italian

---

[4] Quoted in G. Reese, *Music in the Renaissance* (New York, 1954), p. 229.
[5] See *New Oxford History of Music*, III (London, 1960), 262; A. Harman, *Medieval and Early Renaissance Music* (London, 1958), p. 201.

and German texts is in itself not remarkable. What is unusual is the degree to which he could adopt the various national styles and enter into the spirit of the national idioms. As the Duke of Ferrara's secretary suggested, he was an adaptable person and wrote what his patrons wanted. His settings of poems by Lorenzo and Poliziano are in the tradition of the Italian *frottole*, while his German songs seem completely German. The haunting melody of his *Innsbruck ich muss dich lassen* has won for itself an almost unique place in the history of German music. Before the end of the sixteenth century it had been transformed, with some necessary textual changes, into a Lutheran hymn. Later the tune was used by Bach twice in the St. Matthew Passion and once in the St. John Passion. It was also set twice as a choral prelude by Brahms, and it still survives as a favorite hymn tune.

Among the wandering Netherlandish composers, Jacob Obrecht (c. 1450–1505) was unusual in that he spent most of his life at home as choir master in various churches in the Low Countries. He did, it is true, visit Italy at least twice and, in fact, died in Ferrara, but more than any of the others he remained a true Netherlander. He was also the only one who came from the Dutch-speaking Netherlands and who used Dutch texts for some of his secular works. As might be expected from his career as a choir master, however, most of his compositions were sacred rather than secular. In certain respects his Masses and motets are conservative. He revived the almost extinct practice of giving different texts to each voice of motets, and he frequently employed a *cantus firmus* in the almost obsolete form of long note values. On the other hand, his feeling for tonality and clear harmony mark him as progressive, while the flexible grace of his melodies assures him a place of honor among the composers of that brilliant generation.

The prevailing style of the Netherlandish composers around the turn of the century seems designed primarily for vocal production, and from this time on *a capella* performance of church music became increasingly common. With this development came a clearer distinction between vocal and instrumental music, as composers began to write specifically for choir or for such keyboard instruments as the organ, clavichord and virginals, or for the solo lute. The whole question of what parts of medieval and early Renaissance music were intended for vocal or instrumental performance is an extremely complex one and its solution is in many cases still uncertain. It seems fairly clear, however, that polyphonic music until the second half of the fifteenth century, if not later, was performed by voices or instruments more or less indiscriminately, depending on the taste of the performers and the means available. That a great variety of instruments was in common use from the Early Middle

Ages is amply attested by their appearance in illuminations and paintings as well as by contemporary accounts; but there is little evidence of composers writing for specific instruments. It seems to have been taken for granted that any wind or string instrument could follow any voice line in a polyphonic composition, and that instruments might be used either independently or in conjunction with voices in performing almost any piece of music. Even in the sixteenth century, when the development of *a capella* performance on the one hand and on the other the increasing virtuosity of instrumentalists had bred a greater awareness of the differences in style appropriate to either voices or specific instruments, there was still a great deal of music which was labelled by publishers as suitable either for singing or for playing.

Keyboard music furnishes the earliest examples of compositions written especially for instrumental performance. That the organ was apparently the first instrument to attract special attention from composers may be in part due to its prominent place in church music, but also because it was capable of performing several voices of a polyphonic composition simultaneously. By an odd chance nearly all the organ music of the fifteenth century that has survived — the earliest dating from about 1425 — is of German origin, manuscripts of the keyboard music known to have existed in other countries having been lost. One of the largest collections, the *Buxheimer Orgelbuch*, compiled between 1460 and 1470, contains more than 250 examples of organ music, mostly in three parts. Among them are a number of pieces by Conrad Paumann (d. 1473) who, like Landini in the previous century, was born blind but acquired a great reputation as organist and teacher. After the turn of the century collections of keyboard music and also of pieces written specifically for the lute began to be published in Italy and elsewhere. Although the lute was most commonly used to accompany song, composers were beginning to appreciate its independent potentialities. Its strings being plucked rather than bowed, it lent itself, like the keyboard instruments, to the performance of chordal music or polyphonic counterpoint. The first of a series of collections for solo lute was published by the Venetian printer Petrucci in 1507.

Before the turn of the century, indeed, printing was beginning to give wide circulation to music of all kinds and to furnish composers with a public far more extensive than could have been possible otherwise. Despite the difficulties inherent in printing notes on a staff, printers began publishing music less than thirty years after the first appearance of books printed with moveable type. Various experiments, such as engraving the whole page on wooden or metal blocks, proved too expensive for long works. Toward the end of the century the best printers adopted a method calling for a double impression, first of the lines of the staff, then of the notes. This was a difficult enough technique, but when skillfully executed could be very effective. The music printed by Ottaviano de Petrucci (1466–1539) in Venice is exceptionally beautiful. Petrucci's collections — fifty-two issued between 1501 and 1520 — are also our most valuable surviving sources for the music of the period, a very large part consisting of compositions by Netherlandish masters from Ockeghem to Josquin.

The publication of music greatly accelerated the dissemination of musical styles from country to country and thereby helped to end the Netherlandish domination of European music. The polyphonic tradition founded by the great Netherlanders from Dufay to Josquin continued throughout the sixteenth century and, indeed, reached its fullest development only after mid-century with Orlando de Lassus, Victoria and Palestrina. To this development some masters from the Low Countries, like Gombert, Clemens non Papa and Lassus himself contributed, but the polyphonic style had become internationalized and, at the same time, it acquired a distinctively national flavor in the hands of Italian, French, English and German composers. In the two generations after Josquin, music drew increasingly closer to modern tonality, so that until fairly recent times intelligible music was regarded as having begun with Palestrina or perhaps a century later with Bach, and it was not realized that these giants stood at the end of a long tradition stretching back unbroken through the centuries to the distant age when medieval composers first began to add voice to voice, to set note against note and to measure time.

Bibliography

An exhaustive bibliography of all the subjects dealt with in this volume is clearly out of the question. Even the kind of bibliographical essay that now seems fashionable would take an excessive amount of space. The following is intended simply to be a working bibliography, arranged as nearly as possible in accordance with the organization of the book, and including a representative sample of the most important works on each subject. Preference has been given to fairly general works, which in turn will lead the student to the sources and to the more detailed monographs, articles and biographical studies. Only such articles have been included as present new or controversial material not easily available elsewhere. Preference has also been given to works of relatively recent scholarship. Of the older works only those have been included which have established themselves as classics or which for some reason have not been superseded.

GENERAL HISTORY

Barbagallo, C., *Storia universale*, Vol. IV, 1, *L'età della Rinascenza e della Riforma, 1454–1556* (Turin, 1936).

Calmette, J., *Le monde féodal* (Paris, 1934).

Cambridge Medieval History, Vol. VII, *Decline of Empire and Papacy*, ed. J. R. Tanner, C. W. Previté-Orton and Z. N. Brooke; Vol. VIII, *The Close of the Middle Ages*, ed. C. W. Previté-Orton and Z. N. Brooke (Cambridge, 1932–36).

Cheyney, E. P., *The Dawn of a New Era, 1250–1453* (New York, 1936).

Gilmore, M., *The World of Humanism, 1453–1517* (New York, 1952).

Hauser, H., and Renaudet, A., *Les débuts de l'âge moderne* (Paris, 1929) (*Peuples et civilisations*, ed., L. Halphen and P. Sagnac, Vol. VIII).

New Cambridge Modern History, Vol. I, *The Renaissance, 1493–1520*, ed. G. R. Potter (Cambridge, 1957).

Pirenne, H., Renaudet, A., Perroy, É., Handelsman, M. and Halphen, L., *La fin du moyen âge* (Paris, 1931) (*Peuples et civilisations*, ed. L. Halphen and P. Sagnac, Vol. VII).

Bibliography

Propyläen Weltgeschichte, ed. W. Goetz, Vol. IV, *Das Zeitalter der Gotik und Renaissance* (Berlin, 1932).

ECONOMIC HISTORY

General

Boissonade, P., *Life and Work in Medieval Europe (Fifth to Fifteenth Centuries)* (New York, 1927).

Cambridge Economic History, Vol. I, *The Agrarian Life of the Middle Ages*, ed., J. H. Clapham and E. Power; Vol. II, *Trade and Industry in the Middle Ages*, ed., M. Postan and E. E. Rich (Cambridge, 1942–52).

Ferguson, W. K., "Recent Trends in the Economic Historiography of the Renaissance," *Studies in the Renaissance*, VII (1960), 7–26.

Grand, R. and Delatouche, R., *L'agriculture au moyen âge de la fin de l'empire romain au XVIe siècle* (Paris, 1950).

Gras, N. S. B., *Business and Capitalism* (New York, 1939).

Heaton, H., *Economic History of Europe* (New York, 1936).

Koetzschke, R., *Allgemeine Wirtschaftsgeschichte des Mittelalters* (Jena, 1924).

Kulischer, J., *Allgemeine Wirtschaftsgeschichte des Mittelalters und der Neuzeit*, Vol. I, *Das Mittelalter* (Munich and Berlin, 1928).

Lewis, A. R., "The Closing of the Medieval Frontier, 1250–1350," *Speculum*, XXXIII (1958), 475–483.

Lopez, R., "Hard Times and Investment in Culture," *The Renaissance: a Symposium* (New York, Metropolitan Museum of Art, 1953), pp. 19–34.

Lopez, R. and Miskimin, H. A., "The Economic Depression of the Renaissance," *The Economic History Review*, XIV (1962), 408–426.

Mollat, M., Johansen, P., Postan, M., Sapori, A., and Verlinden, C., L'économie européenne aux deux derniers siècles du moyen âge," *Relazioni del X Congresso Internazionale di Scienze Storiche*, III (Florence, 1957), 655–811.

Nef, J. U., "Industrial Europe on the Eve of the Reformation," *Journal of Political Economy*, XLIX (1941), 1–40, 183–224.

Nelson, B. N., *The Idea of Usury* (Princeton, 1949).

Pernoud, R., *Les villes marchandes aux XIVe et XVe siècles. Impérialisme et capitalisme au moyen âge* (Paris, 1948).

Pirenne, H., *Economic and Social History of Medieval Europe* (New York, 1937).

Pirenne, H., *Medieval Cities, their Origins and the Revival of Trade* (Princeton, 1925).

Postan, M., "Some Economic Evidence of Declining Population in the Later Middle Ages," *Economic History Review*, 2nd Series, II (1950), 221–246.

Rörig, F., *Mittelalterliche Weltwirtschaft: Blüte und Ende einer Wirtschaftsperiode* (Jena, 1933).

Sapori, A., "I beni del commercio internazionale nel medioevo," *Archivio storico italiano*, CXIII (1955), 3–44.

Bibliography

Italy

Barbagallo, C., "La crisi economico-sociale dell'Italia della Rinascenza," *Nuovo rivista storica,* XXV (1950), 1–38; 389–411.

Doren, A., *Italienische Wirtschaftsgeschichte* (Jena, 1934).

Fanfani, A., *Le origini dello spirito capitalistico in Italia* (Milan, 1933).

Fiumi, E., "La demografia fiorentina nelle pagine di Giovanni Villani," *Archivio storico italiano,* CVIII (1950), 78–158.

Lane, F. C., *Andrea Barbarigo, Merchant of Venice, 1418–1449* (Baltimore, 1944).

Lane, F. C., *Venetian Ships and Shipbuilding of the Renaissance* (Baltimore, 1934).

Luzzatto, G., *Storia economica d'Italia,* Vol. I, *L'antichità e il medioevo* (Rome, 1949).

Origo, I., *The Merchant of Prato: the Life and Papers of Francesco di Marco Datini* (London, 1957).

Renouard, Y., *Les hommes d'affaires italiens du moyen âge* (Paris, 1949).

Roover, R. de, *The Medici Bank* (New York, 1948).

Sapori, A., *Studi di storia economica medievale* (2nd ed. Florence, 1946). Bibliography, pp. 769–804.

Sapori, A., *La crisi delle compagnie mercantili dei Bardi e dei Peruzzi* (Florence, 1926).

Sapori, A., *Le marchand italien au moyen âge* (Paris, 1952).

Sayous, A.-É., "Les transformations des méthodes commerciales dans l'Italie médiévale," *Annales d'histoire économique et sociale,* I (1929), 161–176.

Netherlands

Dechesne, L., *Histoire économique et sociale de la Belgique* (Paris, 1932).

Doehaerd, L., *L'expansion économique belge au moyen âge* (Brussels, 1946).

Espinas, G., *La draperie dans la Flandre française au moyen âge,* 2 vols. (Paris, 1923).

Houtte, J. A. van, "La genèse du grand marché international d'Anvers vers la fin du moyen âge," *Revue belge de philosophie et d'histoire,* XIX (1940), 87–126.

Laurent, H., *La draperie des Pays-Bas en France et dans les pays méditerranéens, XIIe au XVe siècle* (Paris, 1935).

Lemoine, R. J., *Les étrangers et la formation du capitalisme en Belgique* (Paris, 1933).

Poerek, G. de, *La draperie médiévale en Flandre et en Artois,* 3 vols. (Bruges, 1951).

Roover, R. de, *Money, Banking and Credit in Medieval Bruges* (Cambridge, Mass., 1948).

Sabbe, É., *Histoire de l'industrie linière en Belgique* (Brussels, 1945).

Werveke, H. van, "Industrial Growth in the Middle Ages: the Cloth Industry in Flanders," *The Economic History Review,* 2nd S., VI (1954), 237–245.

Bibliography

England

Carus-Wilson, E. M., *Medieval Merchant Venturers* (London, 1954).

Lipson, E., *The Economic History of England*, I, *The Middle Ages* (London, 1915).

Orwin, C. S., *The Open Fields* (Oxford, 1938).

Power, E., *The Wool Trade in English Medieval History* (London, 1941).

Power, E. and Postan, M. M., eds., *Studies in English Trade in the Fifteenth Century* (London, 1933).

France

Baratier, É., and Reynaud, F., *Histoire du commerce de Marseille*, II (Paris, 1951).

Bloch, M., *Les caractères originaux de l'histoire rurale française* (Paris, 1931).

Boutruche, R., *La crise d'une société. Seigneurs et paysans du Bordelais pendant la Guerre de Cent Ans* (Paris, 1947).

Mollat, M., *Le commerce maritime normand à la fin du moyen âge* (Paris, 1952).

Perroy, É., "Les crises du XIVᵉ siècle," *Annales*, IV (1949), 167–182.

Sée, H., *Histoire économique de la France* (Paris, 1939).

Wolff, P., *Commerce et marchands de Toulouse vers 1350-vers 1450* (Paris, 1954).

Germany

Abel, W., *Die Wüstungen des ausgehenden Mittelalters* (Jena, 1943).

Lütge, F., *Deutsche Sozial-und Wirtschaftsgeschichte* (Jena, 1952).

Pagel, K., *Die Hanse* (Brunswick, 1952).

Planitz, H., *Die deutsche Stadt im Mittelalter* (Graz, 1954).

Rörig, F., *Hansische Beiträge zur deutschen Wirtschaftsgeschichte* (Breslau, 1928).

Strieder, J., *Jacob Fugger the Rich* (New York, 1932).

POLITICAL AND CONSTITUTIONAL HISTORY

Italy

Ady, C. M., *Lorenzo de' Medici and Renaissance Italy* (London, 1955).

Ady, C. M., *The Bentivoglio of Bologna, a Study in Despotism* (Oxford, 1937).

Albertini, R. von, *Das florentinische Staatsbewusstsein im Übergang von der Republik zum Prinzipat* (Bern, 1955).

Brucker, G. A., *Florentine Politics and Society* (Princeton, 1962).

Bueno de Mesquita, D. M., *Giangaleazzo Visconti* (Cambridge, 1941).

Cessi, R., *Storia della Repubblica di Venezia*, 2 vols. (Milan, 1944–46).

Léonard, É., *Les Angevins de Naples* (Paris, 1954).

Muir, D., *A History of Milan under the Visconti* (London, 1924).

Pieri, P., *Il Rinascimento e la crisi militare italiana* (Turin, 1952).

Pieri, P., *I Visconti e l'Italia del secolo XIV* (Turin, 1952).

Pontieri, E., *L'equilibrio e la crisi politica italiana nella seconda metà del secolo XV* (Naples, 1946).

Schevill, F., *History of Florence* (New York, 1936).

Simeoni, L., *Le signorie, 1313–1559* (Milan, 1950).

Valeri, N., *L'Italia nell'età dei principati dal 1343 al 1516* (Verona, 1950).

France and the Burgundian Netherlands

Bridge, J. S. C., *A History of France from the Death of Louis XI*, 5 vols. (Oxford, 1921–23).

Burne, A. H., *The Crécy War* (London, 1955).

Calmette, J., *Les grands ducs de Bourgogne* (Paris, 1949).

Dupont-Ferrier, G., *La formation de l'état français* (Paris, 1929).

Dupont-Ferrier, G., *Les officiers royaux des bailliages et sénéchaussées et les institutions monarchiques locales en France à la fin du moyen âge* (Paris, 1902).

Grosjean, G., *Le sentiment national dans la Guerre des Cent Ans* (Paris, 1927).

Lavisse, E., *Histoire de France, depuis les origines jusqu'à la révolution*, 9 vols. (Paris, 1900–1911). Vols. III to V deal with this period.

Lucas, H. S., *The Low Countries and the Hundred Years' War* (Ann Arbor, 1929).

Perroy, É., *The Hundred Years' War* (New York, 1951).

Pirenne, H., *Les anciennes démocraties des Pays-Bas* (Paris, 1910).

Pirenne, H., *Histoire de Belgique*, Vol. II (4th ed., Brussels, 1947); Vol. III (3rd ed., Brussels, 1923).

Strayer, J. R., "Philip the Fair — a 'constitutional king,'" *American Historical Review*, LXII (1956), 18–32.

England

Chrimes, S. B., *English Constitutional Ideas in the Fifteenth Century* (Cambridge, 1936).

Chrimes, S. B., *Introduction to the Administrative History of Medieval England* (New York, 1952).

Jacob, E. F., *The Fifteenth Century, 1399–1485* (Oxford, 1961). (*Oxford History of England*, Vol. VI).

Lapsley, G. T., *Crown, Community and Parliament in the Later Middle Ages* (New York, 1951).

Mackie, J. D., *The Early Tudors, 1485–1558* (Oxford, 1952). (*Oxford History of England*, Vol. VII).

Bibliography

McKisack, M., *The Fourteenth Century, 1307–99* (Oxford, 1959). (*Oxford History of England*, Vol. V).

Maitland, F. W., *The Constitutional History of England* (Cambridge, 1908).

Myers, A. R., *England in the Later Middle Ages* (Pelican, 1952).

Stubbs, W., *Constitutional History of England*, 3 vols. (Oxford, 1874–78).

Terry, S. B., *The Financing of the Hundred Years' War, 1337–60* (London, 1914).

Wilkinson, B., *Constitutional History of Medieval England*, 3 vols. (London, 1948–58).

Germany

Barraclough, G., *The Origins of Modern Germany* (Oxford, 1949).

Below, G. von, *Der deutsche Staat des Mittelalters* (2nd ed., Leipzig, 1925).

Henderson, E. F., *A Short History of Germany*, Vol. I (New York, 1927).

Hofmann, A. von, *Politische Geschichte der Deutschen*, Vol. III (Stuttgart, 1923).

Kraus, V. von, and Kaser, K., *Deutsche Geschichte am Ausgang des Mittelalters*, 2 vols. (Stuttgart, 1905–12).

Spain

Calmette, J., *La formation de l'unité espagnole* (Paris, 1946).

Merriman, R. B., *The Rise of the Spanish Empire*, Vol. I, *The Middle Ages* (New York, 1918).

The Church and the Papacy

Aubenas, R. and Ricard, R., *L'Église et la Renaissance, 1449–1517* (Paris, 1951). (*Histoire de l'Église*, ed. A. Fliche and V. Martin, Vol. 15).

Boase, T., *Boniface the Eighth, 1294–1503* (London, 1933).

Creighton, M., *A History of the Papacy during the Period of the Reformation*, 5 vols. (London, 1887–94). A classic, the first four volumes of which deal with the two centuries before 1517.

Ferguson, W. K., "The Church in a Changing World," *American Historical Review*, LIX (1953), 1–18.

Flick, A. C., *The Decline of the Medieval Church*, 2 vols. (London, 1930).

Hughes, P., *A History of the Church*, Vol. III (London, 1947).

Lunt, W. E., *Papal Revenues in the Middle Ages*, 2 vols. (New York, 1934).

Mollat, G., *La collation des bénéfices ecclésiastiques sous les papes d'Avignon* (Paris, 1921).

Mollat, G., *Les papes d'Avignon, 1305–1378* (Paris, 1949).

Monticelli, G., *Chiesa e Italia durante il pontificato avignonese* (Milan, 1937).

Partner, P., *The Papal State under Martin V* (London, 1958).

Pastor, L. von, *History of the Popes*, 40 vols. (3rd ed. London, 1905–53). Vols. I to VII of this great work treat the pre-Reformation period.

Bibliography

Renouard, Y., *Les relations des papes d'Avignon et des compagnies commerciales et bancaires de 1316 à 1378* (Paris, 1941).

Seppelt, F., *Das Papsttum im Spätmittelalter und in der Zeit der Renaissance* (Leipzig, 1941).

Ullmann, W., *The Origins of the Great Schism* (London, 1948).

Exploration and European Expansion

Abbott, W. C., *The Expansion of Europe*, 2 vols. (New York, 1918).

Beazley, C. R., *The Dawn of Modern Geography*, 3 vols. (London, 1897–1906).

Hart, H. H., *Sea Road to the Indies* (London, 1952).

Julien, C-A., *Les voyages et découverts et les premiers établissements* (Paris, 1947).

Morison, S. E., *Admiral of the Ocean Sea, a Life of Christopher Columbus* (Boston, 1942).

Sanceau, E., *Henry the Navigator* (New York, 1947).

Sanceau, E., *Indies Adventure* (London, 1936).

SOCIAL HISTORY

Italy

Ady, C. M., "Morals and Manners of the Quattrocento," *Proceedings of the British Academy* (1942).

Boulting, W., *Woman in Italy* (New York, 1910).

Broglio d'Aiano, R., *Lotti sociali in Italia nel secolo XIV* (Rome, 1911).

Cartwright, J., *The Perfect Courtier, Baldassare Castiglione*, 2 vols. (New York, 1927).

Frati, L., *La vita privata in Bologna dal secolo XIII al XVII* (Bologna, 1928).

Herlihy, D., *Pisa and the Early Renaissance* (New Haven, 1958).

Labande, E-R., *L'Italie de la Renaissance: évolution d'un société* (Paris, 1954).

Martin, A. von, *Sociology of the Renaissance* (Oxford, 1944).

Origo, I., "The Domestic Enemy: the Eastern Slaves in the Fourteenth and Fifteenth Centuries," *Speculum*, XXX (1955), 321–366.

Rodolico, N., *I Ciompi* (Florence, 1945).

Salvemini, G., *Magnati e popolani in Firenze dal 1280 al 1295* (Florence, 1899).

France and the Burgundian Netherlands

Bloch, J-R., *L' annoblissement en France au temps de François Ier* (Paris, 1934).

Cartellieri, O., *The Court of Burgundy* (London, 1929).

Defourneaux, M., *La vie quotidienne au temps de Jeanne d'Arc* (Paris, 1952).

Hauser, H., *Travailleurs et marchands dans l'ancienne France* (Paris, 1920).

Kilgour, R. L., *The Decline of Chivalry* (Cambridge, Mass., 1937).

Bibliography

Lefranc, A., *La vie quotidienne au temps de la Renaissance* (Paris, 1938).

Lestocquoy, J., *Patriciens du moyen âge: les dynasties bourgeoises d'Arras du XIe au XVe siècle* (Arras, 1945).

Painter, S., *French Chivalry* (Baltimore, 1940).

Pirenne, H., *La soulèvement de la Flandre maritime de 1323–1328* (Brussels, 1900).

England

Abram, A., *Social England in the Fifteenth Century* (London, 1909).

Abram, A., *English Life and Manners in the Later Middle Ages* (London, 1913).

Bennett, H. S., *Life on the English Manor* (Cambridge, 1937).

Bennett, H. S., *The Pastons and their England* (Cambridge, 1922).

Chadwick, D., *Social Life in the Days of Piers Plowman* (Cambridge, 1922).

Page, T. W., *The End of Villeinage in England* (New York, 1900).

Salzman, L. F., *English Life in the Middle Ages* (London, 1926).

Thrupp, S., *The Merchant Class in Medieval London (1300–1500)* (Chicago, 1948).

Trevelyan, G. M., *English Social History*, Vol. I (London, 1949).

Germany

Borkenau, F., *Der Übergang vom feudalen zum bürgerlichen Weltbild* (Paris, 1934).

Fellner, R., *Die fränkische Ritterschaft von 1495–1524* (Berlin, 1905).

Franz, G., *Die agrarischen Unruhen des ausgehenden Mittelalters* (Marburg, 1930).

Franz, G., *Der deutsche Bauernkrieg*, 2 vols. (Munich and Berlin, 1933–35).

The Clergy

Bennett, R. F., *The Early Dominicans* (Cambridge, 1937).

Capes, W., *The English Church in the Fourteenth and Fifteenth Centuries* (London, 1920).

Coulton, G. G., *Five Centuries of Religion*, Vol. III, *Getting and Spending* (Cambridge, 1936); Vol. IV, *The Last Days of Medieval Monachism* (Cambridge, 1950).

Imbart de la Tour, P., *Les origines de la Réforme*, Vol. II (2nd ed. Melun, 1946).

Knowles, D., *The Religious Orders in England*, Vol. II, *The End of the Middle Ages* (London, 1955).

Moorman, J. R. H., *Church Life in England in the Thirteenth Century* (Cambridge, 1945).

Pantin, W. A., *The English Church in the Fourteenth Century* (Cambridge, 1955).

Power, E., *Medieval English Nunneries, c.1275–1535* (Cambridge, 1922).

Sessevalle, F. de, *Histoire générale de l'ordre de Saint François*, 2 vols. (Paris and Le Puy, 1935–37).

Thompson, A. H., *The English Clergy and their Organization in the Later Middle Ages* (Oxford, 1947).

CULTURAL HISTORY: WORKS OF SYNTHESIS

Andreas, W., *Deutschland vor der Reformation* (Stuttgart, 1932).

Artz, F. B., *The Mind of the Middle Ages* (New York, 1953).

Burckhardt, J., *The Civilization of the Renaissance in Italy* (London, 1878).

Dilthey, W., *Auffassung und Analyse des Menschen im 15. und 16. Jahrhundert. Gesammelte Schriften*, Vol. II (Leipzig and Berlin, 1921).

Haskins, C. H., *The Renaissance of the Twelfth Century* (Cambridge, Mass., 1927).

Huizinga, J., *The Waning of the Middle Ages* (London, 1924).

Olschki, L., *The Genius of Italy* (New York, 1949).

Stadelmann, R., *Vom Geist des ausgehenden Mittelalters* (Halle, 1929).

Symonds, J. A., *Renaissance in Italy*, 7 vols. (London, 1875–86).

Taylor, H. O., *The Medieval Mind*, 2 vols. (New York, 1911).

Taylor, H. O., *Thought and Expression in the Sixteenth Century*, 2 vols. (New York, 1920). Begins with the early fourteenth century.

POPULAR PIETY, MYSTICISM AND HERESY

Angeleri, C., *Il problema religioso del Rinascimento* (Florence, 1952).

Clark, J. M., *The Great German Mystics: Eckhart, Tauler and Suso* (Oxford, 1949).

Denis, É., *Huss et les guerres hussites* (Paris, 1930).

Douie, D., *The Nature and Effect of the Heresy of the Fraticelli* (Manchester, 1932).

Hyma, A., *The Christian Renaissance, a History of the Devotio Moderna* (New York, 1924).

Kelley, C. F., ed., *The Book of the Poor in Spirit by a Friend of God*, with Introduction (New York, 1954).

Lücker, M. A., *Meister Eckhart und die Devotio Moderna* (Leiden, 1950).

Manning, B. L., *The People's Faith in the Time of Wyclif* (Cambridge, 1919).

McDonald, E. W., *The Beguines and Beghards in Medieval Culture* (New Brunswick, 1954).

McFarlane, K. B., *John Wycliffe and the Beginning of English Nonconformity* (London, 1952).

Muzzy, D. L., *The Spiritual Franciscans* (New York, 1907).

Seeholtz, A. G., *The Friends of God, Practical Mystics of the Fourteenth Century* (New York, 1934).

Smith, H. M., *Pre-Reformation England* (London, 1938).

Bibliography

Spinka, M., ed., *Advocates of Reform from Wyclif to Erasmus* (London, 1953).

Steiner, R., *Mystics of the Renaissance* (New York, 1911).

Tenenti, A., *Il senso della morte e l'amore della vita nel Rinascimento* (Turin, 1957).

Troeltsch, E., *The Social Teaching of the Christian Churches*, 2 vols. (London, 1949).

Volpe, G., *Movimenti religiosi e setti ereticali nella società medievale italiana* (Florence, 1926).

VERNACULAR LITERATURE: GENERAL WORKS

Italy

Bargellino, P., *Pian dei giullari. Panoramo storico della letteratura italiana*, Vol. I, *Dalle origini alla fine del Quattrocento* (Florence, 1956).

Flora, F., *Storia della letteratura italiana*, Vol. I, *Dal medio evo alla fine del Quattrocento* (Milan, 1955).

Hall, R. A., *Short History of Italian Literature* (Ithaca, 1951).

Rossi, V., *Storia letteraria d'Italia: il Quattrocento* (Milan, 3rd ed., 1933).

Sanctis, F. de, *History of Italian Literature*, 2 vols. (New York, 1931).

Sapegno, N., *Storia letteraria d'Italia: il Trecento* (3rd ed., Milan, 1938).

Whitfield, J. H., *A Short History of Italian Literature* (Penguin, 1960).

Wilkins, E. H., *A History of Italian Literature* (Cambridge, Mass., 1954).

France

Bossuat, R., *Le moyen âge* (Paris, 1931). (*Histoire de la littérature française*, ed. J. Calvet, Vol. I).

Champion, P., *Histoire poétique du 15e siècle*, 2 vols. (Paris, 1923).

Cohen, G., *La vie littéraire en France au moyen âge* (Paris, 1949).

Doutrepont, G., *La littérature française à la cour des ducs de Bourgogne* (Paris, 1909).

Jeanroy, A., *Les origines de la poésie lyrique en France* (3rd ed., Paris, 1925).

Paris, G., *La littérature française au moyen âge, XIe–XIVe siècle* (Paris, 1913).

Saulnier, V-L., *La littérature du moyen âge* (Paris, 1943).

England

Bennett, H. S., *Chaucer and the Fifteenth Century* (Oxford, 1947).

Cambridge History of English Literature, ed. A. W. Ward and A. R. Waller, Vols. I and II (Cambridge, 1908).

Chambers, E. K., *English Literature at the Close of the Middle Ages* (Oxford, 1945).

Craig, H., *English Religious Drama of the Middle Ages* (Oxford, 1955).

Bibliography

Ker, W. P., *English Literature, Medieval* (Home University Library, 1912).

Ward, A. C., *Illustrated History of English Literature*, Vol. I (London, 1953).

Germany

Petry, K., *Handbuch zur deutschen Literaturgeschichte*, 2 vols. (Cologne, 1949).

Stammler, W., *Epochen der deutschen Literatur*, Vol. II, *Von der Mystik zum Barock* (2nd ed., Stuttgart, 1950).

Stockum, T. C. van and Dam, J. van, *Geschichte der deutschen Literatur*, Vol. I (The Hague, 1934).

HUMANISM

Italian

Baron, H., "Franciscan Poverty and Civic Wealth as Factors in the Rise of Humanistic Thought," *Speculum*, XIII (1938), 1–37.

Baron, H., *The Crisis of the Early Italian Renaissance*, 2 vols. (Princeton, 1955).

Baron, H., *Humanistic and Political Literature in Florence and Venice at the Beginning of the Quattrocento* (Cambridge, Mass., 1955).

Bolgar, R. R., *The Classical Heritage and its Beneficiaries* (Cambridge, 1954).

Garin, E., *L'umanesimo italiano: filosofia e vita civile nel Rinascimento* (Bari, 1952).

Geanakoplos, D. J., *Greek Scholars in Venice* (Cambridge, Mass., 1962).

Gothein, O., *Francesco Barbaro (1390–1454). Frühhumanismus und Staatskunst in Venedig* (Berlin, 1932).

Kristeller, P. O., *The Classics and Renaissance Thought* (Cambridge, Mass., 1955).

Kristeller, P. O., *Studies in Renaissance Thought and Letters* (Rome, 1956).

Nolhac, P. de, *Pétrarque et l'humanisme*, 2 vols. (2nd ed., Paris, 1907).

Sabbadini, R., *Il metodo degli umanisti* (Florence, 1920).

Sabbadini, R., *Le scoperte dei codici latini e greci nei secoli XIV e XV*, 2 vols. (Florence, 1905–14).

Saitta, G., *Il pensiero italiano nell' umanesimo e nel Rinascimento*, 3 vols. (Bologna, 1949–50).

Saitta, G., *L'educazione dell'umanesimo in Italia* (Venice, 1928).

Voigt, G., *Die Wiederbelebung des klassischen Altertums oder das erste Jahrhundert des Humanismus* (Berlin, 1859).

Weiss, R., *The Dawn of Humanism in Italy* (London, 1947).

Woodward, W. H., *Studies in Education during the Age of the Renaissance* (Cambridge, 1906).

Northern

Brandi, K., *Mittelalterliche Weltanschauung, Humanismus und nationale Bildung* (Berlin, 1925).

Bibliography

Bush, D., *The Renaissance and English Humanism* (Toronto, 1939).

Geiger, L., *Renaissance und Humanismus in Italien und Deutschland* (Berlin, 1882).

Hasse, K. P., *Die deutsche Renaissance*, Vol. I, *Ihre Begründung durch den Humanismus* (Meerane, 1920).

Ritter, G., "Die geschichtliche Bedeutung des deutschen Humanismus," *Historische Zeitschrift*, CXXVII (1923).

Schirmer, W., *Der englische Frühhumanismus* (Leipzig, 1931).

Weiss, R., *Humanism in England during the Fifteenth Century* (Oxford, 1941).

Erasmus and Christian Humanism

Allen, P. S., *The Age of Erasmus* (Oxford, 1914).

Bludau, A., *Die beiden ersten Erasmus-Ausgaben des Neuen Testaments und ihre Gegner* (Freiburg im Breisgau, 1902).

Campbell, W. E., *Erasmus, Tyndale and More* (Milwaukee, 1949).

Hermelink, H., *Die religiösen Reformbestrebungen des deutschen Humanismus* (Tübingen, 1907).

Mestwerdt, P., *Die Anfänge des Erasmus: Humanismus und Devotio Moderna* (Leipzig, 1917).

Oelrich, K. H., *Der späte Erasmus und die Reformation* (Münster, 1961).

Phillips, M. Mann, *Erasmus and the Northern Renaissance* (London, 1949).

Renaudet, A., *Érasme et l'Italie* (Geneva, 1954).

Renaudet, A., *Préréforme et humanisme à Paris pendant les premières guerres d'Italie* (Paris, 1916).

Ritter, G., *Erasmus und der deutsche Humanistenkreis am Oberrhein* (Freiberg im Breisgau, 1937).

Smith, P., *Erasmus* (New York, 1923).

PHILOSOPHY

Scholastic

Carré, M. H., *Phases of Thought in England* (Oxford, 1949).

Carré, M. H., *Realists and Nominalists* (Oxford, 1946).

Copleston, F., *A History of Philosophy*, Vols. II and III (London, 1952–53).

Forest, A., Steenberghen, F. van, Gandillac, M. de, *Le mouvement doctrinal du XIᵉ au XIVᵉ siècle* (Paris, 1951). (*Histoire de l'Église*, ed. A. Fliche and V. Martin, Vol. XIII).

Gilson, É., *History of Christian Philosophy in the Middle Ages* (New York, 1955).

Gilson, É., *The Spirit of Medieval Philosophy* (New York, 1936).

Gilson, É., *Reason and Revelation in the Middle Ages* (New York, 1938).

Ueberweg, F., *Grundriss der Geschichte der Philosophie* (11th ed., Berlin, 1928).

Bibliography

Wulf, M. de, *Histoire de la philosophie médiévale*, 3 vols. (7th ed., Louvain, 1947).

Renaissance

Bett, H., *Nicholas of Cusa* (London, 1932).

Cassirer, E., *Individuum und Kosmos in der Philosophie der Renaissance* (Leipzig, 1927).

Cassirer, E., Kristeller, P. O., and Randall, J. H., eds., *The Renaissance Philosophy of Man* (Chicago, 1948).

Garin, E., *Filosofi italiani del Quattrocento* (Florence, 1942).

Kristeller, P. O., *The Philosophy of Marsilio Ficino* (New York, 1943).

Olgiati, F., *L'anima dell'umanesimo e del Rinascimento* (Milan, 1924).

Robb, N. A., *The Neoplatonism of the Italian Renaissance* (London, 1935).

Ruggiero, G. de, *Storia della filosofia*, Parte III, *Rinascimento, riforma e controriforma*, 2 vols. (Bari, 1937).

SCIENCE

Butterfield, H., *The Origins of Modern Science, 1300–1800* (London, 1951).

Crombie, A. C., *Augustine to Galileo. The History of Science, 400–1650* (London, 1952).

Duhem, P., *Le système du monde de Platon à Copernic*, 5 vols. (Paris, 1913–17).

Olschki, L., *Geschichte der neusprachlichen wissenschaftlichen Literatur*, Vols. I and II (Leipzig, 1919–22).

Randall, J. H., "The Development of Scientific Method in the School of Padua," *Journal of the History of Ideas*, I (1940), 177–206.

Thorndyke, L., *History of Magic and Experimental Science*, Vols. III and IV (New York, 1934).

HISTORIOGRAPHY AND POLITICAL THEORY

Baron, H., "Das Erwachen des historischen Denkens im Humanismus des Quattrocento," *Historische Zeitschrift*, CXLVII (1932), 5–20.

Butterfield, H., *The Statecraft of Machiavelli* (London, 1956).

Chabod, F., *Machiavelli and the Renaissance* (London, 1958).

Emerton, E., *Humanism and Tyranny: Studies in the Italian Trecento* (Cambridge, Mass., 1925).

Figgis, J. N., *Political Thought from Gerson to Grotius* (Cambridge, 1907).

Fueter, E., *Geschichte der neueren Historiographie* (Munich, 1936).

Gilbert, F., "The Humanist Concept of the Prince and *The Prince* of Machiavelli," *Journal of the History of Ideas*, XI (1939), 449–83.

Joachimsen, P., *Geschichtsauffassung und Geschichtschreibung in Deutschland unter dem Einfluss des Humanismus* (Leipzig, 1910).

Bibliography

Kingsford, C. L., *English Historical Literature in the 15th Century* (Oxford, 1913).

Lewis, E., *Medieval Political Ideas*, 2 vols. (New York, 1954).

McIlwain, C. H., *The Growth of Political Thought in the West* (New York, 1932).

Meinecke, F., *Machiavellism: the Doctrine of Raison d'État and its Place in Modern History* (London, 1957).

Sabine, G. H., *A History of Political Theory* (New York, 1937).

ART AND ARCHITECTURE

General

Clark, K., *The Nude, A Study of Ideal Form* (New York, 1959).

Gombrich, E. H., *The Story of Art* (London, 1956).

Hauser, A., *Social History of Art*, 2 vols. (London, 1951).

Lassaigne, J. and Argan, G. C., *The Fifteenth Century, from van Eyck to Botticelli* (New York, 1955). (A. Skira, ed., *The Great Centuries of Painting*).

Newton, E., *European Painting and Sculpture* (Penguin, 1941).

Panofsky, E., *Studies in Iconology* (New York, 1939).

Pevsner, N., *An Outline of European Architecture* (Penguin, Jubilee ed., 1960).

Venturi, L., *The Sixteenth Century, from Leonardo to El Greco* (New York, 1956). (A. Skira, ed., *The Great Centuries of Painting*).

Wölfflin, H., *Principles of Art History* (London, 1932).

Italian

Antal, F., *Florentine Painting and its Social Background* (London, 1948).

Berenson, B., *The Italian Painters of the Renaissance* (New York, 1952).

Chastel, A., *Art et religion dans la Renaissance italienne* (Paris, 1945).

Clark, K., *Piero della Francesca* (London, 1950).

Dvořák, M., *Geschichte der italienischen Kunst im Zeitalter der Renaissance*, 2 vols. (Munich, 1927–28).

Gould, C., *An Introduction to Italian Renaissance Painting* (London, 1957).

Meiss, M., *Painting in Florence and Siena after the Black Death* (Princeton, 1951).

Pope-Hennessey, J., *Italian Renaissance Sculpture* (New York, 1958).

Thode, H., *Franz von Assisi und die Anfänge der Kunst der Renaissance in Italien* (Berlin, 1885).

Venturi, L. and Skira-Venturi, R., *Italian Painting: the Creators of the Renaissance*, ed. A. Skira (Geneva, 1950).

Venturi, L. and Skira-Venturi, R., *Italian Painting: the Renaissance*, ed. A. Skira (Geneva, 1951).

Wackernagel, M., *Der Lebensraum des Künstlers in der florentinischen Renaissance* (Leipzig, 1938).

Bibliography

Wittkower, R., *Architectural Principles in the Age of Humanism* (London, 1949).

Wölfflin, H., *Classic Art, an Introduction to the Italian Renaissance* (1903, new ed. New York, 1952).

Northern

Benesch, O., *The Art of the Renaissance in Northern Europe: its Relation to the Contemporary Spiritual and Intellectual Movements* (Cambridge, Mass., 1945).

Dehio, G., *Geschichte der deutschen Kunst*, 3 vols. (Leipzig, 1919–26).

Friedländer, M. J., *Early Netherlandish Painting, from van Eyck to Bruegel* (London, 1956).

Harvey, J., *Gothic England: a Study of National Culture, 1300–1550* (London, 1947).

Mâle, É., *The Gothic Image* (New York, 1958).

Panofsky, E., *Early Netherlandish Painting, its Origins and Character*, 2 vols. (Cambridge, Mass., 1958).

Simson, O. von, *The Gothic Cathedral* (New York, 1956).

Temko, A., *Notre-Dame of Paris* (New York, 1955).

Waetzoldt, W., *Dürer and his Times* (London, 1950).

MUSIC

Apel, W., *The Notation of Polyphonic Music, 900–1600* (Cambridge, Mass., 1950).

Besseler, H., *Die Musik des Mittelalters und der Renaissance* (Potsdam, 1931).

Bukofzer, M., *Studies in Medieval and Renaissance Music* (New York, 1950).

Harman, A., *Medieval and Early Renaissance Music* (London, 1958).

Láng, P. H., *Music in Western Civilization* (New York, 1941).

Leichtentritt, H., *Music, History and Ideas* (Cambridge, Mass., 1938).

Lowinsky, E. E., "Music in the Culture of the Renaissance," *Journal of the History of Ideas*, XV (1954), 509–53.

New Oxford History of Music, ed. J. A. Westrup *et al.*, Vol. II, *Early Medieval Music up to 1300*, ed. A. Hughes; Vol. III, *Ars Nova and the Renaissance*, ed. A. Hughes and G. Abraham (Oxford, 1954–60).

Reese, G., *Music in the Middle Ages* (New York, 1940).

Reese, G., *Music in the Renaissance* (New York, 1954).

Picture Acknowledgments

The following acknowledgments are listed in the order in which the illustrations appear in the book.

Archives Photographiques, Paris
Photo Jean Roubier
Photo T. C. F. Tourisme
Ewing Galloway, N.Y.
Photo Jean Roubier
Alinari — Art Reference Bureau
Alinari — Art Reference Bureau
 (top) Alinari — Art Reference Bureau, (bottom) Photo by Jean Roubier from
  Rapho-Guillumette Pictures
Scala
(top) National Gallery of Art, Washington, D.C. Samuel H. Kress Collection
(bottom) Reproduced by permission of the Syndics of the Fitzwilliam Museum,
  Cambridge
Alinari — Art Reference Bureau
Scala
Scala
Alinari — Art Reference Bureau
Soprintendenza alle Gallerie
Scala
Giraudon
Alinari — Art Reference Bureau
Im Besitz des Wittelsbacher Ausgleichsfond in Verwahrung der Bayer.
  Staatsgemäldesammlungen
Reproduced by courtesy of the Trustees, The National Gallery, London
Scala
Reproduced by courtesy of the Trustees, The National Gallery, London
Alinari — Art Reference Bureau
La Cinescopie s.a. Bruxelles
Scala
Alinari — Art Reference Bureau
Reproduced by courtesy of the Trustees, The National Gallery, London
Musée du Louvre, Paris
Musei Gallerie Pontificie
Scala
Alinari — Art Reference Bureau
Musée du Louvre, Paris
Museo del Prado
Alinari — Art Reference Bureau
Archives Photographiques, Paris
Musée d'Unterlinden, Colmar
Musée d'Unterlinden, Colmar
Reproduced by gracious permission of H. M. Queen Elizabeth II
Photo by George Spearman, Windsor. Reproduced by gracious permission
  of H. M. Queen Elizabeth II
Scala

Index

Index

Index

Index

Heinrich of Langenstein, 231
Henry III, Emperor, 26
Henry IV, Emperor, 26
Henry VI, Emperor, 23
Henry VII, Emperor, 210
Henry I, King of England, 191
Henry II, King of England, 22, 191
Henry III, King of England, 22, 191–193, 199, 217
Henry IV, King of England, 204
Henry V, King of England, 186, 187, 204
Henry VI, King of England, 188, 196, 204, 205, 257, 471, 472
Henry VII, King of England, 421, 440, 461, 473–475, 499, 500, 539
Henry VIII, King of England, 475, 476, 486–488, 499, 501, 536, 546, 573
Henry the Navigator, Prince, 412, 413, 441
Heresy, 60, 61, 217, 232, 234, 353–371, 469, 506. *See also* Sects
Hermandad, the, 468
Hermes Trismegistus, 542
Hermetic Books, The, attributed to Hermes Trismegistus, 542
Heures du Maréchal de Boucicaut, anonymous, 389
Heussgen, Johannes. *See* Oecolampadius
Hexter, J. H., 547n
Hilton, Walter, 353
Hispaniola, 419, 442
History:
  study of, 303, 552
  writing of, 73, 79, 285, 286, 303, 304, 525, 529, 530, 538, 539
History from the Decline of the Roman Empire, Biondo, 304
History of Florence, Machiavelli, 530
History of the Florentine People, Bruni, 296, 304
History of Italy, Guicciardini, 530, 531
Hoccleve, Thomas, 322
Hochstetter, firm of, 434, 438
Hohenstaufen, House of, 23, 24, 140, 147, 163, 168, 170, 207, 217, 218
Holbein, Hans, the Younger, 572, 573
Holland, economy of, 114, 439
Hous of Fame, The, Chaucer, 320
Hugh of St. Victor, 81
Huizinga, Johan, 338
Humanism:
  Christian, 299, 301, 516, 533, 540–554
  clerical, 65, 289, 292
  definition of, 291, 292
  Italian, 288–306, 492, 494, 510–519, 533
  northern, 503, 504, 531–539

Humanists:
  and scholasticism, 301, 515
  as educators, 302
  as historians, 303, 304, 524, 539
  as men of letters, 292, 296, 297, 510–513, 537, 538, 546
  as moralists, 297–301, 513, 541
  as philologists, 294, 295, 510, 511, 536, 537
  as philosophers, 513, 518
  as professional class, 292, 293, 296, 301
  Christian, 534, 540, 541, 545
  Florentine civic, 298, 302
  in conflict with theologians, 535, 543–545
  religious faith of, 300, 301, 540
Hundred Years' War, 181–190, 200
  and royal finance, 107, 109, 124, 180, 266
  devastation caused by, 96, 133, 139
  results of, 130, 155, 197, 471
Hungary, 161, 431, 435
Hus, John, 232, 367–370
Hussites, 232, 234, 369, 370, 507. *See also* Taborites; Utraquists
Hutten, Ulrich von, 503, 540, 545
Hymns, 66, 87, 400
Hythloday, Raphael, 506, 546, 547

Île de France, the, 21
  as center of culture, 80, 85, 388
Illumination, art of, 83, 84, 374, 387–390
Imitation of Christ, The, Thomas à Kempis, 328, 346, 450–452, 540, 550
immorality, as characteristic of Renaissance society, 249, 250, 300
immortality, doctrine of, 69, 326, 515, 518
Imola, 450, 456
Impetus, theory of, 330–332
India, 411, 414–416
  routes to, 98, 407, 410, 413–418, 420, 425
Indian Ocean, 98, 411, 412, 414, 425
Indies, East, 415, 416
Individualism, 248, 249, 299
Indulgences, 339, 340, 364, 368
Industry:
  English, 126, 127, 440
  Italian, 98, 110–113, 163, 164
  medieval, 28, 29
  of Netherlands, 114–119, 438
  regulation of, 12, 202
  See also Metal-working; Mining; Shipbuilding; Silk-weaving; Wool-weaving

612

Index

Infantry, 183, 184, 198, 200, 253, 470, 481.
  See also Archers
Inflation, monetary, 134, 138–141, 214
Innocent III, Pope, 27, 54, 217, 222
Innocent IV, Pope, 411
Innocent VII, Pope, 227
Innocent VIII, Pope, 408, 451, 456
Innsbruck ich muss dich lassen, Isaak, 581
Inquisition, Papal, 61, 217, 355, 358, 359, 469
Institutio oratoris, Quintillian, 302
Investiture Controversy, 23, 27, 28, 31, 32, 207
Isaak, Heinrich, 520, 575, 580, 581
Isabella of Aragon, grand-daughter of Ferrante of Naples, 448
Isabella, Queen of Castile, 410, 418, 464, 467–469, 475, 479
Isidore of Seville, 65
Italia illustrata, Biondo, 304
Italy, 23, 24, 146–170, 445–457, 480–488
  artists visit, 568, 569, 571
  musicians visit, 575–577, 579, 580, 581
  scholars visit, 534, 537, 541, 545, 550
  See also Cities; Communes; States

Jacquerie, the, 183, 267
Jäger, Johannes. *See* Crotus Rubianus
Jamaica, 419, 442
Japan, 417
Jean d'Albret, King of Navarre, 487
Jehan le Bel, 313
Jerome of Prague, 367, 369
Jews, 264, 464, 469, 543, 544
Joachim, father of the Virgin, 377
Joachim of Flora, 344, 355, 358
Joachimites, sect of, 272
Joan of Arc, 188, 458
Joanna, daughter of Ferdinand and Isabella, 479
John XXII, Pope, 210, 221, 224, 230, 325, 341, 345, 357, 358, 396
John XXIII, schismatic pope, 232, 368
John Palaeologus, Byzantine Emperor, 406
John, King of Bohemia, 210, 310
John, King of England, 22, 191, 192, 360
John II, King of France, 107, 180, 182, 183, 185, 186
John II, King of Portugal, 413, 417
John of Gaunt. *See* Lancaster
John of Jandun, 230
John of Paris, 229, 231
John of Salisbury, 65, 292
Joinville, Jean, Sire de, 79, 312
Jongleurs, 74, 78

Jonson, Ben, 538
Josquin des Prez, 575–580, 583
Jubilee, papal, 217–219
Juliana of Norwich, 353
Julius II, Pope (Giuliano della Rovere), 456, 485, 486, 488, 493, 551, 561, 562, 566
Justice, administration of:
  in England, 190, 191, 195, 203
  in France, 177, 178
  See also Courts of law and justice
Justices of the Peace, 203, 253, 475, 499

Kaffa, 425
Khanate of the Golden Horde, 406
Knighthood, honor of, 37, 240, 241, 256, 257
Knights:
  as fighting men, 17, 34, 183–185, 198, 200, 215, 253–256, 259
  as lords, 5, 17, 18, 34
  German, 213, 214, 257
  in Parliament, 195, 197, 200, 201, 252, 314
Knights Hospitallers, Order of, 38, 408
Kraft, Adam, 436, 573
Kublai Khan, 411

La Rue, Pierre de, 575, 578
Labor services, 6–8, 135
  commutation of, 46, 133–141
Lancaster:
  House of, 204, 472
  John of Gaunt, Duke of, 204, 363, 471, 473
Land:
  Church, 25
  clearance of, 7, 95, 133, 142
  enclosure of, 505, 506
  investment in, 143, 243, 492
  See also Landholders; Lords; Tenants; Wealth
Landfrieden, 216
Landholders, 4, 16, 34, 134, 137–140, 146, 173, 197, 215, 251, 252, 497
Landini, Francesco, 248, 398, 581
Landino, Cristoforo, 514, 520
Lando, Michele de, 272
Landsknechte, 470
Landtag. *See* Estates: in Germany
Lane, Frederick C., 104
Langland, William, 317, 318, 338, 342, 354
Language:
  English, 205, 313–315, 318
  French, 75, 310
  Greek, study and use of, 298, 305, 306, 407, 510

Index

Music (*Continued*)
English, 398, 399
French, 397, 398
German, 582
harmonic developments in, 576, 577, 580, 581
imitation as device in, 398, 576, 577, 579, 580
instrumental, 581, 582
Italian, 397, 398, 576, 577
methods of composing, 577, 579
Netherlandish, 398–401, 575–582
notation of, 87–90, 92, 395
performance of, 575–579, 581
polyphonic, 88–91, 395–397, 575, 581, 582
  choral, 577, 578
printing of, 582, 583
sacred, 85–91, 396, 397, 400, 576, 577
secular, 91, 92, 396–398, 401, 579
  See also Choirs; *conductus; Fauxbourdon;* Hymns; Mass, the; Motets; Organum; Songs
Mut, Conrad. *See* Mutianus Rufus
Mutianus Rufus, 536, 538
Mysticism, 55, 56, 344–348, 352, 353, 540, 542
  Neoplatonic, 334, 336, 355, 521, 541, 545

Naples, Kingdom of, 169, 170, 446–451, 456, 457, 461, 467, 480–485, 488
Nauclerus, Johannes, 539
Navarre, 465, 467, 487
  Jean d'Albret, King of. *See* Jean d'Albret
  Marguerite de. *See* Marguerite de Navarre
Navigation Acts, 220, 440
Negroponte, 408, 425
Netherlands:
  area defined, 114
  economy of, 114–119, 436–439
  in possession of Dukes of Burgundy, 186, 187, 477
  in possession of House of Hapsburg, 477, 479
  See also Commerce; Industry; Painting; Music
Newfoundland, 421
Nibelungenlied, anonymous, 75
Niccoli, Niccolò, 293, 304
Nicholas II, Pope, 26
Nicholas III, Pope, 357
Nicholas V, Pope, 235, 294, 295, 510

Nicholas of Cusa, Cardinal, 234, 333–336, 349, 514, 531, 542
Nobility:
  acquisition of, 498
  definition of, 241, 252, 490, 491
  titles of, 240–242, 491, 492
Nobles:
  as arbiters of taste, 307, 531
  as courtiers, 77, 257–259, 462, 467
  as a social class, 34–36, 146, 250–253, 263, 531
  dependent on the monarchy, 193, 497, 498
  English. *See* Barons; Peerage
  French, 140, 185, 497, 498
  German, 23, 502, 503
  Italian, 32, 142, 147–149, 238–241, 491, 492
  Spanish, 464–468, 491, 503
  Venetian, 159, 241
  See also Aristocracy; Birth, noble; Lords
Nogaret, Guillaume de, 175, 176, 219
Nominalism, 70, 71, 324, 327, 332, 353, 541
Nominalists, 70, 71, 328, 332, 392
Normandy, Duchy of, 21, 187
Normans, 21, 23, 75
North Sea, 120, 121
Notre-Dame of Paris, Cathedral of, 89
Novgorod, trade with, 120–122
Nude, in art, 557, 558, 562, 566
Nuns, 42, 43
Nürnberg:
  as center of culture, 535, 568, 571, 573
  economy of, 430, 431, 433, 436

Obrecht, Jacob, 575, 576, 581
Ockeghem, Johannes, 575–579, 583
Ockham, William of, 63, 71, 230, 323, 325–330, 332–334, 360, 363, 364
Oecolampadius, Johannes, 536
Oligarchies, urban, 149, 152, 153, 160, 164, 167, 241, 273, 563
On the Church, Wyclif, 363
On Civil Dominion, Wyclif, 362, 363
On Divine Dominion, Wyclif, 362
On the Immortality of the Soul, Pomponazzi, 518
On the Office of the King, Wyclif, 363
Or San Michele, church of, 382, 384
Oration on the Dignity of Man, Pico, 299, 516, 517
Ordelaffi, House of, 169
Orders, mendicant, 354. *See also* Friars
Ordinances of 1311, 199
Ordinances of Justice, 164, 165, 240, 280